THE EUROPEAN CONVENTION ON HUMAN RIGHTS AND THE CONFLICT IN NORTHERN IRELAND

THE EUROPEAN CONVENTION ON HUMAN RIGHTS AND THE CONFLICT IN NORTHERN IRELAND

BRICE DICKSON

OXFORD
UNIVERSITY PRESS

OXFORD
UNIVERSITY PRESS

Great Clarendon Street, Oxford OX2 6DP

Oxford University Press is a department of the University of Oxford.
It furthers the University's objective of excellence in research, scholarship,
and education by publishing worldwide in

Oxford New York

Auckland Cape Town Dar es Salaam Hong Kong Karachi
Kuala Lumpur Madrid Melbourne Mexico City Nairobi
New Delhi Shanghai Taipei Toronto

With offices in

Argentina Austria Brazil Chile Czech Republic France Greece
Guatemala Hungary Italy Japan Poland Portugal Singapore
South Korea Switzerland Thailand Turkey Ukraine Vietnam

Published in the United States
by Oxford University Press Inc., New York

First published 2010

British Library Cataloguing in Publication Data
Data available

Library of Congress Cataloging in Publication Data
Data available

Typeset by Newgen Imaging Systems (P) Ltd., Chennai, India
Printed in Great Britain
on acid-free paper by
CPI Digital

ISBN 978–0–19–957138–3 (Hardback)

1 3 5 7 9 10 8 6 4 2

Foreword

Professor Brice Dickson has established a highly deserved reputation as a leading academic commentator in the field of human rights law. He has written and lectured widely on the subject and his chapter on Northern Ireland in Lester and Pannick's highly authoritative *Human Rights Law and Practice* is, for practitioners and judiciary alike, an indispensable work of knowledge and erudition. Further, his two terms of office as the first Chief Commissioner of the Northern Ireland Human Rights Commission have provided him with another very useful point of vantage from which to survey the unfolding story of human rights law as it has shaped the law in this jurisdiction.

This latest work seeks to place that story in its historical context by offering a systematic survey of how Strasbourg jurisprudence has evolved – specifically in response to various episodes in the history of the Northern Ireland conflict and the legal challenges to which they gave rise. His detailed and scholarly analysis includes an assessment, from the author's perspective, of the adequacy and effectiveness of current human rights safeguards and occasionally includes the expression of views, some of which are likely to be controversial. It is therefore a work which will both inform and provoke and to that extent it is much more than a mere textbook for lawyers. The author's natural facility for relating the story in comprehensible language will ensure that those working in other disciplines as well as the general reader will find this a thoroughly accessible work.

Professor Dickson has drawn deeply from his well of knowledge in this area and is to be commended for the production of a significant and welcome addition to the growing body of analysis of Convention law and for the contribution which this will undoubtedly make to the continuing debate.

Sir Declan Morgan
Lord Chief Justice of Northern Ireland

Preface

I wrote this book because it deals with a topic which I thought was overdue for detailed exploration. It is rather surprising that there has not before now been a comprehensive assessment of the role played by the European Convention on Human Rights during the conflict in Northern Ireland. The book does not by any means pretend to be a definitive account of that role, but it aims to stimulate further discussion on the matter, largely because lessons can surely be learned from the Northern Ireland experience regarding the way in which international human rights standards should be applied in relation to conflicts in other parts of the world.

Anyone writing in this field is greatly indebted to an array of other authors who have analysed the 'emergency laws' in Northern Ireland over the last generation. Foremost amongst these are David Bonner, Kevin Boyle, Colm Campbell, Des Greer, Tom Hadden, John Jackson, Stephen Livingstone, Fionnuala Ní Aoláin, Michael O'Boyle and, most notable of all perhaps, Clive Walker. I must also acknowledge the assistance provided in various ways – through discussions, comments on draft chapters, or general encouragement – from current and former colleagues such as Les Allamby, Gordon Anthony, Sir Louis Blom-Cooper, Steven Greer, Michael Hamilton, Colin Harvey, Kieran McEvoy, and Dermot Walsh. I am particularly grateful for the information wittingly or unwittingly provided to me in interviews or conversations with Jim Auld, Ed Bates, Kevin Boyle, Lord Carlile of Berriew, Paul Dixon, Padraigin Drinan, Jeff Dudgeon, Brian Garrett, Lord Lester of Herne Hill, and Dawn Oliver.

Staff at Oxford University Press were very supportive from the moment the proposal to write the book was accepted. In this regard special thanks must go to Chris Champion, Alex Flach, Emma Hawes, Natasha Knight, and the compilers of the Tables and Index. I am also very grateful to the current Lord Chief Justice of Northern Ireland, Sir Declan Morgan, for providing such a generous Foreword.

Finally, as always, my particular gratitude must go to my very supportive wife, Patricia Mallon, who assisted with the project in ways too numerous to mention. The book is dedicated to her.

Brice Dickson
Queen's University Belfast
27 November 2009

Contents

Table of Cases

Table of Acts of the British, Northern Irish, and Irish Parliaments

Overseas legislation

Australia

United States Constitution

Table of European Legislation

Table of Statutory Instruments and Statutory Rules

Table of International Treaties

List of Abbreviations

ACPO	Association of Chief Police Officers
AEP	Attenuating energy projectiles
CAJ	Committee on the Administration of Justice
CPT	European Committee for the Prevention of Torture
CSJ	Campaign for Social Justice
DPP	Director of Public Prosecutions
DSAC	Defence Scientific Advisory Council
ECJ	European Court of Justice
EPA 1973	Northern Ireland (Emergency Provisions) Act 1973
EPA 1978	Northern Ireland (Emergency Provisions) Act 1978
EPA 1987	Northern Ireland (Emergency Provisions) Act 1987
EPA 1991	Northern Ireland (Emergency Provisions) Act 1991
FAIR	Families Acting for Innocent Relatives
FEA	Fair Employment Agency
FET	Fair Employment Tribunal
IRA	Irish Republican Army
KPPS	Key Persons Protection Scheme
LCJ	Lord Chief Justice
NICRA	Northern Ireland Civil Rights Association
NIE	Northern Ireland Electricity Services
NIHRC	Northern Ireland Human Rights Commission
Ofcom	Office of Communications
PACE Act	Police and Criminal Evidence Act 1984
PACE Order	Police and Criminal Evidence (NI) Order 1989
PSNI	Police Service of Northern Ireland
PTA 1974	Prevention of Terrorism (Temporary Provisions) Act 1974
PTA 1976	Prevention of Terrorism (Temporary Provisions) Act 1976
PTA 1984	Prevention of Terrorism (Temporary Provisions) Act 1984
PTA 1989	Prevention of Terrorism (Temporary Provisions) Act 1989
RIPA	Regulation of Investigatory Powers Act 2000
RUC	Royal Ulster Constabulary
SACHR	Standing Advisory Commission on Human Rights
SDLP	Social and Democratic Labour Party
UVF	Ulster Volunteer Force

1

Introduction

Today, most people outside Northern Ireland who have spared a thought for the place during the past 10 years probably believe that the conflict there is over. Not having heard much about it on their news bulletins for some time, they will assume that things are relatively quiet and that the people who live there are no longer fighting and killing one another. They might recall that some years ago (in 1994) the most active paramilitary groups in Northern Ireland called a ceasefire, and that a few years after that (in 1998) most of the political parties reached a peace settlement called the Belfast (Good Friday) Agreement.[1] It is also common knowledge that this Agreement ensured that, although Northern Ireland stays a part of the United Kingdom, responsibility for the day-to-day running of the place has to be shared between those who are insistent that Northern Ireland stay British (the unionists) and those who still aspire, at some point in the not too distant future, for Northern Ireland to become part of an all-island Republic of Ireland (the nationalists).

By and large that sketchy picture is an accurate one, but it leaves out of account a number of features of the present situation which suggest that the conflict is in fact far from over. It is by no means as intense as it was, with levels of violence having dropped very significantly since the ceasefires of 1994, but it is still bubbling away beneath the surface of everyday life, with violence erupting now and then as a reminder of how fragile the peace process really is. In March 2009, for example, two British soldiers were shot dead in the town of Antrim by members of the 'Real IRA', and two days later a constable in the Police Service of Northern Ireland (a Catholic, as it happens) was murdered in Lurgan by the 'Continuity IRA'.[2] These were the first murders of members of the security forces in Northern Ireland since 1998, but there had been many non-fatal attacks in the interim and numerous killings had taken place of civilians. In fact, by the time of the murders in March 2009 no fewer than 105 people had been killed in conflict-related incidents in Northern Ireland since the concluding of the Agreement in 1998.[3] That figure can be added to the 3,588

[1] Cm 3883. Available online at <http://www.nio.gov.uk/agreement.pdf>.

[2] The soldiers were Mark Quinsey (23) and Cengiz 'Patrick' Azimkar (21); the police officer was Stephen Carroll (48). 'IRA' stands for Irish Republican Army, an illegal paramilitary/terrorist organization. The 'Real' and 'Continuity' IRA are groups which broke away from the 'Provisional' IRA, which is now committed to the peace process in Northern Ireland and supposedly put all its weapons beyond use in September 2005. The 'Provisional' IRA was itself an offshoot of the 'Official' IRA, formed in 1969, which called a ceasefire in 1972. See generally Kelley (1982), Alexander and O'Day (1984), Bell (1993), Bell, JB (1997), Coogan (2002), Moloney (2002), English (2003), English (2006).

[3] See Rowan (2003), and 'Conflict-Related Deaths in Northern Ireland Since the Ceasefires', a regularly updated database on the website of British Irish Rights Watch, a London-based human rights

who were killed between the outbreak of the conflict in 1968 and the concluding of the Agreement.[4] On top of that there is evidence that the two main communities in Northern Ireland are more segregated than ever,[5] that political attitudes are hardening,[6] and that sectarianism and racism are rife.[7] The conflict is, in a very real sense, still ongoing,[8] albeit in a much more attenuated form than that which prevailed between 1968 and 1998.

Any detailed consideration of what the conflict has been about would require a study of underlying causes, going back centuries, of why these suddenly resulted in the outbreak of serious violence in 1968, of what factors helped to prolong the fighting, of how exactly the Agreement of 1998 sought to resolve matters, and of why there are still deep societal divisions. Theories about the nature of the conflict abound.[9] The more limited purpose of the present book, however, is to examine the extent to which the protection of human rights has featured as an aspect of the conflict. What role was played by the discourse of human rights when the conflict re-ignited in 1968, and what attention has been given to the protection of human rights prior to and in the wake of the Agreement? Did the various measures taken by successive governments to detect and prevent the use of violence for political ends appropriately respect human rights? More particularly, the book focuses on the contribution made during the conflict by the European Convention on Human Rights, the world's most invoked set of international human rights standards, by which the United Kingdom agreed to be bound as early as 1951. Has the European Convention, through its

organization (<http://www.birw.org>). At the time of writing the most recent death was that of Kevin McDaid, a Catholic brutally attacked in Coleraine by Protestant supporters of the Glasgow Rangers football club on 24 May 2009.

4 This figure is taken from McKittrick et al (2004) 1431–2. Sources disagree significantly (by a margin of some 10 per cent) as to whether certain deaths are directly attributable to the conflict. The statistics on the website of the Police Service of Northern Ireland (<http://www.psni.police.uk>; last visited on 3 August 2009) claim that 3,372 people were killed between 1969 and 2008. This figure may be comparatively low because the police do not always categorize as conflict-related the deaths caused by members of the security forces. McKittrick et al (2004), at 1526, claim that exactly 3,700 people were killed between 1969 and 2003. See too Sutton (1994), who records 3,285 deaths between July 1969 and the end of 1993. For a list of conflict-related deaths between 1969 and 1989 see McKeown (1989), and for those since 2002 see the website of the University of Ulster's Conflict Archive on the Internet (CAIN): <http://cain.ulst.ac.uk/issues/violence/deaths2009draft.htm>. For a sociological analysis of the deaths see Smyth and Hamilton (2003) and for an illustration of the anguish caused see Smyth and Fay (2000).

5 There are today some 40 'peace walls' in Belfast, more than in 1998.

6 Electoral support for more extreme political parties has now outgrown that for more moderate ones.

7 Statistics published by the Police Service of Northern Ireland show, for example, that the number of reported racist incidents increased more than fourfold between 2002–3 and 2008–9. In 2008–9 there were also 1,595 sectarian incidents.

8 This is borne out by reports of the Independent Monitoring Commission, the body created in 2004 to report to the British and Irish government on activities by paramilitary groups; see <http://www.independentmonitoringcommission.org>.

9 For an excellent survey see Darby (1976) ch 7 and 198–242 (a useful bibliography). For good historical, political, sociological, and anthropological explorations of the conflict see Barritt and Carter (1962; 2nd edn 1972), Elliot and Hickie (1971), McCann (1974), Burton (1978), Darby (1983), Moxon-Browne (1983), Hewitt (1987), Wilson (1989), O'Leary and McGarry (1993), McGarry and O'Leary (1995), McKittrick and McVea (2000), Millar (2006), Hennessey (2007). For more general guidance on researching the conflict in Northern Ireland see Whyte (1990), Hargie and Dickson (2003).

adjudication and enforcement organs, satisfactorily protected people's human rights during the conflict?[10] Has it helped to bring the conflict to an end, or has it in any way facilitated its prolongation? Whatever the answers to these questions, they lead to two further lines of inquiry: how has the European Convention itself been affected by the issues arising out of the conflict in Northern Ireland, and can the Convention now make a positive contribution to the regulation of conflicts elsewhere in Europe on the basis of what has been learned from dealing with the conflict in Northern Ireland?

In effect, the book is a case study of the European Convention in action. It seeks to explain and evaluate how the Convention—or, rather, its enforcement bodies, the European Commission and European Court of Human Rights—has or has not risen to the challenges which have presented themselves as a result of applications that have been lodged in Strasbourg from Northern Ireland or have been otherwise connected to the conflict there. Given that the conflict has gone on for such a long time, and that the petitions brought to Strasbourg have been so numerous and novel, the story of the enforcement bodies' reaction to those challenges is to a large extent the story of how the Convention itself has developed over the same period. Until the explosion of applications relating to the conflict in Turkey in the late 1980s, no other part of Europe provided as many 'test cases' for the organs of the European Convention as did Northern Ireland. Today that flow has subsided, but many of the principles established in the cases that went from Northern Ireland to Strasbourg still hold good throughout the continent and have been influential further afield too.

The book also looks in some detail at the domestic laws put in place to deal with the civil unrest and with allegations of human rights abuses in Northern Ireland. It assesses how the European Convention's organs have gone about deciding whether the reaction of State authorities to the use of politically motivated violence and to complaints of human rights abuses has been satisfactory. It asks whether sufficient weight has been given to the rights of individuals as opposed to the interests of society. It examines whether too much discretion has been granted to democratic States to devise mechanisms for countering politically motivated violence and whether too passive an attitude has been adopted in the search for concepts and principles to ensure that human rights are better protected during times of crisis. These and other issues are explored with a view to identifying the strengths and weaknesses of the Convention as a tool for policing the protection of human rights in countries experiencing serious conflict.

In the following chapter information is provided about the background to the conflict in Northern Ireland, taking the story to the end of the 1970s. It has been included primarily for those readers who are not already familiar with the situation in Northern Ireland and who may wish to ground their estimation of how the European Convention has dealt with the human rights issues there in a more solid appreciation of the history of the place. Chapter 3 looks at early efforts to invoke the European Convention on Human Rights as a way of redressing some of the grievances raised

[10] For partially complete earlier surveys see Livingstone (1995), Dickson (1996b), Dickson (1997) 143–83.

by disadvantaged groups and individuals in Northern Ireland, almost all of which were entirely unsuccessful. The nine subsequent chapters then examine how the Convention has subsequently been called in aid to protect particular human rights in Northern Ireland, ranging from the right to liberty to the right not to be discriminated against, updating the picture to the present day. A final chapter draws together some of the conclusions emerging from previous chapters and makes a case for the view that the European Convention's adjudication and enforcement organs have not done all that they could have done to ensure that human rights have been fully protected during the Northern Ireland conflict: the Convention is still not completely 'fit for purpose' in that sense.[11] In truth, the Convention has proved itself to be something of a blunt instrument in a highly conflicted society.

[11] For analyses of lessons which may be learned internationally from Northern Ireland's struggle with terrorism, see Campbell (2005) and Campbell and Connolly (2006).

2

The Background to the Conflict and the Rights Discourse

Competing nationalisms

That the nature of the conflict in Northern Ireland is itself a disputed issue is some evidence of how difficult it has been for those with responsibility for governing the territory at any particular time to adopt appropriate strategies for dealing with the conflict. Even the use of the term 'conflict' is contested within Northern Ireland. Until fairly recently, the word customarily employed to describe the unrest was 'the troubles', sometimes dignified with a capital—'the Troubles'. The use of such a euphemistic expression was not just an example of the people of Ulster[1] playing down the importance of their affairs relative to what was going on elsewhere in the world, it was an attempt to label the unrest as a matter that was internal to the United Kingdom—'a little local difficulty' in the phrase used by British Prime Minister Harold Macmillan in a different context.[2] The term 'conflict', by and large, is favoured by those who are more sympathetic to the nationalist or republican perspective on the unrest in Northern Ireland. It connotes something more serious, serves as a reminder that the violence used was politically motivated rather than purely criminal, and helps to internationalize the problem. It also suggests, perhaps, that the unrest in question can be 'managed' in such a way as to hasten its cessation. A specialist field of human endeavour has grown up around the notion of 'conflict resolution' since systematic violence erupted in Northern Ireland in 1968, and it suits both the theories and practices of the professionals in that field to categorize what has gone on in Northern Ireland as typical of many other 'conflict situations' around the world.[3] In addition,

[1] For those not familiar with Irish history it needs to be pointed out that Ulster, one of the four ancient provinces of Ireland, is not coterminous with Northern Ireland: three of the nine counties of Ulster are actually situated in the Republic of Ireland. Hence nationalists often use the term 'the six counties' to describe Northern Ireland.

[2] He made the comment in January 1958 when, abroad at the time, he was asked about the resignation of three of his Treasury ministers back in Britain.

[3] The usual comparator jurisdictions are South Africa and Israel/Palestine: see, eg, Guelke (1988), Byrne (1999), Knox and Quirk (2000), McGarry (2001), Knox and Monaghan (2002), Choudhury (2008). Perhaps because they are less important than South Africa and Israel/Palestine in geopolitical terms, the conflicts in Cyprus and Kashmir tend to be less frequently compared with that in Northern

use of the word 'conflict' makes it easier to invoke international legal standards on the protection of victims of violence. Article 3 of each of the four Geneva Conventions of 1949[4] applies certain of the terms of those Conventions to non-international armed conflicts, requiring, for example, that people who are not taking an active part in the hostilities should be treated humanely, which means, amongst other things, that they must not be subjected to violence, to humiliating and degrading treatment, or to hostage taking. But it is likely that the conflict in Northern Ireland, apart perhaps from a few years in the early 1970s, has never been intense enough to qualify as an 'armed conflict' for the purpose of Article 3.[5] This also makes it unconvincing, in law, for people imprisoned during the conflict to claim the status of 'prisoners of war', because for that to be valid under the Geneva Conventions and Protocols the conflict again has to be an 'armed conflict' and either an international conflict or a conflict in which a people is fighting against colonial domination and alien occupation in the exercise of its right to self-determination.[6] In this book the terms 'troubles' and 'conflict' will be used interchangeably, but the term 'war' will be avoided.

At base the unrest in Northern Ireland is founded on the reality that a sizeable proportion of the population living in the area (which many nationalists prefer to call 'the North of Ireland' in an attempt to give greater emphasis to the fact that the primary unit is the island of Ireland[7]) would rather not be living under a British flag but under an Irish one. The total number of people now living there is close to 1.7 million,[8] of whom some 55 to 60 per cent would be in favour of Northern Ireland remaining part of the United Kingdom and 40 to 45 per cent would be in favour of its becoming part of a united Ireland.[9] The Northern Ireland conflict is thus primarily a conflict about identity, national allegiance and the status of territory.[10] For historical reasons, however, the two sides to the conflict are also divided by religious differences, with pro-British people tending to be Protestants and pro-Irish people tending to be Catholics.[11] But as the conflict has played out since 1968, these religious differences have not been to the

Ireland, even though in some respects their features are more obviously analogous. This book draws on the analogy with Cyprus in ch 13.

[4] These are treaties designed primarily to ensure the humane treatment of people caught up in wars.

[5] Hull (1976) 162–73; Walker (1984) 213. *Ex hypothesi* the conflict would not be serious enough to trigger the application of Protocol 2 to the Geneva Conventions, which was agreed in 1977 and which applies only if the forces opposing the government 'exercise such control over a part of its territory as to enable them to carry out sustained and concerted military operations' (Art 1(2)). ibid, 224. See too Duffy (2005) 217–49.

[6] Protocol 1 to the Geneva Convention, Art 1(4).

[7] Though Protestant unionists old enough to remember a pre-partition Ireland still tended to refer to the area as 'the North of Ireland' for many years after 1920.

[8] 1,685,267 according to the results of the 2001 census: Census (2002) KS01.

[9] In the elections for the European Parliament in June 2009, 49 per cent of those who voted in Northern Ireland gave their first preference vote to a unionist candidate, 42 per cent to a nationalist candidate, and 9 per cent to a candidate who was neither overtly unionist nor nationalist. As for opinion in England, Wales, and Scotland, a poll conducted for *The Guardian* in 2001 showed that 41 per cent of people there are in favour of Northern Ireland becoming part of a united Ireland: see <http://cain.ulst.ac.uk/issues/politics/polls.htm#04> (last visited 3 August 2009).

[10] For a moral philosopher's perspective on what this basic fact entails, see Hughes (1982), which takes Ulster as a case study.

[11] It is difficult to be more precise than this. The last census (2001) revealed that 40 per cent of people in Northern Ireland labelled themselves as Catholics, 40 per cent as Protestant, 6 per cent as having

fore. In that period everyone in Northern Ireland has been free to practise whatever religion they wish and in recent years, as in the rest of the United Kingdom and Ireland, Northern Ireland has increasingly been populated by people who have a religion other than Christianity, as well as by people who have no religion at all.[12]

The jurisdictional dimension to the conflict can be traced back to the twelfth century, when successive Kings of England (a country that had been united under one monarch since the Norman invasion of 1066) sent soldiers to Ireland with a view to subjugating it and imposing English rule through the medium of the 'common law'. Resistance was fierce and prolonged. The whole of the island was never completely conquered in that, even after rule from England was imposed, there were always Irish Chieftains or Lords at work in some parts of Ireland trying to disrupt English governance. The tide of the resistance ebbed and flowed, and was often brutally suppressed. Divisions were exacerbated by the fact that, after King Henry VIII's break with Rome in the sixteenth century, England became a predominantly Protestant country while Ireland remained predominantly Catholic. The Reformation never affected Ireland to the same extent as it did England, Scotland, and Wales, even though many Irish monasteries and churches were destroyed or sacked. During the reign of Queen Elizabeth I (1558–1603), and in succeeding decades, a large migration of Protestant settlers from England and Scotland to the more agriculturally prosperous parts of Ireland radically altered the religious balance of the population so that in the North the majority of the people became Protestant and had some familial or ancestral connection to Britain, while in the South the majority remained Catholic and had no such connections.[13] Throughout Ireland the native Gaels were suppressed and marginalized.

As a means of discouraging people from persisting in heretical religious beliefs, Parliament in London passed a number of 'penal' laws designed to prevent non-adherents of the Church of England (of whom the King or Queen of England was the Supreme Governor) from exercising certain professions or trades and from holding certain offices. While these laws also affected non-conforming Protestants, such as Presbyterians, the main impact was felt amongst the Catholic population, and while this impact was certainly discernible in England, Scotland, and Wales it was even more noticeable in Ireland, where the Reformation had not had the same radical effects. Consequently the degree of resentment built up by the penal laws in Ireland was so much greater.

Attempts were made in the seventeenth and eighteenth centuries to allow Ireland some degree of self-governance by establishing a Parliament in Dublin, and for a short period at the end of the eighteenth century this Parliament had very extensive powers. This Parliament also passed 'penal' laws. But following the 1798 rebellion in Ireland, led by the Protestant Wolfe Tone, the government in London deemed it wiser to abolish the Irish Parliament and to proceed with formalizing the union between Ireland and what was already Great Britain

another religion, and 14 per cent as having no religion: Census (2002) Table KS07a. While the correlation between religious affiliation and political allegiance is very great, it is by no means automatic.

[12] For a discussion of Northern Ireland's laws compelling the collection of information about the religious background of employees and applicants for jobs, see ch 11.

[13] Gallagher (1957) ch 2; de Paor (1970) ch 1; Connolly (1992).

(the name given to the entity created out of the union of England and Wales with Scotland by the Acts of Union of 1707). The new union was called the United Kingdom of Great Britain and Ireland and came into being on 1 January 1801.

The partition of Ireland

The history of nineteenth-century Ireland is primarily a history of land exploitation, famine, migration, and demands for independence (or at least Home Rule).[14] The effects of the famine and emigration in the 1840s and subsequent decades are best illustrated by the fact that in 1841 the census showed the population of the whole island to be 8,175,124, while 160 years later it was still only 5,602,603. The British Liberal Prime Minister, William Gladstone, tried to secure Home Rule for Ireland through two Bills introduced at Westminster in the 1870s and 1880s, but these failed to secure enough votes in Parliament to be enacted. One of Gladstone's Liberal successors, David Lloyd George, ultimately succeeded in getting such a Bill enacted in 1914, but its implementation was thwarted by the outbreak of the First World War later that same year. All of these attempts to impose Home Rule were fiercely resisted by Ulster Protestants. Irish patriots then tried to take things into their own hands by staging an uprising in Dublin at Easter 1916. They failed, and several of those involved were executed by the British for their pains. After the end of the First World War there were three additional years of conflict in Ireland, a period which is now referred to as the War of Independence, culminating in the signing of an Anglo-Irish Treaty in London on 6 December 1921. This in turn partly superseded yet another Home Rule Bill which had been enacted at Westminster as the Government of Ireland Act 1920 and which had proposed the partition of the island of Ireland so that the Protestant northerners, who were mainly pro-British, could govern themselves, and the Catholic southerners, who were much more in favour of independence, could do likewise, although both parts of Ireland were to remain dominions within the British Empire and were to continue to elect representatives to the Parliament at Westminster, where responsibility for reserved matters such as defence and foreign policy was to reside. There was also to be a Council of Ireland which would handle issues of interest to the island as a whole.

The 1920 Act was implemented in what was officially designated as Northern Ireland, but the Anglo-Irish Treaty of 1921 put in place a new regime in Southern Ireland, which became known as the Irish Free State (in Irish, *Saorstat Éireann*), with a Parliament that was independent from, rather than subordinate to, the one in London. While the Head of State remained the King of England, the Irish Free State was no longer a part of the United Kingdom, which from then on has been known as the United Kingdom of Great Britain and Northern Ireland. Even that degree of autonomy was not a satisfactory solution to many Irish republicans and over the course of the next two years there took place a bloody civil war in Ireland, which was eventually won by the pro-Treaty faction. The anti-Treaty faction, led by Eamon de

[14] For a good recent account see English (2006) chs 3 and 4.

Valera, went off to lick its wounds, but within five years it too, under the political party banner of Fianna Fáil (in English, *Soldiers of Destiny*), had accepted the 1921 Treaty and agreed to work within the mechanisms it established.

De Valera's political strategy succeeded, because when he was the President of the Executive Council[15] just a decade later, in 1937, he was able to push through a new Constitution for Ireland (called in Irish *Éire*). Article 2 declared that the national territory consisted of the whole island of Ireland while Article 3 stated that pending the reintegration of the national territory the laws enacted by the Irish Parliament would apply to the same area as before 1937. Until 1938 the Head of State continued to be the King of England, who was represented in the Irish Free State by a Governor-General (selected by the Irish government). From 1938 the Head of State was a President elected by popular vote.[16] It was only in 1949 that Ireland became a completely independent Republic, with no constitutional ties to the United Kingdom at all.[17] Indeed, the new State (called *Poblacht na hÉireann* in Irish) was poor and relatively undeveloped and was dominated by Catholic theology. The Protestant population had diminished significantly since 1920 and in 1939 de Valera declared that his country would not support Britain in its fight against Nazism, preferring to remain officially neutral.[18] In 1949, to the annoyance of many living in the Republic of Ireland, the Parliament at Westminster reaffirmed the status of Northern Ireland as a part of the United Kingdom and said that every part of it would remain so for as long as the Parliament of Northern Ireland so desired.[19] On the other hand, Westminster also declared that for the purposes of any law in force in any part of the United Kingdom (or any territory of the United Kingdom), the Republic of Ireland was not 'a foreign country'.[20] This had implications for matters such as travelling restrictions and voting rights.

Northern Ireland and the Special Powers Act

Northern Ireland on the other hand, since its formation in 1921, had prospered, at least in economic terms.[21] The Government of Ireland Act of 1920 had given it its own bicameral Parliament and a locally elected government, both of which had significant devolved powers. But its relative economic success was at the expense of a lack of pluralism, somewhat mirroring the dominance of Catholicism in the southern

[15] ie head of the government of the Irish Free State.

[16] The first President was Douglas Hyde, the son of a Church of Ireland minister and co-founder of the Gaelic League in 1893, an organization which promoted the study of the Irish language.

[17] This was achieved by the Republic of Ireland Act 1948 (passed by the Irish Parliament) and by the Ireland Act 1949 (passed by the British Parliament). Strangely, no change was made to the Irish Constitution itself at this time.

[18] Nevertheless, well over 100,000 Irish men volunteered to fight in the British army: Wills (2007).

[19] Ireland Act 1949, s 1(2). For further details about the Constitution of Northern Ireland see Calvert (1968), Watt (1981), Hadfield (1989), Morison and Livingstone (1995), Morgan (2000).

[20] s 1(3).

[21] See generally Buckland (1981) esp chs 4 and 5; Hennessey (1997) esp chs 1 and 2. When it was created Northern Ireland had a population of approximately 1.25 million, of whom 820,000 (65 per cent) were Protestant and 430,000 (35 per cent) were Catholic.

jurisdiction. Indeed in 1934, after de Valera had emphasized that his country was a Catholic nation, the first Prime Minister of Northern Ireland, Viscount Craigavon, declared that 'All I boast of is that we are a Protestant Parliament and a Protestant State'.[22] The unionists who were first elected to the Parliament of Northern Ireland in 1921 soon went about trying to make the Union with Great Britain more secure by, for example, insisting that all local elections were run on a first-past-the-post system (rather than proportional representation, as required by the Government of Ireland Act 1920) and ensuring that constituency boundaries were so drawn as to allocate more representatives per head of population to Protestant residents than to Catholic residents.[23] There was also considerable discrimination on religious grounds in both employment and the allocation of social housing.[24] Relatively few Catholics were employed in the civil service or the police and the large private employers (such as the shipbuilding and power-generation companies) tended to exclude Catholics. In rural areas Protestant and Catholic employers each tended to employ their co-religionists rather than people who 'dug with the other foot'.[25] The socio-economic condition of the Protestant and Catholic communities was, on the whole, very differentiated.[26]

In addition to trying to create a fortress province which was dominated by pro-British unionists, the government of Northern Ireland lost little time after the formation of the State in ensuring that legislation was adopted to enable the security forces to effectively counter agitation by pro-Irish nationalists. Some of the measures taken echoed those put in place before partition,[27] but the main piece of legislation—the Civil Authorities (Special Powers) Act (NI) 1922—was the most comprehensive attempt that had been made up until then to secure law and order in part of Ireland. The initial impetus for the legislation was the fact that the rate of killing in Northern Ireland was very high during the first six months of the State's creation (236 people died between 6 December 1921 and the end of May 1922[28]). The 1922 Act contained a sunset clause, ensuring that it would expire in 1923 unless it was renewed. However, it *was* renewed, and again in each of the next four years. In 1928 it was re-enacted for a five-year period and in 1933 the Northern Ireland government decided to make the legislation permanent, although specific powers conferred by it could only be exercised if a government minister approved. A further amendment was made to the Act in 1943 and from then on the legislation became known, officially, as the Civil Authorities (Special Powers) Acts (NI) 1922–43 or, more simply, as the Special Powers Act (SPA).

[22] HC Deb (NI), vol 34, col 1095 (24 April 1934). This is often misquoted as 'a Protestant State for a Protestant people'.

[23] Gallagher (1957) ch 15, which contains a welter of statistics and diagrams to substantiate the point.

[24] ibid, ch 14. Eg, at Queen's University in 1951 there were 36 professors, but only two of them were 'members of the minority'; the minority also occupied only two of the 76 administrative posts in the university (p 215). See too Harris (1972), *passim*.

[25] This is an Ulster euphemism for having a different religion. It supposedly derives from different regional practices regarding the use of spades for digging turf or potatoes.

[26] Birrell (1972).

[27] On which see Townshend (1983), Mulloy (1986).

[28] Donohue (2001) 16. For a detailed exposition of the 'emergency law' applying in Northern Ireland between 1921 and 1925, see Campbell (1994) 268–337.

Surprisingly little has been written about the genesis and actual operation of the SPA, the best account being by Donohue.[29] But even she does not set out in detail the precise content of all the Regulations that were issued under powers conferred by the Act.[30] It was the Regulations that had the most impact on people on the ground, not the provisions of the Act itself. As the years went on, more and more Regulations were issued, some of them amending what had gone before, others adding new material, so by the late 1960s it was extremely difficult for anyone, even police officers, to know the full reach of the powers and duties set out in the Regulations. Even today it takes considerable effort to work out the exact wording of the Regulations that were in force at any particular time. Whatever their content, the Regulations were effectively unchallengeable in the courts. An early attempt to do so, in *R (O'Hanlon) v Governor of Belfast Prison*, failed,[31] ostensibly on the basis that, as there was a law which authorized the applicant's detention,[32] that was enough to supersede the right to bring habeas corpus proceedings. The decision has been much criticized,[33] mainly for failing to take account of the fact that the 'law' in question was made by a subordinate Parliament with limited legislative powers, but it set the tone for future judicial approaches to the Special Powers Act Regulations for the next half-century. In proceedings brought to a court in England in 1972 an argument that the Special Powers Act was *ultra vires* the Parliament of Northern Ireland was rejected.[34]

It was an act of discrimination in the allocation of social housing by the Protestant-controlled Dungannon Urban District Council in County Tyrone that eventually sparked the flame leading to widespread civil unrest in Northern Ireland from 1968 onwards. In June a nationalist politician, Austin Currie, illegally occupied a council house that had been allocated to a 19-year-old unmarried Protestant girl even though there appeared to be many more deserving Catholic families in need of a home. This action was followed by a series of civil rights marches in August and October 1968. Although no-one was killed on any of these occasions, the 'troubles' of Northern Ireland had begun.[35] The severity of the violence quickly escalated. In 1969 there were 10 bomb explosions, 73 shooting incidents and 14 conflict-related killings.[36] By 1972 these figures had risen to 1,853 bomb explosions, 10,631 shooting incidents and 470 conflict-related killings. The average annual death toll for each of the following seven years was 189, with almost 74 per cent of these fatalities being civilians (ie not police officers or soldiers). Throughout the more than 30 years of troubles in Northern Ireland by far the greatest part of the violence was perpetrated by republican paramilitaries,

[29] ibid. Wallace (1971) 91–102; Barritt and Carter (1972) 127–37; Farrell (1976), *passim*.

[30] In Appendices B and C (356–63) she gives an indication of the number and variety of Regulations issued. See too Edwards (1956a); Carroll (1973) 35–7; Hull (1976) 210–3; Bishop (1978) 157–9.

[31] (1922) 56 ILTR 170. See too O'Boyle (1977a) 172.

[32] reg 32B of the Special Powers Act Regs.

[33] Palley (1972) 308; Campbell (1994) 334–6, citing Halsbury's Statutes, 2nd edn, 1950, xvii, 169.

[34] *Re Keenan* [1972] 1 QB 533.

[35] For an extended account of how the troubles emerged in the period 1964–9 see Rose (2000). For an account which draws some comparisons with the situation in the US in the 1950s and 1960s see Bishop (1978) 149–56. For an attempt to learn lessons from Northern Ireland in contemporary America, see O'Connor and Rumann (2002–3).

[36] There were three conflict-related deaths in 1966, but none in 1967 or 1968.

but 'loyalist' paramilitaries—those supposedly 'loyal' to the UK government—and the State's security forces were also responsible for significant acts of violence. According to the most authoritative source, between 1969 and 2003 republican paramilitaries killed 2,158 people (58 per cent of the total), loyalist paramilitaries killed 1,099 (30 per cent), and the security forces killed 365 (10 per cent).[37] The victims of these killings comprised 2,102 civilians (57 per cent), 1,036 members of the security forces (28 per cent), and 562 members of paramilitary organizations (15 per cent).[38]

Direct rule

The government of Northern Ireland struggled to keep the lid on the civil unrest in the late 1960s, and was forced to ask the British Labour government, under Prime Minister Harold Wilson, to authorize the deployment of British soldiers on to the streets of Northern Ireland in August 1969, under what was code-named 'Operation Banner'. The soldiers were at first welcomed by many Catholics, who felt that they would now be better protected against attacks from violent loyalist paramilitaries and what they viewed as one-sided policing by the Royal Ulster Constabulary, as the local police force was known. But in due course disillusionment set in because the British soldiers were perceived by many as being on the same side as the police and not at all sympathetic to the needs and aspirations of Irish nationalists. The soldiers soon became targets.[39] The crisis came to a head in August 1971, when the government of Northern Ireland, using its powers under the Special Powers Act, reintroduced internment without trial as a way of getting dangerous men off the streets.[40] Even that did not reduce the level of violence—on one argument it exacerbated it—and a range of additional measures then had to be devised to deal with the increasingly serious unrest. The British government deemed the Northern Ireland government to be incapable of bringing the unrest under control and so it secured the passing of a Westminster statute which in March 1972 suspended the Northern Ireland government and prorogued the Parliament of Northern Ireland.[41] The British government thereupon became fully responsible for Northern Ireland under what were known as the 'direct rule' arrangements. A Secretary of State for Northern Ireland was appointed, with a seat in the British government (William Whitelaw being the first holder of the post), and most matters that had been previously legislated for by

[37] McKittrick et al (2004) 1528. A further 2 per cent of the victims died in troubles-related accidents or had heart attacks.

[38] ibid, 1529.

[39] Writing in 2006, Peter Rowe noted that since 1969 more British soldiers had been killed while on duty in Northern Ireland than in all the other international armed conflicts in which they had been engaged since then (the Falklands conflict 1982; the Gulf War 1990–91; Kosovo 1999; Afghanistan 2002; Iraq 2003): Rowe (2006) 212.

[40] See further ch 4 below.

[41] Northern Ireland (Temporary Provisions) Act 1972. For details see Hadfield (1989) 100–1. For assessments of the devolved regime in Northern Ireland for all or part of the period 1921–72 see Mansergh (1936), Wallace (1971), Oliver (1978), Birrell and Murie (1980). For assessments of British policy in relation to Northern Ireland at that time see Wallace (1982), Cunningham (1991).

Acts of the Northern Ireland Parliament were instead allowed to be dealt with by Orders in Council—secondary legislation made by senior government ministers in Great Britain who were Privy Councillors, and approved, sometimes with very little if any debate, by Parliament at Westminster. After a frantic search for a new formula to govern Northern Ireland,[42] the Parliament of Northern Ireland was completely abolished by the Northern Ireland Act 1974 and instead the election of a Northern Ireland Assembly was provided for. This sat for the first few months of 1975 but was brought down by a strike organized by the Protestant-dominated Ulster Workers' Council,[43] which was vehemently opposed to a more wide-ranging political settlement reached at a conference in Sunningdale in England in December 1973. Direct rule was reimposed from 29 May 1975 and was to continue until the transfer of some powers to a new Northern Ireland Executive and Assembly on 2 December 1999.

After the initial imposition of direct rule in 1972 the British government announced that it would review all the provisions of the Special Powers Act. In addition it appointed a small group of experts, under the chairmanship of a Lord of Appeal, Lord Diplock, to consider legal procedures to deal with terrorist activities in Northern Ireland.[44] These reviews resulted in the enactment of the first of many pieces of 'emergency' and 'prevention of terrorism' legislation—the Northern Ireland (Emergency Provisions) Act 1973 (EPA). The EPA 1973 retained internment but also created the concept of 'scheduled offences', for which, in serious cases, people could be tried in the absence of a jury in what became known as 'Diplock courts'. Juries were dispensed with because of the risk of jurors being intimidated by members of paramilitary organizations. In the course of the succeeding 25 years, during which the level of violence fluctuated depending on current political circumstances (eg it rose significantly during the hunger strikes by republican prisoners in 1980–81), the British government's preferred approach to 'the troubles' was to devise more and more specialized legislation aimed at the more effective prevention and detection of unlawful paramilitary activities. As we shall see in subsequent chapters, most of this legislation applied only in Northern Ireland,[45] but some of it was applicable throughout the United Kingdom. The legislation was subject to many reviews, including, in more recent years, annual assessments conducted by independent experts appointed under statutory provisions.

Just as the violence in Northern Ireland was diminishing, from the mid-1990s onwards, concerns about terrorism linked to other ideological conflicts were beginning to grow in London. As a result, in the first nine years of the new century Westminster has enacted no fewer than six major pieces of legislation regulating the control of terrorism,[46] two of which contain special provisions applicable in Northern Ireland alone.[47] Under the Justice and Security (NI) Act 2007 some of those special

[42] Hadfield (1989) 102–17.

[43] Anderson (1994).

[44] Cmnd 5185 (December 1972).

[45] As a general rule, legislation which has the words 'Northern Ireland' somewhere in the title applies only in Northern Ireland and not in other parts of the UK.

[46] Terrorism Act 2000; Anti-terrorism, Crime and Security Act 2001; Prevention of Terrorism Act 2005; Terrorism Act 2006; Terrorism (NI) Act 2006; Counter-Terrorism Act 2008.

[47] Part VII of the Terrorism Act 2000; Terrorism (NI) Act 2006.

provisions were repealed, so today most of the 'emergency' and 'anti-terrorism' laws are completely uniform throughout the United Kingdom but there are still a few measures applying only in Northern Ireland.

Human rights discourse in Northern Ireland

It has to be remembered that the emergency legislation enacted to deal with the conflict in Northern Ireland was first and foremost a symptom of that conflict, not the cause of it. Likewise, the violation of the right not to be discriminated against was certainly a key element in raising levels of dissatisfaction within the nationalist community, but in and of itself it cannot be taken as the reason why such serious and protracted violence occurred. Such a denial was, of course, outrageous and needs to be condemned out of hand. There is nothing to be gained by defenders of unionism or other commentators pointing at other contemporary societies and arguing that they were just as bad with regard to discrimination based on race or gender as Northern Ireland was with regard to discrimination based on religious belief or political opinion. All of these forms of discrimination are wrong and should not occur. But discrimination on the basis of political opinion is not exactly a rare phenomenon in the world, given that many political elites seek to maintain power for themselves by adopting policies which members of other political groupings dislike.[48] One might point, for example, to the position of the two main British parties—Labour and Conservative—who for decades have been strongly opposed to using a proportional representation system in elections because they have feared that it might give the balance of power to the third largest British political party, now called the Liberal Democrats. However, in Northern Ireland the exclusion from power of nationalist or republican politicians was not just potentially never-ending, it also had the effect of denying individuals the right to fully enjoy their culture and to express their identity as people who were Irish. As a result of being denied any share in the governing of Northern Ireland, nationalists were indirectly denied other rights. As Amartya Sen has recently emphasized, denying people their national, cultural, religious, or linguistic identity is often a stimulus for violence, though usually unjustifiably so.[49]

While many of those who spoke and wrote about the state of affairs in Northern Ireland between the 1920s and the 1960s did make reference to the denial of equal rights, to discrimination, and to unfair practices, the term 'breach of human rights' was hardly used at all. Such writers and thinkers wanted these practices to stop, but they did not usually couch their calls for reform in terms of better protection of human rights. Many of the people who were doing the discriminating were private individuals, not State officials, and there was a feeling—some of which thrives even today—that in purely private matters there are no such things as human rights. When the discrimination was exercised by State officials the defence often went up that the price of democracy is that majorities must have their way. Parliamentarians at Westminster were precluded from commenting in any substantive way on the affairs of Northern Ireland

[48] See Prince (2007). [49] Sen (2006).

because a constitutional convention had developed whereby discussion of such 'internal' affairs was ruled out of order.[50] There was nothing in the Universal Declaration of Human Rights of 1948, or in any other post-war international document on human rights, to say that people elected to a legislature must share power with their opponents, or indeed that proportional representation should be used in elections, and by the early 1960s there were very few international treaties on human rights which asserted that people had the right to a job or to a home irrespective of their religious or political beliefs. David Schmitt summed up the position quite well in 1976:

> The significance of not exaggerating the degree of repression under the Stormont regime is that it allows consideration of the crucial nature of majoritarian democratic structures in providing a de facto disenfranchising of the minority. Given the absence of pluralistic voting coalitions or autonomous regions in Northern Ireland, as well as the absence of competing government structures such as a powerful upper house or an independent supreme court, democratic processes helped guarantee permanent control of the political system to Protestants. They also served to deceive those in the majority as well as outsiders such as the British authorities, who wanted to believe that the system was essentially democratic.[51]

When agitation first developed around discrimination in Northern Ireland the language commonly used was that of 'civil rights', the term then in vogue in the United States.[52] That phrase is not a term of art, any more so than the phrase 'civil liberties', but it connotes first and foremost a demand for equal protection under the law. In both the United States and Northern Ireland one of the most prominent claims under this heading was for equal protection under electoral law—the right to vote on equal terms with everyone else and the right to be represented on equal terms too.[53] 'Civil rights' also connotes freedom from arbitrary arrest and ill-treatment, the right to a fair trial in both civil and criminal proceedings, and the right to freedom of belief, expression, and assembly. In the Northern Ireland of the 1960s the 'civil rights movement', as it was known, focused on these demands when marching and campaigning for equal protection under the law. At that time the phrase 'human rights' was not on everyone's lips and certainly within legal and academic circles there were not yet the opportunities to study human rights standards. Amnesty International, probably the world's best known human rights organization, was not established until 1961, the United Nations did not promulgate its International Covenants on human rights until 1966 (and these did not come into force for countries ratifying them until 1976), and by the end of the 1960s the European Court of Human Rights, which first sat in 1960, had issued just 10 decisions.[54] The International Commission of Jurists issued an influential report on the human rights situation in Northern Ireland, but only in

[50] Though Calvert thinks it was not as extensive as sometimes claimed to be: Calvert (1968) 94–103.

[51] Schmitt (1976) 17.

[52] See generally Hewitt (1981). An important study on justice in Northern Ireland by Hadden and Hillyard (1973) also spoke mainly of 'civil rights', especially in chs 2, 3, and 4. See too NISLL (1969).

[53] In *Baker v Carr* 369 US 186 (1962), for example, the US Supreme Court established that, in order to comply with the equal protection clause of the US Constitution (Amendment 14), State legislatures had to apportion their electoral districts in a way that ensured approximate population equality.

[54] Of these 10 decisions the first three related to one case (*Lawless v Ireland*, discussed in ch 3 below), three involved Belgium, three Austria, and one Germany. One of the first judges of the Court, who had himself

June 1969.[55] It was very critical of the Northern Ireland government, likening it to the fascist dictatorships then in power in Portugal, Spain, and Greece, and pointing out that the legislation on detention in apartheid South Africa was less draconian than the Northern Ireland Special Powers Act.[56]

Early calls for a Bill of Rights

From time to time, however, the language of human rights *was* used in Northern Ireland, and a few enlightened politicians did try to put in place a general solution to the difficulties rather than seek piecemeal solutions for particular problems.[57] This coincided with agitation in many of Britain's colonies for home-grown Bills of Rights to be adopted there, and from 1962 the government's Colonial Office was in favour of that policy.[58] As early as 3 March 1964 Sheelagh Murnaghan, a Catholic Liberal MP in the Northern Ireland Parliament representing the constituency of Queen's University, gave notice that she was planning to introduce a Human Rights Bill for Parliament's consideration, although she rather over-optimistically suggested that there would be no need in such a Bill for any declaration prohibiting torture.[59] Her Bill received a first reading on 27 May 1964[60] but in June it was rejected by the unionist government.[61] When responding for the government the Attorney General, Ted Jones, began by saying, incredibly:

> When one looks at the world at large I think one is coerced to agree that we are very fortunate that unfair discrimination arising out of race or colour, religion or political belief, is not a serious problem in this community.[62]

And soon afterwards he added:

> Moreover the enforcement of a Bill such as this, as experience has shown in other parts of the world, would almost certainly increase tensions. We feel it would tend to increase tensions here where for political reasons our friends above the Gangway on the other side of the House—the Nationalists, I mean, so as to get it on the record—and those associated with them persistently attribute differences to unfair discrimination, completely ignoring that such differences are in fact attributable to different economic, social and cultural standards.[63]

When a vote was taken on the Second Reading of the Bill, it was lost by 23 to 17.

been involved in negotiating the drafting of the Convention, was worried mid-decade that the Court might cease to exist: Rolin (1965). In the 1970s 24 decisions were issued; 134 in the 1980s. See Gomien (1996).

[55] ICJ (1969).

[56] Rose (2000) 160–1.

[57] Unfortunately these early efforts are not recorded in Michael Zander's otherwise valuable book: Zander (1997) ch 1 ('The History of the Bill of Rights Debate').

[58] Parkinson (2007) ch 9.

[59] HC Deb (NI), 1964, vol 56, cols 1422, 1424. She cited from Maurice Cranston's recently published book, *Human Rights Today* (New York, Basic Books Inc; 1963). A new edition was published in 1974.

[60] HC Deb (NI), 1964, vol 57, col 296.

[61] ibid, col 1989.

[62] ibid, col 2022.

[63] ibid, cols 2023–4.

Similar bills introduced by Murnaghan in February 1966, February 1967 and January 1968 were also lost, as were two Private Members' Bills confined to Northern Ireland introduced simultaneously in the House of Commons and House of Lords on 12 May 1971.[64] Like the 1964 Bill these were all, in effect, anti-discrimination bills rather than fully fledged Bills of Rights,[65] but when introducing her 1968 Bill Murnaghan did refer to the fact that that year was International Human Rights Year[66] and another MP for Queen's University, Bessie Maconachie, explained at some length the elaborate arrangements that were in train to celebrate that special year in Northern Ireland. The Bills even provided for the creation of a Human Rights Commission to supervise and have jurisdiction over the type of unfair discriminatory practices which they would outlaw. But in rejecting the 1968 Bill the then Minister of Home Affairs, William Craig, was quite blunt:

> Essentially our problem is not one of law, but of history. It can be solved not by the expedients of law but by the positive effects of practical action by each member of our community. A distressful past has left us with a deep wound but one which is rapidly healing. I cannot think that that healing process is to be helped by providing an arena where old and imaginary slights can be relived, where disappointed office seekers can air their frustrations and where old agitations can be revived. Like every scar, it will never get well if you pick it. We have come a long way in the past few years and I think that the public would like to have not only less discrimination, but less talk of discrimination; less revival of old antagonisms and more trust in each other and confidence in our future. With that confidence I ask the House to reject this Bill.[67]

When a vote was taken on Sheelagh Murnaghan's 1968 Bill it was lost by 22 votes to eight. Amongst those voting against it were the then Prime Minister of Northern Ireland (Terence O'Neill), two future Prime Ministers (James Chichester-Clark and Brian Faulkner) and Ted Jones, the then Attorney General and a future Lord Justice of Appeal. Despite these setbacks, Sheelagh Murnaghan had planted a seed. As we shall see,[68] that seed has since been extensively watered, but the plant has not yet germinated.

The Standing Advisory Commission on Human Rights

In England, legislative attempts to deal with racial discrimination were enacted in the shape of the Race Relations Acts of 1965 and 1968, and in January 1966 the Cabinet recognized the right of people throughout the United Kingdom to lodge applications with the European Commission of Human Rights if they thought that their rights

[64] By Arthur Latham MP (HC Deb, vol 817, cols 383–94) and Lord Brockway (HL Deb, vol 318, col 1067). See too Harvey and Schwartz (2009) 182–6.

[65] The Bills introduced at Westminster also called for proportional representation to be used in elections in Northern Ireland.

[66] She also referred to the report by Professor Harry Street into the workings of the Race Relations Act 1965, *Anti-Discrimination Legislation* (PEP; November 1967) and to an article by Professor René Cassin in the latest issue of the Journal of the International Commission of Jurists.

[67] HC Deb (NI), vol 68, col 603 (30 January 1968).

[68] In ch 13.

under the European Convention had been breached.[69] Following powerful interventions from the young liberal lawyer Anthony Lester[70] and the eminent High Court judge Sir Leslie Scarman,[71] the campaign for the introduction of a Bill of Rights for the whole of the United Kingdom gathered momentum.[72] One of the most illuminating contributions to the debate was that by Michael Zander, a professor of law at the London School of Economics, whose study has since stretched to three further editions.[73] It ably sums up the pros and cons of enacting a Bill of Rights in the United Kingdom and draws on the experience of other countries, particularly Canada.

Strangely, not much attention was paid in the early literature to the potential benefits of a Bill of Rights in Northern Ireland, even though it was in the mid-1970s that the inter-State case brought by the government of the Republic of Ireland against the United Kingdom in relation to alleged mistreatment of detainees in Northern Ireland by members of the British security forces was wending its way through the Strasbourg system.[74] But the need for more systematic protection of human rights in Northern Ireland was raised in the government's White Paper entitled 'Northern Ireland Constitutional Proposals', published in March 1973.[75] Part 4 of this document, headed 'A Charter of Human Rights', might suggest that the government was indeed in favour of introducing a Bill of Rights for Northern Ireland, but that would be a misreading of the text. The White Paper merely proposed that some additional provisions should be introduced to supplement existing safeguards. The protection of fundamental human rights in Northern Ireland would from then on 'flow from a number of different sources', the principal source remaining 'our parliamentary democratic tradition' and 'the common and statute law'.[76] The White Paper was debated at Westminster,[77] but no government minister gave a commitment to a Bill of Rights for Northern Ireland. When, less than a month later, the Northern Ireland (Emergency Provisions) Bill was debated in the House of Commons, the Secretary of State for Northern Ireland, William Whitelaw, referred more than once to 'the Charter of Human Rights' but did not mention a Bill of Rights. On the other hand, Labour's shadow Secretary of State, Merlyn Rees, did equate the Charter with a Bill of Rights and he regretted the lack of detail about this matter in the Bill in front of him:

> The replacement of the Special Powers Act can only be considered in the context of a Bill of Rights... The lack of legislative proposals on a Bill of Rights, a charter of human rights, not

69 For useful contemporary comments see Simmonds (1966), Beddard (1967), and Gilmour (1968), the last being an examination of whether the UK's Iron and Steel Act 1967 was compatible with the Convention. See also Gearty (1997) 66–71 and Lester (1968).

70 Lester (1968). The author is now Lord Lester of Herne Hill QC.

71 Scarman (1974). Sir Leslie had already chaired a tribunal of inquiry into violence in Northern Ireland in 1969: Scarman (1972). He later served as a Lord of Appeal from 1977 to 1986.

72 For a summary of the debate see Fenwick (2007) 140–56.

73 Zander (1997).

74 This case is considered in detail in chs 4 and 7.

75 Cmnd 5259. This White Paper so antagonized some members of the Ulster Unionist Party that they broke away to form the Vanguard Unionist Progressive Party, led by the former Minister for Home Affairs in Northern Ireland, Bill Craig. David (later Lord) Trimble became a member of this breakaway party too.

76 ibid, para 95.

77 HC Deb, vol 853, cols 1318–1444 (28 March 1973) and 1537–1668 (29 March 1973).

only makes it difficult to do our job today... but also makes it even more necessary for us to look critically at the Bill.[78]

In 1974, when the Prevention of Terrorism (Temporary Provisions) Bill was being rushed through Parliament, one Labour MP reminded the House that at the 1972 annual conference of the Labour Party a resolution had been passed calling for a Bill of Rights for Northern Ireland, and he regretted that, now that Labour was in government, it had not carried forward that commitment. 'Had they done so', he said, 'in my view we would have laid a foundation which would have meant that these proposed powers [in the PTA] and other powers in operation in Northern Ireland would not have been necessary'.[79]

The White Paper's proposals were turned into legislative proposals when the Northern Ireland Constitution Bill was published in May 1973, and it became an Act on 18 July. Section 20 of the Act created the Standing Advisory Commission on Human Rights (SACHR), which was charged with (a) advising the Secretary of State for Northern Ireland on the adequacy and effectiveness of the current law in preventing discrimination on the ground of religious belief or political opinion and in providing redress for persons aggrieved by discrimination on either ground, and (b) keeping the Secretary of State informed as to the extent to which public authorities have prevented discrimination on either ground by persons or bodies not prohibited from discriminating by that law.[80] SACHR can reasonably claim to be the second 'national human rights institution' anywhere in the world, following the establishment of France's National Consultative Commission on Human Rights in 1947. It pre-dated the formation of Human Rights Commissions in Canada and New Zealand by three years.

Much to its credit, SACHR—under the initial chairmanship of Lord Feather and then Lord Plant, both prominent trade union leaders from England—quickly decided to consider whether a Bill of Rights should be put in place for Northern Ireland, even though it realized that this was not strictly within its terms of reference. SACHR was prompted to move in this direction by the fact that the Northern Ireland Constitutional Convention, an elected body, had reported in November 1975[81] and had recommended (in its draft Constitution Bill) that there should be a Bill of Constitutional Rights to guarantee the stability and integrity of the Northern Ireland Constitution and also a general Bill of Rights and Duties to protect the rights of the individual citizen.[82] It appointed Anthony Lester QC (who had already served as a Special Adviser to the Home Secretary in England) and Andrew Donaldson (a former Director of Law Reform for Northern Ireland) as Special Advisers and it published a Discussion Paper on the topic in March 1976.[83] The Commission's subsequent report, *The Protection of*

[78] HC Deb, vol 855, col 293 (17 April 1972). At the 1973 annual conference of the Labour Party a resolution was passed calling for a Bill of Rights for Northern Ireland.

[79] HC Deb, vol 882, cols 683–4 (28 November 1974), per Stan Thorne MP.

[80] See generally Maguire (1981). SACHR itself often called for an extension of its statutory remit: SACHR (1978) paras 65–6; SACHR (1979) paras 32–3; SACHR (1980) paras 28–33; SACHR (1982) paras 51 and 56. For SACHR's own survey of its work from 1973 to 1981 see SACHR (1982) paras 37–56.

[81] Constitutional Convention (1975).

[82] cll 7–8.

[83] *Bill of Rights* (Belfast, Her Majesty's Stationery Office).

Human Rights by Law in Northern Ireland,[84] presented a careful analysis of the issue and recommended that Northern Ireland should have a Bill of Rights based on the European Convention on Human Rights—a Bill, therefore, that would primarily protect civil and political rights, not social and economic rights except the rights to property and to education. But the Commission also suggested that, to avoid the implication that Northern Ireland was somehow being treated as a place apart from the rest of the United Kingdom, the Bill of Rights should be enacted for the whole of the country. Indeed it noted that a Bill of Rights limited to Northern Ireland 'would not be widely welcomed'.[85] Nevertheless, the report concluded that, in the event of legislative and executive functions being devolved to a new government in Northern Ireland (whether before or after the incorporation of Convention rights into UK law):

> it would be desirable for the enabling legislation to include a clear and enforceable charter of rights for Northern Ireland. The guarantees in this charter should be consonant with those which may accompany devolution in other parts of the United Kingdom. This charter of rights could be more comprehensive than the European Convention and should be framed in the light of whatever at the time seem to be the special needs of the people of Northern Ireland.[86]

One member of the Commission, Bob Cooper (a former deputy leader of the bi-confessional Alliance Party of Northern Ireland), dissented from his colleagues to the extent that, while accepting that a Bill of Rights applying to the whole of the United Kingdom was his first choice, if the introduction of a UK Bill were to be long delayed there was no reason why, in the meantime, a Bill should not be enacted for Northern Ireland.[87] A Bill of Rights was not enacted, and nor has it been in the more than three decades that have since elapsed. SACHR itself initiated the cycle of conferences on this theme by organizing a two-day seminar in April 1980.[88] A somewhat sceptical review of the value of a Bill of Rights as a remedy for grievances in Northern Ireland was published the same year.[89] The more recent attempts to create a Bill of Rights for Northern Ireland are considered in the concluding chapter of this book.

Conclusion

Possibly the most significant human rights development in Northern Ireland in the 1970s was the enactment at Westminster of the Fair Employment (NI) Act 1976, the first law anywhere in these islands to make religious and political discrimination unlawful in the

[84] SACHR (1977b); see too SACHR (1978) paras 13–27. Among the members of the Commission at the time were Colin (now Sir Colin) Campbell, later Vice Chancellor of the University of Nottingham; Mrs Brid Rodgers, later an SDLP Minister in the Northern Ireland Executive from 1999 to 2002; and Michael Nicholson QC, later a High Court judge and Lord Justice of Appeal in Northern Ireland from 1985 to 2006.

[85] SACHR (1977b) 75, para 5.

[86] ibid, para 6.15.

[87] ibid, Note of Dissent, at the start of the Report.

[88] The proceedings are recorded in Campbell (1980).

[89] Jaconelli (1980) 226–45, though he observes that 'some notable decisions handed down by the Northern Ireland courts during the most troubled years are far from executive-minded in their approach' (229).

private as well as the public sphere. A Fair Employment Agency was set up to monitor the enforcement of the Act and Bob Cooper left politics to become the Agency's Chief Executive. This attempt to tackle the evil of religious and political discrimination was not immediately successful,[90] but it was a sound beginning. By the end of the 1970s, indeed, the demands of the initial civil rights movement in the late 1960s had effectively all been met: the electoral system had been reformed,[91] the power to allocate public housing had been removed from local councils and given to an unelected body called the Northern Ireland Housing Executive,[92] the Special Powers Act had been repealed and replaced with somewhat less draconian anti-terrorist legislation,[93] and, to complement the work of the Fair Employment Agency, an Ombudsman had been appointed to deal with complaints of 'maladministration' within the public sector, including claims of unfair treatment on the grounds of religious belief or political opinion.[94] Some attempts had been made to reform the Royal Ulster Constabulary—through the appointment of a Police Authority, for example—but these proved to be less successful.

By this time, however, the initial civil rights movement had been usurped by a paramilitary movement that had different aims and used different methods. This is not the place in which to examine how the moderate Northern Ireland Civil Rights Association was overshadowed by the Irish Republican Army,[95] but the consequence of this happening was that perfectly laudable demands for better protection of human rights were dreadfully contaminated by the employment of means to that end—shootings, bombings, kidnappings, and intimidation—which were themselves very grave violations of human rights that were many times worse than the violations being complained about in the first place. One of the unfortunate features of the time was the refusal of many of those who continued to campaign for better human rights protection to recognize that what the paramilitaries were doing (the so-called loyalists just as much as the republicans) was denying the very human rights which the campaigners (quite rightly) were calling upon the government to uphold. It is hard now to remember that, in those relatively early days of human rights work, most of the activists believed that breaches of human rights were things which only governments could commit; atrocities perpetrated by paramilitaries were simply breaches of the criminal law (as if one of the purposes of the criminal law is not to protect the victims of criminality from having their human rights infringed).[96] This was the position adopted by the organization that in practice took over the mantle of campaigning for human rights from the Northern Ireland Civil Rights Association, namely the Committee on the Administration of Justice (CAJ), which was formed in 1981 after a conference in Belfast chaired by a former UK Lord Chancellor,

[90] For more details see ch 12 below.

[91] Electoral Law Act (NI) 1969. See Elliott (1992).

[92] Housing Executive Act (NI) 1971.

[93] Northern Ireland (Emergency Provisions) Act 1973.

[94] Parliamentary Commissioner Act (NI) 1969; Commissioner for Complaints Act (NI) 1969.

[95] See generally Purdie (1990) and Ó Dochartaigh (1997).

[96] In 1978 the European Court made it clear that 'the terrorist activities in the six counties of individuals or of groups . . . are in clear disregard of human rights': *Ireland v UK* (1979–80) 2 EHRR 25, para 149.

Lord Gardiner.[97] Amnesty International did not extend its remit to cover abuses of human rights by armed opposition groups until 1991.[98]

The reality is that human rights, like so many other concepts, had by 1981 become a propaganda tool in a war of words between all sides to the conflict in Northern Ireland. The CAJ, and others, strove to ensure that the government and security forces maintained the highest standards in the administration of justice, and political representatives, especially those from Sinn Féin, echoed many of those calls. But hardly anyone outside political circles was pointing up the hypocrisy in Sinn Féin's stance, given that that party was still refusing to condemn the use of violence to achieve its political goals. In addition, republican and loyalist paramilitary groups were increasingly 'disciplining' people who disobeyed their orders, or who engaged in so-called 'anti-social behaviour', by shooting them in the ankles, knees, or elbows, or by beating them with lumps of wood or iron.[99] At the same time the suggestion was raised in some people's minds that the conflict in Northern Ireland was almost totally focused around human rights and equality issues, when in fact a very large element of it was around whether violence was a justifiable way of seeking political objectives and whether workable arrangements could be made for ensuring power-sharing in what was obviously a deeply divided society. It is safe to assume that when the politicians were discussing these issues very few of them, if any, referred to the European Convention on Human Rights. The role of the European Convention was a much more restricted one, of greater interest to lawyers than to politicians. For the purposes of the subsequent chapters of the present book, what matters is whether the lawyers rose to the challenge of making use of the Convention in a way that was helpful in Northern Ireland. Were applications based on the Convention made in a convincing manner? Did members of the European Commission and Court of Human Rights in Strasbourg react appropriately to the applications lodged with them? Was the Convention itself worded in such a way as to permit human rights to be vigorously protected in a divided society, even in the midst of widespread terrorist activity? These are some of the questions which the rest of this book seeks to address.

[97] The author declares an interest in that he was one of the founding members of the CAJ and served as its Chairman from 1986–7. For an account of the CAJ's challenges see Whelan (1992).

[98] For a discussion of the attitude of non-governmental human rights organizations to violations of human rights by non-State actors see Clapham (2006) 46–53.

[99] For a further discussion of these so-called 'punishment attacks' see ch 7 below.

3

Early Fumblings with the Convention

Any examination of the role played by the European Convention on Human Rights in the conflict of Northern Ireland has to begin with an account of the origins and content of the Convention and with an outline of the situation prevailing in Northern Ireland at the time the Convention came on the scene. This chapter will then examine the first case taken to Strasbourg that was connected with the conflict in Northern Ireland (it was actually a case taken against the government of the Republic of Ireland) and next look at early attempts from within Northern Ireland itself to have recourse to Convention rights. These were challenges to religious and political discrimination, unacceptable police and army behaviour, and the impact of retrospective legislation.

As with the previous chapter, the story is taken as far as the late 1970s.[1] Many of the developments referred to will be mentioned again in the following nine chapters, where the focus shifts to a right-by-right analysis of the involvement of the European Convention in respect of Northern Ireland's troubles. The current chapter sets the scene for that more detailed analysis. In doing so it aims to convey how, for the first quarter century of its applicability in Northern Ireland, the European Convention was fumbled with rather than wholeheartedly embraced. This fumbling occurred mostly in Strasbourg, where the Convention was still being handled very tentatively regardless of the origins of the cases brought there for consideration, but there was also some clumsiness on the part of the applicants and their legal advisers.

The Convention's origins and content

The main mistake made by non-lawyers—and even some lawyers—in relation to the European Convention on Human Rights is to associate it with what is now called the European Union. In fact the Convention has nothing to do with the European Union and pre-dates its earliest incarnation by several years.[2] The Convention is the child of an altogether different inter-governmental organization, the older and larger

[1] For contemporary assessments of the Convention at that time see Vegleris (1973) ch 6 (Northern Ireland is not mentioned in this assessment); Morrisson (1981), where there is an analysis of whether the Court is predominantly activist or restrained (3–27) and comments are made on disagreements between the Commission and the Court (37–42). An important study of the influence of the Convention across Europe, published in 1983, devoted 10 pages to the UK, but, surprisingly, nothing is made of its specific relevance to the conflict in Northern Ireland: Drzemczewski (1983) 177–87.

[2] The Treaty of Rome, establishing the European Economic Community, was signed in 1957.

grouping called the Council of Europe.[3] This was formed shortly after the end of the Second World War, by a treaty signed in London on 5 May 1949. Ten countries participated in the signing ceremony, the United Kingdom and Ireland being among them.[4] The aim of the Council is set out in the first two paragraphs of Article 1 of the founding treaty:

(a) The aim of the Council of Europe is to achieve a greater unity between its members for the purpose of safeguarding and realizing the ideals and principles which are their common heritage and facilitating their economic and social progress.
(b) This aim shall be pursued through the organs of the Council by discussion of questions of common concern and by agreements and common action in economic, social, cultural, scientific, legal and administrative matters and in the maintenance and further realization of human rights and fundamental freedoms.[5]

One of the first tasks the Council set itself was the drawing up of a human rights document which would do for Europe what the United Nations' Universal Declaration of Human Rights, agreed in 1948, had supposedly done for the world as a whole.[6] Brian Simpson has brilliantly mapped the way in which the European Convention on Human Rights and Fundamental Freedoms emerged from this process,[7] a process which, as Geoffrey Marston has shown, was dominated by lawyers and politicians from the United Kingdom[8] and where the elephant in the room was the impact the document might have on the process of decolonization which various European powers were at that time contemplating. The partition of Ireland did raise its head on a few occasions during the discussions[9] and on at least one of these the President of the meeting had to remind the representative of Ireland to keep to the point.[10] On one reading of the *travaux préparatoires*, the negotiations were marked by a polarity between those who wanted the Convention to be simply a guarantee against the threats of fascism and communism and those who were prepared to see it preventing violations of human rights within democracies,[11] but it is abundantly clear that the latter have long since won the day.[12]

[3] For an early account of the development of the Convention by the Council see Robertson (1956) ch 9.

[4] The other eight countries were Belgium, Denmark, France, Italy, Luxembourg, the Netherlands, Norway, and Sweden.

[5] Statute of the Council of Europe, ETS No 001. See too Council of Europe (1970) 8–13.

[6] The Council of Europe paid tribute to the work already done by the Legal Committee of the European Movement, whose Rapporteur was Sir David Maxwell Fyfe. The Committee produced a series of recommendations in July 1949, including a proposal for a European Court of Human Rights: Council of Europe (1952) 2–3. For a longer historical study of the concept of human rights see Ishay (2008).

[7] Simpson (2001).

[8] Marston (1993). See too Wicks (2000).

[9] eg, at the 8th sitting of the Council of Europe's Consultative Assembly held on 19 August 1949: *Travaux Préparatoires* (1975) vol 1, 102–6 (Mr Everett), 138–44 (Mr MacEntee), 150–4 (Sir Ronald Ross).

[10] ibid, 144. 'We must not allow every debate to become the object of a dispute between the Representatives of Ireland and Great Britain.'

[11] Nicol (2005).

[12] The European Court itself has stressed on several occasions that the Convention is 'a living instrument'. Happily Strasbourg has not been dogged by the 'originalism' which on occasions has hampered the work of the US Supreme Court.

The Convention was opened for signature, in Rome, on 4 November 1950. Twelve nations signed it on that day but the United Kingdom was the first nation to ratify it, on 8 March 1951, and Ireland was the fifth, on 25 February 1953. It came into force on 3 September 1953, the day on which the tenth ratification occurred.[13] When Ireland ratified the Convention it also declared that it recognized the competence of the European Commission of Human Rights, under what was then Article 25 of the Convention, to receive petitions brought by individuals against the government of Ireland. The United Kingdom, however, did not recognize this right of individual petition until 13 January 1966, and Anthony Lester has argued that the government of the day may not have fully appreciated the significance of what it was doing even then.[14] From the date of ratification, though, either State could initiate what is referred to by the Convention[15] as an inter-State case against any other State Party to the Convention—no prior acceptance of the competence of the European Commission was required for such inter-State applications. The European Commission was the lower of the two bodies created by the Convention for the adjudication of alleged violations of Convention rights.[16] The higher body was the European Court of Human Rights.[17] It could hear cases referred to it by the Commission or by one of the State Parties to the Convention.[18] Again Ireland accepted the jurisdiction of this Court when it ratified the Convention, but the United Kingdom waited a further 15 years before doing so.

Many people have heard of the European Convention on Human Rights but few could actually say what rights it protects and to what extent it does so. In fact its content is very largely restricted to civil and political rights—the 'traditional' civil liberties such as freedom from torture and arbitrary arrest, and the right to a fair trial, free speech, freedom of belief, and freedom of assembly. The government representatives who negotiated the content could not agree on which of the so-called economic and social rights should be included, such as the right to property, education, health care, and employment. In the end a compromise was reached whereby some of these latter rights were included under the guise of civil and political rights, other such rights were included in add-on Protocols which governments could sign and ratify if they so wished, and remaining economic and social rights were left to be dealt with by a wholly separate treaty. Thus, workers' rights were to some extent protected by provisions in the Convention prohibiting slavery and forced labour and recognizing the

[13] Today the Council of Europe comprises 47 member States, all of which have ratified the Convention on Human Rights. The only European country which is not a member is Belarus.

[14] Lester (1998). It is worth noting that Italy did not accept the right of individual petition until 1973, and France did not even ratify the Convention until 1975 (eventually accepting the right of individual petition in 1981).

[15] Art 24 (now Art 33).

[16] Arts 19–37. For a summary of the Commission's activities up to the end of 1968, see Council of Europe (1970) 266–76. For a perspective on the Commission by an early Registrar of the Court, see Golsong (1986–7).

[17] Arts 38–56. See Council of Europe (1970) 277–81. As Nicol has made clear, the creation of such a court was controversial for those involved in the negotiations around the Convention: Nicol (2005) 164–7. See too Council of Europe (1952) 23–30 and Arold (2007) ch 2. For later overviews of the Court's status and achievements see Walsh (1986–7) and Gearty (1993).

[18] Art 44.

right to form and join trade unions.[19] The right to have one's property protected, and the right to education, were relegated to what became Protocol 1 to the Convention,[20] which was opened for signature on 20 March 1952 and entered into force for those countries which had ratified it on 18 May 1954 (just eight months or so after the Convention itself entered into force).[21] But rights of workers such as the right to a fair remuneration sufficient for a decent standard of living, or the right of everyone to benefit from social welfare services, were enshrined instead in what became the European Social Charter, not opened for signature until 18 October 1961 and not in force for those countries which ratified it until 26 February 1965.[22] However, neither that Charter nor the European Convention protected what are sometimes called 'third generation rights', such as the right to a clean environment or the right to a power-sharing democracy, where, for example, if a society is deeply divided along religious or nationalistic lines power within that society should be shared between the different factions rather than concentrated in one dominant group. The Convention is also silent on the right to self-determination.[23]

As well as having a restricted reach in terms of the rights it protects, the European Convention is restricted in that it qualifies many of those rights by saying that they can be interfered with so long as such interferences are legally provided for (ie 'prescribed by law') and are ones that are necessary in a democratic society in the interests of matters such as national security, public safety, the protection of health or morals, or the protection of the rights and freedoms of others. Some of the rights are defined in limited terms even though no qualifications are then listed; the right to liberty, for example, is not granted to people who are arrested on reasonable suspicion of having committed an offence, and the right to be tried for a criminal offence in public is denied if a court thinks that publicity would prejudice the interests of justice. In addition, all but a few rights in the Convention can be suspended by a government 'in time of war or other public emergency threatening the life of the nation'. By the same provision—Article 15 of the Convention—the measures taken in such circumstances (which are called derogations from the Convention) must be 'strictly required by the exigencies of the situation'. The government must also keep the Secretary General of the Council of Europe informed of the emergency measures it has taken in derogation of the Convention, and why, but the Convention does not actually say that such measures will automatically be in breach of the Convention if no such information is supplied. The wording of Article 15, indeed its very inclusion in the Convention, was heavily influenced by the UK delegates to the committee that drafted the Convention.[24]

19 Arts 4 and 11 respectively.

20 Arts 1 and 2 respectively.

21 The UK ratified on 3 November 1952 and Ireland on 25 February 1953.

22 A Revised Social Charter was agreed in 1996, but not all State Parties to the 1961 Charter (the UK among them) have ratified the Revised Charter.

23 On which, in a Northern Ireland context, see Guelke (1985) and Lee (1995). By way of contrast, Art 1 of each of the two UN Covenants of 1966 (on Civil and Political Rights and on Economic, Social and Cultural Rights) provides: 'All peoples have the right of self-determination. By virtue of that right they freely determine their political status and freely pursue their economic, social and cultural development.'

24 Hartman (1981) 4–5.

The Convention's limitations

There are yet further points to be made about the limitations of the Convention. First, it focuses on the rights of individuals rather than on those of groups or minorities. While there is a provision on the right to be free from discrimination,[25] this is worded in terms which require such discrimination to be linked to the way in which other rights and freedoms listed in the Convention are being protected; it does not confer a more general right to equality before, and equal protection of, the law (such as is found in Article 7 of the Universal Declaration of Human Rights[26]); and it does not allow, say, a religious or political grouping to claim that the way power and economic prosperity are distributed in their country is discriminatory. Unlike the UN Covenant on Civil and Political Rights, there are no rights expressly conferred on ethnic, religious, or linguistic minorities as such.[27]

Second, a complaint can be taken under the Convention only against a State, not against a non-State actor which may have violated human rights. This means that criminals, 'freedom fighting organizations', 'community defence organizations', the media, churches, businesses, companies, trades unions, community groups, and voluntary organizations are all immune from being directly pursued at Strasbourg. A convicted murderer, for example, may complain about a breach of his or her rights when appealing against his or her conviction or complaining about the treatment he or she has received while in prison, but the family of the victim of that murderer cannot complain about the violation of their loved one's rights by the murderer. In such situations the issue can get to the European Court only indirectly, if the representatives of the victim argue that the State has breached their rights by not preventing the murderer from carrying out the crime in the first place or by not properly investigating the killing once it has occurred.

A third restriction within the European Convention is that an individual can have a complaint considered only if he or she (or a personal representative in cases of death or disappearance) can claim to be an actual victim of a human rights violation. A complaint cannot be taken in the abstract alleging that a certain law is inherently in breach of the Convention. And although the Convention requires governments not to hinder in any way the effective exercise of the right of individual petition,[28] in practice governments can do so by restricting the availability of crucial information which might otherwise assist the individual to justify a complaint. There could also be a hindrance in the fact that the legal professionals of the State in question may not be as *au fait* with the Convention as they should be.

[25] Art 14.

[26] 'All are equal before the law and are entitled without any discrimination to equal protection of the law. All are entitled to equal protection against any discrimination in violation of this Declaration and against any incitement to such discrimination.'

[27] Art 27 of that Covenant provides: 'In those States in which ethnic, religious or linguistic minorities exist, persons belonging to such minorities shall not be denied the right, in community with the other members of their group, to enjoy their own culture, to profess and practise their own religion, or to use their own language.'

[28] Art 34, formerly Art 25(1).

Fourth, and crucially, the European Convention explicitly places a number of hurdles in the way of individuals who want to lodge a complaint. These must be successfully negotiated if the complaint is to be considered as 'admissible'. The six most important conditions of admissibility are listed in what is now Article 35:[29]

- the complainant must first have exhausted all domestic remedies within the national legal system where the alleged violation of human rights has occurred;
- no more than six months must have elapsed since the date on which the final decision within the national legal system was taken;
- the complaint must not be anonymous;
- the complaint must not be substantially the same as one that has already been examined by the European Court or by another international procedure;
- the complaint must not be 'an abuse of the right of application'; and
- the complaint must not otherwise be 'manifestly ill-founded', this being a coded expression for a complaint which has little evidence to support it or which is not within the scope of the Convention.

A fairly early study of the way in which the admissibility criteria were handled by the European Commission concluded that:

> Taking into account that ninety-eight per cent of all applications have been rejected so far, it is understandable that it seems to be a broadly accepted view that it is very difficult to force one's way through the extensive system of 'pitfalls' protecting the European protection system or—in a wider sense—the High Contracting Parties.[30]

When assessing the impact of the European Convention it is crucial to bear in mind the built-in limitations to its effectiveness which have been described in the preceding paragraphs. A moment's thought about what these mean in practice leads to a ratcheting down of one's expectations about what the Convention can realistically deliver, especially in a society wracked by complaints of systemic discrimination, civil unrest, and divided national loyalties. This was the kind of society that existed in Northern Ireland when the European Convention became applicable in the area in 1953, as we shall see below. The nature of that society had not changed significantly by the time the right of individual petition became available to people living in Northern Ireland in 1966. In subsequent years the Council of Europe developed a variety of other tools to address conflicts within member States, notably the Convention for the Prevention of Torture and Inhuman or Degrading Treatment or Punishment (agreed in 1987 and in force from 1989), the Charter for Regional or Minority Languages (agreed in 1992 and in force from 1998), the European Commission against Racism and Intolerance (established in 1993 and given greater powers in 2002 and 2005), the European Framework Convention for the Protection of National Minorities (agreed in 1994 and in force from 1998), and the Commissioner for Human Rights (first appointed in 1999). But these were relatively late additions to the Council's toolkit for resolving national conflicts and, even today, none of them can lead to pronouncements by a court that a human

[29] Formerly Arts 26 and 27.
[30] Mikaelsen (1980) 18. For a later but also critical appraisal see Zwart (1994).

right has been violated. The Convention on Human Rights remains the Council of Europe's primary resource for ensuring that, whatever stresses and strains a member State is experiencing, the human rights of the people living there are protected.

The situation in Northern Ireland when the Convention became binding

The IRA was fairly active in Northern Ireland during the period of the Second World War, with several police officers being murdered, but Richard English describes the 1940s as 'quiet by later northern standards'.[31] One IRA man, Tom Williams, was hanged in Crumlin Road prison in 1942 for the murder five months earlier of Patrick Murphy, a Catholic police constable who left behind nine grieving children. Williams is the last member of a paramilitary organization to have been judicially executed in Northern Ireland. After the Second World War the IRA appeared demoralized. As English puts it: 'Their wartime campaigns in Eire, Northern Ireland and Britain alike had produced little progress, and their alliance with the Nazis had proved equally fruitless'.[32]

By 1953, when the European Convention on Human Rights came into force for both the United Kingdom and Ireland (although the UK was not to recognize the right of individual petition for a further 13 years), the main grievances of nationalists in Northern Ireland were based, as alluded to in Chapter 2, on unfair electoral systems, on religious and cultural discrimination, and on one-sided policing. The partition of the island lay at the heart of these grievances, but that was a political reality which no human rights treaty was able to address. More particularly, nationalists were aggrieved at:

- their inability to win any places within the Northern Ireland government because the first-past-the-post electoral system guaranteed a majority of seats to the Protestant-dominated unionist parties;
- a gerrymandered system for electing local councillors, whereby in some areas where the inhabitants were predominantly Catholic the number of seats available for elected representatives was lower than in areas where the inhabitants were predominantly Protestant;
- discrimination against Catholics by local councils when they were exercising their powers to allocate public housing;
- discrimination in the allocation of jobs, with Protestant employers tending to favour Protestant applicants and public authorities doing likewise; and
- suppression of the ideology of Irish nationalism, particularly through the application of the Civil Authorities (Special Powers) Acts (NI) 1922–43, and through the accommodation of anti-Catholic cultural practices such as parades by members of the Orange Order.[33]

[31] English (2003) 70.

[32] ibid, 71.

[33] The Orange Order, named after the Protestant King William III of Orange who defeated the Catholic King James II of England at the Battle of the Boyne, near Drogheda, in 1690, was formed in 1795.

Despite this list of grievances, however, the first application to reach Strasbourg in connection with the affairs of Northern Ireland did not in fact emanate from Northern Ireland but from the Republic of Ireland, reflecting the fact that the Irish government recognized the right of individual petition from the date the Convention came into force, 1953. Before telling the story of how that application fared it is necessary to explain the background to how the application arose in the first place.

The Republic of Ireland's emergency legislation[34]

In Ireland the potential outbreak of war between the United Kingdom and Germany was viewed by some as an opportunity to create even more problems for the British government. The Irish Republican Army (IRA), an unlawful paramilitary force dedicated to the reunification of Ireland and to the establishment of a socialist republic, therefore resumed its violent activities in 1939,[35] a development which was to prove an early and severe test for the new Irish Constitution, promulgated on 29 December 1937. This Constitution explicitly allows for the constitutionality of legislation to be tested in the courts not just after the legislation has been enacted but also before it has been signed into law by the President. To help deal with the IRA, the Irish Parliament (known in Irish as the *Oireachtas*) passed the Offences against the State Act 1939 and the President signed it into law. Just a year later, however, James Burke, who had been interned under Part VI of the 1939 Act, successfully petitioned the High Court in Dublin through his brother Redmond for a ruling that certain of the Act's provisions were unconstitutional. In what was the first legal action arising under the new Constitution, *The State (Burke) v Lennon and the Attorney General*, Gavan Duffy J held that the Act's conferment upon a minister of the power to order the arrest and detention of a person, whenever the minister was 'satisfied' that the person was engaged in activities prejudicial to the peace, order or security of the State, was unconstitutional because it enabled the minister to act judicially and to administer justice, in breach of the separation of powers doctrine enshrined in Article 6 of the Constitution.[36] The Court therefore issued an order of habeas corpus, requiring Burke's release from custody. The Court also held that internment could not be used against citizens of Ireland, and so, when Britain declared war on Germany on 3 September 1939 and, in response, the Dáil passed the Emergency Powers Act 1939 allowing the government to issue emergency orders authorizing internment, the Act specifically excluded 'natural-born Irish citizens' from its reach.

34 See, generally, Hanlon (2008) esp 157–78, and Ó Longaigh (2006).

35 This was in pursuit of 'The S Plan', on which see O'Ballance (1981) ch 5.

36 [1940] IR 136. Article 6 reads: '(1) All powers of government, legislative, executive and judicial, derive, under God, from the people, whose right it is to designate the rulers of the State and, in final appeal, to decide all questions of national policy, according to the requirements of the common good. (2) These powers of government are exercisable only by or on the authority of the organs of State established by this Constitution.' Davis describes Gavin Duffy J's judgment as a *tour de force*: Davis (2007) 80. He goes on to contrast the position adopted by the US Supreme Court in cases concerning the internment of Japanese citizens (ibid, 80–4). It is also difficult to resist contrasting the decision with that of the House of Lords in *Liversidge v Anderson* [1942] AC 206.

The government tried to appeal the decision in *Burke* to the Supreme Court,[37] but it lost on the preliminary point of whether it had any right of appeal in the first place. The Chief Justice and his colleagues followed the precedents laid down by the House of Lords in both *Cox v Hakes*[38] and *Secretary of State for Home Affairs v O'Brien*,[39] which were to the effect that an order of habeas corpus was a final determination of the illegality of detention and could not be reversed on appeal.[40] On the back of this result 53 internees were immediately released and some say that this facilitated the daring raid by the IRA on the Defence Forces' ammunition reserve in the Magazine Fort in Phoenix Park, Dublin, on 23 December 1939, when over one million rounds of ammunition were stolen.[41] The Irish government then set about drafting new legislation that would comply with the Constitution and satisfy the judges. First, the Emergency Powers (Amendment) Act 1940 was passed, under which President de Valera signed the Emergency Powers (No 20) Order 1940 authorizing internment from the following day, 6 January 1940. The purpose of the 1940 Act was to amend the Emergency Powers Act 1939 so as to make it applicable even to 'natural-born Irish citizens'.[42] The 1940 Act was protected from any challenge to its constitutionality by Article 28.3.3 of the Constitution, which had been amended the previous year[43] to allow the Oireachtas to pass laws infringing constitutional rights not only 'in time of war or armed rebellion' but also during national emergencies arising from a conflict in which Ireland was not a participant (such as the Second World War) but as a result of which the 'vital interests' of the State were affected.[44]

Next, the Emergency Powers (Amendment) Act 1940 was supplemented by the Offences against the State (Amendment) Bill 1940, to allow for more permanent internment provisions. This Bill was to remedy the defective wording of the Offences against the State Act 1939 by making it clear that when a minister authorized internment he or she was exercising an administrative function and not a judicial one. The government secured Parliamentary support for the Amendment Bill and then presented it to the President for signature. This time, to be sure of his ground, President Hyde decided that he should first seek a ruling from the Supreme Court that the law was constitutional, and the Supreme Court did indeed so rule.[45] The most important consequence was that, under Article 34.3.3° of the 1937 Constitution, the provision in question was rendered immune from any future challenge to its constitutionality. The resulting Offences against the State (Amendment) Act 1940 conferred on

[37] [1940] IR 157.

[38] (1890) 15 AC 506.

[39] [1923] AC 603.

[40] The Irish Supreme Court changed its mind on this point nearly 30 years later, in *The State (Browne) v Feran* [1967] IR 147.

[41] Davis (2007) 74–7.

[42] s 2 of the 1940 Act.

[43] By the First Amendment of the Constitution Act 1937.

[44] An emergency had been declared on 2 September 1939, the day before the UK and France declared war on Germany, and it remained in place until 1 September 1976, when a new emergency was declared in relation to the conflict in Northern Ireland.

[45] *In re the Offences against the State (Amendment) Bill 1940* [1940] IR 470. For a detailed analysis of this decision see Hogan (2000).

Ministers of State special powers of detention without trial, but only 'if and whenever and so often as the Government makes and publishes a proclamation declaring that the powers conferred by this Part of this Act are necessary to secure the preservation of public peace and order and that it is expedient that this Part of this Act should come into force immediately'.[46] The actual detention power conferred by the Act[47] allowed a Minister of State, if of the opinion that any particular person was engaged in activities prejudicial to the preservation of public peace and order or to the security of the State, to have that person arrested by the police under a warrant signed by the minister and sealed with his or her official seal. Every person so arrested was to be detained in a prison or other place prescribed by regulations made under Part II of the Act until these ceased to be in force or until released under later provisions in the Act. The word internment was not used in the legislation but that is what it provided for.

The IRA and internment in the Republic

After the end of the Second World War—even though the 'emergency' continued in the South of Ireland—the IRA was quiescent: 'almost as insubstantial as the republic it sought'.[48] It was short of weaponry and ammunition, and schisms were beginning to appear between different wings of the movement.[49] But strategizing went on at some level, with most support being given to action north of the border. But there, too, things were relatively quiet.[50] The IRA killed several police officers during the War years, but it had only about four hundred activists throughout Northern Ireland and its leadership frequently had to be renewed because of successful police operations.[51] But after 1945 the IRA appeared demoralized. As English puts it: 'Their wartime campaigns in Eire, Northern Ireland and Britain alike had produced little progress, and their alliance with the Nazis had proved equally fruitless'.[52] At its convention in 1949, so O'Ballance tells us, the IRA decided to prepare for a campaign of terrorism in Northern Ireland and to abstain from any activity in the Republic (as the Irish Free State had by then become).[53] It took considerable time to bring its campaign to a state of readiness, deciding only in December 1956 to engage in actions designed to force the British out of Northern Ireland. Code-named

[46] s 3(2). However, s 3(4) provides that a government proclamation bringing into force the special powers of detention may be annulled at any time by a simple resolution of the Lower House of the Irish Parliament (Dáil Éireann).

[47] s 4.

[48] Bishop and Mallie (1987) 36–7.

[49] English (2003) 71–3; Moloney (2002) 48–51.

[50] English (2003) 70.

[51] O'Ballance (1981) 67–9.

[52] English (2003) 71.

[53] O'Ballance (1981) 73. The Irish Parliament's Republic of Ireland Act 1948 came into effect on 21 January 1949, 30 years to the day since the Declaration of the Irish Republic by the First Dáil (the Lower House of the *Oireachtas*). The UK's Ireland Act 1949, although not given the Royal Assent until 2 June 1949, was deemed to have had effect from 18 April 1949: s 7(3).

Operation Harvest, the campaign largely took the form of incursions from the Republic of Ireland into Northern Ireland by armed units intent on attacking British army depots, police stations, or civil service offices.[54] The government of Northern Ireland, under a regulation introduced on 15 December 1956[55] and untrammelled by any of the constitutional difficulties which the Irish government had encountered during the Second World War, immediately began authorizing the internment of people suspected of being sympathetic to the IRA's campaign. The Irish police also reacted strongly, arresting many leading republicans in their part of the island. Aware that such a hardline approach was attracting some criticism within the population and that, initially at least, there was substantial popular support for the raids into the north, the Irish government's political opponents tabled a censure motion in the Irish Parliament. This was successful, and the coalition government headed by Taoiseach John Costello fell.[56] Ironically, the Fianna Fail government which was elected at the ensuing general election in March 1957, presided over by Eamon de Valera, was prepared to adopt an even tougher line against the extremists than its predecessor.

On 8 July 1957, in reaction to the IRA's murder of a policeman in Northern Ireland a few days earlier, the Irish Minister for Justice followed the lead of his Northern Ireland counterpart and introduced internment in the Republic of Ireland by invoking the special powers of arrest and detention allowed for by the Offences against the State (Amendment) Act 1940.[57] These powers had been revoked by the government shortly after the conclusion of the Second World War and had not been reinvoked since then. The principal difference between the position in the early 1940s and that in the mid-1950s was that by the latter time the European Convention on Human Rights had come into force and Ireland had to ensure that its laws complied with the Convention's requirements. Thus, on 20 July 1957 the Irish Minister for External Affairs wrote to the Secretary General of the Council of Europe informing him of developments in Ireland and adding:

> Insofar as the bringing into operation of Part II of the [1940] Act, which confers special powers of arrest and detention, may involve any derogation from the obligations imposed by the Convention for the Protection of Human Rights and Fundamental Freedoms, I have the honour to request you to be good enough to regard this letter as informing you accordingly, in compliance with Article 15(3) of the Convention.

The letter also indicated that detention of persons under these new powers was considered necessary 'to prevent the commission of offences against public peace and order and to prevent the maintaining of military or armed forces other than those authorised by the Constitution'. It reminded the Secretary General that the 1940 Act provided for the establishment of a Commission to which any detained person could

[54] Flynn (2009).

[55] SR & O 1956/191, issued pursuant to powers conferred on the government by the Civil Authorities (Special Powers) Acts (NI) 1922–43.

[56] In Ireland the Prime Minister is referred to by the Irish word *Taoiseach*.

[57] A Proclamation making the declaration required by s 3(2) of the Act was made on 5 July. Regs were issued on 8 July 1957: Offences against the State (Amendment) Act 1940 (Detention) Regs 1957 (SI 146).

appeal.[58] If the Commission reported that no reasonable grounds existed for the continued detention of any person who had appealed to it, that person would have to be released with all convenient speed.

It was the use of internment in the Republic of Ireland which was to present the first challenge to the ability of the European Convention on Human Rights to play a part in managing the conflict relating to the status of Northern Ireland. As later chapters of this book make clear, and as others such as Connelly[59] and Ní Aoláin and Gross[60] have argued elsewhere, the case of *Lawless v Ireland*,[61] the first case ever to be decided by the European Court of Human Rights, left a deep and not entirely beneficent impact on the jurisprudence subsequently emanating from Strasbourg. One prominent commentator has even suggested the case resulted in a miscarriage of justice.[62] To appreciate its significance we need to remember the context within which the decision was taken, both in Ireland and in Strasbourg.

Lawless v Ireland

Gerry Lawless[63] was a builder's labourer who, by his own admission, joined the IRA in 1956 when he was aged 20. After being acquitted later that year of being in possession of weapons which he conceded were for use in fighting the British occupiers of Ireland, he was found guilty the following year of being in possession of incriminating documents. A few weeks after serving a month's imprisonment for that offence he was rearrested at Dun Laoghaire, a town south of Dublin, while seeking to board a ferry to England and two days later he was detained under the internment provisions of the 1940 Act at the Curragh military camp, also south of Dublin. In August 1957 he was offered release in exchange for a written undertaking 'to respect the Constitution and laws of Ireland' and not to 'be a member of or assist any organization which is an unlawful organization under the Offences against the State Act, 1939', but he refused to give such an undertaking. In September he applied to the Detention Commission to have his case reviewed, but that review was put on hold when he also sought a remedy from the courts on a habeas corpus application. Both the High Court and, on appeal, the Supreme Court, rejected the application,[64]

[58] s 8. The Commission was to consist of three persons, appointed by the government, one to be a commissioned officer of the Defence Forces with not less than seven years' service, and each of the others to be a barrister or solicitor of not less than seven years' standing or a judge or former judge of one of the ordinary courts.

[59] Connelly (1997), 189–91 and 207.

[60] Gross and Ní Aoláin (2001).

[61] As we shall see in the next section, the European Commission held by eight to six that Ireland had taken measures that were strictly required by the exigencies of the situation, but the European Court came to the same conclusion unanimously (1979–80) 1 EHRR 15. In this early period of the Convention's history the Court was often more lenient towards States than the Commission was (see eg *Ireland v UK*, discussed in chs 4 and 7 below).

[62] Doolan (2001). This author also claims (at 232) that the Lawless case 'heralded the beginning of the development of a human rights law in Ireland'.

[63] He sometimes used the Irish form of his name, Gearóid Ó Láighléis.

[64] *Re Ó Láighléis* [1960] IR 93.

mainly on the ground, explained above, that Article 34.3.3° prohibited any further challenge to the constitutionality of the relevant provision in the 1940 Act. Then, on 10 December 1957, just a week after the Supreme Court had given the reasons for its judgment, and at the invitation of the country's Attorney General, Gerry Lawless gave a verbal undertaking to the Detention Commission that he would not 'engage in any illegal activities under the Offences against the State Acts, 1939 and 1940'. He was released the following day.

By then, Lawless's lawyers had already sent an application on his behalf to the European Commission of Human Rights in Strasbourg, arguing that his internment was a breach of the European Convention.[65] Not surprisingly, Lawless wanted those proceedings to continue. The Irish government, meanwhile, decided to phase out internment, the last batch of internees being released on 15 March 1959.[66] It took two years for the European Commission of Human Rights to issue its report on the application,[67] and another 18 months before the European Court delivered its judgment. By that time, July 1961, there had been some 450 IRA operations carried out as part of its border campaign. These had resulted in the deaths of six police officers in Northern Ireland and 12 republicans; hundreds of people had been detained North or South of the border, some (in the North) for nearly four years, and about 200 had been convicted of related crimes. Approximately £1 million worth of damage had been caused, and the extra security costs were about £2.5 million.[68] The IRA did not officially call off its campaign until February 1962, eight months after the European Court had published its decision on the internment question.

The two main questions confronting the European Commission and, later, the European Court of Human Rights were, first, was the notice of derogation issued by the Irish government under Article 15 of the Convention justifiable; in other words, was there indeed 'a public emergency threatening the life of the nation'? Second, if the derogation *was* justifiable, were the measures taken under it 'strictly required by the exigencies of the situation'? The Commission's report on these two issues (and on some subsidiary ones) ran to 200 pages,[69] while the European Court actually issued

[65] One of the counsel representing Gerry Lawless was Sean McBride, who had been a prominent leader of the IRA in the 1920s and 1930s. In 1974 he was awarded the Nobel Peace Prize. He was also leader of a political party, Clann na Poblachta, which had been influential in toppling the Costello government in the confidence vote in 1957. See generally Schabas (2007). One of the senior counsel for the Irish government was Brian Walsh, later a distinguished judge of the Supreme Court of Ireland (1961–90) and of the European Court of Human Rights (1980–98).

[66] Doolan (2001) 103–4. During the period in which internment was employed (1957–59) some 206 people were detained: Davis (2007) 106, citing a file from the Taoiseach's Department.

[67] An attempt to arrive at a friendly settlement between the parties in the wake of the Commission's report failed, allegedly because the Irish government objected to Lawless's suggestion that in exercising powers that it considered to be necessary the government was acting in bad faith: Doolan (2001) 125. The Commission referred the case to the Court on 1 April 1960.

[68] Feeney (2002) 208. The author concludes: 'The whole exercise had achieved nothing.' It has to be remembered, moreover, that the vast majority of the incidents recorded took place during 1957; thereafter they tailed off in both frequency and severity. Donohue says that during this period the Northern Ireland government interned 256 men and one woman: Donohue (2001) 57.

[69] App No 332/57, Report of the Commission (19 December 1959). Doolan (2001), at 130, says that the Commission's report 'made monumental legal history' because '[t]his was the first occasion that an

three sets of judgments, the first two dealing with procedural issues[70] and the third (covering 40 pages) dealing with the substantive merits of the matter.[71] Once it had reported on the application the Commission had a choice whether to refer the case to the Court or straight to the Committee of Ministers. Significantly, it opted for the former route because the case raised issues of fundamental importance to the application of the Convention and the Commission itself had been substantially divided over how to resolve these.

Was there a public emergency in Ireland?

On the first of the two questions mentioned above, after having conducted an investigation into the situation prevailing in Ireland at the time, the European Commission found, by a majority of nine to five, that in July 1957 there *was* 'a public emergency threatening the life of the nation'.[72] Both the Commissioner from Ireland (James Crosbie) and his counterpart from the United Kingdom (Sir Humphrey Waldock) voted with the majority. The nub of the majority's position is apparent from the following extract of the joint opinion of five of the Commissioners:

> When in the present case the IRA made active preparations within the Republic for guerrilla attacks on Northern Ireland and committed armed robberies to obtain explosives for their operations and when, on however minor a scale, cases occurred of apparent attempts by the IRA to threaten judges or witnesses, the situation even within the Republic itself contained some of the elements of a public emergency threatening the life of the nation. When, furthermore, the IRA forces, in defiance of the laws of the Republic and of the repeated injunctions of the lawful Government, launched attack after attack on property and life in the neighbouring territory of Northern Ireland with reckless disregard of the grave consequences that might follow from those attacks, the situation, in our opinion, had clearly become one in regard to which the Government of the Republic might make a determination that a public emergency threatening the life of the nation existed, without being held to have gone beyond the proper limits of a Government's appreciation under Article 15, paragraph 1, of the Convention.[73]

The minority Commissioners focused on the facts that the main activities of the IRA had been carried out in Northern Ireland, not the Republic, that there had been no upset to ordinary life or to the life of the State in the Republic, and that the IRA's campaign was not making it any more likely that there would be a conflict between

international tribunal had adjudicated upon an alleged breach of human rights instigated by an individual against a State that had voluntarily submitted to its jurisdiction'.

[70] The first judgment (1979–80) 1 EHRR 1 (14 November 1960) confirmed that the European Commission has the right to give a copy of its own Report on the case to the persons directly concerned in it (principally the applicant); see Robertson (1960). The second judgment (1979–80) 1 EHRR 13 (7 April 1961) held that the Commission, when giving its observations on the case to the Court, could take into account the views of the applicant. In their own right these were important procedural decisions. They remain laudable even though the third judgment, analysed below, has become so discredited. For a review of the first decade of the operation of the European Convention, and in which the European Court is praised for its careful and thorough handling of the *Lawless* case, see Weil (1963), esp 821.

[71] (1979–80) 1 EHRR 15 (1 July 1961). See Hartman (1981) 4–7.

[72] App No 332/57, Report of the Commission (19 December 1959).

[73] ibid, 90.

the two States of Ireland and the United Kingdom. At the very most, in the words of the Commissioner from West Germany, Professor Süsterhenn, there was a potential or latent emergency, not an actual one.[74]

A year-and-a-half later, however, the European Court, sitting as a bench of seven, unanimously confirmed the majority view in the Commission.[75] The fact that the narrow majority in the Commission became a unanimous majority in the Court turned out not to be an unusual phenomenon, but as this was the first case ever considered by the Court it seems clear that it wished to proceed unitedly and cautiously. The European Convention was still something of an unknown quantity at the time, and the reputation of the Court itself even more so. One can imagine that in the debates amongst the judges there would have been considerable reluctance to send a mixed message to member States of the Council of Europe. They would have wanted to arrive at a clear, reasonably government-friendly, pronouncement. And that is what the Court delivered. In relation to whether there was a public emergency in Ireland the Court said:

> . . . in the general context of Article 15 of the Convention, the natural and customary meaning of the words 'other public emergency threatening the life of the nation' is sufficiently clear; . . . they refer to an exceptional situation of crisis or emergency which affects the whole population and constitutes a threat to the organised life of the community of which the State is composed; . . . the existence at the time of a 'public emergency threatening the life of the nation' was reasonably deduced by the Irish Government from a combination of several factors, namely: in the first place, the existence in the territory of the Republic of Ireland of a secret army engaged in unconstitutional activities and using violence to attain its purposes; secondly, the fact that this army was also operating outside the territory of the State, thus seriously jeopardising the relations of the Republic of Ireland with its neighbour; thirdly, the steady and alarming increase in terrorist activities from the autumn of 1956 and throughout the first half of 1957; . . . the homicidal ambush on the night 3rd to 4th July 1957 in the territory of Northern Ireland near the border had brought to light, just before 12th July—a date, which, for historical reasons is particularly critical for the preservation of public peace and order[76]—the imminent danger to the nation caused by the continuance of unlawful activities in Northern Ireland by the IRA and various associated groups, operating from the territory of the Republic of Ireland . . .[77]

It can be plausibly argued that the European Court too readily accepted that the Irish government was justified in derogating from the European Convention.[78] The Court failed to impose tough enough preconditions on the right to derogate and

[74] ibid, 101.

[75] For contemporaneous comments on the decision see Robertson (1960), O'Higgins (1962), Porter (1963). Doolan (2001) has written an entire book about the case. See too Maguire (2004).

[76] 12 July is the date in 1690 when the Protestant King William III's forces defeated the Catholic King James II's troops at the Battle of the Boyne near Drogheda in County Louth.

[77] (1979–80) 1 EHRR 15, paras 28–30. The Court comprised seven judges, including René Cassin of France as President and Richard McGonigal as the judge from Ireland.

[78] At the hearings on 3 and 4 October 1960 the Irish government reminded the Court that its attitude to derogations could influence States when they were deciding whether to accept the optional jurisdiction of the Court and the right of individual petition.

did not consider alternative standards of scrutiny.[79] It affirmed that the crisis or emergency had to affect 'the whole population' and constitute a threat 'to the organised life of the community of which the State is composed', but there does not seem to have been hard evidence produced to the Court that satisfied these preconditions as regards the situation in Ireland. Indeed at one point the Court admitted that the IRA and its splinter groups 'operated mainly in Northern Ireland, their activities in the Republic of Ireland being virtually limited to the preparation of armed raids across the border'.[80] The Court's approach sent a message to other States, including the United Kingdom, that they retained considerable discretion to develop anti-terrorist laws in whatever ways they themselves thought appropriate.[81] These laws could be challenged in the national courts but if the nation in question, like the United Kingdom, did not confer any power on the national courts to invalidate Parliamentary legislation on the ground that it was unconstitutional, there was no available remedy for people whose human rights were violated by the laws. Even today, when the Human Rights Act 1998 confers a power on higher courts in the United Kingdom to declare primary legislation to be incompatible with European Convention rights, there is still a great reluctance on the part of senior judges to apply a stricter test than that laid down in *Lawless v Ireland* when considering what freedom of action the government of the day enjoys.[82] The legacy of the *Lawless* decision remains a considerable blemish on the face of human rights law throughout Europe and is the principal reason for continuing to doubt the Convention's ability to operate as an effective conflict-regulating tool in societies experiencing serious public disorder.

It should be noted in passing that section 35 of the Offences against the State Act 1939 provides that Part V of that Act (which establishes the Special Criminal Court in Dublin) is to come into force by means of a proclamation by the government made when it is satisfied that the ordinary courts are inadequate to secure the effective administration of justice and the preservation of public peace and order. After the outbreak of the conflict in Northern Ireland in the late 1960s the Irish government made such a proclamation in 1972. It is still in force.

Were the measures taken in Ireland strictly required?

As to whether the measures taken by the Irish government were 'strictly required by the exigencies of the situation', the European Commission in the *Lawless* case was again not as definite as the Court in its conclusions. By eight votes to six the Commission

[79] Hartman (1981) 26. Porter, however, thought that the balance struck by the Court was 'quite reasonable': Porter (1963) 82.

[80] ibid, para 36.

[81] Hull (1976) 233, commenting on *Lawless v Ireland* and writing before the European Commission and Court issued their decisions in *Ireland v UK*, says 'the European Convention would seem to provide Britain with a legal justification for its manifestly inhumane acts and actions... Indeed, it would be surprising, in light of the *Lawless Case*, if Article 15 were not interpreted by the European Commission or European Court to permit derogation from the prescriptions of Articles 5 and 6 of the European Convention.'

[82] *A v Secretary of State for the Home Department* [2005] 2 AC 68. See further ch 4 below.

found that the measures *were* strictly required. Commissioner Erim (from Turkey) had earlier voted in favour of holding that the derogation notice was justifiable, but he switched to the minority camp when considering whether the measures taken were strictly necessary. The minority Commissioners expressed the view that the ordinary criminal law could have been used to deal with the internees. Even Sir Humphrey Waldock, who gave a separate opinion agreeing with the majority, was of the view that the Irish government had not established that Special Criminal Courts set up under the Offences against the State Act 1939 could not have dealt effectively with persons suspected of IRA activities[83] and he noted the contradiction between having recourse to internment for IRA 'desperadoes' and at the same time offering to set those internees free merely on the basis of a verbal undertaking as to their future conduct.[84]

The seven judges in the European Court, however, had fewer qualms about giving their *imprimatur* to Ireland's policy and practice of internment. In essence they gave five reasons for unanimously approving what Ireland had done.[85] First, 'the application of the ordinary law had proved unable to check the growing danger which threatened the Republic of Ireland'. Second, the ordinary criminal courts, and even the special criminal courts or military courts provided for by the Offences against the State Act 1939, could not suffice to restore peace and order. Third, 'the amassing of the necessary evidence to convict persons involved in activities of the IRA and its splinter groups was meeting with great difficulties caused by the military, secret and terrorist character of those groups and the fear they created among the population'. Fourth, 'the fact that these groups operated mainly in Northern Ireland, their activities in the Republic of Ireland being virtually limited to the preparation of armed raids across the border was an additional impediment to the gathering of sufficient evidence'. Fifth, 'the sealing of the border would have had extremely serious repercussions on the population as a whole, beyond the extent required by the exigencies of the emergency'. The European Court's judgment comes close to suggesting that the Irish government had no alternative to act as it did because the ordinary laws were so ineffective, but this is surely to miss a step in the reasoning: had the government actually demonstrated that it had fully considered other 'ordinary' measures short of internment as a way of remedying the inadequacies of the ordinary law?

The European Court added that the 1940 Act was subject to four different safeguards designed to prevent abuses in the operation of the system of administrative detention.[86] First, the Act was subject to constant supervision by Parliament, which 'not only received precise details of its enforcement at regular intervals but could also at any time, by a Resolution, annul the Government's Proclamation which had brought the Act into force'. Second, the 1940 Act provided for the establishment of

[83] App 332/57, Report of the Commission (19 December 1959) 126.

[84] ibid, 133. He added (133–4): 'If the Government considered that action of that kind would suffice to deal with the emergency, it may reasonably be asked whether those men could not equally have been dealt with by being brought before a judge and given the alternative of either entering into a bond to be of good behaviour or remaining in detention by order of the Court—a procedure more consistent with the Convention.'

[85] (1979–80) 1 EHRR 15, 'The Law', para 36. See too O'Boyle (1977a) 178–84.

[86] ibid, para 37.

a Detention Commission and the opinion of this Commission, if favourable to the detainee's release, was binding upon the government. Third, 'the ordinary courts could themselves compel the Detention Commission to carry out its functions'. Fourth, the government had publicly announced that it 'would release any person detained who gave an undertaking to respect the Constitution and the Law and not to engage in any illegal activity, and... the wording of this undertaking was later altered to one which merely required that the person detained would undertake to observe the law and refrain from activities contrary to the 1940 Act'; moreover, persons arrested were informed immediately after their arrest that they would be released following the giving of such an undertaking. In short, the European Court thought that the Irish government had acted reasonably in resorting to internment in the face of a grave threat.[87] As O'Ballance remarks, had the decision gone the other way, 'there would have had to be drastic rethinking in regard to this particular anti-terrorist measure in the Irish Republic, Britain, Northern Ireland, and perhaps elsewhere'.[88]

The detention of persons suspected of terrorist offences in Northern Ireland is an issue which has come before the European Commission and European Court of Human Rights on numerous subsequent occasions, although always, of course, in cases brought against the United Kingdom, not Ireland. Sometimes it was the maximum permitted length of the detention that was challenged, at other times it was the lack of access to legal advice during detention, the conditions in which detainees were held, or the fact that remaining silent in the face of police questioning could be taken as evidence weighing against the detainee. Chapters 4 to 8 of this book provide many examples of the relevant case law, but by and large the rulings of the Commission and Court do not suggest that those bodies saw the European Convention as a means of restricting the actions of governments and their security forces when arresting and confining terrorist suspects. The trend, certainly throughout the 1970s and 1980s, was to allow governments a considerable amount of discretion as to how best to deal with the problem of terrorism. Countries such as Germany, Italy, and Spain also experienced numerous terrorist incidents during this period and the Strasbourg organs were no more fastidious in controlling the actions of those countries' authorities than they were in the case of Ireland or the United Kingdom.[89] However, this was partly because the domestic courts of Germany, Italy and Spain sometimes applied standards derived from their own national constitutions that were more stringent than those contained within the European Convention.

Access by individuals to the European Court

The *Lawless* case was decided at a time when the United Kingdom had not yet accepted the right of individual petition to Strasbourg. That did not occur until 1966. The decision to allow such petitions was taken, it seems, by the then Prime Minister, Harold

[87] It is interesting to note that the Irish government did not rely upon the argument that the use of internment had proved *effective* in countering the IRA's border campaign.

[88] O'Ballance (1981) 88.

[89] See Vercher (1992), which very expertly compares and contrasts the emergency laws in Northern Ireland with those adopted in Spain, France, Italy, and Germany.

Wilson, without even a Cabinet discussion of the issue.[90] The official papers from the time give no hint that the relevance of the European Convention to the situation in Northern Ireland was taken into account before the decision to accept the right of individual petition was taken. Consultations on the proposal took place with all departments in the British government, but not, apparently, with the government in Northern Ireland.[91] Although there had already been numerous complaints about discrimination against Catholics in Northern Ireland, these had not acquired a high profile in the corridors of power at Whitehall or Westminster. Yet a farsighted analyst might have predicted that the new right of petition would at least be the object of experimentation in Northern Ireland. And so it proved to be.[92] For the time being, however, the orthodox position remained that the rights and freedoms listed in the Convention were already secured by domestic law throughout the whole of the United Kingdom.[93] The Convention was not mentioned in a UK court until 1974, in a case about whether a penal provision in the Immigration Act 1971 should be applied retrospectively or not. The House of Lords held that it should not, citing the Convention in support. Having quoted Article 7, Lord Reid said: 'it is hardly credible that any government department would promote or that Parliament would pass retrospective criminal legislation'.[94]

Under the old Article 48 of the Convention (before it was amended by Protocol 9, which came into force in 1994), once the European Commission of Human Rights had transmitted its report on an application to the Council of Europe's Committee of Ministers, the application could go on to be considered by the European Court of Human Rights (still very much a part-time body at this time) only if it was referred to that Court within three months by (a) the Commission itself, (b) the government of the country which may have first referred the case to the Commission, (c) the government of the country whose national was alleged to be a victim of the alleged human rights abuse, or (d) the government of the country against which the application had been lodged. In practice, the majority of cases were referred by the Commission alone.[95] Note that the applicant him- or herself had no right to refer the application to the European Court. Even though the European Convention had supposedly been established to allow every violation of an individual's human rights to be vindicated, the impossibility of individuals insisting on their applications being looked at by the European Court militated against that ideal and this flaw in the enforcement system was not remedied until 1994, when Protocol 9 came into force.

If cases were not referred to the European Court by one of the bodies authorized to do so, they risked languishing within the Committee of Ministers. Under Article 32 of the Convention as it then stood, decisions could be taken by that Committee

[90] Lester (1998).

[91] ibid. Lester makes no explicit reference to Northern Ireland in his analysis of the contemporary documents.

[92] It was also used immediately by various pressure groups in England: Harlow and Rawlings (1992) 255–7.

[93] See Shawcross (1965), Beddard (1967), Daintith (1968), Duffy (1980), Drzemczewski (1983) 177–87.

[94] *Waddington v Miah* [1974] 1 WLR 683, 694E.

[95] Beddard states that of the 252 cases considered by the Court to the end of 1990, 167 had been referred by the Commission alone, 70 by the Commission and then by the respondent State, 10 by the respondent State and then by the Commission, and only five by the respondent State alone: Beddard (1993) 57.

only if two-thirds of the ministers entitled to sit on the Committee so agreed. If they did so agree that there had been a violation of the Convention but the offending State did not then take satisfactory measures to deal with the violation as prescribed by the Committee, a further decision by a two-thirds majority was required on what effect should be given to the original decision. If no such consensuses could be reached, the matter at issue remained unresolved and all efforts made up to that point to reach a conclusion in Strasbourg were rendered fruitless. This is what occurred, for example, in the notorious case of *East African Asians v United Kingdom*,[96] where 31 UK passport holders complained that they had been denied the right to reside permanently in the United Kingdom. The European Commission found that they had been dealt with in a way which breached Article 3 of the Convention (the right not to be ill-treated),[97] but the case was not referred to the European Court. Instead, after hearing that the UK government had granted the applicants indefinite leave to remain in the country, the Committee of Ministers passed a resolution saying that no further action was required.[98] No opportunity was provided to the European Court to give a more definitive ruling in the area.

Complaints of religious discrimination

Despite the hurdles involved in accessing the European Court, the *Lawless* case brought home to people throughout Ireland that the European Convention on Human Rights could be a tool worth resorting to in order to vindicate a human rights claim, although no-one could have been under any illusion that using the tool would easily lead to a resolution of the difficulties. As early as January 1964, two years before the UK government acknowledged the right of individual petition, an organization called the Campaign for Social Justice (CSJ) was formed, based in Dungannon in County Tyrone in Northern Ireland. The leaders immediately stated that they would be prepared to take their grievances to the European Commission of Human Rights in Strasbourg (and also to the United Nations) if they were unable to achieve change through the use of political arguments and prominent publicity within Northern Ireland itself.[99] The philosophy and activities of the CSJ, and of related civil rights groups in Northern Ireland, have since been chronicled in detail by one of its founders, Dr Conn McCluskey.[100] McCluskey was a general medical practitioner who, together with his wife Patricia, was so shocked by the discriminatory way in which

96 (1981) 3 EHRR 76; 13 Ybk 928; 36 CD 92.

97 (1973) 78A DR 5.

98 See comments by Drzemczewski (1978), who refers to this case as a 'non-decision'. He points out that the Commission sent its report to the Committee of Ministers in March 1974 and that the Committee took until October 1977 before deciding to 'remove the examination of the case from its agenda'.

99 *Belfast Telegraph*, 17 January 1964.

100 McCluskey (1989). He discusses 'The Legal System and the Judiciary' at 41–51. Appendix II in that book reprints the CSJ's 1964 pamphlet 'Why Justice Cannot Be Done', which mainly comprises an exchange of letters between the CSJ and the British Prime Minister at the time, Sir Alec Douglas-Home. This is also available on the website of the CAIN archive at the University of Ulster (<http://www.cain.ulst.ac.uk>). See too Carroll (1973) 47–9; Currie (2004) 49–51.

Dungannon Urban District Council was allocating public housing to those in need—regularly giving preference to Protestants over Catholics—that he organized protest marches on the streets. The McCluskeys had apparently been alerted to the discrimination by the fact that more than one of Dr McCluskey's female patients had committed suicide after falling into despair over their housing conditions.

The CSJ was at this time receiving legal advice from Paddy McGrory, a Belfast solicitor, and it also had the support of Kevin Boyle, a young law lecturer who began teaching at Queen's University in 1966.[101] But Boyle would have been only too aware of the fact that the United Kingdom had not yet recognized the right of individual petition and that therefore any application sent to Strasbourg would be automatically declared inadmissible. He would also have known that one of the preconditions for admissibility was the need to exhaust domestic remedies. It was therefore necessary to consider what domestic remedies might be available. In the early 1960s the legal system of Northern Ireland provided few such remedial opportunities, but this was no different from the position in the legal systems of England and Wales, Scotland, or the Republic of Ireland. At that time the British and Irish common law systems contained very few rules or principles allowing actions or decisions by an arm of the State to be declared illegal. Unlike legal systems on the continent of Europe, which derived their rules and principles from the post-revolutionary codes put in place in France in the early nineteenth century, there was no special 'administrative law' in the United Kingdom or Ireland.[102] Ireland did have a written Constitution which, like the Constitution of the USA,[103] permitted courts to declare State actions and decisions to be unconstitutional, but in the first 25 years or so of the new Irish Constitution's life (from 1937) this 'judicial review' power had been extremely rarely exercised,[104] and the idea that it might be applied in order to uphold human rights claims brought against local or central government was as yet wholly foreign. Even if the courts did flex their muscles in this regard, the Irish government, as we have seen, was not averse to having the Constitution altered so that it could, after all, have its way.[105]

In the United Kingdom the only type of judicial review that was tolerated was when an arm of the State had acted 'ultra vires', that is, beyond the powers directly or indirectly conferred upon it by Parliament. The centrality of the notion of Parliamentary sovereignty was such that any action or decision which could reasonably be justified by reference to primary or secondary legislation was effectively immune from

[101] Boyle later became the first Director of the Human Rights Centre at the National University of Ireland, Galway, and later still Director of the Human Rights Centre at the University of Essex. From 2001–02 he served as Senior Adviser to the then United Nations' High Commissioner for Human Rights, Mary Robinson. He was interviewed for the purposes of this book in October 2008.

[102] This was one of the main features of the British Constitution emphasized by Albert Venn Dicey in his *Law of the Constitution* (1885).

[103] As interpreted by the US Supreme Court in *Marbury v Madison* 5 US 137 (1803).

[104] As in *The State (Burke) v Lennon and the Attorney General* [1940] IR 136; see text at n 36 above. Cf McMahon (1979) 87: 'Up to the early 1960s there were very few attempts by Irish lawyers to study the Constitution as a source of legal rights, and Constitutional arguments were rarely urged upon the courts at all.' McMahon attributes the Irish passivity in part to the influence of the English law tradition, where there is of course no written constitution.

[105] See text at nn 42–47 above.

challenge in a British court. This blinkered approach to judicial review of administrative action was not changed until a group of seminal cases was decided by the House of Lords in the 1960s and early 1970s.[106] One such case, *Ridge v Baldwin*, was decided as early as 14 March 1963, but unfortunately it was mainly concerned with the principle of natural justice, according to which a person had the right to know the accusations being made against him or her, not with the right to be free from discrimination. And when the House of Lords did get the opportunity to deal with a discrimination case arising from Northern Ireland it did not deal with the matter at all progressively. In *McEldowney v Forde*, decided on 18 June 1969 by three votes to two, their Lordships upheld the validity of a Special Powers Act Regulation which allowed the Minister of Home Affairs in Northern Ireland to ban any 'Republican club' without being subject to any judicial control beyond ensuring that he or she was acting in good faith.[107] Harry Calvert, in the course of a trenchantly ironic note on this decision, commented:

> By a vote of 2.5+ to 2.1-, the House of Lords has abolished the doctrine of separation of powers ... What is important, and what ought not be lost under the blanket of any particular impact of the decision, is that the powers of governments have been greatly extended and that the individual is much more vulnerable than we had all fondly imagined. Since the political cliques learned how to control Parliament in the nineteenth century the citizen's only protection against tyranny has been those marvellous be-gowned, be-wigged and fearless freedom-fighters on the Bench. When they start to capitulate, even moderate men may start looking to the streets.[108]

In Northern Ireland there was one possible legal channel for claimants like the CSJ which did not exist in other parts of the United Kingdom or, indeed, in the Republic of Ireland. It was provided by section 5 of the Government of Ireland Act 1920, a provision which had been inserted into that Act with the deliberate aim of ensuring that the devolved Parliaments which were to be set up in Belfast and Dublin could not discriminate on religious lines. In the end, because of the Anglo-Irish Treaty of 1921, the 1920 Act never applied in the southern part of Ireland, but section 5 did come into force for the north. It stated that the Parliament of Northern Ireland could not 'make a law so as either directly or indirectly to ... give a preference, privilege, or advantage, or impose any disability or disadvantage, on account of religious belief or religious or ecclesiastical status'. Brigid Hadfield has demonstrated that not much use was made of section 5 in the years of the Stormont regime[109] and it was probably not successfully invoked as part of the campaign to combat discrimination in the

[106] eg *Ridge v Baldwin* [1964] AC 40; *Padfield v Minister of Agriculture, Fisheries and Food* [1968] AC 997; *Conway v Rimmer* [1968] AC 910; *Anisminic Ltd v Foreign Compensation Commission* [1969] 2 AC 147. For an analysis of these and other cognate cases see Griffith (1993) ch 4. For explanations of the modern law on judicial review in Northern Ireland see Anthony (2008) and Larkin and Scoffield (2007).

[107] [1971] AC 632. The majority comprised Lords Pearson, Guest, and Hodson; the dissenters were Lords Pearce and Diplock. Unusually, the majority in the House did not go along with the (dissenting) view expressed in the Court of Appeal of Northern Ireland by their former colleague in the Lords, Lord MacDermott CJ.

[108] Calvert (1970) 191 and 193.

[109] Hadfield (1989) 78–9.

allocation of public housing because it was directed at laws made by the Parliament of Northern Ireland, not at actions taken by local authorities in purported implementation of those laws. Conn McCluskey confirms that the professional legal advice supplied to the CSJ was discouraging on this point, even though the opinions of Jim McCartney and Harry Calvert in the Faculty of Law at Queen's were more optimistic. In late 1965 Northern Ireland acquired its first State-sponsored legal aid scheme (16 years after England and Wales)[110] and an application was made to that scheme by the CSJ for financial assistance with its case. But, dispiritingly, the application was eventually rejected by the Law Society's Legal Aid Committee because the particular applicant in question[111] was not himself claiming to be a victim of discrimination in the allocation of housing. Had the CSJ been able to persuade such a victim to put his or her head above the parapet (not an easy thing to do in the circumstances), the chances of obtaining legal aid would have been greatly enhanced. The CSJ's experience of the legal system demonstrates all too clearly that justice depends on a great deal more than having good laws in place.

Having failed to obtain redress within the domestic legal system, the CSJ was faced with the prospect of applying directly to Europe and, to get round the difficulty that the United Kingdom had not yet recognized the right of individual petition, it sought refuge in the provision within the European Convention which allows one State Party to the European Convention to raise a complaint against another State Party in relation to violations of human rights occurring within the latter State.[112] On 12 August 1964 representatives of the CSJ met with the Minister for External Affairs[113] and the Attorney General in the Republic of Ireland to discuss whether the Irish government would be prepared to take that step. The government rejected such a proposal, on the ground that to rely on the non-discrimination provision in the Convention, Article 14, an applicant had to show that there had been an interference with one of the other rights and freedoms referred to in Articles 1 to 13. A note of the meeting records the Attorney General's view that:

> There was nothing in Articles 1–13 of the Convention with the possible exception of Article 9, on which a complaint could be founded, and it was very much to be doubted if an effective case for breach of Article 9 could be made out.[114]

In some quarters the view was circulated that, as the United Kingdom had not yet recognized the competence of the European Commission or Court under the then Articles 25 and 46 of the Convention, no inter-State application could in fact be brought against it. But, this was not the case. What was then Article 24[115] allowed any State Party to the Convention to refer to the Commission any alleged breach of the Convention by any other State Party. Such cases could not then be subsequently referred to the European Court unless the alleged offending State had accepted the

[110] Under the Legal Aid and Advice Act (NI) 1965 and the Legal Aid (General) Regs (NI) 1965.
[111] Tony Sheridan.
[112] Art 24, now Art 33.
[113] Frank Aiken.
[114] National Archives, Dublin, 2001/43/1304. Art 9 protects freedom of religion, conscience, and belief.
[115] Now Art 33.

compulsory jurisdiction of the Court under Article 46, but the Commission could certainly express its views on the issues raised. This is exactly what happened when Greece lodged two inter-State applications against the United Kingdom as far back as 1956 and 1957 in relation to the way in which detainees in Cyprus were allegedly dealt with by British security forces.[116]

It was not until January 1966 that it became possible for individual applicants to lodge applications against the United Kingdom in Strasbourg and in 1968 a lawyer named James C Heaney, from Buffalo in the State of New York, the founder and president of the American Congress for Irish Freedom, volunteered to assist with the lodging of applications by persons reflecting the interests of the CSJ. Six applications were lodged more or less simultaneously, between April and July 1968. The applicants were drawn from different parts of Northern Ireland—three from County Tyrone, one from County Fermanagh, one from County Londonderry, and one from Belfast. They alleged that the Special Powers Act and Regulations made under it were in breach of several articles in the European Convention, that arrangements for elections in Northern Ireland were in breach of Article 3 of Protocol 1 to the Convention,[117] and that discrimination by the government of Northern Ireland in relation to housing, employment, education, and other areas of public life were also in breach of several articles in the Convention.

On 2 August 1968 Heaney was granted an interview with the Tánaiste, Ireland's Deputy Prime Minister.[118] Heaney asked if the Irish government would be prepared to fund the applications he had lodged in Strasbourg, but the Tánaiste refused, saying, first, that the applications in Strasbourg might fail because the domestic remedies available through the legal system of Northern Ireland had not been exhausted and, second, that the applications needed to be refocused. A note of the meeting records that, after taking advice from the Attorney General, the Tánaiste told Heaney that he should:

> take up for submission to the Commission of Human Rights in Strasbourg a clear case of discrimination in local electoral matters. He felt that there was a possibility of achieving something in this direction in view of the terms of Article 3 of the First Protocol to the Human Rights Convention and he had been pressing nationalists and other groups in the North for some time to take up such a case. If such a case were taken up by proceeding to exhaust domestic remedies all the funds required would be obtained if an advertisement were inserted in the newspapers.[119]

Heaney let it be known that he thought that following the Tánaiste's advice 'would be a waste of time'. He stressed that '[t]here was a widespread feeling... of lack of interest on the part of the Irish Government in these matters' and he noted, in addition, that '[h]e

[116] On these cases see ch 13 below. For summaries of the seven inter-State applications received by the Commission by the end of 1968, see Council of Europe (1970) 269–71.

[117] This provides: 'The High Contracting Parties undertake to hold free elections at reasonable intervals by secret ballot, under conditions which will ensure the free expression of the opinion of the people in the choice of the legislature.' On this and other early applications, see Hannum and Boyle (1972).

[118] Frank Aiken again.

[119] National Archive, Dublin, 2001/43/1304.

found it impossible to interest attorneys with nationalist sympathies to take up discrimination cases, in case it would appear, that their livelihood might be threatened'.[120]

While the European Commission was considering Heaney's applications, further alleged human rights violations were occurring in Northern Ireland. In January 1969 the Northern Ireland Civil Rights Association (NICRA) lodged an application in Strasbourg, as did six other applicants. NICRA had been formed by people closely associated with CSJ, and others, in order to campaign more broadly for civil (as well as social) rights in Northern Ireland.[121] All alleged that their right to demonstrate had been violated by, for example, the banning of a civil rights march in Derry on 5 October 1968 and the failure to protect people lawfully demonstrating in Armagh on 30 November 1968. The six individual applicants each claimed £10,000 by way of compensation, a very large sum for the time, but NICRA itself was hugely more ambitious, claiming £100,000. These extravagant claims no doubt helped to antagonize the natural opponents of the applicants, namely unionist politicians. One such, the MP for South Belfast Rafton Pounder, was reported by the Belfast Telegraph as considering the applications to be 'quite fatuous'. He spoke pejoratively of the 'mouthings' of the European Court of Human Rights and said its outcomes did not 'amount to a rap'.[122]

It is a great pity that all these applications came to nothing in the end, for the simple reason that the lawyers involved in the cases did not, it would seem, do their job properly. The Yearbooks of the European Convention reveal that there was a series of acrimonious correspondence between the Secretary of the European Commission and James Heaney, the American lawyer initially representing the applicants. The Secretary kept requesting more information from the lawyer and the lawyer kept insisting that his expenses were not being adequately reimbursed by the Commission. Eventually the Commission lost patience with Heaney and declared in December 1969 that it would have no further dealings with him. The applicants then requested a solicitor from the Republic of Ireland, Ciaran McAnally, to take over responsibility for the applications but, although McAnally appeared willing to do this, Heaney continued to make matters difficult by threatening to report McAnally to the Law Society of Ireland for having supposedly enticed away his clients. Applicants in Northern Ireland therefore lacked the kind of tenacious lawyering which Sean McBride and others had been able to employ in the Republic of Ireland (as in the *Lawless* case).

In December 1970 the European Commission signified the end of its patience by declaring that the applications were being struck out of the list because 'the applicants have shown a clear lack of interest in pursuing these applications and, in particular, they have failed to take the action necessary to settle the question of their representation and thereby also failed to make the supplementary submissions which were necessary for the final submission of their applications'.[123] The Commission

120 ibid.

121 See generally Purdie (1990) ch 4.

122 30 December 1968.

123 *A and others v UK* (App No 3625 and others), (1970) Ybk 340, 434. A chronology of the proceedings and exchange of correspondence is set out at 358–86.

was fully aware that some of the allegations made by the applicants 'raise problems under the Convention which might extend beyond the interests of the particular applicants and therefore might call for a further examination irrespective of the lack of interest shown by the applicants in the maintenance of their application', but it concluded that, without more precise information from the applicants as regards both the facts alleged and the legal issues involved, it 'cannot adequately continue its examination of these applications even if issues of a general character affecting the observance of the Convention may possibly be involved'.[124] Two-and-a-half years of effort had been wasted. And, even though it may not have been the fault of the organs in Strasbourg, the reputation of the Convention for ensuring that human rights were vindicated took a severe blow.

Bernadette Devlin v United Kingdom

However, just before the European Commission gave up on the CSJ and NICRA applicants, another application was lodged in Strasbourg, this time by the young and feisty Westminster MP for Mid-Ulster, Bernadette Devlin.[125] Interestingly, she chose to be represented by a firm of solicitors in London. In 1969 Ms Devlin had been elected as the youngest ever female MP. In the same year she was convicted in a magistrates' court of indulging in riotous behaviour and of inciting others to commit such behaviour, and was sentenced to six months' imprisonment, the maximum sentence for those offences at that time. Bernadette Devlin had allegedly urged people to set up barricades against the police who were trying to enter the Bogside area of Derry to keep the peace. Her defence was that she was merely trying to prevent illegal actions by the police because past experience had caused her to believe that the police would commit illegal actions if they were given free rein to go where they liked. She wanted to call up to 50 witnesses to support the reasonableness of her belief but the Resident Magistrate would not allow her to do so. On appeal, the Court of Appeal was equally dismissive,[126] and it refused to certify that there was a point of law of general public importance involved, thereby denying Bernadette Devlin the opportunity of applying for permission to appeal to the House of Lords.[127]

After the European Commission received Bernadette Devlin's application it issued a decision within less than four months, but again it declared all aspects of the application

[124] ibid, 434. For contemporaneous comments by key players see Hannum and Boyle (1972).

[125] Now Bernadette McAliskey.

[126] *Devlin v Armstrong* [1971] NI 13 (Lord MacDermott CJ; Curran and McVeigh LJJ). Bernadette Devlin was represented by Sir Dingle Foot QC and Montague Solomon; the State was represented by Brian Hutton QC and Robert Carswell, two future Lord Chief Justices of Northern Ireland and Lords of Appeal.

[127] A comparable point did come before the Lords a generation later, when a protestor in England argued that she had a defence to a charge of criminal damage in that the equipment she had damaged would otherwise have been used in the commission of the international crime of aggression. The Lords dismissed the argument because no such crime of aggression had yet been made part of domestic UK law and it was not within the court's power to make it so: *R v Jones (Margaret)* [2006] UKHL 16, [2007] 1 AC 136.

to be inadmissible.[128] The Commissioners unanimously pointed out that the European Convention, as interpreted to date by the Commission and Court, gave wide latitude to the national authorities of each member State to decide what evidence could or could not be admitted in a trial. Even though Article 6(3)(d) of the Convention expressly conferred the right to 'obtain the attendance and examination of witnesses on [her] behalf', there had been no breach of this right on the facts. No doubt lurking behind the Commission's reasoning was the idea that, even if Bernadette Devlin's witnesses had been heard, their evidence would not have been helpful in deciding whether on the occasion in question Devlin was rioting or inciting rioting. Nor was the Commission impressed by Devlin's allegation that the courts in Northern Ireland were biased against her. She had provided no evidence to substantiate that claim. Her allegation of bias was based solely on the contention that the interpretation of domestic law expressed in the judgment of the Court of Appeal was manifestly wrong, but the Commission stressed that 'it is not competent to consider alleged errors of law or fact committed by domestic courts unless it finds that such errors might have involved a violation of any of the rights and freedoms mentioned in the Convention'.[129] Bernadette Devlin's lawyers had conceded that the evidence she wanted to adduce was only relevant if, having been admitted, it would have supported a valid line of defence.

The Commission's decision to declare the application inadmissible is an early example of the enforcement organs in Strasbourg emphasizing that their role is not to act as a further instance of appeal in relation to a conviction in a domestic legal system: it has a much broader, standard-setting, function. The decision also illustrates the reality that the Strasbourg organs are unwilling to undermine deep-seated traditions in a State's legal system. They shy away from suggesting that a State does not offer a wide enough range of defences to persons charged with criminal offences and they leave the evaluation of evidence almost entirely to the domestic courts.

Miscellaneous complaints

Despite the Commission's bad experience with Heaney in the CSJ-NICRA applications, it accepted him as the legal representative in a series of later applications sent to Strasbourg in 1971 and 1972,[130] although it did cross swords with him again and made it clear that it did not think the way he presented the applications was at all helpful. These applications raised several novel issues. First, whether the Northern Ireland Act 1972, which in response to a decision of the Divisional Court in Northern Ireland[131] had retrospectively legitimized conduct which that court had found to be

[128] App No 4607/70; (1971) Ybk 634; 37 CD 146 (decision of 3 February 1971).

[129] (1971) Ybk, 634, 660.

[130] App Nos 5155/71 *(McMillen v UK, No 1)*, 5459/72 *(McMillen v UK, No 2)*, 5470/72 *(McMillen v UK, No 3)*, 5727/72 *(Montgomery v UK)*, 5744/72 (*Clark v UK*), and 5857/72 (*McPhillip v UK*).

[131] *R (Hume) v Londonderry Justices* [1972] NI 91. For reminiscences by counsel for the government in this case, giving reassurances that the British government did not influence judges in Northern Ireland, see Carswell (1999) 251–2.

illegal since 1921, was in breach of Article 7 of the European Convention, the article which states that no-one can be punished for conduct that was not unlawful at the time when it took place but had been made so later. The Commission declared these applications to be inadmissible because the applicants could not show that they had been victims of the legislation. And if they had been convicted for breaching regulations which had later been held to be illegal, Parliament was still free to declare them to have been legal all along, without violating Article 7. In addition, as non-victims, the applicants could not challenge *in abstracto* the compatibility of a piece of legislation with the Convention.[132]

The second issue raised by these new applications was whether the Special Powers Act in its entirety, and the overall conduct of the security forces in Northern Ireland, were in breach of the Convention. Not surprisingly these complaints were also declared inadmissible because the particular applicant[133] had adduced no specific evidence showing that he himself was a victim of the Act or of the security forces' behaviour and such unspecific allegations could not otherwise be probed in the absence of supporting evidence. Several other allegations relating to detention made by this group of applicants overlapped with those made in the inter-State application lodged by the Irish government (discussed in Chapters 4 and 7 below) and the Commission therefore decided to adjourn further consideration of those allegations until after *Ireland v United Kingdom* had been concluded. On 12 July 1978 it declared them to be inadmissible because in the inter-State decision six months earlier the European Court had held that the detentions in question were justified on the basis of the public emergency threatening the life of the nation at the time.[134]

Two further issues raised by these applicants but not mirrored in the inter-State case were also initially adjourned by the Commission. One was that they had been the victims of discrimination under Article 14 of the Convention because of the way in which public housing had been allocated and access to employment in the public sector had been restricted; the other was that their right to free elections under Article 3 of Protocol 1 had been violated because of the rules on eligibility for voting, the gerrymandering of constituencies, and the small number of MPs allowed to be elected to Westminster from Northern Ireland (at the time there were just 12). The UK government staunchly resisted these claims, arguing that Article 14 was not applicable because it applied only to discriminatory allocation of Convention rights and the rights to housing and employment were not amongst those rights, and that Article 3 of Protocol 1 was not applicable because it did not relate to local government elections and as regards regional and national elections States enjoyed a margin of appreciation as to how they made arrangements for the number of representatives to be elected. On 12 July 1976 the Commission declared the applications to be inadmissible in so far as they alleged a violation of Article 3 of Protocol 1, on the ground that, as the UK

[132] For further discussion of Art 7 see ch 8 below.

[133] Mr McMillen.

[134] Reported under both *MM v UK* and *X, Y and Z v UK*, 14 DR 5 (App Nos 5155/71, 5727/72, 5744/72, 5857/72).

government had argued, the word 'legislature' in that provision was not intended to cover bodies with as few law-making powers as local councils in Northern Ireland.[135] Once the decision was taken that Article 3 of Protocol 1 did not apply, the claim under Article 14 of the Convention, being parasitic upon it, fell away too.

Finally, a complaint by the applicant named McMillen that his correspondence with his legal representative, James Heaney, was being unduly interfered with by the State was also declared inadmissible.[136] The Commission found no evidence that any correspondence had been stopped or the contents deleted or otherwise tampered with. Also, the opening and reading of the correspondence was authorized under regulation 13(2) of the Special Powers Act Regulations, which said that no 'communications may be sent or received by a person interned under the regulations except such as have been examined and passed' by the competent officer. In the alarmingly broad words of the Commission: 'Taking into account the reasons for the first applicant's internment, the Commission further finds that the examination of this correspondence was fully justified "in the interests of national security" or "for the prevention of disorder or crime" within the meaning of Article 8(2).'

Conclusion

Early applications to Strasbourg from Northern Ireland seem to have failed largely because the claims were not formulated and managed carefully enough. Given the youthfulness of the institutions being applied to, there was understandably a degree of uncertainty as to what would or would not pass muster in Strasbourg. Looking back, one might still have hoped that convincing claims by deserving applicants could have been made out. Lawyers and non-lawyers alike in Northern Ireland must have been disillusioned at the apparent powerlessness of the European Convention to eliminate any of the main grievances which were being so commonly experienced in their midst. Boyle, Hadden, and Hillyard, writing in 1974, go some way towards explaining why the domestic legal system of Northern Ireland was failing the people who lived there,[137] but they might also have stressed the apparent uselessness of the European Convention at the same time.[138]

One of the few positive points that can be drawn from the catalogue of failed applications by individuals and organizations considered in this chapter is that they did not relate to claims of ill-treatment while in police or army custody. It was applications alleging breaches of Article 3 of the Convention which first fared well in Strasbourg, thereby indicating that even if the European Commission and Court

135 Reported under *X v UK*, 6 DR 13 (App Nos 5155/71, 5727/72, 5744/72, 5857/72).

136 Reported under *X v UK*, 40 CD 7 (App No 5459/72; 23 March 1972).

137 Boyle, Hadden, and Hillyard (1974) ch 2 ('Civil Rights: The Failure of Law and Lawyers'). Cf the operation of the 'collective legal conscience' at a much later period in the conflict: McEvoy and Rebouche (2007) 284–92.

138 In his long and detailed analysis of the legal aspects of the troubles in Northern Ireland up to 1978, Yale professor Joseph Bishop mentions the Convention only at the very end, when he notes that some have talked of it becoming the basis for a Bill of Rights for Northern Ireland: Bishop (1978) 200.

were proceeding tentatively as regards 'lesser' rights, they were prepared to be more strict when examining allegations of alleged torture or ill-treatment.[139] The story of how those allegations came to be vindicated in Strasbourg, and the consequences of that vindication for law and policy in Northern Ireland, is told in Chapter 7. Before coming to that, however, we need to examine in Chapters 4 to 6 the efforts made to utilize the European Convention as a tool for challenging the draconian laws enacted to deprive people of their liberty in Northern Ireland. It was partly lessons learned from those efforts that led to greater success with applications concerning ill-treatment.

[139] As early as 1972 informed commentators were seeing Art 3 as key: Hannum and Boyle (1972) 339. These authors also made several recommendations as to how the European Convention system could be improved (348).

4

Internment and Restrictions on Movement

We learned in Chapter 3 that the very first case to come before the European Court of Human Rights concerned the practice of internment. Sadly, in *Lawless v Ireland* the European Court concluded that 'in the circumstances prevailing in Ireland at the time' indefinite detention without trial was compatible with the Convention. In this chapter we will examine the use of internment in Northern Ireland, as well as looking at three other powers which interfered with people's freedom of movement to, from, and within Northern Ireland during the conflict there—port powers, powers to stop and question, and powers to issue exclusion orders.

The practice of internment in Northern Ireland

The mechanics of the internment policy used from 1971 to 1975 in Northern Ireland are worth examining because they provide an insight into what kinds of measures the European Court deems necessary and proportionate when they are taken to deal with a public emergency threatening the life of the nation.[1] Internment was invoked by the Minister of Home Affairs of Northern Ireland in exercise of a power vested in him by regulations issued under the Civil Authorities (Special Powers) Acts (NI) 1922–43.[2] The man in question, Brian Faulkner, who was also Prime Minister of Northern Ireland at the time, later explained in his memoirs why the decision was taken to exercise the power on 9 August 1971.[3] He reckoned that a consensus had developed among his security advisers around the need for internment and that they were rapidly running out of arguments against its use.[4] Getting witnesses to testify in open court against alleged terrorists was proving extremely difficult, if not impossible, and special courts, where the accused would not have to face his or her accuser in person, would not be courts of law at all. In his statement to the press Faulkner said: 'I ask those who will quite sincerely consider the use of internment powers as

[1] For an excellent recent account of the early days of internment see Hennessey (2007) ch 4. For a perspective from nearer the time when internment was introduced see Sunday Times Insight Team (1972). Ryder (2000a) chs 4 and 5 vividly describes former internment processes in Northern Ireland as well as the system employed in the 1970s.

[2] SR & O (NI) 1956/191, regs 10 and 11.

[3] Houston (1978) ch 11; and see too Boyd (1972) 76–93.

[4] Though Ní Aoláin (2000) claims (at 41) that '[t]he army command opposed the introduction of internment from the beginning', citing the Sunday Times Insight Team (1972) ch 15.

evil to answer honestly this question: is it more evil than to allow the perpetrators of these outrages to remain at liberty.'[5] A leading personality who seemed to agree with Faulkner's view at the time was Lord MacDermott, the then Lord Chief Justice of Northern Ireland and a former Lord of Appeal.[6]

The decision was taken to strike as severe a blow as possible against the IRA, putting not just its leaders out of circulation but also many of its rank and file members. Some 500 men were therefore targeted on the first day, rather than the 100 or so leaders and organizers. The British Home Secretary, Reginald Maudling, apparently tried to insist that some Protestants should be lifted as well, in order to show a certain even-handedness, but Faulkner claims that the security forces were 'adamant' that there was no evidence of organized terrorism by Protestants. The British army issued a statement on 13 August 1971 asserting that the introduction of internment had inflicted a major defeat on the IRA, but at almost the same time Joe Cahill, the Belfast Commander of the Provisional IRA, was speaking at a press conference in West Belfast saying that internment had been no surprise and that the IRA were still in good shape (he was then secreted out of the country and taken to the USA).[7]

Faulkner explains that he spent nearly two solid days going through the papers of each individual who had been arrested, but that he never saw the full list of targeted names compiled by the security forces. He also says that he 'used quite stringent conditions for the evidence required'—he asked himself whether he was satisfied that the person whose case he was looking at was a member of the IRA, was actively involved in the IRA campaign, or had played a part in promoting violence. He released 97 of the 337 men initially arrested and agreed to detention orders for the remainder. After September 1971 he was assisted in his task by an Advisory Committee comprising senior commanders from the army and police as well as senior intelligence officers.[8] But persons detained had no formal right to have their detention reviewed: they could make representations to the Advisory Committee, and could be given free legal advice to help them with this, but whatever the Advisory Committee said was not binding on the government.

After the suspension of the Northern Ireland Parliament in March 1972 Westminster authorized new secondary legislation governing the processing of such 'detainees', as they became known. The Detention of Terrorists (NI) Order 1972 allowed the Secretary of State for Northern Ireland to make an 'interim custody order', which authorized detention for 28 days. But the Chief Constable could, during that period, refer the case to a Commissioner requesting the issue of a 'final detention order' authorizing indefinite detention. Before issuing such an order the Commissioner had to offer the detainee an oral hearing, where he or she would hear the nature of the case to be answered and could be represented by a lawyer if he or she so wished (this latter right being conferred after the High Court of Northern

[5] Houston (1978) 121.

[6] MacDermott (1972) 487–8, where he objects to the mistreatment of internees but not to the use of internment *per se*. At 492 he writes 'No one would want to raise fine points of constitutional law in the face of organised terrorism . . .'

[7] Bell (1993) 222–3.

[8] This was set up under reg 12 of the Special Powers Act Regulations. For details of how it operated (from the perspective of an internee) see McGuffin (1973) 133–6.

Ireland had ruled in *Re Mackey*[9] that it did not currently exist). The Commissioner also had to be satisfied not only that the detainee was concerned in the commission of acts of terrorism but that detention was necessary for the protection of the public. The detainee could then refer the order to a Detention Appeal Tribunal within three weeks. If the appeal was unsuccessful the detainee was entitled to a review of his or her detention once 12 months had elapsed since the making of the interim detention order, and to six-monthly reviews thereafter.

On the face of it these safeguards against arbitrary deprivation of liberty might seem satisfactory, even 'quite sophisticated',[10] but a moment's thought reveals that they fall far short of what the European Convention requires for such deprivation to be 'lawful'. The nearest Article 5 comes to permitting such detentions is in paragraph (1)(c), which allows detention 'effected for the purpose of bringing [the person] before the competent legal authority on reasonable suspicion of having committed an offence or when it is reasonably considered necessary to prevent [the person] committing an offence'. But the Commissioner and Detention Appeal Tribunal would not have had the independence and security of tenure required for a legal authority to be 'competent' in this context, and detentions based on mere suspicion would not have been objectively enough justified to meet the criterion of 'reasonable suspicion'. This latter point was implicitly recognized by the High Court of Northern Ireland in two decisions, *Re McElduff*[11] and *Kelly v Faulkner*,[12] both of which effectively held that the only way a detention order could be challenged in a court of law was by showing that it had been made in bad faith. As we saw in Chapter 3, in the early 1970s public law was still very underdeveloped in England, Ireland and Northern Ireland: the grounds upon which judges could review the decisions taken by public authorities were very limited. The jurisprudence of the European Court of Human Rights was likewise restricted at this time. The European Court had not yet pronounced, for example, that, in order for the Article 6 right to a fair trial to be satisfied, a judicial body had to have 'full jurisdiction' in relation to the decision being complained about.[13]

The Diplock Commission and the EPA 1973

The second set of internment procedures adopted in 1972 was reviewed as part of the inquiry conducted by Lord Diplock and others into legal procedures to deal with terrorist activities in Northern Ireland.[14] Although the Diplock Commission's terms of reference made it clear that it was to consider legal procedures for bringing individuals involved in terrorism to book 'otherwise than by internment by the Executive', it

[9] (1972) 23 NILQ 113. In mild praise of Gibson J's decision see De Smith (1972).

[10] The term used by Bonner (1985) 154.

[11] [1972] NI 1, critiqued by Boyle (1972) and O'Boyle (1977a). McGonigal J relied on the infamous decision of the House of Lords in *Liversidge v Anderson* [1942] AC 206 when holding that it was not open to the court to inquire into the reasonableness of the belief or decision of a minister of the Crown when making a detention order. This was the era of profound judicial deference to executive discretion.

[12] [1973] NI 31.

[13] This principle was not firmly established until *Albert and Le Compte v Belgium* (1983) 5 EHRR 533.

[14] Diplock (1972) paras 27–34. For commentary, see Twining (1973).

felt itself 'driven inescapably' to the conclusion that internment was still necessary in Northern Ireland.[15] The Commission stressed, however, contrary to Brian Faulkner's assumption, that no one could be interned just because of suspected membership of an unlawful association: '[t]he Commissioner or Tribunal must be satisfied that the detainee has been personally concerned in the use or attempted use of violence for political ends or the direction, organisation or training of others for the purpose of using violence for those ends, and also that his [or her] detention is necessary for the protection of the public'.[16] In relation to his early decisions on whom to intern Brian Faulkner wrote that 'I have no reason to doubt that I made the right decision in nearly all of these cases',[17] but as early as 1972 the Diplock Commission stated (six years before the publication of Faulkner's memoirs) that '[i]t is now recognised by those responsible for collecting and collating this kind of information that when internment was re-introduced in August, 1971, the scale of the operation led to the arrest and detention of a number of persons against whom suspicion was founded on inadequate and inaccurate information'.[18] However, the Diplock Commissioners went on to state that, since the establishment in September 1971 of the Advisory Committee to hear applications for release from internment, they had no reason to think that there had been:

> any intentional misuse of the powers of detention by the security authorities in Northern Ireland upon whose advice the Executive has to rely in taking the initial step . . . The very fact that those responsible for obtaining and collating the inculpatory material know that they will be called upon to justify its sufficiency is in itself a strong deterrent to their acting on suspicions which cannot be supported by convincing facts.[19]

The Diplock Commission went on to recommend other changes to the way terrorist suspects should be tried in Northern Ireland, changes which were implemented by Parliament through the Northern Ireland (Emergency Provisions) Act 1973 (EPA). At the same time, the Detention of Terrorists (NI) Order 1972 was repealed and replaced by almost identical provisions in the 1973 Act.[20] When he was piloting the EPA Bill through the House of Commons, William Whitelaw, as Secretary of State for Northern Ireland, tried to claim that the procedures for detention in the Bill 'are quite different from internment',[21] but Merlyn Rees, the Labour Shadow Secretary of State, was adamant that they were still internment.[22] The House of Commons approved of the continuation of internment by 155 votes to 18, the most vociferous opponents being the Labour MP Kevin McNamara ('we have the Special Powers Act right there in the Emergency Provisions Bill'[23]) and the SDLP's Gerry Fitt.

[15] ibid, para 27. [16] ibid, para 30. [17] Houston (1978) 123.
[18] Diplock (1972) para 32. [19] ibid.
[20] Sch 1, given the force of law by s 10(5) of the Act.
[21] HC Deb, vol 855, col 279 (17 April 1993).
[22] ibid, col 298. [23] ibid, col 356.

The Gardiner Committee and the EPA 1975

These internment provisions were reviewed yet again just two years later, by the Gardiner Committee.[24] Lord Gardiner had been the dissenting member of the Parker Committee, which had reported in 1972 on the procedures for interrogating suspected terrorists.[25] The new seven-member Committee unanimously concluded that, while indefinite detention should not remain as a long-term policy, 'the present level of violence, the risks of increased violence, and the difficulty of predicting events even a few months ahead' made it impossible for them to recommend a precise date by which internment should end. In his note of reservation to the report Lord MacDermott, the former Lord Chief Justice of Northern Ireland,[26] made it clear that he would have preferred stronger language to have been used in support of the retention of internment for the time being: 'The main protection it renders is to keep a substantial body of hard-core terrorists out of circulation. If those were released there was ample evidence to support the view that terrorism would be intensified and intimidation increased.'[27] But the review went on to make a number of criticisms of the way in which the detention procedures actually operated. It said that the hearing before a Commissioner was 'unsatisfactory, or even farcical, if considered as judicial' and that '[t]he use of screens and voice scramblers, the overwhelming amount of hearsay evidence and the in camera sessions are totally alien to ordinary trial procedures'.[28] Commissioners (who came from outside Northern Ireland) varied in quality and consistency and internees had to wait for about six months for an adjudication. The Committee thought that the review system's 'apparent similarity to the ordinary judicial process has had the side effect of tending to bring the ordinary processes of law in Northern Ireland into disrepute'[29] and it therefore recommended that the system should be completely scrapped and replaced by a new scheme. The newly established Standing Advisory Commission on Human Rights, in its first annual report, 'warmly endorsed' the major recommendations of the Gardiner Committee,[30] 'noted' the Committee's opinion that internment could not remain as a long-term policy,[31] and urged the Secretary of State to look further at how an alternative judicial process could take the place of internment.[32]

Hogan and Walker have explained in detail which of the Gardiner Committee recommendations were eventually reflected in Schedule 1 to the Northern Ireland (Emergency Provisions) (Amendment) Act 1975,[33] re-enacted as Schedule 1 to the

[24] Gardiner (1975).
[25] See ch 7 below, at p 141.
[26] He served in that role for 20 years, from 1951 to 1971.
[27] Gardiner (1975) 58.
[28] ibid, para 152.
[29] ibid.
[30] SACHR (1975) para 31.
[31] ibid, para 36.
[32] ibid, para 37. In its report for 1979–80 SACHR suggested that it had always been its view that internment was not a deterrent to terrorists in Northern Ireland: SACHR (1981), para 6(1).
[33] Given the force of law by s 9(1) and (2) of the Act.

Act of the same name in 1978.[34] They point out that, instead of a Detention Advisory Board being established, the Act refers to 'an Adviser', that important time limits recommended by Gardiner were not inserted in the Act (thereby allowing internees to be held for several months on flimsy evidence), that internees were not after all given the right to appear before the Adviser, that the threshold criteria for continuing a period of detention were not raised as Gardiner had proposed (to ensure that a person was detained only if his or her freedom 'would seriously endanger the general security of the public'[35]), that the Secretary of State was not required by the Act to give reasons if an Adviser's recommendation for release was rejected, and that reviews of detention were no longer to be automatic.[36] The authors conclude that the overall effect of the 1975 reforms was to change the character of internment from a quasi-judicial to a more purely executive action, but they note that the workability of the new system was never properly tested because by the time it came into force, on 22 August 1975, the government had already announced that it was going to phase out internment altogether. As David Bonner puts it, Schedule 1 to the EPA 1975 was never operated to detain persons, only to secure their release.[37]

The criminalization policy

The government's decision to end internment followed a number of important developments in the security and political situation in Northern Ireland.[38] Over Christmas 1974 and into January 1975 the Provisional IRA maintained a 25-day ceasefire, and just ten days after the publication of the Gardiner Report in January 1975 it announced a further indefinite ceasefire. The Provisionals issued a statement saying that in return for the ceasefire the British government had agreed (amongst other things) to release 100 internees within two to three weeks and then phase out internment within a specified period. This was not confirmed by the British government but was widely believed to be true. Later, in February, the then Lord Chief Justice of Northern Ireland, Lord Lowry, was appointed as the Chairman of a Constitutional Convention, and elections were held for the delegates to that Convention on 1 May. By that time the IRA had broken the ceasefire (claiming that the British Army had done so first). There was increasing speculation that the Labour government of the day was planning to announce a British withdrawal from Northern Ireland, but what

[34] Given the force of law by s 12 of the Act.

[35] Gardiner (1975) para 166.

[36] Hogan and Walker (1989) 88–91. Ch 3 of that book is the best account yet published of the legal character of the internment regime used in Northern Ireland from 1971 to 1975. But see also Lowry (1975), Lowry (1976), and Spjut (1986). The last piece is based on interviews with two of the Secretaries of State serving in Northern Ireland during the period, William Whitelaw (1972–3) and Merlyn Rees (1974–6). For a contemporary account written from the perspective of an anarchist, the first Protestant to be interned, see McGuffin (1973), available online at <http://www.irishresistancebooks.com/internment/internment.htm>. McGuffin also contributes, along with Joe Diamond, to accounts provided in Van Voris (1975) 203–17.

[37] Bonner (1985) 152.

[38] For an insider's account of this period see Rees (1985) ch 9.

in fact emerged was a determination to treat the Northern Ireland troubles not as political in nature but as essentially criminal.[39] Alongside this approach went a relative inattention to the way in which Northern Ireland's social and economic problems were making it difficult to improve community relations.[40] It was to emphasize this criminalization policy that Secretary of State Merlyn Rees announced on 5 December 1975 that internment was being brought to an end as from that day. In future the government would deal with the use of violence for political ends through the courts (more than 1,200 people had already been processed through the courts in 1975) and a 'hearts and minds' approach to winning the conflict would be adopted, in line with the strategy advocated by a British brigadier serving in Northern Ireland at the time, Frank Kitson.[41] No new person had in fact been interned since February of that year and in April all but three of the men interned before March 1972 (as well as the eight remaining women detainees[42]) had been released. There were just 73 internees still held by 5 December 1975, 27 of whom were also serving prison sentences. The 46 who were not serving sentences were released on that day.

Commentators differ slightly on the overall figures relating to the use of internment between August 1971 and December 1975. Bew and Gillespie say that a total of 1,981 people were interned, of whom 107 (just over 5 per cent) were loyalists and the remainder republicans.[43] Hogan and Walker put the figure at 109 loyalists out of a total of 2,169 internees.[44] Neither source reveals whether any of the people counted were repeat-players, that is, people who were re-interned after earlier being released. In a pamphlet published in 1975 two Catholic priests stated that by 1 August 1975 70 people had been interned more than once.[45] They also listed the names of all those interned on that date, of whom there were 233. Of these, 57 had been interned for more than two years, 11 for more than three years and nine for more than three-and-a-half years.

Opinions also differ as to whether internment reduced or increased the level of violence in Northern Ireland. Paul Wilkinson holds the former view,[46] and Richard Clutterbuck comes close to saying the same.[47] Kevin Boyle, Tom Hadden, and Paddy

[39] For a useful contextualization of this approach see Hadden, Boyle, and Campbell (1988), esp the Table at 4–5; and Ní Aoláin (2000) ch 1, esp 44–56.

[40] O'Duffy (1993). After surveying the religious, economic, political and security dimensions to the conflict he concludes (at 148) that 'The overemphasis upon security policy at the expense of substantial social and economic reforms has not been successful in promoting conditions for consociationalism.'

[41] Kitson (1971); Ellison and Smyth (2000) ch 5.

[42] In all, 31 women were interned at some point (their names are listed in Faul and Murray (1975) 55).

[43] Bew and Gillespie (1993) 107.

[44] Hogan and Walker (1989) 94. Table 3.1, at 93, provides month-by-month figures (supplied by the government) on intakes and releases; it reveals that 27 internees managed to escape, of whom 15 were recaptured; five men died while in captivity. The same information is available in Spjut (1986) at 740.

[45] Faul and Murray (1975) 51.

[46] Wilkinson (1977) 150–8.

[47] Clutterbuck (1975) 127–30, where he emphasizes the IRA's desire to 'make life unbearable' for the people of Northern Ireland and observes that 'even at the height of the violence in 1971–2 the IRA never enjoyed the support of more than 10 per cent of the Catholic population in the six counties of Northern Ireland and by the end of 1972 their apparently mindless bombing of the civilian population had reduced this to around 3 per cent' (128).

Hillyard contend the opposite.[48] They lay particular emphasis on the fact that the system was not judicially, but militarily, based and they point out that:

> The scale of the whole security operation meant that substantial numbers of men and youths in almost every street or estate in the main Roman Catholic enclaves were directly affected. This, when combined with the widespread and deeply felt communal antagonism to the whole system, appears to have ensured that sufficient new recruits were continually available to replace those members of the IRA who were successfully identified and detained.[49]

The plain fact is that after 1971 the level of violence in Northern Ireland rose considerably: in each of the next five calendar years many more people were killed than in 1971. But proving cause and effect in this context is well nigh impossible. John Cole has pointed out that:

> [t]he received wisdom—that internment made a bad situation worse—is probably correct. The number of deaths, the starkest index of security failure, rose from 25 in 1970 to 173 in 1971, and more than four-fifths of these happened after 9 August. But too much ought not to be read into that, for if the principle of *post hoc ergo propter hoc* is applied to either the introduction of direct rule or the ending of internment, both were also failures in terms of numbers of people killed. The apparent truth is that the security situation deteriorated from 1969 to 1977, and that nothing could stop an almost geometric progression of death and destruction.[50]

What is more definite is that the use of internment was something which allowed the republican movement to gain significant publicity around the world and damaged whatever reputation the British State had previously acquired for justice and fairness. In his memoirs, published in 1985, the Secretary of State who ended internment revealed that his security advisers recognized that 'violence had anyway rocketed when internment had been introduced in 1971 and the existence of detention was a good recruiting cry for the paramilitaries'.[51] He went on to say that it became obvious to him that the decisions he was taking to release internees were 'arbitrary': 'In fact the whole system of detention, from my signature of interim custody orders to my signature for releases, was arbitrary. That is why it was wrong and counter-productive'.[52] On the other hand, some of the best and most respected legal minds of the day—people such as Lord Diplock, Lord Gardiner, and Lord MacDermott—were of the view that internment was justified in the prevailing circumstances at the time, and they did not subsequently change their mind on this point, at least not publicly. And it does seem extraordinary, if even the government minister responsible for overseeing internment thought it was so wrong, that the European Convention did not enable a successful challenge to be mounted against it.

[48] Boyle, Hadden and Hillyard (1974) 75–7.

[49] ibid, 76.

[50] 'Security Constraints', in Watt (1981) 122 at 126.

[51] Rees (1985) 225. He had said as much in the House of Commons at the time internment was ended: 'It was a fertile ground for recruitment to the paramilitary organisations . . .' HC Deb, vol 902, col 762 (11 December 1975).

[52] ibid, 243.

Ireland v United Kingdom

We noted in Chapter 3 that efforts made by the Campaign for Social Justice to interest the Irish government in taking up their complaints about discrimination in the allocation of public housing (and in the allocation of seats in local councils) came to nothing. But the introduction of internment on 9 August 1971, in what the British army called 'Operation Demetrius', did so incense the Irish government that—albeit after a few months—it decided to raise a challenge against the phenomenon in Strasbourg.[53] It lodged an inter-State application against the United Kingdom on 16 December 1971.[54] This alleged that internment in Northern Ireland was in breach of Article 5 of the Convention (the right to liberty), Article 6 (the right to a fair trial), and Article 14 (the right to be free from discrimination). The Irish stance was, of course, somewhat ironic, given that the Irish government had a decade earlier successfully defended its own use of internment in the fight against extreme republicans.[55] In addition, although the Irish government had terminated internment in 1959, it had been contemplating the reintroduction of internment as recently as December 1970.[56]

On 1 October 1972 the European Commission declared the bulk of the allegations made by the Irish government to be admissible[57] (it rejected the allegations suggesting that Article 2 of the Convention had been breached in relation to the deaths of certain individuals in Northern Ireland[58]). The findings of the Compton Report, published in November 1971,[59] and of the Parker Report, published in March 1972,[60] both of which had been commissioned by the UK government, made it easy for the European Commission to hold that there was substantial evidence to establish an administrative practice regarding ill-treatment, which meant in turn that there was no need to ask whether the individuals whose experiences were being highlighted by the Irish government should first have exhausted their domestic remedies.[61] An oral hearing took place in Strasbourg from 2 to 5 October 1973 (and resumed on 12 and 13 December 1973 in relation to allegations under Article 3 of the Convention). The Commission then proceeded, through delegated Commissioners, to hear 119 witnesses on behalf of the UK and Irish governments. This process took more than 30 days (with some hearings being held at an air base in Norway, and some in London) and culminated in final oral submissions being made by the two governments to the Commission in Strasbourg from 14 to 20 March 1975.[62] The Commission adopted its report into the

[53] The details of this decision-making process are described by Schabas and O'Sullivan (2009).

[54] App No 5310/71 (1971) 14 Ybk 100.

[55] *Lawless v Ireland* (1979–80) 1 EHRR 15. This was the third of three judgments issued by the European Court in the *Lawless* case; the first two judgments concerned matters of procedure and standing rather than the substantive merits. See ch 3 above, 36 n70.

[56] Schabas and O'Sullivan (2009) 8–9.

[57] (1972) 15 Ybk 76. See Rauch (1973).

[58] This aspect of the litigation is discussed further in ch 9 below.

[59] Compton (1971). This was an inquiry into the violence which occurred on the day internment was introduced, 9 August 1971.

[60] Parker (1972). This was an inquiry into the procedures used for interrogating suspected terrorists.

[61] Schabas and O'Sullivan (2009) 26.

[62] Among the UK's chief legal representatives during all of these hearings were the Attorney General of the day (Sir Peter Rawlinson and then Sam Silkin), and Gordon Slynn QC and Brian Hutton (the last

case on 25 January 1976, more than four years after the application had been lodged. The report ran to 584 pages, 208 of which related to detention without trial.[63] The fact-finding process was therefore extremely thorough, probably more so than in any other case dealt with by the European Commission or Court before or since.[64]

The Commission decided unanimously—including the Commissioner for Ireland, Kevin Mangan[65]—that 'in the situation in Northern Ireland the measures for detention without trial in derogation from Article 5 of the Convention were, during each phase of the operation of the legislation concerned, measures "strictly required by the exigencies of the situation" within the meaning of Article 15(1)'.[66] The Commission rejected the argument that, because improvements to the safeguards against wrongful detentions were introduced in 1972, the detentions prior to then should be seen as excessive, and it pointed out that '[u]nder the Convention the justification of the measures cannot depend on whether they succeeded or failed in their aim of ending violence'.[67] After observing that the British government kept the detention measures under review, the Commission said:

> This development shows that the difficulties in operating these procedures have been recognized and that efforts have been made to overcome them. It does not show that the measures applied at any stage were excessive. In the view of the Commission it rather indicates that the Government has exercised its discretion in a responsible way and on the basis of the experience it has gained.[68]

As to whether the way in which internment had been operated violated Article 14 of the Convention, read in conjunction with Article 5, because it targeted only republicans (the report states that no loyalist was interned until February 1973), the Commission was again unanimous: 'the facts found in relation to the relevant periods do not disclose that the powers of detention and internment have been applied with discrimination, on any ground, contrary to Article 14'.[69] The Commission was not looking at individual cases on this issue, only at the overall picture. It thought it would be justified in holding that the internment power had been exercised in a discriminatory manner on the ground of political opinion only 'if it could be clearly inferred from the facts established that there had been a policy or practice of discrimination by the authorities responsible for applying the powers'.[70] It then considered this issue in relation to four distinct periods: (1) the introduction of the measures on 9 August 1971, (2) the period

two were to become Lords of Appeal many years later). Among the Irish government's representatives were the Attorney General (Declan Costello) and Anthony Hederman (later a Supreme Court judge).

63 (1976) 19 Ybk 512 (extracts); for the Commission's earlier decision on admissibility, which runs to an additional 90 pages, see (1972) 15 Ybk 76.

64 The Commission conducted fact-finding hearings in 74 cases and the post-1998 Court had done so in 18 cases by the end of 2008. For an excellent analysis of the fact-finding missions conducted see Leach, Paraskeva, and Uzelac (2009). The other case from Northern Ireland where fact-finding occurred was *Donnelly and others v UK* (1975) 4 DR 4, discussed in ch 7 below.

65 Another member of the Commission was Torkel Opsahl, from Norway, who was later to chair an influential inquiry into the way forward for Northern Ireland: Pollak (1993).

66 Commission decision (on website of the European Court of Human Rights), p103.

67 ibid, 102.

68 ibid, 102.

69 ibid, 220.

70 ibid, 204.

from their introduction until the introduction of direct rule in Northern Ireland in March 1972, (3) the period from then until the detention of the first loyalist suspects in February 1973, and (4) the period from February 1973 onwards. But for each period the Commission concluded that it could not establish that any such policy or practice of discrimination existed. In fact it thought that there were many other possible explanations for the different approach adopted by the security forces to republicans and loyalists, and it was prepared to give the benefit of the doubt to the security forces:

> Given that the police were largely excluded from Catholic areas and were, on the IRA side, still dealing with a more highly organized and larger campaign of terrorism than that which faced them from the Loyalist side, it would not be surprising if they had viewed their prospects of obtaining sufficient evidence to prosecute Loyalists, as better than their chances of obtaining such evidence against IRA suspects. Whether they were right or wrong in believing this, this was a question of appreciation which had to be judged at the time by the members of the security forces involved in each case. If there was a tendency to make greater efforts to bring Loyalists before the ordinary courts, this does not necessarily indicate an intention to discriminate in their favour in applying the powers of detention . . .[71]

On this point, however, the Commissioner from Ireland, while ultimately concurring with all his other colleagues, expressed some reservations about whether it was indeed 'clear' why the security forces did not arrest more loyalists with a view to internment. Mr Mangan actually went so far as to suggest that the UK government had not fully cooperated with the Commission's investigation:

> While this attitude, in the end, did not prevent the delegates or the Commission from obtaining any evidence which they thought relevant, it amounted, at the time it was adopted, in my opinion, to a failure by the United Kingdom to furnish all necessary facilities within the meaning of Article 28.[72]

Apart from this disquiet over the UK government's lack of cooperation with the investigation, the European Commission seems to have adopted a very indulgent attitude towards the British authorities. Hartman describes the Commission's analysis as neither rigorous nor convincing, and as a 'significant retreat' from the stance taken in *Lawless* on safeguards.[73]

The European Court's decision

The inter-State case was referred to the European Court of Human Rights on 10 March 1976, and almost two more years were to elapse before it issued its judgment on the application.[74] In the interim there were significant political and legal

[71] ibid, 217.

[72] ibid, 494. Art 28 stated that if the Commission accepted a petition it must, if need be, undertake an investigation, 'for the effective conduct of which the States concerned shall furnish all necessary facilities, after an exchange of views with the Commission'.

[73] Hartman (1981) 33.

[74] (1979–80) 2 EHRR 25. One of the counsel for Ireland was John Murray, now the Chief Justice of Ireland; amongst counsel for the UK were Brian Hutton QC (later Lord Chief Justice of Northern

developments within Northern Ireland, including the rise of the Peace People (who were awarded the 1976 Nobel Peace Prize), the ending of 'special category status' for paramilitary prisoners,[75] and the introduction of the Fair Employment (NI) Act 1976.[76] In 1976 and 1977 there were 409 conflict-related deaths, 2,989 bombs were planted, 1,427 weapons and 19.6 tonnes of explosives were found, and 2,584 persons were charged with terrorist offences.[77] It is perhaps no surprise, then, that on 18 January 1978 the European Court confirmed the view of the Commission that the use of internment in Northern Ireland was not a violation of the Convention, just as it had held more than 16 years earlier that internment in the Republic of Ireland in the 1950s, when the violence was much less widespread and severe, was also permissible.

The Court's judgment begins with a long and very useful account of the background to 'the emergency situation' in Northern Ireland,[78] and describes in some detail the mechanics of the internment system.[79] In relation to the latter it held that while, on the face of things, internment breached the right to liberty guaranteed by Article 5 and the right to a fair trial guaranteed by Article 6 (the Commission had held that Article 6 was not engaged), the United Kingdom had validly derogated from the application of those Articles because on 27 June 1957 it had lodged with the Council of Europe a notice under Article 15 of the Convention declaring that there was a 'public emergency threatening the life of the nation',[80] and this notice had never subsequently been withdrawn, even during the years when internment was not practised. From time to time the UK government had notified the Secretary General of the Council of Europe of relevant developments, so, for example, on 25 September 1969 the British Permanent Representative to the Council of Europe had informed the Secretary General that:

> Serious civil disturbances have occurred in various parts of Northern Ireland in the month of August this year as a result of which the Government of Northern Ireland has found it necessary to exercise certain of such emergency powers, to the extent strictly required by the exigencies of the situation. In the course of that month, twenty-four persons were detained in custody without judicial process. Four of such persons have been charged with criminal offences, and the remainder were released from detention within, at most, 14 days of their being first detained.[81]

Likewise, on 20 August 1971, the UK government had informed the Secretary General as follows:

> Over recent months in Northern Ireland there has been a series of acts of terrorism, including murders, attempted murders, maimings, bombings, fire-raising and acts of intimidation, and

Ireland and a Lord of Appeal), Anthony Lester QC (later Lord Lester) and Nicholas Bratza (later the UK's Commissioner on the European Commission of Human Rights and judge on the European Court of Human Rights). Torkel Opsahl represented the Commission at the Court hearing.

[75] See further ch 10 below.

[76] See further ch 12 below.

[77] Figures taken from Bew and Gillespie (1993) 116 and 124. For a good summary of the decision see Bonner (1978).

[78] (1979–80) 2 EHRR 25, paras 11–77.

[79] ibid, paras 78–91.

[80] All the UK's notices of derogation from 1957 to 1975 are collected in SACHR (1977b) 103–7.

[81] (1969) 12 Ybk 72–4. The detentions 'without judicial process' would have been authorized under the Special Powers Act (see chs 2 and 5 of this book).

more recently violent civil disturbances. The Government of Northern Ireland has therefore found it necessary since 9 August for the protection of life and the security of property and to prevent outbreaks of public disorder, to exercise, to the extent strictly required by the exigencies of the situation, powers of detention and internment. Copies of the relevant Regulations under the Civil Authorities (Special Powers) Act (Northern Ireland) 1922 are being sent to you separately. Particular attention is drawn to those provisions of Regulation 12 which provide for the establishment of an Advisory Committee in respect of persons who are the subject of an internment order.

It is part of the European Court's function to ensure that derogation notices are justifiable and that the measures taken under them are, in the terms provided in Article 15(1), 'strictly required by the exigencies of the situation' and 'not inconsistent with [the State's] other obligations under international law'. In this case the European Court did not deem it necessary to spend any time on whether there was in fact an emergency threatening the life of the nation: the Irish government was not suggesting that there was no such emergency and so the Court simply announced that '[t]he existence of such an emergency is perfectly clear from the facts summarized above and was not questioned by anyone before either the Commission or the Court'.[82] Later the Court drew upon its approach in *Lawless v Ireland* and said:

Being confronted with a massive wave of violence and intimidation, the Northern Ireland Government and then, after the introduction of direct rule (30 March 1972), the British Government were reasonably entitled to consider that normal legislation offered insufficient resources for the campaign against terrorism and that recourse to measures outside the scope of the ordinary law, in the shape of extrajudicial deprivation of liberty was called for. When the Irish Republic was faced with a serious crisis in 1957, it adopted the same approach and the Court did not conclude that the 'extent strictly required' had been exceeded.[83]

It is, in retrospect at least, rather remarkable that, at a time when a wide variety of politicians and academics in Britain and Ireland were commenting on the counter-productiveness of internment in Northern Ireland, and when other European countries facing serious terrorist attacks (such as Germany and Italy) were not finding it necessary to resort to internment, the European Court should—with so little detailed analysis—condone the practice in Northern Ireland, partly basing itself on a decision taken in relation to rather different facts more than 16 years earlier. The last internee had been released in Northern Ireland even before the European Commission had adopted its report into the Irish government's application, so it was not as if a finding by the European Court against the United Kingdom's use of internment would have driven a coach and horses through current UK policy in relation to the control of terrorism in Northern Ireland. As we shall see in Chapter 7, the Court did make an adverse finding against the United Kingdom in relation to Article 3. This makes it all the more difficult to understand why there was no adverse finding in relation to Article 5 too. One contemporary commentator summed things up by writing that 'this judgment indicates the limitations of the Convention insofar as proper

[82] (1979–80) 2 EHRR 25, para 205 (referring back to paras 12 and 29–75).
[83] ibid, para 212.

and impartial supervision of the working of the Convention is concerned',[84] and he added that 'a critical onlooker would be justified in concluding that the chances of a state being found guilty of wrongly declaring an emergency are somewhat remote'.[85] Another said that 'The Court's opinion in *Ireland v UK* contains the most extreme statement of the margin of appreciation in Article 15 jurisprudence' and that it represents 'near-total abdication to government discretion'.[86] Mangan reminds us, on the other hand, with some justification, that in this relatively early period of the Court's existence it is conceivable that if it had ruled against the United Kingdom's use of the derogation clause, the government might have reacted 'by refusing to recognize the compulsory jurisdiction of the Court, by entering a reservation to Article 15, or by withdrawing from the European Convention'.[87] He says that such an outcome was not unforeseeable because the government would have been likely to feel less pressure from the international community to uphold human rights than from the majority of its own citizens in Northern Ireland to protect their interests.[88]

The decision in the European Court was taken by 17 judges, but the Irish judge, Philip O'Donoghue, took the courageous step of dissenting on the question whether the steps taken by the United Kingdom to deal with the emergency had gone beyond what was strictly required by the exigencies of the situation. He also felt, and in this respect he was joined by Judge Matscher from Austria, that the UK government had failed to show that the security forces had operationalized internment in a non-discriminatory way. On the derogation point Judge O'Donoghue said:

> The situation did not require the extrajudicial power of arrest and detention to have been employed without two safeguards, viz. informing the person arrested and detained of the grounds therefor, and providing some means of obtaining a review of the extrajudicial action and release if the reviewing body was not satisfied. I regard these safeguards as necessary and indeed the logical principles laid down in the Lawless case. Any such safeguards were not present in the early stages under regulations 10, 11 and 12 [of the Special Powers Act], and to the extent of their absence there was a breach in my opinion of Article 5(4).[89]

On the discrimination point the same judge called the approach adopted by the European Commission of Human Rights 'ill-balanced',[90] adding:

> I see in the selectivity in the enforcement of internment until 1973 the continuance of that element of inherent bias in favour of one community... I am, therefore, obliged to conclude that upon all the evidence in the report that [sic] the respondent Government was guilty of discrimination in its application of extrajudicial steps to deal with the crisis in 1971–73.[91]

[84] Green (1978) 98.
[85] ibid, 100.
[86] Hartman (1981) 34 and 35. It is also possible to criticize the Court for not holding that the UK's use of internment violated the Convention in that the body set up to review the detentions could not make decisions that were binding on the government. Such a weak mechanism would not satisfy the requirements of Article 5.
[87] Mangan (1988) 382. This is not the Mangan who was Ireland's Commissioner on the European Commission from 1971–5.
[88] ibid.
[89] (1979–80) 2 EHRR 25, para 118.
[90] ibid, 117.
[91] ibid, 114–5.

Judge Matscher put the same point more starkly:

A study of the papers seems rather to allow the conclusion that, apart from the *parti pris* of the authorities, which characterizes the general situation in Northern Ireland not only in history but also at the time in question, there was hesitation to proceed against 'loyalist' terrorists in the same energetic fashion with recourse to emergency measures because political repercussions were feared from such conduct. That is not, in my view, a justification based on objective and reasonable grounds.[92]

The majority's rather dismissive treatment of the Irish government's position was, and remains, unfortunate, largely because it sent a signal to member States of the Council of Europe that the Court would be deferential to governments when the latter were weighing up what steps they could take to counter terrorism. There is, alas, little sign of the 'activism' on the Court's part which some have seen as characteristic of at least one wing of the Court from its earliest days.[93] It did not, for example, engage with the (admittedly rather radical) thesis propounded by the International Commission of Jurists that by tolerating a society which discriminated between people on social, economic and political grounds the UK government had somehow forfeited its right to seek to justify in human rights terms the measures it was taking to defend itself against attack.[94]

It is to the credit of other European States that they did not rush to take advantage of the opportunity to issue derogation notices in relation to their anti-terrorism laws, the probable reason for this being the constraints placed upon them by their own constitutional traditions. Today there continues to be little second-guessing by the European Court of a State's own assessment of the seriousness of the situation it is facing, as was made fairly evident in later challenges to derogation notices issued by the government of the United Kingdom in relation to Northern Ireland.[95] The Commission did rule in an early inter-State case taken against Greece that a derogation notice was unjustifiable because there was in fact no 'public emergency',[96] but that was in 1969 and the European Court has never come to such a conclusion.

The decision by the European Court is also disappointing because it did not deal in any detail with the serious allegations made against the UK government to the effect that it had failed properly to cooperate with the European Commission and Court in their consideration of the Irish government's allegations.[97] While the Court rather abstractly stressed the fundamental importance of the duty to cooperate imposed by the Convention, it merely 'regretted' that, according to the Commission, the UK government 'did not always afford it the assistance desirable'.[98] But Judges O'Donoghue and Matscher both criticized the UK government's uncooperative attitude. The former, having upbraided the other judges for conveying 'nothing even approaching disapproval' of this attitude, said that the approach of his fellow judges

[92] ibid, 147.

[93] Nicol (2005) 167–70, where *Ireland v UK* is not mentioned.

[94] ICJ (1983) 217, esp 243–6; see also Mangan (1988) 384–5.

[95] *Brogan v UK* (1989) 11 EHRR 117; *Brannigan and McBride v UK* (1994) 17 EHRR 539; *Marshall v UK* App No 41571/98, decision of 10 July 2001. These cases are discussed further in ch 5 below.

[96] *Denmark, Norway, Sweden and the Netherlands v Greece* (1969) 12 Ybk 1.

[97] This was a duty under Art 28(1)(a) *in fine*, now Art 38(1)(a) *in fine*.

[98] (1979–80) 2 EHRR 25, para 148.

would lead to few inter-State cases being brought in the future (which is indeed what has occurred):

> It would be lacking in candour if I did not state that there is much in the tone and general approach of the Judgment that must discourage States from invoking Article 24. The concept of this being a collective guarantee in that article to secure observance of human rights has been severely damaged.[99]

Further derogations

As already noted, by the time the European Court issued its judgment in *Ireland v United Kingdom*, internment had been phased out, the last detainee having been released more than two years earlier, in December 1975. But the power to reintroduce internment remained on the statute book of Northern Ireland in the sense that all that would have been required to reintroduce the policy would have been the signature of a government minister. No Parliamentary debate, let alone authorization, would have been necessary. Retaining the power in this way was deliberate, although whether it was because the British government and its security advisers genuinely thought that a return to internment might really be necessary or because they wanted to use the continuing existence of the internment power as a bargaining chip in future negotiations over the establishment of peace in Northern Ireland, is unlikely ever to be clear. As the power was never again invoked, its compatibility with the European Convention was not retested. One of the features of the Convention is that it does not allow for abstract assessments of laws which have not been applied in ways that have allegedly breached the rights of particular individuals. The threat of a law's applicability cannot, in general, be subjected to review by the European Court. One has to add 'in general' because occasionally the Court will deem a law to be so inconsistent with the Convention's standards, even though it has not been applied to a particular person, that its very existence will be declared to be in violation of the Convention. This famously occurred in a prominent case taken by a man in Northern Ireland, Jeff Dudgeon, who complained about the continuing existence of a piece of Victorian legislation which made anal sexual intercourse a crime, even between consenting adults.[100]

Even if the European Court had decided against the UK government as regards internment, this would not necessarily have meant that leaving the power to intern on the statute book would have been a continuing breach of Article 5. Given the Court's unanimous acceptance that there was an emergency threatening the life of the nation, the decision in any future case would probably have related to the way in which the power to intern was being exercised, not its existence. The power survived in the form of section 9 of, and Schedule 1 to, the Northern Ireland (Emergency Provisions) (Amendment) Act 1975, which was not allowed to lapse until 24 July 1980, when the last six-month

[99] ibid, 118. Judge Matscher said 'the defendant Government behaved in a very unhelpful manner in the inquiry... such that the full appraisal of the evidence is not in its favour' (ibid, 147).

[100] *Dudgeon v UK* (1983) 5 EHRR 573. See further ch 10 below.

renewal notice for the power expired.[101] Even then the provisions remained 'live', in that they could have been revived at any time by an order of the Secretary of State[102] (although such an order would have required Parliamentary approval, at the very latest within 40 days after having been made[103]). The detention provisions were included in later statutes too[104] and were not finally repealed until 1998.[105] At that point they could be revived only if they were included in a new Bill and approved by a vote in Parliament.

The decision to end the use of detention without trial in Northern Ireland did not mean, moreover, that the United Kingdom could then withdraw its notice of derogation issued under Article 15 of the European Convention. The derogation remained in force because other 'emergency' powers put in place by the British Parliament still applied. These will be examined in more detail in Chapters 5 and 6, but it can be noted here that they required a derogation notice because they authorized arrests on grounds of suspicion, rather than reasonable suspicion. When this anomaly was corrected in 1984 the derogation notice was withdrawn. But in 1988 it became clear that the detention provisions were still in breach of Article 5 (in the absence of a derogation notice) because they allowed arrested persons to be held for up to seven days before being brought before a judge. The derogation was therefore almost immediately reimposed and it was not until the seven-day detention scheme was altered by the Terrorism Act 2000—which came into force in February 2001, more than 25 years after the release of the last internees—that the government was able to notify the Council of Europe that it was at last withdrawing its notice of derogation in relation to detentions connected with terrorism in Northern Ireland.

Within less than a year of that withdrawal, however, the British government contacted the Council of Europe to say that it was submitting a fresh notice of derogation because it had decided, in the wake of the events in the United States on 11 September 2001, to reintroduce internment for a certain category of person anywhere in the United Kingdom. The judicial response to that notice is worth analysing here not only because the notice applied just as much in Northern Ireland as it did in other parts of the United Kingdom but also because the courts have been given a chance to develop the approach to Article 15 of the Convention displayed in *Lawless v Ireland* and *Ireland v United Kingdom*.

The notice of derogation, having cited the events of 11 September 2001, and the Resolution of the UN Security Council requiring all States to take measures to prevent the commission of terrorist attacks, including by denying safe haven to those who finance, plan, support, or commit terrorist attacks,[106] went on to say:

> There exists a terrorist threat to the United Kingdom from persons suspected of involvement in international terrorism. In particular, there are foreign nationals present in the United

[101] The EPA 1975 had provided for six-month renewal orders (s 21(3)(a)), as had the EPA 1978, s 33(3)(a). The EPA 1987, s 26(4)(a), made the renewal period an annual one, in line with a recommendation by Sir George Baker in his report on the review of the EPA 1978: Baker (1984) para 444.

[102] Issued under the EPA 1978, s 33(1)(c).

[103] EPA 1978, s 32(3) and (4).

[104] EPA 1991, s 34 and Sch 3, and EPA 1996, s 36 and Sch 3.

[105] By the EPA 1998, s 3.

[106] Resolution 1373 (2001).

Kingdom who are suspected of being concerned in the commission, preparation or instigation of acts of international terrorism, of being members of organisations or groups which are so concerned or of having links with members of such organisations or groups, and who are a threat to the national security of the United Kingdom.

As a result, a public emergency, within the meaning of Article 15(1) of the Convention, exists in the United Kingdom.

One can see from that final sentence that the UK government felt that it was enough to satisfy Article 15(1) if there were foreign nationals present in the country who were a threat to the national security of the country.

Internment in the twenty-first century

The legislation put in place to deal with this so-called emergency was Part 4 of the Anti-terrorism, Crime and Security Act 2001[107] and the persons in question were non-British nationals in the United Kingdom who were reasonably suspected of involvement in terrorism but against whom there was not enough admissible evidence to convict them in court. The British government actually blamed the European Court of Human Rights for leaving it with no alternative but to intern this category of person because in *Chahal v United Kingdom*[108] the European Court had ruled that, if a member State of the Council of Europe were to deport a person to a country in relation to which there were substantial grounds for believing that he or she would face a real risk of being subjected to treatment contrary to Article 3 of the European Convention,[109] the deportation itself would be a breach of Article 3. Section 23 of the Anti-terrorism, Crime and Security Act 2001 therefore provided that such non-British nationals could be arrested and detained indefinitely.

A group of nine people who were duly detained in Belmarsh prison under this provision challenged the legality of their detention. They won at the level of the Special Immigration Appeals Commission, lost in the Court of Appeal,[110] but won again in the House of Lords.[111] Disappointingly, their Lordships, with the exception of Lord Hoffmann,[112] did not dispute the entitlement of the British government to determine that on the facts there was a public emergency threatening the life of the nation, thereby endorsing the regrettable test on this issue first laid down by the European Court in

[107] Black-Branch (2001), Elliott (2003), Walker (2009) 25–9. See also Brandon (2004).

[108] (1997) 23 EHRR 413.

[109] The UK government has been lobbying to have this legal ruling changed and has adopted the tactic of striking 'Memoranda' with particular countries (such as Jordan and Libya) whereby persons deported to there from Britain will be assured that they will not be ill-treated. Whether such documents will provide a sufficient guarantee that a deportee will be protected against ill-treatment is a question of fact to be decided in the light of all the evidence: *RB (Algeria) v Secretary of State for the Home Department* [2009] UKHL 10, [2009] 2 WLR 512.

[110] [2003] 1 All ER 816.

[111] *A v Secretary of State for the Home Department* [2004] UKHL 56, [2005] 2 AC 68. The decision was welcomed by most commentators (eg Hickman (2005), Dickson (2005a), Bates (2006), Elliott (2006), Fredman (2006a)) but was adversely criticized by Tomkins (2005) and Campbell (2009).

[112] For criticism of Lord Hoffmann's apparent hypocrisy see Dyzenhaus (2005).

Lawless v Ireland[113] and confirmed in *Ireland v United Kingdom*,[114] but the House went on to hold, with only Lord Walker dissenting, that the power to intern in the 2001 Act was a measure that was both improperly discriminatory (because it applied only to non-British nationals) and disproportionate (because it provided for potentially limitless detention). Sandra Fredman has rightly welcomed this part of their Lordships' decision as 'a judicial appreciation of human rights, not as counter-democratic forces, but as constitutive of democracy itself'.[115] She accepts that this in turn requires the judges to articulate the values they see as implicit in the concept of democracy, and the value which emerges as triumphant in this particular decision of the House is that of equality. The Lords held that the internment power was incompatible with both Articles 14 and 15 of the European Convention. But declarations of incompatibility under the Human Rights Act 1998 do not affect the continuing operation of the legislative provision in question and are not binding on the parties to the proceedings in which they are made.[116] Consequently, even though the detainees had won in the House of Lords, they (and two further applicants) proceeded to lodge an application at the European Court of Human Rights a month or so later.[117] The applicants alleged that they had been unlawfully detained, in breach of Articles 3, 5(1) and 14 of the Convention and that they had not had adequate remedies at their disposal, in breach of Articles 5(4) and 13.

On the question whether the UK government had been justified in issuing a notice of derogation because of the existence of a public emergency threatening the life of the nation, the European Court, unfortunately, maintained the stance it had adopted in previous cases concerning the conflict in Ireland.[118] It recalled that in *Lawless v Ireland* it had held that the words 'other public emergency threatening the life of the nation' referred to 'an exceptional situation of crisis or emergency which affects the whole population and constitutes a threat to the organised life of the community of which the State is composed',[119] and it noted that in *Ireland v United Kingdom* the parties were agreed, as were the Commission and the Court, that the Article 15 test was satisfied, since terrorism had for a number of years represented 'a particularly far-reaching and acute danger for the territorial integrity of the United Kingdom, the institutions of the six counties and the lives of the province's inhabitants'.[120] Moreover the European Court observed that (whatever the view of the United Nations Human Rights Committee might be[121]) it had never explicitly incorporated the requirement that the emergency be 'temporary'. It again referred to the cases relating to the security situation in Northern Ireland to demonstrate that it

[113] (1979–80) 1 EHRR 15. See ch 3 at 34–40.

[114] (1979–80) 2 EHRR 25.

[115] Fredman (2006a) 60.

[116] s 4(6).

[117] *A v UK* (2009) 49 EHRR 29 (Grand Chamber). The Fourth Section of the Court relinquished jurisdiction in favour of the Grand Chamber of the Court on 11 September 2007. Two London-based NGOs, Liberty and Justice, were given leave by the President of the Court to make written interventions in this case.

[118] ibid, paras 173–81.

[119] ibid, para 176. The quotation is from the judgment in *Lawless v Ireland* (1979–80) 1 EHRR 15, para 28.

[120] ibid, quoting from paras 205 and 212 of the judgment in *Ireland v UK* (1979–80) 2 EHRR 25.

[121] ibid, para 178.

is possible for a 'public emergency' to continue for many years. Summing up its position, the European Court reaffirmed its reluctance to second-guess the assessment made by national authorities as to whether a public emergency existed:

> ... the national authorities enjoy a wide margin of appreciation under Article 15 in assessing whether the life of their nation is threatened by a public emergency. While it is striking that the United Kingdom was the only Convention State to have lodged a derogation in response to the danger from al'Qaeda, although other States were also the subject of threats, the Court accepts that it was for each Government, as the guardian of their own people's safety, to make their own assessment on the basis of the facts known to them. Weight must, therefore, attach to the judgment of the United Kingdom's executive and Parliament on this question. In addition, significant weight must be accorded to the views of the national courts, who were better placed to assess the evidence relating to the existence of an emergency.
>
> On this first question, the Court accordingly shares the view of the majority of the House of Lords that there was a public emergency threatening the life of the nation.[122]

At first glance this stance by the European Court has a certain attraction, because in accordance with the principle of subsidiarity (more commonly referred to in discussion of European Community law) it locates responsibility for decision-making at the level where there is greatest awareness of the relevant factors that need to be taken into account—in this context the national courts. But whenever national courts hold, as the House of Lords did (with the exception of Lord Hoffmann), that whether there is a public emergency is effectively beyond their purview and should instead be decided by the national government without any judicial input whatsoever, the European Court's stance means that responsibility bypasses the national courts altogether: they do not 'assess the evidence relating to the existence of an emergency'.

However, the European Court, like the House of Lords, went on to hold that the measures taken in response to the emergency were disproportionate. It rejected the UK government's contention that the detention provision was in fact an immigration measure rather than a national security measure.[123] It upheld the complaints by four of the 11 applicants that they had not been able to challenge the lawfulness of their detention (a breach of Article 5(4)) and the complaint by nine of the applicants that they had been denied the right to compensation (a breach of Article 5(5)). But in time-honoured fashion the Court then held that, in view of its findings on Article 5, it was not necessary for it to consider whether there had been a breach of Articles 6, 13 or 14 of the Convention.[124] As regards the alleged breach of Article 3, the Court held that the applicants had not exhausted their domestic remedies on this issue.[125]

[122] ibid, paras 180–1.

[123] ibid, para 186. In the previous year the European Court had been more open to allowing extended detention in an immigration context: *Saadi v UK* (2008) 47 EHRR 17 (Grand Chamber). In *A v UK* the UK government, perhaps surprisingly, did not expressly rely on Art 16 of the European Convention, which reads: 'Nothing in Articles 10, 11 and 14 shall be regarded as preventing the High Contracting Parties from imposing restrictions on the political activity of aliens'. In *Piermont v France* (1995) 20 EHRR 301 the Court was very narrowly split (five to four) in favour of holding that the French government could not rely upon Art 16 when deporting a German MEP from French Polynesia.

[124] (2009) 49 EHRR 29, paras 233, 225, and 192 respectively.

[125] ibid, para 133. In a report on visits to the detainees in February 2002 and March 2004 the European Committee for the Prevention of Torture and Inhuman or Degrading Treatment or Punishment had

Following the House of Lords' decision in *A v Secretary of State for the Home Department* in December 2004, the government allowed section 23 of the 2001 Act to lapse when it came up for renewal in February 2005. To replace it the government persuaded Parliament to enact the Prevention of Terrorism Act 2005, which allowed persons who would formerly have been detained indefinitely to be subjected instead to 'control orders', severely limiting their freedom of movement, their freedom of association and their right to conduct a private life. Not surprisingly the legality of these control orders was also challenged in the courts, again reaching the House of Lords. In October 2007 the House held, by three to two,[126] that the control orders in six of the appeals were in breach of the controlees' right to liberty under Article 5 of the Convention.[127] But in three other appeals the House did not think that Article 5 was breached.[128] One of the key factors distinguishing the cases was that in the first group the 'curfew' imposed on the controlees lasted for more than 16 hours—they were not permitted to leave their small flats for more than six hours a day—while in the other cases the curfew lasted 16 hours or less. Lord Brown of Eaton-under-Heywood laid particular emphasis on this point.[129] To comply with the judgment the government had to relax some of the restrictions imposed on six of the suspected terrorists. And in a follow-up case taken by some of the same controlees less than two years later, the House of Lords held, in a unanimous nine-judge decision, that their Article 6 rights were being breached because they were not being given enough information about the reasons why the control orders were being issued to allow them to instruct their lawyers effectively on how to challenge them.[130] In the case of one of these controlees the Secretary of State has since decided that more information cannot safely be disclosed to the individual, so a High Court judge has now quashed the control order.[131]

The 2005 Act allows control orders to be issued, if necessary, in derogation of the European Convention, but to date no such derogating order has been issued. There is currently no derogation notice in place in relation to any of the United Kingdom's laws. The Act also requires an independent reviewer to report to the Secretary of State each year on how it has been operated.[132] In his four reports to date,[133] Lord Carlile of Berriew QC has said that he agrees with all the decisions taken so far to issue control orders. He notes developments in the courts but does not himself analyse the control

concluded that 'their situation at the time of the visit could be considered as amounting to inhuman and degrading treatment'.

126 Lords Bingham and Brown, and Lady Hale in the majority; Lords Hoffmann and Carswell dissenting.

127 *Secretary of State for the Home Dept v JJ* [2007] UKHL 45, [2008] 1 AC 385.

128 *Secretary of State for the Home Department v MB and AF* [2007] UKHL 46, [2008] 1 AC 440 (Lord Hoffmann dissenting); *Secretary of State for the Home Department v E* [2007] UKHL 47, [2008] 1 AC 499 (unanimously). In the former case the House found a breach of Art 6 of the Convention and referred the applications back to the High Court to be reconsidered in the light of the requirements of that provision.

129 *Secretary of State for the Home Dept v JJ* [2007] UKHL 45, [2008] 1 AC 385, para 108.

130 *Secretary of State for the Home Department v AF* [2009] UKHL 28, [2009] 3 WLR 74.

131 *Secretary of State for the Home Dept v AN* [2009] EWHC 1966 (Admin).

132 Prevention of Terrorism Act 2005, s 14(2)–(8). Every three months the Home Secretary must also prepare his or her own report for Parliament on how the control order powers have been exercised: s 14(1).

133 Available on the website of the Home Office: <http://www.homeoffice.gov.uk>, and the links to 'security'.

order powers with respect to their compatibility with the European Convention. The Joint Parliamentary Committee on Human Rights has also issued reports on control orders[134] but in its response to these the government has not shifted its ground on any Convention points.[135] The power to issue control orders has to be renewed each year; so far that renewal has occurred with little controversy in Parliament.[136]

In the immediate aftermath of the House of Lords' judgment in the first group of appeals there was again speculation that the British government was thinking of reintroducing internment and not limiting it to non-British nationals. This was said to be a result of the government's frustration at the courts' apparent willingness to declare unlawful whatever measure the government came up with to combat what it perceived as a real terrorist threat. But it seems very unlikely that the desperate step of reintroducing internment will in fact be taken in the current 'war on terrorism': it would be hugely risky in terms of the government's popularity and international reputation, and the measure would be highly vulnerable to challenge in the courts as a disproportionate response to the threat of terrorism. Even if the European Court were minded to uphold such a practice, it might not get the chance to rule on the matter because the highest domestic court (from October 2009, the UK Supreme Court) might strike down the measure as disproportionate and the government could not then 'apply' to Strasbourg to challenge this, since applying to Strasbourg is a privilege reserved for individuals and non-governmental organizations. Yet the European Court *needs* another chance to review the approach it adopted in *Lawless v Ireland* nearly 50 years ago and in *Ireland v United Kingdom* more than 30 years ago. Given that the Court has admitted that the Convention is 'a living instrument' and that its jurisprudence must evolve to keep pace with the times, one would hope that, if allowed the opportunity, the Court would greatly tighten the requirements for a valid derogation notice. It is highly regrettable that Northern Ireland's unfortunate experiment with internment did not persuade the Court to abandon its 1960 stance much sooner. It is also unfortunate that no serious attempt seems to have been made within the Council of Europe to alter the wording of Article 15 so as to make it a more effective control mechanism for derogations during emergencies. One commentator has drafted a Protocol to the Convention that would allow the Strasbourg Court to play an advisory role in commenting on a proposed derogation before it begins operating, but this has attracted little attention.[137]

Port powers

Article 5 of the European Convention permits detention in a number of situations other than when a person is reasonably suspected of involvement in a criminal offence. Article 5(1)(b) lists one of these as detention 'in order to secure the fulfilment

[134] 2008–9, 5th Report, HL 37 / HC 282; 2007–8, 10th Report, HL 57 / HC 356; 2006–7, 14th Report, HL 106 / HC 539; 2006–7, 8th Report, HL 60 /HC 365; 2005–6, 12th Report, HL 122 / HC 915.

[135] See, eg, Cm 7625 (May 2009).

[136] The most recent renewal order is the Prevention of Terrorism Act 2005 (Continuance in force of sections 1 to 9) Order 2009 (SI 554), effective from 11 March 2009.

[137] Mangan (1988) 387–94.

of an obligation prescribed by law'.[138] On one reading, this authorizes detention in any situation where a person does not comply with the law. It suggests that if anyone does not do what is required by law he or she can be detained. Fortunately, the European Court has stressed that the key words in the sub-paragraph are 'to secure the fulfilment' of any obligation: the arrest must occur to enable the obligation to be carried out, not to punish a person for not carrying it out. With regard to the conflict in Northern Ireland the application of the provision came into question in relation to the obligation to submit oneself to an 'examination' if requested to do so by officials at a port or airport. Paddy Hillyard examined both the nature and the impact of these port powers in 1993, commenting that they were much more insidious than purely random investigations of travellers because they discriminated against people who were Irish.[139] But how often this occurred in practice, and whether it was justifiable given that most of the terrorist attacks taking place in Great Britain at the time were being perpetrated by people who were Irish, he does not discuss.

The obligation to submit oneself to an examination at a port or airport was first imposed by the Prevention of Terrorism (Temporary Provisions) Act 1974 (PTA 1974)[140] but it was first considered in Strasbourg when the relevant Act was the 1976 successor to that Act (PTA 1976). Schedule 13 to the PTA 1976 empowered the UK government to issue an Order providing for the examination of persons arriving in or leaving Great Britain or Northern Ireland and also for the arrest and detention of persons who were subjected to such examination. The government duly issued such an Order,[141] Article 5 of which empowered 'examining officers' to examine persons for the purpose of determining three things: (a) whether they appeared to be, or to have been, concerned in the commission, preparation, or instigation of acts of terrorism, (b) whether they were the subject of an 'exclusion order' (these were orders authorized by another part of the PTA 1976, and are discussed in a separate section of this chapter, below), and (c) whether there were grounds for suspecting that the persons had committed one of a number of offences listed elsewhere in the PTA 1976. 'Examining officers' were usually police officers working in the 'Special Branch', or customs and excise officers. Article 6 of the Order went on to impose a duty on persons who were being examined to furnish the examining officer with all such information as he or she may require. Article 7 permitted the searching of people being examined, and Article 10 permitted their detention (pending their examination or pending consideration of whether they should be issued with an exclusion order) for a period of up to two days on the authorization of an examining officer and for up to a further five days if the Secretary of State so directed. To avoid any doubt, Article 11 said that a person liable to be detained under Article 10 could be arrested without warrant. Another provision in the PTA stated that where a person was detained under Article 10 any examining

138 Second limb of Art 5(1)(b).

139 Hillyard (1993) chs 2 and 3, esp at 19.

140 s 8 and Sch 3, and see Prevention of Terrorism (Supplemental Temporary Provisions) Order 1974, SI 1975 (and (NI) Order 1974, SI 2038). For an account of how the port powers were exercised, see Bonner (1985) 170–82.

141 Prevention of Terrorism (Supplemental Temporary Provisions) Order 1976, SI 1976/465 (for Great Britain); SI 1976/466 (for Northern Ireland).

officer, constable, or prison officer could take all such steps as may be reasonably necessary for photographing, measuring, or otherwise identifying him or her.[142]

An attempt was made in the English courts to challenge the use of these port powers in *Re Boyle, O'Hare and McAllister*[143] but, as with challenges to the use of internment powers in Northern Ireland nearly a decade earlier, it failed. The Divisional Court had to admit that the wording of the legislation was quite explicit and that the only basis upon which a challenge might be successfully mounted against the use of the powers was if the applicants could show that there had been bad faith on the part of those who were using the powers, a very difficult thing to prove. As Lord Donaldson MR put it:

> An officer has to satisfy himself of the only matter upon which he must be satisfied, namely, that the person whom he seeks to examine is in the category of person where he can say to himself bona fide 'I wish to find out whether this person has, for example, information which he or she should have disclosed...'[144]

McVeigh, O'Neill and Evans v United Kingdom

Given the near impossibility of challenging port powers through the domestic courts, it was inevitable that a challenge would quickly reach the European Convention organs in Strasbourg. Sure enough, in *McVeigh, O'Neill and Evans v United Kingdom* the European Commission of Human Rights was asked to consider the position of three men who, having been in Ireland on a holiday in 1977, returned by ferry to Liverpool and were then detained for 45 hours for the purposes of examination under the 1976 Order. During that period they were questioned, searched, photographed, and fingerprinted, but at the end of it they were not issued with an exclusion order or charged with any offence. At the admissibility stage in Strasbourg, the arguments presented by the applicants focused on the fact that they were arrested without being suspected of anything, and the European Commission declared the applications admissible because there had not been a failure to exhaust domestic remedies (those that existed being ineffective).[145] But in its report on the merits of the applications, adopted on 18 March 1981,[146] the Commission expressed the opinion by 13 votes to one that there had been no breach of Article 5(1) or (3), by 13 votes to one abstention that there had been no breach of Article 5(2), by 12 votes to two abstentions that there had been no breach of Article 5(4), by 13 votes to one abstention that there had been no breach of Article 5(5), unanimously that

[142] Sch 3, para 5(3).

[143] 30 October 1980, unreported, but discussed in the Jellicoe report (Jellicoe (1983) para 119).

[144] Quoted in Hillyard (1993) 18.

[145] Sub nom *X, Y and Z v UK* (App Nos 8022/77, 8025/77, and 8027/77; decision of 8 December 1979). Amongst the applicants' legal representatives were Cedric Thornberry, a native of Northern Ireland who later had a distinguished career at the United Nations, and Paul O'Higgins, then a lecturer, later a professor, at the University of Cambridge.

[146] The Commission's report is not available through the European Court's website but is printed at (1983) 5 EHRR 71 and (1981) 25 DR 15. Extracts also appear in Mowbray (2007) 263–7.

the measures such as fingerprinting taken during the applicants' detention had not been in breach of Article 8, by 11 votes to one and two abstentions that the retention of records after release had not been in breach of Article 8, and unanimously that the fact that two of the applicants had been prevented from joining their wives involved no breach of Article 8. The only part of the applicants' complaint which was upheld by the Commission—by 12 votes to two—was that the alleged failure to allow two of the applicants to contact their wives while they were detained was a breach of Article 8. The British government contested whether these two applicants had ever actually requested that their wives be contacted, but for the avoidance of future doubt it secured the enactment of section 62 of the Criminal Law Act 1977 (in force from June 1978) to ensure that from then on there would be a full record of all requests for notification of the fact of detention to a person named by persons detained by the police (and also a full record of the reasons for any refusal of such immediate notification).

In the course of its report the Commission stressed that the detention was justifiable not under Article 5(1)(c) but under Article 5(1)(b). In response to the applicants' argument that Article 5(1)(b) could be invoked only if a person had voluntarily refused to comply with the obligation in question, the Commission said that it found much force in this point and that this part of Article 5(1)(b) 'is primarily intended... to cover the case where the law permits detention as a coercive measure to induce a person to perform a specific obligation which he has wilfully or negligently failed to perform hitherto'.[147] But it went on to point out that the wording of the subparagraph 'does not expressly require that there should have been such deliberate or negligent failure on the part of the detainee',[148] while adding that there must be 'specific circumstances such as to warrant the use of detention as a means of securing the fulfilment of an obligation before detention on this ground can be justified'.[149] On the facts of this case the Commission thought that the provisions in the PTA and in the Order made under it did 'create an overall obligation arising in specified circumstances, to submit to "examination"'[150] and that the obligation was 'a specific and concrete obligation' (the test previously laid down by the European Court in *Engel v The Netherlands*[151]).

To justify its view that there were specific circumstances warranting the use of detention in this case the Commission stated:

> In considering whether such circumstances exist, account must be taken... of the nature of the obligation. It is necessary to consider whether its fulfilment is a matter of immediate necessity and whether the circumstances are such that no other means of securing fulfilment is reasonably practicable. A balance must be drawn between the importance in a democratic society of securing the fulfilment of the obligation in question, and the importance of the right to liberty. The duration of the period of detention is also a relevant factor in drawing such a balance.
>
> The Commission has already noted that the obligation imposed on the applicants in the present case was, in essence, an obligation to submit to a security check on entering Great Britain, the scope of the check being limited (broadly speaking) to the prevention of terrorism. The importance in present day conditions of controlling the international movement of

[147] ibid, para 173. [148] ibid, para 174. [149] ibid, para 175. [150] ibid, para 178.
[151] (1976) 1 EHRR 647, para 69.

terrorists has been widely recognised in Western Europe, in particular by the Parliamentary Assembly of the Council of Europe... In the particular context of the UK there is also evident importance in controlling and detecting the movement of terrorists not only between the UK and the Republic of Ireland but also between Great Britain and Ireland as a whole, including Northern Ireland. The necessary checks must obviously be carried out as the person enters or leaves the territory in question and there is a legitimate need to obtain immediate fulfilment of the obligation to submit to such checks.[152]

Following the production of the Commission's report, the case was not referred to the European Court (by either the Commission or the British government), so it fell instead to be considered by the Committee of Ministers.[153] The Committee endorsed all the Commission's views and, because of the changes introduced by the Criminal Law Act 1977, it decided that no further action needed to be taken in the case.[154] One commentator nevertheless sees the case as a prime example of the way in which the UK government and Parliament ignored the European Commission when it was considering later draft legislation: in the very long debates on what became the Police and Criminal Evidence Act 1984 no reference at all was made to the *McVeigh* case even though (in Kinley's view) the European Commission had suggested that waiting up to 48 hours before allowing some friend or relative of the detainee to be informed about the detention was a breach of Article 8 of the Convention.[155]

The *McVeigh* case raises fundamental questions about the degree to which, in practice, the European Convention can protect people of any nationality against arbitrary arrest. It can be seen as a break in the trend that was emerging in Strasbourg to give greater protection to the right to liberty.[156] For that reason alone it is regrettable that the case did not benefit from consideration by the European Court. It left the legal position in the United Kingdom internally inconsistent: while people could not be arrested on the streets unless there was some reasonable suspicion that they were involved in terrorism, they could be arrested at ports and airports even though they were full UK citizens and had left the country for a short holiday. To its credit, the European Commission stressed that on the facts before it the detention had lasted 45 hours, thereby leaving open the question whether detentions for longer periods (the maximum permitted under the PTAs 1974 and 1976 being seven days) would be justifiable. When, as we shall see in Chapter 6, the European Court came to view four days as the maximum permitted period of detention under Article 5(1)(c),[157] it would surely not have tolerated a longer maximum for detention under Article 5(1)(b).

152 (1983) 5 EHRR 71, paras 191–2.

153 As in *Arrowsmith v UK* (1978) 19 DR 5.

154 Resolution of the Committee of Ministers of 24 March 1982, available on the European Court's website.

155 Kinley (1993) 61–2: 'The *McVeigh* case again demonstrates the evidently unsatisfactory operation of the present arrangements for the screening of legislation for compliance with the European Convention'. See also 92.

156 Warbrick (1983b) 758–9, where the outcome is described as demonstrating the 'minimum' nature of the Convention's safeguards.

157 In *Brogan v UK* (1989) 11 EHRR 117.

The Shackleton and Jellicoe reviews

Lord Shackleton reviewed the PTA 1976 in a report published in 1978, long before the Commission decided the *McVeigh* case.[158] He reminded readers that the number of people detained under the port powers was very small—of the nearly four million people who passed through six of Britain's major ports and airports in 1977, only 308 were detained, fewer than one in 10,000; and of the 2,299 people who were detained at some time between the introduction of the powers on 19 November 1974 and 1 June 1978, only 300 were held for more than 48 hours.[159] He noted that in some people's eyes these statistics suggested not that the powers were too intrusive but that they were not as intrusive as they needed to be! He also stated that he had no reason to doubt the judgement of the police that exclusion 'has made a significant contribution' in the fight against terrorism.[160] But, in a comment still relevant today, given the ongoing debates about the need for identity cards in the United Kingdom, he rejected the suggestion that the system of exclusion orders could be replaced by a system of identity cards, such as existed during the Second World War, saying it was doubtful whether such cards would make any significant contribution to the prevention of terrorism.[161] The one change Lord Shackleton did recommend was that the maximum period during which a person detained under the port powers could be held should be 48 hours, not seven days.[162] But the government refused to accept this proposed change.[163]

Earl Jellicoe, in his review published in 1983, also recommended retention of the powers and suggested some minor changes to the way they should be exercised, including their extension to 'suspected international terrorists of any group, cause or nationality'.[164] The only major change made as a result of the Jellicoe review was introduced by the Prevention of Terrorism (Supplemental Temporary Provisions) Order 1984,[165] issued under the PTA 1984, which itself replaced the PTA 1976. Under the new Order a person could not be examined at a port for longer than 12 hours unless an examining officer had 'reasonable grounds for suspecting that the person examined is or has been concerned in the commission, preparation or instigation of acts of terrorism' and unless the person had been required in writing to submit to further examination.[166] But Article 10 of the new Order simply repeated the wording of the previous Article 11, so that persons liable to be detained under the port powers for any period could still be arrested without warrant by an examining officer. This meant that, for up to 12 hours, a person could be arrested even though there were no reasonable grounds for suspecting him or her of any offence or of any

158 Shackleton (1978).
159 ibid, para 98.
160 ibid, para 130.
161 ibid, para 152.
162 ibid, paras 153–4.
163 The seven-day detention power was re-enacted in the PTA 1984, s 12(4)–(5).
164 Jellicoe (1983), para 144. See Walker (1983).
165 SI 1984/418 (for Great Britain); SI 1984/417 (for Northern Ireland).
166 Art 4(2).

involvement in terrorism. The Standing Advisory Commission on Human Rights (SACHR) found Earl Jellicoe's failure to discuss the operation of the port powers in Northern Ireland 'somewhat disturbing' and recommended that the government should repeal the powers in so far as they apply to UK citizens.[167] If the government was unwilling to do that (and it was) SACHR then recommended that the maximum detention period under the port powers should be just four hours, with detention beyond that time requiring an arrest based on reasonable suspicion of involvement in a specific terrorist offence.[168] Detaining people for longer than that without arresting them under a pre-existing legal power was, said SACHR, 'a fundamental departure from the hallowed principles of the common law'.[169] But there do not seem to have been any further applications to Strasbourg challenging an arrest on this basis.

The *McVeigh* case concerned three men who were trying to enter Great Britain, but later a challenge to the port powers was raised by Paul Lyttle, who in 1985 was detained while he was trying to *leave* Great Britain—from the port of Cairnryan in Scotland on a ferry to Northern Ireland. He was detained at Stranraer police station for 31 hours. Not surprisingly, the European Commission adopted exactly the same approach as it had done in *McVeigh*, and ruled the application to be inadmissible.[170] The Commission pointed out that Lyttle could have challenged his detention by bringing habeas corpus proceedings, so there was not even a breach of Article 5(4) of the Convention, which guarantees everyone who has been deprived of his or her liberty by arrest or detention the right to take proceedings by which the lawfulness of the detention can be decided speedily by a court and his or her release ordered if the detention is not lawful. But this ignores the reality that had Lyttle brought such proceedings the domestic court would almost inevitably have rejected his claim because under the doctrine of Parliamentary sovereignty it would have had to apply the provisions of the prevention of terrorism legislation.

Powers to stop and question

Detention for the purpose of securing the fulfilment of an obligation prescribed by law was again at issue in relation to the stop and question powers conferred on the police and army by emergency legislation in Northern Ireland, but again there was no successful challenge to these legislative provisions in Strasbourg.

Starting with section 16 of the Northern Ireland (Emergency Provisions) Act 1973,[171] a person could be arrested in Northern Ireland for failing to answer certain questions when stopped (whether while on foot or in a vehicle) by a police officer or soldier. The provision was re-enacted several times throughout the period of the civil unrest in Northern Ireland, ending up as section 89 of the Terrorism Act 2000, which

[167] SACHR (1984) 11.
[168] ibid, 12.
[169] ibid.
[170] *Lyttle v UK* (1987) 9 EHRR 381.
[171] When read in conjunction with s 11(1) of the same Act.

ceased to have the force of law in Northern Ireland only on 31 July 2007. It allowed a police officer or soldier to stop a person 'for so long as is necessary' to question the person to ascertain (a) his or her identity and movements, (b) what he or she knows about a recent explosion or another recent incident endangering life, and (c) what he or she knows about a person killed or injured in a recent explosion or incident. It was an offence, punishable (by 2001) with a fine of up to £2,000, to refuse to stop when required to do so under this section, to refuse to answer questions addressed under the section, or to refuse to answer questions to the best of one's knowledge and ability.

Despite the very extensive use of this power throughout the years after 1973, its compatibility with Article 5(1)(b) was never fully tested in either the domestic courts or the European Court. It is at least arguable that the obligation in question is not 'specific and concrete', as required by *Engel v The Netherlands*,[172] because terms such as 'movements' and 'recent' are so vague. Whether there were specific circumstances in Northern Ireland justifying the use of the power is also dubious, since it applied in all places and at all times, without reference to any particular goal other than the unstated one of disrupting the movements of terrorists within Northern Ireland. In retrospect it is difficult to make any assessment of whether the existence and/or use of such a power did in fact appreciably assist the security forces in their fight against the terrorists; no official statistics were ever published on how many of the arrests resulting from these powers to stop and question led to people being convicted of involvement in terrorism. There is some anecdotal evidence on the other side of the line, namely that excessive use of the power, in a manner which to some was harassment, so alienated parts of the community in Northern Ireland that it made the security forces' efforts to defeat terrorism more, not less, difficult. But no hard evidence was ever produced comparable to that relating to the more general security force harassment of Irish nationalists within Northern Ireland[173] or within Great Britain.[174]

In 2006 an opportunity did arise, though not in a case directly concerning Northern Ireland, for the House of Lords to consider the compatibility of anti-terrorist stop and search powers with European Convention rights. In *R (Gillan) v Commissioner of Police for the Metropolis*[175] two people were stopped near an arms fair in London's Docklands and their belongings were searched by police officers acting under powers conferred by the Terrorism Act 2000.[176] Nothing untoward was found and they were allowed to go about their business after some minutes (about 30 minutes in the estimate of one of the persons searched, a journalist). In a typically thoughtful and well-crafted lead judgment, Lord Bingham of Cornhill upheld the legality of the stop and search power, even though it was not based on reasonable suspicion of any offence. He explained that Parliament must have thought that the power was an appropriate measure to protect the public against the grave risks posed by terrorism, provided it was subject to effective constraints.[177] Lord Bingham then listed no fewer than 11 such constraints. First, an authorization under the Act could be given only if the person giving it considered it expedient 'for the prevention of acts

[172] (1976) 1 EHRR 647. [173] McBride (1995). [174] Hillyard (1993).
[175] [2006] UKHL 12, [2006] 2 AC 307. [176] s 44.
[177] [2006] UKHL 12, [2006] 2 AC 307, [14].

of terrorism'. Second, it could be given only by a very senior police officer. Third, it could not extend beyond the boundary of a police force area. Fourth, it could last no longer than 28 days. Fifth, it had to be reported to the Secretary of State immediately. Sixth, it lapsed after 48 hours if not confirmed by the Secretary of State. Seventh, the Secretary of State could shorten or cancel an authorization. Eighth, a renewed authorization was subject to the same confirmation procedure. Ninth, the powers conferred could be exercised only to search for articles of a kind which could be used in connection with terrorism. Tenth, reports on the working of the Act had to be made to Parliament at least once a year.[178] Last, it was clear that any misuse of the power to authorize or confirm or search would expose the authorizing officer, the Secretary of State, or the constable, as the case may be, to corrective legal action. The other four Law Lords reached the same conclusion as Lord Bingham,[179] namely that the stop and search power was not incompatible with Article 5, 8, 10, or 11 of the European Convention. Lords Hope and Brown also examined the potential for the power to be used in a discriminatory fashion.[180] When one contrasts the long list of constraints cited to justify the proportionality of the police power examined in the *Gillan* case with the almost complete absence of constraints on the stop and question power applicable in Northern Ireland that began as section 16 of the EPA 1973 and ended up as section 89 of the Terrorism Act 2000, one is left wondering how the latter managed to escape judicial scrutiny at the highest level for so long. Questioning someone about what he or she knows concerning recent incidents endangering life or recent victims may not be as intrusive as searching his or her belongings, and the threat of terrorism in Northern Ireland may have been higher in Northern Ireland during most of that period than it was in Great Britain in the lead up to and in the years following after 9/11,[181] but the disparity in approaches is still remarkable.

Exclusion orders

Amongst the other situations in which the European Convention permits detention (and, indeed, arrest) other than for involvement in a criminal offence is where a person can be arrested 'to prevent his [or her] effecting an unauthorised entry into the country'.[182] It is accepted within international law that States have the right to control who is allowed to enter their territory, and on what conditions, but it is also accepted that one of the attributes of citizenship of a State is the right freely to enter and leave that State. The true extent of the latter right was called into question

[178] Terrorism Act 2000, s 126.

[179] Lords Hope, Scott, Walker, and Brown. The applicants also lost in the Divisional Court ([2003] EWHC 2545 (Admin)) and in the Court of Appeal ([2004] EWCA Civ 1067, [2005] QB 388).

[180] For criticism of the dicta in the case concerning ethnic profiling see Moeckli (2007).

[181] Although very few people seemed to know this, because the authorizations were not published, authorizations under s 44 had been in place for the whole of London for consecutive 28-day periods ever since the 2000 Act had come into force on 19 February 2001: [2006] UKHL 12, [2006] 2 AC 307, [16], per Lord Bingham.

[182] The first limb of Art 5(1)(f).

during the conflict in Northern Ireland by the use made of so-called 'exclusion orders'. As early as 1922, one of the Special Powers Act Regulations allowed the Minister of Home Affairs of Northern Ireland to prohibit any person from residing in, or entering, any part of Northern Ireland, or to grant permission to reside or enter on certain conditions.[183] This was one of the Regulations which was roundly condemned by the Commission of Inquiry into the Special Powers Act held by the London-based National Council for Civil Liberties in 1936. The Commission argued that, in so far as exclusion orders interfered with a person's 'domicile', they were unconstitutional because the Government of Ireland Act 1920 specifically precluded the Parliament of Northern Ireland from passing laws regarding a person's domicile.[184]

Exclusion orders were also issued during the Second World War in an effort to disrupt IRA activity in Great Britain while efforts were there being focused on the fight against Nazism. In fact the Prevention of Violence (Temporary Provisions) Act 1939 remained in force for 15 years, during which time 268 expulsion and prohibition orders were issued by successive Home Secretaries.[185] But exclusion orders were not part of the emergency laws put in place for Northern Ireland in 1973 as a substitute for the Special Powers Act. The power to issue them in relation to terrorism connected with Northern Ireland was introduced by the PTA 1974, supplementing laws on immigration which had by then been added to the statute book. In other words, exclusion orders were seen as a way of keeping mainland Britain free from terrorists, even if this meant using Northern Ireland as, effectively, a dumping ground for those who were excluded. The 1974 Act allowed people to be excluded only from Great Britain but, recognizing the asymmetry and inherent racism in such a law, the British government ensured that, under the PTA 1976, people could be excluded from Northern Ireland too. Nevertheless, there continued to be what the Standing Advisory Commission on Human Rights referred to as 'one way traffic into Northern Ireland' and as 'internal exile'.[186]

'Exclusion orders' could endure for up to three years at a time and could be issued 'in such a way as appears to the Secretary of State expedient to prevent acts of terrorism connected with the affairs of Northern Ireland'.[187] The Secretary of State had to be satisfied that the person to be excluded was or had been concerned in the commission, preparation, or instigation of acts of terrorism connected with Northern Ireland *or* that he or she was attempting or might attempt to enter the territory with a view to being concerned in such activities. No British citizen could be excluded from the whole of the United Kingdom and, initially at any rate, no British citizen could be excluded from Great Britain or from Northern Ireland if he or she had been ordinarily resident in that part of the country for the previous 20 years[188] (the PTA 1974 followed the 1939 legislation in this respect). It was only when the PTA 1989 was

[183] reg 23A, added to the Regs in 1922.

[184] NCCL (1936) 7 and 19. 'Domicile' is here used in its strict legal sense (as a concept in private international law).

[185] HC Deb, vol 493, col 1209 (15 November 1951), cited by Hillyard (1993) 198.

[186] SACHR (1983), para 9.

[187] PTA 1974, s 3(1). For further details on how exclusion orders operated, see Bonner (1985) 191–209.

[188] PTA 1974, s 3(4)(a); PTA 1976, s 4(3)(a).

enacted, following recommendations in the review conducted by Earl Jellicoe,[189] that this 20-year qualification period was drastically reduced to just three years.[190]

There were, it seems, three direct challenges in Strasbourg to the legality of PTA exclusion orders in Strasbourg.[191] No doubt other potential applicants received legal advice to the effect that any such challenge would be bound to fail. The European Convention, as originally agreed, does not prohibit States from imposing limitations on entry to and exit from their territories. But Protocol 4 to the Convention, agreed on 16 September 1963 and in force from 2 May 1968, does contain some relevant provisions.[192] Article 2 begins by conferring on everyone lawfully within the territory of a State the right within that territory to liberty of movement and freedom to choose his or her residence, and it adds that everyone must be free to leave any country, including his or her own. But the Article also makes it clear that restrictions can be imposed on these rights if conditions similar to those found in the second paragraphs of Articles 8 to 11 in the parent Convention are satisfied. Moreover, the rights to liberty of movement and freedom to choose one's residence may be subject 'in particular areas' to restrictions justified by the public interest in a democratic society.[193] Even more pertinently, Article 3 of Protocol 4 prohibits States from expelling any of their nationals from the territory of the State, whether by means of an individual measure or a collective measure, and adds that no national can be deprived of the right to enter the territory of the State of which he or she is a national. These Article 3 rights are unqualified.

Unfortunately, the United Kingdom has never ratified Protocol 4, although it signed it on the day it was agreed. It is one of only four of the 47 member States of the Council of Europe not to be bound by the Protocol,[194] one part of the government's reasoning being that Article 3(2) would cause it severe difficulty in that it confers on people the unrestricted right to be admitted to the State of which they are nationals: there are innumerable people living in former British possessions who can make a sustainable claim to British nationality but to allow them unrestricted entry into the United Kingdom would, it is thought, be potentially overwhelming. The non-applicability of Protocol 4 meant that no-one 'excluded' from a part of the United Kingdom under the PTA 1974 (or by subsequent Acts[195]) was able to challenge the exclusion under that head.[196]

Attempts to challenge exclusion orders in the courts

In *M v UK*[197] the applicant was a UK citizen who from 1975 to 1984 was imprisoned in England for conspiracy to cause explosions. Upon his release he was immediately

[189] Jellicoe (1983).

[190] PTA 1989, ss 5(4)(a) and 6(4)(a).

[191] See the next section of this chapter, which also mentions two indirect challenges.

[192] The effect of the jurisprudence on these provisions is summarized in Van Dijk et al (2006) chs 20–23.

[193] Art 2(4).

[194] The other three are Greece, Switzerland, and Turkey. Several States have entered reservations or declarations relating to the Protocol, including Ireland, which acceded to the Protocol on 29 October 1968.

[195] PTA 1989, ss 4–8 and Sch 2.

[196] On exclusion orders more generally see Bonner (1990) 92–9; Finn (1991) 134.

[197] App No 11517/85, decision of 3 March 1986.

served with an exclusion order under the PTA 1984 and was put on a plane to Dublin. While he was content to live in Ireland, he wanted to be able to make occasional visits to Great Britain, so he applied to have the exclusion order declared a breach of his rights under the European Convention. He lodged his application directly in Strasbourg because he believed that he had no effective domestic remedies which he should first exhaust: he would have to show bad faith on the part of the Secretary of State, but as he did not know the case against him this would not be possible. In Strasbourg he argued that his Article 6 rights had been breached: he had effectively been charged with a criminal offence and was presumed to be guilty of that offence, yet he had not been told the details of the case against him and had not been given any opportunity to examine witnesses whose evidence motivated the Secretary of State's decision to issue the exclusion order; nor did the 1984 Act provide him with an independent and impartial tribunal to consider the charge against him. The European Commission ruled, however, that the applicant's exclusion from Great Britain was not 'a criminal penalty' but rather 'a security measure', so Article 6 was not engaged at all. For the same reason the applicant could not engage Article 7, which prohibits the retrospective imposition of criminal sanctions on what was non-criminal behaviour at the time it took place. As regards Article 8, the Commission observed that this provision does not confer a right to reside in any particular part of a Convention country and that in any event the applicant had not substantiated his allegation that he was prevented from seeing elderly members of his family who lived in Great Britain. Nor was Article 9 breached (the right to freedom of belief), and Article 13 (the right to an effective remedy) was of no assistance to the applicant because that provision 'does not guarantee a remedy in respect of complaints directed against legislative provisions as in this case'.[198] The European Commission, in short, gave the applicant short shrift, declaring his application to be 'manifestly ill-founded'.[199] There were no dissenting voices among the 13 Commissioners, who included Brendan Kiernan from Ireland. The simple truth was that the European Convention was no help at all in challenging the use of the power to exclude. As the Commission perhaps unwittingly conceded (in relation to Article 9, but the point applies more generally):

> It is clear... that the applicant has been excluded from Great Britain because of his involvement with a terrorist organisation, albeit that the precise facts or information on which the order is based are not known. The Commission does not consider that in these circumstances there can be said to be an interference with his rights...[200]

In *McGlinchey (Paul), Quinn and Barrow v UK*[201] and in *O'Neill (Peter) v United Kingdom*[202] the complainants focused on the fact that their release from detention had been delayed while applications for orders excluding them from Great Britain were applied for. In the former case the applicants won at the Commission on the basis that their detention exceeded the four-day maximum allowed by the European

198 ibid, para 15.
199 Under Art 27(2) of the Convention, now Art 35(3).
200 *M v UK*, App No 11517/85, decision of 3 March 1986, para 14.
201 App 15096–15008/89, decision of 29 March 1989.
202 App 19748/92, decision of 30 January 1992.

Court in *Brogan v United Kingdom*,[203] which meant that the Commission did not have to comment on the compatibility of exclusion orders with the Convention. In the *Peter O'Neill* case the Commission was again relieved of that obligation for the simple reason that the application was inadmissible on the ground that it had not been brought within the six-month time limit. It is worth noting in passing that when the Home Secretary was introducing the second reading of the PTA 1974 he suggested that the seven-day detention power was being created specifically to allow time for the government to consider whether to make exclusion orders.[204] In *McCullough v United Kingdom*[205]the Court reiterated its position in *M v United Kingdom*,[206] that exclusion orders did not even engage Article 6 and did not interfere with family life in a way that breached Article 8(1). Nor was the applicant able to adduce evidence to show that there was a discriminatory aspect to the use of exclusion orders based on religious belief or political opinion.

The most interesting Strasbourg decision on exclusion orders is probably *Adams and Benn v United Kingdom*,[207] where the President of Sinn Féin argued that the order excluding him from Great Britain was unjustified in that it prevented him from attending an event in Parliament, organized by Tony Benn MP, at which the prospects for peace in Northern Ireland were to be discussed. Gerry Adams had previously been issued with an exclusion order in 1982 but this had been revoked six months later when he was elected to Westminster (he lost his seat in the election of 1992). When Tony Benn informed the Secretary of State that he had invited Gerry Adams to the meeting in 1993 the Secretary of State issued an exclusion order against him the next day. Adams then challenged the order through judicial review proceedings, but lost on the domestic law because the Divisional Court recognized that there were political sensitivities at stake, the Secretary of State was not obliged to give reasons, and 'the desirability of an effective remedy must yield to the higher interest of the state'.[208] But the court did refer a number of questions to the European Court of Justice (ECJ) because issues arose as to the interpretation of European Community law. Before the ECJ could deal with the case, however, the IRA announced a ceasefire in August 1994 and the Secretary of State revoked the exclusion order against Gerry Adams in October 1994. The government then persuaded the Divisional Court to withdraw the reference it had made to the ECJ. In his application to the European Commission Adams claimed a breach of Article 6 in that the Divisional Court had ultimately refused to hear his case, of Article 10 in that the exclusion order prevented him from speaking at a meeting, and of Article 13 in that the dismissal of his judicial review proceedings meant that he had been denied the right to an effective remedy.

[203] (1989) 11 EHRR 117; this case is discussed in more detail in ch 6.

[204] 'The powers of arrest in Clause 7 largely concern matters closely related to the powers to make exclusion orders which essentially depend upon decisions of the executive. Accordingly, it would not be appropriate to make these matters dependent on any form of judicial determination.' HC Deb, vol 882, col 641 (28 November 1974), per Roy Jenkins MP.

[205] (1998) 25 EHRR CD 34.

[206] App No 11517/85, decision of 3 March 1986.

[207] App Nos 28979/95 and 30343/96, decision of 13 January 1997.

[208] Cited in the decision of the European Commission, p 3.

Tony Benn, the second applicant, argued that his own rights under Articles 10 and 13 had been breached, including his right to receive information and ideas.

The European Commission, amazingly, ruled that the interference with the applicants' rights to freedom of expression were both 'necessary in a democratic society' and 'proportionate'. On the former point it repeated the mantra that 'it is in the first place for the national authorities to assess whether there is a pressing social need for a restriction and in making their assessment they enjoy a certain margin of appreciation'.[209] On the latter point it recalled 'the sensitive and complex issues arising in the context of Northern Ireland where there have been ongoing efforts to establish a peace process acceptable to the various communities and parties involved and where the threat of renewed incidents of violence remains real and continuous'.[210] The Commission also ruled that Article 6 was not engaged because the right to free movement within EC law is not a 'civil right or obligation' for the purposes of that article. And Article 13 only applies when an individual can be said to have an 'arguable claim' of a violation of the Convention, which the applicants here, in the Commission's eyes, did not have.

There is perhaps no better example of the pusillanimity of the Strasbourg enforcement organs than this decision in *Adams and Benn v United Kingdom*, especially given that the Commission was deciding the case more than three years after the events which triggered the applications. By that time the IRA ceasefire of August 1994 had come and gone, having been shattered by a massive car bomb in the docklands of London in February 1996, and, although all-party talks had begun in June 1996 under the chairmanship of Senator George Mitchell from the USA, they excluded Sinn Féin because no new ceasefire had yet been put in place. But rather than take a risk for peace in the name of human rights (as President Clinton had done in 1994 by issuing a visa to Gerry Adams), and recognizing, for example, that Adams was already free to speak his mind on the peace process in Northern Ireland itself, it seems extraordinary that the Commission allowed an exclusion order to be clamped on a party political leader to prevent him travelling to another part of the same State to speak at a meeting with other elected representatives. The order looks as if it was imposed for purely political purposes.[211]

People subjected to exclusion orders could have recourse to an 'adviser', but the adviser's opinion on the issue was not binding on the Secretary of State and, as Anne Grimes and David Bonner pointed out in 1997, despite a ruling by the European Court of Justice in the *Gallagher* case,[212] exclusion orders were still not subjected to 'a binding process of review by an independent judicial body'.[213] In 1983 John Gallagher

[209] App Nos 28979/95 and 30343/96, decision of 13 January 1997, p 7.

[210] ibid.

[211] Others would argue that political manoeuvring is, in the end, the best way forward in peace processes, even if this means not acting in a wholly moral way. See, eg, Powell (2008).

[212] *R v Secretary of State for the Home Dept, ex p John Gallagher* [1995] ECR I-4253. The Court saw nothing wrong in the mere fact that the person giving advice to the Secretary of State was appointed by the Secretary of State; what really mattered was whether the adviser could act with absolute independence, and only the national court could assess that.

[213] Grimes and Bonner (1997) 136.

had been sentenced in Ireland to three years' imprisonment for possessing two rifles for unlawful purposes. In 1991 he was arrested in England under the PTA 1989 and was served with an exclusion order. He challenged this in the English High Court and, on appeal, in the Court of Appeal. He relied on Article 9(1) of EC Directive 64/221, which concerned the coordination of special measures relating to movement and residence of foreign nationals that are justified on grounds of public policy, public security, or public health. Article 9(1) reads:

> Where there is no right of appeal to a court of law, or where such appeal may be only in respect of the legal validity of the decision, or where the appeal cannot have suspensory effect, a decision . . . ordering the expulsion of [a person allowed to reside in the territory] . . . shall not be taken by the administrative authority, save in cases of urgency, until an opinion has been obtained from a competent authority of the host country before which the person concerned enjoys such rights of defence and of assistance and representation as the domestic law of that country provides for.

Mr Gallagher acknowledged that he had the right under the PTA 1989 to make representations in writing to the Secretary of State setting out the grounds of his objection to the exclusion order, and to request a personal interview with the person or persons nominated by the Secretary of State for that purpose. Such an interview did indeed take place, in Dublin, but when the Secretary of State reconsidered his decision in light of that interview he confirmed what he had previously decided. Mr Gallagher argued that Article 9(1) required the nominated person's view of the matter to be given *before* the decision to expel a person was taken. The Court of Appeal, uncertain of the preferred interpretation of Article 9(1), referred the issue to the European Court of Justice in Luxembourg. That Court agreed with Mr Gallagher's view of Article 9(1) and stressed that any other interpretation would eliminate the distinction between Articles 9(1) and (2), the latter covering situations where an expulsion order is made against someone who has not yet been permitted to reside in the territory. The case was then referred back to the Court of Appeal in England for this ruling to be applied to the facts. Presumably domestic practice then changed on this point, although by late 1995 very few new exclusion orders were being made in any event. David Bonner observes that the decision in *Gallagher* did not prove 'a catalyst for subjecting [exclusion orders] to a binding process of review by an independent judicial body'.[214] Instead, as a response to the European Court of Human Rights' judgment in *Chahal v United Kingdom*,[215] the British government set up the Special Immigration Appeals Commission to deal with such cases.[216] But by that time the power to exclude had been suspended.

It was, as we saw in the case involving Gerry Adams, extremely difficult to get an exclusion order revoked or overturned in the domestic courts. An attempt to do so by Sean Stitt, who had been excluded from Great Britain since 1978, failed in 1987 because the Divisional Court in England would not order the Home Secretary to

[214] Bonner (2000) 60.
[215] (1997) 23 EHRR 413.
[216] Special Immigration Appeals Commission Act 1997.

disclose to the applicant the information he was relying upon to make the order.[217] The information supposedly raised issues of national security and the court deferred to the Home Secretary's exclusive right to use it as he thought best. As Antonio Vercher points out,[218] this reflected the more general attitude of English courts at that time to issues of national security, as illustrated by *R v Secretary of State for the Home Department, ex p Hosenball*.[219] Even European Community law, which protects the free movement of workers, the right of establishment, and the right to provide and receive services, allows for an exception to these rights on public policy and public security grounds. This was confirmed in 1974 in a case brought by a member of the Church of Scientology who had been refused entry into the United Kingdom.[220] And in another case the European Court of Justice suggested that restrictions operating within the borders of a member State were outside its purview.[221] But the British government was also able to cite public policy grounds for *revoking* exclusion orders, as it did vis-à-vis Gerry Adams and Martin McGuinness in 1994, just a few weeks after the announcement of the IRA's ceasefire. Seventy other exclusion orders, however, were left in place. Later that year a court in England did scrutinize more closely a decision by the Home Secretary to issue an exclusion order against a man from Northern Ireland who claimed that requiring him, in effect, to live in Northern Ireland would put his life at risk, but in the end the challenge again failed because the court would not compel the Home Secretary to reveal any of the information which prompted him to make his decision.[222]

Criticisms of the power to exclude

Even if Protocol 4 to the European Convention had been in force for the United Kingdom, this would not have guaranteed that exclusion orders issued under the PTA would have been held invalid by the European Court. The control of the movement of suspected terrorists could well be seen as justified by the public interest in controlling crime, and the wording of Article 3 of the Protocol does not mean that nationals have a right to enter any particular part of the territory of the State. Human rights campaigners did of course complain about the operation of exclusion orders, especially as they seemed to result in many suspected terrorists being confined to Northern Ireland, as if other people living there were not as deserving of protection against terrorism as people living elsewhere in the United Kingdom. It is likely, as well, that a number of people were subjected to exclusion orders even though there

217 *R v Secretary of State for the Home Department, ex p Stitt, The Times*, 3 February 1987.

218 Vercher (1992) 46.

219 [1977] 1 WLR 766 (CA). In this case an American journalist failed in his attempt to obtain further information from the British Home Secretary as to why he was to be deported from the UK. Lord Denning MR, citing *R v Halliday* [1917] AC 260 and *Liversidge v Anderson* [1942] AC 206, said (at 778F): '... this is no ordinary case. It is a case in which national security is involved: and our history shows that, when the state itself is endangered, our cherished freedoms may have to take second place. Time after time Parliament has so enacted and the courts have loyally followed.'

220 *Van Duyn v Home Office* [1974] 1 WLR 1107.

221 *R v Saunders* [1979] 2 CMLR 216.

222 *R v Secretary of State for the Home Dept, ex p McQuillan* [1995] 3 All ER 400.

were in fact no reasonable grounds for suspecting them of being involved in terrorism. But despite widespread dissatisfaction with the system of exclusion orders, the power to issue them remained in existence for many more years.

In the first two reviews of the PTAs, conducted by Lord Shackleton in 1978[223] and by Earl Jellicoe in 1983,[224] the power was deemed to be necessary as a measure of last resort, but the Standing Advisory Commission on Human Rights in Northern Ireland was consistently of the view that it was unnecessary, pointing out that it violated the spirit (if not the letter) of Article 8 of the European Convention, which protects the right to a family life.[225] Even the official reviewer of the PTAs in the mid-1980s, Sir Cyril Philips, declared the power to be 'objectionable in principle' and thought that 'the strategy of transferring suspected terrorists from one part of the United Kingdom to another appears to have diminishing relevance and application'.[226] He recommended that the power to exclude be phased out and this view was repeated by his successor in the post of official reviewer, Viscount Colville, both in his report on the operation of the PTA during 1986[227] and in his more general review of the PTA published in 1987.[228] Even though Lord Colville was considered quite conservative by human rights activists, he made a sober assessment of this power, though without referring once to the European Convention on Human Rights:

I have to agree that it is probably an effective way of getting rid of people from an area where otherwise they might cause great trouble; and that it disrupts terrorist lines of communication and supply of arms, ammunition and explosives. However I am not convinced that the ends justify the means... The Home Secretary announced earlier this year that after careful consideration he had decided it would not now be wise to discontinue this power. I recognise that the alternative is a hard decision, but I express the view that it would be the correct one both in terms of civil rights in the United Kingdom and this country's reputation in that respect among the International Community.[229]

In the campaign to get rid of exclusion orders, references were often made to the effect of such orders on the rights guaranteed by the European Convention. Paddy Hillyard made much of these effects in his seminal 1993 study,[230] where he argued that exclusion orders involved 'a serious deprivation of civil liberties', adding:

They affect people's freedom of movement, the right to family life, the right to associate freely with others, the right to participate in public affairs and the right to seek work.

[223] Shackleton (1978). Lord Shackleton noted (at para 126) that 'it has always been the case that the Secretary of State has revoked an exclusion order where an Adviser has recommended that it should be revoked', and (at para 130) that 'the police have no doubt that exclusion has made a significant contribution to [the prevention of terrorism]. On the basis of the cases I have seen I have no reason to doubt their judgment.'

[224] Jellicoe (1983). Earl Jellicoe concluded 'with some reluctance' that 'for the present at least a residual power to exclude must remain' (para 200).

[225] See, eg, SACHR (1985), para 40. Similar views were expressed in SACHR (1986), paras 61–2; SACHR (1987), pp 13–4, para 2(a); and SACHR (1988) 55–8.

[226] Philips (1986), para 20.

[227] para 2.3.7.

[228] Colville (1987).

[229] ibid, para 11.6.1.

[230] Hillyard (1993) chs 10 and 11.

> Exclusion orders not only affect the person on whom they are served. The partner and children of the subject of the exclusion order also suffer considerable disruption. If they accompany the excludee, they suffer all the loss of rights that he or she has suffered. If they do not, family life is broken up.[231]

But the European Court was of the view, as we have seen, that exclusion orders were not incompatible with Article 8, or with any other article, in the Convention. The Court did not say that there was interference but that it was justified: it did not think there was any interference in the first place.

The UK government eventually altered its policy on exclusion orders in the late 1990s. In 1997 it revoked all existing orders and from 22 March 1998 it suspended the powers to make new orders,[232] doubtless because of the need to put in place 'confidence building measures' to facilitate the party political talks that were to culminate in the Belfast (Good Friday) Agreement of 10 April 1998.[233] By that time several hundred people had been excluded from Great Britain since 1974, the vast majority to Northern Ireland; 34 people had been excluded from Northern Ireland.[234] Hogan and Walker say that 'exclusion might be depicted as a rather draconian and inflexible alternative to internment' and they suggest that the Special Powers Act Regulations were more imaginative in that they permitted orders to be issued prohibiting residence in, or entry into, specified areas or imposing conditions as regards reporting regularly to the police.[235] But it seems likely that the latter measures were not deemed to be enforceable within Northern Ireland after the civil unrest became so widespread in the early 1970s. To the UK government exclusion was seen as an acceptable, if rather unsubtle and only partly effectual, halfway house between internment and complete freedom. The fact that it was not contrary to EC law or to the European Convention made it an all the more attractive weapon against terrorism.

In 2005, by way of response to the House of Lords' decision that detention without trial of non-British nationals reasonably suspected of involvement in international terrorism was discriminatory and disproportionate, the government persuaded Parliament to authorize the use of 'control orders' to inhibit the movements of persons against whom there was such reasonable suspicion but who could not be deported because they would be at risk of ill-treatment in their home country and could not be charged because the evidence against them was not strong enough to support a conviction in a court of law. As alluded to earlier, the legality of these control orders has itself been successfully challenged in some cases, a lot turning on the precise restrictions which they place on the activities of the controlees.[236] Here it is worth

[231] ibid, 237.

[232] Prevention of Terrorism (Temporary Provisions) Act 1989 (Partial Continuance) Order 1998, SI 768.

[233] *Agreement reached in the Multi-Party Negotiations in Northern Ireland*, Belfast, Her Majesty's Stationery Office, Cmnd 3883.

[234] For a Table representing the picture up to the end of 1991, see Hillyard (1993) 208. In the three years 1992–4 there were just nine new exclusion orders issued and by the end of 1994 there were 58 in total still in force, compared with 238 at the end of 1984: *Home Office Statistical Bulletin on the Operation of the Prevention of Terrorism Legislation 1994*, para 8 and Table 1. For exclusions from Northern Ireland see the quarterly statistics issued by the Northern Ireland Office, 2nd quarter 1998, Table 7.

[235] Hogan and Walker (1989) 96.

[236] See 73–4 above.

emphasizing that such control orders were never resorted to specifically to deal with terrorism in Northern Ireland. Given the resources required to enforce such orders, it is likely that they would not have been a feasible option in a society which had so many individuals who might have been made subject to them.

Conclusion

It is clear from the analysis of the powers considered in this chapter that the European Convention singularly failed to control them effectively. The UK government was able to exploit loopholes in the wording of the Convention and push to the limits the qualifications on the right not to be deprived of liberty that is conferred by Article 5. There was nothing in existing Strasbourg jurisprudence to facilitate successful challenges to these powers. Through issuing a derogation notice the government was able to lock people up indefinitely without trial, and even without having to rely on any such derogation it could detain people at ports and airports in the absence of any suspicion about their past or future activities, restrict their movements on the streets, and exclude them from travelling within the United Kingdom on grounds that could not in practice be scrutinized in a court of law.

A case can be made for saying that all of these powers were in fact necessary, and that their exercise helped to prevent even more violence occurring in connection with the affairs of Northern Ireland than actually took place. Many would argue that the detention of people at ports and airports, or at pedestrian or vehicle check points within Northern Ireland, was not an issue worthy of much attention: if it constituted an interference with human rights at all, it was justifiable on the basis that the interest of society in preventing disorder or crime outweighed the inconvenience experienced by a small minority of people. Some might even suggest that excluding people from one part of the country, or locking them up indefinitely without trial, was a price worth paying given that those people were thereby prevented from committing violent acts for the duration of their exclusion or detention. But the wider point is that a legal system based on the rule of law cannot afford to have 'blind spots' within which legal scrutiny does not operate. If there has to be interference with people's human rights, there needs to be a host of safeguards put in place to ensure that the interference does not become too deep or too broad. Giving so much power to executive agencies, while neutering the power of the courts, is a sure way of undermining people's confidence in the rule of law and their support for democratic values. To that extent it does the work of terrorists for them. In the next chapter we will see that similar comments can be made in relation to the more general powers of arrest in Northern Ireland. The lack of insistence upon such safeguards either in the European Convention itself or in the judgments of the European Court is a matter for considerable regret.

5

Powers of Arrest

The scope of Article 5 of the Convention

The right to liberty is protected by Article 5 of the European Convention, but not in the absolute or quasi-absolute terms that are used in Articles 2, 3, and 4.[1] Indeed, as with Article 6 on the right to a fair trial,[2] Article 5 provides a degree of protection which is midway between the practically absolute protection guaranteed by the first few articles of the Convention and the much more qualified protection guaranteed by Articles 8 to 11 of the Convention. The approach of Article 5(1) is first of all to state categorically that 'Everyone has the right to liberty and security of person', but then to provide a long list of exceptions to that right which eat into it considerably. The list begins with the most obvious exception—where a person has been convicted of an offence by a competent court—and proceeds through increasingly less evident situations, culminating in the detention of a person against whom action is being taken with a view to his or her deportation or extradition. The thrust of Article 5(1) can be summarized by saying that it aims to protect people against being deprived of their liberty in an arbitrary fashion, but whether it actually achieves this is a moot point, especially in situations where a country is experiencing serious civil unrest.

After conferring the right in paragraph (1), restricted though it be, Article 5 continues in paragraph (2) by conferring an additional right on everyone who has been arrested, namely the right to be informed promptly, in a language which the person understands, of the reason for his or her arrest and of any charge against him or her. Article 5(3) is addressed specifically at people who, as allowed by Article 5(1)(c), have been arrested or detained with a view to being brought before a competent legal authority on reasonable suspicion of having committed an offence or because it is reasonably considered necessary to prevent them from committing an offence or from fleeing after having done so. Article 5(3) says that these people have to be brought promptly before a judge or other officer authorized by law to exercise judicial power and that they are entitled to be tried within a reasonable time or to be released

[1] See generally Murdoch (2002); Ovey and White (2006) ch 7; Leach (2005) 220–41; Janis, Kay, and Bradley (2008) ch 12.

[2] See ch 8 below.

pending their trial. Article 5(4) supplements this right—and confers it on all persons who have been arrested or detained for whatever reason—by saying that they are entitled to take proceedings by which the lawfulness of their detention shall be decided speedily by a court and their release ordered if the detention is not lawful. Finally, Article 5(5) specifically confers on everyone who has been the victim of arrest or detention in contravention of Article 5 the right to compensation. Surprisingly, this is the only right to compensation guaranteed by the Convention, which is some indication of the importance attributed to the right to liberty by the Convention's framers. Not even the right not to be tortured carries with it the automatic right to compensation if torture nevertheless occurs. Article 13 of the Convention says that everyone whose rights and freedoms as set forth in the Convention are violated must be given an effective remedy before a national authority, but this does not necessarily mean that compensation has to be paid.

A further indication of the importance of the right to liberty is that, more so than any other Convention article, Article 5 is replete with use of the word 'lawful'. Each of the six sub-paragraphs in Article 5(1)—where the exceptions to the right to liberty are listed—requires the arrest or detention in question to be 'lawful'. To many casual readers of the Convention this may seem odd, for surely the whole point of the Convention itself is to determine what is or is not lawful? But the crucial feature to bear in mind is that the Convention is actually a default, or subsidiary, document: it provides protection for rights in situations where member States themselves fail to do so. Putting this differently, the Convention allows member States to protect rights to whatever extent they wish, but insists that certain minimum standards must not be undercut. The Convention requires member States to protect rights 'by law' (Article 2), in a 'lawful' way (Article 5), 'in accordance with the law' (Article 8), subject to limitations 'prescribed by law' (Articles 9, 10, and 11), or 'according to national laws' (Article 12). All of these circumlocutions are intended to indicate that the primary source of protection for rights in Europe is the national law of each State and that it is only if no such laws exist, are not of the minimum standards, or are breached, that the European Convention's organs need to step in.

Curiously, the Convention itself does not provide any guidance as to what 'law' actually means in this context. What really counts as 'law'? Does it have to be an Act of the national Parliament? Can a ministerial order suffice? Or a judicial precedent? What if the law has not been officially published or is difficult to look up, or is retrospective in nature, very vague, or difficult to comprehend? Over the years the European Court of Human Rights has devised answers to questions such as these, thereby producing a definition of law which helps to clarify the precise extent to which Convention rights are protected. There are at least three requirements which a norm must satisfy to be a 'law' for Convention purposes: it must be formulated with sufficient precision (so that, for instance, if it confers a discretion the scope of that discretion and how it is to exercised must be indicated with sufficient clarity); it must be accessible; and it must be applicable in a foreseeable way.[3]

[3] See, eg, *Sunday Times v UK* (1979–80) 2 EHRR 245; *Silver v UK* (1983) 5 EHRR 347; *Olsson v Sweden (No 1)* (1989) 11 EHRR 259.

We shall be examining some of the controversial aspects of this definition later in this chapter, but for now it is enough to stress one corollary to the subsidiary nature of the Convention. This is that if a member State wishes to exceed the minimum protection of rights guaranteed by the Convention it is free to do so, and if for some reason the State fails to meet its own higher standards in a particular case the victim of that failure can then take his or her case to Strasbourg arguing that he or she has not been treated 'lawfully'. The European Court of Human Rights, when dealing with such a complaint, will judge the lawfulness of what has happened not just by looking at whether the minimum protection guaranteed by the Convention has been assured but also by asking whether the State's own, more demanding, laws have been complied with. It is in relation to Article 5 that this approach to Convention rights is most apparent, for States differ quite a lot in the laws they have in place concerning the deprivation of people's liberty and the rights of such people if they have been arrested.

Having stressed the strengths of Article 5 it is worth noting some of its limitations. For a start, it is relatively silent on what rights must be guaranteed to people once they have been deprived of their liberty. It says nothing, for example, about the environment within which they must be detained, their access to fresh air and to nutritious food, their ability to consult with a lawyer, their freedom to communicate with a member of their family, a friend or the outside world, their right to have interrogation sessions audio- or video-recorded, or their access to reading materials. Some of these claims may be protected by other rights guaranteed by the Convention, such as the right not to be ill-treated (Article 3), the right to a fair trial (Article 6), or the right to respect for one's private and family life and for one's correspondence (Article 8), but they are not protected by Article 5 and so the right to compensation conferred by Article 5(5) does not apply if they are violated. Nor, as we shall see in Chapter 8, does Article 5 fully explain how, if at all, the right to liberty is to be protected after a person has been charged with a criminal offence.

The right to security

Article 5 is headed 'Right to liberty and security' and the opening words of Article 5(1) state bluntly that 'Everyone has the right to liberty and security of person'. But the word 'security' does not appear at any later point in the Article, nor in any other provision of the Convention, and the European Court has chosen not to develop its meaning in any significant way. The Court has not accepted, for example, that the right to security of person means that the State is under an obligation to protect people against dangers, or that the State is required to treat detainees in a particular way. When it has expanded upon such an obligation it has done so by interpreting the right to life in Article 2 as carrying with it further positive duties on State authorities to protect people against crimes and accidents, or by construing the right not to be subjected to inhuman or degrading treatment in Article 3 as entailing that certain facilities must be provided in places of detention. Moreover, in so far as 'security of person' might be taken to refer to a person's need to feel protected against non-violent but still intrusive interference with his or her personal life, this is much more likely to be dealt with by the Court under the aegis of Article 8 rather than Article 5.[4]

Some might think that the European Court has missed an opportunity to develop Article 5 in a way that would raise people's sense of safety and bodily integrity. Doing so would certainly help to counter the perception that the European Convention is all about protecting the rights of criminals and that it ignores the plight of victims or potential victims of crimes. Throughout the troubles in Northern Ireland it was difficult for supporters of the Convention to sell its message to many ordinary members of the public because the latter did not think the Convention could do much to protect them against the scourge of violence, from whatever source it emanated, but especially violence perpetrated by illegal paramilitary organizations. We will see in Chapters 7 and 9 how, respectively, Articles 3 and 2 of the Convention have not been actively developed by the European Court in a way which helps to protect people's right to life in the face of terrorism. Likewise, the Court has always supported the view that Article 5 should be confined to protecting people against deprivations of liberty. It has taken 'security of person' to mean 'security against arbitrary arrest', not 'security against criminals'. And, as we saw in the previous chapter, deprivation of liberty is not the same thing, in the eyes of the European Court, as restrictions on freedom of movement. Drawing a line between the two concepts—deprivation of liberty and restrictions on movement—is not always easy.

Arrests in connection with criminal offences

As mentioned in Chapter 4, the ending of internment in Northern Ireland in 1975 did not mean the lifting of the UK's derogation notice under Article 15 of the Convention, because the 'emergency' arrest powers still in force would otherwise have been in breach of Article 5. But the ending of internment did increase the pressure on the British government and its security forces to make the other counter-terrorism powers fully effective.[5]

Of the six exceptions to the right to liberty listed in Article 5(1)(a) to (f) of the Convention, only three refer to arrest powers. Sub-paragraph (b) allows the lawful arrest of a person 'for non-compliance with a lawful order of a court or in order to secure the fulfilment of any obligation prescribed by law'.[6] Sub-paragraph (c) allows the lawful arrest of a person 'for the purpose of bringing him [or her] before a competent legal authority on reasonable suspicion of having committed an offence or when it is reasonably considered necessary to prevent his [or her] committing an offence or fleeing after having done so'. And sub-paragraph (f) envisages the lawful arrest of a person 'to prevent his [or her] effecting an unauthorised entry into the country' or if

[4] On the relevance of Art 8 to the conflict in Northern Ireland, see ch 10 below.

[5] See, generally, Walsh (1983) ch 2.

[6] We saw in ch 4 that this provision was held not to be breached by the UK's laws on 'port powers': *McVeigh, O'Neill and Evans v UK* (1983) 5 EHRR 71.

he or she is a person 'against whom action is being taken with a view to deportation or extradition'.[7] During the troubles in Northern Ireland the first two of these subparagraphs were at issue in several complaints taken to Strasbourg. In all but one of the applications, however, the complaint was not upheld. We have dealt with Article 5(1)(b) already.[8] The focus here is on Article 5(1)(c), and to explain the law's development and the role played in it by the European Convention it is first necessary to distinguish between 'ordinary' arrest powers and 'special' arrest powers and then between the army's special arrest powers and the police's special arrest powers.

'Ordinary' and 'special' arrest powers

At the start of the troubles in 1968 there was an 'ordinary' power of arrest in Northern Ireland but also two 'special' powers of arrest. The ordinary power was conferred by section 2 of the Criminal Law Act (NI) 1967, which exactly mirrored section 2 of the Criminal Law Act 1967 applying in England and Wales. Section 2(1) defined an arrestable offence as one which carried a potential penalty of at least five years' imprisonment and section 2(4) went on to say that a police officer could arrest without warrant anyone whom he or she reasonably suspected to be guilty of an arrestable offence which the police officer reasonably suspected to have been committed. Section 2(5) also allowed a police officer to arrest without warrant anyone who was, or whom he or she reasonably suspected to be, about to commit an arrestable offence.

Each of the special arrest powers were conferred by regulations issued under the Civil Authorities (Special Powers) Acts (NI) 1922–43. They allowed a vast array of people to be 'authorized' to carry out arrests, without requiring any formal process to be gone through for such authorization to occur. The first of the powers was conferred by regulation 10, as substituted in 1957. This stated that:

> Any officer of the Royal Ulster Constabulary, for the preservation of the peace and maintenance of order, may authorise the arrest without warrant and detention for a period of not more than 48 hours of any person for the purpose of interrogation.[9]

While a period of detention for 48 hours is not *per se* a breach of Article 5, that Article does not envisage the arrest of someone merely so that he or she can be interrogated. The arrested person must at least have been reasonably suspected of having committed an offence, or the arrest must have been 'reasonably considered necessary' to prevent his or her committing an offence. This regulation 10 arrest power was, therefore, clearly incompatible with Article 5. It could have been approved by the European Court only on the basis that the UK government had issued a derogation notice under Article 15 of the Convention indicating that from time to time it might have to arrest people in such circumstances.

[7] Again we saw in ch 4 that this provision provided no protection to people who were the subject of exclusion orders: *M v UK* App No 11517/85, decision of 3 March 1986. Extradition is discussed in ch 8 below.

[8] See ch 4, in the section on port powers.

[9] Substituted by the Civil Authorities (Special Powers) Acts (Amending) (No 6) Regs (NI) 1957, SR 132.

The second special arrest power was conferred by regulation 11(1), as substituted in 1956. This stated:

> Any person authorised for the purpose by the civil authority, or any police constable, or member of any of Her Majesty's forces on duty when the occasion for the arrest arises may arrest without warrant any person whom he suspects of acting or of having acted or of being about to act in a manner prejudicial to the preservation of the peace or maintenance of order . . . [10]

This effectively gave *carte blanche* to police officers and soldiers to arrest anyone whom they felt was acting suspiciously. Again, though, mere suspicion, even of a serious offence, is not enough to justify deprivation of liberty under Article 5 of the European Convention, so this power too would have fallen foul of that provision had it not been for a derogation notice in place under Article 15. Even if there had been reasonable suspicion in a particular case, the arresting officer would have needed to show, if wishing to comply with Article 5, that the prejudice to 'the preservation of the peace or maintenance of order' was equivalent to a criminal offence, which would not always have been easy to do. Regulation 11(1) shares with regulation 10 this reference to the preservation of the peace and the maintenance of order, no doubt partly because the Parliament of Northern Ireland was empowered to make laws only for the peace, order, and good government of Northern Ireland.[11] It is the kind of very general phrase which authoritarian governments around the world like to use in their legislation in order to allow their security forces to perpetuate the government's view of what peace and order mean in practice.

Clearly there was enough uncertainty surrounding the appropriateness of arrest powers in Northern Ireland when direct rule was imposed in March 1972 to justify a formal review, although it does not seem that the requirements of the European Convention were at the forefront of the British government's mind at that time. A review duly occurred in 1972, when the Diplock Commission was tasked with considering the legal procedures to deal with terrorist activities in Northern Ireland.[12] Very oddly, the Commission's report made recommendations only in relation to the arrest powers of the army, not the police, so we shall begin our analysis with the army powers.

Special army arrest powers

Normally, members of the army have no greater arrest powers than ordinary citizens have. But when the army is called upon to help the police control civil unrest it is usual—and sensible—for Parliament to confer special, but limited, arrest powers on soldiers.[13] After very little explanation of the current state of the law in this field, and no discussion of the pros and cons of the various options available for reforming the

[10] Civil Authorities (Special Powers) Acts (Amending) Regs (NI) 1956, SR 191. Regs 11(2) and (5) confirmed that persons arrested under reg 11(1) could be detained indefinitely without trial.

[11] Government of Ireland Act 1920, s 4(1).

[12] Diplock (1972).

[13] For an account of an alternative model, martial law, see Bishop (1978) 148, Gross and Ní Aoláin (2006) 30–5. For clear insights into the position in Northern Ireland see Walker (1989).

law (this section of the report covers just nine paragraphs), the Diplock Commission recommended in December 1972 that the powers of soldiers to carry out arrests in Northern Ireland should be simplified.[14] It said they should be empowered to arrest without warrant *any* person suspected of having committed or being about to commit *any* offence, or of having information about *any* offence, whether already committed or not, and regardless of who might be responsible for it. This recommendation, had it been implemented, would have greatly extended the regulation 11(1) arrest power which, although still very wide, restricted soldiers to arresting people only if they suspected them of acting, or of having acted, or of being about to act, 'in a manner prejudicial to the preservation of the peace or maintenance of order'. Moreover the Diplock Commission proposed that arrests under the new power should not be unlawful just because the soldier gave no reason, or a wrong reason, for the arrest. The Commission did say, on the other hand, that persons arrested should be released once their identity had been established satisfactorily, unless they were wanted by the police on suspicion of having committed an offence or for interrogation about any terrorist organization or activities, in which case they should be rearrested on that basis and told of the ground for the further detention. Although the Diplock Report is not explicit on this point, the presumption must be that the regulation 10 arrest power, in so far as it allowed *soldiers* to be authorized to conduct arrests purely for the purpose of interrogation, was going to be allowed to lapse, and that is indeed what occurred.

The Diplock Commission's recommendations in this area were translated into law only in part, via the Northern Ireland (Emergency Provisions) Act 1973 (the EPA). Section 12 of that Act permitted a soldier to arrest without warrant any person whom the soldier suspected of committing, having committed or being about to commit any offence, and to detain that person for up to four hours. But it did not limit the questioning to which that person could be subjected during the four-hour period to the establishment of his or her identity, and nor did the arrest have to be for the purpose of handing the person over to the police. It is arguable that detention just for the purposes of establishing identity would have been a breach of the European Convention (had there been no derogation notice in place) and, more definitely, that arresting someone *with no intention* of handing that person over to a competent legal authority would also have been a breach. Section 12(2) also differed slightly from the Diplock Commission's recommendation in that it exempted the arresting soldier from having to state the reason for the arrest, provided only that he or she stated that it was being effected by the soldier as a member of Her Majesty's forces. Diplock's recommendation had gone even further, suggesting that the soldier could get away with saying nothing at all. And of course section 12 did at least require suspicion relating to a particular offence, whereas the police's special power of arrest, as we shall see, extended to people suspected of 'involvement in terrorism', whether the police had a specific offence in mind or not. As Hogan and Walker point out,[15] this meant that

[14] Diplock (1972) paras 42–50. At para 47 the Commission says that reg 11(1) authorized the arrest of persons suspected of four different alternative offences, but it does not say what these are. The wording of reg 11(1) in force at that time (see the wording in the text) would suggest that there were six possible grounds for arrest. For a contemporary critique of the Diplock Report see Twining (1973).

[15] Hogan and Walker (1989) 53–4.

the police could arrest someone for associating with a member of an unlawful organization, which was not in itself a crime, but that the army could not.

It is clear from the differences between the provisions in the EPA 1973 and the recommendations in the Diplock Report that a good deal of thought was given both within government and by Parliamentarians as to how exactly the special arrest powers should be formulated in Northern Ireland. Doubtless what counted most were the views of the commanders in the army and the police, as it was those forces which would have to operate the powers. This was certainly the case as regards the Diplock Report, as the Commissioners themselves recognized. They admitted that, during their inquiry, which lasted only two months, they received only three written representations:

> The bulk of our evidence has been oral and was taken from people with responsibility for the administration of justice in Northern Ireland, but we have also heard from representatives of the Civil and Armed Services. Almost all the evidence was heard in London, but our Chairman made two visits to Northern Ireland, each lasting two days, during which he met members of the security forces on the ground. Like those responsible for inquiries in the past in which there has been considerations of security, we do not intend to publish the evidence we have received nor the names of those who submitted it.

In the Parliamentary debates on the Bill that became the EPA 1973, there is little evidence that the requirements of the European Convention on Human Rights played much part in the thinking of MPs and peers. Derogation notices were in place regarding Article 5,[16] and it would have been assumed that if internment was a proportionate step to take under those notices then the much less draconian special arrest powers could hardly have been disproportionate. Nevertheless, aspects of the legality of the army's arrest powers were in due course challenged in Northern Ireland's courts, as we shall see.

The Baker Review and the EPA 1987

The army arrest powers conferred by the EPA 1973 were re-enacted by the EPA 1978 and after a further six years they were closely examined in a review of that Act commissioned by the British government from Sir George Baker, a former President of the Family Division of the High Court in England and Wales.[17] Having acknowledged that the arrest powers contravened the European Convention and were only saved by the United Kingdom's derogation, Sir George stated: 'Any action which can be taken to avoid the UK having to rely on the notice of derogation to excuse breaches of the Convention is desirable'.[18] The Baker Report listed no fewer than eight respects in which the army arrest power was thought to be questionable,[19] but in the end Sir George accepted only three of them and made corresponding recommendations for reform. He thought it was beyond doubt that the army still needed

[16] The notices applicable at the time are set out in SACHR (1976) 103–5.
[17] Baker (1984). See comments by Bonner (1984).
[18] ibid, para 264. See too para 340.
[19] ibid, para 340.

a power of arrest, and even Northern Ireland's Standing Advisory Commission on Human Rights agreed that there should be an 'appropriate' power.[20]

First, while Sir George noted that the number of army arrests had declined dramatically since 1976, when the army began to operate in more of a secondary role in aid of the police, he recommended that the army's power to arrest should be limited to situations where 'reasonable suspicion' existed. The GOC and his staff officers voiced strong disquiet about this, because they thought it 'would pose enormous training difficulties, create uncertainty among soldiers and a disposition on the part of those antagonistic to the Army to dispute the grounds of arrest'.[21] But Sir George thought that in practice it would make little difference to the way in which the military went about its business, because normally a soldier would be arresting someone on the back of an order to do so and it would be reasonable to obey such an order and to assume that that order was based on reasonable suspicion. He did, though, hope that the tightening up of the arrest power would prevent people like local councillors being arrested just so that they could be asked questions about how people might react to the locating of an army base in their area.[22]

Baker was even stronger in his second recommendation that the army arrest power should be limited to specific offences rather than available for 'any' offence. He said it was nonsense that a member of Her Majesty's forces was less well able to recognize a terrorist or certain acts of terrorism than a constable or an ordinary citizen and he therefore suggested that the arrest power should extend only to persons whom a soldier 'reasonably suspects of being a terrorist or a member of a proscribed organisation or of committing, having committed or being about to commit any act of terrorism or violence or of rioting or an offence involving the use of an explosive, explosive substance or firearm, or of making or possessing a petrol bomb'.[23]

The third change recommended by Baker was that the arresting soldier should tell the arrested person at the time of the arrest which of the grounds was being used to justify the arrest. Baker reasoned that if a soldier needs to explain to a police officer to whom he is handing over an arrested person the circumstances of the arrest (eg 'he was throwing petrol bombs'), it was not too burdensome to require the soldier to give the same kind of information to the arrested person.[24] The force of this reasoning was somewhat undermined, however, by the immediately following paragraph in the report, where Baker indicated that he was prepared to accept that as many as three-quarters of people arrested by the army may not be later handed over to the police: 'is it not better that the Army should have the ability to question and release quickly than to keep and hand over a person who will be released later by the police?'[25] Baker would have done better to justify the army's duty to give reasons for the arrest squarely on Article 5(2) of the European Convention.[26] Baker also recommended no change to the army's power to detain the arrested person for up to four hours, though he was prepared to accept the case made by the National Council for Civil Liberties and

[20] ibid, para 343. [21] ibid, para 347. [22] ibid.
[23] ibid, para 348. [24] ibid, para 351. [25] ibid, para 352.
[26] Art 5(2) reads; 'Everyone who is arrested shall be informed promptly, in a language which he understands, of the reasons for his arrest and of any charge against him.'

SACHR that the law should require the army to hand over the detainee to the police 'as soon as possible and within a maximum period four hours'.[27] He appeared to think that the hours spent in army custody should count against the maximum periods of 48 or 72 hours during which the detainee could then be held by the police,[28] but he made no specific recommendation to that effect.

The only one of the Baker recommendations which the then Conservative government accepted, and implemented, through an amendment to section 14 brought about by the Northern Ireland (Emergency Provisions) Act (EPA) 1987, was the first. From 15 June 1987, therefore, soldiers could arrest a person only if they had reasonable grounds to suspect that he or she was committing, had committed, or was about to commit, any offence.[29] The army arrest power contained in section 14 of the EPA 1978, as amended by the EPA 1987,[30] was later re-enacted in section 18 of the EPA 1991, with the addition of the power to seize, and detain for up to four hours, anything which the soldier had reasonable grounds to suspect was being, had been, or was intended to be used in the commission of offences concerning interference with works executed or equipment used by the army.[31] The provision survived to find a place in the EPA 1996[32] and then the Terrorism Act 2000.[33] The power was eventually terminated on 31 July 2007, when Part VII of the 2000 Act expired.[34] Today the army has no special arrest powers in Northern Ireland. 'Operation Banner', which was the codename given to the transfer of troops to Northern Ireland in August 1969, officially came to an end 38 years later.[35] There are still some British soldiers in Northern Ireland, but they are in barracks, as they were prior to August 1969. During their time on the streets of Northern Ireland the European Convention, rightly or wrongly, did little to place constraints on their arrest and detention powers, as we shall now see.

Margaret Murray v United Kingdom

In *Walsh v Ministry of Defence*[36] Lord Chief Justice Lowry, in the High Court of Northern Ireland, awarded a young woman exemplary damages of £4,000 after she had been arrested by the army under the power conferred by section 12 of the EPA

[27] Baker (1984) para 353.

[28] 48 hours under the PTA 1974, s 7(2), PTA 1976, s 12(2), and PTA 1984, s 12(4); 72 hours under the EPA 1973, s 10(3), EPA 1978, s 11(3).

[29] The army could enter and search any premises where such a person was, but they could enter and search any premises where they reasonably suspected that person to be only if they reasonably suspected him or her to be a terrorist or an offender involved in the use of explosives. On the EPA 1987 see Jackson (1988).

[30] s 25(1) and Sch 1, para 2. [31] s 18(4). [32] s 19.

[33] s 83. Part VII of the 2000 Act (ss 65–113) was the final incarnation of the special anti-terrorist powers enacted for Northern Ireland. Most of these were allowed to lapse on 31 July 2007: see Justice and Security (NI) Act 2007; but some (including the army's arrest and search powers) were retained.

[34] As provided by the Terrorism (NI) Act 2006, s 1(2).

[35] <http://www.operationbanner.com> is a website which provides a network of information, services and advice for security forces and civil servants involved in the troubles of Northern Ireland. The Ministry of Defence issued a lengthy report analysing Operation Banner in 2006: see <http://wikileaks.org/leak/uk-operation-banner-2006.pdf>, last visited 4 August 2009.

[36] [1985] 4 NIJB 1.

1973, detained for about two hours, and asked questions at a police station only about her association with others. The judge found that the arresting female soldier had acted in good faith but that the fault lay with her superiors in not being able to demonstrate that they had grounds for suspecting Mrs Walsh's involvement in anything (it seems to have been a case of mistaken identity). But in *Murray v Ministry of Defence*, where the facts were similar to those in *Walsh*, neither the High Court[37] nor the Court of Appeal of Northern Ireland[38] held the arrest to be unlawful because the officer who briefed the arresting soldier did in fact have grounds for suspecting that the woman in question had committed an offence, namely the collecting of money for a proscribed organization, the IRA. The fact that later questioning focused exclusively on her associations with others—intelligence gathering—was irrelevant. Dermot Walsh, writing in 1983, also thought that persons arrested under the section 12 power had the common law right, the existence of which was confirmed in *Re McElduff*,[39] to be told precisely under which power they were being arrested.[40] But in *Murray v Ministry of Defence* the courts in Northern Ireland rejected such a view, and when the case went on further appeal to the House of Lords the point was not raised.[41] The House did, however, make it clear that, although there is a general rule, established by the House's own previous decision in *Christie v Leachinsky*,[42] that a person must be told the reason for his or her arrest at the time the arrest is made, or within a reasonable time of the arrest, the army in Northern Ireland were entitled not to give the reason for an arrest until after they had finished conducting a search of the house where the person was located because otherwise 'there is a real risk that the alarm may be raised and an attempt made to resist arrest, not only by those within the house but also by summoning assistance from those in the immediate neighbourhood'.[43] With respect, this seems a flimsy point: if an arrest was to take place during the course of a search, the likelihood of its being resisted was hardly going to be significantly enhanced just because the reason for the arrest was given before the search of the house was completed.

Stephen Livingstone criticized the decision in *Murray*, saying that it showed the House of Lords 'declined to read emergency powers strictly to uphold only clear derogations from common law principles' and missed an opportunity 'to assert the values of the rule of law even in an extreme situation'.[44] He pointed out that when Mrs Murray, with her husband and four children, took their case to the European Commission of Human Rights in Strasbourg after losing in the House of Lords, she won.[45] The Commission held in her favour as regards a breach of Article 5(1) of the Convention by 11 votes to three, and as regards a breach of Article 5(2) by 10 votes to four. The UK Commissioner, Sir Basil Hall, voted with the minority; the Commissioner from Ireland, Jane Liddy, was the only one of the 14 Commissioners

[37] [1985] 12 NIJB 1 (Murray J).

[38] [1987] NI 219 (Gibson and Kelly LJJ, who themselves granted leave to appeal to the House of Lords). The Court of Appeal did, however, award the plaintiff £250 for an illegal 'pat' search of her body. Later in 1987 Gibson LJ and his wife were murdered by the IRA; he was the most senior judge to be killed during the Northern Ireland troubles.

[39] [1972] NI 1. [40] Walsh (1983) 29. [41] [1988] 1 WLR 692.

[42] [1947] AC 573. [43] [1988] 1 WLR 692, 700G. [44] Livingstone (1994) 346.

[45] App No 14310/88, decision of 17 February 1993.

to find that there had also been a breach of Article 8 of the Convention as regards the entry into Mrs Murray's home, the recording and retention of her personal details, and the secret photographing of her. Yet six months after Livingstone's article was published, and no doubt to his dismay, the Grand Chamber of the European Court of Human Rights overturned the Commission's decision. It held *against* Mrs Murray on Article 5(1) by 14 votes to four and on Article 5(2) by 13 votes to five.[46] The UK judge, Sir John Freeland, voted with the majority. The four judges who dissented on the Article 5(1)(c) point thought that the government had not demonstrated that the police had had reasonable suspicion for their arrest:

> The conviction in the United States of Mrs Murray's two brothers of offences connected with the purchase of weapons for the Provisional IRA, her visit to her brothers there and the reference to the collaboration with 'trustworthy' persons residing in Northern Ireland implied by such offences are not, in our opinion, sufficient grounds for reasonably suspecting the first applicant of involvement in the offence of collecting funds in Northern Ireland to buy arms in the United States for terrorist purposes. Family ties cannot imply a criminal relationship between the author of the offence and his or her relatives; nor can the 'co-operative' nature of the crime be considered a valid basis for a reasonable suspicion of complicity on the part of members of the family or friends of the criminal. These circumstances may give rise only to a bona fide suspicion of such complicity. They do not give rise to a 'reasonable' suspicion such as to justify the serious measures taken against the applicants unless they are connected with other facts in direct relation to the offence. No facts of this kind have however been furnished by the respondent Government, although, in our opinion, they could have been supplied without jeopardising the confidentiality of the source of information which is necessary to protect the life and personal safety of that source...[47]

The four dissenting judges—who thought the arrests were unlawful—could not distinguish the claims from those made in *Fox, Campbell and Hartley v United Kingdom* where, as we shall see shortly, an arrest carried out by the police was held by the European Court (albeit by just four votes to three) to be invalid because the reasonableness of the suspicion in question had not been demonstrated by the government.

This turnaround in the thinking at Strasbourg between the Commission's decision in February 1993 and the Court's decision in October 1994 tells us a lot about the dynamics of the adjudication process there at that time and about the prevailing mood concerning State efforts to combat terrorism. Some would say that it betokened a greater realism, an appreciation that when security forces are dealing with very difficult security situations they may need to have the freedom to cut some corners and to take advantage of exceptions to general rules, provided of course that the rights of individuals are not disproportionately affected. On this view the rule of law does not mean that those exercising powers in relation to others must dot every 'i' and cross every 't': the interests of society are seen as a good excuse for not having to satisfy all legal technicalities. The alternative view is that the European Court's approach marked a retrogressive step in Strasbourg's promotion of the rule of law. 'Technical'

[46] (1995) 19 EHRR 193.

[47] Joint dissenting judgment of Judges Loizou (Cyprus), Morenilla (Spain) and Makarczyk (Poland) (1995) 19 EHRR 193, 238–9, para 3; Judge Jambrek (Slovenia) also associated himself with these views.

requirements are there for a reason: they are a link in what might be a long chain, but if they are loosened the whole chain risks falling asunder. It is clear that a large majority of judges in the European Court were prepared to run that risk.

Special police arrest powers

For a police arrest to be valid under regulation 11(1) of the Special Powers Act Regulations it had to be carried out as such. It was not enough for the police simply to receive in custody someone who had been arrested by the army under regulation 10. This was made clear by McGonigal J in *Re McElduff*, a case already mentioned, where the judge also held that the arrest was invalid because the person in question had not been informed under what power he was being arrested or the general nature of the suspicion leading to his arrest.[48] In *Kelly v Faulkner* there was also a failure to inform the arrested person—later to become a prominent solicitor in Belfast, and the husband of a Queen's Counsel—of the grounds for his arrest, but Gibson J held that a subsequent detention order issued in relation to Oliver Kelly was nevertheless still lawful.[49] In *Re Close*, however, O'Donnell J conceded that if a detainee was granted bail in relation to a criminal charge laid against him, this would render his continuing detention under regulation 11 in relation to the same matter unlawful.[50] We can see, then, that even without having to rely on the European Convention, judges in Northern Ireland did sometimes uphold challenges to the legality of arrests by relying on common law rights and standard principles of statutory interpretation. Indeed the European Court of Human Rights referred in passing to these safeguards in its judgment in the inter-State case.[51]

In 1972 the Diplock Commission made no recommendations regarding police powers of arrest, but changes were nevertheless provided for by sections 10 and 11 of the EPA 1973. The former was supposedly a specific power (whose marginal note read 'Arrest and detention of terrorists'), while the latter was a more general one ('Constables' general power of arrest and seizure'). The section 10(1) power was obviously intended to be used in situations where a person's internment was envisaged, even if its wording, when looked at out of context, was more broad.[52] The Act defined 'terrorist' as 'a person who is or has been concerned in the commission or attempted commission of any act of terrorism or in directing, organising or training persons for the purpose of terrorism', and it defined 'terrorism', in turn, as 'the use of violence for political ends and [including] any use of violence for the purpose of putting the public or any section of the public in fear'.[53] Interestingly, the latter definition was not confined to political ends connected with the affairs of Northern Ireland. Section 11(1), on the other hand, empowered any constable to arrest without

[48] [1972] NI 1 (12 October 1971), discussed in Walsh (1983) 25–6.
[49] [1973] NI 31.
[50] [1972] NI 27.
[51] *Ireland v UK* (1979–80) 2 EHRR 25, paras 198, 217, and 219.
[52] 'Any constable may arrest without warrant any person whom he suspects of being a terrorist.'
[53] EPA 1973, s 28(1).

warrant any person whom he or she suspected of committing a scheduled offence or an offence under the EPA which was not a scheduled offence. On the recommendation of the Diplock Commission the EPA 1973 introduced the concept of 'scheduled offence' as a way of triggering special trial procedures in the absence of a jury. The offences listed in Schedule 4 to the 1973 Act were very wide-ranging and the Act itself created several new offences, including failing to stop when required to do so by a police officer or soldier, failing to answer to the best of one's knowledge and ability questions put after being stopped, interfering with works executed by the police or army, and belonging to a proscribed organization.

The section 10 and 11 arrest powers were, as far as the police were concerned, narrower in scope than the arrest powers conferred by the Special Powers Act Regulations, and indeed that was the government's intention.[54] They no longer permitted arrests merely 'for the purpose of interrogation' (as regulation 10 had done) and they did not permit arrests of persons merely suspected of acting 'in a manner prejudicial to the preservation of the peace or maintenance of order' (as allowed by regulation 11(1)). During the Second Reading debates on the Emergency Provisions Bill in April 1973, the Secretary of State tried to suggest that the new legislation was actually putting an end to 'internment' and substituting 'detention',[55] but this was obvious sophistry. It did not fool the Labour opposition,[56] who nevertheless voted in favour of the new provisions, or the MP for West Belfast, Gerry Fitt, who remained 'vehemently opposed to the Bill'[57] and said that the new arrest powers were 'almost an exact repetition of the most offensive and obnoxious sections of the Special Powers Act'.[58] Kevin McNamara, a Labour MP, protested as well about what became section 24 of the EPA 1973, which he said meant that the Special Powers Act was being preserved. Section 24(1) allowed the Secretary of State free rein to issue regulations which 'make provision additional to the foregoing provisions of this Act for promoting the preservation of the peace and the maintenance of order'; by section 24(2) anyone failing to comply with the regulations issued under section 24(1) was liable to be sent to prison for up to six months and/or to be fined up to £400. Despite these and other protestations the Emergency Provisions Bill completed its Second Reading stage by 155 votes to 18.

The new police arrest powers were more clearly targeted on particular forms of serious anti-social behaviour, namely, the use of violence for political ends. The use for the first time of the words 'terrorism' and 'terrorist' was no doubt deliberate: those who were using violence in relation to the politics of Northern Ireland would not have wanted to be branded with the same mark as the pro-communist Red Army Faction in West Germany (officially formed in 1970), the Red Brigades in Italy (also formed in 1970), and the Tupamaros guerrillas in Uruguay (who were at their most active in 1970 and 1971), although the IRA did to some extent model itself on the

[54] HC Deb, vol 855, col 285 (17 April 1973), per William Whitelaw MP.

[55] '[T]he procedures for detention are quite different from internment': ibid, col 279, per William Whitelaw MP.

[56] The Shadow Secretary of State, Merlyn Rees, recognized what became the s 10 provision as still internment: ibid, col 298.

[57] ibid, col 327.

[58] ibid, col 330.

Popular Front for the Liberation of Palestine (formed in 1967 out of the Palestinian Liberation Front and two other organizations).[59] For the vast majority of people living in Northern Ireland, Catholic as well as Protestant, the IRA did at the time strike terror into their hearts, so, whatever the political motivation for their exploits might have been, 'terrorism' does not seem to be an inaccurate description of their behaviour.

The use of the word 'terrorism', though, was potentially problematic from the point of view of Article 5 of the European Convention. Article 5(1)(c) requires the arrest to be in relation to an offence, whereas section 10 of the EPA 1973 referred only to 'terrorist'. 'Terrorism', as such, was not (and is not) an offence; it is a word which describes a type of motivation for a range of actions which are themselves offences. It might have been argued, therefore, that an arrest for 'being a terrorist' was not an arrest that complied with the conditions of Article 5(1)(c). Moreover, both sections 10 and 11 of the EPA 1973 allowed arrests based on mere suspicion. An honest belief on the part of the arresting police officer was enough, even though the belief was not objectively justifiable. Only if the arrested person could prove that the arresting police officer had acted in bad faith could he or she have sued for wrongful arrest (mere negligence would not have sufficed). All of this was a breach of Article 5(1)(c), which requires 'reasonable suspicion', and also of Article 5(5), which requires an enforceable right to compensation for persons arrested in breach of Article 5. Nevertheless, sections 10 and 11 were later re-enacted, without any significant amendments, as sections 11 and 13 of the Northern Ireland (Emergency Provisions) Act 1978. The legality of this new section 11 power was tested in two important cases, one decided by the House of Lords and the other by the European Court of Human Rights, but, before either of those courts could issue their judgments, the review of the 1978 Act conducted by Sir George Baker was published. In addition, the police had by then been given yet a further arrest power by the Prevention of Terrorism (Temporary Provisions) Act 1974 (the PTA 1974).

The PTA 1974 was rushed through Parliament because of the widespread outrage at a series of pub bombings that had occurred in England and for which the IRA claimed responsibility. On 5 October 1974 five people were killed in Guildford, on 7 November 1974 two were killed in Woolwich, and, worst of all, on 21 November 1974, 21 were killed in Birmingham. Four days later Roy Jenkins, the Home Secretary in the then Labour government, informed Parliament that he would be asking his fellow MPs to approve draconian powers, unprecedented in peacetime.[60] Within a further five days a compliant Parliament had duly enacted the Bill, with hardly any amendments; it passed through the Commons in an all-night debate between 28 and 29 November, and was nodded through the Lords and given Royal Assent by 9.30am on 29 November. In the House of Commons' debates comparatively little attention was paid to what became section 7 ('Powers of arrest and detention'), with the few comments that were made on it being mostly focused on the power it gave to the Secretary of State to extend 48-hour detention by the police by up to a further five

[59] Most of these other terrorist groups engaged in political kidnappings, something which the IRA tended to avoid. See Clutterbuck (1975) ch 2.

[60] HC Deb 1974–5, vol 882, col 35 (25 November 1974).

days (this is further discussed in Chapter 6 below).[61] This was a power which went considerably beyond the 72-hour detention power already available to the police in Northern Ireland. But the standards set by the European Convention on Human Rights did not feature in the parliamentary debates. When one MP asked why the pre-charge detention period was 'only' seven days, and not 14, the reply from the Minister of State was not that that would have been incompatible with the European Convention but that the police had said that seven days would be long enough to make a proper investigation.[62]

Clive Walker has shown that much of the Bill had been drafted in secrecy after bombings in London during the previous year, when the Conservatives were still in power,[63] and David Bonner, following Owen Lomas's analysis of the genesis of the Prevention of Violence (Temporary Provisions) Act 1939,[64] has brought to light the intra-governmental thinking of the day in 1974.[65]Bonner indicates how the government's obligations under the European Convention on Human Rights, which was not on the scene in 1939, 'helped intensify the focus on civil liberties aspects, but rather more in the internal work of the Home Office and Foreign Office, particularly on the Conservative proposals, than in the Labour Cabinet which considered the Bill that quickly became law as PTA 1974'.[66] The Home Office's legal advisers did not think that the PTA's provisions on arrest and extended detention were in conflict with the European Convention, but they were worried that the exclusion order power (discussed in Chapter 4 above) might breach Article 3 (the prohibition on inhuman treatment) as well as Article 5. Nevertheless both the Home Secretary (Roy Jenkins) and the Foreign Secretary (James Callaghan) were of the view that a derogation from the Convention would be politically unwise, and in any event it was not possible as far as Article 3 was concerned. Bonner quotes the departmental advisers as saying: 'We are not persuaded that the weight of legal argument as to the likelihood of our being in breach of the Convention is such as to outweigh the political arguments against derogating'[67] and he himself concludes that 'the papers show possible breach of human rights as not being a determinative factor in decision-making, but a risk that would have to be run or circumvented if that could be done without political embarrassment'.[68]

Challenging arrests in domestic courts

A person arrested under the new arrest powers in the EPA 1973 and PTA 1974 could, in theory, apply for a writ of habeas corpus, but such writs were almost impossible to obtain because they depended on showing that the detention was unlawful. As

[61] ibid, cols 900–6.
[62] ibid, cols 900–1, per Alexander Lyon MP.
[63] Walker (1986) 22–4 and 29–30.
[64] Lomas (1980). [65] Bonner (2006). [66] ibid, 603.
[67] ibid, 621, citing (it seems) National Archives catalogue reference FCO 87/396.
[68] ibid, 628.

both Acts explicitly permitted detention if the specified grounds for arrest existed, and as those grounds included one as vague as suspicion or, in the case of the PTA, reasonable suspicion that the person was 'concerned in the commission, preparation or instigation of acts of terrorism', a habeas corpus application was usually futile. In English law there is no 'constitutional right' to a writ of habeas corpus. In any event, a person arrested under the anti-terrorism laws was often not made aware of what information the police were acting on when they carried out the arrest (because this would have compromised the identity of informants, who would then have been liable to attack by paramilitary organizations), so it was well nigh impossible to argue that that information was inaccurate. The applicant could also try to challenge the arrest on the basis that it was conducted in bad faith, but bringing forth credible evidence to substantiate such a claim is always very difficult.

A writ of habeas corpus was not even available in situations where a person was arrested under one power, questioned and released, and then arrested under another power. This is what happened in *Ex parte Lynch*,[69] but the Divisional Court of Northern Ireland (through Lord Lowry CJ in particular) rejected the application for habeas corpus. One of the arguments put on behalf of Mr Lynch was that, when he was arrested for the second time, under the PTA, he was not told what specific offence he was reasonably suspected of, contrary to the common law's requirement—laid down by the House of Lords as far back as 1946[70]—that an arrested person had to be told as soon as practicable the nature of the offence he or she was suspected of, otherwise the arrest would be unlawful (not that this necessarily meant that the person would be entitled to be released, only that he or she could sue for compensation for the tort of false imprisonment). Lord Lowry answered this argument by saying that in the case before him there was no need to specify the suspected offence because an arrest under the PTA 'is usually the first step in the investigation of the suspected person's involvement in terrorism'.[71] Dermot Walsh has incisively critiqued this rather question-begging conclusion, arguing that the police process of accumulating evidence to ground the reasonable suspicion for the arrest should be the first step in the investigation process, not the arrest itself:

> If, as the Lord Chief Justice seems to be suggesting, the police can use [section 7 of the PTA] as the first step in that process then they can use it to arrest anyone simply for the purpose of checking whether they are involved in terrorism.[72]

In *McKee v Chief Constable of the RUC*[73] Gerard McKee had been arrested under section 11(1) of the EPA 1978 early one morning in September 1981 and had been released without charge some 18 hours later the same day. He sued the police for unlawful arrest, assault, trespass, and false imprisonment. MacDermott J upheld the validity of the arrest but the Court of Appeal of Northern Ireland (with one

[69] [1980] NI 126.
[70] *Christie v Leachinsky* [1947] AC 573.
[71] [1980] NI 126, 131.
[72] Walsh (1983) 27. Later (at 108) Walsh says that the court's decision in *Ex parte Lynch* 'gave the green light to many of the misuses and abuses' which he identified in the opening chapter of his book.
[73] [1985] 1 All ER 1.

dissenter[74]) disagreed. Kelly J, for the majority, pointed out that section 11(1) requires an honest suspicion that the person to be arrested is indeed a terrorist as defined in section 31 of the EPA. Having cited that definition he said:

Both limbs of the definition require activity, active involvement and not only active involvement but a particular kind of active involvement. Neither limb brings into its definition the person for example who is merely a member of a proscribed organisation, nor one whose activity is no more than soliciting support for such organisation.[75]

The House of Lords, however, decided unanimously in favour of the police, with only Lord Roskill giving a judgment and the other four Law Lords concurring. The task of the Lords was to interpret words in an Act of Parliament and therefore it is not very surprising that they could see nothing in those words which meant that an arresting officer had to have a reasonable suspicion rather than just an honest suspicion. What the case really turned on was whether an arresting officer was entitled to form an honest suspicion merely on the basis of what his or her superior officer had told the officer about the person to be arrested (in this case, that he was 'a suspected terrorist'). The House held that the officer was so entitled, especially as a junior police officer is not able in practice to challenge instructions given by a superior officer. Livingstone is again critical of this decision:

In deciding that, so long as the arresting officer genuinely held a suspicion that someone was a terrorist, even if this was based on no evidence or a legally mistaken definition of terrorism, the decision displays a deference to government decision making that compares with the infamous decision of the majority in *Liversidge v Anderson*.[76]

As I have stated elsewhere, there is a major difference between the power of a police officer to arrest someone for short-term questioning and the power of a government minister to order someone's indefinite detention (which is what was at issue in *Liversidge v Anderson*),[77] but there is still much to be said for Walker's suggestion that, to reduce the risk of arrest powers being abused, junior police officers should be given an outline of the evidence which has prompted their superior to instruct them to arrest someone.[78] Livingstone also says that the House of Lords found the view of the Court of Appeal of Northern Ireland, that suspicion of IRA membership was different from suspicion of terrorism, to be 'too subtle'. In fact the Lords expressly stated that they did not have 'any view whatever' on the question whether suspicion of IRA membership would without more justify arrest under section 11(1).[79] They said there

[74] Jones LJ.

[75] [1983] 11 NIJB (pages not numbered).

[76] Livingstone (1994) 345. *Liversidge v Anderson* [1942] AC 206 is the wartime decision by the Lords which upheld the Home Secretary's power to detain someone whom he had 'reasonable cause' to believe to be of hostile origin or associations. Only Lord Atkin dissented. Lest anyone think that the decision in *McKee* represents a peculiarly British position on arrest powers it is worth observing, as Walker does in his commentary on the case (Walker (1985) at 149), that Ireland's Court of Criminal Appeal came to the same conclusion in *The People (DPP) v McCaffrey* (1984) 2 ILT 191.

[77] Dickson (2006a) 399.

[78] Walker (1985) 150.

[79] [1985] 1 All ER 1, 4g.

was no evidence that such suspicion was a factor in the mind of the arresting police constable in this case.

What is peculiar about the Lords' decision in *McKee* is that at no point did it make reference to the fact that earlier that year (in March) Parliament had approved the Prevention of Terrorism (Temporary Provisions) Act 1984 (the PTA 1984), section 12 of which re-enacted, with slight amendments, previous provisions in PTAs. All of those provisions qualified the arresting power of police officers in a terrorism context by stipulating that the officer had to have reasonable suspicion. Those provisions applied in Northern Ireland as they did elsewhere in the United Kingdom. Why did the Lords not comment on this unsatisfactory state of the Northern Ireland statute book, which was allowing two contradictory arrest powers to coexist—the EPA requiring only honest suspicion and the PTA requiring reasonable suspicion? Given that the arrest powers in the EPA were not amended so as to require *reasonable* suspicion until the EPA 1987 was enacted, it is also difficult to understand why the British government was so sure in August 1984 that the law throughout the United Kingdom was now fully in conformity with the European Convention's standards. In that month the government sent a letter to the Secretary General of the Council of Europe withdrawing the notice of derogation that had been in place since 1957.[80] This was done without publicity,[81] and apparently in ignorance of the fact that there was another dimension to the arrest powers (namely the length of time an arrested person could be detained before being brought before a judge) which still violated Article 5 of the Convention.

In his review of the EPA 1978 Sir George Baker could not ignore the anomaly between the wording of the EPA arrest powers and the PTA arrest power. He therefore recommended, as he also did for the army arrest powers, that police arrests under the EPA should require 'reasonable suspicion', though he did not expressly say that this was to ensure that the law was brought into line with the European Convention. He seems to have been persuaded to make the recommendation because the police themselves (unlike senior army officers) were telling him that the reasonableness requirement would not make any practical difference to the way they went about their business, and because the police were in any event making more and more use of the arrest power they had been given under the PTA. The ordinary arrest power in the Criminal Law Act (NI) 1967 also required reasonable suspicion. Baker noted that in the first nine months of 1983, the latest statistics available at that time, 47.8 per cent of arrests for terrorism in Northern Ireland were conducted under the PTA power and not the EPA power. The government was convinced by this point and so when the EPA came to be re-enacted in 1987 the police's section 11 power was

[80] Notice dated 22 August 1984: see Information Bulletin on Legal Activities within the Council of Europe and in Member States, vol 21, (2 July 1985).

[81] The lack of publicity accorded to the notice of withdrawal may be one reason why it is not referred to in Hogan and Walker (1989), even though that was published five years later. But those authors did speculate (at 37) that '[e]specially after the reforms in 1987, it is now quite likely that the Emergency Provisions Acts would by and large pass the test' of whether the steps taken to deal with the emergency were strictly required by the exigencies of the situation.

dropped altogether,[82] leaving the police with the arrest power in what by then had become section 12 of the PTA 1984. Of course the EPA still retained the more general police arrest power in section 13, but this power was hardly ever used and, when the EPA 1987 came into force on 15 June 1987, it too was qualified by the insertion of words requiring a reasonable suspicion.

Between 1974 and 1987 almost 8,000 people were detained under the PTA in Northern Ireland, and significant numbers were also arrested under the two EPA arrest powers. Compared with the practice concerning those arrested for non-terrorist offences, relatively few of these terrorist suspects were later charged with an offence, a matter which caused the Standing Advisory Commission on Human Rights some concern as early as 1980.[83] The arrest power under the ordinary law effectively fell into disuse, even though it would have been perfectly adequate in many situations, thereby giving the lie to ministerial assurances that the emergency laws would be resorted to only where the ordinary laws could not do the job. By 1987, the need to resort to emergency laws almost appeared to be taken for granted in Northern Ireland.[84] Three cases which went all the way to the European Court of Human Rights, each analysed in the following two sections, can be cited as evidence to support that proposition.

Fox, Campbell and Hartley v United Kingdom

Gerard McKee did not lodge an application in Strasbourg after losing in the Lords on 22 November 1984, but about 18 months later three other arrested persons chose to challenge the section 11 EPA arrest power in that forum. Bernard Fox and Maire Campbell (husband and wife, but separated) were arrested by the police in Belfast on 5 February 1986. They were told that it was because they were suspected of being terrorists. After being questioned, they were released without charge some 44 hours later. During that time their solicitor actually initiated proceedings for habeas corpus, but they were released before the applications could be heard by a judge. A third person, Samuel Hartley, was arrested by the police in Waterfoot, County Antrim and, after being questioned, was released without charge some 30 hours later. In June 1986 all three of these people lodged applications with the European Commission of Human Rights alleging that their rights under Article 5 of the Convention had been violated. Their primary argument was that there had been no reasonable grounds for suspecting them of any offence when they were arrested, but they also argued that they had not been informed of the reasons for their arrest and that they had had no effective remedy for those two breaches of Articles 5(1)(c) and 5(2), itself a violation of Articles 5(5) and 13 of the Convention.

The Commission held in their favour on all three points by seven votes to five, one of the dissenters again being Sir Basil Hall, the UK Commissioner. The dissenters

[82] A new s 11 was substituted (by the EPA 1987, s 6) conferring on the police a power to enter and search any place where they reasonably suspected to find a person who was reasonably suspected of being concerned in acts of terrorism.

[83] SACHR (1980), para 10(2).

[84] Dickson (1992).

thought that there had been reasonable grounds for suspecting the three applicants of an offence because the government stated that it had information from intelligence sources about their involvement in terrorist activities and the first two applicants had previous convictions for terrorist offences. The Commission then referred the case to the European Court of Human Rights,[85] which agreed with the Commission by four votes to three on the first point and on part of the third point raised by the applicants, but held unanimously that there had been no breach of Article 5(2) as regards informing the applicants of the grounds for their arrest.[86] Again the UK judge, Sir Vincent Evans, was one of the three dissenters. The dissenting judges were of the view that '[i]n cases such as these it is not possible to draw a sharp distinction between genuine suspicion and reasonable suspicion',[87] though they did not fully explain why this was so. They sided with the security forces, noting that even the four majority judges had agreed that the police had had a bona fide suspicion that the persons they were arresting were terrorists.

Again, as in *Murray v United Kingdom*, we see here deep divisions within the adjudicating bodies in Strasbourg. Of the 19 Commissioners and judges who looked at the arguments raised by *Fox, Campbell and Hartley v United Kingdom*, 11 thought there had been no reasonable suspicion justifying the arrest while eight thought that there had been. Of course the real locus for the disagreement was the leeway that should be given to security forces to rely on information provided to them by informers which they cannot, for security reasons, make known to the persons arrested or to anyone else. It seems strange, though, that the police are not required to justify their actions in general terms by saying what it is that the arrested person is suspected of having done and why they have that suspicion (eg 'we suspect you have been writing down the numbers of police officers' cars because you have been seen doing so'). When considering whether, in accordance with Article 5(2) of the Convention, the applicants were informed promptly of the reasons for their arrest, in a language which they understood, all seven European Court judges agreed that it would not have been enough merely to tell them that they were suspected of being terrorists, but, because all of the applicants had been interrogated by the police about their suspected involvement in specific criminal acts and their suspected membership of proscribed organizations, the judges held that there was 'no ground to suppose that these interrogations were not such as to enable the applicants to understand why they had been arrested. The reasons why they were suspected of being terrorists were thereby brought to their attention during their interrogation.'[88] If the reasons for an arrest can be inferred in this way from questions put to the detainees, one wonders why it is ever necessary to tell people why they have been arrested and why it is so difficult to infer the reasonableness of the grounds for an arrest in the first place.

[85] Where amongst counsel for the government were Nicolas Bratza QC (later himself a judge in the European Court) and Brian Kerr QC (later Lord Chief Justice of Northern Ireland and a Lord of Appeal); counsel for the applicants were Reg Weir QC and Seamus Treacy, both now High Court judges in Northern Ireland.

[86] (1990) 13 EHRR 157. For a negative assessment of this decision see Finnie (1991).

[87] Joint dissenting opinion by Judges Evans (UK), Bernhardt (Germany) and Palm (Sweden).

[88] (1990) 13 EHRR 157, para 41.

The European Court, however, unanimously confirmed its position in a subsequent case from Northern Ireland, *Kerr v United Kingdom*,[89] where a terrorist suspect had been arrested and interrogated over a seven-day period about his suspected involvement in a recent bomb explosion at a military barracks, his alleged membership of the IRA, and the use he was making of items seized from his house, especially material stored on a computer there. He was told that he was being arrested under the PTA 1989 because there were reasonable grounds for suspecting that he had been concerned in the commission, preparation, or instigation of acts of terrorism, but he was not told what specific offences he was suspected of until he was charged at the end of the seven-day period. The Court declared that there was 'no reason to suppose that these periods of questioning were not such as to enable the applicant to understand why he was arrested and why he was suspected of being concerned in the commission, preparation or instigation of acts of terrorism'.[90]

It is difficult to read the decision of the European Court in *Fox, Campbell and Hartley v United Kingdom* without thinking that the majority simply wanted the UK government to comply more transparently with the European Convention by expressly limiting the police arrest power to situations which mirrored Article 5(1)(c), with its explicit reference to 'reasonable suspicion'. By the time the Court came to decide the case in August 1990 it would have been well aware that Sir George Baker had already recommended the insertion of a reasonableness requirement in the relevant section of the EPA and that the government had accepted that recommendation in 1987. However, Baker had also recommended a change to the subsection dealing with the giving of reasons for an arrest, a recommendation which the British government did not accept, yet the European Court did not follow Baker on that point. This is another example of the European Court adopting a rather minimalist approach to the interpretation of Article 5.

O'Hara v United Kingdom

After 15 June 1987, when the EPA 1987 came into force, all police (and army) arrest powers in Northern Ireland could be exercised only on the basis of reasonable suspicion. But still some people felt that the powers were still not carefully enough worded, thereby giving free rein to police officers to arrest people merely in order to question them so as to gather intelligence, not to inquire into specific offences they were believed to have committed. One of the challenges raised was brought by Gerry O'Hara in a case, which, like the *Margaret Murray* case, went all the way to the House of Lords and then to the European Court.[91] O'Hara had been arrested in the city of Derry three days after Christmas 1985 on suspicion of involvement in the murder five weeks earlier of a 38-year-old German-born businessman, Kurt König, a supplier of catering to the British army. The arrest was conducted under section 12(1)

[89] (2000) 29 EHRR CD184.

[90] ibid, CD188.

[91] Dickson (2006a) at 398–400; Hunt (1997).

of the PTA 1984, which allowed a police officer to arrest a person whom he or she had reasonable grounds for suspecting of being concerned in the commission, preparation, or instigation of acts of terrorism. O'Hara was held in detention until 3 January 1986,[92] when he was released without charge. We will examine in the next chapter the permitted length of such detentions, but for the moment our focus is on whether O'Hara was lawfully arrested in the first place. He argued that he was not, because there had to be a real factual basis for the reasonable suspicion in an arresting officer's mind. The Chief Constable of the RUC, on the other hand, argued that an arresting officer's reasonable suspicion could be based purely on the order to arrest given to him by a superior officer.

In the High Court of Northern Ireland McCollum J held against the plaintiff (who had sued, amongst other things, for wrongful arrest). As things turned out, none of the three judges in the Court of Appeal of Northern Ireland, or of the five judges in the House of Lords, thought differently. And in the European Court of Human Rights only one of the seven judges, Judge Loucaides from Cyprus, who has a reputation for an anti-UK stance,[93] held in favour of the applicant. In the Lords the court adopted a midway position between those advocated by the plaintiff and the Chief Constable. They said that an arrest under section 12 of the PTA was lawful if there was a reasonable suspicion in the officer's mind; this suspicion did not have to be based on his or her own observations but could be based on what he or she had been told, whether or not he or she knew that what he or she had been told was true. But an order from a superior officer was not by itself enough—it had to be accompanied by more information. In the words of Lord Hope: '[t]he question whether [the information] provided reasonable grounds for the suspicion depends on the source of his information and its context, seen in the light of the whole surrounding circumstances'.[94]

The European Court of Human Rights, in effect, endorsed the House of Lords' position (which in any event had been grounded in what the European Court had said in *Fox, Campbell and Hartley v UK*).[95] Having reviewed the outcome in the two previous cases in this area considered by the European Court—*Fox, Campbell and Hartley* and *Murray*—the main judgment in *O'Hara v United Kingdom* continued:

> There may thus be a fine line between those cases where the suspicion grounding the arrest is not sufficiently founded on objective facts and those which are. Whether the requisite standard is satisfied and whether the guarantee against arbitrary arrest laid down by Article 5(1)(c) is thereby satisfied depends on the particular circumstances of each case.
>
> The suspicion in the present case was based on information passed on at a police briefing by informers who identified the applicant as one of a number of persons suspected of involvement in a specific terrorist event... There is no basis in the material provided for the Court to reject the Government's submissions on this point. The arrest was therefore a pre-planned operation, more akin to the arrest in Murray, and was based on slightly more specific detail

[92] This release date is misprinted as '13 January' in [1997] 1 All ER 129, 135g and [1997] AC 286, 294E (Lord Hope).

[93] For a recent collection of extracts from his European Court judgments, see Tulkens et al (2008).

[94] [1997] 1 All ER 129, 139d.

[95] (2002) 34 EHRR 812.

than in Fox, Campbell and Hartley. In these circumstances, and having regard to additional distinguishing elements referred to above,[96] the Court considers that the domestic courts' approach—that the judge was entitled on the sparse materials before him to infer the existence of reasonable grounds of suspicion—was not incompatible with the standard imposed by Article 5(1)(c) of the Convention.[97]

At the end of the day the history of this particular litigation is a monument to the preparedness of the Northern Ireland legal aid system to fund challenges based on potential human rights arguments. But it does at least serve to confirm the legal position as stated in *Fox, Campbell and Hartley*. Police officers in Northern Ireland—and elsewhere in Europe—now know what standard of suspicion they must have before carrying out an arrest and no doubt the training which they receive makes them aware of the tests laid down by the European Court.

In a later case, *Brogan v United Kingdom*, about which more is said in the next chapter, the European Court again held that on the facts there had been reasonable suspicion justifying the arrests of the four applicants.[98] Moreover, their argument that they were suspected not of having committed specific offences but of involvement in unspecified acts of terrorism, something which could not be regarded as an 'offence' for the purposes of Article 5(1)(c), was dismissed. The Court noted that in the inter-State case of *Ireland v United Kingdom* it had previously indicated that the definition of acts of terrorism used in the PTA and EPA was 'well in keeping with the idea of an offence'.[99] The Court also mentioned that all of the applicants had been questioned within a few hours of their arrest about their suspected involvement in specific offences and their suspected membership of proscribed organizations, suggesting that that was a further ground for holding that they had been arrested in compliance with Article 5(1)(c). The applicants argued that the section 12 arrest power in the PTA 1984 amounted in effect to a power of administrative detention exercised for the purpose of gathering information, for otherwise an ordinary arrest power could have been employed. But the European Court was not convinced by this argument either, although it has to be said that its dismissal of it was not particularly convincing and even perhaps rather naïve:

There is no reason to believe that the police investigation in this case was not in good faith or that the detention of the applicants was not intended to further that investigation by way of confirming or dispelling the concrete suspicions which, as the Court has found, grounded

[96] ibid, paras 38–40. These elements included the fact that the legality of O'Hara's arrest had already been considered by three levels of domestic courts; his counsel had not taken steps to have the briefing officer give evidence as to what took place at the session where the arresting officer was briefed; the applicant had not made any requests for discovery in relation to the existing documentary evidence concerning the arrest; the information which led the police to arrest the applicant was obtained independently from four separate informers, who had proved previously reliable and whose information concerning the murder was consistent; and no challenge had been made by the applicant in the domestic proceedings to the good faith of any of the officers involved in the arrest or detention, despite the fact that after a previous incident in March 1993 the applicant had succeeded in proving that his arrest had been motivated by malice and he had been awarded damages.

[97] ibid, paras 41–42.

[98] (1989) 11 EHRR 117.

[99] (1979–80) 2 EHRR 25, para 196.

their arrest. Had it been possible, the police would, it can be assumed, have laid charges and the applicants would have been brought before the competent legal authority.[100]

Conclusion

In summary, we can see that the European Court exercised a fairly 'light touch' control over army and police arrest powers in Northern Ireland under the emergency legislation in force during the troubles. Beyond insisting, in *Fox, Campbell and Hartley v United Kingdom*, that arrests had to be grounded in *reasonable* suspicion, not just suspicion, the Court gave more or less *carte blanche* to arresting officers to act on whatever their superior officers told them to do, provided only that those superior officers were acting on what to them seemed reliable information. But before we protest too loudly that the European Court thereby abrogated its responsibility to control over-zealous police officers, one has to remember that formulating more precisely the limits of ideal arrest powers is extremely difficult, especially if the police are not to be unduly hamstrung in their efforts to solve crimes. There are societal interests involved in the solution of crime and the police are the officials appointed to protect those interests. They have to be granted some leeway to arrest people against whom they have, on an objective basis, reasonable suspicion. And that leeway may need to be greater when the crimes in question are particularly heinous. To offset the risk that people may be arrested who in fact have nothing to do with the crime, a range of safeguards needs to be in place to protect them while they are in police custody and at any subsequent trial, matters which will be addressed in Chapters 7 and 8 of this book. In Chapter 6, meanwhile, consideration will be given to the extent to which the European Convention was able to regulate the period during which arrested persons could be kept in detention in Northern Ireland while awaiting charge or trial. This is a topic which is still very much at the forefront of discussions about current UK laws on combating terrorism.

[100] (1989) 11 EHRR 117, para 53.

6

Detention Pending Charge or Trial

Chapter 4 examined the unsuccessful efforts made to use the European Convention on Human Rights as a tool—in the context of the conflict in Northern Ireland—for limiting powers of internment, powers to conduct examinations of travellers at ports, powers to stop and question people on the streets, and powers to issue exclusion orders. Chapter 5 looked more generally at powers of arrest in Northern Ireland and revealed that, although there was a slightly better success rate when challenges to those powers were raised in Strasbourg, the European Convention remained no real obstacle to the reduction in human rights which those special arrest powers inevitably entailed. Both chapters considered in some detail the precise wording of Article 5 of the Convention, which seeks to protect people against arbitrary deprivation of liberty by strictly limiting the situations in which they can be lawfully detained or arrested. The Article makes it clear that detention may occur even if no arrest ensues (as with powers to examine travellers at ports, or to stop and question people on the streets), but it does not explicitly say how long detention can lawfully continue, whether before or after an arrest has occurred. In this chapter, two particular aspects of that issue are addressed. First, for what period can detention continue without the detainee having to appear before a judge? Second, for what period can detention continue after the person has appeared before a judge? This second question can be further subdivided, focusing initially on the maximum period that can be permitted to elapse before the detainee has to be charged with an offence or released, and then on the period that can be permitted to elapse after the detainee has been charged but before his or her substantive trial begins.

The right of detainees to be brought before a judge

Article 5(3) of the Convention states that everyone who has been arrested or detained for the purpose of being brought before a competent legal authority on reasonable suspicion of having committed an offence (or because arrest or detention was reasonably considered necessary to prevent his or her committing an offence or fleeing after having done so) has the right, first, to be brought promptly before a judge or other officer authorized by law to exercise judicial power and, second, to be tried within a reasonable time or to be released pending trial. Restricting our attention for the moment to the first limb of Article 5(3), what does 'promptly' mean in this context?

The Special Powers Acts that applied in Northern Ireland from 1922 to 1973 allowed for internment to be introduced by ministerial regulation. But they did not otherwise extend the time during which people who were arrested on suspicion of having committed specific offences could be detained before being brought before a judge. The so-called 'ordinary' law applied in such situations. When serious civil unrest broke out in 1968 this ordinary law was enshrined in the Magistrates Courts Act (NI) 1964,[1] which allowed detention after arrest for just 24 hours, but that period could be extended to 48 hours on the say-so of a senior police officer. The arrested person then had to be brought before a court or released. The Northern Ireland (Emergency Provisions) Act 1973 (EPA)—which was enacted in the wake of the Diplock Commission's report in 1972 and the government's more general review of the Special Powers Act Regulations—retained internment in section 10, supplemented by Schedule 1. Arrests under that section were obviously intended to be the preliminary stage in what could well be indefinite detention. Section 10(3) authorized the detention of persons arrested under section 10(1) for a maximum of 72 hours—not just the 48 permitted by the then ordinary law. The thinking behind this was that it might take as long as 72 hours for the Secretary of State to decide whether to make an interim custody order in relation to the person arrested, this being the first step in the formal internment process.[2] As we saw in Chapter 5, the EPA 1973 also conferred another arrest power on the police, in section 11(1). This did not extend the maximum period during which an arrested person could then be detained without being brought before a court, so in those instances that period remained at 48 hours.

Internment was phased out two years after the EPA 1973 came into force, but unfortunately the power of arrest conferred by section 10 was still very frequently invoked. It was a much more general power than that conferred by section 11, so police officers naturally resorted to it as a matter of course. But this meant that the section 10 power was being used for a purpose for which it was never intended and that people were being arrested without the police having to show that they were suspected of any specific offence—suspicion of being a terrorist was enough. It also meant that people who were arrested could be detained for up to 72 hours before having to be brought before a court. Almost by stealth the ordinary law's standard on being brought 'promptly' before a court was thereby subverted.

When, in the wake of the Birmingham and Guildford pub bombings in 1974, Westminster enacted the Prevention of Terrorism (Temporary Provisions) Act 1974 (the PTA), a further arrest power was conferred on the police, by section 7. For some reason this power was included in a Part of the Act which was extended to the whole of the United Kingdom, not just England, Wales and Scotland. This meant that the police in Northern Ireland had a third arrest power at their disposal, one which was really an amalgam of the two existing powers in terms of the grounds which could be used to justify the arrest. Section 7(2) said that a person arrested under section 7(1) could not be detained in right of the arrest for more than 48 hours, but one of the novel features of

[1] s 132. This later became the Magistrates' Courts (NI) Order 1981, art 131, which was in turn replaced by the Police and Criminal Evidence (NI) Order 1989, art 42(1).

[2] See EPA 1973, Sch 1, para 11.

the PTA was that it allowed the police to apply to the Secretary of State for permission to prolong the detention by up to a further five days. This meant that arrested persons could be held in police custody for a total of seven days before having any right to appear before a court. While this was not as bad as the internment provisions which at that time still operated in Northern Ireland (though only for a few more months), it was otherwise a draconian step within the context of Great Britain (ie England, Scotland, and Wales). There, it authorized a kind of 'mini-internment'. When he was introducing the seven-day detention power in Parliament the then Home Secretary intimated that its primary justification was to allow him and his successors time to consider whether to issue exclusion orders against detainees, which in turn was why it would be inappropriate to make the length of the detention dependent on a judicial determination.[3]

Given the panic to enact the PTA, it is perhaps understandable that little attention was paid to the provisions which allowed executive detention for up to seven days. During the Parliamentary debates on the Bill and, it seems, the intra-governmental discussions of the Bill,[4] no serious attention appears to have been given to the requirement in Article 5(3) of the Convention that arrested persons must be brought 'promptly' before a judge or other officer authorized by law to exercise judicial power. The assumption was made that a seven-day delay would not breach this requirement. The corollary to this was that the British government did not believe that a derogation notice was required in relation to the seven-day detention power. A series of derogation notices had been lodged with the Council of Europe some years earlier in relation to the emergency in Northern Ireland.[5] The first three of those notices—submitted in 1957, 1969, and 1971—referred only to actions taken by the government of Northern Ireland, while the last four—submitted in 1973 and 1975, two in each year—referred to laws passed at Westminster which applied only in Northern Ireland and not elsewhere in the United Kingdom. No additional notice of derogation was issued when the PTA 1974 was enacted. Kinley has suggested that in later years, when the government and Parliament were renewing or replacing the PTA 1974, they should have anticipated what Strasbourg's reaction to the retention of the seven-day detention power was likely to be: he calls the government's unwillingness to investigate the relevance of the Convention 'inadequate'.[6] Others might use a much stronger adjective. It was when the PTA came to be replaced in 1979 that the relevance of the European Convention to the seven-day detention power was mentioned in Parliament for the first time: a backbench MP reminded her colleagues that the National Council for Civil Liberties was currently supporting six applicants at Strasbourg who were challenging the power.[7] A former Attorney General, Sam Silkin, told the House two years later that he had the gravest doubts whether the power was consistent with Article 5 of the Convention, especially given that the derogation notice which then applied covered only Northern Ireland, not Great Britain.[8]

[3] HC Deb, vol 882, col 641 (28 November 1974), per Roy Jenkins MP.
[4] Bonner (2006).
[5] They are set out in SACHR (1977b) 103–7.
[6] Kinley (1993) 60.
[7] HC Deb, vol 964, col 1607 (21 March 1979), per Joan Maynard MP. Cited in Kinley, ibid, 89.
[8] HC Deb, vol 1, col 368 (18 March 1981). Cited in Kinley, ibid, 90.

Brogan v United Kingdom

It is clear, then, that the PTA's seven-day detention power was applied in Northern Ireland without much thought being given to its compatibility with the European Convention. The authorities may have taken some comfort from the findings by the European Commission of Human Rights, in a 1966 case concerning ordinary criminal offences, that a period of four days satisfied the requirement of promptness in Article 5(3)[9] and, in an 'exceptional' 1972 case, where the applicant's state of health required him to be hospitalized, that a period of five days was considered acceptable.[10] But a challenge to the PTA detention system was then lodged by four men who had been detained in Northern Ireland in 1984 for periods ranging from four days and six hours to six days and 16-and-a-half hours. Supported by their solicitors in Belfast,[11] they applied to Strasbourg just a few weeks after being released from detention without charge. They had no domestic remedies to pursue because a UK court cannot rule that a provision in an act of the Westminster Parliament is somehow unlawful. In May 1987 the European Commission made it clear that it was examining the applications against the background of a continuing terrorist threat in Northern Ireland and the particular problems confronting the security forces there in bringing those responsible for terrorist acts to justice; it had to remain vigilant 'that a proper balance was struck between the protection of individual rights and the need to defend democratic society against the threats posed by organised terrorism'.[12] It also took into account 'that the struggle against terrorism may require a particular measure of sacrifice by each citizen in order to protect the community as a whole against such crimes'.[13]

In the event, the majority of the European Commission drew the dividing line somewhere between four days and 11 hours, which they said was acceptable, and five days and 11 hours, which they said was not. Consequently they upheld by 10 votes to two the applications by Terence Brogan and Dermot Coyle but rejected by eight votes to four the applications by William McFadden and Michael Tracey.[14] Four prominent members of the Commission, holding that all of the applications should have been upheld, were not prepared to make concessions to the terrorist background to the arrests:

The question arises in the present case whether the combat against terrorism justifies an interpretation of the word 'promptly' in a more lenient way than in the case of ordinary criminal offences... In the opinion of the majority, the struggle against terrorism justifies that all citizens should accept the risk of being detained for some time beyond four days without being

[9] App No 2894/66, decision of 6 October 1966, 9 Ybk 564.

[10] App No 4960/71, decision of 19 July 1972, 42 CD 49.

[11] J Christopher Napier & Co.

[12] App Nos 11209/84, 11234/84, 11266/84, and 11386/85, decision of 14 May 1987, para 80.

[13] ibid, para 106.

[14] There were corresponding findings regarding whether Art 5(5) (the right to compensation) had been breached, although one of the Commissioners who held that Art 5(3) had been breached in relation to Brogan and Coyle then held that Art 5(5) had not been breached.

brought before a judge. We cannot accept this position. It is precisely in situations where wider powers of arrest are conferred on the authorities to cope with an organised terrorist threat that the need for judicial control against the abuse of power is greatest. It cannot be said that the need for judicial control is less than in respect of detention for ordinary criminal offences.

The Government has alluded to special problems which exist when suspected terrorists are arrested and detained... We agree that account must be taken of these problems but it has not been shown that they exclude judicial control of detention.[15]

On the other hand, and not for the first time, the UK Commissioner, Sir Basil Hall, felt unable to join his fellow Commissioners in condemning the UK government in any way:

In the four cases before the Commission, the Commission has concluded that four days 6 hours and four days 11 hours satisfied the requirement of promptness; but that five days 11 hours and six days 16 hours did not.

I do not agree with this conclusion. The legislature of the respondent State has provided that, in cases of a reasonable suspicion, a person who has been concerned in terrorism may be detained for 48 hours, but the Secretary of State may, in any particular case, extend the period by a further period or periods specified by him, the further period or periods not to exceed five days in all. Having regard to the need to strike a balance between the interests of the individual and the general interest of the community, I do not consider that the legislature has prescribed an obviously excessive period.[16]

The case then went on to be considered by the European Court,[17] which on 29 November 1988 held by 12 votes to seven that Article 5(3) had been breached in relation to all four applicants,[18] a rare example of the European Court going further than the Commission in protecting human rights.[19] Like the Commission, the Court acknowledged that the investigation of terrorist offences undoubtedly presented the authorities with special problems. It took 'full judicial notice' of the factors adverted to by the UK government in this connection and noted that in Northern Ireland 'the referral of police requests for extended detention to the Secretary of State and the individual scrutiny of each police request by a minister do provide a form of executive control'.[20] It also took into account that the need for the continuation of the

[15] Joint partly dissenting opinion of Commissioners Frowein, Trechsel, Schermers, and Thune.

[16] Partly dissenting opinion of Sir Basil Hall.

[17] Astonishingly, the PTA was renewed earlier that year without any mention being made in either House of Parliament of the decision by the European Commission in May 1987. See HC Deb, vol 127, cols 925–49 (16 February 1988) and HL Deb, vol 483, cols 565–85 (16 February 1988). In the debate in the House of Commons, Alex Carlile MP did note that 'the legislation is contrary to the European Convention on Human Rights' (col 936), but he was not specific and the Home Secretary did not address the point.

[18] (1989) 11 EHRR 117. By 13 to 6 the Court held that Art 5(5) had also been breached in relation to each applicant. See Roche (1989–90).

[19] On this phenomenon see Tomkins (1997) 23: 'If all the cases where the Court and Commission have come to different conclusions as to whether or not there has been a violation of the Convention are listed, up to the end of 1990 that list would contain 52 cases. In only 12 of these cases did the Court find a violation where the Commission did not, and in the remaining 40 the Court found no violation whereas the Commission did.' He lists the 12 cases, only two of which were against the UK—*Brogan*, the case discussed here, and *Soering v UK* (1989) 11 EHRR 439. For a later example of this occurrence in a case connected to the conflict in Northern Ireland see *McCann, Farrell and Savage v UK* (1996) 21 EHRR 97.

[20] (1989) 11 EHRR 117, para 61. See too Finnie (1989); Livingstone (1989).

special powers was constantly monitored by the UK Parliament and their operation regularly subjected to independent reviews. It even accepted that the context of terrorism in Northern Ireland had the effect of prolonging the period during which the authorities may keep a person suspected of serious terrorist offences in custody before bringing him or her before a judge or other judicial officer. Nevertheless, despite all these 'concessions', the European Court held that:

> To attach such importance to the special features of this case as to justify so lengthy a period of detention without appearance before a judge or other judicial officer would be an unacceptably wide interpretation of the plain meaning of the word 'promptly'. An interpretation to this effect would import into Article 5(3) a serious weakening of a procedural guarantee to the detriment of the individual and would entail consequences impairing the very essence of the right protected by this provision.[21]

Seven judges dissented. Six of them wrote a joint opinion saying that, in view of the exceptional situation in Northern Ireland, and given that a period of four days was acceptable in normal situations, it seemed reasonable to regard periods of detention for less than a week as acceptable: 'Such a view fits in with the case-law and is justified by the wholly exceptional conditions obtaining in Northern Ireland'.[22] Sir Vincent Evans, the UK judge, delivered a separate dissenting opinion in which he pointed out that more than 30,000 people had been killed, maimed, or injured in Northern Ireland as a direct result of terrorist activity in the previous 20 years. He also noted that in the most recent year, 1987, of 83 persons detained in excess of five days, 39 had been charged with serious terrorist offences, and he added that in his report on the operation of the PTA 1984 during 1987 Viscount Colville had concluded that if a High Court judge were to be asked to grant extensions to detention this would have to be done in camera, without any effective representation of the detainee, a procedure that 'could lead to unanswerable criticisms of the judiciary'.[23]

The European Court's decision in *Brogan v United Kingdom* undoubtedly came as a shock to the British government and also, it must be said, to other regular observers of the enforcement of the Convention. The government quickly had to decide how to react so as to avoid future adverse judgments and it opted again for officially derogating from the Convention. It had lifted its previous derogation more than four years earlier, in August 1984, at a time when it had decided to accept many of the recommendations contained in the Baker Review published in April 1984, including that special police arrest powers should be premised not just on 'suspicion' but on 'reasonable suspicion'. Now the derogation was imposed specifically to allow extended detention periods after arrest. It was notified to the Secretary General of the Council of Europe on 23 December 1988 and in a further notice dated 12 December 1989 the UK government informed the Secretary General that a satisfactory procedure

[21] ibid, para 62. In a separate judgment, delivered on 30 May 1989, the Court held unanimously that no compensation should be awarded to any of the applicants. By way of exemplary damages they had each claimed £2,000 per hour of excess detention.

[22] Judges Thór Vilhjálmsson (Iceland), Bindschedler-Robert (Switzerland), Gölcüklü (Turkey), Martens (Netherlands), Matscher (Austria), and Valticos (Greece).

[23] para 4 of Sir Vincent Evans' dissenting judgment.

for the review of detention of terrorist suspects involving the judiciary had still not been identified and that the derogation would therefore remain in place for as long as circumstances required. A month earlier a Minister of State had informed the UK Parliament why judges could not be used to consider applications for extensions to periods of detention in Northern Ireland:

> Decisions to authorise the detention of terrorist suspects for periods beyond 48 hours may be, and often are, taken on the basis of information, the nature and source of which could not be revealed to a suspect or his legal adviser without serious risk to individuals assisting the police or the prospect of further valuable intelligence being lost. Any new procedure which avoided those dangers by allowing a court to make a decision on information not presented to the detainee or his legal adviser would represent a radical departure from the principles which govern judicial proceedings in this country and could seriously affect public trust and confidence in the independence of the judiciary. The Government would be most reluctant to introduce any new procedure which could have this effect.[24]

Ten years later the new derogation notice was specifically set out in the Human Rights Act 1998,[25] but the relevant provision was repealed by the Human Rights Act (Amendment) Order 2001 when Part VII of the Terrorism Act 2000 came into force in 2001.[26] The UK government had issued a consultation paper on extensions to detention in December 1998, and the 2000 Act conceded that it was now possible, even in Northern Ireland, for a High Court judge to determine whether a terrorist suspect's detention should be extended. While it is undeniable that the security situation in Northern Ireland improved immeasurably between 1988 and 2001, a case can certainly be made for saying that the power to order extensions to detentions should have been transferred from the Secretary of State to local judges much sooner. Conflict-related fatalities tailed off significantly in Northern Ireland after 1994, the year in which ceasefires were called by the IRA and by major loyalist paramilitary organizations. One cannot help but assume that the measure was kept in place because it allowed the security forces to cause disruption to the activities of persons suspected of involvement in paramilitary activities. It also gave them an opportunity to try to recruit more informers from amongst the persons arrested.

Further challenges to the derogation notice

In a further case brought to Strasbourg by two men who had been detained for more than four days in Northern Ireland—Peter Brannigan and Patrick McBride—the legality of the government's derogation notice of 1988 was itself challenged. The applicants had each been arrested within two weeks of the notice having been sent to Strasbourg, Peter Brannigan having been detained for six days and 14-and-a-half hours and Patrick McBride for four days and six-and-a-half hours.

[24] HC Deb, vol 160, col 210W (14 November 1989), per David Waddington MP.

[25] Sch 3, Pt I. This sets out the text of the notification sent on 23 December 1988 and also of a supplementary notice sent on 23 March 1989 to take account of the replacement of the PTA 1984 by the PTA 1989.

[26] SI 2001/1216.

Their applications, supported by their solicitors Madden and Finucane, were submitted before the end of January 1989.[27] On 3 December 1991 (an indication of how slow the proceedings can be at Strasbourg) the European Commission held by eight votes to five that there had been no breach of Article 5(3) because of the UK government's derogation notice of 23 December 1988, which was perfectly valid. Commissioner Hall repeated what he had said in *Brogan* about there not being a breach of Article 5(3) in the first place, so there was no need for him to rely on the derogation notice. Commissioner Frowein also maintained his previous position that the UK government had not demonstrated to his satisfaction why it was not possible to allow judges to determine whether to allow detentions to be extended.[28] Three other Commissioners agreed with Commissioner Frowein, pointing out that judges might in any event be involved in assessing the legality of detention through judicial review or habeas corpus proceedings and that courts often have to decide cases which require examination of sensitive confidential information. However minimal the judicial safeguards, they said, some judicial control is better than none.

The case was then referred to the European Court and decided on 26 May 1993.[29] Amnesty International had intervened to argue that the Court should apply a particularly strict approach when examining the legality of derogations from fundamental procedural guarantees in times of emergency. Likewise, Liberty, Interights, and the Committee on the Administration of Justice intervened to argue that, if States are to be allowed a margin of appreciation when derogating from the Convention, this margin should be narrower the longer the emergency goes on, and they contended that by early 1989 there was no evidence of an exceptional situation of crisis in Northern Ireland. They said the situation had not demonstrably deteriorated since August 1984, when the UK's previous derogation was withdrawn. The Standing Advisory Commission on Human Rights in Northern Ireland, however, accepted in its intervention that there was a sufficient emergency in Northern Ireland to justify the government's derogation. The Court, making its own assessment of the situation, held by 22 votes to four that 'in the light of all the material before it as to the extent and impact of terrorist violence in Northern Ireland and elsewhere in the United Kingdom... there can be no doubt that such a public emergency existed at

[27] On 12 February 1989 one of the partners in this firm, Patrick Finucane, was murdered by loyalist gunmen. Although one man, Kenneth Barrett, was convicted of the murder in 2003, an investigation by a retired Canadian Supreme Court judge, Peter Cory, concluded that there was good cause to hold a public inquiry into the killing on account of the alleged collusion between loyalist paramilitaries and elements of the British security forces: Cory (2004). The UK government is content for such an inquiry to occur, but only under the Inquiries Act 2005, a statute which many think was enacted specifically to allow the State to conceal from the Finucane inquiry information which is particularly sensitive from a security point of view. So far no inquiry has been established and the Finucane family has said that it will not cooperate with one held under the 2005 Act. See too O'Brien (2005) and Requa (2007).

[28] He was joined in this view (although they issued a separate joint dissenting opinion) by Commissioners Loucaides, Thune, and Rozakis.

[29] (1994) 17 EHRR 539. By this time one of the applicants, Patrick McBride, was dead. He was shot when a police officer ran amok at Sinn Féin's headquarters in 1992.

the relevant time',[30] a categorical position reminiscent of that adopted by the same court in the inter-State case 15 years earlier.[31]

As to whether the measures taken were strictly required by the exigencies of the situation, and in particular whether the absence of judicial control of extended detention was justified, the Court held by the same majority that the United Kingdom 'had not overstepped their margin of appreciation in this regard'.[32] It accepted the UK government's view that it was essential to prevent the disclosure to the detainee and his legal adviser of information on the basis of which decisions on the extension of detention are made and that, in the adversarial system of the common law, the independence of the judiciary would be compromised if judges or other judicial officers were to be involved in the granting or approval of extensions.[33] It then added:

> In the context of Northern Ireland, where the judiciary is small and vulnerable to terrorist attacks, public confidence in the independence of the judiciary is understandably a matter to which the Government attach great importance.[34]

The Court was also of the view, contrary to that put forward by the intervening NGOs, that the safeguards in place to prevent abuse of the detention power were adequate. The applicants could take habeas corpus proceedings, they had an absolute and legally enforceable right to consult a solicitor (though only 48 hours after being arrested!),[35] their right to consult with a solicitor before then could be delayed only if there were reasonable grounds for doing so and any such decision to delay access was susceptible to judicial review where the burden of establishing reasonable grounds for the delay would rest on the police, the applicants were entitled to inform a relative or friend about their detention and to have access to a doctor, and the operation of the legislation was kept under regular independent review.[36]

The European Court therefore held that the applicants could not complain of a breach of Article 5(3), nor indeed of Articles 5(5) or 13. Among the dissenters was Judge Brian Walsh from Ireland, who roundly condemned his fellow judges for being taken in by the British government's arguments. Having pointed out that the

[30] ibid, para 47. The Court referred back to para 12 of its judgment, where it had noted that between 1972 and 1992 organized terrorism had continued to grow in Northern Ireland. There had been over 3,000 deaths and 35,104 people injured as a result of terrorist acts (many injuries involving loss of limbs and permanent physical disability). There had been a total of 41,859 terrorist shootings or bombings.

[31] *Ireland v UK* (1979–80) 2 EHRR 25, para 205.

[32] (1994) 17 EHRR 539, para 57.

[33] ibid, para 58.

[34] ibid, para 59.

[35] It is an indication of how quickly the European Court can change its standards that in this case, decided in 1993, the Court unequivocally envisaged a delay of 48 hours in giving a detainee access to a solicitor, yet in *Murray (John) v UK*, decided in 1996, it viewed immediate access to a solicitor as essential, at least in situations where inferences could be drawn from a detainee's silence in response to police questioning. See further ch 8 below.

[36] Amnesty International had relied on the UN's Body of Principles for the Protection of All Persons under Any Form of Detention or Imprisonment (1988), which rule out incommunicado detention, and it had submitted that habeas corpus was in practice an ineffective remedy since the decision to detain is taken in complete secrecy. The independent reviews referred to by the Court were conducted by Sir Cyril Philips in 1984 and 1985 and by Viscount Colville from 1986 to 1991. A broader review of the PTA 1984 was conducted by Viscount Colville in 1987: Colville (1987).

adversary procedure of the common law does *not* require confidential police sources to be disclosed at a remand hearing, and that it was 'unfortunate' that the majority judges had 'been allowed to believe' that habeas corpus was a realistic alternative remedy open to detainees,[37] he continued in equally strong language:

> The Government's plea that it is motivated by a wish to preserve public confidence in the independence of the judiciary is, in effect, to say that such confidence is to be maintained or achieved by not permitting them to have a role in the protection of the personal liberty of the arrested persons. One would think that such a role was one which the public would expect the judges to have. It is also to be noted that neither Parliament nor the Government appears to have made any serious effort to rearrange the judicial procedure or jurisdiction, in spite of being advised to do so by the persons appointed to review the system,[38] to cater for the requirement of Article 5(3) in cases of the type now under review. It is the function of national authorities so to arrange their affairs as not to clash with the requirements of the Convention. The Convention is not to be remoulded to assume the shape of national procedures.[39]

There matters rested for the remainder of the 1990s, even though the level of violence in Northern Ireland declined considerably during the decade. While 94 people were killed in 1991, only nine died in 1995 and seven in 1999.[40] From 1993 to 1998 annual reviews of the operation of the PTA 1989 in Northern Ireland were conducted and published by John Rowe QC. On more than one occasion he stated that he favoured involving judges in decisions to grant extensions to detentions, but he never actually recommended that the legislation should be amended to allow this to happen.

In *Marshall v United Kingdom* the Committee on the Administration of Justice, a human rights non-governmental organization based in Belfast, represented a man who, in February 1998, had been held in Castlereagh Holding Centre in East Belfast for six days and two hours before being released without charge. While in detention the applicant saw his solicitor on 10 occasions and during the first 48 hours the detention was regularly reviewed by senior police officers not directly involved in the case, as required by the Code of Practice issued under the Northern Ireland (Emergency Provisions) Act 1996.[41] When arguing before the European Court that the derogation from Article 5 was no longer justified, Paul Mageean (a solicitor employed by the Committee on the Administration of Justice) submitted that at the time of Marshall's detention the security situation in Northern Ireland had changed beyond recognition. The main paramilitary groups had called a ceasefire in 1994 and since then there had been a marked decline in the use of emergency powers of arrest,

[37] (1994) 17 EHRR 539, para 6 of Judge Walsh's dissenting opinion.

[38] This appears to be a reference to suggestions made by the most recent independent reviewer, John Rowe, in his report for 1993.

[39] (1994) 17 EHRR 539, para 10 of Judge Walsh's dissenting opinion. Judge Walsh also said, as his predecessor as an Irish judge at the European Court, Philip O'Donoghue, had said in the inter-State case of *Ireland v UK* (1978) 2 EHRR 25, that a threat to the life of the nation, in the words of Art 15, ought to mean a threat to the whole nation, not just to one small part of it (para 2 of his opinion).

[40] Admittedly 62 died in 1994 and 55 in 1998.

[41] s 52. The Code reflected standards laid down for non-terrorist suspects by the Police and Criminal Evidence (NI) Order 1989.

search, and detention,[42] less frequent recourse to extended periods of detention,[43] the closure of army bases, and the running down of the number of army personnel involved in operational duties. He argued that the government should not be permitted to impose a permanent state of emergency on Northern Ireland with the pernicious consequences which that would entail for respect for the rule of law. The Court, he said, should apply a 'strict scrutiny test' with regard to the government's claim as to the existence of a public emergency and to the legality of the measures taken thereunder. He maintained that the power of extended detention was not strictly required by the exigencies of the situation, since statistics showed that at the material time most individuals detained under section 14 of the 1989 Act were released without charge. The annual reviews of the PTA and EPA, moreover, did not examine the capacity of the ordinary criminal law process to deal with the security situation.

The European Court nevertheless unanimously held that the application should be declared 'manifestly ill-founded' because the detention was justified under the derogation notice issued by the United Kingdom. Amazingly, the judges did not think the security situation in Northern Ireland had sufficiently improved in the almost nine years since the detentions in *Brannigan and McBride* to justify a conclusion that there was no longer a public emergency threatening the life of the nation. The Court recalled that 'by reason of their direct and continuous contact with the pressing needs of the moment, the national authorities are in principle better placed than the international judge to decide both on the presence of such an emergency and on the nature and scope of the derogation necessary to avoid it'.[44] On the government's refusal to countenance judicial involvement in decisions to extend detentions, the Court added:

> As to the decision to prolong the applicant's detention in the absence of judicial intervention, the Court observes that the Government rely on the same justifications for this measure which they advanced in the Brannigan and McBride case. Those justifications were accepted by the Court in that case on the basis that it was not its role to substitute its view as to what measures were most appropriate or expedient at the relevant time in dealing with an emergency situation for that of the Government which have direct responsibility for establishing the balance between the taking of effective measures to combat terrorism on the one hand, and respecting individual rights on the other. The Court considered that in the context of Northern Ireland, where the judiciary was small and vulnerable to terrorist attacks, public confidence in the independence of the judiciary was understandably a matter to which the Government attached great importance.[45]

The decision in *Marshall v UK* was issued on 10 July 2001, by which time the derogation notice of 1988 had been withdrawn (as from 1 April 2001). The Terrorism Act 2000 came into force in February 2001. As of then a person detained under

[42] In 1992, 1993, and 1994 the numbers of persons detained in Northern Ireland under the PTA were, respectively, 1795, 1641, and 1503. In 1995, 1996, and 1997 the numbers were 443, 569, and 504. See Northern Ireland Office, *Research and Statistical Bulletin 6/2001*, Table 1.

[43] In 1992, 1993, and 1994 the numbers of applications for extensions to detention that were granted in Northern Ireland were, respectively, 441, 455, and 384. In 1995, 1996, and 1997 the numbers were 12, 60, and 72. ibid.

[44] *Marshall v UK* App No 41571/98, decision of 10 July 2001, p 12.

[45] ibid.

anti-terrorism legislation has had to be brought before a judge no later than 48 hours after being arrested, but the judge can authorize extensions. The permitted length of those extensions has been a matter of great controversy, which is addressed in the next section, but in the years 2002, 2003, and 2004, the number of persons detained in Northern Ireland under the detention power[46] was, respectively, 236, 359, and 230. The number of applications for extensions to detention that were granted in each of those years was, 12, 23, and 16.[47]

As far as the ordinary (non-terrorist) law is concerned, the Police and Criminal Evidence (NI) Order 1989 (PACE Order), in force since 1 January 1990, had already provided that the police in Northern Ireland could detain an arrested person for a maximum of 36 hours. If they wanted that period to be extended they again had to go to a magistrate, who could lengthen it to 96 hours if persuaded that there were reasonable grounds for believing this to be necessary in order to secure evidence.[48] By 2001, therefore, the domestic laws of Northern Ireland dealing with 'ordinary' suspects and terrorist suspects were pretty much aligned as far as the detainee's right to be brought before a judge was concerned—it was just that in terrorist cases the police had a further 12 hours in which to question the arrested person before having to bring him or her before a judge.

The right of detainees to be charged or released

We now turn to consider the rights of detainees after they have been brought before a judge. How is their position protected by the European Convention? Strange as it may seem, even though the permitted maximum detention period for suspected terrorists has been one of the hottest issues in UK politics in recent years, it is not a matter on which either the European Convention or the European Court has given much guidance. This is because the Convention was largely drafted with European civil law systems in mind, rather than Anglo-Saxon common law systems. Article 5 pays very little attention to the concept of a criminal 'charge', referring to it only in paragraph (2), which states that everyone who has been arrested must be informed promptly, and in a language which he or she understands, of the reasons for the arrest 'and of any charge against him'. When Article 5(3) addresses the length of detention periods it does so in relation to only two key events—appearance before a judge (which must occur 'promptly') and trial (which must occur 'within a reasonable time'). There is no indication of how much time can be allowed to elapse before a detained person is charged.

To some extent this is because Article 5(4) gives every detained person the right to take proceedings by which the lawfulness of his or her detention can be decided 'speedily' by a court, with his or her release being required if the detention is found not to be lawful. If a State wishes to detain someone while an investigation is conducted into his or her involvement in criminal activities, such 'provisional detention' (*détention*

46 Terrorism Act 2000, s 41.

47 Northern Ireland Office, *Research and Statistical Bulletin 9/2005*, Table 3.

48 See, generally, Leigh (1989).

préventive in a French-based legal system) is not in itself a breach of Article 5, whether or not any formal 'charge' has already been laid against the detainee. Unfortunately, recent comparative studies of law and practice in this field, whether conducted for the UK government[49] or leading non-governmental organizations,[50] do not fully enough elucidate the differences between common law systems (where being charged is a crucial stage in the administration of criminal justice) and civil law systems (where a distinction is made between police custody—*garde à vue*—and judicial investigations—*mise en examen*). In countries such as France and Italy people can be held in detention during the latter stage as well as during the former, even though they have not yet been informed that they are going to be tried for a particular offence.

As we have seen, when the PTA 1974 was introduced it required persons arrested under section 7 to be brought before a judge within 48 hours (the same period that the ordinary law then allowed), but it provided that the Secretary of State could extend the period of 48 hours by a further period not exceeding five days. When it condemned this seven-day maximum detention period in *Brogan v United Kingdom* the European Court did so because it breached the first limb of Article 5(3)—the requirement that a detainee must be brought promptly before a judge or other officer authorized by law to exercise judicial power. The Court did not suggest that if the detainee were to be brought promptly before a judge he or she would have to be charged within seven days (or any other stipulated period). Nor did the Court refer to any such pre-charge detention limits in *Brannigan and McBride v United Kingdom* or *Marshall v United Kingdom*. When, therefore, the UK government eventually withdrew its notice of derogation in this context in 2001, requiring detainees to be brought before a judge within 48 hours of being arrested, it had no qualms about retaining seven days as the maximum period that could elapse before the detainee would need to be charged with an offence or released.[51] Three years later it felt comfortable in extending the maximum pre-charge detention period from seven days to 14 days,[52] and in 2005 it tried to extend it to 90 days, but a defeat in a vote in the House of Commons persuaded it to compromise on 28 days.[53] In 2008, during a debate on the Counter-Terrorism Bill, the government again tried to lengthen the maximum period to 42 days, but on this occasion a defeat in a vote in the House of Lords led it to withdraw the proposal (while saying that it would hold the power in reserve in a draft Bill, ready to be enacted if and when required).[54]

[49] See FCO (2005). This report is available on the FCO's website, last visited 3 August 2009.

[50] Russell (2007). This report is available on Liberty's website, last visited 3 August 2009.

[51] Terrorism Act 2000, s 41 and Sch 8, para 29(3).

[52] Criminal Justice Act 2003, s 306, which inserts new paras (3A) and (3B) into the Terrorism Act 2000, Sch 8.

[53] MPs voted by 322 to 291 against the government's proposal for 90-day detentions and by 323 to 290 in favour of 28 day detentions: HC Deb, vol 439, cols 325–385 (9 November 2005). The result was the Terrorism Act 2006, s 23, which amends the Terrorism Act 2000, Sch 8. For an argument that in the first situation where the 28-day power was used—the aircraft liquid bomb case—a 14-day power would have been adequate, see Bajwa and Duke (2006).

[54] HL Deb, vol 704, cols 491–541 (13 October 2008); the majority in the vote, taken during the Committee stage of the Bill, was 191. Two hours after the vote the Home Secretary, Jacqui Smith, announced in the House of Commons: 'I have prepared a new Bill to enable the police and prosecutors to

There is disagreement over how long a period of pre-charge detention needs to be in order to constitute a violation of Article 5. The European Court of Human Rights has never intimated what is an acceptable maximum. Instead its approach has been to look at whether the detention is reasonable and proportionate in the circumstances, and at whether there are adequate safeguards to ensure that at any hearing into whether the detention should be extended the detainee is given a full opportunity to hear the case against him or her and to challenge the reliability of the information which the prosecution is relying upon. In *Garcia Alva v Germany*, for example, the Court said:

> A court examining an appeal against detention must provide guarantees of a judicial procedure. The proceedings must be adversarial and must always ensure 'equality of arms' between the parties, the prosecutor and the detained person. Equality of arms is not ensured if counsel is denied access to those documents in the investigation file which are essential in order effectively to challenge the lawfulness of his client's detention.[55]

But it should be noted that that case was about remand in custody, not about pre-charge detention, and the Court pronounced only on Article 5(4), not Article 5(3). In *Kerr v United Kingdom*, a case brought by a suspected terrorist in Northern Ireland who had been held for seven days under the PTA 1989 before being charged, the European Court seemed particularly aware of the flexibility available to States in this area when it noted that:

> the fact that the applicant was only notified about the charges against him [seven days after being arrested] does not in itself raise an issue under Article 5(2) from the standpoint of the requirement of promptness. It is to be recalled that that requirement only comes into play if there is 'any charge' against the applicant.[56]

Further guidance from the Court is awaited on whether, even if the safeguards mentioned in *Garcia Alva v Germany* are provided, a lengthy period of pre-charge detention can nevertheless be a breach of Article 5(3) *per se*. Current indications are, unfortunately, to the contrary.[57]

The right of detainees to be released pending trial

The word 'bail' is not mentioned at all in Article 5, but when Article 5(3) says that a detainee has the right to a trial within a reasonable time or to release pending trial it is obviously alluding indirectly to the concept. This is made even clearer by the last phrase in that paragraph: 'Release may be conditioned by guarantees to appear for trial.' In Northern Ireland two main issues have arisen in relation to the compatibility

do their work—should the worst happen, and should a terrorist plot overtake us and threaten our current investigatory capabilities... The Counter-Terrorism (Temporary Provisions) Bill now stands ready to be introduced if and when the need arises.' HC Deb, vol 480, col 624 (13 October 2008).

[55] App No 23541/94 (judgment of 13 February 2001), para 39.

[56] (2000) 29 EHRR CD184, CD188.

[57] Dickson (2009b).

of its domestic law on bail with the requirements of Article 5. The first, discussed in this section, is whether the special rules on bail put in place for terrorist cases in Northern Ireland are compliant with the European Convention. The second, discussed in the next section, is whether the more generally applicable rules on bail are compliant.

The first issue has itself two aspects: are the criteria for granting bail in terrorist cases in Northern Ireland consistent with the Convention, and is the fact that only senior judges can grant bail in those cases also consistent? The former question arises from the fact the EPA 1973, and also the EPA 1978, did not permit the courts to grant bail to a person charged with a scheduled offence unless satisfied that the accused person would comply with certain conditions, some of which were specified (for example, that the person would not commit any offence while on bail) and others of which could be imposed at the discretion of the court.[58] This in effect meant that the onus was on the accused to show why bail should be granted rather than on the prosecution to show why it should not be. The Standing Advisory Commission on Human Rights (SACHR) felt that this was improper and in its submission to Parliament for the renewal debate of the EPA in July 1979 it recommended that the section on bail should not be renewed.[59] It repeated this recommendation the following year[60] and called for the law in Northern Ireland to be brought into line with that created for England and Wales by the Bail Act 1976, whereby the accused must be granted bail unless the judge is satisfied by the prosecution that the accused will not meet certain conditions. It recognized that the judges were not disadvantaging defendants as often as they might have done, but added: 'That the sub-section operates fairly in practice is not the point at issue, rather the provision in section 2(2) is contrary to precept and practice.'[61] And it did submit that 'the evidence suggests that rather more persons might safely be admitted to bail'.[62] When Walsh conducted his survey of 170 Diplock court trials in the first three months of 1981 he did not comment on the bail criteria: he noted that 36 per cent of all the defendants in the survey were released on bail, that defendants under the age of 19 were more likely to receive bail, and that, surprisingly perhaps, the success rate in bail applications for republican defendants was twice as high as it was for loyalist defendants (42 per cent as opposed to 21 per cent).[63]

Sir George Baker looked at the issue during his review of the EPA 1978. He acknowledged that '[i]t is generally accepted by those who have studied the question of bail in depth that the NI judges have interpreted section 2 liberally and sensibly',[64] but he doubted whether Northern Ireland was yet ready to adopt the wording of England's Bail Act 1976—'A person shall be granted bail ... unless.'[65] He

[58] EPA 1973, s 3(2) and (3); EPA 1978, s 2(2) and (3).

[59] SACHR (1980) para 10(4).

[60] SACHR (1981) para 6(2).

[61] Submission on file with the author, para 27.

[62] ibid, para 68.

[63] Walsh (1983) 83–4. He suggested that the reason for the disparity might have been that republican defendants at the time were more likely to have better criminal records, to be younger, and to be charged with less serious offences.

[64] Baker (1984) para 75.

[65] ibid, para 80.

recommended an amalgam of the Bail Act approach and the EPA approach, whereby judges would be given a wide discretion, with guidelines on how to exercise it.[66] The government accepted almost all of Baker's draft new clause, except the initial statement that 'There shall be a presumption in favour of bail'. It specified the circumstances to which the judge had to have regard when exercising his or her discretion, such as 'the character, antecedents, associations and community ties' of the accused.[67] This provision remained in force until the bulk of the emergency law apparatus was repealed in Northern Ireland on 31 July 2007.[68] It was challenged in the High Court of Northern Ireland in 2003, but to no avail: in *Re Shaw's Application*[69] an argument that section 67(3) of the Terrorism Act 2000 was incompatible with Article 5 of the European Convention did not convince Kerr J, as he then was, nor did the contention that the Secretary of State's failure to introduce regulations on bail similar to those in force in England and Wales discriminated against unconvicted defendants in Northern Ireland contrary to Article 14 of the Convention.There are now no special laws in place in Northern Ireland on bail for terrorist suspects.

The question of whether only senior judges should be allowed to grant bail was not so controversial. The thinking behind the rule, which was introduced following the report of the Diplock Commission in 1972,[70] was that to allow magistrates to take such decisions would be to expose them to too much danger—they could easily be targeted by republican paramilitaries and, given that the magistracy was quite numerous, they could not be easily protected. As there were only a few Supreme Court judges, who in any event received round the clock police protection, it was deemed wiser to task them with the responsibility of deciding whether or not to grant bail to such suspects. Boyle, Hadden, and Hillyard argued that there was a strong case for restoring the right of magistrates to grant bail for scheduled offences,[71] but Baker was unconvinced, mainly because he had been assured that restricting the power to High Court judges did not in practice cause any delays. In these debates, however, no-one thought of examining whether restricting the right to grant bail to senior judges might actually be contrary to the European Convention. The issue eventually came before the European Court in *McKay v United Kingdom*.[72]

Mark McKay, having been arrested on 6 January 2001 on suspicion of having carried out a robbery of a petrol station, admitted his guilt the next day and was officially charged with the offence. On 8 January 2001 he appeared in a magistrates' court and applied for release on bail. The police gave evidence that the robbery was not connected with terrorism and that they would have no objection to bail being granted, but the

[66] ibid, para 81.

[67] EPA, s 2(4), as substituted by the EPA 1987, s 1.

[68] EPA 1978, s 2 (as amended) was replaced in turn by EPA 1991, s 3, EPA 1996, s 3, and Terrorism Act 2000, s 67.

[69] [2003] NIQB 68.

[70] Diplock (1972). A magistrate was in fact murdered in 1973, and another in 1974. Three other, more senior, judges were also killed in the Northern Ireland conflict (in 1974, 1983, and 1987).

[71] Boyle, Hadden and Hillyard (1980) 67. SACHR recommended no change to the law on this point: SACHR (1981) para 6.

[72] (2007) 44 EHRR 41.

magistrate indicated that because the offence in question was a scheduled offence (ie one liable to be committed for terrorist purposes) he did not have the power to order McKay's release.[73] Later that same day McKay applied to the High Court for bail and he was granted it the next day. He immediately applied for judicial review, seeking a declaration that the anti-terrorist legislation was in this regard incompatible with Articles 5 and 14 of the European Convention. On 3 May (three weeks after McKay was sentenced to two years' detention in a young offenders' institution, followed by a year of probation, for the offence to which he had pleaded guilty) Kerr J, as he then was, rejected his judicial review application.[74] In relation to the Article 14 argument, the judge did not accept that accused members of the security forces were treated more favourably than other accused people concerning bail. The judge, the Divisional Court, and the House of Lords itself, all refused leave to appeal any further.

After the application had been held admissible by the European Court it was deemed important enough to be referred to the Grand Chamber of 17 judges rather than to a mere Chamber of seven judges. The Grand Chamber held by 16 votes to one that there had been no breach of Article 5(3).[75] Citing its earlier decision in *TW v Malta*,[76] the Court acknowledged that Article 5(3) conferred two distinct rights which were not on their face logically or temporally linked.[77] Noting that in relation to the second right there is no express requirement of 'promptness' as there is in relation to the first, the Court nevertheless said that 'such consideration, whether on application by the applicant or by the judge of his or her own motion, must take place with due expedition, in order to keep any unjustified deprivation of liberty to an acceptable minimum',[78] and it added, tellingly:

> In order to ensure that the right guaranteed is practical and effective, not theoretical and illusory, it is not only good practice, but highly desirable in order to minimise delay, that the judicial officer who conducts the first automatic review of lawfulness and the existence of a ground for detention, also has the competence to consider release on bail. It is not however a requirement of the Convention and there is no reason in principle why the issues cannot be dealt with by two judicial officers, within the requisite time-frame. In any event, as a matter of interpretation, it cannot be required that the examination of bail take place with any more speed than is demanded of the first automatic review, which the Court has identified as being a maximum four days.[79]

On the facts of the case before it the Court stressed that no element of possible abuse or arbitrariness arose from the fact that it was another tribunal or judge that

[73] EPA 1996, s 3(2), replaced in February 2001 by the Terrorism Act 2000, s 67(2). Robbery involving any explosive, firearm, imitation firearm, or weapon of offence, was specified as a scheduled offence by EPA 1996, Sch 1, Pt I, para 10(b) (when read with Note 3(a)); this was replaced by the Terrorism Act 2000, Sch 9, para 10(b).

[74] [2002] NIQB 31, 3 May 2002 (Kerr J).

[75] (2007) 44 EHRR 41.

[76] App No 25644/94, decision of 29 April 1999, para 49.

[77] (2007) 44 EHRR 41, para 21. The two rights were, first, to be brought promptly before a judge or other officer authorized by law to exercise judicial power and, second, to be tried within a reasonable time or to be released pending trial.

[78] ibid, para 46.

[79] ibid, para 47, citing *Brogan v UK* (1989) 11 EHRR 117.

considered whether to release the applicant, nor from the fact that that consideration was dependent on the applicant himself taking the initiative. It did not appear that the system prevented weak or vulnerable people from taking such an initiative. Even though the applicant was in effect detained for a day longer than he would otherwise have been, 'the procedure in this case was conducted with due expedition, leading to his release some three days after his arrest'.[80]

It is worth stressing, however, that no fewer than five of the 17 judges, while concurring in the ultimate result, differed from the majority in their reasoning.[81] In their opinion the majority's reasoning placed insufficient emphasis on the principle laid down in Article 5(1) read in conjunction with Article 5(3), namely that at the pre-trial stage an arrested person has the right to prompt and full judicial control and the right to be set free immediately unless there are still sufficient grounds to keep him or her in custody. These five judges concurred in the result only because McKay was released less than 72 hours after his arrest, within the maximum period of four days laid down in *Brogan v United Kingdom*: in the circumstances, the requirements of both *promptness* and *speediness* had in fact been satisfied. The judge who dissented was the Norwegian, Judge Jebens. In his view the speedy release of the applicant made no difference: the fact remained that the applicant had instructed his solicitors to apply for release on bail, and a request to that effect was actually put before the magistrate, with even the police officer who appeared in the magistrates' court having no objection to bail, provided proper conditions were set.

General rules on bail

As regards the more general rules on bail, it is again remarkable that during all the years of the conflict in Northern Ireland the compatibility of the judges' attitude to bail (which was, in brief, to grant bail if the offences alleged against the accused were not serious but to deny it if they were[82]) was never directly challenged before the European Court. Instead, it was the approach adopted in England in relation to non-terrorist offences which produced the first such ruling. In *Caballero v United Kingdom*[83] the Grand Chamber considered section 25 of the Criminal Justice and Public Order Act 1994, under which Clive Caballero had been automatically refused bail because of an earlier serious conviction. He was again convicted and sentenced to life imprisonment, and his appeal to the Court of Appeal failed. When he challenged the automatic denial of bail the UK government conceded that there had been a breach of Articles 5(3) and

[80] ibid, para 50.

[81] Judges Rozakis (Greece), Tulkens (Belgium), Botoucharova (Bulgaria), Myjer (Netherlands), and Ziemele (Latvia).

[82] In the seven-year period 1978 to 1984, an average of 46 per cent of persons charged with scheduled offences were on bail at the time of their trial, compared with an average of 83 per cent of persons charged with non-scheduled offences (see Northern Ireland Information Service, *Statistics on Northern Ireland Emergency Legislation*, Table 2; dated 28 June 1988). In the 10-year period 1985 to 1994 the contrasting percentages were 53 per cent and, again, 83 per cent (extrapolated from Northern Ireland Office, *Statistics on the Operation of the Northern Ireland (Emergency Provisions) Act, Annual Statistics 1994*, Table 2).

[83] Including Sir Robert Carnwath, the *ad hoc* UK judge.

5(5) and the European Court held unanimously that £1,000 should be awarded to the applicant as compensation.[84] This decision was followed by the Court in the indistinguishable case of *SBC v United Kingdom*.[85] To avoid any future such decisions the UK government secured a change in domestic law by amending section 25 of the 1994 Act so as to make the refusal of bail discretionary.[86]

The provisions on bail in the 1994 Act were never extended to Northern Ireland, and in all the 'emergency' laws devised for dealing with the conflict in Northern Ireland there was never a statutory provision which automatically denied bail, even for a charge of murder. In *Kerr v United Kingdom*,[87] already mentioned,[88] the applicant had been arrested on 7 November 1996, charged with terrorist offences on 14 November 1996, and released from custody on 30 August 1997 when all charges against him were withdrawn. He complained that he had not been brought to trial within a reasonable time or released pending trial, in breach of Article 5(3). But the European Court declared the complaint inadmissible on account of the applicant's failure to exhaust domestic remedies (he had never made a bail application even though he had been brought before a magistrates' court on several occasions during his remand in custody) and it observed that:

> A period of detention of nine months cannot be considered unreasonable in length in the context of a person charged with serious terrorist offences, especially having regard to the fact that the need for the applicant's continued detention was the subject of periodic review over that period.[89]

It was the application of the judicial discretion to deny bail in a non-conflict-related case which first provided the European Court with an opportunity to comment in detail on the law in Northern Ireland in this area. In *Gault v United Kingdom* the applicant, Lesley Ann Gault, had been charged with aiding and abetting the murder of her husband. She was released on bail pending her trial (she had six-year old triplets to look after) and the trial judge permitted her to remain on bail throughout the trial itself. After the jury in the trial failed to agree on a verdict, she remained on bail while the prosecution decided whether to prosecute her again, which it did. During this second trial she again remained on bail, but at the end of it she was convicted of murder and sentenced to life imprisonment. The next year, however, she won an appeal against her conviction on the basis that the second trial judge had misdirected

[84] (2000) 30 EHRR 643.

[85] (2002) 34 EHRR 21. The five judges in *McKay v UK* who issued a separate concurring judgment thought that the decision in *SBC v UK* 'provides persuasive authority for finding that the first obligatory appearance before a judicial officer must encompass bail' ((2007) 44 EHRR 41, concurring judgment of Judges Rozakis et al, para 2), but the other 10 judges in the majority disagreed.

[86] See Crime and Disorder Act 1998, s 56, which entered into force on 30 September 1998.

[87] (2000) 29 EHRR CD180.

[88] See 131 above.

[89] (2000) 29 EHRR CD180, CD189. In relation to the applicant's claim that his Art 5(4) rights had been violated in that he had not been entitled to take proceedings by which the lawfulness of his detention could be decided, the Court reiterated (also at CD189) its controversial position in *Brannigan and McBride v UK* (1994) 17 EHRR 539, para 63, that the availability of the remedy of habeas corpus had not been affected by the existence of the UK's derogation notice. For further discussion of the right to trial within a reasonable time, see ch 8 below.

the jury as to the state of mind necessary to make the applicant an accessory to murder. But the Court of Appeal ordered a further retrial and required her to remain in detention until then, seemingly on the basis that the next trial would take place soon and that the applicant's position was different from what it had been after the first trial because then she had never been convicted while after her second trial she had been. Two months later the judge at the third trial granted her bail. She remained on bail throughout that third trial, and a month later was acquitted of all charges. In her subsequent application to the European Court, she alleged that the decision to place her in detention on remand pending her third trial had not been supported by relevant and sufficient reasons. The European Court unanimously upheld her complaint,[90] saying that neither of the reasons given for denying bail to the applicant was both relevant and sufficient: even if reasonable suspicion of the applicant's guilt persisted, this was not enough to infer that there was a greater risk of the applicant's absconding before the third trial than had been the case before the previous two trials.[91] The Court awarded Mrs Gault 7,500 euros by way of compensation.

Conclusion

Of the three issues discussed in this chapter the European Court has been most active on the first and third. It has limited to four days the period during which a person can be detained by the police without being brought before a judge, and it has ensured that there is, in effect, a presumption of bail once a person has been told that he or she is going to be prosecuted for a criminal offence, a presumption which the prosecution has to work hard to rebut on the particular facts of each case. It is in relation to the second issue—how long a person can be detained before having to be charged or released—that the Court has been comparatively silent. After the enactment of the PTA 1974 that period could be seven days, both in Northern Ireland and in Great Britain, and even after a further derogation notice was sent to the Council of Europe at the end of 1988, that remained the maximum period. When the derogation notice was withdrawn, pursuant to the reforms introduced by the Terrorism Act 2000, the maximum period again remained untouched, even if the detention now had to be authorized by a judge rather than a government minister. No-one challenged the compatibility of that period with Article 5(3) either in a domestic court or in the European Court, and nor, apparently, has anyone challenged the later extensions of that maximum period to 14 days in 2003 and to 28 days in 2006. As yet, very few people have in fact been detained for anything like 28 days, but it is likely that challenges will be raised in the courts in due course. In a recent case in Northern Ireland, arising out of the murder of two British soldiers in March 2009, the local Divisional Court held that when a judge is considering whether to extend detention beyond 14 days he or she must ensure not only that the extension is justified but also that the original arrest

[90] App No 1271/05, decision of 20 November 2007.
[91] ibid, para 22.

was legally justified.[92] In coming to this decision the court relied upon Article 5(3) of the European Convention, a good example of a domestic court applying Convention standards in advance of the European Court itself.[93] Alas, that is not what transpired during the earlier years of conflict in Northern Ireland, and the European Court itself was not always proactive in ensuring that Convention standards kept pace with government attempts to combat terrorism. It could have done so much more.

[92] *Re Colin Duffy's Application* [2009] NIQB 31 (Kerr LCJ, Higgins and Coghlin LJJ).

[93] The court adjourned until later in the year a hearing into the question whether any of the provisions in the Terrorism Act 2000 regulating extensions to periods of pre-charge detention were incompatible with the European Convention.

7

The Right Not to be Ill-treated

Article 3 of the Convention

Of all the provisions in the European Convention on Human Rights, Article 3 is the simplest and clearest in its wording: 'No one shall be subjected to torture or to inhuman or degrading treatment or punishment.' Evans and Morgan have summarized the process by which this article came to be drafted in the way that it is, giving particular credit to the contribution made by a British member of the Consultative Assembly of the Council of Europe in 1949, Mr Seymour Cocks, and pointing out that the inclusion of the word 'degrading' and the omission of the word 'cruel' were not at the time seen as significant by any of the people involved in the drafting.[1] There was no controversy over the absolute nature of the prohibition—it was not qualified or limited in any way—but there does not appear to have been any discussion of what the consequences should be if torture or inhuman or degrading treatment or punishment nevertheless occurred. No suggestions were made, for example, that information obtained through such practices should be inadmissible as evidence in a court. There was not even a proposal that a victim of these practices should be automatically entitled to compensation.[2]

Perhaps more seriously, there was not much consensus at the time (1950) as to what behaviour terms such as 'torture', 'inhuman treatment', and 'degrading treatment' actually encompassed. The *travaux préparatoires* of the Convention do not expressly state that the drafters envisaged a hierarchy of ill-treatment within the phraseology of Article 3, but when the provision first came to be considered by the European Commission of Human Rights in the *Greek* case in 1969 that was the approach which

[1] Evans and Morgan (1998) 69–73. 'Cruel and unusual punishments' are outlawed not only by the English Bill of Rights of 1689 but also by the US Bill of Rights of 1791 (8th Amendment); neither mentions cruel treatment. The French Declaration of the Rights of Man of 1789 prohibits punishments that are not strictly and obviously necessary (cl 8) and states that 'if arrest shall be deemed indispensable, all harshness not essential to the securing of the prisoner's person shall be severely repressed by law' (cl 9). Art 5 of the Universal Declaration of Human Rights (1948) reads: 'No one shall be subjected to torture or to cruel, inhuman or degrading treatment or punishment.' Art 7 of the International Covenant on Civil and Political Rights reads: 'No one shall be subjected to torture or to cruel, inhuman or degrading treatment or punishment. In particular, no one shall be subjected without his free consent to medical or scientific experimentation.'

[2] Only Art 5 of the Convention, protecting the right to liberty, guarantees the right to compensation in the event of a breach (see Art 5(5)).

was taken. The Commission said that all torture must at the same time be inhuman and degrading treatment, and that all inhuman treatment must also be degrading.[3] It went on in the same paragraph to characterize degrading treatment as treatment which grossly humiliates a person before others or which drives a person to act against his or her will or conscience. Inhuman treatment was described as 'at least such treatment as deliberately causes severe suffering, mental or physical, which, in the particular situation is unjustifiable'. Torture, said the Commission, 'is often used to describe inhuman treatment which has a purpose such as the obtaining of information or confessions, or the infliction of punishment, and it is generally an aggravated form of inhuman and degrading treatment'.

This is how matters stood at the time when allegations of police and army brutality began to emerge in Northern Ireland less than two years later. The standards set by Article 3 would have been well known to commanders in both the police and the army. The question taxing contemporary lawyers was whether they could make use of the Convention system in a way that would make it very difficult, if not impossible, for brutality to occur with impunity. Efforts made in that regard were valiant but, alas, ultimately unsuccessful. Matters were not helped by the approach taken by the committee headed by Sir Edmund Compton, the first ever Ombudsman for the United Kingdom,[4] which on 31 August 1971 was tasked by Home Secretary Reginald Maudling with investigating allegations by some of those arrested on the day internment was introduced, 22 days earlier, that they have suffered 'physical brutality' while in the custody of the security forces prior to being released, charged, or officially detained. The Compton Report,[5] described by one commentator as 'not only... a ludicrous mockery of common sense, but also... a perversion of justice',[6] does not refer at any point to Article 3 of the European Convention. Instead of using international standards as a touchstone, the committee applied its own subjective standards when deciding whether a substantiated allegation of ill-treatment contained 'any element of brutality as we understand the term'.[7] In relation to the use of the infamous 'five techniques' against 11 individuals—hooding, exposure to loud noise, enforced posture against a wall, deprivation of sleep, and deprivation of food and drink—as well as to allegations of beatings, the committee concluded that, while physical ill-treatment took place, it would not make a finding of brutality on the part of those who handled the complainants:

> We consider that brutality is an inhuman or savage form of cruelty, and that cruelty implies a disposition to inflict suffering, coupled with indifference to, or pleasure in, the victim's pain. We do not think that happened here.[8]

The Home Secretary was therefore able to trumpet, in November 1971, that the Compton Committee 'have found no evidence of physical brutality, still less of torture

[3] *Denmark, Norway, Sweden and the Netherlands v Greece* (1969) 12*bis* Ybk 186 (Report of the Commission), para 2.

[4] He served as Parliamentary Commissioner for Administration from 1967–71.

[5] Compton (1971).

[6] Hull (1976) 181.

[7] Compton (1971) para 20.

[8] ibid, para 105.

or brain-washing'.[9] He pointed to the fact that the methods employed during interrogation were 'the same as those employed in all emergencies of this kind in which Britain has been involved in recent years', the relevant rules having been issued in 1965 and revised in 1967 as a result of recommendations made by Roderick Bowen QC in a report on procedures for the arrest, interrogation, and detention of suspected terrorists in Aden.[10] The Home Secretary conveniently neglected to mention the allegations of violations of Article 3 which had been raised by Greece in relation to the way British forces had treated some detainees in Cyprus. Maudling summed up the UK government's position by saying:

> the security forces have discharged their onerous duties with the utmost restraint despite the provocations of which the Press and other public media give us daily evidence. The Government do not regard the findings of the Committee as in any way reflecting adversely on the responsibility and discipline with which the security forces in Northern Ireland are conducting their fight against a vicious and ruthless enemy.[11]

The UK government was to receive a rude awakening, but not for a few more years. Just three months later, in February 1972, the Parker Committee—established to consider in general the authorized procedures for interrogating suspected terrorists (not just in Northern Ireland)—held by a majority of two to one that the five techniques in use in Northern Ireland were legally and morally justified provided they were not applied too intensely and that there were proper safeguards in place.[12] The majority was able to come to this conclusion because, given that the inter-State case was pending before the European Commission of Human Rights, it conveniently left out of account whether the techniques contravened Article 3 of the European Convention. Perhaps with an eye to influencing the Commission to see things its way, the majority stated:

> ... we think that such expressions as 'humane', 'inhuman', 'humiliating' and 'degrading' fall to be judged by [a dispassionate] observer in the light of the circumstances in which the techniques are applied, for example, that the operation is taking place in the course of guerrilla warfare in which completely innocent lives are at risk; that there is a degree of urgency; and that the security and safety of the interrogation centre, of its staff and of the detainees are important considerations.[13]

In support of its stance the majority cited figures purporting to show that, as a direct result of the techniques employed, the interrogation of terrorist suspects had been very effective: 700 (sic) further members of the IRA had been identified, over 40 sheets giving details of IRA units and sub-units had been uncovered, and individual responsibility for about 85 incidents on police files had been revealed.[14] The majority also claimed that the marked increase in the rate at which arms, ammunition,

[9] ibid, Introduction by the Home Secretary, Reginald Maudling MP, para 14.

[10] ibid, para 16, and see Bowen (1966).

[11] ibid, para 18.

[12] Parker (1972), majority report, para 34. The majority comprised Lord Parker himself (who had served as Lord Chief Justice of England from 1958 to 1971) and Mr John Boyd Carpenter, a former Chief Secretary to the Treasury in a Conservative government, who was given a life peerage three months after the publication of the Parker Report.

[13] ibid, para 30.

[14] ibid, para 20.

and explosives had been found in Northern Ireland after internment was introduced had 'resulted directly or indirectly from information obtained by interrogation in depth'.[15] The member of the Parker Committee who dissented, Lord Gardiner,[16] found that the use of the techniques could not be justified in terms of their physical and mental effect on the detainees, their effects on the obtaining of information (a dramatic increase in intelligence information was only to be expected given that there was a considerable increase in the number of people questioned after 9 August), their effect on the hearts and minds of the local population, and their effect on the world-wide reputation of the United Kingdom. On this last point Lord Gardiner said:

> For many years men and women and a number of international organisations have been engaged in trying patiently to raise international moral standards, particularly in the field of human rights [he cited the European Convention as an example at this point] . . . If . . . we now depart from world standards which we have helped to create, I believe that we should both gravely damage our own reputation and deal a severe blow to the whole world movement to improve human rights.[17]

How right he was.

Donnelly v United Kingdom

While some earlier applications to the European Commission of Human Rights had raised questions concerning the lawfulness of arrest and internment powers in Northern Ireland, the first case to raise issues concerning the alleged mistreatment of detainees was *Donnelly and others v United Kingdom*.[18] There were seven applicants involved[19] and their applications were jointly coordinated by two local non-governmental organizations—the Association for Legal Justice and the Northern Ireland Civil Rights Association. Their legal representatives were Kevin Boyle and Hurst Hannum, the former a law lecturer and the latter a legal researcher, both at Queen's University Belfast.[20] By this time lessons had been learned about how difficult it was to ensure that an application to the Commission would be both procedurally admissible and substantially meritorious. Thus, the applicants were carefully selected on the basis of their actual victimhood—they were not complaining about some abstract injustice but about the treatment they as individuals had suffered. They were also drawn from across Northern Ireland so as to emphasize that the complaints related

[15] ibid, para 21. The Committee stated, eg, that from 1 January to 8 August 1971 the security forces had discovered 193 weapons, 41,000 rounds of ammunition, and 1,194 lbs of explosives. From 9 August (the day internment was introduced) to 31 December 1971 the figures were 413 weapons, 11,500 rounds of ammunition and 2,541 lbs of explosives.

[16] A former Labour Lord Chancellor from 1964–70.

[17] Parker (1972), minority report, para 20.

[18] Boyle and Hannum (1974); Hannum and Boyle (1977).

[19] Gerard Donnelly (29), Gerard Bradley (20), Edward Duffy (17), all resident in Belfast; John Carlin (24), from Derry; Francis McBride (26) from Rasharkin, County Antrim; and Anthony Kelly (24) and Thomas Kearns (20) from Newry, County Down.

[20] Kevin Boyle is now a professor at the Human Rights Centre in the University of Essex, while Hurst Hannum is a professor at Tufts University in the USA.

to systemic malpractice and not just to isolated incidents. And the applicants did not make a claim for compensation under Article 13 because otherwise they could easily have been turned away on the ground that they had not first exhausted their domestic remedies by seeking damages in a Northern Ireland court.

Each of the seven men alleged that he had been beaten while in police custody—some alleged that they had received blows to the head and body, others that they had been kicked in the genitals or given electric shocks to their genitals. Three of the applicants even alleged that against their will they had been administered 'truth drugs' to make them confess to crimes. Six of them alleged that they had been forced into signing confessions, which they later retracted. But the purpose of making these allegations was not only to seek a ruling that in particular cases Article 3 had been violated. It was also to try to show that such practices constituted a systematic administrative pattern of brutality. To support their allegations the applicants submitted the Compton and Parker Reports[21] and a report by Amnesty International.[22] In all they referred to 157 specific cases of alleged ill-treatment.[23] The applicants asked for a temporary injunction to put a halt to such practices pending the outcome of their applications. They also asked for their applications to be given expedited consideration and for a full investigation to be conducted into the alleged systemic brutality. It seems that the lawyers involved also deliberately confined their attention to alleged brutality occurring after the introduction of direct rule in Northern Ireland on 24 March 1972. In this way they could focus attention on the failure of the central UK government to uphold human rights, rather than on the policies of the (by then defunct) government of Northern Ireland.

With commendable speed the European Commission issued its first decision in relation to the applications on 14 July 1972, just seven weeks after they had been lodged. The Commission decided that it would indeed expedite its handling of the applications[24] but that it had no power to issue a temporary injunction of the kind requested (only to take 'interim measures' in relation to particular applicants, which was not the same thing). The applicants' lawyers were given an oral hearing on 3–5 March 1973, and a month later, on 5 April 1973, the Commission declared the applications to be admissible.[25] This in itself was a significant triumph for the applicants, not only because the Commission was prepared to proceed with the case even though similar allegations were still pending before the European Commission in the inter-State application lodged by the Irish government on 16 December 1971,[26] but mainly because it established two propositions which have since become firm rules within

[21] Compton (1971); Parker (1972). These reports are valuably critiqued in Evans and Morgan (1998) 33–9. See too Brownlie (1972).

[22] Amnesty International (1972).

[23] (1973) Ybk 212, 216. They also relied on a booklet prepared by the Association for Legal Justice entitled 'The Mailed Fist' and on a booklet prepared by two Catholic priests, Denis Faul and Raymond Murray, entitled 'British Army and Special Branch Brutalities'.

[24] Under rule 38(1) of its Rules of Procedure.

[25] (1973) Ybk 212; 43 CD 122.

[26] The Commission decided to allow the overlapping allegations to be considered because under Art 27(1)(b) of the Convention an application is to be excluded from consideration if it is substantially the same as a matter which has 'already been examined', and the inter-State case had not yet been examined. The inter-State case is analysed in ch 4 and also in the next section of this chapter.

the European Convention system, even if they have not been exploited by applicants (and their lawyers) to the extent that they might have been.

The first of these was the ruling that an individual applicant could raise a complaint 'in respect of an alleged administrative practice in breach of the Convention provided that he brings *prima facie* evidence of such a practice and of his being a victim of it'.[27] It was not necessary for the applicant to attain any higher standard of proof at that stage, contrary to what might have been surmised from earlier Commission pronouncements in inter-State cases.[28] This means that, contrary to the normal rules, complaints about human rights abuses being suffered by other (perhaps anonymous) people can be adduced by an applicant provided that he or she is also a victim of the alleged systemic abuse. The second ruling was that when an individual applicant is alleging the existence of such an administrative practice he or she does not first have to exhaust domestic remedies in relation to that issue. Instead the question of the effectiveness of those domestic remedies will be considered at the same time as, and as part of, the merits of the application. In this regard the Commission quoted what it had said in the *Greek* case,[29] where Denmark, Norway, Sweden, and the Netherlands had alleged in an inter-State application that Greece's security forces had been systematically abusing detainees:

> [w]here, however, there is a practice of non-observance of certain Convention provisions, the remedies prescribed will of necessity be side-stepped or rendered inadequate. Thus, if there was an administrative practice of torture or ill-treatment, judicial remedies prescribed would tend to be rendered ineffective by the difficulty of securing probative evidence, and administrative enquiries would either not be instituted, or, if they were, would be likely to be half-hearted and incomplete.[30]

It followed that it would be inappropriate to require the applicants to exhaust their domestic remedies in relation to alleged violations which they had experienced, since they would be likely to encounter difficulties in being able to win those remedies. This is a remarkably realistic conclusion for its day and marks a somewhat underplayed coming-of-age on the part of the European Commission in its handling of applications under the Convention. Boyle and Hannum (who were counsel for the applicants) said at the time that the decision 'may herald a new era in human rights enforcement by the European Commission'.[31]

However, the triumph at the initial admissibility stage in the *Donnelly* case turned out to be something of a pyrrhic victory. After the Commission had examined the merits of the claim, it decided on 15 December 1975 that the alleged administrative practice could not be considered to be a violation of the Convention because evidence had not in the end been adduced to show that domestic remedies were ineffective or inadequate.[32] Three of the seven applications (by Carlin, Kelly, and Kearns) were held

[27] (1973) Ybk 212, 260; 43 CD 122, 146.

[28] Boyle and Hannum (1974) 451.

[29] App No 3321–3/67; (1968) 11 Ybk Pt I, ch II; 11 Ybk Pt II, ch II; (1969) 12 *bis* Ybk.

[30] (1973) Ybk 212, 262; 43 CD 122, 147; each citing the *Greek* case (1969) 12 *bis* Ybk 194.

[31] Boyle and Hannum (1974) 440.

[32] (1975) 4 DR 4. As Hannum and Boyle (1977) 319 put it: 'It now appears that the prima facie proof of an administrative practice produced by an applicant at the admissibility stage raises a rebuttable presumption only that remedies are inadequate.'

in the end to be inadmissible because the applicants had not exhausted the local remedies available to them within the legal system of Northern Ireland: they had instituted civil proceedings against the Ministry of Defence, the Chief Constable of the RUC, and a particular police officer, but had not yet taken those proceedings any further. The four remaining applications were declared inadmissible because the applicants had already received financial settlements in respect of their claims (Duffy had received £6,000; Donnelly and Bradley had each received £5,000, and McBride had received £301; moreover they had all also received their legal costs). The applicants all alleged that any remedies which existed were subject to such delays as to render them illusory and that any appeal to the courts might be frustrated by 'the inherent bias of the system in favour of the security forces'. To its credit the European Commission examined these allegations carefully,[33] but it ultimately rejected them. Indeed the Commission was of the view that it had been shown that the machinery for providing compensation had worked effectively in practice in the cases of Duffy, Donnelly, Bradley, and McBride, particularly as regards the first three, to whom high sums of compensation had been paid, including a substantial element of punitive damages in the form of aggravated and exemplary damages.

The Commission went on to consider at some length the applicants' wider argument that, in the circumstances prevailing in Northern Ireland, compensation was not an adequate remedy for their complaints, since they were allegedly the victims of an administrative practice.[34] Indeed, the applicants claimed that 'the sums paid in compensation are simply treated as a necessary cost of the respondent government's policies in Northern Ireland'. This argument required the Commission to assess the effectiveness of the procedures in place to prevent the occurrence or repetition of the acts complained of. It concluded that there was no middle level in the chain of command which tolerated and had knowledge of the ill-treatment of suspects, noting that the applicants' allegations had all been investigated reasonably promptly when they came to the notice of the authorities, that two police officers and a soldier had been prosecuted for inflicting grievous bodily harm on three of the applicants (although they had been acquitted), and that four of the applicants had refused to cooperate with the officer who investigated their complaints. While the investigations were open to criticism on certain grounds—the significance of some of which the Commission seems to have too easily glossed over[35]—the Commission found that they were effective enough for the purposes of the Convention. Disappointingly, the Commission noted that:

> [t]he fact that ill-treatment may be tolerated, at the middle or lower levels of the chain of command, for example at the level of an officer in charge of a police station or military post, does not

[33] ibid, 70–7.

[34] ibid, 77–85.

[35] eg, that soldiers present at a military post at one of the relevant times refused to cooperate with an investigating officer, that an investigating officer failed to check records concerning the presence of Special Branch officers at a police holding centre, that an investigating officer allowed members of the Military Police to take statements from soldiers rather than taking them himself, and that an investigating officer was too categorical in his finding that there was 'no evidence' of ill-treatment in the light of medical evidence that two men did in fact bear some injuries.

in the opinion of the Commission necessarily mean that the state concerned has failed to take the required steps to comply with its substantive obligations under Article 3 of the Convention.[36]

Somewhat irrelevantly, moreover, the Commission highlighted the fact that a considerable length of time had been spent investigating these complaints at a period when the security forces were under attack and the police were under considerable pressure. The Commission speculated that complainants might have been more co-operative with investigating officers if the latter had been completely independent. In fact, it was to be many years before such a truly independent system was put in place.[37]

All in all the *Donnelly* case presented a further lesson to applicants and lawyers alike. Proving that a State is systematically failing to comply with its Convention obligations is extremely difficult. It requires a lot of hard evidence. Suggestions that the State is failing in its obligations can be easily defeated by the State showing that it is making its best effort to prevent abuses of rights or that the failings, even if widespread, are at the level of low or middle management. If these efforts and failings are not out of line with best practice elsewhere in Europe, the enforcement bodies in Strasbourg will be loath to condemn them as inadequate. It will always be very difficult for an applicant to prove that there was 'official tolerance' of ill-treatment at a high level of government, and in the *Donnelly* case itself the Commission did not specifically ask for evidence about such tolerance (even though it heard from 45 witnesses) and in the end it merely inferred a lack of tolerance from the evidence about remedies.[38] Moreover, it is almost always fatal to an applicant's case that he or she has started civil legal proceedings in the domestic legal system. If these have resulted in the award of compensation (whether through a settlement or a judgment) the applicant will usually be deemed to have already received just satisfaction. If the proceedings have not yet been concluded domestic remedies will be deemed to have not yet been exhausted.[39]

Ireland v United Kingdom

A great deal has already been written about the efforts made by the government of Ireland to hold the United Kingdom to account in Strasbourg for the behaviour of its security forces when dealing with the civil unrest in Northern Ireland.[40] As Simpson has observed in his masterly study of the origin and early years of the European Convention,[41] it did not seem probable in 1950, when the Convention was agreed,

[36] (1975) 4 DR 4, 85.

[37] Not until the establishment of the office of the Police Ombudsman of Northern Ireland, created by the Police (NI) Act 1998, ss 50–65. See Dickson (2005b) 222–6.

[38] Hannum and Boyle (1977) 320.

[39] At the second reading of what became the EPA 1973 the Attorney General, Sir Peter Rawlinson, revealed that by then about 150 civil actions had been brought against the Crown for alleged assaults by members of the security forces and that there had been directions for prosecution against 37 members of the security forces on charges of bodily harm: HC Deb, vol 855, col 388 (17 April 1973).

[40] See, eg, O'Boyle (1977b), Spjut (1979), Hartman (1981), Boyle (1982–3), Mangan (1988), Delmas-Marty and Chodkiewicz (1992) 259–68.

[41] Simpson (2001) 4.

that other European States would want to take cases against the United Kingdom, as was allowed by Article 24.[42] Yet in 1956 proceedings were brought against the United Kingdom by Greece in respect of measures taken by the British to suppress an insurrection in Cyprus (then a British colony). This was followed by a second application by Greece in 1957, alleging that the United Kingdom was complicit in the use of torture in Cyprus. As Simpson remarks:

> It was not possible for the British government to take no notice of these embarrassing proceedings; they were a major headache and led to modifications in the use of emergency powers. In the event only the first of these applications led to a concluded report by the Commission; this remained secret, at least in theory, until 1998. The proceedings in the second case were discontinued in 1959. Yet life was never to be quite the same again.[43]

Beddard reminds us that, since neither Greece nor the United Kingdom recognized the right of individual petition at this time, the victims of the abuse in Cyprus had no mechanisms for continuing their fight for a remedy after the European Commission allowed the applications to be withdrawn following a political settlement of the Cyprus problem.[44]

No doubt emboldened by the example of cases taken both by and against[45] Greece, the government of the Republic of Ireland lodged two applications against the United Kingdom in 1971 and 1972. As we noted in Chapter 3, the Irish government had come under strong pressure from Northern nationalists to do more to support their plight. The first application, which was lodged with the Commission on 16 December 1971,[46] was prompted by the reintroduction of internment in Northern Ireland on 9 August 1971. The Irish government claimed internment was in breach of Articles 5 and 6 of the Convention, and also that it was being practised in a discriminatory manner, in breach of Article 14, because it was directed in the main at alleged republican rather than loyalist terrorists. We saw in Chapter 4 how this part of the application was rejected by the Strasbourg enforcement organs. The application also accused Britain, because of the way the Special Powers Acts, and the regulations made under them, were being implemented in Northern Ireland, of failing to

[42] Art 24 read: 'Any High Contracting Party may refer to the Commission, through the Secretary-General of the Council of Europe, any alleged breach of the Convention by another High Contracting Party.'

[43] Simpson (2001) 7. Simpson looks in great detail at the first and second Cyprus cases in chs 17 and 18 of his book. Between 1967 and 1970 the government of Greece was itself on the receiving end of five inter-State applications brought by Denmark, Norway, Sweden, and the Netherlands, in respect of security force practices tolerated by the Greek colonels' regime. The Greek government withdrew from the Council of Europe and denounced the Convention before the Committee of Ministers could comment on the report submitted to it by the European Commission, but the newly restored democratic government acceded again to the Convention in 1974. After Cyprus acquired its independence in 1960 it lodged applications against Turkey in respect of that country's invasion of the northern part of the island in 1974. These eventually led to what has so far been the most significant of all the inter-State applications lodged at Strasbourg: *Cyprus v Turkey* (2002) 35 EHRR 30. Further applications were lodged against Turkey by Denmark, France, the Netherlands, Norway, and Sweden in 1982. The cases concerning Cyprus are further discussed in ch 13 below.

[44] Beddard (1980) 6.

[45] See nn 3 and 43 above.

[46] App No 5310/71 (1971) 14 Ybk 100; (1972) Ybk 76. Beddard says the application 'seemed, to a great extent, to be politically motivated': Beddard (1993) 9.

comply with its obligation under Article 1 of the Convention to secure to everyone within its jurisdiction the rights and freedoms defined in Article 2 to 18. To boot, the application submitted that nine deaths which had occurred in Northern Ireland in August and October 1971[47] were in breach of Article 2 and that persons interned under the Special Powers legislation had been ill-treated in breach of Article 3. In this last regard, the plight of 14 men was examined, not with a view to treating them as individual applicants but in order to try to demonstrate that the United Kingdom was engaging in a State practice regarding 'in-depth investigations'. In particular the Irish government alleged that detainees were being hooded, spread-eagled against walls, deprived of food, water, and sleep, and exposed to continuous loud or monotonous noises. Significantly, all of the 14 individuals had already received compensation of between £10,000 and £25,000 from the United Kingdom authorities for the treatment they had endured.

On 25 February 1972 the Irish government submitted supplementary material referring to deaths in Derry in July 1971 and on Bloody Sunday in January 1972, and the Commission decided to treat this as part of the original application. But in further supplementary material submitted on 6 March 1972 the Irish also alleged that the Northern Ireland Act 1972 (retrospectively legitimating actions by security forces which a court had held to be unlawful[48]) was a breach of Article 1 because it denied to residents of Northern Ireland the rights defined in Article 7 of the Convention. This was deemed by the Commission to constitute a second, separate, application.[49]

The British government was obviously disturbed by all of these applications but, to avoid any further embarrassment, the then Prime Minister, Edward Heath, wasted little time in announcing that the use of the five interrogation techniques which were impugned in the applications had been abandoned; at the same time, however, he stated that 'interrogation in depth' would continue.[50] The Parker Report had noted that the same interrogation techniques had been used by British soldiers in many previous campaigns—in Malaya, Palestine, Kenya, Cyprus, Cameroons, Brunei, British

[47] These were the deaths of Seamus Cusack and Desmond Beattie (both on 8 July 1971), Hugh Mullan (a Catholic priest) and Francis McGuinness (9 August 1971), William McKavanagh (11 August 1971), Eamonn McDavitt (18 August 1971), Robert Anderson, Thomas McLaughlin and Sean Ruddy (23 October 1971). The deaths of Cusack and Beattie were informally investigated shortly afterwards by an inquiry comprising Lord Gifford QC, Paul O'Dwyer, and Albie Sachs. The death of Thomas McLaughlin was the focus of a further application brought by his widow to the European Commission on Human Rights (*Farrell v UK* (1983) 5 EHRR 466), which led to a 'friendly settlement' whereby the British government paid the claimant £37,000. For accounts of all of these deaths, including references to the British and Irish governments' perspectives on what occurred, see McKittrick et al (2004).

[48] *R (Hume) v Londonderry Justices* [1972] NI 91.

[49] App No 5451/72. For discussion of this application see ch 8 below.

[50] HC Deb, vol 832, col 744 (2 March 1972). Heath also stated that the five techniques had not been used in cases other than those mentioned in the Parker report, namely, the 12 cases in August 1971 and the two in October 1971, and he added that 'if any Government did come to the decision, after the most careful thought, that it was necessary to use some or all of these techniques, it would be necessary to come to the House first before doing so'. This Prime Ministerial commitment was in the news again 37 years later during the first day of the Inquiry into the Death of Baha Mousa in Iraq: see <http://www.bahamousainquiry.org> (evidence given on the morning of 13 July 2009).

Guiana, Aden, Borneo, and the Persian Gulf.[51] It was almost as if the mere constancy with which they had been employed was itself enough to constitute evidence of their current legality.

An oral hearing into both the first and second application lodged by Ireland was held in Strasbourg on 25–29 September 1972. Amongst those representing the parties were, for the Irish government, Colm Condon SC (the Attorney General), John Murray (a future Chief Justice of Ireland) and Anthony Hederman (a future justice of the Irish Supreme Court), and, for the British government, Sir Peter Rawlinson QC (the Attorney General), Brian Hutton QC (a future Lord Chief Justice of Northern Ireland and Lord of Appeal), Gordon Slynn (a future Advocate General at the European Court of Justice and Lord of Appeal) and Nicholas Bratza (a future British judge at the European Court of Human Rights). On 1 October 1972 the Commission declared the first application to be admissible, except as regards the complaints relating to Article 2 of the Convention.[52] It decided that it should not proceed with these because the Irish government had not offered substantial evidence to show that an administrative practice existed as alleged, and in such circumstances the 22 deaths could not be examined unless and until it were shown that the domestic remedies available under the law of Northern Ireland had been exhausted.[53] Moreover, the second application was struck off the Commission's list of cases when it was withdrawn by the Irish government following the British Attorney General's undertaking at the oral hearing before the Commission that no one would be held guilty by reason of the 1972 Act of any act or omission which did not constitute a criminal offence at the time it was committed.[54]

For the following three years the allegations continued to be investigated, through extensive fact-finding hearings. Then there was a dramatic development. The European Commission of Human Rights, in its report on the merits of the applications issued on 9 February 1976,[55] unanimously found that the techniques employed during the detaining and interrogating of suspects amounted to 'torture'. This was less than two months after the Commission's decision in *Donnelly v United Kingdom*,[56] where it had rejected the allegation that there was an administrative practice to mistreat detainees and that there were no effective domestic remedies available to address complaints of mistreatment. It looked like a startling U-turn. The Commission decision in the inter-State case was exhaustively analysed—and approved—by Michael O'Boyle, then a junior lecturer at Queen's University Belfast, today a Registrar at the European Court.[57] The crucial question is, why was the result so different from that in *Donnelly*? The most obvious reason is that in *Donnelly* the UK government made no admissions concerning the alleged ill-treatment expe-

[51] Parker (1972) para 10 of the majority report; see too Compton (1971) paras 43–105 ('Interrogation in Depth').
[52] (1972) 15 Ybk 76, 80 (decision summarized at 254–6).
[53] ibid, 242.
[54] ibid, 254.
[55] Published in (1976–78) ECHR, Ser B, vol 23-I, 377–90; extracts appeared in (1976) 19 Ybk 512.
[56] Discussed in the previous section of this chapter.
[57] O'Boyle (1976).

rienced by the seven applicants,[58] whereas in the inter-State case the UK government did not dispute that the five techniques in question had been employed and had been officially authorized.[59] Indeed, it argued that because of its admission and the abandonment of the techniques the case did not need to proceed any further. But the Commission rejected that argument. Coupling what had been revealed in the Compton and Parker Reports, the Commission was able to say 'that there can be no doubt that the employment of these interrogation techniques constituted an "administrative practice"',[60] which in turn meant that the rule about needing to exhaust domestic remedies did not apply.

Despite their admissions, one of the most regrettable aspects of this litigation remains the uncooperative stance of the British authorities regarding the complaints about the impugned interrogation techniques. Brian Simpson describes it thus:

> The British declined to identify either the locations where they had been used or the senior individual who authorized their use. The British did not produce Brigadier Kitson, the military officer in command in Belfast at the time, as a witness. Witnesses who were produced were instructed to answer no questions about the practice of interrogation.[61] Plainly, there was something deeply embarrassing to conceal, though the squalid details of what was done were already public knowledge. One can only speculate as to what else had to be concealed.[62]

The Commission itself, in its report, indicated that the United Kingdom government 'did not always afford it the assistance desirable'.[63]

It took a further two years for the Commission's decision to be reviewed by the European Court.[64] When the Court finally issued its judgment on 18 January 1978 it was the first occasion on which it had pronounced on an inter-State matter (and in the 30 years that have since elapsed it has pronounced in only one further inter-State case).[65] As we have already seen, the Court concluded that the use of internment in Northern Ireland did not violate any Convention right.[66] And by 13 votes to four the Court held that the five techniques did *not* amount to torture—instead, by 16 votes to one, it held that they were inhuman and degrading treatment, at least so far as they were used at the Palace Barracks in Holywood, County Down, not at the army camp at Ballykinler, further south in County Down.

Judges at the European Court are, self-evidently, meant to be completely neutral when they are considering applications involving their own country, but sadly

58 (1975) 4 DR 4, 20.

59 (1972) 15 Ybk 76, 244.

60 ibid.

61 (1976–78) ECHR, Ser B, vol 23-I, 496.

62 Simpson (1995–96) 707 (footnote in the original). Simpson concludes this long article by saying that 'the United Kingdom's record of failure under the European Convention, with the high point reached in *Ireland v United Kingdom*, can only be regarded as lamentable' (708). Brigadier Frank Kitson was one of the prime designers of the counter-insurgency tactics employed in Northern Ireland: see Kitson (1971) and, for a critique of his thinking, Faligot (1983).

63 This is how the European Court summarized the substance of the Commission's view on how the UK government behaved: (1979–80) 2 EHRR 25, para 148.

64 (1979–80) 2 EHRR 25. See Andrews (1978).

65 *Cyprus v Turkey* (2002) 35 EHRR 30.

66 See ch 4 above, 63–8.

there is room for doubt about this when one considers the position of the British and Irish judges in some of the early applications to Strasbourg relating to the conflict in Northern Ireland. The one judge out of the 17 involved in this inter-State decision who thought that the use of the five techniques in August and October 1971 did not even amount to degrading treatment was Sir Gerald Fitzmaurice, the UK judge, who issued a 23-page dissenting opinion. In his words:

> ...a breach of Article 3 under this head [degrading treatment] requires not only degrading treatment but a certain kind or degree of such treatment. As to this, and subject to the possible exception of the wall-standing element, it does not seem to me that the use of the five techniques was of that order or attained that degree of gravity. Three of them involved no degradation at all in the proper sense of the term, a fourth (hooding) might be a border-line case. Thus, only the wall-standing could be said without much exaggeration or distortion to fall on the far side of the line.[67]

Amongst the four European Court judges who agreed with the European Commission that what had happened in Northern Ireland was torture was the Irish judge, Philip O'Donoghue, who had worked on Convention cases in Strasbourg since 1965.[68] If Fitzmaurice displayed a particularly pro-British attitude, it is perhaps fair to say that O'Donoghue was particularly pro-Irish. He thought that his colleagues on the Court had 'strained beyond breaking point their conception of the margin of appreciation in [the United Kingdom's] favour'[69] and, in relation to whether the British notice of derogation was justified (as the Irish notice had been held to be in *Lawless v Ireland* in 1961), he said:

> It is erroneous to seek to establish a parallel with the Lawless case where the threat was to a small unitary State, not long recovered from a civil-war situation, whereas in this case the threat must relate to the existence of the United Kingdom and not to the Six Counties only.[70]

On the issue of whether the UK government had properly cooperated with the Commission's investigations of the alleged incidents, the European Court said it 'regrets this attitude on the part of that Government; it must stress the fundamental

[67] (1979–80) 2 EHRR 25, 136. It is not clear what Fitzmaurice meant by the 'proper sense' of the term 'degradation'.

[68] He was the Irish member of the European Commission from 1965 to 1971 and was the Irish judge on the Court from 1971 to 1980. When appointed to the Commission he was 69, so when he retired from the Court he was 84. He had been called to the Bar before the partition of Ireland, in 1919, and was made State Counsel in 1939. The other three judges who agreed with the Commission were Judges Zekia (Cyprus), Evrigenis (Greece), and Matscher (Austria). Judges Zekia and Evrigenis would have had definite views about the behaviour of UK forces in Cyprus, which had been the object of Greece's applications against the UK in 1956 and 1957 (see text at n 43 above). The dissenting judgments of Judges Evrigenis and Matscher were praised at the time by one commentator in the USA, who saw them as 'bold attempts to condemn, in the strongest terms, resort to sensory deprivation during interrogation': Spjut (1979) 272. He added that the majority, by their narrow view of the meaning of torture, had 'relegated the applicability of [Article 3] to ancient forms of barbarity' (ibid).

[69] (1979–80) 2 EHRR 25, 119.

[70] ibid, 118. This attitude to the phrase 'threatening the life of the nation' in Art 15 was to be repeated by the Irish Judge Brian Walsh 15 years later when he dissented in *Brannigan and McBride v UK* (1994) 17 EHRR 539: see ch 6 above, 126–7.

importance of the principle, enshrined in Article 28(a) *in fine*, that the Contracting States have a duty to cooperate with the Convention institutions'.[71]

The ramifications of the European Court's decision in this inter-State case were significant, but more perhaps at the political level than at the human rights level.[72] While the ultimate result did not vindicate all of the concerns raised by the Irish government, it nevertheless served to put the Northern Irish conflict on the European, if not the world, legal stage. The UK government was doubtless mightily relieved to be spared the ignominy of being the first member State of the Council of Europe to be condemned by the European Court for using torture (that dubious honour was to go to Turkey in 1996,[73] the first EU member State to be so condemned being France[74]), and also to have got away with its use of internment, but it did not appreciate being condemned for interrogation practices which it had not contested and which had been terminated six years earlier. The Court, to its credit, refused to be fobbed off by the UK's argument that the allegations had become of academic interest only. For a start, there were alleged instances of ill-treatment which the government was not admitting to.[75] In addition, the Court's judgments 'serve not only to decide those cases brought before the Court but, more generally, to elucidate, safeguard and develop the rules instituted by the Convention, thereby contributing to the observance by the States of the engagements undertaken by them as Contracting Parties'.[76] For Kevin Boyle, who had experienced previous disappointments at Strasbourg, both the Commission and the Court had done a good job:

> [t]he painstaking and lengthy investigation into the facts undertaken by the Commission stands in striking contrast to the role of the domestic common law courts and the Committees of Enquiry... The real significance of the findings in Ireland v United Kingdom concerning ill-treatment in police or military custody was the emphasis placed by the Commission and Court on the inadequacy of remedies during the period it was examining. The Commission

[71] (1979–80) 2 EHRR 25, para 148.

[72] Harlow and Rawlings (1992), at 255, claim that after the Court's judgment 'some 300 applications were received from N. Ireland', but if this is so there is no record on the European Court's website as to how they were dealt with.

[73] *Aksoy v Turkey* (1997) 23 EHRR 553. In that case the Turkish judge, Judge Gölcüklü, dissented as he felt that the applicant had not exhausted his domestic remedies.

[74] *Selmouni v France* (2000) 29 EHRR 403. The French judge, Judge Jean-Paul Costa, a future President of the Court, did not dissent.

[75] There were also practices indulged in by the British army which were not included in the evidence submitted to the Commission and Court for the simple reason that they were deemed to be too 'incredible'. One of these involved forcing blindfolded detainees to jump out of a helicopter which, unknown to the detainees, was just a few feet off the ground. (Statement by Jim Auld, former detainee, at Queen's University, 18 February 2009, on file with the author.) See also Compton (1971) paras 106–19.

[76] (1979–80) 2 EHRR 25, para 154 (citing Art 19 of the Convention in support, the provision which created the Court 'to ensure the observance of the engagements undertaken by the High Contracting Parties in the present Convention'). Judge Fitzmaurice, in his dissent, disagreed with this invocation of Art 19, which he said attributed to the Court a teleological role which it was not originally intended to have (para 6 of his opinion). He thought the Court was right to adjudicate on the points conceded by the UK government in case it wished to come to a different conclusion on them from that reached by the Commission (which of course is what occurred): para 5 of his opinion. Fitzmaurice was well known for his 'non-activist' approach to the Convention: see Nicol (2005) 167–70.

expressed particular concern about the failure to carry out internal police inquiries and to prosecute or discipline those found guilty of misconduct.[77]

As for the European Court itself, in later cases it seems to have felt that it was unduly generous to the United Kingdom in the inter-State case. In *Selmouni v France*, having referred to *Ireland v United Kingdom* two paragraphs earlier, it stated that, 'having regard to the fact that the Convention is a "living instrument which must be interpreted in the light of present-day conditions" the Court considers that certain acts which were classified in the past as "inhuman and degrading treatment" as opposed to "torture" could be classified differently in future'.[78] This was a clear sign that, 20 years after the inter-State case, the Court recognized that its decision should have been different.

Diplock, the EPA, and the Bennett Inquiry

While the inter-State case was wending its way through the Strasbourg system some changes were being made to Northern Ireland's law concerning the admissibility of confessions. In English and Irish common law the general rule is that in criminal cases evidence is admissible even though it has or may have been obtained illegally. The unlawfulness of its procurement might affect the weight to be given to the evidence, but it does not in itself make the evidence inadmissible. The thinking behind the rule is that there are ways in which the illegality that has been perpetrated can be sanctioned other than through rendering the evidence inadmissible: separate criminal, civil, or disciplinary proceedings may be initiated to deter the objectionable behaviour in future. American law, on the other hand, tends to adopt the 'fruits of the poisoned tree doctrine', according to which any information resulting from an illegal act is itself tainted by that illegality and must not be used in a court of law.[79] In England, as a way of mitigating the harshness of the general rule, the judges gradually developed a set of what became known as 'the Judges' Rules', first formulated in 1918, whereby evidence would not in fact be admissible if it was not given 'voluntarily'.[80] The judges in Northern Ireland readily adopted these English rules, but when the English relaxed them a little in 1964 the judges in Northern Ireland did not follow suit. The net result was that when the troubles started the judges in Northern Ireland were more willing to exclude statements made by defendants as 'involuntary' than their counterparts in England and Wales would have been. The Diplock Commission, which had as one of its members the leading English expert on the law of evidence, Professor Rupert Cross, thought that the judges in Northern Ireland had carried the situation too far and were actually making it too difficult to convict guilty people:

> Although not strictly rules of law but rules of general guidance from which the judge who tries a case has a discretion to depart, [the Judges' Rules] appear to have been applied in Northern

[77] Boyle (1982–83) 166–7 (footnotes omitted). The Committees of Enquiry referred to in this quotation are those chaired by Sir Edmund Compton (1971) and Lord Parker (1972).

[78] (2000) 29 EHRR 403, para 101.

[79] America's 'exclusionary rule' was first established by the US Supreme Court in *Weeks v UK* 217 US 349 (1910).

[80] See also the section on access to a solicitor in ch 8 below.

Ireland with considerable rigidity as if they were a statutory requirement from which no departure is permissible. In a recent decision the Court of Criminal Appeal of Northern Ireland has ruled that the mere creation by the authorities of any 'set-up which makes it more likely that those who did not wish to speak will eventually do so', renders involuntary and therefore inadmissible in a court of law any confession subsequently made even though the actual statement sought to be relied upon was made in writing after the accused had been expressly cautioned and notwithstanding that its contents are such that no man who was not guilty could have had knowledge of the facts that it discloses . . . [81]

While not condoning the sorts of interrogation practices which were described (and justified) in the Compton and Parker Reports, the Diplock Commission thought that the way in which the judges in Northern Ireland were applying the rules on admissibility was hampering the course of justice and compelling resort to detention without trial instead. It therefore recommended that an inculpatory statement made by an accused may be used as evidence against the accused 'unless it is proved on a balance of probabilities that it was obtained by subjecting the accused to torture or to inhuman or degrading treatment'.[82] The wording of Article 3 of the European Convention was deliberately chosen in this context because 'it is a simple concept which we do not think the judiciary in Northern Ireland would find it difficult to apply in practice'.[83] The wording also left the police free to create in some other way 'a situation in which a guilty man is more likely than he would otherwise have been to overcome his initial reluctance to speak and to unburden himself to his questioners'.[84] The Commission expressly gave the green light to interrogators to 'build up a psychological atmosphere in which the initial desire of the person being questioned to remain silent is replaced by an urge to confide in the questioner, or [in which] statements [are] preceded by promises of favours or indications of the consequences which might follow if the person questioned persisted in refusing to answer'.[85] Albeit these words were written 37 years ago, they still seem quite shocking, authorizing (even encouraging) the holding out of rewards or the issuing of threats. It is surely very doubtful whether, as the Commission claimed, no fair-minded man would be against such an approach to the questioning of people in custody.

The Diplock Commission's recommendation, framed around Article 3 of the Convention, found its way into section 6 of the EPA 1973, and was re-enacted in later versions of the EPA.[86] But a substantial change was made to it by section 5 of the EPA 1987, following a recommendation made by Sir George Baker in his review of the operation of the 1978 Act published in 1984.[87] Baker said there was a very large measure

[81] Diplock (1972) para 83. The case referred to by the Commission was probably *R v Flynn and Leonard* [1972] NIJB, but that was a decision of Lowry LCJ sitting in the Belfast City Commission (forerunner of the Crown Court), not a decision of the Court of Criminal Appeal: see *Re Russell's Application* [1996] NI 310, 318c, per Hutton LCJ.

[82] ibid, para 89.

[83] ibid, para 90.

[84] ibid, para 91.

[85] ibid.

[86] EPA 1978, s 8(2) (inserted by s 5 of the EPA 1987); EPA 1991, s 11(2); EPA 1996, s 12(2); Terrorism Act 2000, s 76(3). The last provision was repealed as from 26 July 2002 by the Terrorism Act 2000 (Cessation of Effect of Section 76) Order 2002 (SI 2141), art 2.

[87] Baker (1984). The change had also been urged upon the government some years earlier, to no avail, by the Standing Advisory Commission on Human Rights: SACHR (1979) para 36; SACHR (1980)

of agreement that the Northern Ireland judges had interpreted the admissions section of the EPA 'with such good sense that a declaratory redraft would gain overwhelming approval'.[88] Yet in one of those decisions, *R v McCormick*,[89] a judge had said that the EPA still left it open to a police officer who was interviewing a suspect to use 'a moderate degree of physical maltreatment to induce the making of a statement'. The judge in question had (fairly enough) drawn support for this stance from the European Commission of Human Rights which, in both the *Greek* case[90] and *Ireland v UK*, had stated that a distinction had to be drawn between acts prohibited by Article 3 of the Convention and 'a certain roughness of treatment... [which]... may take the form of slaps or blows of the hand on the head or face'.[91] Baker could not go along with that approach and so he recommended that the view expressed by Lord Chief Justice Lowry in *R v O'Halloran*[92] should prevail, namely that it is 'difficult in practice to envisage any form of physical violence which is relevant to the interrogation of a suspect in custody and which, if it had occurred, could at the same time leave a court satisfied beyond reasonable doubt in relation to the issue for decision'. As a result, the wording of the legislation was changed to require the prosecution to prove (if there was *prima facie* evidence of the contrary raised by the defendant) not only that Article 3 had not been violated but also that there had been no violence or threat of violence (not amounting to torture).[93] This is a clear example of domestic law going further than is required by the European Convention in protecting human rights. It is a sad reflection on the European Commission and Court of Human Rights that this was felt to be necessary.

In 1978, after visiting the province for a week towards the end of 1977, Amnesty International published a damning report on the way the police in Northern Ireland were treating people who had been arrested on suspicion of involvement in terrorism.[94] One of the report's recommendations was that a public inquiry should be established to investigate the allegations made to Amnesty. While he refused to establish such an inquiry, the Secretary of State for Northern Ireland in the then Labour government, Roy Mason, did immediately announce that he was setting up a Committee of Inquiry, chaired by a county court judge from England (Judge Bennett), with two other members (James Haughton and John Marshall).[95] Its terms of reference were:

> To examine police procedures and practice in Northern Ireland relating to the interrogation of persons suspected of scheduled offences; to examine the operation of the present procedures for dealing with complaints relating to the conduct of police in the course of the process of interrogation; and to report and make recommendations.

paras 11–19; SACHR (1981) para 6(3); SACHR (1983) p 10 (where the Advisory Commission describes the current admissibility test in the EPA 1978 as 'grossly unfortunate').

[88] And he expressed indebtedness to an article by Greer (1980b). See also Greer (1973).

[89] [1977] NI 111.

[90] (1969) 12 Ybk 1.

[91] *Ireland v UK*, Commission Report, 25 January 1976, p 377. The Commission went on to say: 'This underlines the fact that the point up to which prisoners and the public may accept physical violence as being neither cruel nor excessive varies between different societies and even between different sections of them.'

[92] [1979] NIJB.

[93] EPA 1987, s 5, inserting a new s 8 into the EPA 1978.

[94] Amnesty International (1978).

[95] HC Deb, vol 951, cols 229–34W (8 June 1978).

The inquiry lasted about nine months, reporting in March 1979.[96] It did not inquire into individual allegations of maltreatment, and nor did Amnesty International pass the allegations it had received about cases of abuse to the Director of Public Prosecutions for further investigation. The Bennett Inquiry also did not look generally at the operation of section 6 of the EPA 1973—because that was already being reviewed by Lord Shackleton as part of his general consideration of the Prevention of Terrorism (Temporary Provisions) Acts 1974 and 1976[97]—and it did not look at the overall fairness of criminal procedures because that was being examined, albeit only for England and Wales in the first instance, by the Royal Commission on Criminal Procedure.[98] The Committee received some views from a number of solicitors in Northern Ireland, but nothing from the Bar Council or from individual barristers. It took oral evidence from 58 witnesses over 14 days, and it visited the police offices (ie holding centres) at Castlereagh and Gough as well as a number of other police stations.

The Bennett Committee carried out its assessment of police interrogation practices and the handling of complaints against a background of considerable mayhem on the streets of Northern Ireland. Although no-one could have known it at the time, the troubles were to continue for twice as long as they had already lasted, with as many deaths and injuries still to occur as had already occurred. By the end of 1978 more than 1,800 people had been killed since 1969, including more than 370 soldiers and 117 police officers; 21,000 people had been wounded, including more than 3,000 soldiers and 3,250 police officers. There had been more than 6,000 bombings. As we noted in Chapter 4, in pursuance of the British government's 'criminalization policy' the police had taken over prime responsibility for security from the army in January 1977, with the army available to give support when needed. According to Bennett this change of policy had been 'steadily successful, as is evidenced by the large numbers of crimes detected, the large number of criminals brought to trial and convicted, and the decline in the numbers of serious crimes committed'.[99] The Committee wisely acknowledged that there was 'abundant evidence of a co-ordinated and extensive campaign to discredit the police' but it stated that 'any misconduct by an individual member of the force concerned with the interrogation of prisoners... strengthens the propaganda campaign and provides ammunition for the enemies of society who are adept and experienced in inventing allegations against the police, even without any justification'.[100]

In all, the Bennett Committee reached 64 conclusions and recommendations. It noted that it was not always entirely clear how the Judges' Rules were applied in Northern Ireland (they had been re-adopted in 1976, in the same version as England and Wales had acquired in 1964), and that the European Court's judgment in *Ireland v United Kingdom* meant there was a need for continuing vigilance regarding the interrogation of prisoners. Damages had been awarded or settlements made out of court in civil claims brought against the Royal Ulster Constabulary, but although criminal proceedings had occasionally been undertaken against police officers too, no final

96 Bennett (1979).
97 Published on 24 August 1978.
98 Which did not report until 1981: Philips (1981).
99 Bennett (1979) para 18.
100 ibid, paras 19–20.

conviction had yet occurred in any case. The Committee's examination of medical evidence revealed 'cases in which injuries, whatever their precise cause, were not self-inflicted and were sustained in police custody'.[101] It therefore recommended, amongst other things, that a training programme for interrogation should be devised for detectives, that interviews should not normally last longer than the interval between normal meal times or continue after midnight, that not more than two officers at a time, or six in all, should interview one prisoner, that officers should identify themselves by name or number, and that a code of conduct should be drawn up for interviewing officers.

To help prevent mistreatment, senior police officers should be given responsibility for the good conduct of interviews, with changes in police procedures being made to allow any misconduct to be detected at once and dealt with without delay. It was noted that existing supervisory measures in the RUC went further than in any other police force in the United Kingdom at the time but that further improvements should be considered, with, for example, an increase in the number of uniformed supervisory inspectors on duty throughout the day at Castlereagh holding centre. Perhaps most importantly of all, there was a recommendation that viewing lenses should immediately be installed in all remaining rooms where interviews were taking place and that closed-circuit television cameras should also be installed in all interview rooms used for interrogation, with the monitor screens being scrutinized by uniformed supervisory staff. While medical examination did not need to take place after each interview, uniformed police should ask each prisoner after each interview whether he or she had any complaint and wished to be examined by a medical officer (and examinations by a doctor chosen by the prisoner should continue to be allowed). Each prisoner should be given a printed notice of his or her rights, and should be allowed to retain this. The Committee also felt that the consistent refusal to allow access to a solicitor throughout the whole period of detention was unjustifiable; it recommended that an unconditional right of access to a solicitor should be given after 48 hours, as well as every 48 hours thereafter. Solicitors should still not be permitted to be present at interviews, but some provision should be made for the attendance of parents when interviews were taking place with children and young persons. Some reforms were, however, rejected by the Bennett Committee. It did not think it was practical to introduce civilian supervisors into police offices and police stations, it did not want medical officers to be given a wider invigilatory role, Northern Ireland was not the best place to begin experimenting with the tape-recording of interviews, and video-recording should also not occur.

As regards the complaints system, the inquiry discovered that, while there had in recent years been an increase in the numbers of complaints against members of the RUC, no disciplinary proceedings had been brought in respect of interrogations. There was disquiet about the effectiveness of the complaints procedure in this regard and to help improve matters the inquiry suggested that much more use should be made of officers from other police forces. Complainants should be notified every three months of how their complaint was progressing. Responsibility for considering the prosecution of police officers should remain with the Director of Public Prosecutions (DPP), who should continue to look at all cases in which criminal conduct by a police

[101] ibid, para 163.

officer was alleged, and after reaching his or her decision the DPP should indicate to complainants whether it was reached on evidential or other grounds and explain to the Police Authority and Police Complaints Board the reasons for deciding against a prosecution. The Police Authority should make appropriate use of its power to require a complaint to be referred to a tribunal and consideration should be given to enhancing the powers of such a tribunal.

In general, the report of the Bennett Committee was well received in civil liberties circles, although looking back with the benefit of 30 years' hindsight it is still extraordinary how cautious some of its recommendations appear to be, such as those relating to tape- and video-recording, access to and involvement of solicitors, and effective complaint-handling mechanisms. Nevertheless, the report is credited with greatly reducing the incidence of police brutality in holding centres and police stations in Northern Ireland. Statistics in this field are often unreliable, but officially they show a marked drop in the post-Bennett years in the number of complaints of assault by the police. In the four years between 1975 and 1978 the average number of recorded complaints alleging assault by a police officer during interview was 391; in the four-year period 1980–83 the figure was still 409, but that included allegations of assault occurring during arrests as well as those occurring during interviews. The annual average in the period 1989–92 was 282.[102]

The fact that the Bennett Committee found it necessary to make such a large number of recommendations clearly shows that it believed ill-treatment of detainees was still common. In other words, while the European Court's judgment in *Ireland v United Kingdom* may have put an end to certain techniques used by the interrogators at military barracks, it does not seem to have curtailed ill-treatment in the police holding centres. The violence which was accepted by Compton,[103] but which was not in his eyes 'brutality', was clearly continuing. Those few detainees who were able to provide convincing proof that such ill-treatment had occurred could, and did, seek damages from a local court; none of them appear to have taken a case to Strasbourg and no organization was able to mount a case alleging that there was a pattern and practice of ill-treatment. Without applications to consider, the European Commission and Court were powerless to raise standards in Northern Ireland's police stations. It would be another decade before the Council of Europe established another mechanism for dealing with ill-treatment for detainees, the European Convention for the Prevention of Torture and Inhuman or Degrading Treatment or Punishment, which was agreed in 1987. This established a Committee which had the power to make unannounced visits to States to inspect their facilities for holding people in custody (CPT). But such visits did not commence until 1990, too late to address the problems in Northern Ireland during the 1980s.

In its comments submitted to Parliament prior to the renewal debate on the EPA 1978 in July 1979, the Standing Advisory Commission on Human Rights submitted what it called 'a radical proposal' to help ensure that police officers who used or

[102] Figures extrapolated from the annual reports of the Police Complaints Board (until 1977) and the Independent Commission for Police Complaints.
[103] See 140–1 above.

threatened to use violence were effectively punished.[104] This amounted to insisting that hearings about the admissibility of statements made by an accused person should be separated from the actual trial of that person: if a preliminary *voir dire* ('a trial within a trial') certified that a statement had been obtained through ill-treatment, this would be regarded as final and steps could then be taken to deal with the officers who were responsible for the ill-treatment. However the government did not accept this recommendation, perhaps because it seems to assume that if a statement is declared inadmissible because the prosecution cannot show that ill-treatment was not used this automatically means that ill-treatment must have been used, which is a non sequitur and a denial of the police officers' right to be considered innocent until proven guilty.

The holding centres

After the Bennett inquiry, use continued to be made of the so-called 'police offices' at Castlereagh in East Belfast, Gough Barracks in Armagh, and Strand Road in Derry/Londonderry. The statutory authorization for these 'holding centres', as they were more commonly known, was supposedly located in the Prevention of Terrorism (Temporary Provisions) Acts,[105] but there was no equivalent authorization in the Northern Ireland (Emergency Provisions) Acts. The justification given for their establishment was that ordinary police stations were not secure enough places in which to detain and question hardened terrorists. Given the apparent ease with which some prisoners were able to escape from prisons, there was a feeling in government quarters that keeping suspected terrorists in ordinary police stations, even ones fortified against attack, would be too risky. Besides, the accommodation in most of these stations was just not adequate (even for police officers).

There was not, however, any system in place for allowing independent checks to be made on the conditions under which detainees were held in the holding centres. Many allegations of poor conditions were made by people who experienced them at first hand, but no official body could verify these. For years they remained places where there was little or no oversight of what took place inside. Allegations proliferated that detainees were beaten up in the centres, either during or between interrogation sessions.[106] It was not until 1992 that the British government appointed, on a non-statutory basis, an Independent Commissioner for the Holding Centres. Though there was by then less concern about army ill-treatment of detainees (who could only be held for up to four hours) legislation did provide for the appointment

[104] SACHR (1980), para 17.

[105] PTA 1974, Sch 3, para 6(1); PTA 1976, Sch 3, para 5(1); PTA 1984, Sch 3, para 5(1); PTA 1989, s 15(6); Terrorism Act 2000, Sch 8, paras 1(1) and 5. All of these state, in effect, that a terrorist suspect may be detained in such place as the Secretary of State may direct, and they add that a person so detained shall be deemed to be in legal custody. Whether this latter provision is compatible with Art 5 of the Convention was called into question by the Divisional Court of Northern Ireland in *Re Colin Duffy's Application* [2009] NIQB 31, but was left to be resolved at a future hearing.

[106] Because such detainees had to be taken to an ordinary police station to be charged, lay visitors sometimes encountered them there. But very few complaints of ill-treatment were relayed by the detainees on such occasions. For the role of lay visitors see 164 below. See too CAJ (1993).

of an Independent Assessor of Military Complaints Procedures,[107] who could supply some independent oversight of the army's own mechanisms for dealing with complaints about ill-treatment or other matters.

The courts of Northern Ireland did not do much to ensure that conditions for detainees in the holding centres were improved—they refused to overturn the chief constable's decisions to disallow detainees access to writing materials, for example.[108] The European Commission and Court likewise never commented to any significant extent on the regime used for holding suspected terrorists in Northern Ireland prior to their being charged. In *Kerr v United Kingdom*,[109] the Court did say that the conditions in the Castlereagh holding centre were 'austere', but it held the complaint under Article 3 to be manifestly ill-founded because the applicant had not disclosed any physical or mental ill-treatment such as to attain the minimum level of severity required for a violation of that provision. Just six months later, though, in *Magee v United Kingdom*,[110] where the applicant relied on the harsh conditions under which he was detained in the Castlereagh holding centre as further evidence that his will had been undermined when he was questioned by the police before being allowed to consult with a solicitor, the European Court referred specifically to those conditions, which had been criticized in a report produced by the CPT after a visit to Castlereagh in July 1993.[111] That report remarked on the lack of natural light and exercise facilities at Castlereagh, where detainees might be held for up to seven days, and concluded:

> the existing material conditions of detention at Castlereagh Holding Centre render it inappropriate as a place in which to detain persons for extended periods. The deficiencies as regards access to natural light for detainees and the absence of exercise facilities were the principal failings, but the mediocre ventilation system and the cramped and rather dilapidated nature of the facilities should also be mentioned. All these factors contributed to create a distinctly claustrophobic atmosphere... Even in the absence of overt acts of ill-treatment, there is no doubt that a stay in a holding centre may be—and is perhaps designed to be—a most disagreeable experience. The material conditions of detention are poor (especially at Castlereagh) and important qualifications are, or at least can be, placed upon certain fundamental rights of persons detained by the police (in particular, the possibilities for contact with the outside world are severely limited throughout the whole period of detention and various restrictions can be placed on the right of access to a lawyer). To this must be added the intensive and potentially prolonged character of the interrogation process. The cumulative effect of these factors is to place persons detained at the holding centres under a considerable degree of psychological pressure. The CPT must state, in this connection, that to impose upon a detainee such a degree of pressure as to break his will would amount, in its opinion, to inhuman treatment.[112]

In its judgment in *Magee v United Kingdom* the European Court said the 'austerity' of the conditions of the applicant's detention, and his exclusion from outside

[107] EPA 1996, s 51 and Sch 4; Terrorism Act 2000, s 98 and Sch 11. The post was created as a result of a proposal made by Viscount Colville: Colville (1991) ch 5.

[108] *Re Floyd's Application* [1997] NI 414 (Div Ct: Carswell LCJ and Kerr J).

[109] (2000) 29 EHRR CD184.

[110] (2001) 31 EHRR 35.

[111] See generally Shaw (1999) 267–8.

[112] Paras 45 and 109. The report was dated 19 November 1994.

contact, 'were intended to be psychologically coercive and conducive to breaking down any resolve he may have manifested at the beginning of his detention to remain silent'.[113] As a matter of procedural fairness, therefore, the applicant should have been given access to a solicitor at the initial stages of the interrogation, 'as a counterweight to the intimidating atmosphere specifically devised to sap his will and make him confess to his interrogators'.[114] The Court also referred in passing to the reports of the Independent Commissioner for Holding Centres published between 1993 and 1996,[115] and the conclusions and recommendations of the United Nations Committee against Torture in its report on the United Kingdom issued in 1995. Thus, in 2000, two years after the Belfast (Good Friday) Agreement, the European Court did finally speak out to condemn the regime in Northern Ireland's holding centres. The regret is that this did not occur much sooner.

Developments since 1989

The Police and Criminal Evidence (NI) Order 1989 (in force from 1 January 1990) radically improved the rights of people arrested and detained under the 'ordinary' law. It ensured, for example, that there were clear rules as to the questioning and treatment of persons by the police,[116] and it provided for codes of practice on this and other matters to be issued by the Secretary of State.[117] A breach of these codes would generally be a breach of police discipline[118] and, while it would not of itself render a police officer liable to any criminal or civil proceedings,[119] it had to be 'taken into account' by any court of tribunal conducting such proceedings.[120] Perhaps the most significant reform resulting from the PACE legislation was the requirement that police interviews with people who had been arrested because they were suspected of committing a criminal offence had to be tape-recorded.[121]

None of these changes applied to persons arrested in Northern Ireland on suspicion of involvement in terrorism, even though some of the equivalent provisions in the PACE Act 1984 did apply to suspected terrorists arrested in England and Wales.[122] But two of the rights—the right of access to legal advice, and the right to have someone informed of one's detention—had in fact already been conferred on terrorist suspects in Northern Ireland by the EPA 1987,[123] in furtherance of the recommendations

[113] (2001) 31 EHRR 35, para 43.
[114] ibid.
[115] These were written by Sir Louis Blom-Cooper QC, who served in that role from 1992 to 2000.
[116] PACE (NI) Order 1989, arts 53–64.
[117] ibid, art 65.
[118] ibid, art 66(7).
[119] ibid, art 66(9).
[120] ibid, art 66(10).
[121] ibid, art 60(b). A code of practice was to be issued on this matter too: art 60(a).
[122] eg the provisions on right of access to a solicitor: see further ch 8 below. For more details on the rights of detainees under both PACE and the anti-terrorism laws applicable in Northern Ireland in 2003, see Jackson (2003).
[123] ss 14 and 15; later re-enacted as EPA 1991, ss 44 and 45 and as EPA 1996, ss 46 and 47.

of the Bennett Committee eight years earlier.[124] The taking of terrorist suspects' fingerprints was also regulated by the PTA 1989.[125] Interviews with terrorist suspects were not required to be tape-recorded, but in 1996 a requirement was introduced that such interviews be silently video-recorded.[126] This was described as 'an acceptable compromise between ensuring that persons being questioned under the anti-terrorism legislation at holding centres should be protected from threats or from the use of violence, while preserving the anonymity of such individuals, who could otherwise be recognised by terrorists or those sympathetic to terrorists by their voices'.[127]

The PACE provisions in England and Wales were amended by the Criminal Justice and Police Act 2001,[128] one of the most notable reforms being the introduction of video-recording of police interviews with non-terrorist suspects,[129] though provisions requiring the destruction of fingerprints were also amended at that time so as to allow the prints to be kept indefinitely in many more cases.[130] There was then a review of the PACE legislation jointly conducted by the Home Office and the Cabinet Office in 2002, and a further review by the Home Office in 2004. These led to 'modernizing' powers being introduced by the Criminal Justice Act 2003 and the Serious Organised Crime and Police Act 2005. In Northern Ireland provision was made as far back as the Police (NI) Act 2000 for the video-recording of police interviews with non-terrorists suspects,[131] but this provision did not actually come into force until April 2002.[132] A review of the PACE legislation in Northern Ireland was announced in 2004, the intention being to bring law and practice there more into line with the amended regime in England and Wales. The initial intention was to have the new law and codes of practice operational by the summer of 2005 but in fact the amendments did not come into effect until March 2007, through the Police and Criminal Evidence (Amendment) (NI) Order of that year. Then, in January 2009, the Northern Ireland Office issued yet more proposals for amending the law.[133] While the Foreword to the latest review talks of the need to strike the right balance between the powers of the police and the rights of the individual, and to maintain the

[124] Bennett (1979) paras 277 and 281. On the latter right Bennett noted that there was satisfactory provision in the RUC Code of Practice for notice to be given to relatives, but he recommended that greater publicity should be given to the proper places at which families should make inquiries.

[125] s 15(9) and (10). The EPA 1991, s 46, substituted a new art 61(4) into the PACE (NI) Order 1989 to deal with situations where a police officer was taking a suspected terrorist's fingerprints under the PTA 1989: this meant that, as in England and Wales under the PTA 1989, s 15(10), the fingerprints of terrorist suspects could not be taken without consent unless this was authorized by an officer of at least the rank of superintendent. However, fingerprints taken under this provision could be retained indefinitely even though no charges were brought against the suspect or, if charged, the suspect was then acquitted, while fingerprints taken from non-terrorist suspects under the PACE (NI) Order 1989, art 61, had to be destroyed in such circumstances 'as soon as is practicable' (art 64).

[126] EPA 1996, s 53(1)(b). A code of practice on video-recording had to be issued too: art 53(1)(a).

[127] Scanlan and Gale (1997), general note to s 53. See too Hill (1991).

[128] Pt 3, ss 71–86.

[129] PACE Act 1984, s 60A, inserted by Criminal Justice and Police Act 2001, s 76.

[130] PACE Act 1984, s 64, amended by Criminal Justice and Police Act 2001, s 82.

[131] s 72 inserted s 60A into the PACE (NI) Order 1989.

[132] Police (NI) Act 2000 (Commencement No 4) Order 2002 (SR 146).

[133] Available on the website of the Northern Ireland Office: <http://www.nio.gov.uk>, last visited 24 August 2009.

safeguards and protections for those suspected of involvement in crime, the review itself does not mention the European Convention even once.[134]

Meanwhile, on 10 December 1999 an official announcement was made that the Castlereagh holding centre was to close by the end of that year. Later the holding centres in Armagh and Derry were also closed. After using an interim facility at Lisburn police station, a new purpose-built custody suite for terrorist suspects was eventually constructed in the police station in Antrim, and that is now where all such suspects are taken on arrest. The Northern Ireland Human Rights Commission has criticized the facilities there, in particular the lack of access to exercise and fresh air,[135] but it has not gone as far as to say that the conditions amount to a breach of Article 3 of the Convention, and the government's official reviewer of anti-terrorism legislation, Lord Carlile, appears to think the facilities are acceptable.[136] The conditions are certainly immensely better than the conditions in the holding centres, and there is reason to believe that the behaviour of the police officers who interrogate suspects has greatly improved too.

Many of the provisions of the EPA 1996 were re-enacted in Part VII of the Terrorism Act 2000, which was made subject to annual renewal by the affirmative resolution procedure.[137] Part VII was to lapse completely, however, after five years.[138] In April 2003 a Joint Declaration of the British and Irish governments committed the former to repealing Part VII within two years, provided there was evidence of a definitive transition to exclusively peaceful and democratic means by the IRA.[139] Following a statement by the IRA on 28 July 2005 that it was formally declaring its armed campaign to be over, the British government repeated its 2003 commitment and said that Part VII would be repealed by 1 August 2007.[140] In order to ensure that Part VII did not lapse before then it was specifically kept in force by the Terrorism (NI) Act 2006, which received the Royal Assent two days before the deadline.[141] The Secretary of State for Northern Ireland described it as 'a measured approach . . . necessary to ensure the proper functioning of the criminal justice agencies under normalised conditions'.[142] But just in case the timetable were to slip again, the 2006 Act allowed for an order to be made keeping Part VII of the 2000 Act in force for yet another year, until 1 August 2008. In the end this extension was not required, so Part VII did indeed lapse on 31 July 2007. However, rather than simply allowing all the anti-terrorism provisions applicable in England, Wales, and Scotland to then apply to Northern Ireland too, the government deemed it necessary to enact further legislation just for Northern Ireland. This came in the form of the Justice and Security (NI) Act 2007. As well as permitting juryless courts to continue for some terrorist cases, and conferring more

[134] The CAJ thinks some of the proposals may conflict with Arts 5, 6, and 14 of the Convention: see its newsletter, *Just News*, May 2009, p 2.

[135] See NIHRC press statements dated 23 and 24 March 2009.

[136] Carlile (2008) para 111.

[137] s 112(1) and (2), and s 123(4).

[138] s 112(4).

[139] Available on the website of the Northern Ireland Office: <http://www.nio.gov.uk>.

[140] In a report published on 26 September 2005 the Independent International Commission on Decommissioning reported that the IRA had decommissioned its weapons.

[141] Part VII would have lapsed on 18 February 2006, since it came into force on 19 February 2001.

[142] HC Deb, vol 438, col 636 (31 October 2005).

legal and investigative powers on the Northern Ireland Human Rights Commission, this Act sets out a range of police powers to stop, question, arrest, enter, search, and seize,[143] all of which were brought into force on 1 August 2007.[144] The provisions do not otherwise impinge upon the treatment of terrorist suspects who are detained in Northern Ireland; the rules in that area are now the same as those applying in England and Wales.[145] On their face they seem to be not only consistent with the European Convention but even to go beyond its requirements in certain respects (as regards the taking of fingerprints and samples, for example).

All of these post-1989 developments meant that complaints of assault by police officers from people held in custody in Northern Ireland gradually tailed off during the 1990s. In the early part of that decade the oversight body for the RUC, the Police Authority, appointed 'lay visitors' on a non-statutory basis and allowed them to visit people held in police stations (but not the holding centres) at any time of the day or night to check on their well-being.[146] In 2000 this scheme was made statutory[147] and responsibility for running it was transferred to the new Northern Ireland Policing Board. A new and powerful Police Ombudsman's Office also began functioning in 2000, replacing the rather discredited Independent Commission for Police Complaints,[148] and in the four years between 1997 and 2000 the average number of complaints by persons arrested under the emergency laws (not all of which alleged assaults by the police) fell to 73. In 2005 the role of the Independent Commissioner for Detained Terrorist Suspects was brought to an end.[149] But persons mistreated in the holding centres in years gone by are not, it seems, giving up on their attempts to get justice: in 2008 it was reported that some 300 former members of the IRA were planning to sue the British government for compensation for being wrongly convicted on the basis (amongst other things) of confessions forced from them by police coercion.[150]

A novel context in which the right not to be ill-treated by police officers arose after the Belfast (Good Friday) Agreement was that of the so-called Holy Cross dispute in 2001. This concerned the shocking attempt by loyalists to prevent Catholic schoolgirls[151] and their adult companions from walking daily to and from the Holy Cross

143 ss 21–32. There are supplementary provisions (dealing with codes of practice, compensation, etc) in ss 33–42. These too all came into force on 1 August 2007: see s 53(1) and Justice and Security (NI) Act 2007 (Commencement No 1 and Transitional Provisions) Order 2007 (SI 2045).

144 s 53(1).

145 Terrorism Act 2000, Sch 8, paras 6–15. There are slightly different rules for Scotland: Sch 8, paras 16–20.

146 The lay visiting scheme was modeled on one already in place in England and Wales. Visitors inspected police custody suites in pairs, were able to talk to any detainees who were willing to be interviewed, and could ask questions of the officer in charge of the custody suite.

147 Police (NI) Act 2000, s 73.

148 Hayes (1997).

149 This was the new title given to the Independent Commissioner for the Holding Centres in 2001. Dr Bill Norris occupied the post from 2000 to 2005. See Walker (1998).

150 *The Guardian*, 25 August 2008 (Henry McDonald), *The Daily Telegraph*, 25 August 2008 (Jon Swaine). See too *An Phoblacht*, 3 December 2009.

151 Though, with reference to the Holy Cross dispute, Richard Dawkins prefers not to describe children as being of any religion unless they are old enough to decide for themselves which if any religion to adopt: Dawkins (2006) 339.

Primary School in the Ardoyne area of North Belfast. The police took steps to protect the children and adults from the protestors, some of whom were hurling missiles as well as verbal insults. One mother persuaded a High Court judge to grant her leave to take judicial review proceedings against the chief constable challenging his decision not to police the protest in a way that better protected the right of her daughter and herself not to be subjected to inhuman and degrading treatment. The case went all the way to the House of Lords, but was unsuccessful every step of the way.[152] The judges confirmed that, while courts should not defer completely to professional experts when decisions have to be taken as to how best to police a protest, they should nevertheless recognize that experienced police officers are usually in a better position to judge the merits of operational tactics. In another case which went to the House of Lords, not from Northern Ireland, *Austin v Metropolitan Police Commissioner*,[153] the Law Lords held that the police's tactic of 'kettling' a demonstration in London on 1 May 2001 did not amount to a deprivation of liberty under Article 5 of the European Convention. They said that, even in relation to fundamental rights, in relation to which no limitation is permitted by the Convention, the courts had to adopt a pragmatic approach which took full account of all the circumstances. The claimant in that case did not rely upon any alleged violation of Article 3, but it seems that the principle underlying the decision is just as applicable to Article 3 claims as it is to those arising under Article 5.

Punishment attacks

Quite apart from the ill-treatment meted out by members of the security forces during the conflict in Northern Ireland, there was widespread and extremely violent ill-treatment perpetrated by members of paramilitary organizations. Obviously this often took the form of murderous sectarian attacks against 'the other side', when, often quite randomly, young men walking in areas known to be predominantly Catholic or Protestant would be singled out for a beating or a shooting by paramilitaries supposedly representing the opposing side of the community. In addition, however, numerous attacks were committed by paramilitary organizations against individuals from their 'own' side. These were usually individuals who had disobeyed a command from the organization that they desist from engaging in certain 'anti-social behaviour', such as burglaries of homes and businesses, thefts of cars, or incidents of criminal damage. Members of the organizations who refused to undertake missions on behalf of the organization were also often 'disciplined', and the usual punishment for giving information to the security forces about paramilitary activities was in fact execution. It is estimated, for example, that the IRA killed about 60 alleged informers.[154]

[152] *E v Chief Constable of the Royal Ulster Constabulary* [2008] UKHL 66, [2008] 3 WLR 1208. For further discussion see ch 9 below. An application to the European Court is pending.

[153] [2009] UKHL 5, [2009] 2 WLR 372.

[154] Liam Clarke, *The Sunday Times*, 27 November 2005. See generally Knox and Monaghan (2002) and Feenan (2002).

In the early days of the troubles a common punishment exacted on those who displeased the paramilitaries was tarring and feathering (girls who fraternized with British soldiers were often subjected to this). Sometimes the victim would be tied to a lamp-post with a placard round his or her neck proclaiming what wrong he or she was alleged to have committed. In later years the punishment began to take the form of shootings or beatings. Victims would be shot in the ankles, knees, or elbows[155] or, allegedly because gunshot wounds left too many forensic traces that could be linked back to particular weapons, they would be beaten with clubs, such as baseball bats or hurling sticks. Often the victims of these horrendous attacks were teenagers. Many of them suffered injuries that would remain with them for the rest of their lives.[156] In addition to being maimed several were ordered to leave their localities, or to quit Northern Ireland altogether—they were 'exiled'.

According to police statistics[157] (and bearing in mind that many incidents were never officially reported) the numbers of such punishment attacks averaged 71 per year between 1973 and 1986 but went up to 194 per year between 1987 and 1997. The 'peace process', which many date from 1988, when Gerry Adams of Sinn Féin and John Hume of the SDLP began having secret talks, did not seem to have any influence on the rate of attacks, except inversely. The paramilitaries obviously saw the use of such repressive tactics as a means of maintaining power over communities.[158] Even after the Belfast (Good Friday) Agreement was concluded in 1998 the incidence of punishment attacks *rose*: the average number per year between 1998 and 2005 was 255.[159]

Unfortunately these attacks did not feature much in the campaigning of human rights NGOs because, not having been committed by agents of the State, they were not viewed as human rights abuses.[160] One of the first differences of opinion that emerged between the members of the Northern Ireland Human Rights Commission when it was established in 1999 was over what kind of statements, if any, the Commission should be making about such attacks. Some political leaders also equivocated over the phenomenon, pleading for it to be 'understood'. Occasionally they even pointed to alleged community support for the attacks, as if that was itself a justification for them. The police, for their part, were not successful at bringing to justice many of the alleged perpetrators, partly of course because the victims were too frightened to give evidence about what happened to them in case they were again 'punished' for disobeying orders not to reveal any such information. There are no police statistics available on the proportion of attacks that led to a successful prosecution, but the number must be tiny. The failure to bring perpetrators to court is evidence of

155 The gruesome slang expression used for a punishment consisting of shots to both ankles, both knees, and both elbows was 'a six-pack'.

156 Thompson and Mulholland (1995).

157 Available on the website of the PSNI: <http://www.psni.police.uk/ps_attacks_cy.pdf> (last visited 18 October 2009). The police did not begin gathering statistics on punishment *beatings* until 1982.

158 Kennedy (1995).

159 The rate fell to an average of 67 per year between 2005 and 2009 (to the end of August). The Northern Ireland Association for the Care and Resettlement of Offenders has a unit (Base 2) which gives people advice and support if they are threatened by paramilitaries (see <http://www.niacro.co.uk>).

160 An honourable exception was Helsinki Watch (1992), though they characterized the behaviour of paramilitary organizations as violations of international humanitarian law, not of human rights standards.

a policing vacuum in certain parts of Northern Ireland, although what has grown up to supplement the policing system in some of those areas—locally based restorative justice schemes—has gone some way towards remedying the situation.

The European Convention was as irrelevant to this aspect of paramilitary illegality as it was to most other aspects, for the simple reason that the Convention is directed at acts and omissions by States, not by other organizations or individuals. Only if it could have been shown that the UK authorities, contrary to the positive obligations imposed on them through Article 3 of the Convention, were failing to protect people who were under a real and immediate threat of punishment attacks could the State have been brought to book in Strasbourg. It would have been very difficult to demonstrate such a degree of threat against any particular victim, and again any litigation would have been dependent on that victim wishing to publicize the matter. The local political leaders who appeared to tolerate the attacks (and who seemed able to have their frequency drastically reduced whenever it was politically opportune, because, say, of an imminent visit by a US president) were likewise unamenable to the European Court's jurisdiction.

Conclusion

Without doubt, the European Court's decision in *Ireland v United Kingdom* was a disappointing turning point in the application of the European Convention to the conflict in Northern Ireland. In reversing the European Commission's decision as to whether the 'five techniques' employed by the security forces in Northern Ireland amounted to torture, the European Court sent a subliminal message to the UK government that it could continue to tolerate heavy-handed interrogation tactics without having to worry too much about international opprobrium. In addition, the European Court failed to adequately condemn the systemic nature of the malpractices which had been officially authorized in Northern Ireland. These two green lights, coupled with the failure of the European Court to lay down positive obligations on the State to ensure that proper accountability mechanisms for dealing with complaints against the security forces were in place, meant that for a generation British soldiers and police officers could behave disgracefully towards detainees without risking a finding of torture at the international level. Small wonder that the infamous 'torture memos' produced by the Bush administration in the first decade of the new century would use the European Court's judgment in the inter-State case as authority for the proposition that certain interrogation practices would not contravene the ban on torture in international law.[161] No surprise, too, to find that the five techniques condemned as inhuman treatment were still being employed by British soldiers in Iraq 30 years later.

[161] Greenberg and Dratel (2005) 196–8.

The European Court's decision in *Ireland v United Kingdom* was, quite simply, a wasted opportunity for the world's premier international human rights court to speak out loudly and clearly against police and army brutality of all kinds. Not only did the judgment set the tone for the relatively 'hands-off' attitude displayed by the Court to many of the anti-terrorism measures in Northern Ireland coming before it in the ensuing 20 years, it also delayed for a similar period the Court's willingness to set a lower threshold for a definition of torture throughout Europe.[162] The fact that the men who were subjected to ill-treatment in *Ireland v United Kingdom* had been in custody at the time should have prompted the European Court to impose positive obligations on the State to show that the detainees were not mistreated, but this too was a position which the European Court was not to adopt until almost 15 years later.[163]

Somewhat paradoxically, it was only after the terrorist organizations called a ceasefire in Northern Ireland in 1994 that the Court began to impose more stringent duties on the British authorities. The context in which this occurred was that of security force ambushes of suspected terrorist operatives. Later chapters in this book, particularly Chapter 9 on the right to life, will make it clear that by the end of the twentieth century—in time for the half-centenary of the coming into force of the European Convention in 2003—there had been a very significant change in the way in which the European Court was prepared to 'police' the actions of Council of Europe States when dealing with serious law and order problems in their societies. This may be partly attributable to the creation of a full-time European Court, and the abolition of the European Commission, at the end of 1998, a reform brought about by Protocol 9 to the Convention, which at a stroke not only made the Court more productive and more self-confident but also conferred on applicants the right to take their case to the Court rather than have to wait for it to be referred by the Commission or the respondent State. Having by then examined so many applications from Northern Ireland, the Court was beginning to apply the principles it had developed in those cases when considering numerous applications brought against Turkey with respect to the actions of that country's security forces in combating the violent campaign waged by Kurdish separatists. Today, with relative peace having been brokered in Turkey, attention has shifted again to a plethora of cases brought against Russia with respect to the manner in which it has handled the rebellion in Chechnya. Thus has the Convention truly come of age.

162 The breakthrough came in *Selmouni v France* (2000) 29 EHRR 403, where the Court took the view (at para 101) 'that the increasingly high standard being required in the area of the protection of human rights and fundamental liberties correspondingly and inevitably requires greater firmness in assessing breaches of the fundamental values of democratic societies'. For a good overview of the still inadequate state of the law on Article 3 in the wake of *Selmouni v France* see McBride (2000).

163 In *Tomasi v France* (1993) 15 EHRR 1. For comments on how Art 3 does not, in practice, confer an 'absolute' right, see Addo and Grief (1998).

8

The Right to a Fair Trial

Article 6 of the European Convention, which protects the right to a fair hearing, is the most frequently invoked Convention article, not just in the United Kingdom but in Strasbourg too. Not surprisingly, it has featured prominently in some cases arising out of the conflict in Northern Ireland, though perhaps not as often as one might have imagined, especially if one considers that the European Court of Human Rights, when judging whether a defendant has received a fair hearing for the purposes of Article 6, examines the entire criminal justice process from the moment of arrest to the moment of sentence. When the UK government was devising changes to pre-trial procedures in Northern Ireland to take account of the difficulties encountered in dealing with suspected terrorists, it therefore had to be sure that the new procedures were not themselves so special as to make the whole trial unfair. By and large it seems to have succeeded in that goal, for here too the European Commission and Court have been prepared to grant the UK government considerable freedom of action.

For persons suspected of terrorist offences in Northern Ireland the government allowed the prosecution to insist on the holding of a 'preliminary enquiry' prior to the full trial, rather than a 'preliminary investigation'.[1] The latter would have necessitated a full hearing, with witnesses attending to give oral testimony, whereas the former could be conducted very largely on a documents-only basis. This change was made in order to reduce the need for witnesses to expose themselves to the risk of intimidation. There is nothing contrary to the European Convention about it unless subsequent disclosures in the trial indicate that there has been unfairness contrary to Article 6.[2] Nor was the Convention breached on the few occasions when the prosecution dispensed altogether with pre-trial proceedings and went straight to trial through what was called the 'voluntary bill of indictment' procedure.[3] Moreover, as we saw in Chapter 6, the rule that only a High Court judge could grant bail to someone charged with a scheduled offence was also found not to be contrary to the Convention, although this was not finally determined until 2006.[4] There were, however, several other issues which raised much more starkly the risk that Article 6 was

[1] Northern Ireland (Emergency Provisions) Act (EPA) 1978, s 1. No such recommendation was made by the Diplock Commission and the provision was not included in the EPA 1973. It eventually became the Terrorism Act 2000, s 66, and is now to be found in the Justice and Security (NI) Act 2007, s 3. In his report on the operation of the Terrorism Act 2000 during 2007, Lord Carlile said he had received no adverse representations on the provision: Carlile (2008) para 187.

[2] See *Re Kerr's Application* [1997] NI 225. See too Walsh (1983) 85–8.

[3] See further SACHR (1984) paras 14–9 and Appendix A; Walsh (1983) 88–90.

[4] *McKay v UK* (2007) 44 EHRR 41.

being breached, whether pre-trial or at the trial. These are discussed below. Once again the story is one of the European Convention having had little real influence on the way in which the criminal justice system was adjusted in Northern Ireland to cope with the difficulties thrown up by paramilitary threats. It did not prevent some serious abuses of human rights from occurring.

Access to a solicitor

The European Convention does not, on its face, guarantee the right of access to a lawyer to persons who have been arrested on suspicion of a criminal offence. The closest it comes to doing so is in Article 6(3), where it states that everyone charged with a criminal offence has the rights 'to have adequate time and facilities for the preparation of his defence' and 'to defend himself in person or through legal assistance of his own choosing or, if he has not sufficient means to pay for legal assistance, to be given it free when the interests of justice so require'.[5] In 1984, in *Can v Austria*,[6] where the applicant was not complaining about being denied access to a lawyer but about that access being subjected to supervision by police officers, the European Commission of Human Rights summed up the current position under the Convention:

> The Commission first observes that the Convention does not expressly guarantee the right of an accused to freely communicate with his defence counsel, for the preparation of his defence or otherwise. In this respect the Convention differs from other international provisions in the field of human rights and in particular from Art 14, para 3(b) of the United Nations Covenant on Civil and Political Rights where this right is expressly mentioned alongside with the right to have adequate time and facilities for the preparation of the defence. Rule 93 of the Standard Minimum Rules for the Treatment of Prisoners (Resolution (73) 5 of the Committee of Ministers of the Council of Europe) provides that 'an untried prisoner shall be entitled, as soon as he is imprisoned, to choose his legal representation... and to receive visits from his legal adviser with a view to his defence and to prepare and hand to him, and to receive, confidential instructions. At his request he shall be given all necessary facilities for this purpose... Interviews between the prisoner and his legal adviser may be within sight but not within hearing, either direct or indirect, of a police or institution official'...
>
> The fact that this right is not specifically mentioned in the Convention does not mean that it may not implicitly be inferred from its provisions, and in particular those of Art 6(3)(b) and (c). The Commission has in fact recognised that the possibility for an accused to communicate with his lawyer is a fundamental part of the preparation of his defence. However, the Commission has added that in the absence of an express provision, it cannot be maintained that the right to have conversations with one's lawyer and exchange confidential instructions or information with him, as implicitly guaranteed by Art 6(3), is not susceptible of any restriction...[7]

[5] Art 6(3)(b) and (c).

[6] (1986) 8 EHRR 14. See generally Reid (2008) 151–9. The parties in *Can* reached a friendly settlement, so the European Court did not have the opportunity to rule upon the matter.

[7] ibid, paras 51 and 52, citing *Bonzi v Switzerland* App No 7854/77, 12 DR 185; *Schertenleib v Switzerland* App No 8339/78, 17 DR 180; *Kröcher and Möller v Switzerland* App No 8463/78, 26 DR 24; and *G v UK* App No 9370/81, 35 DR 75. In this last case, decided on 13 October 1983, the Commission recalled (at p 6) that 'although there are differing practices as to the availability of access to legal advice

Throughout the conflict in Northern Ireland the inadequacy of the European Convention in this respect meant that thousands of terrorist suspects did not receive the immediate legal advice that was guaranteed to them under the UN Covenant and that might have assisted them to raise a stronger defence against the accusations they were facing.

When the troubles broke out in Northern Ireland in 1968 it was not entirely clear whether, in domestic law, an arrested person had an immediate right to consult a lawyer. There was certainly no such right conferred by statute, any more than there was in England and Wales (or in the Republic of Ireland), but there was also some doubt over whether any such right existed under the common law. The right was not included in the so-called Judges' Rules of 1918, which still applied in Northern Ireland. In 1976 a new version of these rules, first adopted in England and Wales in 1964, was extended to Northern Ireland with the consent of the Lord Chief Justice and the Chief Constable of the RUC.[8] This version acknowledged the principle that:

> every person at any stage of an investigation should be able to communicate and to consult privately with a solicitor. This is so even if he is in custody provided that in such a case no unreasonable delay or hindrance is caused to the processes of investigation or the administration of justice by his doing so.[9]

But no court had ever said that this principle was a fundamental right under the common law.[10] In 1979 the Bennett Committee reported that the RUC had adopted a policy of refusing terrorist suspects any access to a solicitor,[11] sometimes justifying this on the basis that the principle in the Judges' Rules was inapplicable to a situation where a society was facing the type of terrorist activity Northern Ireland was experiencing and sometimes on the basis that the proviso in the Judges' Rules expressly allowed for exceptions to the principle.[12] At any rate the police openly admitted that access was refused because 'the only advice a solicitor could give to his client was

for persons arrested, but not yet charged with a criminal offence, in the various member states of the Council of Europe, and, as to the sufficiency of a confession as evidence for a conviction, the European systems of criminal law all incorporate various safeguards, either controlling the manner of obtaining evidence, or for assessing its subsequent probative value at the trial, where a defendant makes a substantial allegation of its impropriety'. On the facts of the case before it the Commission felt able to hold that adequate safeguards had existed in that the admissibility of the applicant's statement had been considered separately in a voir dire (a trial within a trial).

[8] HC Deb, vol 917, col 134W (13 October 1976) per James Dunn MP.

[9] [1964] 1 WLR 152, 153 at para (c). The same principle (but without the words 'or hindrance') was contained in the revised Judges' Rules included in a later Home Office Circular No 89/1978. The Administrative Directions accompanying those Rules added (at para 7(a)) : 'A person in custody should be allowed to speak on the telephone to his solicitor or to his friends provided that no hindrance is reasonably likely to be caused to the processes of investigation, or the administration of justice by his doing so . . . '

[10] In *R v Chief Constable, ex p McKenna* [1992] NI 116, at 140g, Kelly LJ said: 'At common law a suspect held in police custody had no right to consult a solicitor'. But in *R v O'Kane* (16 June 1995, unreported, at p 34), cited by himself in *Re Russell's Application* [1996] NI 310, at 325h, Hutton LCJ said, on behalf of the Court of Appeal of Northern Ireland, '[w]e think that the common law position was accurately stated in the Home Office Circular No 89/1978 setting out the Judges' Rules'.

[11] Bennett (1979) paras 123 and 268.

[12] ibid, paras 270–2.

not to admit anything'.[13] Bennett was clearly uncomfortable with the status quo, noting that '[t]he exercise of this particular discretion of the police is... in practice virtually uncontrolled by the courts'.[14] But no reference was made to the European Convention. Bennett recommended that access to a solicitor should be a right after 48 hours, and after every further period of 48 hours if the detention continues that long.[15] Until legislation could be passed implementing the recommendation, Bennett proposed that the RUC's own Code should be amended to confer this right. That change did occur, so that from 1979 onwards a right of access after 48 hours was in practice guaranteed. However, in the survey he conducted of 60 persons who had been arrested, interrogated, and released without charge between September 1980 and June 1981, Walsh records that only 50 per cent had asked to see a solicitor: 'of these 76 percent claimed that they were refused and of the remainder who were allowed access none saw their solicitor inside the first 48 hours'.[16]

The report of the Royal Commission on Criminal Procedure in England and Wales, published in 1981, ultimately led to the enactment of the Police and Criminal Evidence Act 1984, which, for the first time, conferred on detained persons in England and Wales the statutory right to legal advice after 36 hours.[17] Presumably for the avoidance of doubt, the right conferred was expressly applied to persons detained under the terrorism provisions,[18] but for them the right became live only after 48 hours[19] and allowances were made for the special nature of terrorist investigations in the provisions dealing with the grounds available to the police for delaying access to a solicitor.[20] When, in 1987, the government was considering replacing the Northern Ireland (Emergency Provisions) Act (EPA) 1978, which applied only in Northern Ireland, it decided to replicate the PACE provisions on access to legal advice for terrorist suspects,[21] even though this meant giving such suspects in Northern Ireland greater rights than non-terrorist suspects (who did not gain equality until the PACE (NI) Order 1989[22] came into force in 1990). Bennett's recommendation had taken eight years to be translated into

[13] ibid, para 272.

[14] ibid, para 276.

[15] ibid, paras 277–8.

[16] Walsh (1983) 66. In some cases suspects were told that they had no right of access at all until 48 hours had elapsed, which Walsh (at 67) rightly describes as 'a blatant contradiction of the Bennett recommendations'.

[17] s 58(1) read 'A person arrested and held in custody in a police station or other premises shall be entitled, if he so requests, to consult a solicitor privately at any time.' As Lords Bingham and Steyn pointed out in *Cullen v Chief Constable of the RUC* [2003] 1 WLR 1763, at 1767F, discussed below, the protection conferred by this section could be described as the most important in the whole Act. Research for the Royal Commission had revealed that only about 11% of all suspects in police custody asked to see a solicitor.

[18] s 58(12).

[19] s 58(13)(a).

[20] PACE Act 1984, s 58(13)(c), adding two grounds to those made available in non-terrorist cases by s 58(8). Also, by s 58(14)–(18) a direction could be given by the police that a person may consult a solicitor only in the sight and hearing of another police officer.

[21] EPA 1987, s 15.

[22] Art 59. In one respect this provision did not go as far as the EPA 1987, s 15, in that it contained no equivalent to s 15(2), which required a person to be informed of the right conferred on him or her by s 15(1) as soon as practicable after being detained. Art 59 was expressly made inapplicable to persons arrested or detained for terrorist offences, but this did not mean that those persons had no right of access to a solicitor; it merely reflected the fact that their position was already covered by the EPA 1987.

statutory form ('prescribed by law' in the terminology of the European Convention). During that period, and after 1987 too, the police were allowed to delay access during the initial 48-hour period if certain conditions were fulfilled[23] and they did routinely exercise that power to delay. Failure to have the right of access made a reality was also a problem in England and Wales, as the Royal Commission on Criminal Procedure discovered, but there was never a comprehensive policy to delay access in the way that occurred in Northern Ireland.[24] In 1984, when Sir George Baker was reviewing the EPA 1978 prior to its replacement,[25] he had considered whether to get rid of the power to delay access for up to 48 hours, but he rejected this:

> Having, as was to be expected, had several submissions that any person arrested under the EPA or PTA should have an immediate and unconditional right to have a solicitor present, and the 48 hours period should be abolished I have discussed this fully with senior officers of the RUC. I am satisfied that the isolation of a prisoner is often necessary for several reasons, as indeed Bennett recorded. I conclude that an unqualified right of access to a solicitor would defeat the purpose of interrogation, the object of which is to discover the truth. I have here no recommendation to make.[26]

The regrettable point to be emphasized here is that at no stage in the discussions on access to a solicitor for terrorist suspects in Northern Ireland (including in the Bennett and Baker Reports) does any reference seem to have been made to the requirements of the European Convention on Human Rights, for the every good reason that even by 1989 the European Court had not stated categorically that all suspects, including terrorist suspects, had the right of access to a solicitor immediately upon arrest. More precisely, while the Court was prepared to allow such a right to be inferred from Article 6(3), it was also prepared to countenance wide-ranging restrictions on that right. This meant that any further litigation about the precise extent of the right of access conferred by domestic legislation could not be usefully informed by European Convention standards. The UK government certainly did not feel that it was under any pressure to grant detainees immediate access to a lawyer, even though the very first judgment issued by the European Court of Human Rights in a case from the United Kingdom (in 1975) had been one in which the right of prisoners to correspond privately with their lawyers was upheld in strong terms.[27] In the discussion which follows in the next two sections, two discrete aspects of the right of access to a solicitor will be further considered: first, the right of access immediately upon arrest; second, the right of access during interviews with the police.

[23] These were set out in s 15(8) and included situations where, eg, the police had reasonable grounds for believing exercise of the right 'will lead to interference with the gathering of information about the commission, preparation or instigation of acts of terrorism' (s 15(8)(d)).

[24] Philips (1981) para 4.95. In their joint dissenting judgment in *Cullen v Chief Constable of the RUC* [2003] 1 WLR 1763, 1768C, discussed below, Lords Bingham and Steyn pointed out that applying for relief in judicial review proceedings when access to a solicitor was denied was 'largely ineffective, notably because cross-examination on an application for judicial review, although not excluded, was in practice rarely permitted'. See too 1773D.

[25] Baker (1984).

[26] ibid, para 323.

[27] *Golder v UK* (1979–80) 1 EHRR 524 (decision of 21 February 1975).

The right of immediate access

The conferment of a right of access to a solicitor by the EPA 1987 did not, unfortunately, mean that in practice such access was then usually granted. More often than not access was delayed by the police on one or more of the grounds set out in the Act itself.[28] In fact, in the first four full years of the Act's applicability, 58 per cent of requests made for access to a solicitor were delayed.[29] It seems, moreover, that routine denial of access to a solicitor for the first 48 hours of detention was unchallenged in the courts of Northern Ireland until the early 1990s.[30] The problems facing a detainee are vividly illustrated by *R v Harper*,[31] where in the Court of Appeal of Northern Ireland Hutton LCJ carefully considered the arguments put on the defendant's behalf to the effect that his access to a solicitor should be denied only if the police were able to show that there was evidence that the anticipated adverse consequences 'will' occur.[32] The defendant's lawyers relied upon a dictum from the English Court of Appeal in *R v Samuel*,[33] but Hutton LCJ expressed disagreement with that dictum and instead preferred the views of Lord Lane CJ in *R v Alladice*.[34] He said it was enough if the police could show that they had reasonable grounds for believing that one of the adverse consequences will occur. Even though the police admitted in *Harper* that no suspicion attached to the solicitor whose access to the defendant was being delayed,[35] the court was prepared to affirm the police's right to delay access on the tenuous ground that the solicitor might unwittingly convey information to others after having consulted with his client. This was on the basis of evidence given by at least one senior police officer that this had indeed occurred in the past and by two others (including an Assistant Chief Constable) that it *could* happen.

The denial of access was again an issue a year or so later, in *Re O'Neill's Application*,[36] where Carswell J refused leave to apply for judicial review to an applicant who had been denied access to a solicitor while in police custody even though the offence about which he was being questioned (the planting of a hoax car bomb outside a police station) had occurred two years before his arrest. The main basis for the judge's conclusion was that it would be more appropriate to deal

[28] s 15(8). The commonest ground cited seems to have been that in para (d)—that access to a solicitor 'will lead to interference with the gathering of information about the commission, preparation or instigation of acts of terrorism'.

[29] *Statistics on the Operation of the EPA*, Belfast, Northern Ireland Information Service (Table 12, aggregated). See too Dickson (1992) 615–6.

[30] For a contemporary review see Colville (1991) para 4.2.

[31] [1990] 4 NIJB 75 (Hutton LCJ, MacDermott LJ, and McCollum J). The defendant was charged with supplying information that led to the murder of a UDR soldier, Alan Johnston, on 15 February 1988.

[32] These consequences were enumerated in the EPA 1987, s 15(8)(a)–(e). The one in question in this case was (d)—see n 28 above.

[33] [1988] QB 615.

[34] (1988) 87 Cr App R 64 (CA).

[35] Gerald Trainor, of Newry.

[36] 1991, unreported, but summarized in Hutton LCJ's judgment in *R v Chief Constable, ex p McKenna* [1992] NI 116, 126–8.

with this denial of a right at the criminal hearing itself rather than through satellite judicial review proceedings. The applicant had specifically alleged that what had happened to him was a regular occurrence, part of a consistent pattern of abuse of the statutory power conferred on the police to deny access,[37] but still the court was not prepared to address it head-on.

Another year elapsed before, in *R v Chief Constable of the RUC, ex p McKenna*,[38] the Divisional Court of Northern Ireland held that a police officer's decision to delay access to a solicitor[39] could be subjected to judicial review, but it said that the test to be applied in that review was whether the police officer had acted in good faith and had reasonable grounds for believing in respect of a particular suspect that the prompt exercise of the right to consult with a solicitor would lead to one of the results specified in the legislation.[40] Even though the solicitor in this case[41] had given a written undertaking not to disclose anything said during an interview with the applicant, this was still not enough to make the officer's decision unreasonable. Hutton LCJ said he was satisfied that there were reasonable grounds for the officer's decision because:

> the Provisional IRA is a completely ruthless and unscrupulous terrorist organisation which would be fully prepared by force or threat, against him or his family, to compel Mr McGrory, against his will and in breach of his undertaking, to disclose to it what the applicants had told him in the course of consultations.[42]

There is much truth in the learned judge's claim about the ruthlessness of the IRA, but one has to wonder whether that organization would have risked its future relationship with the legal professions in Northern Ireland by threatening a previously trusted solicitor who had promised to keep information secret.[43]

None of the cases so far considered reached the House of Lords, presumably because the lower court in Northern Ireland refused to certify (if indeed it was asked to do so) that a point of law of general public importance was raised, this being a prerequisite to any application for leave to appeal (which can then be granted either by the lower court or by the House itself). What did happen, however, is that no fewer than five cases from Northern Ireland touching upon the right of access to a solicitor were decided by the European Court of Human Rights. The first and most important of these, *Murray (John) v United Kingdom*,[44] was primarily about the right of silence, and is discussed in that context below. But at the Commission stage it was held, by 13 votes to four, that the denial of access to a solicitor during the first 48 hours of his detention was a violation of the applicant's right to a fair trial under

[37] EPA 1987, s 15(5)–(9).

[38] [1992] NI 116.

[39] Under powers then contained in EPA 1991, s 45.

[40] In s 45(8).

[41] Barra McGrory, the son of P J McGrory, who had acted for many people arrested under the emergency laws in the 1960s and 1970s. Barra later became the first solicitor to be appointed a QC in Northern Ireland.

[42] [1992] NI 116, 140c.

[43] For more general accounts of the dangers facing defence lawyers in Northern Ireland see Lucy (2003) and Flaherty (1994).

[44] *Murray (John) v UK* (1996) 22 EHRR 29. See Dickson (1996a) 1.

Article 6(1), taken in conjunction with Article 6(3)(c). One of the dissenters was the UK's Commissioner, Nicolas Bratza, who said:

> While I accept that the guarantees of Article 6 may require that an accused has the assistance and support of a lawyer at a pre-trial stage including during his police interrogation, the question in each case is whether a restriction on access to legal advice is such as to prejudice the position of the defence at trial and thereby deprive the accused of a fair hearing.
>
> In the present case there is nothing in my view to suggest that the restrictions had this effect. The applicant remained steadfastly silent at all stages of the proceedings from the moment of his initial arrest. His stance throughout his police interview remained unchanged even after access to a solicitor had been granted. In these circumstances I can find no indication that the rights of the defence were in the present case affected by the inability of the applicant to consult a solicitor at an early stage or by the absence of a solicitor during his police interviews.[45]

When the case reached the Grand Chamber of the European Court the Chamber's decision was endorsed by 12 votes to seven, but entirely on the basis that:

> ...the scheme contained in the [Criminal Evidence (NI) Order 1988, which affected the right to silence] is such that it is of paramount importance for the rights of the defence that an accused has access to a lawyer at the initial stages of the police interrogation... To deny access to a lawyer for the first 48 hours of police questioning, in a situation where the rights of the defence may well be irretrievably prejudiced, is—whatever the justification for such denial—incompatible with the rights of the accused under Article 6.[46]

The seven judges who dissented, including the UK judge, Sir John Freeland,[47] did so on the basis that on the facts of this specific case no unfairness had arisen:

> ...we conclude that the applicant has failed to establish that, in the circumstances of his case, the drawing of an inference against him by reason of conduct on his part before he obtained access to legal advice caused any unfairness in his trial and conviction. We therefore do not agree that the delay of access involved a violation of Article 6. We consider that the majority of the Court, in making the linkage at paragraph 66 between 'the scheme contained in the Order' and the right of access to a lawyer, strays unjustifiably far from the specific circumstances of the instant case.[48]

Post-*Murray* it was hard to see how the police in Northern Ireland could question someone in the absence of a solicitor and still then seek to draw inferences from the detainee's silence.[49] The judgment was issued just at the time when the Northern Ireland (Emergency Provisions) Bill was going through Parliament in February 1996; the Labour opposition tried to take advantage of the opportunity to urge the government to amend the Bill in order to bring the law into compliance with the judgment,

[45] ibid, 55.

[46] ibid, paras 66 and 67.

[47] The others were Judges Ryssdal (from Norway, President of the Court), Matscher (Austria), Palm (Sweden), Foighel (Denmark), Wildhaber (Switzerland, a future President of the Court), and Jungwiert (Czech Republic). Cf Dickson (1996a).

[48] (1996) 22 EHRR 29, 72 (para 9 of the judges' joint partly dissenting opinion).

[49] In its intervention at the European Court in the *Murray* case the Standing Advisory Commission on Human Rights had pressed for recognition of the immediate right of access to a lawyer in such circumstances and attendance of that lawyer at any interview with the police: SACHR (1998b).

but the government prevaricated.[50] It was not until 1998 (when Labour were in government) that the Attorney General issued new guidance to prosecutors advising them that 'they will not be able to attach any weight to the accused's failure to reply to questions in an interview conducted at the police station when access to legal advice has been delayed but that inferences may be drawn... if the suspect remained silent when re-interviewed after legal advice was obtained'.[51] But of course answers given by the detainee during those interviews *could* be used as evidence, so the police did continue their practice of questioning in the absence of a solicitor. This was despite the fact that in *Murray* the European Court had highlighted the problem facing a detainee in such a situation:

> ...at the beginning of police interrogation, an accused is confronted with a fundamental dilemma relating to his defence. If he chooses to remain silent, adverse inferences may be drawn against him in accordance with the provisions of the [Criminal Evidence (NI)] Order. On the other hand, if the accused opts to break his silence during the course of interrogation, he runs the risk of prejudicing his defence without necessarily removing the possibility of inferences being drawn against him.[52]

This scenario was precisely the one which confronted the European Court in the second of the Northern Irish cases to be decided on this topic, *O'Kane v United Kingdom*.[53] The applicant did not rely upon his right to silence but argued that statements he made before getting access to a solicitor (some of them before he had even asked for a solicitor) should not have been admitted in evidence. The Court accepted the UK government's argument that the case was different from Murray and consequently declared the application inadmissible, a clear sign that even in 1999 the Court did not consider that arrested persons had a fundamental right to immediate access to a lawyer. In the next two cases, *Magee v United Kingdom*[54] and *Averill v United Kingdom*,[55] the European Court confirmed that denying access to a lawyer without good cause to a person who is being questioned by the police is a breach of Article 6(1), taken in conjunction with Article 6(3)(c), but again this was in a context where adverse inferences might have been drawn from the applicant's silence during the police questioning. In both cases Sir Nicolas Bratza, now a judge in the European Court, went along with the unanimous decisions, despite his dissent at the Commission stage in *Murray*. In *Averill* the denial of access had been for only 24 hours but still the Court was adamant that Article 6(3)(c) had been breached. It repeated that it did not matter whether the applicant would have behaved differently if he had received legal advice, and it did not see any inconsistency between its stance

[50] HC Deb, vol 272, cols 83–4 (19 February 1996), per Tony Worthington MP and Sir John Wheeler MP.

[51] Home Office Circular 53/98 to Chief Officers of Police, referring to the guidance issued by the Attorney General to prosecutors.

[52] (1996) 22 EHRR 29, 67.

[53] App No 30550/96, decision of 6 July 1999. Sir Nicolas Bratza had by now become a judge of the Court. Even Judge Loucaides agreed that the application should be declared inadmissible.

[54] (2001) 31 EHRR 35.

[55] (2000) 31 EHRR 36. Mr Averill escaped from prison in December 1997 and is still unlawfully at large.

on this issue and its view that allowing adverse inferences to be drawn from a detainee's silence is not *per se* a violation of Article 6(2). Clearly the Court saw the right of access as a trade-off for the interference with the right to silence.[56]

In the fifth of the Northern Irish cases in Strasbourg, *Brennan v United Kingdom*,[57] the applicant's access to a solicitor had also been delayed for just 24 hours, this time on the ground that there was a risk of alerting other persons suspected of involvement in the offence in question, a murder, or of making it more difficult to secure the apprehension of such persons.[58] He was questioned by the police during those 24 hours but he made no incriminating admissions until after his request to see his solicitor had been granted (though before the solicitor arrived, more than a day later). In these circumstances, as in *O'Kane*, the European Court (again with Sir Nicolas Bratza amongst the judges) decided that Article 6(3)(c) had not been violated, although it did find a violation in the fact that the applicant's conversation with his solicitor in the period up to 48 hours after his arrest had taken place within sight and earshot of a police officer. That the Court came to a contrary decision to that reached in *Averill* is curious, the only material difference between the two cases being that in *Averill* the trial judge drew an adverse inference from the applicant's silence (though this was just one of the elements which the judge relied upon when finding that the charges against the applicant had been proved beyond reasonable doubt), while in *Brennan* no such inference was drawn. The Court had the opportunity to rule that the police had not sufficiently demonstrated a justification for delaying access to a solicitor for 24 hours, but it did not take it.

Eventually a case dealing with the right of immediate access to a solicitor (at least tangentially) did reach the House of Lords. In *Cullen v Chief Constable of the RUC*[59] the question was whether a terrorist suspect who, contrary to the requirements of the EPA 1987,[60] had not been told why his access to a solicitor was being delayed, was entitled to claim damages. At both the High Court and the Court of Appeal in Northern Ireland, where the four most senior judges heard the case, the plaintiff lost.[61] He also lost in the Lords, but only very narrowly in the face of a strong dissenting judgment submitted jointly by Lords Bingham and Steyn. The majority of the Lords,[62] which now included Lord Hutton, who had been made a Lord of Appeal in 1997, held that the duty on the police to give reasons for delaying access to a solicitor was a public law duty, for which the appropriate remedy was an application for judicial review, not a private law duty which could give rise to a claim for damages

[56] Merrills (1996b) 622: 'In effect, the Court's decision was a compromise... investing the right to silence with a relative character, but stipulating access to a lawyer as a necessary safeguard.'

[57] (2002) 34 EHRR 18. Judge Loucaides from Cyprus was also a judge in this case, but on this occasion he did not dissent on any of the points on which the UK government was exonerated.

[58] EPA 1991, s 45(8)(b) and (e).

[59] [2003] UKHL 39, [2003] 1 WLR 1763. Also discussed in Dickson (2006b) 403–6.

[60] s 15(9)(a). The facts of this case arose as far back as October 1989; even after it was decided by the Court of Appeal of Northern Ireland a further four years were to elapse before the decision of the House of Lords in July 2003 (the Northern Ireland Human Rights Commission assisted in the funding of the case to the Lords).

[61] MacDermott LJ in the High Court; Carswell LCJ, Nicholson and Campbell LJJ in the Court of Appeal: [1999] NI 237. Rather unusually, none of the three Lords of Appeal who gave leave to appeal (Lords Nicholls, Hobhouse, and Scott) ultimately heard the appeal.

[62] Lords Hutton, Millett, and Rodger.

if harm was suffered. Lord Hutton based his decision on the availability of judicial review, giving as an example of the lengths the courts are prepared to go to in that regard the speed with which hearings were conducted in *R v Chief Constable, ex p McKenna*.[63]

Consideration of the standards laid down in this field by the European Convention on Human Rights was, in *Cullen*, left to Lord Millett. He said that the right of a person detained in custody on suspicion of an offence to have access to a lawyer was 'implicit' in Article 6 and that serious consequences could follow the denial of the right (eg the person's detention may be unjustifiably prolonged in breach of Article 5, or his or her defence to a criminal charge may be compromised, resulting in a trial that was unfair under Article 6). Moreover in a memorable phrase he noted that, although Article 6 is stated as applying in the determination of a criminal charge, it nevertheless 'casts its shadow before it', by which he meant that 'it is engaged in relation to events which take place even before a charge is brought if they may affect the fairness of the trial'.[64] He observed, however, that, in *Murray (John) v United Kingdom*[65] the Grand Chamber of the European Court had explained the extent of an accused person's immediate right of access to a lawyer thus:

> National laws may attach consequences to the attitude of an accused at the initial stages of police interrogation which are decisive for the prospects of the defence in any subsequent criminal proceedings. In such circumstances Article 6 will normally require that the accused be allowed to benefit from the assistance of a lawyer already at the initial stages of police interrogation. However, this right, which is not explicitly set out in the Convention, may be subject to restrictions for good cause. The question, in each case, is whether the restriction, in the light of the entirety of the proceedings, has deprived the accused of a fair hearing.[66]

Lord Millett then referred to the fact that the delay in granting access to a solicitor, and the failure to explain the reasons for the delay, had not caused the claimant in the case before him any prejudice, because he made no admission until after he had eventually had an unsupervised consultation with his solicitor, whereupon he freely admitted his guilt.[67] Yet in *Murray v United Kingdom* the European Court had stressed that 'it is not for the Court to speculate on what the applicant's reaction, or his lawyer's advice, would have been had access not been denied during this initial period'. Lord Millett did not advert to that point in his judgment. Instead he rather presumptuously concluded that if the matter before him were to reach the European Court 'it would be bound to conclude that there was no breach of Article 6(1) or (3)(c) of the Convention'.[68] And, he said, even if there had been a breach, he would strongly set his face against making an award of damages:

> It would seriously undermine public confidence in the administration of criminal justice if an offender who pleaded guilty to a criminal offence and received an appropriate sentence,

[63] [1992] NI 116, discussed above.

[64] [2003] 1 WLR 1763, 1782F.

[65] *Murray (John) v UK* (1996) 22 EHRR 29.

[66] ibid, para 63.

[67] [2003] 1 WLR 1763, 1783H–1784A.

[68] ibid, 1784B, citing *Imbrioscia v Switzerland* (1993) 17 EHRR 441, on which see Merrills (1994), who favours the view of the three dissenting judges that, on the facts, Art 6(3)(c) had been breached.

after having already had the costs of his defence funded by the state, were in addition to receive a monetary award because of an error on the part of the police which had no adverse consequences to him. I think that the public would see the payment as rewarding the offender for his offence, and would ridicule a justice system which tended to be more solicitous of the offender than of his victim.[69]

Lord Millett did not make any reference to the *Magee*, *Averill*, and *Brennan* decisions, even though *Magee* and *Averill* had been cited by the appellant's counsel.

It is worth noting that in their dissenting judgment in *Cullen* Lords Bingham and Steyn were not able to draw upon any jurisprudence of the European Convention to back up their conclusion, even though they were able to cite support in the jurisprudence of the United States, Canada, and Ireland.[70] They also described the right of access to a solicitor conferred by the EPA 1987 as 'a fundamental right' and labelled the distinction drawn in the court below by Carswell LCJ between this right and 'constitutional' rights as 'fragile'.[71] Although not given much attention by academic commentators at the time, the *Cullen* case surely illustrates a deep division between the attitudes of judges in the House of Lords, even at a period when, under Lord Bingham's leadership as Senior Law Lord, the House was once again enjoying a high reputation for principled, thoroughly reasoned, and consistent adjudication.[72] What is more, the case illustrates the peculiar influence that can sometimes be exercised by a Scottish judge when adjudicating upon English or Northern Irish law: in *Cullen* Lord Rodger of Earlsferry said that he was reluctant to call the right of a detainee to consult a solicitor a 'constitutional' right because in Scotland, his home country, those detained for questioning by the police have no right to consult a solicitor at all (principally because in most cases such detention can endure for no longer than six hours).[73]

The Scottish rule, though, is now under review because in the interim the European Court has further developed its stance on the right of access to a lawyer. In *Salduz v Turkey*,[74] where a 17-year-old was detained and questioned about pro-PKK activities,[75] and then convicted on the basis of the statements he made during that time even though he did not then have access to a lawyer, the Court held that Article 6(3)(c) had been violated. Although the applicant's age played a part in this conclusion the main reason given seems to be that under the Turkish law

[69] ibid, 1790B–C.

[70] ibid, 1772G–H.

[71] ibid, 1772H–1773B.

[72] Dickson (2007b); Dickson (2009c).

[73] [2003] 1 WLR 1763, 1790H–1791B. Under the Criminal Procedure (Scotland) Act 1995, s 15(1)(b), a detained person has the right 'to have intimation of his detention and of the police station or other premises or place sent to a solicitor . . . without delay or, where some delay is necessary in the interest of the investigation or the prevention of crime or the apprehension of offenders, with no more delay than is so necessary'. Lord Rodger pointed out that recent attempts in Scotland to use Convention rights to challenge the leading of evidence of incriminating statements made by detainees before they obtained access to a solicitor had failed: *Paton v Ritchie* 2000 JC 271 and *Dickson v HM Advocate* 2001 JC 203.

[74] (2009) 49 EHRR 19 (Grand Chamber).

[75] The PKK is the Kurdistan Workers' Party, a militant group campaigning in Turkey for an independent Kurdistan.

then applicable there was an automatic exception made, in cases involving alleged breaches of State security laws, to the normal rule of domestic law that persons in police custody should have immediate access to a lawyer:

> In the present case, the applicant's right of access to a lawyer was restricted during his police custody, pursuant to section 31 of Law no. 3842, as he was accused of committing an offence falling within the jurisdiction of the State Security Courts. As a result, he did not have access to a lawyer when he made his statements to the police, the public prosecutor and the investigating judge respectively. Thus, no other justification was given for denying the applicant access to a lawyer than the fact that this was provided for on a systematic basis by the relevant legal provisions. As such, this already falls short of the requirements of Article 6 in this respect ...[76]

It seems that the European Court is creeping ever closer to affirming that the right of immediate access to a lawyer is almost absolute. There must now be 'compelling reasons' which 'exceptionally justify denial of access'.[77]

A side issue which arose during these attempts to copper-fasten the right of immediate access to a solicitor was whether a detainee has the right to insist that the solicitor giving advice is someone that the detainee has personally chosen. The question became controversial mainly because the man who was appointed, in 1992, as the first Independent Commissioner for the Holding Centres in Northern Ireland, Sir Louis Blom-Cooper QC, proposed that a State-sponsored scheme of 'duty solicitors' should be set up to ensure that when people were arrested they could very quickly be provided with legal advice. This was an attempt to blow a hole in the police's policy of delaying access to a solicitor on the pretext that there could be interference in the investigation of the crime. The Committee on the Administration of Justice and British Irish Rights Watch were not supportive of Sir Louis's proposal, and nor was the Law Society of Northern Ireland, and it was never implemented. But in the course of the debate it became clear that neither domestic law nor the European Convention guaranteed that a person should have absolute freedom of choice over which solicitor to be advised by (always assuming the solicitor was willing and able to act for the person making the request).

In sum, attempts to ensure that persons arrested in Northern Ireland on reasonable suspicion of terrorist offences should have a right of immediate access to a solicitor all failed in the courts. Neither Convention rights nor the common law went far enough to guarantee that such detainees would not be routinely denied such access. The right of immediate access remains fettered in Northern Ireland even today, but not more so than it is in England and Wales.[78] The EPA 1996 had allowed delays on the ground that access to a solicitor would 'make it more difficult ... to prevent an act of terrorism',[79] but that wide let-out has now been repealed.

In the past few years a number of cases have been brought to the Court of Appeal of Northern Ireland by persons who have managed to persuade the Criminal Cases Review Commission that their convictions for terrorist offences imposed many

[76] (2009) 49 EHRR 19, para 56.
[77] ibid, para 55.
[78] Terrorism Act 2000, Sch 8, paras 7–8.
[79] EPA 1996, s 47(8)(e).

years ago now deserve to be reviewed. Many of these have involved scenarios where incriminating statements were made by the suspect before he or she had access to legal advice. When considering these cases today the courts apply the statute law and codes that were in force at the time of the original trial, but modern standards of fairness and the current common law.[80] In at least two of the cases in which the Court of Appeal has quashed the earlier convictions the court seems to have felt that, even if other factors were not taken into account, such as allegations of police brutality or concessions by the prosecution that the person in question could not have committed the offence, the denial of access to a solicitor was itself enough to give 'a distinct feeling of unease about the safety of the convictions'. In *R v Mulholland*,[81] for example, the conviction by Lord Lowry CJ in 1977 of a 16-year-old youth for membership of a proscribed organization, an offence for which the youth then spent 12 months in borstal training, was quashed, with the Court of Appeal saying, rather disingenuously perhaps, that if Lord Lowry CJ had been aware of the breach of the Judges' Rules which had occurred at the time he would not have convicted the appellant. Likewise, in *R v McMenamin*[82] the applicant had served a period of borstal training after admitting to offences in the absence of a solicitor back in 1979, and again the Court of Appeal quashed the conviction. The best that can be said about such cases is that justice is better served late than never.

The right of access during police interviews

If access to a solicitor was not guaranteed during the first 48 hours of a person's detention, it was always going to be unlikely that the law of Northern Ireland or the Convention would accord the detainee the right to have a solicitor present during interviews with the police. It was hardly a surprise then, in 1995, when the Court of Appeal of Northern Ireland issued two decisions, both unfortunately unreported, confirming that an arrested terrorist suspect does not have that latter right.[83] The following year the matter came before the Divisional Court (which is bound by Court of Appeal decisions) in *Re Russell's Application*.[84] On that occasion there were in fact nine applicants, who collectively argued that the Chief Constable had adopted an unlawful policy, or practice, of not permitting solicitors to be present during police interviews of terrorist suspects. The court's decision, alas, is the epitome of how

[80] *R v Gordon* [2002] NIJB 50, following *R v Bentley* [2001] 1 Cr App R 21 (CA), where at [4] the court sets out clearly the four principles it thinks should be adhered to in such cases.

[81] [2006] NICA 32 (Kerr LCJ, Nicholson and Campbell LJJ). The appellant's counsel, Barry Macdonald QC, argued that denial of access to legal advice was in itself a violation of Art 6 of the Convention and that this alone should lead to the conclusion that the conviction was unsafe, but the judgment of the Court of Appeal does not express a view on that argument.

[82] [2007] NICA 22 (Campbell and Girvan LJJ; Gillen J).

[83] *R v Dougan* (15 June 1995); *R v O'Kane* (16 June 1995).

[84] [1996] NI 310. *R v Dougan* and *R v O'Kane* are briefly summarized at 335 and long extracts from the judgments of MacDermott LJ in the former and of Hutton LCJ in the latter appear, respectively, at 336e–340f and 340f–343d. This *O'Kane* case is the same as the one which later went to the European Court of Human Rights (see text at n 52 above).

deferential, even as recently as the mid-1990s, courts in Northern Ireland could be to police and government anti-terrorism policies. Hutton LCJ noted the number of people killed and injured during more than 25 years of 'the troubles' and he cited decisions of the European Court of Human Rights to support the view that 'a democracy, faced with the threat of terrorism on the scale which has existed in Northern Ireland, is entitled to amend its laws and to derogate to some extent from rights normally accorded to those within its jurisdiction'.[85] Having quoted at length from an affirmation submitted to the court by British Irish Rights Watch,[86] and to the affidavit of the then Chairman of the Criminal Law Committee of the Law Society of England and Wales,[87] the learned judge nevertheless concluded that to allow solicitors to be present during police interviews with terrorist suspects would be contrary to the general intent of Parliament when it provided for the admissibility of statements:

> The general intent of Parliament was that a statement would be admissible even though it was 'obtained as a result of building up a psychological atmosphere in which the initial desire of the person being questioned to remain silent is replaced by an urge to confide in the questioner'. I further consider that it was the general intent of Parliament that the police should be able (other than by improper treatment) to create 'a situation in which a guilty man is more likely than he would otherwise have been to overcome his initial reluctance to speak and to unburden himself to his questioners'.[88]

On the interesting question of whether the police had acted unlawfully in adopting a general practice to deny access to a solicitor, Hutton LCJ held that the decision of a chief constable to allow a solicitor to be present at an interview with a suspect was not comparable to the exercise of a discretion entrusted to a public body by statute: 'It is merely a decision to permit something which a person has no right to claim.'[89] That meant that it did not particularly matter whether the chief constable was operating, on the one hand, a fixed policy or, on the other, a general practice subject to some exceptions. The Chief Constable of the RUC seems to have operated a fixed policy in this context until January 1996 but thereafter each request was considered on its particular merits.[90] At all times, thought the judge, the chief constable was entitled to adopt the position he did.[91]

At the time when the *Russell* case was decided the judges involved would have known (although they did not mention it in their judgments) that 10 days earlier the Court of Appeal of Northern Ireland had certified in a different case that there was a point of law of general public importance involved concerning the admissibility of confessions made by terrorist suspects before they had access to a solicitor. The House

[85] ibid, 316e, citing *Ireland v UK* (1978) 2 EHRR 25, *Brannigan v McBride v UK* (1993) 17 EHRR 539 and *Murray (Margaret) v UK* (1994) 19 EHRR 193.

[86] ibid, 331g–333j.

[87] ibid, 334g–335a. The Chairman at that time was Robert Roscoe.

[88] ibid, 336b–c. The quotations are from Diplock (1972) paras 90 and 91, cited by Hutton LCJ at 321e–g.

[89] ibid, 358h.

[90] ibid, 359f.

[91] Campbell LJ and Kerr J delivered judgments agreeing with Hutton LCJ, though Kerr J said that if the chief constable had an inflexible policy of refusing access to a solicitor this would be unlawful: ibid, 365j.

of Lords later granted leave to appeal in that case and it was decided in October 1997 as *R v Chief Constable of the RUC, ex parte Begley and McWilliams*.[92] The House took into account a recent review of the EPA 1991 conducted by the then independent reviewer of terrorism legislation in Northern Ireland, John Rowe QC. Mr Rowe seemed to be supportive of current practice:

> Section 11 [of the EPA 1991], and the courts' interpretation of it, permit lengthy and persistent questioning, probably more so than PACE (NI): to allow solicitors to be present at interviews would be contradictory. Putting it another way, the regime of the holding centres contemplates that kind of questioning; but solicitors, quite legitimately, by advising their clients not to answer, would impair that regime.[93]

Apart from ignoring the point that the questioning of terrorist suspects could be just as lengthy and persistent in England and Wales, where solicitors could be present at interviews, this passage suggests that the reviewer saw solicitors as something of a nuisance in the context of aggressive police questioning. The sophistry was compounded in the judgment delivered by Lord Browne-Wilkinson when he commented that, because Parliament had re-enacted in the EPA 1996 the same provisions on this point as were in the EPA 1991, '[t]he conclusion is inescapable that it is the clearly expressed will of Parliament that persons arrested under section 14(1) of the PTA should not have the right to have a solicitor present during interview'.[94] With respect, such a conclusion is not at all inescapable, mainly because the point was not expressly addressed at any stage during the debates on the enactment of the EPA 1996. In any event, the EPA 1996 did not expressly ban access to a solicitor during interviews: John Rowe himself had explicitly said in his 1995 review that '[t]here is no express rule against it'.[95] It was, therefore, surely disingenuous of Lord Browne-Wilkinson to say that '[the] differential treatment of persons suspected of having committed offences under the terrorism provisions in Northern Ireland is plainly part of a *legislative* policy'.[96] It if *was* legislative policy, how was it possible for the then Chief Constable of the RUC, in 2000, to announce that he was changing police practice and allowing solicitors, as a general rule, to be present during interviews? Was he flying in the face of legislative authority: if so, why could he do so, but not the highest court in the land?

The latest issue to arise in this context is whether private conversations between detainees and their lawyers can ever be 'bugged' by police or security services. The very suggestion seems anathema, given the high value normally placed on the confidentiality of the lawyer-client relationship. In English common law the concept of 'legal professional privilege' is long-standing and revered.[97] But events in Northern Ireland have made it clear that the privacy of the relationship is not so sacrosanct after

[92] [1997] 1 WLR 1475. Also discussed in Dickson (2006a) 400–3.

[93] Rowe (1995) para 130. Later in the same paragraph he said the regime of the holding centres 'may be a breach of Article 6 of the European Convention. I am not asserting that it is.'

[94] [1997] 1 WLR 1475, 1481G.

[95] Rowe (1995) para 130.

[96] [1997] 1 WLR 1475, 1481C (emphasis added).

[97] It dates back to the sixteenth century.

all. In February 2006 a solicitor was charged with incitement to murder and perverting the course of justice, the evidence against him being based on covert electronic surveillance conducted by the police of conversations he had had with loyalist clients who were consulting him while they were held at Antrim police station. When this came to light other people held in custody who wanted to consult their lawyers (or, in one case, a consultant psychiatrist) asked the police to assure them that no such surveillance of those consultations would take place. When the police would not give such assurances, applications were made by way of judicial review for declarations that such covert directed surveillance would be unlawful. The Divisional Court of Northern Ireland[98] held that they would indeed be unlawful, but only because the requisite authorizations would not have been obtained under the Regulation of Investigatory Powers Act 2000 (RIPA). The applicants wanted a more far-reaching declaration to the effect that, even under RIPA, the surveillance would be unlawful, and they obtained leave from the Divisional Court to appeal to the House of Lords on that issue.

However, in *McE v Prison Service of Northern Ireland*[99] the applicants all lost, the House holding that, provided the surveillance was carried out in accordance with RIPA, the Code of Practice issued under RIPA, and the European Convention, communications between detainees and their legal or medical advisers *could* be bugged. The four judges in the majority relied heavily upon the fact that the relevant section of RIPA said that covert surveillance carried out in accordance with the Act 'shall be lawful for all purposes'.[100] This meant that the Convention's requirement that something be 'in accordance with the law' (the so-called principle of legality) was satisfied, but its other requirements (eg as to a fair trial) would also need to be met. Only Lord Phillips, the Senior Law Lord, dissented, because he felt that the wording of RIPA 2000 did not compel the interpretation that the statutory rights of access to a solicitor conferred by the PACE legislation were being qualified;[101] in other words, he preferred to apply the maxim *generalia specialibus non derogant*.[102] Given that the UK's constitution does not give a clear answer to the question whether later legislation that is inconsistent with earlier legislation should take precedence or not, the European Court of Human Rights, if faced with the conundrum, is likely to defer to the views of the highest domestic court on this point. The commencement of the Human Rights Act 1998 was, after all, delayed until October 2000 partly to ensure that by the time it started to apply RIPA 2000 would already be in force. It would be ironic, though, if, just at the time when the European Court seems on the brink of recognizing an almost absolute right of access to have a solicitor present during police interviews, it were to pronounce that this right can be qualified through covert surveillance conducted 'in accordance with the law'.

[98] [2007] NIQB 101 (Kerr LCJ, Campbell and Girvan LJJ).

[99] [2009] UKHL 15, [2009] 2 WLR 782.

[100] s 27(1): ibid, Lord Hope [63]–[66], Lady Hale [68], Lord Carswell [100]–[105], Lord Neuberger [107].

[101] ibid, [40].

[102] General provisions cannot qualify specific provisions.

Judicial review of prosecutorial decisions

In the early 1970s, when detainees complained that they had been subjected to ill-treatment while in police custody, their complaint was first considered by the complaints unit of the police themselves. Evidence could be passed to the office of the Director of Public Prosecutions if there was a suspicion that a criminal offence had been committed, but this rarely occurred.[103] In 1977 a Police Complaints Board was established[104] with a remit to oversee the handling of complaints by the police, but it led to little rise in the number of police officers being disciplined or prosecuted. The Board was replaced in 1988 by the Independent Commission for Police Complaints,[105] which was given increased powers to supervise the investigation of complaints, but these were still the primary responsibility of the police themselves. In 1997 an important report on the topic was published by Dr Maurice Hayes, a former Ombudsman for Northern Ireland,[106] and this led to the creation of the office of the Police Ombudsman for Northern Ireland.[107] For the first time complaints could be investigated completely independently by non-serving police officers. Still, however, prosecutions of police officers could take place only if the office of the DPP decided to proceed after having considered whatever evidence was passed to it by the Police Ombudsman.

Ensuring that errant police officers who used violence against terrorist suspects were brought to justice was a problem throughout the years of conflict in Northern Ireland, as we saw in Chapter 7, and, sadly, the European Convention did little to alter that. This was mainly for two reasons. First, the enforcement organs in Strasbourg took quite some time to impose an obligation on States to show that injuries suffered by a detainee in police custody were not sustained at the hands of the police. This obligation did not clearly emerge until the Court's decision in *Tomasi v France* in 1992,[108] where the French government could give no explanation as to the cause of injuries suffered by an alleged terrorist detained in Corsica and so was found to have violated Article 3 of the Convention. The applicant successfully argued that special vigilance was required of the Court in view of the fact that under French law he had not been allowed access to a lawyer during the interrogations, nor any other contact with the outside world.[109] Second, the enforcement organs in Strasbourg took even

[103] Under the Prosecution of Offences (NI) Order 1972, art 6(3), the DPP could specify the alleged offences with respect to which the Chief Constable of the RUC was under a duty to supply the DPP with facts and information, but there is no evidence that the DPP ever specified offences allegedly committed by police officers.

[104] See the Police (NI) Order 1977. Cf Walsh (1983) 109–11.

[105] See the Police (NI) Order 1987.

[106] Hayes (1997).

[107] Police (NI) Act 1998, Pt VII. For more details see Dickson (2005b) 223–6 and the website of the Police Ombudsman.

[108] (1993) 15 EHRR 1. The applicant alleged that he had been slapped, kicked, punched, given forearm blows, made to stand for long periods without support and with his hands cuffed behind his back, spat upon, made to stand naked before an open window, deprived of food, and threatened with a firearm. Amazingly the applicant claimed that this was just inhuman and degrading treatment, not torture, and the Court did not demur to that.

[109] ibid, para 112.

longer to impose a positive obligation on States to conduct a thorough investigation of allegations of serious ill-treatment, one that is capable of leading to the identification and punishment of those responsible for the ill-treatment. This was finally enunciated in 1998, in *Assenov v Bulgaria*,[110] some three years after a similar positive obligation had been imposed by the Court in a case relating to killings in Gibraltar connected with the Northern Ireland conflict.[111] The Court observed that if no such obligation were imposed:

> ...the general legal prohibition of torture and inhuman and degrading treatment and punishment, despite its fundamental importance...would be ineffective in practice and it would be possible in some cases for agents of the State to abuse the rights of those within their control with virtual impunity.[112]

Even with these (late) developments in Convention law there was still a problem in the domestic law of Northern Ireland in that if the office of the DPP decided not to prosecute a police officer for alleged brutality it was very difficult for the victim of the mistreatment to have that decision reviewed, let alone reversed. In *Re Adams*[113] the applicant had been hospitalized for three weeks after suffering serious injuries while in police custody in 1994.[114] He was then tried for serious offences, including conspiracy to murder and possession of explosives, and in 1995 he was convicted and sentenced to 25 years' imprisonment. By that time he had already lodged an application in Strasbourg, claiming not just a breach of Article 3 of the Convention, but also of Articles 5, 6, 13, and 14. While that application was being processed he also issued a civil claim for the assaults perpetrated by the police and in 1998 Kerr J awarded him no less than £30,000 in damages. Having been informed of this success the European Commission sought information from the applicant and his solicitors on whether he intended to continue with his application. But it received no reply, so the 30 Commissioners struck off the application from the list on the basis that the matter was already resolved.[115] It is unfortunate that the solicitors did not try to keep the proceedings alive, as they might have prompted the European Court into making a ruling on whether, for example, information obtained by the police from someone who was as badly injured as this applicant should have been usable against him at his trial.

Moreover, Adams had another complaint which was never even raised at Strasbourg. The DPP had considered whether to prosecute the officers who caused the applicant's injuries, but had decided not to do so. No reasons were given for that decision and the applicant was given no access to the investigation file on his case. He tried to judicially review the DPP's decision but failed, both in the High Court

110 (1999) 28 EHRR 652. Earlier cases, such as *Aydin v Turkey* (1998) 25 EHRR 251, had dealt with the matter as if it were solely an issue under Art 13 (the right to an effective remedy).

111 *McCann v UK* (1996) 21 EHRR 97.

112 (1999) 28 EHRR 652, para 102.

113 [2001] NI 1. The Northern Ireland Human Rights Commission was allowed to intervene at the High Court stage but not at the Court of Appeal stage (although that court did read the Commission's written submission): ibid, 4h–5b.

114 These included a broken leg, a punctured lung, two broken ribs, extensive bruising to the body, and cuts to the head.

115 *Adams v UK* App No 25526/94, decision of 29 June 1998.

and in the Court of Appeal. Those courts did not consider whether the Convention could assist in this context, but the uncomfortable truth is that it probably could not, given that the decision, not being one concerning the applicant's civil rights or obligations or determining a criminal charge against him, did not have to comply with the requirements of Article 6. In relation to the applicant's supposed right of access to the investigation file, the judges in Northern Ireland pointed out that the European Court had not yet said that such a right always existed and so denial of access did not of itself mean that an otherwise thoroughly conducted investigation had to be regarded as deficient.[116]

A few months after the decision of the Court of Appeal in *Re Adams* the European Court of Human Rights issued its judgments in a quartet of cases from Northern Ireland concerning the right to life,[117] and as a result the DPP's office changed its practice slightly with respect to the disclosure of reasons for not proceeding with a prosecution, but only in cases where conduct of the agents of the State had, or might have, occasioned a person's death.[118] The exception did not extend to cases where agents of the State might have breached Article 3 rather than Article 2. Article 3 cases are still governed by the DPP's general policy, which is to give reasons for decisions not to prosecute only in the most general terms, such as that there is insufficient evidence to afford a reasonable prospect of a conviction or that it would not be in the public interest to prosecute. If a request for the provision of more detailed reasons is made, the Prosecution Service will consider what further information may reasonably be given, taking into account the factors which militate against providing detailed reasons (such as the interest of victims and witnesses, damage to the reputation or other injustice to an individual, the danger of infringing someone's presumption of innocence or other human rights, and the risk of jeopardizing the safety of individuals) together with any other considerations which seem material to the particular facts.[119]

In practice, therefore, the lack of transparency in this context is as great today as it was during the years of serious conflict in Northern Ireland. Decisions of the DPP are just about as inscrutable now as they were then. For its part, the European Convention has not done much to ensure that people who are beaten up by the police can see the perpetrators brought to justice in a criminal court. What can be said, however, is that in recent years the Police Ombudsman's Office has brought a new broom to the scene. In the five years between 2003 to 2008 the Ombudsman recommended prosecutions of police officers in a total of 44 cases, many of these being cases where the officers had allegedly used violence; in nearly all of these cases the Prosecution Service did prosecute, and several convictions were secured.[120]

[116] ibid, 22c.

[117] *Jordan v UK* (2003) 37 EHRR 52; *Kelly v UK* App 30054/96, decision of 4 May 2001; *McKerr v UK* (2002) 34 EHRR 553; *Shanaghan v UK* App 37715/97, decision of 4 May 2001. These decisions are discussed in detail in ch 9 below.

[118] This is now set out in the Code for Prosecutors of the Public Prosecution Service of Northern Ireland, at para 4.12.4 (available on the PPS's website).

[119] ibid, para 4.12.2–3.

[120] Source: annual reports of the office of the Police Ombudsman. Unfortunately it is not possible to calculate from either the Ombudsman's annual reports or those of the police and prosecution services exactly how many of these prosecutions resulted in convictions.

The presumption of innocence and the burden of proof

Every non-lawyer is familiar with the adage that a person must be presumed innocent until proven guilty, and for once the adage reflects pretty accurately a golden rule of English law. Even when someone is caught *in flagrante delicto*—'red-handed'—the prosecution has to prove that the ingredients of the offence in question do exist.[121] In particular it has to prove that the accused person did the act which is an offence (the *actus reus*) and did it with the requisite state of mind (the *mens rea*). The prosecution does not have to show that the person knew that what he or she was doing was an offence (the adage that ignorance of the law is no excuse is also very largely true), but it must prove that the person acted with the state of mind required by law for that offence (eg intentionally, recklessly, or carelessly). The criminal law uses a wide range of different states of mind depending on the type of behaviour it wishes to deter.

When a legal system wants to make it easier to convict people of criminal offences one tactic it can adopt is to shift the burden of proving the *actus reus* and/or *mens rea* away from the prosecution, thereby requiring the accused person to demonstrate why he or she should not be found guilty. Another tactic is to allow the defendant to rely upon certain defences only if he or she proves that they are applicable, the best example of this in English common law being the rule that if a defendant wishes to rely upon the defence of insanity the burden is on him or her to show (albeit on the balance of probabilities only, not beyond reasonable doubt) that he or she was in fact insane at the time of the offence. There are obvious dangers associated with these tactics, because the person (if innocent) may be ill-equipped to make the demonstration in question. For example, if prohibited goods have been found under the floorboards in a rented flat, the tenant may be genuinely at a loss to explain how they got there.

The European Convention on Human Rights states categorically in Article 6(2) that 'Everyone charged with a criminal offence shall be presumed innocent until proved guilty according to law.' The reference to 'proved guilty according to law' leaves open the possibility that a State may create a law which allows guilt to be proved by a failure of the accused person to explain away certain facts. Before the troubles in Northern Ireland, legislation both in the United Kingdom and in the Republic of Ireland had long provided that if a person were found to be in possession of firearms or explosives the burden of proving that the possession was for a lawful purpose rested on that person. But the prosecution still had to show that the person knew that the firearms or explosives were present or knew that they were likely to be present and had deliberately avoided ascertaining whether they actually were or not. If, for example, a gun was found in a house occupied by four people, none of those people could be convicted of unlawful possession of the gun unless the prosecution proved such knowledge on his or her part.

121 *Woolmington v DPP* [1935] AC 462. Even today the fact that Woolmington was acquitted may seem remarkable to some. For a reminder of the case's significance see Hooper (2009).

It was to get round this prosecutorial difficulty that in its 1972 report the Diplock Commission recommended that '[t]he onus of proof as to the possession of firearms and explosives should be altered so as to require a person found in certain circumstances to prove that he did not know and had no reason to suspect that arms or explosives were where they were found'.[122] At the point where it discusses this recommendation the Diplock Report does not once refer to whether such a provision would run counter to the European Convention on Human Rights, but earlier, in a section headed 'Minimum Requirements of a Judicial Process', the Commissioners expressly stated that 'we would find ourselves unable to recommend any changes in the conduct of a criminal trial of terrorist offences in a court of law in Northern Ireland which would have the result that it no longer complied with the minimum requirements of Article 6 of the European Convention.'[123] They must therefore have assumed that such a reversal of the burden of proof would have been Convention-compliant. In 1972 there was little Strasbourg case law to verify the view that the proposed change to the law of Northern Ireland would not violate Article 6(2) of the Convention, and later case law has probably vindicated the Commission's position.[124] As we shall see in the next section, the House of Lords has also had to consider the influence of the Human Rights Act on so-called 'reverse onus' provisions and has largely endorsed their compatibility with Convention rights. The leading decision by the European Court in this context is *Salabiaku v France*,[125] where it said that States must confine such provisions 'within reasonable limits which take into account the importance of what is at stake and maintain the rights of the defence'.[126]

The Diplock Commission's recommendation concerning the burden of proof in relation to offences of possession was put into effect by the EPA 1973,[127] and was later re-enacted many times, not ceasing to have effect until 2002.[128] The provision said that a court may accept proof that a person and a prohibited article (eg a gun, ammunition, explosives, or a petrol bomb) were both present in any premises, or that the article was present in premises of which the person was the occupier or an habitual user, as sufficient evidence of the person's possession of that article at that time, 'unless it is further proved that he did not at that time know of its presence in the premises in question, or, if he did know, that he had no control over it'.[129] This provision was considered in *R v Killen*, where the Court of Appeal of Northern Ireland, through Lord Chief Justice Lowry, stressed that because the section 'erodes the protection of the ordinary criminal law... its application must be viewed in the most circumspect manner'.[130] The court therefore held that the section does not, in law, reverse the burden of proof. As soon as the defendant raises a doubt over his or her 'possession' of the article in question, the burden of proof shifts firmly back to the

[122] Diplock (1972) para 7(*j*), summarizing the discussion at paras 61–72.
[123] ibid, para 14.
[124] See, eg, *Salabiaku v France* (1991) 13 EHRR 379.
[125] ibid
[126] ibid, para 28.
[127] s 7.
[128] See EPA 1978, s 9; EPA 1991, s 12; EPA 1996, s 13; Terrorism Act 2000, s 77.
[129] EPA 1973, s 7(1).
[130] [1974] NI 220, 224.

prosecution to show beyond reasonable doubt that the *actus reus* and the *mens rea* of the offence do exist. This is an illustration of the ability of the common law to supply a degree of human rights protection even in situations where legislation seems to require otherwise. It was not until 2000 that Parliament formally endorsed the judicial position,[131] no doubt conscious that the statutory provision might otherwise be found to contradict, on its face, Article 6 of the European Convention.

During the troubles many people were convicted of possessing explosives, an offence under the Explosive Substances Act 1883. That Act provides that: 'Any person who... knowingly has in his possession... any explosive substance, under such circumstances as to give rise to a reasonable suspicion that he... does not have it in his possession... for a lawful object, shall, unless he can show that he... had it in his possession... for a lawful object, be guilty of a felony.'[132] No-one from Northern Ireland appears to have challenged the compatibility of this provision with the European Convention but a man sentenced to five years in prison in Ireland for the offence did do so,[133] having first failed to persuade the domestic courts that the provision breached his constitutional rights to the presumption of innocence.[134] He lost, with the Commission noting that in Irish law the 'persuasive' burden of proof remained on the State and, in those situations where an 'evidential' burden is transferred to the accused (as in the 1883 Act) it was in a 'saving or excusatory context', the maximum obligation on the accused in such circumstances being merely to 'raise a doubt of substance in relation to the prosecution's case'. This decision was a vindication of the common law's approach already advocated by the courts within Northern Ireland.

Proof of membership of unlawful organizations

A further context in which the placing of the burden of proof becomes important is where membership of certain organizations is unlawful. At the time when the Diplock Commission was deliberating, in 1972, Special Powers Regulation 24A was still in force in Northern Ireland. This made it an offence to become or remain a member of any of the 'unlawful associations' listed in the regulation, or to do anything to promote the objects of any such association. All of the organizations listed were ones which advocated the use of violence for political ends. The Diplock Report noted that the practical effect of listing organizations as unlawful was evidential: 'It relieves the prosecution of the necessity to prove in court each time that an individual member of one of the named organisations is charged that its objects or the means

[131] Terrorism Act 2000, s 118(2), which says that, in relation to s 77 of that Act (see n 128 above): 'If the person adduces evidence which is sufficient to raise an issue with respect to the matter the court or jury shall assume that the defence is satisfied unless the prosecution proves beyond reasonable doubt that it is not'. In *R v Shoukri* [2003] NICA 53 the Court of Appeal of Northern Ireland quashed the defendant's conviction on one count of possession because the trial judge, McCollum LJ, had not been referred to the change effected by s 118.

[132] s 4.

[133] *Hardy v Ireland* App 23456/94, decision of 29 June 1994.

[134] *Hardy v Ireland* [1994] 2 IR 550.

by which it seeks to attain them are unlawful.'[135] The Report indicated that the offence created was comparable to the common law offence of conspiracy,[136] where in every case the objective of the conspiracy would need to be proved by evidence. Proscribing certain associations—'provided that the power to name organisations as "unlawful associations" for the purpose of the Regulation is not abused by the [Home Secretary]'[137]—was a way of condensing the criminal process. Regulation 24A did not otherwise make it easier for the prosecution to show beyond a reasonable doubt that an accused person was a member of a proscribed organization, but it did say that when documents 'relating... to the affairs of any [unlawful] association' were found in a person's possession, or on premises in a person's occupation or control at which he or she was found or had resided, the burden of proving that he or she was not a member of the association was cast upon that person. This particular provision was not carried over into the EPA 1973, which simply said that possession of such documents 'shall be evidence of that person belonging to the organisation at the time when he had the document in his possession'.[138]

The Diplock Commission considered how else the law could be changed so as to make it easier to convict someone of membership of a proscribed organization, but it rejected two specific suggestions in that regard. The first was that evidence from a high-ranking police officer that he or she believed the accused to be a member of such an organization should have the effect of shifting to the accused the burden of proving the contrary. The Diplock Commission felt that this change to the law would be compatible with Convention rights provided the police officer was obliged to answer questions put on behalf of the accused concerning the grounds for his or her belief so that the credibility of the assertion could be assessed. But it went on to reject the proposal because:

> The need to preserve the lives of those who had provided the information upon which the police officer's belief was founded in our view makes it impracticable under existing conditions in Northern Ireland to permit the only kind of investigation of its validity which would be useful unless that investigation could be conducted in the absence of the accused and of his lawyers and without informing the accused of any matters which might reveal the sources from which information had been obtained about what the accused had actually done. But an investigation undertaken under those conditions would not satisfy the requirements [of the European Convention].[139]

Interestingly, the government of the Republic of Ireland did not wholly share these qualms. Under a provision of the Offences against the State (Amendment) Act 1972 in that jurisdiction (still in force) a statement of belief by an officer of the Garda Síochána not below the rank of chief superintendent 'shall be evidence' that the person believed to be a member of an unlawful organization was such a member.[140]

[135] Diplock (1972) para 21.

[136] Later largely codified within the Criminal Attempts and Conspiracy (NI) Order 1983.

[137] Diplock (1972) para 21.

[138] s 19(6); this later became EPA 1978, s 21(6), then EPA 1991, s 28(5), then EPA 1996, s 30(5). It was dropped from the Terrorism Act 2000. Irish law continues to have a similar provision, contained in the Offences against the State Act 1939, s 24.

[139] Diplock (1972) para 22.

[140] s 3(2)(b).

If this evidence is uncontested it may suffice to convict the defendant, although in practice the court will require corroboration.

The United Kingdom eventually succumbed to the temptation to enact such a law in 1998, in the aftermath of the bomb planted in Omagh by members of the so-called 'Real IRA', which killed 29 people as well as unborn twins. The Criminal Justice (Terrorism and Conspiracy) Act 1998 provided that if a police officer of or above the rank of superintendent states in oral evidence that in his or her opinion the accused (a) belongs to an organization which is specified, or (b) belonged at a particular time to an organization which was then specified, the statement is admissible as evidence of the matter stated, but the accused must not be committed for trial, be found to have a case to answer, or be convicted, solely on the basis of the police officer's statement.[141] There was considerable scepticism at the time as to whether this change would have any real effect (even David Trimble, the then leader of the Ulster Unionist Party, said in Parliament that he did not think any judge in Northern Ireland would convict someone of a membership offence simply on this basis[142]) and indeed no-one ever appears to have been convicted in this way. Kent argued that the Act as a whole would neither reduce terrorist activity in the United Kingdom nor bolster the peace process in Northern Ireland.[143] When the Terrorism Act 2000 consolidated the United Kingdom's anti-terrorism legislation the provision was dropped for Great Britain. It was retained for Northern Ireland,[144] but disappeared even there when most of the emergency measures ceased to have effect on 31 July 2007.[145] In the Republic of Ireland the law on membership of unlawful organizations was further amended in 1998 (again as a response to the Omagh bomb) to allow inferences to be drawn from a person's silence in the face of pre-charge questioning,[146] and this remains in force.

The second suggestion considered by the Diplock Commission for facilitating prosecution for membership of a proscribed organization was that certain kinds of conduct by a person should be taken as proof of his or her membership unless and until he or she proves the contrary; examples of the kind of conduct in question would be contributing to or collecting funds for the organization, distributing statements on its behalf, attending its meetings, or omitting to deny a published report that the person is indeed a member. The Commission noted that the first two forms of conduct were already criminal offences in themselves and that nothing would be gained by making them *prima facie* proof of another offence. Drawing inferences from the other two forms of conduct was just too impracticable (though the

[141] s 1(1) made the change for Great Britain by inserting s 2A into the PTA 1989; s 2 made it for Northern Ireland by inserting s 30A into the EPA 1996. See Walker (1999).

[142] HC Deb, vol 317, col 790 (2 September 1998). Trimble observed that, ever since republican defendants began recognizing the courts in the mid-1970s and simply denying that they were members of the IRA, convictions of membership, even in the Republic of Ireland, had fallen considerably. Trimble also said, at col 792, that he wanted to see the power to intern restored to the statute book.

[143] Kent (2000) 221.

[144] s 108. As Walker points out, the provision did not assist with later prosecutions for the Omagh bombing: Walker (2009) 277.

[145] Lord Carlile called for the repeal of s 108 in his report on the operation of the Terrorism Act 2000 in 2003: para 19.7.

[146] Offences against the State (Amendment) Act 1998, s 2.

Commission failed to note that the second of them had just been expressly permitted in Irish law[147]). So the Commission made no recommendations for changing the law in this area, even though the steps discussed would not have constituted violations of the European Convention. This shows that the constraints imposed on criminal justice systems by the Convention are sometimes not as great as those which exist within the systems' own national traditions, or those which are imposed by reality and common sense.

The proscription of organizations has been a legal tool used in Ireland, North and South, since the late nineteenth century.[148] But when the tool was fashioned for Great Britain too, in the wake of the Birmingham and Guildford pub bombings in 1974, a slightly different approach was adopted. The legislation in question said that it was a defence for a person charged with belonging or professing to belong to a proscribed organization to prove that (a) the organization was not proscribed on the last (or only) occasion on which he or she became a member or began to profess to be a member, and (b) that he or she has not taken part in the activities of the organization at any time while it was proscribed. The burden of proving these facts was expressly placed upon the defendant, whereas the legislation in place in Northern Ireland and the Republic of Ireland did not require the defendant to prove anything. It merely stated that a person was not guilty of membership of a proscribed organization if he or she had not taken part in any activities of the organization since the organization was proscribed.

This difference in wording between the two sets of provisions became very important in a case brought to court under the Terrorism Act 2000. Section 11(2) of that Act adopts the PTA approach—the defendant must prove the exonerating facts—even though neither the Lloyd Report, which the government commissioned prior to that legislation,[149] nor the joint Home Office and Northern Ireland Office consultation paper which was issued in response to the Lloyd Report,[150] gave any hint that this would be the case.[151] In *Attorney General's Reference (No 4 of 2002)*[152] the House of Lords held by three to two[153] that this provision created an evidential burden on the defendant, not a legal burden. This was because it may well be all but impossible for a defendant to show that he or she had not taken part in the activities of an organization at any time while it was proscribed. The majority of the Lords ruled that the defendant had to raise only a *prima facie* case that the defence was available before

[147] By the Offences against the State (Amendment) Act 1972, s 3(1)(b). At least one Irish judge thought that this provision was 'not consistent with the presumption of innocence or the burden of proof otherwise imposed on the prosecution in criminal trials' (Gannon J in *The People (DPP) v Cull* (1980) 2 Frewen 36) but the Court of Criminal Appeal in *The People (DPP) v Ferguson* (1975, unreported) seems to have adopted a different view. See Hogan and Walker (1989) 248–50.

[148] The *fons et origo* is the Criminal Law and Procedure (Ireland) Act 1887: see Townshend (1983) 207–21; Mulloy (1986) 10–12; Hogan and Walker (1989) 12–14.

[149] Lloyd (1996). This particular burden of proof point is not adverted to in para 6.12, the only paragraph in the report dealing with proscription of organizations within the UK. Ch 12 of the report touches on the proscription of organizations overseas.

[150] Home Office and NIO (1998).

[151] Nor do the Parliamentary debates of the time provide any enlightenment.

[152] [2004] UKHL 43, [2005] 1 AC 264.

[153] The dissenters were two of the House's most expert criminal judges, Lords Rodger and Carswell; they thought that s 11(2) created a legal burden but that it was still compatible with Art 6.

the burden shifted back to the prosecution to prove that no such defence was available. They came to this view by reading and giving effect to the provision as they were directed to do by section 3 of the Human Rights Act 1998, namely, '[s]o far as it is possible to do so . . . in a way which is compatible with the Convention rights'.[154] Despite the fact that the Terrorism Act 2000 had expressly set out a list of reverse onus provisions which were intended to create only an evidential burden of proof, and had excluded section 11(2) from that list,[155] the majority of their Lordships 'read down' section 11(2) to make it create only that kind of burden. In other words, had it not been for the duty imposed on them by the Human Rights Act these judges would have held the provision to be contrary to the European Convention.

This reasoning suggests that had the predecessors of section 11(2)[156] been challenged in Strasbourg the European Court would have found them to be in breach of Article 6(2). That they were not challenged is doubtless due to the fact that there were very few convictions for the offence in Great Britain. The government admitted in 1998 that there had been no convictions for proscription-related offences in Great Britain since 1990.[157] During the same period there were 195 convictions in Northern Ireland ('usually as the second count on the charge sheet')[158] but, as noted, the applicable legislation there did not require the defendant to prove anything.[159]

The subject of 'reverse onus' provisions is likely to remain a highly contentious one in the fight against terrorism. Continental European systems, as pointed out by Lord Rodger in *Attorney General's Reference (No 4 of 2002)*, do not recognize the common law distinction between 'legal' and 'evidential' burdens, so the locus for future contention will probably be when is it fair, reasonable, and proportionate to expect a defendant to prove something rather than the prosecution? Ordinary members of the public who are otherwise highly committed to the adage that everyone is innocent until proven guilty may nevertheless think it is not unfair, unreasonable, or disproportionate, in a context where what the State is trying to combat is extreme and highly dangerous terrorism, for persons who are very reasonably suspected of certain offences (because of the weight of evidence against them) to have to show, on the balance of probabilities (ie that it is more likely than not) that, for example, their possession of certain goods or their involvement in certain events was for an innocent purpose. As has recently been confirmed by the Court of Appeal of Northern Ireland,[160] current law (in both Northern Ireland and England) expects people who rely on the defence of insanity to raise *prima facie* evidence of their insanity before the burden of disproving it reverts back to the prosecution, so is it going much further to expect defendants to

[154] Lord Rodger [66] placed considerable store by the statement of the European Court in *Salabiaku v France* ((1991) 13 EHRR 379, para 27) that 'Contracting States may, under certain conditions, penalise a simple or objective fact as such, irrespective of whether it results from criminal intent or from negligence'.

[155] See s 118(5).

[156] PTA 1989, s 2(3); PTA 1984, s 1(7); PTA 1976, s 1(6); PTA 1974, s 1(6).

[157] Home Office and NIO (1998) para 4.8.

[158] ibid.

[159] EPA 1996, s 30(6); EPA 1991, s 28(6); EPA 1978, s 21(7); EPA 1973, s 19(7).

[160] *R v McQuade* [2005] NICA 2, in which the Court noted that in *Robinson v UK* App No 20858/92, decision of 5 May 1993, the European Commission of Human Rights declared a similar argument to be 'manifestly ill-founded'.

present a higher level of evidence when they are accused on strong grounds of having done something which is characteristic of the behaviour of a terrorist?

The admissibility of evidence

As we saw in Chapter 7, the European Convention on Human Rights is defective in the way that it deals with the right not to be tortured or subjected to inhuman or degrading treatment or punishment because it gives no indication of what the consequences should be if torture or ill-treatment is in fact used. Banning such practices is one thing, as is punishing those who use or turn a blind eye to them, but ensuring that the victims of torture or ill-treatment are not prejudiced as a result of their use is quite a different issue. Besides requiring in Article 13 that people whose Convention rights are violated have the right to 'an effective remedy', the Convention itself is silent about whether the victims of ill-treatment should, for example, be released from custody immediately, allowed to sue for compensation, or have any evidence obtained as a result of the ill-treatment declared inadmissible. The Convention does not even say that an accused person who has been ill-treated while in custody awaiting trial has the right to have the trial declared unfair under Article 6 of the Convention, though that may indeed be the outcome if the ill-treatment was serious and undermined the credibility of any subsequent conviction.

The silence of Article 6 is even more deafening in relation to the whole question of what quantity and quality of evidence must be adduced before a person can legitimately be convicted of a criminal offence. The term 'criminal offence', because it is expressly mentioned in Article 6(1), *has* been interpreted by the European Court, so we now know what characteristics an accusation must display in order to qualify, in the Court's eyes, as such an offence.[161] Some breaches of prison, police or army discipline, for example, will fall into that category. But the Court has not developed a set of standards around the type of evidence which a national court is entitled to bear in mind when finding someone guilty of an offence. Instead it leaves the determination of that matter to each State, just as it leaves to each State the choice as to what forms of behaviour to make punishable in the first place. In the words of Karen Reid:

> The admissibility and assessment of evidence is, primarily, a matter for the domestic courts. Whether or not the courts have correctly assessed the evidence is largely outside the competence of the Court.[162] There has only been a limited supervision by the Convention organs, having regard to their position that they are not a fourth instance, nor in an appropriate position to overrule the opinion of the local court who have first-hand knowledge and experience.[163]

The European Court does not even follow the rule that evidence which has been obtained illegally must be excluded from consideration by the national court.[164] The

[161] These are the so-called *Engel* criteria, taken from *Engel v Netherlands* (1979–80) 1 EHRR 647.

[162] *X v UK* App No 6172/73; 3 DR 77 (decision of 7 July 1975).

[163] Reid (2008) 119. The reference to 'a fourth instance' emphasizes that the European Court is not a further court of appeal that can hear a case even after it has been heard by a trial court and two appeal courts within a domestic legal system.

[164] *Khan v UK* (2001) 31 EHRR 45.

only question which the European Court asks is whether, in the round, bearing in mind all the circumstances of the case, the trial in question has been 'unfair'.[165] As John Jackson has pointed out, the Court has developed its own autonomous concept of 'unfairness' in this context, one which is different from what may be understood by that term in both common law and civil law systems.[166]

The EPA 1973 included a provision the purpose of which was to make it more difficult for judges to exclude confessions made by persons interrogated by the police in Northern Ireland.[167] It borrowed the language of Article 3 of the Convention, which was a clever ploy because it gave the impression that basic human rights standards were not being ignored. It is not so clear, though, whether even in 1973 the European Court would have agreed with the Diplock Commission's elucidation of what was meant by that language. Diplock said it:

> would not render inadmissible statements obtained as a result of building up a psychological atmosphere in which the initial desire of the person being questioned to remain silent is replaced by an urge to confide in the questioner, or statements preceded by promises of favours or indications of the consequences which might follow if the person questioned persisted in refusing to answer.[168]

In addition, Diplock did not justify imposing the burden of proof in this matter on the accused, but when the government implemented the recommendation it adjusted it so as to require the accused to adduce only *prima facie* evidence of the alleged ill-treatment, leaving it to the prosecution to then satisfy the court that such ill-treatment had not occurred.[169] In 1987, as a result of the Baker Report's recommendations in 1984, the provision was adjusted so as to trigger it in all cases where any violence was used or threatened.[170]

The Baker Report also recommended that the section on admissions[171] should be supplemented by a provision expressly recognising that judges still have discretion to exclude such evidence even if the prosecution proves that it was not obtained by the use of practices outlawed by Article 3. This had already been made clear by Lord Chief Justice Lowry in *R v Corey*,[172] where he said that 'there is always a discretion, unless it is expressly removed, to exclude any admissible evidence on the ground that (by reason of any given circumstance) its prejudicial effect outweighs its probative value and that to admit the evidence would not be in the interests of justice'. Whether Parliament, after its endorsement of most of what was recommended by the Diplock Commission, intended such a discretion to continue in existence, is a moot point, but

[165] Leach (2005) 254.

[166] Jackson (2005), especially 749–50.

[167] s 6(2).

[168] Diplock (1972) para 90.

[169] EPA 1973, s 6(2). The provision was re-enacted as the EPA 1978, s 8(2).

[170] EPA 1987, s 5, inserting a new s 8 into the EPA 1978, effective as from 15 June 1987. See also ch 7 above.

[171] The heading to EPA 1973 s 6, and its successors, refers to 'Admissions by persons charged with scheduled offences', but the sections themselves all refer to 'statements made by the accused', a much wider category of evidence.

[172] 1973, but not reported until [1979] NI 49.

the government did not act on the recommendation of Lord Gardiner's Committee, in January 1975, that the Act should be amended to make the discretion explicit. Baker thought this was because this might have made it look as if the exercise of judicial discretion up to that time had been unauthorized, but that is surely fanciful. In any event, the amended EPA 1978 permitted judges to exercise their exclusionary discretion 'if it appears to the court that it is appropriate to do so in order to avoid unfairness to the accused or otherwise in the interests of justice'.[173] This is very close to the draft provision included in Appendix J of the Baker Report and reflects the gist of the test proposed by Lord Lowry in *R v Corey*.

Surprisingly, although very contentious debates about how to amend the ordinary law in England and Wales on criminal evidence were taking place around the time that Sir George Baker was compiling his report, he does not refer to them. They resulted in the Police and Criminal Evidence Act 1984, which was later mirrored in the Police and Criminal Evidence (NI) Order 1989. That legislation, which does not apply to terrorist suspects, expressly confers a discretion on judges to exclude otherwise admissible evidence in certain circumstances, but it distinguishes between confession evidence and other evidence. In relation to the former, the PACE legislation says that a court must not allow a confession to be given in evidence except in so far as the prosecution proves (if the defendant suggests otherwise) that the confession was not obtained (a) by oppression of the person who made it, or (b) in consequence of anything said or done which was likely, in the circumstances existing at the time, to render the confession unreliable.[174] In relation to other evidence, the PACE legislation says that a court may refuse to allow it to be given if it appears to the court that, 'having regard to all the circumstances, including the circumstances in which the evidence was obtained, the admission of the evidence would have such an adverse effect on the fairness of the proceedings that the court ought not to admit it'.[175] Both of these are wider than the EPA provision, because the EPA provision does not talk about 'oppression', 'unreliability', or 'unfairness'. But as far as the European Convention is concerned these differences are immaterial. The Convention does not require the same rules of evidence to be applied across the whole criminal justice system and does not prohibit differential treatment of defendants depending on the nature of the charges they are facing. Being a terrorist suspect is not a 'status' for the purposes of the non-discrimination provision in Article 14 of the Convention, and therefore special criminal evidence rules for terrorist cases do not need to be justified unless they have been introduced in furtherance of some derogation to the Convention.

The right to remain silent

We have already alluded to the fact that one of the changes made to the criminal justice system of Northern Ireland in an attempt to make it more effective in combating the terrorist problem was to allow courts to draw inferences from a suspect's

[173] EPA 1978, s 8(3), as inserted by EPA 1987, s 5.
[174] PACE Act 1984, s 76(2); PACE (NI) Order 1989, art 74(2).
[175] PACE Act 1984, s 78(1); PACE (NI) Order 1989, art 76(1).

silence when faced with police questioning.[176] The change was made quite suddenly by the Criminal Evidence (NI) Order 1988[177] and was a direct response to specific terrorist incidents that year in which a high number of security force personnel had been killed.[178] The change applied only in Northern Ireland, and only in terrorist cases, but many felt at the time that the change would later be applied in England and Wales too, and be extended to non-terrorist cases, and that is indeed what happened.[179] It was also rightly predicted by Ashworth and Creighton that 'the most powerful effect of the curtailments of the right of silence in Northern Ireland and in England and Wales is likely to be felt in police-suspect encounters, before any legal advice is forthcoming and before the tape-recorder has started to run'.[180]

The compatibility of the Order with the Convention was ultimately tested in *Murray (John) v United Kingdom*,[181] which has already been referred to above in the discussion of the right of access to a solicitor.[182] It was found compatible at the Commission level by 15 votes to two,[183] and at the Court level by 14 votes to five.[184] The Court acknowledged that in many parts of Europe the conduct of the accused could be freely taken into account in the assessment of the evidence and so it refused to say that the right of silence was absolute, adding that it was obvious that the right to remain silent under police questioning and the privilege against self-incrimination 'cannot and should not prevent that the accused's silence, in situations which clearly call for an explanation from him, be taken into account in assessing the persuasiveness of the evidence adduced by the prosecution'.[185] The decision set out for the first time the European Court's preferred test to be applied in this field:

> Whether the drawing of adverse inferences from an accused's silence infringes Article 6 is a matter to be determined in the light of all the circumstances of the case, having particular regard to the situations where inferences may be drawn, the weight attached to them by the national courts in their assessment of the evidence and the degree of compulsion inherent in the situation.[186]

The *quid pro quo* for this decision, however, was an insistence, as explained above, that the suspect must have had the benefit of access to legal advice before any inferences from his or her silence could be drawn.

[176] See p 176 above.

[177] Ashworth and Creighton (1990) 122: 'The procedure was marked by lack of prior consultation and publicity, a dearth of evidence to justify the changes and the absence of any mechanism for detailed or effective Parliamentary scrutiny.' At 137 the authors describe the Criminal Evidence (NI) Order 1988 as 'a dog's breakfast'.

[178] A bomb in Lisburn on 15 June 1988 killed six off-duty British soldiers engaging in a charity fun run, and another in Ballygawley on 20 August killed eight British soldiers.

[179] Criminal Justice and Public Order Act 1994, ss 34–9. See Jackson (1991).

[180] Ashworth and Creighton (1990) 137.

[181] (1996) 22 EHRR 29. See Reid (2008) 152–3.

[182] See 175–7 above.

[183] The dissenters were Commissioners Busuttil and Loucaides.

[184] One of the five dissenters was Judge Walsh (Ireland).

[185] (1996) 22 EHRR 29, para 47.

[186] ibid.

The European Court's stance on inferences from silence was confirmed in both *Magee v United Kingdom*[187] and *Averill v United Kingdom*,[188] in each of which there was again a finding that Article 6 had not been breached except in so far as the inferences were drawn (or could have been drawn) at a time when the detainees had been denied access to a solicitor. In *Magee* a further relevant factor was the nature of the conditions in the Castlereagh holding centre where the applicant had been detained.[189] In other cases, not from Northern Ireland, the Court has gone on to stress that the right to silence is in fact an aspect of the right to be presumed innocent until proven guilty:

> The right not to incriminate oneself in particular presupposes that the prosecution in a criminal case seek to prove their case against the accused without resort to evidence obtained through methods of coercion or oppression in defiance of the will of the accused. In this sense the right in question is closely linked to the presumption of innocence contained in Article 6(2) of the Convention...[190]

As so often happens, the UK government took some considerable time to respond to the European Court's judgment in the *Murray* case, so much so that, more than 10 years later, it was still being criticized by a prominent Parliamentary watchdog on that score. In 2007 the Joint Committee on Human Rights noted that an interim solution had initially been put in place in the form of non-statutory guidance but that the statutory provision implementing the judgment[191] had entered into force only on 1 March 2007, after the completion of a review of the application of the PACE legislation in Northern Ireland.[192] By then there had been three further Northern Ireland-related cases on this issue dealt with in Strasbourg, two of them brought against Ireland and one against the United Kingdom. They were preceded by the European Court's decision, some nine months after its ruling in the *Murray* case, in *Saunders v United Kingdom*.[193] Taken together, as we will now see, these cases show that the European Court has come to adopt quite a strict approach to the right to remain silent—too strict for the likes of some prominent UK judges.

Saunders was an application by a chief executive who had been convicted in England of conspiracy, false accounting, and theft at the time when the Guinness company was being taken over by Distillers. The conviction was based partly on information he had given to government inspectors who had investigated the takeover, and whose questions he had been compelled by statute to answer on pain of committing a criminal offence. The European Court decided that his trial had therefore been unfair. Although this did not mean that the conviction was quashed,[194] and

[187] (2001) 31 EHRR 35.

[188] (2001) 31 EHRR 36. Judge Loucaides, from Cyprus, dissented. For him the right to silence is absolute.

[189] Mr Averill had been detained in the slightly better conditions at Gough Barracks holding centre.

[190] *Weh v Austria* App No 38544/97 (2005) 40 EHRR 37.

[191] Criminal Evidence (NI) Order 1999, art 36.

[192] 16th Report of 2006–7, HL 128 / HC 728, para 97.

[193] (1996) 23 EHRR 313. The decision was 16 v 4; this time the UK judge, Sir John Freeland, voted with the majority, against the UK.

[194] Three of Mr Saunders' co-defendants also won their case in Strasbourg: *IJL, GMR and AKP v UK* (2000) 33 EHRR 225. When they then tried to argue in the English courts that their convictions should

the applicant was not even awarded any compensation (having claimed £1 million), Lord Hoffmann has attacked the decision for not taking into account the history of the law on company fraud in England and for not articulating 'why it was improper, let alone a gross violation of human rights, for Mr Saunders to have to tell the inspectors about his actions during the take-over'.[195]

In the first of the European Court's cases related to the conflict in Northern Ireland, *Heaney and McGuinness v Ireland*,[196] the two applicants had been arrested in a house in Ireland a short distance over the border from where, a few hours earlier, a bomb had exploded killing five British soldiers and a civilian. In 1991 they were each convicted in the Special Criminal Court in Dublin of failing to provide an account of their movements during a specified period, contrary to the Offences against the State Act 1939, and were sentenced to six months' imprisonment. The relevant section of that Act provides that, if a person is detained in custody under the Act, the police may demand of him or her at any time 'a full account of [his or her] movements and actions during any specified period and all information in his possession in relation to the commission or intended commission by another person of any offence' under the Act.[197] It goes on to say that if the detainee 'fails or refuses to give . . . such account or any such information or gives . . . any account or information which is false or misleading', he or she shall be guilty of an offence and liable to up to six months' imprisonment.[198] The applicants challenged the constitutionality of this provision in Ireland, but the Supreme Court rejected their arguments,[199] holding that the right to silence was a corollary to the qualified right to freedom of expression conferred by Article 40.6.1° of the Irish Constitution and that the restriction imposed by the 1939 Act was a proportionate one: 'the State is entitled to encroach on the right of the citizen to remain silent in pursuit of its entitlement to maintain public peace and order'.[200]

The European Court, however, took a different view. Having noted that, at the time of their interrogation Irish law was still unclear as to whether statements made by the accused could later be used in evidence against them, but not making its decision hang on that specific point, the Court concluded that the degree of compulsion imposed on the applicants by the 1939 Act with a view to compelling them to provide information relating to charges against them under that Act 'in effect destroyed the very essence of their privilege against self-incrimination and their right to remain silent'.[201] Moreover, the government's security concerns could not justify a provision

be quashed as unsafe they lost (Lord Hoffmann being one of the judges hearing the case in the House of Lords): *R v Lyons* [2002] UKHL 44, [2003] 1 AC 976.

[195] Hoffmann (2009) 16.

[196] (2001) 33 EHRR 12. For an unspecified reason the Irish judge on the Court, Judge Hedigan, withdrew from sitting in the case and the Irish government nominated Judge Vajić, from Croatia, as his replacement.

[197] s 52(1).

[198] s 52(2).

[199] *Heaney v Ireland* [1992] 1 IR 580.

[200] ibid, 590. The High Court (see [1994] 3 IR 593) had held that the right to silence was protected under Article 38(1), which states, very generally, that 'No person shall be tried on any criminal charge save in due course of law', but the Supreme Court left that point open.

[201] (2001) 33 EHRR 12, para 55.

which extinguishes the very essence of the applicants' rights,[202] and in support of this view the Court referred to its decision in the Northern Irish case of *Brogan v United Kingdom*, where 'the fact that the arrest and detention of the applicants were inspired by the legitimate aim of protecting the community as a whole from terrorism was not, on its own, sufficient to ensure compliance with the specific requirements' of the Convention.[203] Each applicant in *Heaney and McGuinness v Ireland* was awarded IR£4,000 by way of compensation.

On the same day that it decided *Heaney and McGuinness* the European Court issued an almost identical judgment in *Quinn v Ireland*,[204] where the same issues had arisen, this time following an IRA armed robbery in Limerick which had left one police officer dead.[205] The decisions in *Heaney and McGuinness v Ireland* and *Quinn v Ireland* were a clear and bold signal to European States that in the fight against terrorism and other serious crime they cannot, in effect, shift the burden of proof on to the accused to explain their innocence, even when they have been found in very suspicious circumstances. Even the Irish Supreme Court's view of constitutional rights in Ireland seems to have been gainsaid.[206] But it has to be admitted, surely, that the provision in Ireland's 1939 Act did eat too far into a suspect's right to be presumed innocent. Even the UK government never went that far in the legislation it devised for dealing with terrorism in Northern Ireland.

The final case in the story is *Shannon v United Kingdom*, in which the applicant, who was the chairman of the Irish Republican Felons Club in Belfast,[207] had been fined £200 for failing to reply to questions about specific offences put to him by financial investigators under the Proceeds of Crime (NI) Order 1996. At the time the questions were put he had already been charged with the same offences, and the European Court consequently found that there had been a violation of Article 6(1).[208] The UK government argued that the right not to incriminate oneself could not be at issue in the present case because there had in fact been no later substantive proceedings in which the evidence could have been used in an incriminating way, but the Court dismissed that argument.[209] It also ruled that the security context ('the special problems of investigating crime in Northern Ireland'[210]) could not justify the application of the 1996 Order in the present case any more than could the security context in *Heaney and McGuinness*. And what also turned the Court in the applicant's

[202] ibid, para 58.
[203] ibid, para 57.
[204] App 36887/97, judgment of 21 December 2000. The same judges sat in both cases.
[205] This was Garda Detective Jerry McCabe. Four IRA men were convicted of his manslaughter. They were not released early from prison under the terms of the Belfast (Good Friday) Agreement 1998, which Morgan (2002) thinks was a breach of Ireland's international obligations (at 319).
[206] Given Lord Hoffmann's stringent criticisms of the European Court's decision in *Saunders v United Kingdom*, which was relied upon in *Heaney and McGuinness v Ireland*, one can but imagine what he thinks of the way in which Strasbourg supplanted Dublin's appreciation of its own legal culture: see Hoffmann (2009).
[207] Membership is limited to persons who have been 'imprisoned for their Irish Republican beliefs'.
[208] *Shannon v UK* App No 6563/03, decision of 4 October 2005. The Court awarded the applicant 1,750 euros as compensation.
[209] ibid, paras 33–5.
[210] ibid, para 38.

favour were the facts that it would have been open to the investigators to forward any information revealed by the applicant in his interview with them to the police, and also that any information revealed could have been used at a subsequent criminal trial if the applicant had relied on evidence which was inconsistent with it.[211]

From the quintet of decisions by the European Court examined in this section we can see that the Court has adopted quite a distinct approach in favour of protecting a suspect's right not to incriminate him- or herself. The approach is somewhat at odds with the Court's relative lack of concern over whether other types of evidence should be admissible or not, and it may seem rather counter-intuitive in a situation where other evidence against a suspect cries out for an explanation. The Court has, however, balanced its preference for the right to remain silent by acknowledging that it can be compromised if there are other safeguards in place to ensure a fair trial (eg access to legal advice, the need for corroboration, or restrictions on the use that can be made of information revealed).

The use of informers

The fight against terrorism relies a lot upon the work of informers—people who reveal information to the police about someone suspected of involvement in a crime. Informing the police about crimes is in fact a civic duty, and in some instances it is a legal duty. In English and Irish law, the information provided may be admissible in court, but the weight to be given to it by the jury or judge will depend on all the circumstances. Information supplied by an informer who is actually an accomplice of the person to whom the information relates—in slang such a person is called a 'grass'—is obviously not always as reliable as that provided by an informer who is not an accomplice. An accomplice's information may need to be treated with a pinch of salt because he or she may be trying to divert attention from his or her own wrongdoing and/or to receive a promise that he or she will not be prosecuted for that wrongdoing or, if prosecuted, will receive a lighter than usual sentence for it. In Northern Ireland informer evidence from accomplices and non-accomplices began to be used in the early years of the troubles, in line with Brigadier Kitson's theories about low intensity counter-insurgency operations.[212] In his valuable account of this period Steven Greer says that 'throughout 1971–5 the army became the eyes and ears of the law enforcement system in Northern Ireland, especially in republican areas which were too dangerous for the police to penetrate alone'.[213]

The traditional common law rule concerning the admissibility of evidence given by an accomplice to a crime was that it can be admitted but that it would be dangerous (although not impossible) to convict someone solely on the basis of accomplice evidence and in the absence of some other corroborative evidence. In 1954 the House of Lords said that a rule of law had by then become firmly established whereby judges were under a duty to warn juries that it would be dangerous to convict someone on uncorroborated accomplice evidence.[214] Strangely, none of the committees appointed to consider

[211] ibid, paras 39–40. [212] See Kitson (1971) and Newsinger (2002).
[213] Greer (1995) 35. See too Greer (1986); Hillyard and Percy-Smith (1984).
[214] *Davies v DPP* [1954] AC 378.

the legal measures that should be put in place to deal with terrorism in Northern Ireland considered the possibility of changing this common law rule on informers, just as Parliament and the government steered away from considering changes to other areas of the law, such as when it is lawful to discharge a firearm knowing it might kill someone.[215] In the absence of special laws on the use of informers the prosecution service in Northern Ireland (a new such service, independent of the police, had been established in 1972[216]) decided in the late 1970s and early 1980s that it would make greater use of informers. The police and army handlers of informers somehow persuaded a number of prominent paramilitaries to provide evidence against their erstwhile colleagues in exchange for immunity from prosecution for their own crimes or for a reduction in sentence if tried and found guilty. The story of these 'supergrass' trials has been thoroughly told elsewhere,[217] and in the end the reputation of the Northern Ireland legal system was restored through the Court of Appeal quashing the convictions of most of the individuals who were convicted in the Crown Court on the word of a supergrass.[218] It did so on the basis that the evidence was simply not credible enough to leave no reasonable doubt about the guilt of the people who were accused by the informers.

The European Convention seems to have played virtually no part in the challenges raised against the supergrass system by the victims of it or by external campaigning groups. Steven Greer argues that a human rights perspective provides the best normative critique of the supergrass system, yet at no point does he suggest that a useful specific source for that normative critique could be the European Convention. That document was, quite simply, irrelevant to the supergrass phenomenon. It seems that none of those defendants whose convictions were not quashed on appeal decided to lodge an application in Strasbourg alleging that their trial had been unfair under Article 6 of the Convention. Given that the European Court expressly denies that it is a further tier of appeal in criminal cases, and that it is very reluctant to second-guess the way a national court weighs up the evidence put in front of it, it is unlikely that any such application would have been declared admissible, let alone ultimately successful. In all of these cases it would appear that there was other evidence against the accused which might have been enough to produce a conviction even in the absence of the supergrass evidence.[219] The European Commission has held that if the

[215] See ch 9 below.

[216] Pursuant to the Prosecution of Offences (NI) Order 1972, the first Order in Council to be made under the 'direct rule' arrangements in Northern Ireland (see ch 2). Remarkably, only two individuals have held the post of Director of Public Prosecutions in the 37 years of the post's existence—Sir Basil Shaw (from 1972 to 1989) and Sir Alasdair Fraser (from 1989 to the present).

[217] See Greer (1995); Gifford (1984); Boyd (1984); Jackson (1985).

[218] eg, in *R v Graham* (the Joseph Bennett case, named after the supergrass involved) 14 of the original 16 defendants were convicted in April 1983, but all 14 had their convictions quashed on appeal in December 1984; in *R v Donnelly* (the Christopher Black case) 35 of the original 38 defendants were convicted in August 1983, but 18 of these had their convictions quashed in July 1987; and in *R v Steenson* (the Harry Kirkpatrick case) all of the original 27 defendants were convicted in December 1985 but 24 of these had their convictions quashed in December 1987.

[219] See Appendix C in Greer (1995) 287. He suggests that of the 79 guilty verdicts which survived an appeal, there was confession evidence against the accused in 55 cases, in 12 cases the accused was arrested at the scene of the crime, in six cases there was forensic evidence implicating the accused, in six cases the accused's silence was taken as corroboration, and in four cases there was a guilty plea.

testimony of an informer is open to challenge but is not the only evidence against the accused, the trial is likely to be fair.[220]

In cases where witnesses in terrorist trials or inquiries in Northern Ireland have sought protection from being publicly identified, the right of the defendant or of others to a fair hearing can clash with the right to life of the witnesses, because many of them fear being personally attacked by allies of the defendant. These cases are discussed in the following chapter of this book.

The right to jury trial

The most memorable recommendation in the Diplock Commission report of 1972 was that people charged with terrorist offences in Northern Ireland (since known as 'scheduled' offences, because they were listed in a Schedule to the EPA 1973[221]) should be tried in the absence of a jury. The twin justification for this recommendation was that jurors would be intimidated by paramilitary organizations and would be tempted to deliver biased verdicts depending on which side of the community they came from. The Commission also pointed out that the property qualification for jury service meant that the pool of potential jurors was dominated by Protestants to an even greater extent than the population as a whole, and that the right of the defence and prosecution to peremptorily challenge the suitability of a potential juror was exercised more vigorously in Northern Ireland than in England. It suggested, too, that with increasing loyalist violence there was a risk of loyalist defendants being perversely acquitted, with more use therefore having to be made of detention without trial as a way of combating terrorism. The Commission concluded: 'The jury system as a means for trying terrorist crime is under strain. It may not yet have broken down, but we think that the time is already ripe to forestall its doing so.'[222]

Lord Diplock and his colleagues therefore proposed that trials of suspected terrorists should be conducted without a jury (but that counts for scheduled and non-scheduled offences should not be joined in the same indictment). They preferred having a single judge as opposed to a collegiate bench because:

> [i]t would gravely inconvenience the progress of the trial and diminish the value of oral examination and cross-examination as a means of eliciting the truth, if a plurality of judges had to consult together, albeit briefly, before each ruling [on admissibility of evidence and other matters of procedure] was made.[223]

The Commission recommended that the trial judge should indicate how he has directed himself on the law relating to the offence charged, and that the existing rights of appeal should apply.

[220] *Baragiola v Switzerland* App No 17265/90 (1993) 75 DR 76; see generally Emmerson, Ashworth and Macdonald (2007) 611–5.

[221] EPA 1973, Sch 4; later re-enacted as EPA 1978, Sch 4; EPA 1991, Sch 1; EPA 1996, Sch 1; Terrorism Act 2000, Sch 9.

[222] Diplock (1972) para 37.

[223] ibid, para 39. For later views on 3-judge courts see Jackson (1986).

When the resultant EPA emerged from Parliament (coming into force on 9 August 1973), it more or less mirrored what the Diplock Commission had recommended.[224] Counts alleging non-scheduled offences were to be disregarded if mixed with counts alleging scheduled offences, trials were to be conducted without a jury, there was to be one judge per trial rather than a plurality of judges, and when convicting a defendant the judge had to give a judgment stating the reasons for the conviction. But the Act went further than the Diplock Commission as regards appeal rights: convicted defendants were given the right to appeal, against conviction and/or against the sentence imposed, without first having to obtain any permission to appeal, as defendants in non-terrorist cases had to do. In addition, while the Act specified a long list of scheduled offences it allowed the Attorney General for Northern Ireland to certify that in any particular case the offences of murder, manslaughter, or causing grievous bodily harm should not be treated as such—they could be 'de-scheduled'.[225] Robbery and aggravated burglary were declared to be scheduled offences only where an explosive, firearm, imitation firearm, or offensive weapon was used in the course of the offence.[226] This still meant, for example, that armed bank robbers with no connection whatsoever to paramilitary organizations still had to be tried in the absence of a jury. One researcher calculated that 40 per cent of all Diplock cases involved defendants whose actions were not taken on behalf of paramilitaries.[227]

The removal of trial by jury was not a breach of Article 6 of the European Convention, because the Convention does not guarantee the right to jury trial, even in countries where such a form of trial has a long and honourable tradition.[228] Continental European countries have little experience of juries, and jury trials are certainly not a part of their legal heritage. Even though British lawyers were centrally involved in the drafting of the Convention, they did not argue for the inclusion of jury trial as a basic requirement of a fair trial. It would in any event have been difficult to sustain such an argument since in the United Kingdom the vast majority of criminal offences were even then, as they still are, tried in magistrates' courts without a jury.[229] Attempts to suggest that a person has received an unfair trial as guaranteed by Article 6 of the Convention because he or she has been tried in a juryless Diplock court are bound to fail, provided the domestic law's requirements for the use of the court in that particular case have been satisfied. Nor can it be argued that having one kind of criminal trial for terrorist suspects and a different kind for non-terrorist suspects is a breach of Article 14 of the Convention, the non-discrimination provision, because the two sets of defendants could not be said to have a different 'status' within

[224] EPA 1973, s 2; later re-enacted as EPA 1978, s 7; EPA 1991, s 10; EPA 1996, s 11; Terrorism Act 2000, s 75.

[225] Sch 4, Pt I, Notes 1 and 2.

[226] ibid, Note 4. Walsh (1983) 82 comments that of the 55 individuals in his survey who were accused of robbery, 'over 87 per cent appeared to have been carried out for ordinary criminal motives'.

[227] Walsh (1983) 59–60.

[228] Reid (2008) 143–6.

[229] In the US, Art III (2)(3) of the Constitution states categorically that '[t]he trial of all Crimes, except in Cases of Impeachment shall be by Jury', but even there 'petty' crimes can be dealt with in the absence of a jury, a petty crime being one that does not carry a possible prison sentence of more than six months: *Baldwin v New York* 399 US 66 (1970; US Sup Ct).

the terms of that provision. An argument that the Diplock court system was applied in a discriminatory way because it was used disproportionately to try republican rather than loyalist defendants would not have convinced the European Commission or Court, because no convincing evidence can be produced to substantiate such a claim. Walsh did find in his 1981 survey that republicans were almost three times more likely than loyalists to receive a non-custodial sentence, but he suggested this may have been due to the fact that republicans were more likely to be charged with relatively minor or peripheral offences, and to be first-time offenders.[230] He was also very guarded in his findings regarding discrimination in the length of custodial sentences.[231] Likewise, it is not possible to argue that an appeal should take place before a jury because a jury was used at the trial itself: this is what the Birmingham Six claimed when the Court of Appeal first looked at new evidence in their case, but the European Commission rejected the argument.[232]

The Convention also does not prohibit the establishment of special courts for special kinds of suspects, provided only that the courts established are impartial and independent. The Republic of Ireland, with its Special Criminal Court in Dublin,[233] has taken advantage of this permissive attitude just as readily as the United Kingdom, and this arrangement is as immune from challenge under the European Convention as the Northern Irish system is. When two applicants complained about being tried by the Special Criminal Court on the basis that the offences with which they were charged were not 'political', they too failed in Strasbourg.[234] In that case the Commission said:

> The Commission is satisfied that the Special Criminal Court sitting in the applicant's case was independent and impartial...The Commission does not feel called upon to determine the question, disputed between the parties, whether the bank robbery of which the applicants were convicted constituted a political offence. It notes that the Special Criminal Court is competent not only for the trial of persons charged with offences scheduled in the Offences against the State Act but, under the conditions set out in section 46 of the Act, also for the trial of persons charged with non-scheduled offences, as in the applicants' case.[235]

Interestingly, the Special Criminal Court has not been immune from challenge under the International Covenant on Civil and Political Rights. Article 26 of that Covenant begins by saying: 'All persons are equal before the law and are entitled without any discrimination to the equal protection of the law', and from 8 March 1990 the Irish government has accepted the jurisdiction of the UN's Human Rights Committee to hear complaints brought by individuals alleging that their rights under the Covenant have been violated by the Irish State.[236] In *Kavanagh v Ireland* the Human Rights Committee found that Ireland had violated the complainant's right

[230] Walsh (1983) 101.

[231] ibid, 102–4.

[232] *Callaghan and others v UK* App No 14739/89, 60 DR 296 (decision of 9 May 1989).

[233] See, generally, Davis (2007).

[234] *X and Y v Ireland* App No 8299/78, 22 DR 51 (decision of 10 October 1980). See also the section on extradition, below.

[235] ibid, paras 19–20.

[236] The UK has still not recognized such a right.

under Article 26 because it had failed to demonstrate that the decision to try him before the Special Criminal Court for the offences of false imprisonment, demanding money with menaces, and possession of a firearm was based upon reasonable and objective grounds.[237] Regrettably, no comparable decision could be taken by the European Court of Human Rights. In 2005 a man from North Africa who was accused of terrorist offences in Northern Ireland which were not connected with the conflict there was tried and convicted in a Diplock court. Neither at the trial stage[238] nor at the appeal stage[239] (where the accused again lost) was there a challenge based on the European Convention to the State's right to use a Diplock court to try a type of case it was not originally designed to deal with. Jackson and Doran have also highlighted the fact that the 'presumption against jury trial' in the EPAs meant that numerous defendants were tried in Diplock courts even though their offences did not have paramilitary connections.[240]

The key question in this context is whether trials without a jury are any less reliable than trials with a jury when it comes to determining whether the accused is guilty of the offence charged. If there were clear evidence to show that one type of trial was significantly less fair than the other this would help to sustain a claim that the former is unfair in terms of Article 6 or that there was improper discrimination in terms of Article 14. But the largest study undertaken on this issue, by Jackson and Doran, supplies little such evidence.[241] They demonstrate that the two forms of trial mean that the judges and the lawyers involved behave differently, but it is difficult if not impossible to deduce from this that one form of behaviour tends to lead to greater unfairness. Moreover, while the analysis by Jackson and Doran of appeals against convictions between 1987 and 1993 shows that a greater proportion of Diplock defendants than 'ordinary' defendants appealed but that their success rate was much lower (16 per cent as opposed to 32 per cent), these facts tell us nothing about the relative fairness of the two forms of trial. A study conducted a decade earlier, by Steven Greer and Antony White, is no more informative on this point, focusing as it does on what they see as the lack of any continuing justification or need for the Diplock system and on a practical scheme that could be put in its place whereby juries could be restored but the risk of perverse verdicts and the intimidation of jurors avoided.[242] An analysis based on a study commissioned by Amnesty International, published in 1984, showed that the single most important issue affecting the fairness

[237] Communication No 819/1998 (view adopted 4 April 2001), CCPR/C/71/D/819/1998, available at <http://www1.umn.edu/humanrts/undocs/819–1998.html>.

[238] *R v Abbas Boutrab* [2005] NICC 36 (Weatherup J).

[239] [2007] NICA 23.

[240] Jackson and Doran (1992). Challenging the Attorney General's refusal to de-schedule an offence in a particular case was difficult because the Attorney General's discretion on prosecution issues is generally deemed to be non-justiciable: see the line of cases beginning with the decision by the Court of Appeal of England and Wales in *Gouriet v Union of Post Office Workers* [1977] 1 QB 729 (the case went on to the House of Lords, but not on this point), discussed in Miller and Feldman (1997).

[241] Jackson and Doran (1995). For a much briefer, more politically grounded appraisal, which still concludes that the Diplock courts gained a degree of acceptance among nationalists in Northern Ireland, see Carlton (1981). A contrary view is expounded by Harvey (1981).

[242] Greer and White (1986).

of Diplock trials was the reliability of confessions obtained during interrogation—the trials themselves, as opposed to pre-trial procedures, were found to be in accordance with fundamental international principles safeguarding the right to a fair trial, though the effect of 'case-hardening' on the objectivity of the judges was noted as a concern.[243]

In jury trials, when a challenge is made to the admissibility of some evidence, the jury is dismissed from the courtroom and a hearing, called a *voir dire*, takes place in front of the judge alone, allowing him or her to focus on the legal rules applicable to admissibility. If the evidence is declared inadmissible the jury never gets to hear it and so cannot be prejudiced by it, consciously or subconsciously. In non-jury trials a separate hearing dealing with admissibility can still take place, but if the evidence is declared inadmissible, and the case resumes under the same judge, there is the possibility that he or she will nevertheless be influenced by what was revealed at the hearing—even though judges are supposedly trained to put extraneous considerations out of their mind. The EPA 1973 made provision for (but did not require) a trial to be restarted before a differently constituted court in situations where evidence had been received in evidence which the prosecution could not show had not been obtained through the use of torture or inhuman or degrading treatment, but in practice it seems that that discretion was rarely exercised and in any event it did not apply to other situations where the judge had had to give a ruling on the admissibility of evidence. In one of the most high profile cases involving a *voir dire*, *R v Brophy*, where the defendant had been charged with 12 murders and 36 offences connected with explosives or firearms, the trial judge was not satisfied that the statements made by him while he was in custody had not been induced by torture or inhuman or degrading treatment. The judge therefore acquitted him of those offences[244] but, on the basis that during the *voir dire* Brophy had confessed to being a member of the IRA, the judge convicted him of that offence. The Court of Appeal allowed Brophy's appeal,[245] and an attempt by the Crown to have this reversed in the Lords was unsuccessful, though without reference to Article 6 of the Convention.[246] Lord Diplock was himself a member of the court that decided that appeal. Had the Crown won that appeal it is possible that Brophy could have lodged an application in Strasbourg and eventually obtained a judgment that his trial had been unfair.

In the year of the Belfast (Good Friday) Agreement the UK government gave a commitment to phase out the Diplock courts,[247] and two years later it issued a consultation paper on the topic.[248] But no steps were actually taken until a further seven years had elapsed, mainly because the security and political situations were not deemed to be stable enough to cope with an alteration to the system. Following a further consultation

[243] Korff (1984) 99–100.
[244] 1 April 1980 (unreported) (Kelly J).
[245] 27 March 1981 (unreported) (Lord Lowry CJ, Gibson LJ, and MacDermott J).
[246] [1982] AC 476.
[247] Home Office and NIO (1998) para 13.8.
[248] NIO (2000).

paper in 2006[249] legislation was eventually introduced the following year.[250] It was to last initially for two years,[251] but there was a renewal power[252] and this has since been exercised, continuing the provisions in force until August 2011.[253] The legislation permits the DPP (not, as before, the Attorney General) to certify, prior to the arraignment of the defendant in the Crown Court, that the trial is to take place without a jury.[254] Northern Ireland, like England and Wales, also now has legislation which allows a trial that has already started with a jury to proceed without a jury if the case involves complex fraud or if there is evidence of a real and present danger that jury tampering will take place and, notwithstanding any steps which might reasonably be taken to prevent jury tampering, the likelihood that the tampering will take place is so substantial as to make it necessary in the interests of justice for the trial to be conducted without a jury.[255] This latter provision has already been used in Northern Ireland,[256] but the provisions in the 2007 Act have been used much more frequently.[257]

The right to a trial within a reasonable time

Article 6 expressly states that everyone charged with a crime has a right to a fair and public hearing 'within a reasonable time'. In Northern Ireland concerns were expressed quite early in the conflict that trials before the juryless Diplock courts were taking far too long to come to court.[258] The government responded by establishing a sixth such court.[259] The following year SACHR seemed ready to accept that there were understandable reasons for the delays in cases coming to trial, such as the unavailability of key witnesses or of the counsel of the accused's choice.[260] A year later SACHR felt able to express relief at the progress that had been made with regard to the problem of remand.[261] Of the indictable cases referred to the DPP in October 1977, the average length of time spent prior to trial was 45 weeks, made up of about 15 weeks between the start of the police investigation and the submission of papers to the DPP, about 15 weeks between the submission of papers to the DPP and the committal proceedings, and a further 15 weeks between the committal proceedings and

[249] NIO (2006), available on the NIO's website: <http://www.nio.gov.uk>, last visited 24 August 2009.

[250] Justice and Security (NI) Act 2007, ss 1–9.

[251] ibid, s 9(1).

[252] ibid, s 9(2).

[253] Justice and Security (NI) Act 2007 (Extension of Duration of Non-Jury Trial Provisions) Order 2009 (SI 2090).

[254] For further details see Walker (2009) 281–6.

[255] Criminal Justice Act 2003, ss 43–50; it is s 50 which extends these provisions to Northern Ireland.

[256] See *R v Mackle* [2007] NICA 37.

[257] In 2008 there were 15 cases disposed of in the Crown Court of Northern Ireland that were tried under the 2007 Act: see NICS (2009) Table C.2.

[258] SACHR (1979) 14–5.

[259] HL Deb, vol 394, col 1280 (6 July 1978), per Lord Melchett.

[260] SACHR (1980) para 24.

[261] SACHR (1981) para 16.

the start of the trial.[262] SACHR regarded 45 weeks as a reasonable period, but was glad to report that by September 1980 the average delay between arrest and trial had been reduced still further—to 30 weeks.[263]

In 1983 the European Commission considered a case on delay brought from Northern Ireland, *Orchin v United Kingdom*.[264] The applicant, a loyalist, had been arrested and charged with firearms offences in December 1972. He was then charged with three murders, but two of these murder charges were later dropped and he was acquitted of the third charge in February 1974. He was released on bail later that month in relation to the original firearms offences and was not notified until March 1978 that the Attorney General had decided not to proceed with these. After examining the conflicting accounts given by the applicant and the UK government, the Commission held that most of the applicant's allegations as to the authorities' motives for keeping the charges hanging over him were not supported by any evidence but that nevertheless the last three years of the four-year delay in notifying him that the firearms charges were not being proceeded with was unreasonable. The Commission noted that the government had taken steps to reduce such periods in future by, for example, ensuring that the DPP was given regular reports on all cases in which a trial had not begun within six months of the accused's committal for trial. This was a timely warning shot across the authorities' bows, and it does seem to have helped speed up the processing of Diplock cases over the ensuing years.

In 2000 the Secretary of State for Northern Ireland was empowered to issue regulations setting down the maximum periods during which the prosecution must complete a preliminary stage of proceedings for a scheduled offence and the accused may be held in custody.[265] Three years later a similar power was conferred in relation to the trial of non-scheduled offences.[266] But in fact neither power has ever been exercised, doubtless because there is a concern that the time limits set may not in practice be met, and in fact the former power expired when Part VII of the Terrorism Act 2000 lapsed on 31 July 2007. In 2006, the last full year for which published statistics are available, the average time elapsing between a defendant's remand for scheduled offences and his or her committal proceedings was 42 weeks; between the committal proceedings and arraignment it was seven weeks, and between arraignment and the start of the trial it was 25.5 weeks, making a total average period between remand and trial of 74.5 weeks.[267] The Northern Ireland Court Service's statistics do not reveal the average time elapsing between a defendant's remand for *non-scheduled* offences and his or her committal proceedings in 2006, but they do say that the average time elapsing between the committal proceedings and the start of the trial was 19 weeks, considerably less than the average time in scheduled cases.[268] While the waiting times

[262] ibid, para 12.
[263] ibid, para 13.
[264] (1984) 6 EHRR 391.
[265] Terrorism Act 2000, s 72(1).
[266] Criminal Justice (NI) Order 2003, ss 11–7.
[267] Carlile (2008) 79, Table NIO/D.
[268] NICS (2007) Table C.4. That Table gives the average period for scheduled cases as 37 weeks, whereas Carlile gives it as 32.5 (7 + 25.5). In 2008 the average waiting time for all Crown Court defendants

in cases of scheduled offences are often unduly long, they are probably not so long as to violate the requirements of Article 6 concerning a trial within a reasonable time. The European Court has laid down no fixed rules in this context, even for criminal trials, saying that everything depends on the particular circumstances, including the complexity of the crime, the manner in which it has been handled by the national authorities, and the conduct of the accused.[269] This is another field where practices in Northern Ireland, though generally not good, have not run the risk of regularly contravening the rather lax standards of the European Convention.

Today there is now a gap in the annual review arrangements for the juryless trials of terrorist suspects in Northern Ireland. One independent reviewer reviews the permanent provisions on terrorism which apply in Northern Ireland as much as in the rest of the United Kingdom and another reviews the provisions in the Justice and Security (NI) Act 2007 dealing with police and army powers and the army's procedures for dealing with complaints,[270] but no-one reviews the temporary provisions in the 2007 Act allowing for juryless trials. The Secretary of State has the power to request the latter independent reviewer to review these,[271] but so far he has not exercised that power.

The right to no punishment without law

Article 7 of the European Convention guarantees the right not to be held guilty of an offence if the act or omission in question was not an offence under national or international law at the time it was committed, nor must a heavier penalty be imposed than the one that was applicable at the time the offence was committed. We saw in Chapter 3 that the European Commission of Human Rights declared inadmissible complaints about the Northern Ireland Act 1972 which, by way of a response to an unexpected court decision,[272] had retrospectively legitimized conduct which that court had found to be illegal since 1921.[273] The Bill was introduced in Parliament on the evening of the day on which the court issued its judgment (with only Bernadette Devlin MP voting against its introduction) and it acquired the Royal Assent at 2.11am the next day—

between committal and the start of their trial was over 19 weeks: NICS (2009) Table C.5, but this figure does not differentiate defendants facing scheduled offences from those facing non-scheduled offences.

269 Reid (2008) 160–7.

270 The first report on these matters by Robert Whalley, covering the period August 2007 to July 2008, was published in December 2008: Whalley (2008). It is available on the website of the Northern Ireland Office, <http://www.nio.gov.uk>.

271 Justice and Security (NI) Act 2007, s 40(3).

272 *R (Hume) v Londonderry Justices* [1972] NI 91 (Div Ct). The applicant later became leader of the Social and Democratic Labour Party and a Nobel peace prize winner alongside David Trimble. This decision was of immense significance since it held that all the actions taken by British soldiers in Northern Ireland since 1920 under regulations issued by the Northern Ireland Parliament were ultra vires: the Government of Ireland Act 1920, s 4(1), had prohibited that Parliament from making laws 'in respect of the army'. Ackner J had come to a different conclusion in September 1971 in an English case: *Re Keenan* [1972] 1 QB 533.

273 App Nos 5155/71 (*McMillen v UK, No 1*), 5459/72 (*McMillen v UK, No 2*), 5470/72 (*McMillen v UK, No 3*), 5727/72 (*Montgomery v UK*), 5744/72 (*Clark v UK*), and 5857/72 (*McPhillip v UK*). For contemporary comments on the 1972 Act, see O'Higgins (1972).

the court had given leave to appeal to the House of Lords but the government wanted the law clarified without having to wait for that appeal to be heard. In the somewhat Orwellian words of the Home Secretary, '[t]he sole effect of the Bill will be to declare that the law so far as the powers of the Armed Forces are concerned is and always has been what it has hitherto been believed to be'.[274] When explaining the impact of the Bill the Attorney General for England and Wales, Sir Peter Rawlinson, reported that his counterpart in Northern Ireland had given an undertaking that no-one would be prosecuted for actions that would have been legal under the terms of the Divisional Court's judgment but illegal in the eyes of the new Bill.[275] Before the European Commission the applicants could not show that they had been victims of the legislation and, even if they had been convicted for breaching regulations which were later held to be illegal, it would not have been a violation of Article 7 for Parliament to declare them to have been legal all along.[276] This is a further illustration of the fact that the European Convention does not police the rule of law, only the protection of basic rights, at least in cases that are brought by individuals. In the inter-State case of *Ireland v United Kingdom*, as we saw in Chapter 7, Ireland did submit additional material complaining about the Northern Ireland Act less than two weeks after it was passed, but when Sir Peter Rawlinson repeated his assurance that that no-one would be held guilty by reason of the Act of any act or omission which did not constitute a criminal offence at the time it was committed the Irish government withdrew that particular complaint. In *R v Gorman*[277] Lowry LCJ held that a man who had been arrested by a solider and then escaped before the Northern Ireland Act 1972 came into force was nevertheless guilty (after it came into force) of the offence of escaping from lawful custody. The defendant then lodged an application with the European Commission of Human Rights, but the application was declared inadmissible because he had not raised any argument about the 1972 Act at his trial and had not appealed against his conviction; he had therefore not exhausted his domestic remedies.[278]

Oddly, Article 7 was the first Convention provision to be relied upon by a court in Northern Ireland, as far back as 1977. In *R v Deery* the appellant had been sentenced in January 1977 to six years' imprisonment for possession of firearms. He had committed the offences in April 1976 but in August 1976 the maximum penalty for those offences had been increased from five years to 10 years by the Firearms (Amendment) (NI) Order 1976. The Court of Criminal Appeal held that that Order had to be interpreted in a way which did not breach the UK's international treaty obligations, including Article 7 of the European Convention, and accordingly it reduced the defendant's sentence to three years.[279] Since then Article 7 has not had to be

[274] HC Deb, vol 831, col 1285 (23 February 1972), per Reginald Maudling MP.

[275] ibid, col 1370.

[276] This somewhat undermines the point made by the Labour MP A W Stallard during the second reading debate on the Northern Ireland Bill when he said: 'Twelve months ago, hon. Members on this side tried to introduce a Bill of Rights. It would have taken care of all the points raised tonight, and many more besides.' ibid, 1402.

[277] [1974] NI 152. In *R v Meehan* [1973] NIJB McGonigal J had acquitted a defendant in similar circumstances.

[278] *X v UK* (1981) 3 EHRR 302.

[279] [1977] NI 164 (Lowry LCJ and Jones LJ). Counsel for the appellant was Kevin Boyle.

considered at length in relation to any aspect of the Northern Ireland conflict. In one of the cases on exclusion orders, *M v United Kingdom*,[280] the applicant tried to argue that to penalize him with such an order for something he had allegedly done in the past was a breach of Article 7, but the Commission said Article 7 was not engaged because the exclusion order did not amount to a 'penalty'.

Extradition

At various times during the troubles in Northern Ireland requests have been made by the British authorities to have someone extradited from another jurisdiction so that he or she can be prosecuted in the United Kingdom for offences connected with the Northern Ireland conflict. Two of the arguments the authorities have often had to counter in those situations are, first, that the person should not be extradited because the alleged offence was a 'political' offence, and, second, that the person should not be extradited because he or she would not receive a fair trial in the United Kingdom, especially if the trial were to be in a juryless Diplock court in Northern Ireland. The two jurisdictions in which controversies have most often arisen are the United States and the Republic of Ireland. The United Kingdom has separate extradition arrangements with each of those countries.

Extradition arrangements with the USA

When the troubles broke out in 1968 extradition between the United States and the United Kingdom was governed by a series of treaties between the two nations, the last of which had been negotiated in 1905. Since 1889 each country had agreed that they would not extradite anyone for 'political offences', a common feature of extradition treaties the world over. In 1972 a new treaty on extradition was agreed and it too exempted offences 'regarded by the requested Party as one of a political character'.[281] This new treaty came into force early in January 1977.[282] In 1979, on the first occasion when the United Kingdom sought the extradition of an alleged IRA bomber, Peter McMullen, the US courts refused the request on the grounds that bombing a British army barracks in England was an offence of a political character.[283] Two years later the Second Circuit of the US Court of Appeals reached the same conclusion regarding a British request to have Desmond Mackin extradited for the alleged attempted murder of a British soldier in Belfast.[284] And in a third case, in 1984, a

[280] App No 11517/85 (decision of 3 March 1986): see ch 4 above.

[281] Extradition Treaty Between the Government of the United States of America and the Government of Great Britain and Northern Ireland, 8 June 1972, Cmnd 5040, Art V.

[282] See the United States of America (Extradition) Order 1976 (SI 2144).

[283] McElrath (2000) 47–8; Branick (2001–2) 182. McMullen, a former British army soldier himself, was later deported back to the UK: 788 F 2d 591 (9th Cir 1986): <http://cases.justia.com/us-court-of-appeals/F2/788/591/300514>, last visited 20 August 2009, as supplemented by McElrath, ibid.

[284] *Re Requested Extradition of Mackin* 668 F 2d 122: <http://openjurist.org/668/f2d/122>, last visited 20 August 2009. McElrath (2000) 46–7; Branick (2001–2) 182–3.

district court in New York refused to extradite Joe Doherty, who had been convicted in his absence of murdering a British soldier.[285] A fourth man, James Barr, was not extradited in 1986 because the evidence against him—allegations by a supergrass—was not deemed to be compelling enough.[286] It was not until 1986 that the UK government won its first claim to have a person extradited from the US in connection with offences related to the conflict in Northern Ireland. William Quinn was sought for the alleged murder of a police officer in London and conspiracy to cause explosions in England, but because these offences occurred in England the Ninth Circuit of the US Court of Appeals held, by a majority, that they could not be classified as offences of a political character as there was no political uprising in England at the time, only in Northern Ireland.[287] Quinn was returned to England, convicted of murder, and given a life sentence; he was later transferred to a prison in the Republic of Ireland and released in 1999. Quinn was actually an American citizen but the US, unlike some countries, does not exempt its own nationals from extradition.

In none of these five cases was it suggested that the accused person would risk being ill-treated or receiving an unfair trial if he were sent back to the United Kingdom, and no mention was made of rights conferred by the European Convention. None of the individuals could claim the protection of the Convention because they were living in the US at the time and the Convention applies only to people present in Council of Europe States or in other parts of the world under the control of such States.[288] They might have considered lodging applications in Strasbourg once they returned to the United Kingdom (having been extradited or deported), but they would have had to exhaust domestic remedies first and it is hard to see what rights under the Convention they could claim were breached.

Nor was this situation altered by the fact that at the end of 1986 an amendment to the US–UK treaty on extradition took effect[289] whereby the 'offence of a political character' defence was replaced by a provision which allowed a defence if the accused was able to show, on a preponderance of the evidence, that the extradition request was politically motivated or that, if returned to the requesting State, he or she would be prejudiced at trial or punished on account of race, religion, nationality, or political opinion. In addition, the sorts of offences which were 'scheduled' offences in the Northern Ireland (Emergency Provisions) Act 1978 were declared *not* to be offences of a political character, and the US government was for the first time given the right to appeal against a lower court's decision not to extradite someone. What is more, these amendments were made retroactive.[290] It seems that the changes were made

[285] *Re Requested Extradition of Doherty* 559 F Supp 270: <http://www.uniset.ca/other/cs4/599FSupp270.html>, last visited 20 August 2009. Kelly (1992); McElrath (2000) 53–5; Branick (2001–2) 183. Like McMullen, Doherty was eventually deported back to the UK, losing his challenge to this in the US Supreme Court: 502 US 314 (1992). For Doherty's full story see Dillon (1992).

[286] McElrath (2000) 50–1.

[287] *Quinn v Robinson* 783 F 2d 776: <http://www.uniset.ca/other/cs4/783F2d776.html>, last visited 20 August 2009. McElrath (2000) 48–50; Branick (2001–2) 184–5.

[288] *Bankovič v Belgium* (2007) 44 EHRR SE5.

[289] Cmnd 9565 (1985). See the United States of America (Extradition) (Amendment) Order 1986 (SI 2020).

[290] For full details see Lubet (1987).

by the Reagan administration as part of a deal with Mrs Thatcher which included Britain being used as a staging post for aircraft on their way to bomb Libya.[291]

A day after the 1986 amendments to the extradition arrangements came into effect the US authorities, at the UK government's request, rearrested Peter McMullen, who had already won his fight against extradition but was awaiting deportation. This blatant attempt to subvert the rule of law failed, because the US courts saw the new arrangements as amounting to a 'bill of attainder', that is, an attempt by legislators or the government to do the work of courts by targeting laws at a particular individual, a practice that was explicitly contrary to Article I(9)(3) of the US Constitution.[292] In this respect Mr McMullen should have been grateful that he was living in the US, because it is hard to see a British or a Strasbourg court taking the same attitude to such specific legislation (unless it were deemed, in the UK, to be contrary to the abuse of process doctrine at common law).

At the time when peace talks were ongoing in Northern Ireland, in the early 1990s, requests were made to the US for the extradition of four men who had escaped from the Maze prison in 1993. The first request, for Jimmy Smyth, was successful before the Ninth Circuit of the US Court of Appeals, and Smyth was returned to Northern Ireland to serve two more years of his sentence before being released in 1998 under the terms of the Belfast (Good Friday) Agreement.[293] The American court said that evidence of general discrimination against nationalists in Northern Ireland could not be used to show that Smyth himself would be discriminated against. In October 1998 the same American court threw a lifeline to the three other members of the 'H-Block Four', Barry Artt, Pól Brennan, and Terence Kirby, by directing a lower court to examine more closely whether they had received fair trials in Northern Ireland,[294] a decision which angered unionist politicians there. But in September 2000, before the lower court could complete its reconsideration of the case, the UK government decided to drop its extradition requests, acknowledging that if the men were to be returned to Northern Ireland they would be eligible for release under the Agreement.[295]

In the wake of the 9/11 atrocities yet another extradition treaty between the United Kingdom and the United States was agreed in 2003.[296] This retains the 1986 approach to the political offence defence but repeats that each State must refuse to extradite if the competent authority (which, in the US, is the government) determines that the request is politically motivated. The most controversial aspect of the

[291] Kelly (1992); Thatcher (1993) 449, where the change to the extradition treaty is said to have been regarded as vital in bringing IRA terrorists back from America.

[292] 953 F.2d 761 (2nd Cir, 1992): <http://openjurist.org/953/f2d/761/mcmullen-v-united-states>. Branick (2001–2) 188.

[293] *Re Requested Extradition of Smyth* 61 F 3d 711: <http://openjurist.org/61/f3d/711/in-the-matter-of-the-requested-extradition-of-james-joseph-smyth>.

[294] 106 F.3d 855: <http://cases.justia.com/us-court-of-appeals/F3/183/944/529746>. Artt and Kirby had been convicted in Diplock court trials of murdering, respectively, a prison governor and a petrol station attendant. Brennan had been convicted of possessing explosives.

[295] Deportation proceedings continued against Brennan, and on 21 August 2009 he was returned to the Republic of Ireland: *Irish Times*, 22 August 2009.

[296] Cm 5821. The treaty was given effect in the UK by the Extradition Act 1993, in force from 1 January 1994, but it was not ratified in the US until September 2006.

new treaty is that it allows the US to request the extradition of persons in the United Kingdom without having to show a *prima facie* case against them, whereas it still requires the United Kingdom to show such a case when it is requesting the extradition of persons from the United States. While this anomaly has proved problematic in a number of instances,[297] the new arrangements have not so far had to be used in relation to extradition requests connected with the conflict in Northern Ireland.

As regards extradition *to* the United States, in the late 1980s the European Commission and Court of Human Rights took a principled stand (though not in a case coming from Northern Ireland) when in *Soering v United Kingdom*,[298] they, first, each issued interim measure orders against the United Kingdom requiring the government not to complete the extradition of the applicant to the United States before his application had been dealt with in Strasbourg, and, second, found that the United Kingdom would be violating the applicant's rights under the Convention if it extradited him to the state of Virginia in the United States where, if convicted of the murder of his girlfriend's parents, he could be sentenced to death and have to wait on death row for some time. The Commission, in a split decision, found a violation of Article 13 (the right to an effective remedy), but not of Article 3 or 6. The Plenary Court, on the other hand, held unanimously (18 to 0) that extradition would be a breach of Article 3, but not of Article 6 or 13:

> ... in the Court's view, having regard to the very long period of time spent on death row in such extreme conditions, with the ever present and mounting anguish of awaiting execution of the death penalty, and to the personal circumstances of the applicant, especially his age and mental state at the time of the offence, the applicant's extradition to the United States would expose him to a real risk of treatment going beyond the threshold set by Article 3.[299]

The position remains, however, that the European Court has not yet enunciated a principle that a State cannot extradite a person unless it is satisfied that none of the person's Convention rights will be breached in the receiving State.[300] The Court will find a violation only if the breach would amount to a 'flagrant denial' of the accused person's rights.[301]

Extradition arrangements with Ireland

Extradition between the United Kingdom and Ireland,[302] when the troubles broke out, was governed by the UK's Backing of Warrants (Republic of Ireland) Act 1965[303] and by Ireland's Extradition Act 1965. These allowed for a warrant of arrest to be issued in one of the countries and endorsed for execution in the other without the

[297] eg, in relation to the 'Nat West Three', who in 2006 lost their appeal in England against extradition ([2006] EWHC 200 (Admin)) and failed to persuade the European Court to issue an interim measure order requiring the extradition to be postponed, and computer-hacker Gary McKinnon, who took his case, unsuccessfully, as far as the House of Lords: *McKinnon v Government of the USA* [2008] UKHL 29, [2008] 1 WLR 1739.

[298] (1989) 11 EHRR 439.

[299] ibid, para 111.

[300] Reid (2008) 321.

[301] ibid, 321–2.

[302] See generally Connelly (1982); McGrath (1983); Connelly (1985); Campbell (1989).

[303] This Act was prompted by a decision by the House of Lords finding flaws with the earlier extradition system. See *R v Metropolitan Police Commissioner, ex p Hammond* [1965] AC 810.

requesting State having to make any further attempt to justify the warrant—there was no requirement, for example, that the requesting State make a *prima facie* case against the accused. The Acts included the 'political offence defence' but did not define what a political offence was. In the Republic it was usually taken to include offences committed by the IRA,[304] which was a very unpopular and, some would say hypocritical,[305] stance in the eyes of people who felt they were living in the midst of terrorism in Northern Ireland. The issue was then referred to a special Anglo-Irish Commission, which reported in 1974.[306] While the British and Irish members of that Commission could not agree on the way in which the political offence defence should be interpreted, the report did lead to the two States agreeing that each of them could prosecute persons in their own jurisdiction for crimes committed in the other, and legislation was enacted in each country to put that agreement into effect.[307] Paradoxically, this legislation seems to have helped persuade the Irish courts to adopt a less stringent line as regards the political offence defence, for in several subsequent cases the Supreme Court authorized the extradition to Northern Ireland of Irish republicans.[308] On the other hand, many requests were turned down by the Irish courts on the basis that the strict letter of the law had not been complied with by the requesting authorities.[309] And in a decision in 1990 the Supreme Court reversed its general approach and held that the IRA was not a group acting 'unconstitutionally' (even though it was unlawful) and so people doing things on its behalf could not be extradited.[310] This decision, criticized by Gilbert for one,[311] was moderated by the Supreme Court in *Sloan v Culligan*,[312] where it said that the particular charges laid against the accused had to be scrutinized to see if they furthered unconstitutional aims.

The Council of Europe, meanwhile, was taking its own steps to try to harmonize the law on extradition amongst member States. It had produced a Convention on Extradition as early as 1957, which Ireland ratified in 1966 but which the United Kingdom did not ratify until 1991 because it did not approve of its rather wide provisions on political offences and the discretion it gave States not to extradite their own nationals.[313] In 1977 the Council issued a Convention on the Suppression of

[304] See, in particular *The State (Magee) v O'Rourke* [1971] IR 205. And cf Farrell (1985).

[305] Dickson (1991) 169.

[306] Law Enforcement Commission (1974). See McCall, Smith and Magee (1975).

[307] Criminal Jurisdiction Act 1975 (UK); Criminal Law (Jurisdiction) Act 1976 (Ir). Evidence could also be taken in one jurisdiction for a trial taking place in the other.

[308] *McGlinchey v Wren* [1982] IR 15; *Shannon v Fanning* [1984] IR 569; *Quinn v Wren* [1985] IR 323; *Russell v Fanning* [1988] ILRM 333 (though in this last case two Supreme Court judges dissented, saying that the murder of a police officer in Northern Ireland was a political offence). For a Unionist perspective on the extradition arrangements with Ireland in the early 1980s, see Graham (1982). See also Hadden and Boyle (1989) 59–66.

[309] See the Table of 20 cases in Campbell (1989) 601–3.

[310] *Finucane v McMahon* [1990] IR 165. The decision is difficult to reconcile with *Russell v Fanning*, n 307 above, since Russell and Finucane were both escapees from the Maze. Finucane was not extradited because he feared ill-treatment by the prison officers if he were returned to the prison, but it was accepted that Russell, after his return, had not been ill-treated.

[311] Gilbert (1992) 79–80.

[312] [1992] 1 IR 223.

[313] Arts 3 and 6.

Terrorism, which downplayed the political offence defence to some extent,[314] so the United Kingdom ratified that in 1978 but Ireland did not do so until 1989.[315] Even then the Irish legislation required the Attorney General of Ireland to certify in each case where a request was made by another State that there was in fact a clear intention to prosecute the accused person.[316] In 1988, in the infamous case involving the UK's request for the extradition of Father Ryan, who was suspected of involvement in the murder of three off-duty British soldiers in Amsterdam, the Attorney General did so certify, but he nevertheless went on to refuse the request because he was not satisfied, given the amount of adverse publicity about him, that Father Ryan could receive a fair trial in the United Kingdom.[317] Consideration was then given to prosecuting Father Ryan in Ireland itself, but in 1989 a decision was taken not to do so.

With both Ireland and the United Kingdom being bound by the European Convention on Human Rights, the scope for its application is obviously greater than in the US–UK cases, yet in fact very few applications seem to have been lodged in Strasbourg. One reason for this is that, rather bizarrely, extradition proceedings in a member State of the Council of Europe are not themselves required to comply with Article 6 of the Convention because they do not involve 'the determination of civil rights and obligations or of any criminal charge'.[318]

One case that was brought is *X and Y v Ireland*,[319] where two brothers, British citizens, had been arrested in England for their suspected involvement in a bank robbery in Dublin in 1972. The English courts granted the Irish government's request for their extradition in 1973, the extradition hearings being held in camera because of national security considerations. The men claimed to be British secret service agents who had infiltrated the IRA and been sent to Dublin to commit a bank robbery in order to put pressure on the Irish authorities to take more effective action against the IRA in the Republic. They fought extradition on the basis that the offences with which they were charged were political offences, but Ireland's Attorney General issued an affidavit saying that they were not. When they were returned to Dublin, however, they were brought before the Special Criminal Court for trial without a jury and were convicted, one brother receiving a prison sentence of 20 years and the other a sentence of 15 years. After exhausting their appeal rights in Ireland they applied to the European Commission, pointing out, not unreasonably perhaps, that until then all IRA offences had been regarded by English courts as non-political but Irish courts had always regarded them as political. They claimed that this difference in approach between the two countries 'went beyond reasonable variance in interpretation' and was therefore 'contrary to the concept of reciprocal protection of human rights and

314 Campbell (1989) 594.

315 Pursuant to the Extradition (European Convention on the Suppression of Terrorism) Act 1987 (Ir), as amended by the Extradition (Amendment) Act 1987.

316 ibid, s 44B.

317 The Attorney General was John Murray, later a judge at the European Court of Justice from 1992 to 1999, a judge of the Supreme Court of Ireland from 1999, and the Chief Justice of Ireland from 2004 to the present.

318 Art 6(1), as interpreted, eg, in *Mamatkulov v Turkey* (2005) 41 EHRR 494.

319 App No 8299/78, decision of 10 October 1980.

freedoms as accepted in international law regarding extradition between two treaty countries'.

Unfortunately (from a legal point of view, as well as from the applicants'), the Commission found it quite easy to declare the applications inadmissible, for two reasons. First, because the applications had been brought only against Ireland, not against the United Kingdom, where the alleged unfair 'trial' had taken place, and where there was evidence to show that the decision to extradite was not influenced by what Ireland's Attorney General had said. Second, because as regards the trial in Ireland the applicants had never been given a guarantee that they would not be tried in the Special Criminal Court, the Convention does not guarantee the right to trial in any specific domestic court or trial by jury, and the European Commission and Court have no competence to deal with allegations that errors of law or fact have been made by domestic courts unless those alleged errors might involve a possible violation of a Convention right. Besides, the Special Criminal Court dealt with non-terrorist as well as terrorist cases and the applicants had been tried for the very offences for which they had been extradited. The European Commission also said that it could find no basis in the Convention for an authoritative interpretation of the widely disputed notion of 'political offence'.[320] The applicants had also alleged a violation of Article 3 in that the conditions under which they were confined in Mountjoy Prison in Dublin were inhuman and degrading but, rather harshly, the Commission found these complaints to be inadmissible because the applicants had not sought leave to appeal out of time against the dismissal of their application for a writ of habeas corpus in the Irish courts.

This case illustrates well that extradition is more an administrative matter than a judicial one and that applying human rights standards to the administrative process is difficult. The same can be said of a challenge that was raised in Strasbourg to the Criminal Jurisdiction Act 1975.[321] The complainant was an Irish republican prisoner in England who argued that his rights under Article 6 had been breached by the fact that for his trial in England the UK government had used exhibits which the Irish authorities had supplied. He pointed out that he had no standing to appear before the Irish Court of Criminal Appeal when the British DPP applied there for access to the exhibits (which were being used at the trial of another man), nor could he get legal aid in respect of those proceedings. The Commission said the application was inadmissible *ratione materiae* because the proceedings in Ireland did not 'determine his civil rights or obligations' under Article 6(1) and it was beyond the powers of the UK government, against which his complaint was lodged, to confer a right of audience in an Irish court. The Commission observed that in any event there was nothing to show that the exhibits had been contaminated in any way by being transferred from and to Ireland.

The highly technical nature of the extradition process—and of the admissibility requirements in Strasbourg—are also demonstrated by a further high-profile case involving the courts on both sides of the Irish border. In *McGlinchey v Ireland*[322]

[320] Which suggests that it is unrealistic to think, as one commentator does, that the European Court could serve as a model for an international court created for the purpose of adjudicating claims that the political offence defence should apply to an extradition claim: Branick (2001–2) 195.

[321] *M v UK* App 10386/83, decision of 12 May 1983. The origins of the Act are explained at 218 above.

[322] *McGlinchey (Dominic) v Ireland* App 16751/90, decision of 19 January 1990.

the applicant, one of the most notorious terrorists throughout the Northern Ireland conflict,[323] complained that when he was extradited by Ireland to Northern Ireland in 1984 his rights under Articles 5, 6, 13, and 14 had been breached. He had first been arrested in 1982, on the back of an arrest warrant issued in Northern Ireland in 1981 and endorsed for execution in the Republic under that country's Extradition Act 1965. An Irish court ordered his extradition less than a week later but he was released on bail while he challenged that decision. He then vanished (his challenge being lost in the meantime[324]), until he was again arrested in the Republic in 1984, this time for firearms offences. Almost immediately he was sent to Northern Ireland pursuant to the 1982 extradition order. He was initially found guilty of murder there, but he won his appeal against that conviction and was then extradited back to the South to stand trial for the firearms offences. In his application to Strasbourg McGlinchey argued that his arrest in 1984 had been unlawful and that his subsequent extradition to the North was therefore also unlawful. But the Commission did not have to deal with the full substance of his complaints because they were found to be inadmissible on the grounds that they had been lodged two months after the six-month time limit set by the Convention.[325] The Commission did add, however, that there was in fact no evidence to show that McGlinchey's 1984 arrest had been unlawful, and it pointed out that Article 5(1)(f) of the Convention specifically permits the arrest or detention of a person against whom action is being taken with a view to extradition.[326]

Extradition arrangements with other countries

The United Kingdom did not succeed in persuading the French or Belgian authorities to extradite IRA suspects,[327] but it did manage to get two escapees from the Maze sent back from the Netherlands, notwithstanding their application to the European Commission of Human Rights. In *K and F v The Netherlands*[328] the applicants argued that they would be subjected to inhuman or degrading treatment if they were returned to the Maze prison, or that the trial they would undergo for offences committed during their escape from prison would be unfair. They failed on both counts because they could not supply the Commission with any evidence to support their claims. The Commission relied heavily on the fact that, as the applicants were being returned to a country where the Convention itself applied, they would be able

[323] Holland and McDonald (1994) 211–32.

[324] *McGlinchey v Wren* [1982] IR 154.

[325] Art 26, now Art 35(1).

[326] McGlinchey was himself shot dead in 1994, a crime not claimed by any organization and for which no-one has yet been prosecuted.

[327] Campbell (1989) 604, n 65, and 611, n 98.

[328] App No 12543/86, 51 DR 272 (decision of 2 December 1986). Both applicants had been serving sentences for bombings, and in the second applicant's case also for murder, when they escaped from the Maze in September 1983. The applicants were Gerry Kelly (currently a Minister in the Northern Ireland government) and Brendan McFarlane (who had been the Provisional IRA Officer Commanding in the Maze at the time of the 1981 hunger strike by republican prisoners). In 2008 the latter's trial in Dublin for the kidnapping of the supermarket executive Don Tidey in 1983 collapsed due to lack of evidence.

to complain of violations of their Convention rights in that country if these did in fact occur.

In one extradition case concerning the conflict in Northern Ireland the United Kingdom was not the requesting country but the requested country. This was in 1997, when the German government asked for the extradition of Roisin McAliskey[329] to face prosecution for her alleged involvement in a bombing at an army base in Osnabrück the previous year. No-one was killed or injured by the bomb, but the base was extensively damaged. A court authorized her extradition, but the Home Secretary, Jack Straw, then vetoed the move because Ms McAliskey was in bad health at the time.[330] Two years later the government announced that no prosecution would be launched against Ms McAliskey within the United Kingdom.[331] However, following the introduction of a new system of 'European arrest warrants' in 2003—a post-9/11 EU initiative to which the United Kingdom gave effect through its Extradition Act 2003[332]—Germany renewed its request for Ms McAliskey's extradition in 2007. A court in Northern Ireland then refused that request, saying it would be oppressive to carry out the extradition because so much time had elapsed since the Home Secretary's first refusal.[333]

If future requests are made within the 27 member States of the EU for the 'transfer' of persons suspected of involvement in offences connected with the conflict in Northern Ireland, whether to or from the United Kingdom, they are likely to be made through the new European arrest warrant system, which was designed to speed up the transfer process and to make it an entirely judicial process, involving no politicians. This is how, for example, Osman Hussain, who was suspected of involvement in the bombs in London on 21 July 2005, was very quickly transferred to England from Italy in September of that year.[334] Although there are some concerns about European arrest warrants, one safeguard is that all EU countries have to comply with the European Convention on Human Rights. If the fairness of a person's trial is somehow tainted by the way in which the European arrest warrant system is applied, he or she is free to cite the Convention rights and to lodge an application in Strasbourg if necessary. But of course the European Court has no power to quash the applicant's conviction even if it finds that his or her trial was grossly unfair. There are still several dozen people, the so-called 'on-the-runs', who are wanted in Northern Ireland

[329] Roisin McAliskey is the daughter of Bernadette Devlin, who lodged a doomed application in Strasbourg back in 1970: see ch 3 above. For a non-legal account of Ms McAliskey's experience see Sullivan (1999) ch 1.

[330] HL Deb, vol 587, col WA32 (10 March 1998), per Lord Williams of Mostyn. Lord Williams said the decision was made in exercise of the Home Secretary's duty, under the Extradition Act 1989, s 12, not to extradite someone if this would be unjust or oppressive. He added: 'It does not reflect in any way on the fairness of the German legal system or on the quality of the German extradition request.'

[331] HL Deb, vol 615, col WA76 (18 July 2000), per Lord Williams of Mostyn, who explained that 'the Crown Prosecution Service has concluded that there is not a realistic prospect of convicting Miss McAliskey for any offence arising out of the Osnabrück bombing. It has reached that conclusion having taken into account the available evidence and the likely result of any argument that may be put forward by Miss McAliskey that to prosecute her now would be an abuse of process.'

[332] It results from a Framework Decision of the Council of Ministers adopted on 13 June 2002.

[333] *Federal Public Prosecutor, Germany v McAliskey* [2007] NICty 1 (Judge Burgess).

[334] In 2007 Hussain was convicted of conspiracy to murder and was sentenced to life imprisonment with a recommendation that he serve at least 40 years.

because they have not yet stood trial there, or anywhere, for offences they allegedly committed during the conflict, or because they escaped from custody in Northern Ireland before completing their sentences. For political reasons it is unlikely that extradition requests will now be made in respect of these individuals,[335] but sooner or later some legal provision is going to have to be made for regularizing their position.

Conclusion

This chapter has demonstrated that, despite alterations to the trial process being at the heart of the government's strategy for dealing with terrorist violence in Northern Ireland, the European Convention on Human Rights played a very small role in regulating those alterations. It was ineffective as regards guaranteeing detainees the right of access to a solicitor, especially during interviews with the police, at least until the European Court decided in 1996 that a court could draw inferences from a detainee's silence only if he or she had first been granted access to legal advice. Nor did the Convention make any significant contribution to ensuring that police officers who used violence against detainees during interrogation sessions would face criminal prosecutions. It was domestic courts rather than the European Court which maintained the integrity of the principle that the burden of proving a person's guilt rests entirely on the prosecution, and the Court has displayed a distinctly 'hands off' attitude as regards interfering with domestic rules concerning the admissibility of evidence. Fortunately, the Court of Appeal of Northern Ireland was able to put paid to the supergrass phenomenon, because the European Court might not have done so had any of the people convicted solely on the word of a supergrass lodged an application in Strasbourg. The cornerstone of the 'emergency' response to the troubles—the juryless Diplock court—was never in any danger of being the focus of an adverse ruling by the European Court, regardless of what some courts in the United States and elsewhere might have thought about the fairness of the justice dispensed in those courts.

It remains true that, whatever criticisms have been made of the conflict-related criminal justice system in Northern Ireland,[336] the number of allegations of miscarriages of justice has been comparatively low.[337] The major disasters in this area occurred in England, where juries were retained for trials of suspected terrorists. It is unlikely that a stricter application of the European Convention standards would have prevented even those egregious miscarriages of justice from occurring, for they were the result of police or forensic malpractice rather than of defective trial procedures *per se*. The so-called Guildford Four were convicted in 1975 and did not succeed in getting their convictions quashed until 1989;[338] the Maguire Seven were convicted

[335] Harrington (2009) 32.

[336] eg, Hunt and Dickson (1983); Dickson (1992).

[337] Jackson and Doran (1995) 29; Dickson (1999a).

[338] *R v Richardson and others*, *The Times*, 20 May 1993. The individuals were Paul Hill, Gerry Conlon, Paddy Armstrong, and Carole Richardson. Paul Hill's conviction for the separate murder of a British soldier was later quashed by the Court of Appeal of Northern Ireland in 1994.

in 1976 and had to wait for justice until 1991;[339] the convictions of the Birmingham Six occurred in 1975 and were also not overturned until 1991.[340] These tragedies led to the establishment of a Royal Commission on Criminal Justice, whose report in turn resulted in the creation of a specialist body to examine alleged miscarriages of justice, the Criminal Cases Review Commission (CCRC).[341]

The CCRC has referred several cases to the Court of Appeal of Northern Ireland, and many of these references have resulted in convictions being quashed. In *Re Boyle's Application*, for example, compensation was granted for a miscarriage resulting from the police's false denial that there was another version of their notes of an interview with the claimant: electrostatic detection analysis (ESDA) had revealed the existence of that other version.[342] In *R v McCartney* and *R v MacDermott* convictions were quashed because the Court of Appeal had a 'distinct feeling of unease' about how safe they might be, given the allegations that had been made about police brutality.[343] In *R v Walsh* the Court of Appeal was even prepared to grant an application to have a second appeal re-opened.[344] Notoriously, the European Convention does not even guarantee *one* appeal in a criminal case. The fact that the Diplock court system allowed every convicted person to appeal without having to seek permission to do so shows that in that respect too the domestic system was in advance of minimum European human rights standards. Alas, the same cannot be said for the way in which the domestic system protected the right to life, as we shall see in the next chapter.

[339] *R v Maguire and others* [1992] 2 All ER 433. The victims of the injustice here were Anne Maguire, her husband Patrick, sons Patrick and Vincent, brother William Smyth, brother-in-law Giuseppe Conlon, and family friend Patrick O'Neill.

[340] *R v McIlkenny and others* [1992] 2 All ER 417. These individuals were Hugh Callaghan, Patrick Hill, Gerry Hunter, Richard McIlkenny, William Power, and John Walker.

[341] Criminal Appeal Act 1995.

[342] [2008] NICA 35.

[343] [2007] NICA 10.

[344] *R v Walsh* [2007] NICA 4. The appellant had been sentenced to 14 years in prison for possession of a coffee jar bomb in 1992; the Court of Appeal allowed his second appeal to be re-opened because the previous court had failed to have regard to relevant new evidence.

9

The Right to Life

Given the appalling loss of life in Northern Ireland during the years of conflict—the 2004 edition of *Lost Lives*[1] lists 3,697 deaths between 11 June 1966 and 21 November 2003, and at least a further 22 have died since then[2]—it is obvious that Article 2 of the European Convention, which supposedly guarantees the right to life, should be at the very heart of any study of the part played by the Convention in Northern Ireland over that period. This chapter tells the story of the extent to which Article 2 was in fact relevant to the conflict. It explains that the provision was not frequently invoked during the early years, that the applicants who did invoke it were not successful, and that the Article has come into its own only during the last 10 or 15 years. It will show that cases connected with Northern Ireland have been extremely important in the development of the European Court's jurisprudence on the right to life, even if that jurisprudence has not significantly benefited the families of the victims of killings in Northern Ireland itself. In particular, applications from Northern Ireland have contributed hugely to the outworking of standards concerning the investigation of killings.

With the incorporation of Convention rights into the domestic law of Northern Ireland through the Human Rights Act 1998, there have also been many occasions on which Article 2 has been invoked in cases coming before the local courts. Several of these have progressed as far as the House of Lords. With the benefit of hindsight one can say that these court decisions did not do much to stop the violence in Northern Ireland but they did contribute, eventually, to ensuring that the role of the State in such violence was brought to light to a greater extent than would otherwise have been the case. Sadly, however, there are still respects in which the State does not appear to be wholly fulfilling its responsibilities under Article 2 in Northern Ireland and there are limits to what the European Court itself has required under that provision. The result is that the right to life under the Convention cannot be equated to any substantial degree with the right to truth or the right to accountability.[3]

[1] McKittrick et al (2004).

[2] According to the Police Service of Northern (PSNI) website, the annual number of post-2003 fatalities has been five (2004), five (2005), three (2006), three (2007), one (2008), and five (2009, to 31 August).

[3] Discussions are currently taking place on whether there should be a 'Legacy Commission' established in Northern Ireland. This follows proposals put forward by the government-appointed Consultative Group on the Past. See CGP (2009); Simpson (2009). For a victim-centred analysis see Morrissey and Smyth (2002).

The wording of Article 2 of the Convention

It is sensible to begin with the actual wording of Article 2, which reads as follows:

(1) Everyone's right to life shall be protected by law. No one shall be deprived of his life intentionally save in the execution of a sentence of a court following his conviction of a crime for which this penalty is provided by law.

(2) Deprivation of life shall not be regarded as inflicted in contravention of this article when it results from the use of force which is no more than absolutely necessary:

- (a) in defence of any person from unlawful violence;
- (b) in order to effect a lawful arrest or to prevent the escape of a person lawfully detained;
- (c) in action lawfully taken for the purpose of quelling a riot or insurrection.

Initially the wording seems relatively straightforward, but there are hidden nuances.[4] Five points can immediately be noted. First, unlike some other international human rights treaties,[5] Article 2 of the European Convention does not in so many words confer the right to life. Instead it simply says that the right to life 'shall be protected by law'. This is an invitation to each member State of the Council of Europe to protect the right to life through laws of its own choosing. A constraint is placed on States by the sentence which says that the only situation in which a State can authorize the intentional deprivation of life is when it executes someone after he or she has been duly convicted of a crime. Somewhat contradictorily, but presumably to avoid doubt, the Article then lists some further situations which will not be taken to amount to a deprivation of life in breach of the Article whether or not the deprivation was intentional. The absence of a clear statement that everyone has the right to life makes it more difficult for someone in a novel situation to argue that his or her Article 2 right has been breached. It makes it harder to claim, for example, that a person has the right to end his or her own life,[6] that a person should not be denied artificial nutrition and hydration if suffering from a degenerative brain condition,[7] or that the State has a duty to protect a person from committing suicide. During the various hunger strikes conducted by prisoners in Northern Ireland at different times during the conflict,[8] none of the prisoners ever argued that they had a right to die that was protected by the European Convention. Nor could anyone counter that the State was under some kind of obligation to ensure that they did not die: it simply had to provide appropriate medical care and attention. To have force-fed the prisoners would itself have been a breach of their rights under Articles 3 and 8 of the Convention, unless it could have

[4] See, generally, Reid (2008) 542–59. For a clear and straightforward account of the meaning of Art 2 in practice see Kelly (2005). For a prescient overview prior to the flowering of jurisprudence on the article see Harris (1994). See too the incisive critique by Bell and Keenan (2005).

[5] See, eg, Art 6(1) of the UN's International Covenant on Civil and Political Rights, which begins 'Every human being has the inherent right to life.'

[6] *Pretty v UK* (2002) 35 EHRR 1. But see now *R (Purdy) v DPP* [2009] UKHL 45, [2009] 3 WLR 403.

[7] *Burke v UK* App No 19807/06, decision of 11 July 2006.

[8] eg by republican prisoners in 1980 and 1981 and by loyalist prisoners in 1985. See McEvoy (2001) ch 4.

been shown that the prisoner in question was too mentally incompetent to take a decision on whether or not to die.[9]

Second, notwithstanding what has just been said, the European Court has stressed on several occasions that Article 2 must be strictly interpreted and must be applied in a way that makes the safeguards it provides *practical* and *effective*. It categorizes Article 2 as one of the most fundamental provisions in the Convention, enshrining, together with Article 3, a basic value of the democratic societies making up the Council of Europe.[10] Yet there are provisions within the Convention itself which militate against the effectiveness of the safeguards it provides. In particular, the requirements that applicants must themselves be victims (rather than, say, organizations representing victims),[11] and that they must lodge their application within six months from the date on which the final decision has been taken in relation to the last remedy available in the national legal system,[12] are inbuilt obstacles to ensuring that the European Court can get to the bottom of alleged abuses of the right to life. The Convention uses the same application and admissibility criteria regardless of the seriousness of the allegations being made in an application. One might have imagined that, when faced with applications from a region where protracted and serious unrest has broken out, the European Court would have been able to adopt less demanding criteria for receiving and dealing with allegations of really serious human rights abuses.[13] But the Convention does not allow for that kind of differentiated approach.

Third, the phrase 'Everyone's right to life shall be protected by law' is in one sense more positive than those used in other articles of the Convention. By this I mean that Article 2 expressly requires States to use the law to protect the right. A State cannot simply do nothing and then provide a remedy when the right is violated, which is largely the scheme of Article 3 of the Convention (the right not to be ill-treated). The European Court of Human Rights, alive to this point, has recently been keen to read into Article 2 certain positive obligations on the part of the State.[14] These include, as is explained in more detail below, the obligation to protect people against threats to their life and the obligation to thoroughly investigate actual or attempted killings. In these two respects cases from Northern Ireland have played a very significant role in the development of standards for the whole of Europe. It is through further development of the concept of positive obligations that the potential for Article 2 to play an even more significant role in modern society mainly lies.

Fourth, Article 2(2) does not primarily define instances where it is permitted intentionally to kill an individual, but describes 'the situations' where it is permitted to 'use

[9] Mental ill-health is the reason given for the force-feeding of the moors murderer, Ian Brady, which has been continuing since 1999. In 2000 Kay J declared the force-feeding to be lawful: *R v Collins and Ashworth Hospital Authority, ex p Brady* [2000] 8 Lloyd's Med Rep 355. See Keown (2002) 228–30.

[10] These points are all made in *McCann v UK* (1996) 21 EHRR 97.

[11] This requirement is now in Art 34 of the Convention.

[12] This requirement is now in Art 35(1) of the Convention.

[13] The effectiveness of the European Convention in the conflict zones of Turkey and Russia could also be said to have been affected by these inbuilt limitations, although in the case of Turkey the European Court has from time to time adopted a rather relaxed attitude towards the requirement to exhaust domestic remedies.

[14] See generally Mowbray (2004).

force' which may result, as an unintended outcome, in the deprivation of life.[15] The use of force, however, must be no more than 'absolutely necessary' for the achievement of one of the purposes set out in sub-paragraphs 2(a), (b), or (c). The use of the term 'absolutely necessary' shows that a stricter and more compelling test of necessity must be employed from that normally applicable when determining whether State action is 'necessary in a democratic society' under Articles 8(2), 9(2), 10(2), or 11(2) of the Convention. In particular, the force used must be strictly proportionate to the achievement of the aims set out in sub-paragraphs 2(a), (b), and (c). Amongst the factors to take into account when assessing this proportionality are 'the nature of the aim being pursued, the nature of the risk to life inherent in the particular case, and the extent of the risk that loss of life might be caused'.[16] So the European Court subjects deprivations of life to the most careful scrutiny, particularly where deliberate lethal force is used, taking into consideration not only the actions of the agents of the State who actually administered the force but also all the surrounding circumstances, including such matters as the planning and control of the actions in question.

Fifth, the strength of Article 2 is confirmed by the fact that under Article 15(2) of the Convention no derogations from Article 2 can be made under Article 15(1), which otherwise permits derogations in time of war or other public emergency provided the measures taken are strictly required by the exigencies of the situation and are not inconsistent with the State's other obligations under international law. The Irish and UK governments did, as we have seen in earlier chapters,[17] derogate from Article 5 of the European Convention in relation to the conflict in Northern Ireland, but they could not derogate from Article 2. In fact at no stage did either country put in place any special laws regulating the use of lethal force by members of the State security forces. In Northern Ireland the ordinary law of murder and manslaughter was applied throughout, an approach which suited the UK government because that law made it very difficult to secure the conviction of a police officer or soldier for murder as the judge (or jury, if there was one) took some persuading that the accused was not at the time acting either in self-defence or in defence of others. Concrete proposals for reform of this aspect of domestic law in Northern Ireland were repeatedly ignored by the UK government.[18]

The death penalty

Mercifully, the use of the death penalty as an official State punishment was never an issue during the years of the conflict in Northern Ireland from the late 1960s. The last execution took place there in 1961[19] and the death penalty was officially abolished for all but a few esoteric crimes by section 1(1) of the Northern Ireland (Emergency

[15] *Stewart v UK* App No 10044/82, decision of the European Commission, 10 July 1984, paras 14–15.

[16] Leach (2005) 183.

[17] Chs 3 and 4.

[18] Doran (1987); Hadden (1993).

[19] Robert McGladdery (aged 25) was hanged at Belfast's Crumlin Road prison for the murder of Pearl Gamble in Newry. This was not a conflict-related killing. See Ryder (2000a) 25.

Provisions) Act 1973, some eight years after this occurred in England and Wales.[20] It was reassuring to see this provision inserted at the very beginning of an Act whose purpose was otherwise to replace the notorious Civil Authorities (Special Powers) Acts (NI) 1922–43.[21] It sent out a clear message, from the then Conservative government in London, that whatever other steps might be taken to deal with the terrorist problem in Northern Ireland, application of the death penalty would not be one of them. Other States going through crises comparable to that experienced by Northern Ireland—notably South Africa—*have* resorted to the death penalty.[22] In the wake of several horrific terrorist atrocities in England in 1974 there were strong calls both within and without Westminster during the following 12 months for the death penalty to be reintroduced for terrorist murders, but these were resisted by the then Labour government.[23] Likewise, even though treason remained an offence for which the mandatory punishment was death (subject to an exercise of the Royal prerogative of mercy), no-one was ever prosecuted in Northern Ireland for that crime.[24] Throughout the United Kingdom the maximum penalty for treason was not changed to life imprisonment until the enactment of the Crime and Disorder Act 1998.[25]

The European Convention has itself been supplemented by two Protocols dealing with the death penalty. Protocol 6 was ratified by the United Kingdom in 1999 (and by Ireland in 1994). Article 1 of this Protocol abolishes the death penalty, but Article 2 says that a State may still provide for the death penalty in respect of acts committed in time of war or of imminent threat of war. The situation in Northern Ireland has never amounted to a 'war', so from 1999 the UK government could not introduce the death penalty for terrorist activities in Northern Ireland unless it denounced Protocol 6. Protocol 13 was ratified by the United Kingdom in 2003 (and by Ireland in 2002). It completely abolishes the death penalty, allowing of no exceptions whatsoever. Such is the extent of the prohibition of the death penalty throughout Europe today that in the recent case of *Őcalan v Turkey*[26] the Grand Chamber of the European Court agreed with a statement made by a Chamber of the Court that 'capital punishment in peacetime has come to be regarded as an unacceptable, if not inhuman, form of punishment which is no longer permissible under Article 2'.[27] The Grand Chamber

[20] Through the Murder (Abolition of Death Penalty) Act 1965, s 1. The last people executed in Britain were Peter Allen and Gwynne Evans on 13 August 1964.

[21] Edwards (1956b).

[22] The Republic of Ireland executed six men under emergency powers legislation during the period of the Second World War. See generally O'Brien (2006).

[23] Bishop (1978) 147. Bishop expressed himself to be in favour of the death penalty for terrorist murderers: 175.

[24] Though it has been suggested that Sir John Donaldson, who tried the Guildford Four in 1975, expressed regret that the defendants had not been charged with treason, because then the death penalty would have been available if they had been found guilty. When the PTA 1974 was going through the House of Commons Michael Mates, a Conservative MP, in his maiden speech, called for the law of treason to be updated and applied 'to the new sort of enemy that exists in our midst': HC Deb, vol 882, col 654 (28 November 1974). See too cols 661–3, per Sir Peter Rawlinson MP; cols 691–2, per William Rees-Davies MP; col 742, per Sir Michael Havers MP.

[25] s 36. [26] (2005) 41 EHRR 45.

[27] (2003) 37 EHRR 10, at para 163 (citing the Chamber's judgment of 12 March 2003 at para 196). In *Hussein v Albania and others* (2006) 42 EHRR SE16 Saddam Hussein's lawyers argued that 20 European

was a hair's breadth away from concluding that Article 2 of the Convention has been amended in so far as it permits the death penalty in times of peace.[28] Notwithstanding this position, at the end of 2008 the UK government delivered into the custody of the Iraqi High Tribunal two Iraqi civilians who were accused of the murder of two British soldiers, even though the government knew that, if convicted, the two men could well be sentenced to death. Despite the European Court's issue of an interim measure order requiring the UK government not to proceed with the handover, the government did so.[29] It remains to be seen whether either the Iraqi High Tribunal or the European Court will take further steps to ensure that the European antipathy to the death penalty is adhered to in this case.

It is conceivable that courts in Northern Ireland could still have to consider the impact of the death penalty when deciding whether to deport someone. In *Bader and Kanbor v Sweden*[30] the European Court held that if Sweden were to go ahead with its decision to deport a Syrian man to Syria, where he had been convicted of murder and sentenced to death, this would be a breach of Article 2. The Court noted that it is contrary to the Convention, even if Article 2 were to be construed as still permitting the death penalty in Europe, to implement a death sentence following an unfair trial, as an arbitrary deprivation of life is prohibited. In this case there had been a flagrant denial of the right to a fair trial because Bader's trial had taken place in his absence, no oral evidence had been submitted, all the evidence examined had been presented by the prosecutor, and not even the accused's lawyer had been in court. Moreover, the European Court held that to impose a death sentence on a person after an unfair trial would generate, in circumstances where there exists a real possibility that the sentence will be enforced, a significant degree of human anguish and fear on the part of the person found guilty and his or her family, bringing the treatment within the scope of Article 3 of the Convention. The Court therefore held that it would also have

States (including the UK and Ireland) had breached his rights under Arts 2, 3, 5, and 6 of the European Convention, together with Art 1 of Prots 6 and 13. He maintained that those States had had jurisdiction over him and that the European Court's previous decision in relation to when occupying forces have control over people (*Banković v Belgium and others* (2007) 44 EHRR SE5) was incorrect. But the Court declared his application to be inadmissible because his arguments around jurisdiction were based on assumptions which had not been substantiated. He had not specified each respondent State's precise role and responsibility or the division of power between them and the United States. Most importantly, he had not indicated which respondent State had had any involvement in his arrest, detention and handover to the Iraqi Interim Government on 30 June 2004 and he had not shown how those States had thereafter *de facto* remained in power in Iraq. The Court also held that there was no basis in the Convention's jurisprudence, or in any established principle of international law, which meant that he fell within the respondent States' jurisdiction on the sole basis that the European States allegedly formed part (at varying unspecified levels) of a coalition with the US. It noted that the impugned actions had been carried out by the US, that security in the zone in which those actions took place was assigned to the US, and that the overall command of the coalition was vested in the US. Saddam Hussein was executed on 30 December 2006.

[28] (2003) 37 EHRR 10, para 164.

[29] *Al-Saadoon and Mufdhi v UK* App No 61498/08, decision of 30 December 2008. A judicial review application in the English High Court also failed: [2009] EWCA 7, [2009] 3 WLR 957. For the views of the Parliamentary Joint Committee on Human Rights on this case see its Press Notice No 58, 30 July 2009 (revealing an exchange of correspondence with the Secretary of State for Defence).

[30] App No 13284/04, decision of 8 November 2005. See too *Öcalan v Turkey* (2003) 37 EHRR 10, paras 165–75.

been a breach of the Article 3 rights of Bader and his wife and two children to deport them all to Syria. In *F v United Kingdom*,[31] on the other hand, an Iranian seeking political asylum in Britain argued that he should not be deported to Iran because he might be in danger of execution there on account of his homosexuality. But the European Court was not convinced by the materials presented to it that this outcome was likely and it therefore found the application to be inadmissible. In such cases it is obviously crucial to be able to put before the Court highly persuasive evidence of the actual state of affairs in the non-European country in question.

Apart from issues to do with the death penalty, the case law of the European Court of Human Rights suggests that there are three distinct aspects of the right to life protected by Article 2, each of which will be examined separately below. They are the right to be protected against risks to life, the right not to be killed, and the right to a thorough investigation of a killing or attempted killing. We shall see that cases from Northern Ireland have contributed significantly to the European Court's jurisprudence in the first and third of these areas, but not, surprisingly, in the second.

The right to be protected against risks to life

Early attempts to secure from the European Commission and Court of Human Rights a commitment to impose a duty on States to protect people living in those States against risks to their lives failed. The risks did not directly emanate from organs of the State, as they had done during the Nazi regime in Germany, but from criminal elements in society whom the State organs were trying (but largely failing) to detect and punish.

In *JPB v Ireland*[32] a man living in Dublin who had previously received the protection of a bodyguard complained that the refusal of the Irish authorities to continue this protection was a breach of his rights under Article 2 of the Convention. In July 1969 an attempt on his life had been made by three members of the IRA. He had been shot in the back and the leg but was able to escape and to identify his attackers to the police. One man was arrested and convicted but the two other men involved were not caught. Following that incident the claimant was placed under police protection, in the form of a personal armed escort and a 24-hour uniformed police officer watching his home. This protection apparently continued even after he moved to work in London in May 1972, but when he returned to Dublin in December 1972 he was told that he would no longer receive special police protection. He was nevertheless warned by the police that there was a still a great danger to his life, so he decided to live separately from his family and he complained that the Irish State was not doing enough to protect him. In Strasbourg the European Commission declared his application inadmissible because Ireland did have some laws in place to protect the right to life and Article 2 could not be interpreted as imposing a duty on a State to supply

[31] App No 17341/03, decision of 22 June 2004.

[32] App No 6040/73, decision of 20 July 1973, also known as *X v Ireland*, 16 Ybk 388.

a constant personal bodyguard, 'at least not for an indefinite period of time'.[33] The applicant also sought to rely on Article 5(1) of the Convention, which protects the right to security of person as well as the right to liberty but, as we saw in Chapter 5, the Commission (and Court) have consistently chosen not to develop the right to security in any significant way.

Several further applications were made to Strasbourg by people living in Northern Ireland who alleged that the UK government was not doing enough to protect the lives of Protestants living in terrorized areas (particularly those areas close to the border with the Republic of Ireland) or the lives of persons employed in the security forces.[34] Some applications were lodged against Ireland as well as against the United Kingdom, but they were declared inadmissible against Ireland on the ground that the deaths in question had occurred outside that country's jurisdiction, ie within Northern Ireland.[35] Two of those cases were in any event brought outside the six-month time limit.[36] Likewise, the United Kingdom could not be held responsible in relation to deaths occurring in the Republic of Ireland, even if the victim had travelled there from Northern Ireland for a brief visit.[37] In one case the applicant's husband, William Elliott, was killed by the Provisional IRA while he was visiting a cattle mart in the Republic in 1980;[38] he was a member of the governing body of the Ulster Unionist Party and (until 18 months before his death) a member of the Ulster Defence Regiment, a regiment of the British army. The victim was held not to have been 'within the jurisdiction' of the United Kingdom at the time he died, although the European Commission did also consider whether any active measures by the UK authorities could have contributed to his murder in the Republic, which suggests that if this had been the case the jurisdictional point would not have been an obstacle to a finding that Article 2 had been violated.[39]

In *W v United Kingdom* Mrs Elliott also complained of a breach of Article 2 on behalf of herself and her two dependent children (she had three other children, who were older), this time in relation to the murder of her brother, Jack Donnelly, who was killed by republican paramilitaries while he was having a drink in a pub in

[33] ibid, 'The Law', para 1. The Commission also found that there was no breach of Arts 8 or 14 of the Convention.

[34] Much of the legal work associated with these applications was conducted by Brian Garrett and Neil Faris, two Belfast solicitors, and by Edgar Graham, a young university lecturer and barrister who was also active in the Ulster Unionist Party. Mr Garrett was interviewed for this book in July 2009. In December 1983 Edgar Graham was himself murdered by an IRA gunman in the grounds of Queen's University Belfast. No-one has yet been convicted of his murder. This whole aspect of Art 2 is ignored in Liberty's account of Art 2 concerns in Northern Ireland: NIHRA (1993) 13–29.

[35] eg *M v UK and Ireland* App No 9837/82, 47 DR 27.

[36] *H v UK and Ireland* App No 9833/82, 42 DR 53, where a mother argued that both governments had not done enough to prevent terrorists murdering her daughter in 1977, but she did not lodge her application until four years after the death; see too *X v UK and Ireland* (1986) 8 EHRR 49.

[37] *W v UK* (1983) 5 EHRR 504, 'The Law', para 5.

[38] For more details see McKittrick et al (2004) 831.

[39] In *M v UK and Ireland* App No 9837/82, 'The Law', para 29, the Commission again stressed that 'in the concrete circumstances of her case' the right to life of a widow whose husband had been murdered in Northern Ireland had not been affected by any specific act or omission of the Irish State.

Northern Ireland in 1981.[40] She alleged that the UK government had not adopted adequate or effective measures to protect her and her children against a concerted terrorist campaign being waged with the calculated genocidal intent of driving members of the Protestant community from their lands, homes, and businesses in certain border areas. The European Commission of Human Rights acknowledged that Article 2 of the Convention may indeed give rise to positive obligations on the part of a State but noted that this did not mean that there was a positive obligation to exclude any possible violence. Curiously, the Commission then added that '[it] does not find that it can be its task, in its examination of the present applicant's complaint under Article 2, to consider in detail, as she appears to suggest, the appropriateness and efficiency of the measures taken by the United Kingdom to combat terrorism in Northern Ireland'.[41] Without going into those details the Commission nevertheless felt able to hold that the United Kingdom was not 'required under the Convention to protect the applicant's brother [nor the applicant] by measures going beyond those actually taken by the authorities in order to shield life and limb of the inhabitants of Northern Ireland against attacks from terrorists'.[42] The only 'evidence' it referred to in support of this conclusion was that, 'while the peacetime army strength in Northern Ireland was 4,000 men, it currently stands at about 10,500 and that, between August 1969 and December 1981, several hundred members of the armed and security forces lost their lives there combating terrorism'.[43] Applying the rather blunt admissibility criterion in what was then Article 17(2) of the European Convention, the Commission declared the applicant's application to be 'manifestly ill-founded'.

The approach taken by the Commission in this Northern Irish case is indicative of a reluctance on its part to 'second-guess' the decisions of governments, and of military authorities, when they are combating terrorism. There seems to be an acceptance that effectively combating terrorism is extremely difficult and that States should be left to get on with the task as they judge best, even if in practice they are not very successful in preventing terrorist attacks. This attitude remained in place throughout virtually the entire conflict in Northern Ireland and is still apparent today as regards the anti-terrorist strategies adopted in countries such as Turkey and Russia. Other branches of the Council of Europe may be attempting to make States more effective in their counter-terrorism work,[44] but the approach of the European Court has consistently been cautious. As yet it has not been confronted with an inter-State application alleging that the respondent State is not doing enough to prevent terrorists travelling from that State to the applicant State in order to commit terrorist acts.[45]

[40] McKittrick et al (2004) 854.

[41] *W v UK* (1983) 5 EHRR 504, 'The Law', para 14.

[42] ibid, paras 15–16.

[43] ibid, para 16.

[44] See, eg, the Council's Convention on the Prevention of Terrorism 2005 and the work of its Committee of Experts on Terrorism (CODEXTER).

[45] There is no record of the UK government ever considering such an application against Ireland in the early years of the troubles. For a plea for a new approach to the rules on State responsibility for terrorism see Becker (2006).

Several cases have also been taken to Strasbourg around the denial of special protection measures to individuals. In *M v United Kingdom and Ireland*,[46] already referred to, the applicant's husband, Hugh McGinn, a Catholic who was a part-time sergeant-major in the Territorial Army, had been shot dead in the doorway of his Armagh home three days after Christmas in 1980 by six men for whose actions the Irish National Liberation Army claimed responsibility.[47] McGinn had asked the Territorial Army to issue him with a personal protection firearm but it had refused, supposedly on the rather specious basis that if he were given such a weapon he would become even more of a target. He and his six children lived in a strongly republican area in County Armagh and had been seriously intimidated in the past: their house had been stoned and petrol-bombed, his children had been attacked and abused in the street, and slogans had been written on the gable of his house during the republican prisoners' hunger strike in 1981. Unfortunately the complaint concerning the murder of the applicant's husband was declared inadmissible by the European Commission because it had been lodged more than 11 months after the killing, contrary to the Convention's requirement that applications be lodged 'within six months from the date on which the final decision was taken'.[48] An opportunity was lost, therefore, to obtain from the Commission, and possibly the Court, a more detailed exposition of the more general obligations resting on States to ensure that people are protected against this kind of violent and highly personalized harassment. Later case law, both domestic and European, would suggest that a remedy may now lie under Article 8 of the European Convention—partly because the harassment is often not such as to amount to what is required (as we shall see) for a breach of Article 2, namely 'a real and immediate risk to *life*' (as opposed to *a private and family life*), but also because the concept of positive obligations has gained a firmer foothold in the context of Article 8 than it has in the context of Article 2.

As regards Mrs McGinn's complaint concerning her own situation in Northern Ireland, the Commission adopted virtually identical language to that which it had used in *W v United Kingdom*.[49] The applicant tried to argue that the mass breakout of republican prisoners from the Maze Prison in 1983, and the failure of the security

[46] App No 9837/82, 47 DR 27.

[47] The INLA was another republican paramilitary organization, separate from the IRA; see generally Holland and McDonald (1994). For more details of McGinn's murder and the ensuing prosecutions see McKittrick et al (2004) 844.

[48] Then Art 26, now Art 35(1), of the Convention. In this case there was no domestic remedy available for the applicant to exhaust and the Commission followed its ruling in an earlier case that 'where no domestic remedy is available, the act or decision complained of must itself normally be taken as the "final decision" for the purposes of Art 26' (*X v UK* App No 7379/76, 8 DR 211, 212–13). This is a rather harsh approach to take, especially when one considers that it may take at least six months for the victim of a human rights abuse to discover that there is no domestic remedy which he or she can pursue. There is a strong case to be made for introducing a rule that in cases where there is no such domestic remedy the applicant should have 12 months in which to lodge an application in Strasbourg. This would, incidentally, coincide with the usual time limit imposed by the Human Rights Act 1998 for claims made in UK courts in respect of breaches of Convention rights allegedly committed by public authorities (s 7(5)(a)), though that Act goes on to say that such proceedings can be brought even after one year if the court considers this to be 'equitable having regard to all the circumstances' (s 7(5)(b)).

[49] See text at nn 37–43 above.

forces to block border crossings effectively, were indications that the State was not doing enough to protect people against terrorists, but the Commission could not accept that this tipped the balance in favour of finding a breach of Article 2 on the part of the UK government.

At the end of the 1980s, therefore, the position was that the European Commission and Court of Human Rights were extremely reluctant to impose any kind of specific obligation on States to protect life. The furthest they would go was to require States to have in place a system of criminal law enforcement, essentially a reactive rather than a preventative approach to the protection of life by law.[50] And while the Strasbourg organs seemed prepared to take into account the special features of terrorism when considering whether States had violated their negative obligations under the Convention (such as the obligation not to deprive someone of his or her liberty except in accordance with Article 5[51]), they did not seem to think that the phenomenon of terrorism placed a greater burden on the State to protect people against such acts. Moreover, little has emerged from the Strasbourg organs since the 1980s to suggest that today's European Court of Human Rights would be much more willing to closely examine the anti-terrorist policies of Council of Europe States from this angle. In so far as the European Court has significantly developed its standards at all in this area, it has been in the context of increasing the effectiveness of the right to have a killing or attempted killing thoroughly investigated[52] not the context of enhancing the right to be protected against risks to life in the first place.

Eventually, however, a step-change was taken by the European Court in *Osman v United Kingdom*,[53] not a case involving the conflict in Northern Ireland, where it stressed that the first sentence of Article 2(1) requires a State not only to refrain from the intentional and unlawful taking of life but also to take appropriate steps to safeguard the lives of those within its jurisdiction. This meant, said the Court, that a State must put in place not just effective criminal law provisions to deter the commission of violent inter-personal crimes but also effective law enforcement machinery for the *prevention*, suppression, and sanctioning of breaches of such provisions. In other words, Article 2 implies in certain well-defined circumstances a positive obligation on the authorities to take preventative operational measures to protect an individual whose life is at risk from the criminal acts of another individual.

In *Osman v United Kingdom* itself a male school-teacher who was besotted with a young boy at his school eventually shot the boy and his father (as well as another boy and his father) in March 1988. The two boys survived but the two adults died. The widow and son of the first man then sued the Metropolitan Police in London for their negligence in not protecting the family against the crazed stalker (who was convicted of manslaughter and sentenced to be detained in a secure mental hospital without limit of time) but in the Court of Appeal the police succeeded in getting the claim struck out as disclosing no reasonable cause of action.[54] The

50 See *X and Y v The Netherlands* (1986) 8 EHRR 235.

51 See chs 5 and 6 above.

52 See 268–74 below.

53 (2000) 29 EHRR 245. See McBride (1999).

54 *Osman v Ferguson* [1993] 4 All ER 344.

Court of Appeal said it would be against public policy to impose a duty of care on the police to apprehend potential offenders, as this would significantly divert police resources from the investigation and suppression of crime. Leave to appeal to the House of Lords was refused. The family then took their case to Strasbourg, where 20 judges in the Grand Chamber of the European Court held unanimously, more than 10 years after the killing, that English law's blanket exclusion of a duty of care on the part of the police towards potential victims of crime was a breach of the right to access justice, guaranteed by Article 6 of the Convention. Each of the applicants was awarded £10,000 to compensate them for the denial of an opportunity to obtain a ruling from the English courts on the merits of their claim for damages against the police.[55]

As regards Article 2, the European Court formulated the duty to protect life in the following way:

> In the opinion of the Court where there is an allegation that the authorities have violated their positive obligation to protect the right to life... it must be established to its satisfaction that the authorities knew or ought to have known at the time of the existence of a real and immediate risk to the life of an identified individual or individuals from the criminal acts of a third party and that they failed to take measures within the scope of their powers which, judged reasonably, might have been expected to avoid that risk. The Court does not accept the Government's view that the failure to perceive the risk to life in the circumstances known at the time or to take preventive measures to avoid that risk must be tantamount to gross negligence or wilful disregard of the duty to protect life. Such a rigid standard must be considered to be incompatible with the requirements of Article 1 of the Convention[56] and the obligations of Contracting States under that Article to secure the practical and effective protection of the rights and freedoms laid down therein, including Article 2. For the Court, and having regard to the nature of the right protected by Article 2, a right fundamental in the scheme of the Convention, it is sufficient for an applicant to show that the authorities did not do all that could be reasonably expected of them to avoid a real and immediate risk to life of which they have or ought to have knowledge. This is a question which can only be answered in the light of all the circumstances of any particular case.[57]

On the facts of the case before it, however, the European Court (by 17 to three) was not persuaded that the police at any decisive stage knew or ought to have known that the lives of the applicants' family were at real and immediate risk from a third party. The Osmans therefore lost on Article 2[58] but the principle established in the case remains applicable throughout Europe. The 'real and immediate risk' test is the one which has to be applied in all jurisdictions, including Northern Ireland.

[55] By 19 to one the Court held that the requirements of Art 13 of the Convention—which confers the right to an effective remedy for violations of human rights—were less strict than, and so here absorbed by, those of Art 6, which meant that it was not necessary for the Court to examine Art 13 in more detail in this case.

[56] Art 1 reads: 'The High Contracting Parties shall secure to everyone within their jurisdiction the rights and freedoms defined in Section 1 of the Convention.' Section 1 comprises Arts 2 to 18 of the Convention.

[57] (2000) 29 EHRR 245, para 116 (references omitted).

[58] For the same reason, and by the same majority, the Court also held that there was no breach of Art 8 of the Convention.

Post-*Osman* cases relating to Northern Ireland

In Northern Ireland there have been several post-*Osman* cases on the right to be protected against risks to life, most of them brought by people who want their anonymity protected when giving evidence in court or who want access to better personal protection after having received death threats. There have also been recent decisions in England which might well have ramifications for this area of the law in Northern Ireland.

In *Re A's Application*[59] the applicant challenged the refusal by the Chief Constable of the RUC to release certain information concerning a find of material held by loyalist paramilitaries. His name had been discovered on a piece of paper, as had a poor photocopy of his photograph. The applicant suspected that the documents in question originated from the police or army and that they had been 'leaked' to the loyalist paramilitaries. He wanted to see the documents so that he could assess the nature of the threat against him. In his judgment Kerr J, as he then was, referred to what Lord Hope had said a few months earlier in *R v DPP, ex parte Kebeline*, namely that there is a 'discretionary area of judgment' within which the judiciary should defer, on democratic grounds, to the considered opinion of the executive or legislature.[60] Lord Hope continued:

> It will be easier for such an area of judgment to be recognised where the Convention itself requires a balance to be struck, much less so where the right is stated in terms which are unqualified. It will be easier for it to be recognised where the issues involve questions of social or economic policy, much less so where the rights are of high constitutional importance or are of a kind where the courts are especially well placed to assess the need for protection. But even where the right is stated in terms which are unqualified the courts will need to bear in mind the jurisprudence of the European Court which recognises that due account should be taken of the special nature of terrorist crime and the threat it poses to a democratic society.[61]

Kerr J noted that in the case before him the decision under challenge had not been taken by an elected body and that therefore 'the degree of deference due to it is commensurately less', but he added that:

> an appropriate level of discretion must be available to the police authorities in deciding what measures are required to afford the applicant adequate protection in fulfilment of his Article 2 rights. The police are inevitably in a better position than is the court to assess the level of threat to the applicant and to judge the degree of risk that would accrue if the information sought by the applicant were released to him. They are also aware whether further arrests are likely and whether future prosecutions might be jeopardised if the information was disclosed. These considerations do not relieve the court of its supervisory duty but the court should be conscious of them in exercising superintendence of the respondent's decision.

Kerr J then held that, although (as we shall see below) the State authorities are under a duty to ensure that a thorough investigation of the risk to the applicant is

[59] [2001] NIQB 21.

[60] [2000] 2 AC 326, 379. Lord Hope acknowledges that the phrase was coined by Lords Lester and Pannick in their *Human Rights Law and Practice* (1st edn, 1999) para 3.21.

[61] ibid, citing *Murray v UK* (1994) 19 EHRR 193, 222, para 47.

undertaken, and that as part of that investigation the applicant needs to be informed of the find of material relating to him, he does not need to be told everything about the find. He added:

Nor do I consider that he is entitled to access to the information that he has sought in order to take proceedings against those responsible for releasing information about him unless it is shown that such a facility is required in order to provide him with adequate safeguards under Article 2 and I do not consider that this has been established in the present case.

This decision was not 'appealed' to Strasbourg, no doubt on legal advice that the European Court would probably be no more sympathetic to the applicant's arguments than the Northern Irish court had been.

In another case, arising long after the supergrass tactic had been abandoned in Northern Ireland,[62] a man who was outed as being an alleged informer for the British security forces while still operating at a high level within the IRA went to court to seek a declaration that he was not an informer. He relied upon Article 2 of the Convention because he knew that the IRA murdered people who were informers and he feared for his life. His attempt to get a declaration failed, because the court would not go behind the government's policy of neither confirming nor denying rumours about the identity of its informers (the 'NCND' policy).[63] Even though Article 2 is 'a right fundamental in the scheme of the Convention',[64] Carswell LCJ clearly thought that protection of the right to life under Article 2 did need to be 'balanced' against other competing interests. He summed up his position as follows:

My conclusion on this part of the case is that the Minister's decision did not constitute a breach of the positive obligation placed upon her as a public authority and upon the Government to take appropriate steps to safeguard the applicant's life. In reaching this conclusion I have taken into account the several factors which I have mentioned, the risk to the applicant's life, the extent to which a statement from the Minister would protect him, the risk that departure from the NCND policy in this case would endanger the lives of agents on other occasions and the effect on the Government's ability to continue to obtain intelligence in order to combat terrorism. Having weighed these matters, I am of the firm opinion that the Minister's decision not to depart from the NCND policy did not constitute a breach of Article 2.[65]

Doubtless unimpressed by the ability of the European Convention to protect his right to life (and aware that, in any event, a court order in his favour was hardly likely to dissuade his enemies from exacting their 'revenge'), the applicant in this case reportedly fled Northern Ireland and is now living abroad. He later obtained an injunction from the High Court preventing anyone from disclosing his whereabouts.[66]

[62] On which see ch 8 above.

[63] *In re Scappaticci's Application* [2003] NIQB 56, a decision impliedly criticized by Anthony (2008) at para 1.09, n 40.

[64] See the extract from the European Court's judgment in *Osman v UK* cited at n 57 above.

[65] ibid, [20]. For a general account of the interrelationship between human rights and issues of national security see Cameron (2000).

[66] *Scappaticci v Independent News and Media Ltd*, decision of 29 June 2006, unreported (Weir J). For a copy of the injunction see <http://cryptome.org/scappaticci-gag.htm>, last visited 16 August 2009. In another case involving a prominent Sinn Féin activist who was outed as a government agent, Denis

In *Re Anderson's Application*[67] a prisoner wanted to be transferred to a part of Maghaberry Prison which was 'separate accommodation' for loyalists.[68] He argued that the State's obligations under Article 2 required him to be moved there for his own protection, but the judge ruled that even if the applicant was under a real and immediate risk to his life in one part of the prison (which was far from clear) this did not mean that he had to be moved to the loyalist accommodation. Insufficient evidence had been produced to show that the Prison Service should have considered him to be a member or a supporter of a loyalist paramilitary organization, despite his protestations to that effect.

It seems, then, that the right to a thorough investigation of a killing or of an attempted killing extends in the law of Northern Ireland to a situation where someone is under a threat, but that the information which the threatened person is entitled to receive in such a situation is not as wide-ranging as that which would be available if there has already been an attempt on his or her life. In brief, Article 2 is better at vindicating the rights of people who are dead than the rights of those who are in grave peril of their lives. The later cases on the right to a thorough investigation of a killing, which are examined in the next section, do not, regrettably, correct this apparent anomaly. It is worth noting, moreover, that in *Re A's Application* Kerr J did not address the conundrum which would arise if, during the investigation of a threat, the police were to discover that other police officers may have been implicated in the threat (eg by providing information about the threatened person). If the police were to continue with their investigation the threatened person might well argue that the investigation is not independent and impartial, as now required under Article 2. An obvious way out of this conundrum would be for the Policing Board or the Secretary of State to transfer the responsibility for such investigations to the office of the Police Ombudsman for Northern Ireland.[69]

The Key Persons Protection Scheme

A claim for protection next came before the courts of Northern Ireland in *Re Meehan's Application*,[70] where the applicant wanted to be allowed to have a personal protection weapon. The court refused an application for judicial review of the decision not to grant such a weapon and in doing so Carswell LCJ, as he then was, set out the four

Donaldson, a Sunday newspaper did give some indication of where he was hiding; less than a month later, in April 2006, he was found murdered there, the Real IRA claiming responsibility for the killing.

[67] [2005] NIQB 61 (Weatherup J).

[68] In 2003, following a report by a Safety Review Team, the Secretary of State for Northern Ireland authorized the official separation of loyalist and republican paramilitary prisoners in the interests of safety.

[69] This power is available under the Police (NI) Act 1998, s 55(1): 'The [Policing Board] or the Secretary of State may refer to the Ombudsman any matter which (a) appears to the [Board] or the Secretary of State to indicate that a member of the police force may have (i) committed a criminal offence or (ii) behaved in a manner which would justify disciplinary proceedings, and (b) is not the subject of a complaint, if, after consultation with the Ombudsman and the Chief Constable, it appears to the [Board] or the Secretary of State that it is desirable in the public interest that the Ombudsman should investigate the matter.'

[70] [2004] NIJB 53.

factors which should be weighed up by the court when deciding whether the State has been in breach of its duties under Article 2 of the European Convention:

> The court should ascertain the extent or degree of risk to life, take into account whether or not that risk has been created by some action carried out (or proposed) by the State, determine whether it would be difficult for the State to act to reduce the risk and whether there are cogent reasons in the public interest why it should not take a course of action open to it which would reduce the risk.

Again, as in the *Scappaticci* case just discussed we see the Chief Justice openly admitting that there may be 'reasons in the public interest' not to protect an individual's life. The implication is that factors such as 'national security', public expenditure, or, perhaps, previous life-style, can be used to lessen the right to life even of someone who is under a real and immediate threat.

Thereafter there was a flurry of cases around personal protection systems decided towards the end of 2004, three by Weatherup J and one by Girvan J. They all concerned what is known as the Key Persons Protection Scheme (KPPS), which is a non-statutory scheme operated by the Secretary of State for Northern Ireland with the aim of protecting those whose death or injury as a result of terrorist attack could damage or seriously undermine the democratic framework of government, the effective administration of government and/or the criminal justice system, or the maintenance of law and order. Persons occupying certain jobs qualify for the scheme if they are assessed by the Chief Constable as being under serious or significant threat, but other persons also qualify if they are performing a wider public role which makes a positive and helpful contribution to the realization of the objectives of the scheme or if there are compelling political reasons for extending the scheme's protection.[71] Even if people do not qualify under the scheme, the Secretary of State sometimes agrees (pursuant to a policy introduced only in January 2002) to provide home protection measures outside the scheme.[72] At the time of these cases the Chief Constable operated a threat level assessment which distinguished between six different levels of threat—imminent, serious, significant, moderate, low, and negligible.

[71] In 2002 the Northern Ireland Human Rights Commission published a report prepared in June 2001 on the compatibility of the government's Key Persons Protection Scheme in Northern Ireland with the European Convention on Human Rights: see NIHRC (2002). A Freedom of Information request has also revealed how much the KPPS cost the government in the years 1998 to 2006. The figures were: 1998–99: £5.2m; 1999–00: £6.6m; 2000–01: £4.9m; 2001–02: £4.9m; 2002–03: £11m; 2003–04: £13m; 2004–05: £7.5m; 2005–06: £4.6m (est). The increased expenditure in 2002–05 resulted from the need to provide physical home security measures for prison officers whose personal details were compromised in 2002 when data relating to 1,426 prison staff were found on a computer which had fallen into the hands of the Provisional IRA (HC Deb, vol 396, col 53W, 9 December 2002), whereupon all compromised officers were given the option of applying for enhanced security measures to be installed at their home under the KPPS or the Prison Service Protection Scheme; alternatively, officers could apply for financial assistance to move home under the Prison Service Assisted Home Removal Scheme, and arrangements were also put in place with the Northern Ireland Housing Executive to facilitate the purchase of an officer's house under the Scheme for the Purchase of Evacuated Dwellings (HL Deb, vol 654, col WA357, 20 November 2003). The website of the Northern Ireland Prison Service reveals that 669 of the 1,426 prison officers received help under the KPPS.

[72] As mentioned in n 7 above, the Northern Ireland Housing Executive also runs a scheme which allows the purchase of homes which have been evacuated because of intimidation of the current occupants.

In *Re W's Application*[73] the applicant was told by the police that the level of threat against her was 'significant' but she was refused protection under the KPPS because she did not otherwise meet the scheme's eligibility criteria. Later the police's threat assessment was raised to 'severe' (even though this was not one of the six recognized levels) and the applicant again applied for protection but was refused. She was however provided with some home protection by the Northern Ireland Housing Executive (and advised by the police to move house). Weatherup J applied the balancing test enunciated by Carswell LCJ in *Re Meehan's Application*, summing it up by saying:

> The approach to Article 2 obligations is not based on an applicant reaching a threshold of risk set at different levels in different contexts, but rather about balancing the risk against reasonable measures to reduce the risk.

Applying that balancing test in conjunction with the 'real and immediate threat' test laid down by the European Court in *Osman v United Kingdom*,[74] the learned judge held that the Secretary of State's approach in the case before him was flawed because, according to his officials, it excluded from home protection measures those people who were subject to a real and immediate threat that was less than 'imminent'. The judge was not prepared to accept that this flaw was cured by the fact that public authorities were at liberty to provide protective measures not covered by the KPPS or the home protection scheme; nor was it cured by the fact that the authorities had 'an area of discretionary judgment' when reaching a determination as to the extent of the measures required to meet Article 2 obligations from case to case. In other words, Weatherup J applied what amounted to strict scrutiny of the authorities' discretion in this field. He admitted that the decision taken by the authorities might have been the same even if they had taken into account that people under a 'serious' threat in the police's eyes could still be under a 'real and immediate threat' in the Convention's eyes, but as the approach taken by the officials left out of account this relevant consideration, the judge quashed their decision. He did not, however, accept that the way the protection system operated was a breach of Article 14 of the European Convention (the right not to be discriminated against): the system, whether flawed or not in the way already described, did not treat people differently on any of the grounds listed in Article 14.[75] One's lack of importance as a public person is apparently not a 'status' which can ground a discrimination claim within the terms of that provision.

Weatherup J delivered two other judgments in this field on the same day in *Re Frazer's Applications*[76] and *Re Brolly's Application*.[77] In the police's assessment the

[73] [2004] NIQB 67. [74] (2000) 29 EHRR 245.

[75] This was not the view of the NIHRC, which said: 'If the state is failing to provide protection under the KPPS based on occupational criteria then this constitutes a "ground" which is not defensible under Article 14 ... The value of a person's life has never been interpreted by the Court to be based on a person's social status, the occupation they profess or their ascribed external contribution to the society. The opposite is true. The Court has consistently looked beyond such descriptive assessment and focused on the inherent dignity and equality of each person regardless of social occupation or status' (NIHRC (2002) 14).

[76] [2004] NIQB 68. Mr Frazer was, and is, a prominent campaigner for the rights of the victims of republican paramilitary groups, primarily through the pressure group FAIR (Families Acting for Innocent Relatives).

[77] [2004] NIQB 69.

level of threat in the former case was 'significant' and in the latter it was 'moderate'. It followed from his analysis in *Re W's Application* that in both cases Weatherup J found the authorities' approach to be flawed because it left out of account the relevant consideration that, even if the level of threat was only 'significant' or 'moderate' there could still have been a real and immediate threat to life in Convention terms. In *Re Frazer's Applications* the judge went on to consider, and reject, a challenge to the Secretary of State's decisions not to issue the applicant with a personal protection weapon and to revoke his existing firearms certificate for a shotgun. He held that Mr Frazer was entitled to be told the gist of the information considered by the Secretary of State which was adverse to his application but that on the facts of the case it was acceptable for the Secretary of State to rely on the intelligence information furnished by the police as there were no indications that called into question his reliance on that information:

> Officials sought confirmation that there was intelligence that the applicant's contacts were illegitimate and that the information was considered reliable and both matters were confirmed. There will be cases where circumstances require that further enquiries be undertaken, but no such circumstances are evident in the present case.[78]

Procedural fairness was also an issue in *Re Brolly's Application*, where the same judge repeated the points he made in *Re Frazer's Application* concerning disclosure of information about the threat assessment. He was able to imagine cases where there would be grounds for concluding that fairness required greater disclosure than that provided by the police in this case. He went on to hold, however, that even in such cases the process available to someone dissatisfied by the decision in question was judicial review and that those proceedings would provide a sufficient hearing for the purposes of Article 6 of the European Convention.[79] Weatherup J also followed the ruling by the Court of Appeal of Northern Ireland in *Re Brown's Application*,[80] which was to the effect that neither Article 8 (the right to a private life) nor Article 1 of Protocol 1 to the European Convention (the right to peaceful enjoyment of one's possessions) was engaged in situations where eligibility for a firearm certificate was being considered.

A further challenge to a refusal by the Secretary of State to order personal protection measures was made in *Re Patrick Murray's Application*,[81] where the applicant was the Chairman of Sinn Féin in the town of Antrim but was allegedly under threat from both loyalist paramilitaries and dissident republican paramilitaries. He was told that he could avail himself of extra security arrangements put in place by the Housing Executive (worth at least £1,500) but was otherwise refused protection. Girvan J agreed with the approach to Article 2 adopted by Weatherup J in *Re W's Application* but, even though the level of threat against the applicant was, in police terms, 'severe', he did not quash the decision to refuse protection on the ground that the police had

[78] [2004] NIQB 68, para 48.

[79] In this the judge followed the House of Lords' approach to the meaning of 'civil rights and obligations' in Art 6 in *Runa Begum v Tower Hamlets* [2003] UKHL 4, [2003] 2 AC 430.

[80] [2003] NIJB 168.

[81] 2004, unreported.

failed to take into account a relevant consideration (namely, that people under severe threats could also be under a 'real and immediate threat'). He expressly said that the applicant had failed to demonstrate that the minister's decision was infected by a failure to take into account relevant considerations.[82] Instead, he moved to consider whether in all the circumstances of the case what the State authorities were doing about the risk was 'all that could be reasonably expected of them to avoid a real and immediate risk to life of which they have or ought to have knowledge'.[83] In undertaking that consideration the learned judge reminded us that what is 'reasonable' must to an extent take account of cost and expense. He cited what the European Court had said in *Kiliç v Turkey*, namely:

Bearing in mind the difficulties in policing modern societies, the unpredictability of human conduct and the operational choices which must be made in terms of priorities and resources, the scope of the positive obligation must be interpreted in a way which does not impose an impossible or disproportionate burden on the authorities.[84]

And he added, for his own part:

If manpower and funds were unlimited the applicant's house could be fully fortified and the house guarded throughout the day. However, funds are not unlimited nor is unlimited manpower available. Substantial diversion of funds for the type of work the applicant demands, if applied in all analogous situations, would have a major impact on government budgetary considerations... The court has limited qualification to determine issues involving the best use of resources which raise wider democratic issues... It is possible for the court to envisage other and theoretically better ways that the state could pursue to reduce the risks to the applicant... But it is not the function of the court in a judicial review application to conduct a policy review.[85]

In so far as Girvan J's judgment in *Re Patrick Murray's Application* may be inconsistent with Weatherup J's three earlier judgments, in that Girvan J was more concerned with whether the decision made actually resulted in a breach of rights rather than with whether the right test had been applied by the decision maker when making the decision, more recent case law is on the side of Girvan J. The House of Lords, in both *R (SB) v Head Teacher and Governor of Denbigh High School*[86] and *Re Misbehavin' Ltd v Belfast City Council*,[87] has suggested that the nature of the outcome is more important than the nature of the process prior to the outcome. As Lord Bingham put it in the first of those two cases:

[T]he focus at Strasbourg is not and has never been on whether a challenged decision or action is the product of a defective decision-making process, but on whether, in the case under consideration, the applicant's Convention rights have been violated... This pragmatic approach is fully reflected in the [Human Rights Act 1998]. The unlawfulness proscribed by section 6(1)

[82] ibid, para 21.
[83] *Osman v UK* (1998) 29 EHRR 245, para 18.
[84] (2001) 33 EHRR 58, para 63. The Court borrows here from what it said in *Osman v UK* (2000) 29 EHRR 245, para 116.
[85] *Re Patrick Murray's Application* (2004, unreported) [17] and [19].
[86] [2006] UKHL 15, [2007] 1 AC 100.
[87] [2007] UKHL 19, [2007] 1 WLR 1420.

is acting in a way which is incompatible with a Convention right, not relying on a defective process of reasoning, and action may be brought under section 7(1) only by a person who is a victim of an unlawful act.[88]

With respect, such an approach seems to be unfortunate on two fronts. First, it makes a distinction between judicial review claims based on the Human Rights Act and judicial review claims based on other grounds, because in the latter context the chief inquiry is indeed into whether the appropriate decision-making processes were adopted, regardless of the outcome. Second, it disincentivizes public authorities from putting in place proper decision-making processes which are more likely to produce outcomes that are compliant with Convention rights, and it thereby diminishes the chances of developing a human rights 'culture' within those authorities. This is another area where the domestic courts in the United Kingdom might have gone beyond the basic requirements of the European Convention but chose not to do so. The failure may not be too significant in the context of alleged breaches of the right to a fair hearing, but in the context of the right to life it can have much more far-reaching consequences.

The accountability of the police has been considerably improved in Northern Ireland since the establishment of the office of the Police Ombudsman in 2000. One of the complaints investigated by that office was brought by the family of William Stobie, a loyalist who was shot dead outside his home in Belfast in 2001 by a loyalist paramilitary group, the Red Hand Defenders. The murder occurred just 10 days after the police had warned Stobie about his personal security and 16 days after he had been acquitted of aiding and abetting the murder of Belfast solicitor Pat Finucane in 1989. The victim's family alleged that the police had failed to adequately protect him from threats to his life. The Ombudsman's report, without (unfortunately) expressly referring to the standards required by Article 2 of the European Convention, reveals that police officers had alerted Stobie to the threat against him and had offered him support to move house and advice on what steps he could take to increase his safety, but that Stobie had declined such help. On those facts there was, implicitly, no violation of Article 2.[89] There may at times be a duty on the State to protect individuals' lives, but those individuals still retain the right to put themselves at risk if they so wish.

A Northern Ireland Committee on Protection has recently been established, with Lord Carlile of Berriew QC as its chairperson. The Committee determines the UK government's policy concerning the provision of close armed protection to individuals living in Northern Ireland and decides what degree of protection, if any, should be made available to those who apply for it. The Committee must obviously pay close attention to the standards set by the European Court of Human Rights in this regard.

Claims by witnesses to anonymity

The European Court of Human Rights does not take an absolutist position regarding the need for witnesses in criminal or civil trials to be openly identified. For the

88 [2007] 1 AC 100, [29], approved by Lord Hoffmann in the *Misbehavin'* case, [2007] 1 WLR 1420, [14].
89 Police Ombudsman press release dated 4 July 2004.

purposes of the Article 6 right to a fair trial the Court will look at all the circumstances before deciding whether maintaining the anonymity of the witnesses has introduced an unacceptable element of unfairness into the proceedings. One of the most important of those circumstances will be whether maintaining the anonymity was necessary in order to give effect to the Article 2 right to have someone's life protected by law. Article 2 is a non-derogable right, while Article 6 is merely an unqualified right. This means that, in a situation where both are in play but they point towards different outcomes, it is Article 2 which must be given priority.

This is precisely the kind of situation which arose during the course of the second Bloody Sunday Tribunal of Inquiry,[90] which began in 1998 and had still not been completed by the time this chapter was being finalized in 2009. The story of the litigation resulting from an early ruling by the Tribunal concerning anonymity for soldier witnesses and the venue of the hearings has been well told by Brigid Hadfield, who suggests on the basis of these events that the purposes served by Tribunals of Inquiry need to be re-evaluated.[91] In *R v Lord Saville of Newdigate, ex parte A*,[92] retired and serving soldiers who were due to give oral evidence to the inquiry challenged a ruling by the Tribunal in May 1999 that they should be identified by their full names.[93] The Tribunal had accepted that the 17 soldiers who had fired live rounds on Bloody Sunday were 'more attractive targets than the generality of soldiers', and that they thus faced a higher likelihood of terrorist attack if identified. But it also accepted that this increased threat did not move those soldiers from the 'significant level of threat' category' to a higher category, so the danger to the soldiers did not outweigh or qualify the Tribunal's duty to conduct a public open inquiry. In the Divisional Court the 17 soldiers succeeded in getting this decision overturned,[94] and when the Tribunal appealed the Court of Appeal upheld the Divisional Court's decision. On behalf of the Court of Appeal Lord Woolf MR said that:

> when what is at stake is the safety of the former soldiers and their families . . . the risk is extremely significant . . . After all, the individual's right to life is, as Lord Bridge stated in *Bugdaycay v Secretary of State for the Home Department*,[95] the most fundamental of all human rights. It does appear that the tribunal may well have failed to attach sufficient weight to this.[96]

[90] This is the Inquiry into the deaths of 14 people shot by British soldiers in Derry on 30 January 1972. See <http://www.bloody-sunday-inquiry.org.uk>. The first inquiry had been conducted by the then Lord Chief Justice of England: see Widgery (1972). For an excellent account see Walsh (2000).

[91] Hadfield (1999a) 680. She added: 'The difficult question . . . remains as to whether a . . . Tribunal of Inquiry is the most appropriate means to an end.' (ibid, 681).

[92] [2000] 1 WLR 1855. The fact that the judicial review of the Tribunal's decision was heard by courts in England and not by courts in Northern Ireland (where there might have been more awareness of *all* the sensitivities involved in the matter) was itself controversial. It seems that, in law, the applicants had a choice as to where to lodge their judicial review application. See Hadfield (1999a) 674–6.

[93] There had been earlier judicial review proceedings concerning a ruling by the Tribunal given in December 1998: see Hadfield (1999) 670–3.

[94] Decision of 17 June 1999, *The Times* 22 June 1999 (Roch LJ and Maurice Kay J, Hooper J dissenting). The views of these judges are summarized by Lord Woolf MR at [2000] 1 WLR 1855, [45]–[51].

[95] [1987] AC 514, 531.

[96] [2000] 1 WLR 1855, [68(5)].

The Tribunal was held to have failed to demonstrate that there were compelling reasons for naming the soldiers, notwithstanding their fears.[97] But in coming to this conclusion the Court of Appeal applied the test laid down by a previous Court of Appeal (largely in the judgment of Bingham MR, as he then was) in *R v Ministry of Defence, ex parte Smith*.[98] That test said that, '[t]he more substantial the interference with human rights, the more the court will require by way of justification before it is satisfied that the decision ... [is] ... beyond the range of responses open to a reasonable decision-maker'.[99] Even on that test, however, it is difficult to see how a strong enough case had been made out to show that the risk to the life of the soldiers was 'real and immediate'. In fact the Court of Appeal did not cite any judgments by the European Court of Human Rights[100] and proceeded on the basis that 'the increased real risk'[101] faced by the soldiers was enough (coupled with the assurance of anonymity given by Lord Widgery 27 years earlier and the soldiers' feeling of unfairness) to lead to the conclusion that no decision was possible other than to grant anonymity to the soldiers.[102]

The English Court of Appeal had an opportunity to reconsider some of the same issues when another appeal concerning a ruling by the Bloody Sunday Tribunal came before it in 2001, this time on whether the Tribunal should hear evidence from soldiers in Derry or in London.[103] The Tribunal wanted to hear them in Derry, but the Ministry of Defence objected. Both the High Court and the Court of Appeal held for the Ministry. In the Court of Appeal Lord Phillips MR said that this was not a case where the *Osman* test was appropriate. Instead he likened the situation to one where a public authority was carrying out an operation which was going to invite an armed response from criminals and where, therefore, according to the European Court's decision in *Ergi v Turkey*,[104] there was a duty to do all that was feasible to ensure that civilians are not thereby harmed. As Lord Phillips put it:

> The degree of risk described as 'real and immediate' in Osman, as used in that case, was a very high degree of risk calling for positive action from the authorities to protect life. It was 'the real and immediate risk to the life of an identified individual or individuals from the criminal acts of a third party' which was, or ought to have been, known to the authorities. Such a degree of risk is well above the threshold that will engage Article 2 when the risk is attendant upon some action that an authority is contemplating putting into effect itself. It was not an appropriate test to invoke in the present context.[105]

[97] There was never any objection raised to keeping secret the present addresses, telephone numbers and occupations of the soldiers: [1999] 4 All ER 860, 867a.

[98] [1996] QB 517.

[99] ibid, 554.

[100] The Human Rights Act 1998 had been passed on 9 November 1998 but had not yet come into force (and would not until 2 October 2000).

[101] [1999] 4 All ER 860, 878g.

[102] ibid, 882e.

[103] *Lord Saville of Newdigate v Widgery Soldiers* [2001] EWCA Civ 2048, [2002] 1 WLR 1249. The case is sometimes referred to as the 'Widgery soldiers' case to distinguish it from the earlier Court of Appeal decision about witness anonymity.

[104] (2001) 32 EHRR 18. This duty to plan operations carefully was first imposed by the European Court in *McCann v UK* (1996) 21 EHRR 97, but the Court of Appeal did not refer to that case, even though it too involved likely activities by Irish republican paramilitaries. It is discussed at 255 below.

[105] [2002] 1 WLR 1249, para 28.

Once again, then, the relatives of the Bloody Sunday victims were disappointed by a decision of the Court of Appeal taken in England, and one needs to ask whether that court leant too readily in favour of upholding the Ministry of Defence's arguments. Even if the court was right to apply a less demanding test than that laid down in *Osman*, was its threshold met, bearing in mind that the police assessment of the threat to soldier witnesses was 'moderate' and that in the previous 30 years there had been no attack, whether successful or unsuccessful, on parties or witnesses to legal proceedings in Northern Ireland? The Court of Appeal placed considerable emphasis on the scale of the security operation that would be required to protect between 200 and 400 soldier witnesses travelling day after day to the Tribunal for more than six months, but that scale was going to be just as great if the soldiers' testimony were to be heard in London (even if it would be more difficult for dissident republican paramilitaries to operate in England than in Northern Ireland).

The lower test approved in the Widgery soldiers case for the application of Article 2 duties was, as we have seen, the one applied by the Court of Appeal of Northern Ireland in *Re Meehan's Application*[106] in the context of claims for Key Person Protection. But the previous section has indicated how the courts have since moved away from that test, and that is now also the case in the context of witness anonymity. The opportunity to do so came in *Re Officer L*,[107] where former and current police officers who were due to be called to attend the inquiry into the killing of Robert Hamill in Portadown in 1997 challenged a ruling by the inquiry denying them anonymity. The police officers won their challenge in the High Court[108] and Court of Appeal[109] of Northern Ireland but this time the inquiry took the matter one step further, to the House of Lords, and was able to persuade that court to reverse the Court of Appeal's decision. Oddly enough, Lord Carswell himself, who as the former Lord Chief Justice of Northern Ireland had set the lower standard in *Re Meehan's Application*, gave the sole judgment in the Lords. His reasoning, with respect, sometimes appears overly subtle, but his conclusion is clear—that the 'real and immediate risk' threshold is a high one to reach, requiring objective evidence rather than just subjective fears, and the fact that the State was requiring witnesses to give evidence did not allow that threshold to be reached unless it raised a pre-existing risk of death to the 'real and immediate' category.[110] In particular, the standard to be applied did not drop 'when the risk is attendant upon some action that an authority is contemplating putting into effect itself'.[111] The judge did not avert to the fact that that was one of the factors which, in *Re Meehan's Application*, he had said *should* be taken into account.

That the Court of Appeal misstated the law in the second Saville Inquiry case was again acknowledged by the House of Lords in *Van Colle v Chief Constable of the Hertfordshire Police*,[112] where the family of a man who was murdered because

[106] [2004] NIJB 53.
[107] [2007] UKHL 36, [2007] 1 WLR 2135.
[108] A decision of Morgan J (who became Lord Chief Justice of Northern Ireland in June 2009).
[109] A decision of Kerr LCJ, Campbell and Girvan LJJ.
[110] [2007] 1 WLR 2135, [20], [23]–[25].
[111] ibid, [20].
[112] [2008] UKHL 50, [2008] 3 WLR 593; see Anthony (2009).

he was about to be a prosecution witness in the trial of a man charged with theft failed to convince the judges that Article 2 had been breached. Lord Bingham questioned whether the Court of Appeal had been correct to impose a lower test where a threat to the life of an individual derives from the State's decision to call that individual as a witness,[113] Lord Hope said he would confine the decision in the *Saville* case to its own facts,[114] and Lord Brown believed that the decision in the *Saville* case 'was amply justified without resort to Article 2, merely by the application of ordinary public law principles of fairness, reasonableness and proportionality'.[115] Lord Phillips (who as Lord Chief Justice also sat in the *Van Colle* case) did not comment on his own previous ruling in the *Saville* case.[116] In view of the position adopted by the House of Lords in both *Re Officer L* and *Van Colle*, it is perhaps unfortunate that the Saville Tribunal chose not to appeal against either of the two decisions taken by the Court of Appeal on that Tribunal's rulings some years earlier. A cynic might suggest that the distinguishing feature was the fact that the Saville Tribunal cases involved potential threats against British soldiers (as opposed to police officers in Northern Ireland or members of the public in England), but that would be improper. In any event, the test reinforced by the House of Lords is now applied in Northern Ireland, as a recent decision by the new Lord Chief Justice of Northern Ireland indicates.[117]

The right not to be killed

It is a remarkable fact that, despite all the controversy over the alleged use of excessive force by the police and army during the conflict in Northern Ireland,[118] not to mention the more than 3,000 deaths caused by illegal paramilitary organizations, the European Commission and Court of Human Rights has never once conclusively ruled that the force used in a particular case violated Article 2. All the cases on Article 2 have concerned secondary matters, such as whether proper planning has preceded the use of force and whether proper investigations has taken place in the wake of killings. The primary reason for this absence of rulings is that domestic law allowed civil claims to be taken in relation to the use of allegedly excessive force. Such domestic remedies have to be exhausted before any complaint can be ruled admissible

[113] ibid, [35]. But Lord Bingham had no doubt that the Court of Appeal's decision was correct on the facts.

[114] ibid, [69].

[115] ibid, [116].

[116] Nor did Lord Carswell, who, being from Northern Ireland himself, might have been expected to have a view on the *Saville* case.

[117] *Re GL's Application* [2009] NIQB 67. Morgan LCJ rejected an application to overturn a Minister of State's decision not to admit the applicant to the Limited Home Protection Scheme (a variant of the Key Persons Protection Scheme) because the threats against him did not amount to a 'real and immediate risk' to his life.

[118] For further information about the prosecutions brought against members of the security forces see Jennings (1988b) 105 and Hadden (1993) 173.

in Strasbourg,[119] and the Strasbourg organs are unlikely to overturn findings of fact made by a domestic court in such cases[120] or to rule that an award of compensation by a domestic court is inadequate.[121] Moreover, proving systemic failings to meet human rights standards, such as a concerted practice to 'buy off' victims of a shoot-to-kill policy, requires hard evidence to be adduced, and this is inherently very difficult to come by.[122] Other hurdles got in the way too. The families of the victims of Bloody Sunday, for instance, waited until long after the six-month limitation period before complaining in Strasbourg that they had no effective remedy in domestic law.[123] In at least one other case the UK government was able to prevent it from going to the European Court by agreeing a friendly settlement with the widow of a man who had been killed by the army.[124] And for a long time the government kept secret the instructions that were issued to members of the police and army as to when it was acceptable for them to use firearms: these were not even disclosed to the Standing Advisory Commission on Human Rights until 1982.[125]

In another respect, too, the European Convention system showed itself to be a far from complete protector of the right to life during Northern Ireland's conflict. It did not at any time require the UK government to put in place more precise laws regarding the use of force by the State's security forces. The principal law was enshrined in the Criminal Law Act (NI) 1967, which simply stated that '[a] person may use such force as is reasonable in the circumstances in the prevention of crime, or in effecting or assisting in the lawful arrest of offenders or suspected offenders or of persons unlawfully at large'.[126] This test of reasonableness seems vague, and does not necessarily suggest a test of proportionality, as required by the jurisprudence based on Article 2.[127] A further rule of the common law is that to be guilty of murder an accused person has to have intended to kill or to cause serious personal harm to the deceased; if the accused did not have that intention there can be no conviction for murder, and if the accused did have that intention then he or she is not guilty of murder (or of any crime) if the action was taken in self-defence or in defence of others and did not involve the use of force that was unreasonable in the circumstances.[128] Throughout the conflict in Northern Ireland those laws remained unchanged, and they applied to members of the police and army in just the same way as they did to everyone else.

[119] This is why the complaints relating to 22 deaths included in the inter-State application were declared inadmissible: *Ireland v UK* (1972) 15 Ybk 76.

[120] *Stewart v UK* (1985) 7 EHRR 453; *Kelly v UK* (1993) 16 EHRR CD 20, on which see Smith (1994). These cases are discussed further below.

[121] *Caraher v UK* (2000) 29 EHRR CD 119, where the Court rejected a complaint that payment of £50,000 for the death of the applicant's husband was not an adequate remedy.

[122] ibid.

[123] *McDaid v UK* (1996) 22 EHRR CD 197.

[124] *Farrell v UK* (1983) 5 EHRR 466. Discussed at 253 below.

[125] SACHR (1984) para 24. The army's 'Yellow Card' was reprinted in Jennings (1988b) 127. A photstat copy also appeared on the front page of *The Times* two days after Bloody Sunday, on 1 February 1972.

[126] s 3(1). This provision was identical to the Criminal Law Act 1967, s 3(1), applicable in England and Wales.

[127] Cf SACHR (1984) para 13: 'The difficulty stems from the fact that section 3(1) does not explicitly contain an element of proportionality.'

[128] See, generally, Ormerod (2008) 473–87.

The security forces were not placed under any 'higher' duty as regards resorting to the use of force. In fact, the danger they confronted was one of the circumstances that could be taken into account under the Criminal Law Act when determining if they had used reasonable force. The consequences of this attitude became clear quite early in the conflict, in 1976.

This was when the House of Lords decided the *McElhone* case.[129] Here a 22-year-old man had been shot dead in 1974 as he ran away from an army foot patrol in South Armagh.[130] The soldier who fired the fatal shot was tried for murder and, on the assumption that he knew the target was unarmed but honestly believed him to be a member of the IRA, was acquitted, MacDermott J holding (somewhat mysteriously) that there was no evidence that the soldier had intended to kill or seriously injure the victim.[131] The Crown was unhappy with this acquittal but had no power to appeal against it. Instead the Attorney General referred the case to the Court of Criminal Appeal of Northern Ireland, using his powers under the Criminal Appeal (NI) Act 1968,[132] which permitted that court to clarify the law for the future without changing the outcome of the trial giving rise to the reference. The Court of Criminal Appeal endorsed the trial judge's view that, if a soldier fired to kill or seriously wound a person whom he reasonably believed to be a member of the IRA and in circumstances where he felt that there was no other way of apprehending the person, this could be 'such force as is reasonable in the circumstances' within the meaning of the Criminal Law Act (NI) 1967.[133] One of the appeal judges strongly dissented,[134] but when the case was referred again to the House of Lords there was unanimous endorsement of the majority's ruling.

The lead judgment was given by Lord Diplock, who had conducted the inquiry four years previously that had led to the retention of internment and the introduction of juryless courts in Northern Ireland.[135] He pointed out that on the assumed facts the only options open to the accused had been either to let the victim escape or to shoot at him; a reasonable man would know that shooting at him would be likely to kill him or injure him seriously, but a reasonable man would also know that if the victim escaped the kind of harm that might ensue would be even greater, namely:

> the killing or wounding of members of the patrol by terrorists in ambush, and the effect of this success by members of the Provisional IRA in encouraging the continuance of the armed insurrection and all the misery and destruction of life and property that terrorist activity in Northern Ireland has entailed.[136]

[129] Reported under *Attorney General for Northern Ireland's Reference* [1977] AC 105. See Jennings (1988b) 107–9; Livingstone (1994) 336–8.

[130] The killing provoked great concern at the time. See: <http://www.nuzhound.com/articles/irish_news/arts2005/jan3_Irish_government_shocked_at_shooting.php> (last visited 28 July 2009).

[131] *R v Jones* [1975] 2 NIJB.

[132] s 48A, inserted by the Criminal Justice Act 1972, s 63(3) and Sch 4. The Attorney General himself, Sam Silkin QC, assisted by Brian Hutton QC (a future Lord Chief Justice of Northern Ireland and Lord of Appeal), argued the case for reform of the law.

[133] [1976] NI 169, 171 (Jones, McGonigal and Gibson LJJ).

[134] McGonigal LJ. He pointed out that the maximum prison sentence a person could receive for being a member of the IRA was five years.

[135] Diplock (1972).

[136] [1977] AC 105, 138F.

Viscount Dilhorne and Lords Simon, Edmund-Davies, and Russell of Killowen all agreed with Lord Diplock. The contrast with the court's refusal some years earlier to allow Bernadette Devlin to rely upon a defence of necessity when using force against police officers who she believed were about to break the law is quite stark.[137] The Law Lords all also agreed that if the force used had been unreasonable then the charge of murder would have had to stand: the law at that time was quite clear that the charge could not be reduced to one of manslaughter:[138]

> If a plea of self-defence is put forward in answer to a charge of murder and fails because excessive force was used though some force was justifiable, as the law now stands the accused cannot be convicted of manslaughter. It may be that a strong case can be made for an alteration of the law to enable a verdict of manslaughter to be returned where the use of some force was justifiable but that is a matter for legislation not for judicial decision.[139]

Despite the elapse of more than 30 years since those words were written, the law today remains just as it was then. Judges and juries were, and still are, reluctant to convict a member of the security forces of murder because the penalty for that crime is mandatory life imprisonment (even if the sentencing judge can set a low 'tariff', after which the convicted person can be released if deemed not to be a danger to the public). Sentences for manslaughter, on the other hand, can vary from absolute discharge to life imprisonment.

The *McElhone* decision is possibly the most baneful of all the domestic judicial decisions relating to the conflict in Northern Ireland, not perhaps because the soldier in question was acquitted of murder but because he got off scot-free. No reference at all was made to the standards flowing from Article 2 of the European Convention and, unfortunately, no application was later lodged on behalf of Mr McElhone at Strasbourg.[140] As a result, for the next 20 years or more the security forces were able to operate with virtual impunity when applying lethal force against suspected terrorists.[141] Doran says that the House 'declined to offer wholly authoritative guidance on the matter when one might have expected it to do so',[142] Livingstone notes that the ruling 'provided little reassurance that the higher judiciary would prevent the security forces from acting

[137] *Devlin v Armstrong* [1971] NI 13. See ch 3 above, 48.

[138] There was some discussion of whether to follow recent Australian case law which had allowed a charge of murder to be reduced to manslaughter if excessive force had been used in self-defence (eg *R v Howe* (1958) 100 CLR 448), but this option was rejected, as it had already been by the Privy Council (in *Palmer v The Queen* [1971] AC 814) and by the Court of Appeal (in *R v McInnes* [1971] 1 WLR 1600): ibid, 139E–F (per Lord Diplock); 152G–153C (per Lord Simon).

[139] [1977] AC 105, 148 (per Lord Diplock).

[140] Had it been it may well have petered out in the way that *Farrell v UK* did, through a friendly settlement: (1983) 5 EHRR 466.

[141] One case that came to court soon after *McElhone* was *R v Bohan and another* [1979] 5 NIJB, where soldiers shot dead a man who, having reported that he had found an arms cache, went back to the scene and supposedly lifted a rifle and pointed it at the soldiers. The soldiers were acquitted of murder because Lowry LCJ accepted their defence of self-defence. For an insightful critique (though without reference to Art 2) see Stannard (1980).

[142] Doran (1987) 295. Doran goes on to make recommendations for reform that take account of Art 2 of the Convention, but this was some years before decisions such as *McCann v UK* (1995) 21 EHRR 97.

beyond the rule of law,[143] and Jennings goes so far as to label the decision 'a licence to kill'.[144] For a period in the 1980s the Standing Advisory Commission on Human Rights tried to persuade the government to amend the law, but in vain.[145] Sir George Baker did not consider the issue during his review of the EPA 1978, even though for the purposes of his report he chose to expand and define the right to life as: 'A right to life and to live free from the fear of terrorist violence, coercion and threats, and from injury, loss or damage by their criminal activities'.[146] When a soldier *was* eventually convicted of murder, in 1984,[147] Lord Lowry CJ, in the Court of Appeal, agreed that the law on the use of force in Northern Ireland was unclear and he stated that 'the obvious solution of this problem . . . is for Parliament to decide what the law ought to be and to declare or amend it accordingly'.[148] However, he and his fellow appeal judges refused to grant a certificate that a point of law of general public importance was at stake,[149] so no appeal was possible to the House of Lords.[150] A decade later, when Private Lee Clegg was convicted of the murder of Karen Reilly,[151] a passenger in a car driven by a joyrider who also died, the Court of Appeal of Northern Ireland was able to distinguish the case from previous decisions because on the facts before it there was no evidence that Private Clegg had thought that the driver of the car was a terrorist or that if the driver were to escape he would commit terrorist offences in the future. The House of Lords endorsed that view[152] and cast doubt on the legality of the army's 'yellow card' instructions, which appeared to suggest that a soldier could open fire on a car if someone had been injured by that car in even a minor way. But the House once again refused to develop the common law so as to create a new type of manslaughter offence,[153] mainly because the government had had the option of introducing legislation to that effect but had so far not done so.[154] Nevertheless, Home Secretary Michael Howard ordered Private Clegg's release from prison less than two years after his conviction.[155]

143 Livingstone (1994) 338.

144 Jennings (1988b) 109.

145 SACHR (1984), paras 20–8 and App B; SACHR (1985) paras 67–71; SACHR (1986) para 71(d); Hadden (1993).

146 Baker (1984) para 48.

147 Private Ian Thain was convicted of murdering Thomas 'Kidso' Reilly, road manager of the pop group, Bananarama. See Jennings (1988b) 121–2.

148 (1985) 11 NIJB 31, 40.

149 (1985) 11 NIJB 76. This is a rare example of a Court of Appeal decision on such an application being reported.

150 See Criminal Appeal (NI) Act 1980, s 31(2). But on the orders of the Home Secretary Private Thain was released from prison in 1988 after serving just 26 months of his life sentence.

151 No relation to Thomas 'Kidso' Reilly (n 147 above). Her father, James McGrillen, had been shot dead by the army in 1976 while he was engaged in an IRA gun attack on Protestant teenagers: McKittrick et al (2004) 627.

152 [1995] 1 AC 482. See Dickson (2006a) 389–92.

153 The Australian High Court had by then refused to follow *R v Howe* (see n 138 above): *Zecevic v DPP (Victoria)* (1987) 162 CLR 645.

154 But there is no evidence that the government had actively considered the proposal and rejected it; it was more a case of a passive omission to legislate rather a conscious decision not to do so.

155 Later, supporters of Private Clegg succeeded in getting his case referred back to the Court of Appeal by the Criminal Cases Review Commission, on the basis that there was new evidence suggesting that

The *McElhone* decision, and the failure to get a ruling from the European Court on whether making such a broad defence available to members of the security forces when charged with the excessive use of force was compatible with the victim's right to life under Article 2 of the Convention, must be seen as indirectly responsible for what seems to have been the tolerance of a 'shoot to kill policy' on the part of those forces in the early 1980s, with 23 people being shot dead between 1982 and 1985.[156] In response to much pressure (and in the aftermath of the acquittal of a police officer on a double murder charge) the UK government appointed the Deputy Chief Constable of Greater Manchester, John Stalker, to investigate six of these killings.[157] Before he could complete his investigation, which many believed was beginning to unearth matters which the government would have preferred to keep secret, he was removed from his post because of a complaint against him on an unrelated matter. His investigation was completed by Colin Sampson, of the West Yorkshire Police. The Stalker-Sampson Report was delivered to the government in 1986 but has never been made public. Stalker himself, and others who were involved in the production of the report, have denied that they found any shoot-to-kill 'policy' as such, but they have suggested that the police may have deliberately turned a blind eye to certain dubious practices.[158]

There are several other instances of how the right to life in Northern Ireland was inadequately protected by law in this period, and of how the courts missed opportunities to reform the law. One of these is the killing of Thomas McLaughlin in 1971. He and two others were shot dead by British soldiers as they tried to rob two men who were inserting money at a night safe outside a bank in Newry, County Down. The soldiers had been tipped off that the IRA were going to plant a bomb at the bank that night and mistakenly thought that the robbers were bombers. In the preceding two months there had been 35 bomb explosions in Newry and just two days earlier a bomb had been placed outside another bank in Newry. Mr McLaughlin's widow (now Mrs Farrell) sued the Ministry of Defence for their negligence but at the High Court (where there was a civil jury) she lost. The judge, however, refused to put to the jury any evidence relating to the way the operation had been planned, because the plaintiff's allegations were being made only against the four soldiers involved in the incident. The Court of Appeal of Northern Ireland overturned this decision,[159] holding that there should be a new trial and that when deciding whether, under the Criminal Law Act (NI) 1967, the force used had been reasonable in the circumstances, the jury should be allowed to take account of the way the operation was planned by superior officers. But the House of Lords reversed the Court of Appeal, and also held that it was too late to change the pleadings in the case so as to allow the plaintiff to sue the commanding officers.[160] One is left with the impression that,

he had not fired at the car after the threat had passed. In 1998 the Court of Appeal of Northern Ireland acquitted Clegg of the murder charge and he returned to the army.

[156] Jennings (1988b); Davies (1999); Ellison and Smyth (2000) ch 7, esp 129–33.

[157] One was that of Gervaise McKerr, whose death was later to be the subject of an important ruling by the European Court: *McKerr v UK* (2002) 34 EHRR 20, discussed later in this chapter.

[158] See, eg, Stalker (1988).

[159] [1978] 7 NIJB.

[160] [1980] 1 WLR 172.

while the House was prepared to take a very wide view of what was meant by 'the circumstances' in the *McElhone* case, where this favoured the State, so it was prepared to take a very narrow view, in the *Farrell* case, where this also favoured the State. Greer has characterized this decision as one that 'missed a unique opportunity to reassert the primacy of the rule of law'[161] and he argued that the Criminal Law Act (NI) 1967 should be given an interpretation 'which attempts to balance the conflicting rights of arrestor and arrestee and which starts from the proposition that the use of lethal force is *prima facie* unreasonable'.[162] Mrs Farrell then lodged an application in Strasbourg, claiming a violation of Articles 2, 6, and 13. The Commission held it to be admissible as far as Article 2 was concerned, though not on the other grounds.[163] But then a friendly settlement was reached between the parties, with the government agreeing to pay Mrs Farrell £37,500 by way of compensation as well as something towards her legal costs.[164] This might have been satisfactory to Mrs Farrell, but it deprived the European Court of the chance to elucidate the meaning of the relevant phrase in Article 2(2)(b) of the Convention, namely, 'use of force... no more than absolutely necessary to effect a lawful arrest'. That could have had a profound impact on how courts in the United Kingdom were required to interpret the Criminal Law Acts.

Yet a few years later, when the Commission did get the opportunity to interpret those Acts in a way which promoted the right to life, it failed to do so. This was in *Kelly (John) v United Kingdom*, where the applicant's 17-year-old son had been shot dead by a soldier while driving a stolen car which tried to evade a security checkpoint at a roundabout in Belfast. Having failed, like Mrs Farrell, in his civil action against the Ministry of Defence in the domestic courts,[165] the victim's father petitioned the European Commission of Human Rights but without success.[166] The Commission declared his application inadmissible because the force used against the driver of the car was considered to be justified in the attempt to effect an arrest. In words that are ominously reminiscent of those used by Lord Diplock in the *McElhone* case, the Commission said:

> [The soldiers'] conduct must also be assessed against the background of the events in Northern Ireland, which is facing a situation in which terrorist killings have become a feature of life. In this context the Commission recalls the judge's comments that, although the risk of harm to the occupants of the car was high, the kind of harm to be averted (as the soldiers reasonably thought) by preventing their escape was even greater, namely the freedom of terrorists to resume their dealing in death and destruction.[167]

The Commission's decision prompted one of the UK's foremost experts in criminal law, John Smith, to point out that it would have been beyond the powers of the soldiers to arrest these joyriders (or even if they had been terrorists) because the EPA

[161] Greer (1980a) 159. See too Walker (1980).
[162] ibid, 155.
[163] (1983) 5 EHRR 466.
[164] App 9013/80, Commission decision of 2 October 1984.
[165] [1989] NI 341.
[166] (1993) 16 EHRR CD20.
[167] (1993) 16 EHRR CD20, 'The Law'.

1978 permits soldiers to arrest only those persons who are suspected 'of committing, having committed or being about to commit any offence',[168] not persons who are likely, even very likely, to commit a crime at some remote time in the future.[169]

Thus, domestic criminal law as well as European Convention law proved unequal to the challenge of holding the security forces properly to account during the conflict in Northern Ireland, primarily because insufficient emphasis was given to the State's duty to protect the right to life and also because too subjective an approach was taken to judging the actions of soldiers and police officers on the ground.[170] The criminal law did recognize the concept of conspiring to commit crimes, but generally speaking it tended to foreclose inquiry into the plans surrounding a criminal act, especially one in which agents of the State may have been complicit.[171] Arguably that deficiency in the common law still exists today.[172] No attempt seems to have been made to persuade the European Commission of Human Rights to look more broadly at Northern Ireland's law on the use of lethal force, probably because the enforcement organs in Strasbourg are notoriously reluctant to examine a State's general approach to the protection of a right by legislation: the Convention protects a minimum floor of rights, nothing more. In later years the Court has spoken out against 'blanket' rules which fail to distinguish between deserving and undeserving individuals (for example, in relation to prisoners' voting rights,[173] or prisoners' access to fertility treatment[174]) but this was not an approach which was common in the 1970s and 1980s.

At the European Convention level, however, a major breakthrough eventually occurred when the European Court issued its judgment in *McCann v United Kingdom*, where the families of two men and a woman shot dead by undercover British soldiers in Gibraltar in 1988 claimed that the victims' right to life had been violated. This was a high profile case, given that the deceased were all members of the IRA on active operations at the time. They were not actually in possession or control of a bomb when they were killed but they were on a reconnaissance mission for the planting of a bomb which was already located in a car in Marbella in Spain. Their ultimate objective was to murder a number of British soldiers at the changing of the guard in Gibraltar. At an inquest into the deaths, held in Gibraltar, and for which the UK government issued 'public interest immunity certificates' to prevent the disclosure of certain categories of information such as the nature of the soldiers' training and their previous operational activities,[175] the jury found by nine to two that the killings had been lawful. In doing so they took into account domestic Gibraltarian law which, as set out in Article 2 of the colony's Constitution, protects the right to life in terms comparable but not identical to those of Article 2 of the European

[168] s 14.

[169] Smith (1994) 356.

[170] Ní Aoláin (2000) 96–116, where she refers to 'the insidious assault of reasonableness' (102).

[171] Bell, C (1997) para 6.4.

[172] The failure to hold any individuals to account under the criminal law for the death of Jean Charles de Menezes at Stockwell tube station in 2005 provides some evidence for such a view.

[173] *Hirst (No 2) v UK* (2006) 42 EHRR 41.

[174] *Dickson v UK* (2008) 46 EHRR 41.

[175] For more details see (1996) 21 EHRR 97, 123–4.

Convention. One of the differences in wording related to the circumstances in which lethal force is allowed, the test in Gibraltar being whether the force used was 'reasonably justifiable', as opposed to the Convention's test of whether it was 'absolutely necessary'. To that extent the test in Gibraltar was modelled on the Criminal Law Acts applicable in England, Wales, and Northern Ireland. The families then tried to sue the Ministry of Defence in the High Court in Belfast for the loss and damage suffered by the estates of the deceased as a result of their deaths, but that action had to be abandoned because the government issued certificates under the Crown Proceedings Act 1947,[176] thereby rendering conclusive its assertion that 'any alleged liability of the Crown arises otherwise than in respect of His Majesty's Government in the United Kingdom', which meant that the Crown was immune from being sued in the United Kingdom in respect of actions committed outside the United Kingdom.

When the applicants took their complaints to the European Commission of Human Rights[177] it voted by 11 to six to reject the claim that Article 2 had been breached.[178] Neither the actions of the soldiers who fired the shots nor those of the officers who planned the operation were deemed to be defective. The UK Commissioner (Sir Basil Hall) formed part of the majority, but the Irish Commissioner (Ms Jane Liddy) joined the minority.[179] When the case was referred to the European Court it was the first occasion on which that Court had had to consider Article 2 in detail.[180] To many people's surprise, the Court reversed the Commission decision, but the judges were even more divided than the Commissioners, with 10 finding for the applicants and nine against.[181] There was no Irish judge on the Court, but the UK judge, Sir John Freeland, still held in favour of his own government's position. Even the majority judges, however, did not think that the soldiers who fired the fatal shots had breached Article 2, and they all agreed that the test for the lawful use of force in domestic Gibraltarian law (and, by implication, in the Criminal Law Acts applicable in England, Wales, and Northern Ireland) was not sufficiently different from the Convention's standard to justify a finding of a violation of Article 2 on that ground alone.[182] The violation of Article 2 lay instead in the way the operation had been controlled and organized, with the majority judges pointing to the facts that the three deceased could have been arrested immediately after their entry into Gibraltar, that at the briefing meeting prior to the operation the idea that the three visitors were on

[176] ss 40(2)(b) and (3)(a).

[177] They were represented by Belfast solicitor Barra McGrory (whose father, P J McGrory had represented the families at the inquest in Gibraltar) and by the Dutch lawyer Douwe Korff, author of a report on the Diplock Courts published a decade earlier: Korff (1984).

[178] Decision of 4 March 1994, extracted at (1996) 21 EHRR 97, 135–59.

[179] Who also comprised Commissioners Trechsel, Ermacora, Reffi, Nowicki, and Loucaides (between them they gave three dissenting judgments).

[180] It had indirectly considered Art 2 in *Soering v UK* (1989) 11 EHRR 439 and *Open Door Counselling and Dublin Well Woman Centre v Ireland* (1992) 15 EHRR 244.

[181] *McCann, Farrell and Savage v UK* (1996) 21 EHRR 97. The judges in the majority were from Estonia, Greece, Italy, Lithuania, Luxembourg, Malta, Poland, Portugal, Slovakia, and Spain. The judges in the minority were from Finland, Germany, Hungary, Iceland, Norway, Slovenia, Sweden, Turkey, and the UK. No judge supported the payment of compensation to the applicants (beyond the reimbursement of costs and expenses). For comments see Joseph (1996).

[182] ibid, para 155.

a reconnaissance mission was not regarded as a serious possibility, that the unlikelihood of the three visitors detonating a bomb when many civilians were present was not properly considered, that one soldier too readily concluded that the suspect car in Gibraltar definitely had a bomb in it, and that there was no evidence to show that the soldiers had been instructed to assess whether the use of firearms to wound their targets may have been warranted by the specific circumstances that confronted them at the moment of arrest. The nine dissenting judges[183] issued a joint judgment concluding that in all the circumstances the use of lethal force did not exceed what was 'absolutely necessary'.

I have explained elsewhere that in many ways this decision by the Grand Chamber of the European Court was a turning point in the Court's own development: it 'helped the Court to earn its jurisprudential spurs and to assert itself more firmly on the European stage'.[184] Reaction to the decision within official circles in Britain was, on the contrary, 'a mixture of outrage and bafflement',[185] the more so as it came in the midst of a series of judicial decisions which severely irked the politicians of the day.[186] There were even suggestions that it would lead the UK government to refuse to renew the right of individual petition to Strasbourg when that came up for consideration in January 1996.[187] The then Prime Minister, John Major, reportedly said the decision 'defied common sense', while the Deputy Prime Minister, Michael Heseltine, commented that the government would ignore it:

> We shall do nothing. We will pursue our right to fight terrorism to protect innocent people where we have jurisdiction, and we will not be swayed or deterred in any way by the ludicrous decisions of the Court.[188]

Bell claims that this assertion of inaction was more an act of defiance than a serious appraisal of the Convention obligations,[189] but the fact remains that the British army's training methods for undercover soldiers are still secret today and that British police forces still adhere to policies which tend to suggest a 'shoot first, ask questions later' approach.[190] Moreover, the Committee of Ministers of the Council of Europe noted on 22 March 1996 that the UK government had paid the applicants' costs and expenses as required by the judgment of 27 September 1995 and declared that it had

[183] Who included the Court's President, Judge Ryssdal, from Norway.

[184] Dickson (1997) 154. See too Ní Aoláin (2001) 28–34.

[185] Merrills (1996a) 611.

[186] Woodhouse (1996) 426–31.

[187] In the event the government renewed the right of individual petition permanently rather than just for the usual five years: see HL Deb, vol 567, col 117 (14 December 1995).

[188] 'Tory anger as European Court condemns Gibraltar killings' *The Independent*, 28 September 1995. This article also quotes David Trimble, the then leader of the Ulster Unionist Party, as saying 'the decision would strike dismay into all police forces in Europe and could seriously hamper peace-keeping activities and the maintenance of law and order'.

[189] Bell, C (1997) para 7.2.

[190] Cf 'Operation Kratos', the operational name for a wide range of tactics that London's Metropolitan Police Service uses to protect the public from the potential threat posed by suicide bombers (see <http://www.met.police.uk/communities_together/docs/v_05–11-08_srb_anna_de_vries_1_.pdf>, last visited 28 July 2009). It was applied when Jean Charles de Menezes, an innocent man, was killed at Stockwell tube station in 2005.

then fully exercised its enforcement functions under the Convention. This is further evidence, if it were needed, that the enforcement mechanisms of the European Convention are far from satisfactory.[191]

The importance of the Gibraltar case lies in the standards it lays down for the 'control and organization' of operations that result in deaths. In the case of the so-called Loughgall massacre, where eight IRA terrorists and one civilian were killed when undercover members of the British army surprised the attackers of a police station in County Armagh in 1987, the European Court was concerned only with whether there had been a proper investigation of the killings.[192] Seven of the nine applicants had begun civil proceedings against the Ministry of Defence; one of these (the widow of the civilian victim) had settled the claim out of court,[193] one had chosen to drop the case, and the other five were still proceeding with their case by the time their application reached Strasbourg. The European Court held in relation to these five applicants that it could not deal with this aspect of their applications because they had not exhausted their domestic remedies and this precluded the Court from examining the applicants' complaints of a substantive violation of Article 2 due to the alleged excessive use of force or negligence in the planning or control of the operation. Moreover, the Court was not prepared to conduct 'on the basis largely of statistical information and selective evidence, an analysis of incidents over the past thirty years with a view to establishing whether they disclose a practice by security forces of using disproportionate force'.[194] To do so would have required the Court to go 'far beyond the scope of the present application'[195] (though presumably the applicants felt that their application did, in terms, extend that far). On the other hand the Court rejected the UK government's argument that the mere availability of civil proceedings meant the Court did not have to examine the case further under Article 2: the Court recalled that 'the obligations of the State under Article 2 cannot be satisfied merely by awarding damages... The investigations required under Articles 2 and 13 of the Convention must be able to lead to the identification and punishment of those responsible.'[196]

Since the conclusion of the Belfast (Good Friday) Agreement on 10 April 1998 the police have killed only two persons in Northern Ireland, and the army has killed no-one. The Police Ombudsman has completed an investigation into the first fatality (that of Neil McConville in 2003) and concluded that, while the police operation in question had been poorly managed by senior police officers,[197] the officer who fired the fatal shots was justified in using his firearm to protect the life of a colleague who he thought was about to be run over by the driver of a car.[198] The Police

[191] See, generally, Bates (2005) 51–62.

[192] *Kelly v UK* App 30054/96, judgment of 4 May 2001. See further 268–70 below.

[193] She accepted a payment of £100,000 from the government: ibid, para 43.

[194] *Kelly v UK* App 30054/96, judgment of 4 May 2001, para 104.

[195] ibid.

[196] ibid, para 105, citing *Kaya v Turkey* (1998) 28 EHRR 1, para 105 and *Yaşa v Turkey* (1999) 28 EHRR 408, para 74.

[197] The Ombudsman also expressed 'grave concern' at sensitive intelligence being deleted from a police computer during her investigation and at the failure of officers who were in the Control Room on the day in question to cooperate with her investigation.

[198] Police Ombudsman's press release dated 4 October 2007.

Ombudsman did not recommend any prosecutions, and (disappointingly) made no explicit comment on whether any of the Article 2 standards may have been breached, for example, the requirement that police operations be carefully controlled and organized. But she did say that the commanding officers had not properly considered alternative methods for apprehending the suspects they had chased:

> The tactic of pursuing a vehicle and stopping it from behind is inherently dangerous and placed both officers and suspects at risk... This was a high-risk strategy with a high likelihood of requiring the use of potentially lethal force. There are occasions when such a tactic is necessary, but only after careful consideration of other options.[199]

The Ombudsman suggested that alternative strategies could have included mounting a vehicle checkpoint ahead of the suspect vehicle, stopping the car earlier when it went to collect a weapon, disrupting the exchange of the weapon at that time, or stopping the suppliers of the weapon on their way to that exchange. Whatever strategy is adopted, the Ombudsman stated categorically that, due to the potential for loss of life, police firearms operations should be managed in accordance with clear rules and procedures.[200] The Ombudsman's investigation into the second fatal shooting by the police since the Belfast Agreement, that of Steven Colwell in 2006, is still ongoing.[201]

The Police Ombudsman has also undertaken occasional investigations into the way some deaths occurring during the conflict between 1969 and 1998 were previously investigated by the police and has unearthed evidence of distinctly unsavoury behaviour on the part of the security forces as regards collusion with loyalist paramilitaries. In 2001 the Ombudsman issued a report on the death of Samuel Devenny, who died three months after he and members of his family and friends were attacked in his home by members of the RUC as far back as April 1969. Given the disputed medical evidence, the Ombudsman was unable to come to a conclusion on whether Mr Devenny's death was a direct result of what had happened to him on the night in question, but she was at least able to disclose to the family the report of an investigation conducted at the time by London's Metropolitan Police.[202]

In a 160-page statement issued in 2007 on what was called Operation Ballast[203] Mrs O'Loan looked at the activities between 1991 and 2003 of one particular police informant, and at those of his associates, many of whom were also police informants and members of the Ulster Volunteer Force, an illegal paramilitary group. She discovered that police informants were linked to the murders of 10 (or possibly 15) people, 10 attempted murders, 10 'punishment shootings', 13 'punishment attacks', a bomb attack in Monaghan, 17 instances of drug dealing, and numerous incidents of

[199] ibid.

[200] Cf Police Ombudsman's press release dated 21 March 2007 relating to the non-fatal shooting of a bomber in Belfast in 2002, where she described as inadequate the fact that the 'policy log' for the operation in question comprised just two A4 pages and did not provide a full account of the options considered, decisions taken, and rationale for the operation.

[201] Mr Colwell was one of six people travelling in a stolen car which failed to stop at a checkpoint in Ballynahinch, Co Down, at 11.30 one Sunday morning.

[202] Police Ombudsman press release 4 December 2001.

[203] Statement by the Police Ombudsman for Northern Ireland on her investigation into the circumstances surrounding the death of Raymond McCord Junior and related matters, 22 January 2007.

criminal damage, extortion, and intimidation. The Police Ombudsman's report contained 20 recommendations, the last of which was that the Northern Ireland Policing Board should establish a mechanism to regularly review the police's response to the other recommendations. The Policing Board asked its two expert Human Rights Advisers to perform this oversight role and three separate reports were produced by those advisors between July 2007 and September 2008. By that time all of the recommendations were well on their way to being implemented in full[204] and Her Majesty's Inspectorate of Constabulary had assured the Board that the procedures and practices now adopted by the PSNI were in line with guidelines issued by the Association of Chief Police Officers (ACPO) for use across the whole of the United Kingdom. These developments should go a long way towards ensuring that breaches of the European Convention by handlers of intelligence agents—particularly breaches of Article 2—should not occur in the future, though it has to be said that the guidelines issued by ACPO do not seem to have been applied at all satisfactorily when Jean Charles de Menezes was shot at Stockwell tube station in London in 2005.[205]

Rubber and plastic bullets

During most of the period of the troubles in Northern Ireland great controversy has been caused by the security forces' use of rubber and plastic bullets, or 'baton rounds' to use the official parlance.[206] Supposedly intended as a means of deterring rioters, these weapons were responsible for 17 deaths—three people died as a result of being hit by a rubber bullet and 14 by a plastic bullet. The first death occurred in 1972 (the victim was an 11-year-old boy, Francis Rowntree), the last in 1989. Sixteen of the victims were from the Catholic community (11 were killed in West Belfast); only one was a Protestant. No fewer than seven of the victims were killed between April and August in 1981, in the wake of disturbances following the hunger strikes by republican prisoners.

Rubber bullets were first used in Northern Ireland in 1970. They had been developed as a result of research conducted at the Chemical Defence Establishment at Porton Down in England into the production of a relatively safe alternative to wooden baton rounds, which had been used by British soldiers in other parts of the world but were deemed to be too dangerous for use within a part of the United Kingdom. By the time they were withdrawn from use, in 1975, more than 55,000 rubber bullets had been fired. As well as causing three fatalities, they blinded two people[207] and deprived seven others of the sight of one eye. It seems that no claims were taken in the courts to challenge the general use of rubber bullets, though some claims for compensation brought by individuals were probably settled out of court.

[204] For the third report see <http://www.nipolicingboard.org.uk/operation_ballast_interim_report_3_final_21_oct_2008.pdf>.

[205] See n 190 above.

[206] For a good earlier account see Jennings (1988c).

[207] Richard Moore and Emma Groves. For their own accounts of what happened to them, see 'Blinded by Rubber Bullets' in Murray (1998) 135–40.

Rubber bullets were gradually replaced by plastic (or PVC) bullets from 1973 onwards. These were supposedly a safer weapon, in that their impact was meant to be less severe. Rubber bullets were designed to be fired at the ground so that they could ricochet towards their target, whereas plastic bullets were to be fired directly at the target. But experience soon demonstrated that safety was improved only if the baton round was fired strictly in accordance with the instructions issued to the security forces. A senior surgeon at the Royal Victoria Hospital in Belfast, Lawrence Roche, writing in *The Lancet*, confirmed that plastic bullets tended to cause more severe injuries to the skull and brain than did rubber bullets, and therefore more deaths.[208] At the time he wrote those words, plastic bullets had already killed 11 people. This is because on many occasions the instructions for the use of the bullets were disobeyed. Proving this in court, however, was difficult, because the instructions were actually *secret*. The first time they were widely publicized was when someone leaked them to an 1984 inquiry[209] into the lethal use of firearms in Northern Ireland, chaired by Kader Asmal.[210] These 'rules for engagement' of baton rounds made it clear that they were to be used 'to disperse a crowd whenever it is judged to be minimum and reasonable force in the circumstances'. They were to be fired 'at selected persons and not indiscriminately at the crowd'. They were to be aimed 'so that they strike the lower part of the target's body directly (ie without bouncing)' and 'must not be fired at a range of less than 20 metres except when the safety of soldiers or others is seriously threatened'.

In the late 1970s and throughout the 1980s and 1990s some people who were struck by plastic bullets, and the families of some of those who were killed, did bring legal actions against the firers of the bullet—the police or army. On occasions the legal actions were successful because the security forces could not prove to the satisfaction of a judge that they had kept within the law.[211] The 'rules of engagement' were not themselves 'the law'. That was to be found in the Criminal Law Act (NI) 1967, referred to earlier in this chapter.[212] This allowed the police to use 'such force as is reasonable in the circumstances' in order to prevent crime or to effect a lawful arrest.[213] While comparable to the wording of the rules of engagement, the Act envisaged the use of plastic bullets even in situations where the force (although reasonable) was not 'minimum' and where the purpose was not just to disperse a crowd but to prevent crime or to effect an arrest. Whether their use for those purposes is compatible with Articles 2 and 3 of the European Convention is at least questionable.

No member of the security forces has ever been convicted of a crime as a result of firing a rubber or plastic bullet. Indeed it seems that only one of the 17 deaths caused by the bullets led to the prosecution of the police or army personnel involved.[214]

[208] *The Lancet* 23 April 1983. See too Millar et al (1975).

[209] Shoot to Kill (1985) 63. They were also revealed in the decision of the European Commission in *Stewart v UK*. See too n 125 above.

[210] Asmal, a South African, was then living and teaching in Dublin but he later served as a minister in the government of South Africa from 1994 to 2004.

[211] eg *Wasson v Chief Constable of the RUC* [1987] NI 42.

[212] See 249 above.

[213] s 3(1).

[214] Constable Hegarty was acquitted of the manslaughter of Sean Downes in 1987: see discussion below.

The facts of many of the incidents are contested, but it seems clear that several of the individuals who were killed were not rioting at the time. A particularly worrisome case is that of Norah McCabe, a 33-year-old mother of three, who was hit by a plastic bullet fired from a police Land Rover as she was walking to a shop to buy cigarettes; she died in hospital the next day from the skull fracture and brain injuries sustained in the hit.[215] At a coroner's inquest into the death a jury concluded that there was no clear evidence to suggest that there was a legitimate target to be fired at in the street in question and nor was there clear evidence to support the view that Mrs McCabe was anything other than an innocent party. The jury had no power, however, to recommend that one or more police officers should be prosecuted in relation to the killing and in due course the Director of Public Prosecutions directed that no prosecution of any police officer should take place. No police officer was even disciplined in relation to the incident. But the McCabe family did bring a civil claim in respect of the death and in an out-of-court settlement more than £25,000 was allegedly paid by the police. The Chief Constable at the time was Sir John Hermon. Such a settlement meant that no application concerning the case could then be declared admissible before the European Commission of Human Rights in Strasbourg. In December 1981, though, the European Parliament of what was then the European Community, by a large majority, condemned the use of plastic bullets.

The reluctance to choose the Strasbourg route may well have had something to do with the fact that a few years earlier another application concerning a plastic bullet fatality had been unsuccessful. It was lodged by Kathleen Stewart, whose 13-year-old son was killed by a baton round in 1976 (the only such death to occur in the five years between August 1975 and August 1980). Brian Stewart died six days after having his skull fractured by a baton round fired by a soldier in Turf Lodge in West Belfast. Apparently the soldier had been aiming at the legs of a ringleader of a riot going on at the time but had been jolted by two missiles just as he fired, thereby hitting the head of Brian Stewart, who was standing next to the ringleader. At an inquest into the death a jury found that young Brian had actually himself been rioting at the time and that therefore the firing of the plastic bullet was a reasonable action in the circumstances, but it nevertheless delivered an open verdict (indicating that it did not know whether the killing was lawful or not). Mrs Stewart sued the Ministry of Defence for £1,000 compensation but was unsuccessful both in the county court in 1979 and on appeal to the High Court in 1982. Jones LJ, in the High Court, said that:

> there was a riot at the material time and up to about 150 people were doing their best to make life unbearable for the 8 soldiers. And those actions of the rioters included throwing missiles which in fact found their target, on occasions at any rate. When one considers the risks to which the army were subject in those circumstances, namely the risk of serious injury from direct contact and the risk of sniper attack, I take the view that it was fully justified on the part of the Patrol Commander to order a baton round to be fired.[216]

[215] McKittrick et al (2004) 870.
[216] Cited in the Commission's decision, (1985) 7 EHRR CD453, CD454.

In other words, the courts in Northern Ireland found that the firing of the plastic bullet was reasonable for the prevention of crime in accordance with section 3(1) of the Criminal Law Act (NI) 1967. It was then that Mrs Stewart lodged an application with the European Commission of Human Rights alleging a breach of Article 2 of the European Convention (as well as breaches of Article 3—the right not to be ill-treated—and Article 14—the right to be free from discrimination).[217] However, the European Commission decided that the application should not proceed because the finding of the courts in Northern Ireland—which the Commission would not disturb as its job is not primarily to investigate the facts of cases—had been that Brian had been rioting at the time he was shot and no new evidence had been brought before the European Commission to suggest that the trial judge had incorrectly evaluated the evidence placed before him.[218] The applicant had argued, in essence, that plastic bullets were an inappropriate weapon to deal with civil disturbances in Northern Ireland, but the Commission disagreed. It said that it had to bear in mind that Northern Ireland was:

> facing a situation of continuous public disturbance that has given rise to much loss of life [citing Ireland v UK]. Moreover, rioting of the kind which occurred in the present case is a frequent occurrence and gives rise to the apprehension, as adverted to by Lord Justice Jones, that the disturbance will be used as a cover for sniper attack, although no claim has been made in the present case that the patrol actually came under such attack... [T]he Commission must also observe, in this context, that the Convention specifically envisages, in sub-paragraph (c), the right of the authorities to take action to quell a riot without imposing any requirement of retreat or avoiding action in the face of mounting violence... The Commission notes that the use of the plastic baton round in Northern Ireland has given rise to much controversy and that it is a dangerous weapon which can occasion serious injuries and death, particularly if it strikes the head. However, information provided by the parties concerning casualties, compared with the number of baton rounds discharged, shows that the weapon is less dangerous than alleged... The Commission is of the opinion, taking due account of all the surrounding circumstances, referred to above, that the death of Brian Stewart resulted from the use of force which was no more than 'absolutely necessary' 'in action lawfully taken for the purpose of quelling a riot...' within the meaning of Article 2(2)(c).[219]

The Commission went on to hold that, as the use of force was justified in this case, no issue of treatment in breach of Article 3 could arise. Moreover, the claim based on Article 14 was rejected because the applicant had in no way substantiated it by adducing evidence to support her allegation of discrimination.

What this decision by the European Commission illustrates are two central deficiencies in the European Convention system. First, that the system is almost entirely based on the consideration of complaints from individuals whose rights have allegedly been breached: it cannot easily deal with more general complaints to the effect that, for example, an inappropriate weapon has been deployed for use by a country's security forces or that the instructions for its use do not take proper account of the likelihood

[217] She was represented by the London-based National Council for Civil Liberties and the barrister Lord Gifford QC.

[218] *Stewart v UK* (1985) 7 EHRR CD453.

[219] ibid, paras 27, 28, and 30.

of young children being struck by the weapon. To that extent the Convention is, we see again, a reactive rather than a preventative system. Second, the adjudicating bodies sometimes express themselves in ways which do not measure up to thorough scrutiny. In the passage cited above, for instance, it is alarming that the Commission can deduce from the small number of casualties in relation to the number of plastic bullets fired that the weapon is therefore not sufficiently dangerous to constitute more force than is 'absolutely necessary' in a particular case. And it is surely illogical to suggest that just because there has been no breach of Article 2 there can therefore be no breach of Article 3: the scope of the prohibitions contained in those articles is quite different and it is not irrational to suggest that, while the use of what turns out to be lethal force may not be inappropriate under Article 2, the suffering which that force causes (not least to bereaved families)), or the risk that it constitutes for young children who are in the vicinity of the person being targeted by the force, is inhuman or degrading. Nevertheless, the attitude of the European Court in recent times has not altered from that of the European Commission in 1984. It would be just as difficult today to obtain a ruling from Strasbourg that, for example, Tasers[220] or CS gas are automatically beyond the pale as far as Article 2 is concerned.

As Jennings has noted, '[t]he Stewart decision is not a blanket endorsement of the use of plastic bullets, but it is unfortunate that the only case in which an inquest had found that a plastic bullet victim was a "rioter" was selected as the test case'.[221] Subsequent to the European Commission's decision three more people were killed by plastic bullets. Three months later the European Parliament again supported the withdrawal of the weapon. Calls for their ban increased, with a group co-led by Emma Groves, the United Campaign Against Plastic Bullets, being to the fore in this regard. In relation to the killing of Sean Downes,[222] which was captured on television, a reserve police constable was prosecuted for manslaughter. The incident occurred at a Sinn Féin anti-internment rally in West Belfast addressed by Martin Galvin, the Director of Noraid in the United States. Constable Hegarty said that he had discharged his baton round gun in order to protect two of his colleagues whom he thought were going to be struck by Mr Downes as he ran up wielding a stick. After a trial without a jury Hutton J held that the police officer should be acquitted because he had acted 'almost instinctively to defend his comrades without having time to assess the situation in the light of his knowledge of the police regulations'.[223] Spjut interpreted this decision as conferring on police officers a residual discretion to decide when to use force notwithstanding the relevant police regulations (and he argued that those regulations should be made public),[224] but a serving police inspector replied that the police regulations were drawn up by civil servants, not police officers, and that to regard them as determinative of whether reasonable force has been used 'involves a usurpation... of the roles of judge,

220 An electroshock weapon.
221 Jennings (1988a) 140.
222 McKittrick et al (2004) 993.
223 *R v Hegarty* (1986) 12 NIJB 25, 42.
224 Spjut (1987) 37 and 40.

jury and ultimately Parliament'.[225] He makes a convincing case for saying that Constable Hegarty was faced with a stark choice: fire a baton gun or risk someone being seriously injured.

The use of potentially lethal force today

It was not until the late 1990s that resort to plastic baton rounds significantly diminished. In 2000 only 26 were fired. The Report of the Independent Commission on Policing (the Patten Report) devoted less than three pages to the weapon.[226] The Commission said that it would like to see the use of such baton rounds discontinued as soon as possible but that it did not want a situation where the police would have no option but to resort to live rounds. It therefore recommended 'that an immediate and substantial investment be made in a research programme to find an acceptable, effective and less potentially lethal alternative to the PBR'.[227] In a Table the Commission listed 10 other pieces of equipment for public order policing which are in use or under review, such as 'bean bags' and pepper sprays, and it proposed that the police in Northern Ireland should be equipped with a broader range of such equipment so that a commander would have a wide range of options at his or her disposal.[228] It particularly suggested that personal protection CS sprays and water cannon might be suitable in some situations. If plastic baton rounds were to continue to be deployed, 'their use should be confined to the smallest necessary number of specially trained officers, who should be trained to think of the weapon in the same way as they would think of a firearm, that is a weapon which is potentially lethal'.[229] Also, 'guidance governing the deployment and use of PBRs should be soundly based in law, clearly expressed and readily available as public documents'.[230]

The first research report produced by the new Northern Ireland Human Rights Commission established in 1999 was into the system used by the police for recording the use of plastic bullets.[231] It was based on a study of 20 files chosen at random from those held by the police concerning incidents where a total of 122 plastic bullets were fired by police officers during the period 1997 to 2000, apparently striking 48 people. The report found, amongst other things, that the files in question often took months to complete and were poorly maintained. The principal form used by Sub-Divisional Commanders was inadequate and witness statements were often presented in an overly standardized manner and not properly signed by the police officers making them. Documents contained in the files did not give a full enough picture about the level of violence being used at the time the plastic bullets were fired and in many

[225] Robertson (1988) 15. He points out, too, that the relevant police regulations in England are just as 'secret' as those in Northern Ireland, though he agrees with Spjut that they should all be made public.
[226] Patten (1999) 54–6.
[227] ibid, para 9.15.
[228] ibid, p 55 and para 9.16.
[229] ibid, para 9.17.
[230] ibid, para 9.20.
[231] NIHRC (2001a).

files the chain of authority for the carrying and firing of plastic bullets was not made clear. Perhaps most damningly of all, several of the files were closed even though by any meaningful standard of accountability they should not reasonably have been closed. Based on these findings the Human Rights Commission recommended that new forms should be designed, that witness statements should provide more specific details than at present, and that files should be completed more quickly.

A further report by the Human Rights Commission reviewed the human rights implications of the introduction and deployment of a new type of baton round—the L21A1—which was introduced in place of the old L5A7 in 2001.[232] The report found that the new round travelled faster and hit harder than the one it replaced and it concluded that the lack of accuracy of the new round made it potentially more lethal. The researchers discovered that over 10 per cent of the new baton rounds fired had caused injury, compared with a 1.14 per cent injury rate with the previous round. The new round was also 2.5 times more likely to penetrate the skin.[233] Medical reports commissioned from the Defence Scientific Advisory Council (DSAC) to examine the biomedical effects of the new round suggested that if the new projectile hit a skull end-on, the risk was that it would lodge in the brain with fatal effect. The higher velocity of the round also meant that it had a greater potential for ricochet, thereby endangering innocent bystanders. But the government still refused to release full details of the DSAC research. The researchers ended by calling for the British government to commit to the withdrawal of baton rounds and for truly independent research to be conducted into safe alternatives. In the meantime they thought that no chemical irritant device should be deployed by the police in Northern Ireland until it had undergone a testing regime that was as rigorous as if the irritant were a drug (thereby ruling out CS spray), no type of electroshock weaponry should be introduced, and no other technology should be selected until a full and independent evaluation of its possible biomedical effects had been published. Nevertheless, the PSNI has continued to add new weaponry to its arsenal. It now has both CS spray and Tasers at its disposal. The Police Ombudsman's office has retrospectively approved the use of CS sprays during no fewer than 23 incidents.[234]

The Northern Ireland Police Ombudsman is now 'immediately informed' after the discharge of a plastic bullet. The Ombudsman conducts an investigation of each firing, if possible, which includes an examination of whether there was compliance with guidelines issued by the Association of Chief Police Officers (ACPO) and whether the use of force was proportionate. The Ombudsman has access to all documentation and can conduct forensic tests, attend debriefs, and view CCTV footage held by the police. This mechanism for allowing independent review of the justifiability of resorting to plastic baton rounds has gone a long way towards providing reassurance to those who are very uncomfortable at the weapon being deployed at all,

[232] NIHRC (2003).

[233] ibid, section 2.1.3.

[234] Police Ombudsman press releases dated 7 and 8 June 2005, 2 and 3 August 2006, 8 and 13 November 2006, and 22 March 2007.

for even they have to recognize that, in situations where the police may be justified in using real bullets in self-defence, firing plastic baton rounds is a better option.[235]

The Police Ombudsman can also choose to investigate matters arising more than 12 months prior to a complaint being lodged. Because of the gravity of the allegations made in relation to one of the plastic bullet deaths—that of 15-year-old Paul Whitters in 1982—and no doubt in order to demonstrate that the phenomenon of plastic bullets deserved to undergo at least one representative investigation, the Police Ombudsman has produced one detailed report into an 'old' fatality. In the case of Paul Whitters the Police Ombudsman concluded that there was no new evidence to show that the police officer who fired the bullet intended to kill Paul, but she added:

> In my view, the firing of the baton gun on that occasion was wrong and unjustifiable. The gun was used in contravention of the rules in place at the time. No warning was given by loud-hailer, and it was fired at less than the permissible range of 20 metres. The police justification for the shooting was that the baton gun was used to prevent a lorry being hijacked, and they said that the rules permitted this. We have found no evidence that Paul intended to hijack the lorry, or that the safety of officers was at risk. Police officers did not say that the gun was fired because there was a serious risk of injury to anyone.[236]

At the end of 2005 the Police Ombudsman reported on the firing of 299 baton rounds by the police during 2001 and 2002, finding that in all of the 24 riots in question the use of baton rounds was a justified and proportionate response to the serious violence directed at police officers, though the Ombudsman did recommend informal disciplinary action against six officers who were found to have breached police procedures during the incidents. The Ombudsman noted that on a number of occasions the police had acted with considerable restraint, but she made no fewer than 43 recommendations to address matters such as public warnings about the imminent use of baton rounds, records of rounds issued to officers, the videoing of discharges, and the use of baton gun assistants.[237] A close analysis of the Police Ombudsman's reports on the firing of plastic bullets in 2001 and 2002 has been conducted by British Irish Rights Watch, a human rights non-governmental organization based in London. It expresses concern that the Police Ombudsman is heavily reliant on the reports made out by police officers after plastic bullets have been fired and it documents discrepancies between police reports and reports received by solicitors from people who claim to have been hit by a bullet.[238] The Ombudsman suggests that none of the people hit were innocent bystanders, but solicitors dispute that.

In the wake of the Patten Commision Report a Steering Group led by the Northern Ireland Office was set up in July 2000 to take forward the recommendations on plastic

[235] See, eg, Police Ombudsman press releases dated 28 May 2002, 24 June 2003, and 2 September 2003. The Independent Assessor of Military Complaints Procedures also published a review of the military use of baton rounds in 2002.

[236] Police Ombudsman press release dated 16 April 2007. In 2002, the UN Committee on the Rights of the Child had called for the abolition of the use of the baton round as a means of riot control: CRC/C/15/Add 188, paras 27 and 28.

[237] Police Ombudsman press release dated 15 December 2005. See also the press releases dated 28 May 2002, 24 June 2003, 2 September 2003, and 25 February 2004, relating to seven riots in 2001 and three in 2002.

[238] BIRW (2006) text at n 105 in the report.

bullets. By the autumn of 2006 the 'Steering Group on Alternative Policing Approaches to the Management of Conflict' had published five reports on less lethal weapons[239] and a year earlier, in June 2005, the PSNI had formally replaced plastic bullets with 'attenuating energy projectiles' (AEPs), which are similar to plastic bullets except that they have an air pocket in the tip which collapses on impact, thereby supposedly making them safer. There was no consultation with the Policing Board, let alone with the general public or human rights groups, before AEPs were purchased and deployed, but within a month they were being fired during riots connected with contested marches in Belfast. PSNI officers were under instructions to comply with the operational guidance on the use of AEPs issued by ACPO.[240] So far there appear to have been no serious adverse consequences from the firing of AEPs in Northern Ireland, but the risks are still great, as British Irish Rights Watch has indicated.[241] But even that organization cannot point to a violation of the European Convention in the fact that AEPs are available: whether they are used in violation of Articles 2 or 3 of the Convention, as with the rubber and plastic bullets which preceded them, will depend on the circumstances of each firing. In 2008 the UN Committee on the Rights of the Child welcomed the abolition of plastic baton rounds as a means of riot control in Northern Ireland but expressed concern that the less harmful nature of AEPs had not been proven and that the use of Tasers had been authorized even on children. It called on the UK government to 'put an end to the use of all harmful devices on children': CRC/C/GBR/C04, para 30.

The right to a thorough investigation

Perhaps the single most important development in European human rights standards attributable to applications resulting from the conflict in Northern Ireland is that relating to the investigation of killings. But even this turning point came as late as 4 May 2001, when judgments were issued at Strasbourg in four separate cases, involving a total of 12 deaths dating from as far back as 1982: *McKerr v United Kingdom*,[242] *Kelly and others v United Kingdom*,[243] *Shanaghan v United Kingdom*,[244] and *Jordan v United Kingdom*.[245] All but one of these deaths had been directly caused by members

[239] Available at <http://www.nio.gov.uk/less_lethal_weaponry_steering_group_phase_4_report.pdf> (last visited 18 November 2009). There is also a European Working Group on Non-Lethal Weapons: see <http:www.non-lethal-weapons.com/index.html>.

[240] These are available on the website of the West Mercia Constabulary: <http://www.westmercia.police.uk>, last visited 12 August 2009.

[241] ibid. See too Police Ombudsman press releases dated 16 November 2008.

[242] (2002) 34 EHRR 20. Gervaise McKerr was killed by the police in 1982. Two other men were killed in the same incident, but no applications were taken to Strasbourg on their behalf.

[243] App No 30054/96, judgment of 4 May 2001. This case was about nine men killed by the British Army's SAS in 1987. See 258 above.

[244] App No 37715/97, judgment of 4 May 2001. Patrick Shanaghan was killed by a loyalist gunman in 1991.

[245] (2003) 37 EHRR 2. Pearse Jordan was killed by the police in 1992. No death in Northern Ireland has led to such extensive litigation as this one (including a decision by the European Court, another by the House of Lords, and several by the Court of Appeal and High Court of Northern Ireland), but still the full truth of what happened on the day of the killing does not seem to have emerged. At the time of writing the inquest into the death is still incomplete.

of the security forces in Northern Ireland, the exception being the death of Patrick Shanaghan, who was killed by a loyalist gunman but in circumstances suggesting there might have been collusion between a loyalist paramilitary organization and the police. In relation to all of the deaths the families of the victims argued that the State had not done enough to investigate the killings with a view to determining whether any laws had been broken by State agents.

In many respects the substance of all of these judgments is the same: in holding that the UK government had failed to satisfy the 'procedural' aspects of Article 2,[246] the European Court set out a list of requirements for Convention-compliant investigations. In doing so it drew upon the general duty imposed upon States by Article 1 of the Convention, namely to 'secure to everyone within [its] jurisdiction the rights and freedoms defined in [the] Convention', inferring from this that there should be some form of effective official investigation when individuals have been killed as a result of the use of force.[247] The Court (here I take its judgment in *Jordan v United Kingdom* as representative of the four cases) added:

> The essential purpose of such investigation is to secure the effective implementation of the domestic laws which protect the right to life and, in those cases involving State agents or bodies, to ensure their accountability for deaths occurring under their responsibility. What form of investigation will achieve those purposes may vary in different circumstances. However, whatever mode is employed, the authorities must act of their own motion, once the matter has come to their attention. They cannot leave it to the initiative of the next of kin either to lodge a formal complaint or to take responsibility for the conduct of any investigative procedures.[248]

In more detail, the requirements imposed by the Court were as follows:

(1) the people who investigate killings must be independent from the people who are implicated in them; this means 'not only a lack of hierarchical or institutional connection but also a practical independence';[249]

(2) the investigation must be effective 'in the sense that it is capable of leading to a determination of whether the force used in such cases was or was not justified in the circumstances . . . and to the identification and punishment of those responsible'; no such outcomes have to be guaranteed, but the authorities 'must have taken the reasonable steps available to them to secure the evidence concerning the incident, including *inter alia* eye witness testimony, forensic evidence and, where appropriate, an autopsy which provides a complete and accurate record of injury and an objective analysis of clinical findings, including the cause of death';[250]

(3) the investigation must occur with reasonable expedition; there may be obstacles or difficulties which prevent progress, but 'a prompt response by the authorities

[246] But there were no findings that any other article of the Convention had been violated.

[247] *Jordan v UK* (2003) 37 EHRR 2, para 105, citing *McCann v UK* (1995) 21 EHRR 97, para 161, and *Kaya v Turkey* (1998) 28 EHRR 1, para 86.

[248] ibid, citing *İlhan v Turkey* (2002) 34 EHRR 36, para 63 (Grand Chamber).

[249] ibid, para 106. [250] ibid, para 107.

in investigating a use of lethal force may generally be regarded as essential in maintaining public confidence in their adherence to the rule of law and in preventing any appearance of collusion in or tolerance of unlawful acts';[251] and

(4) there must be 'a sufficient element of public scrutiny of the investigation or its results to secure accountability in practice as well as in theory' and 'the next-of-kin of the victim must be involved in the procedure to the extent necessary to safeguard his or her legitimate interests'.[252]

These ground-breaking judgments of the European Court were prompted, to some extent, by the submission made to it as an intervener by the Northern Ireland Human Rights Commission (NIHRC), established by statute just a year earlier.[253] Although the judgment does not expressly rely upon the arguments contained in that submission, it is clear from a comparison of the two documents that it was influential on the judges. The submission was largely based on the standards concerning the right to life contained in the case law of the Inter-American Court of Human Rights[254] and in the findings of the UN Human Rights Committee. In particular, the NIHRC argued that it was not sufficient for a State to declare that, 'while certain mechanisms were inadequate, a number of such mechanisms regarded cumulatively could provide the necessary protection'.[255] Attention was drawn to 'the problematic role of the RUC in Northern Ireland, the allegedly serious deficiencies in the mechanisms of police accountability, the limited scope of and delays in inquests, and the lack of compellability of the members of the security forces who have used lethal force to appear at inquests'.[256] Finally, the NIHRC urged the Court to seize the opportunity to give precise guidance as to the form which investigations into the use of lethal force by State agents should take.

In each of the cases decided on 4 May 2001 the Court awarded the applicants £10,000 by way of compensation for the State's failure to conduct an effective investigation into the deaths in question. This award added to the embarrassment, not to say outrage, displayed by UK government representatives at the time, although in due course the government did pay up. Things were made worse for the government by the fact that in two later cases, the second of which was a particularly high-profile one, the European Court again condemned the United Kingdom for not having properly investigated suspicious deaths. In *McShane v United Kingdom*[257] the victim had been run over by an army personnel carrier during a riot in Derry in 1996; in *Finucane v United Kingdom*[258] the victim was a prominent solicitor who was killed by

[251] ibid, para 108.

[252] ibid, para 109. See generally Mowbray (2002).

[253] Northern Ireland Act 1998, ss 68–72. The submission was largely drawn up by Professor Fionnuala Ní Aoláin, of the University of Ulster, who has published extensively in this field: Ní Aoláin (2000), Ní Aoláin (2001), Gross and Ní Aoláin (2001), Ní Aoláin (2002), Gross and Ní Aoláin (2006).

[254] In particular, *Velásquez Rodriguez v Honduras*, judgment of 29 July 1988. This was a case about a man's disappearance: paras 174–7 spell out the duties which were later elaborated upon by the European Court.

[255] *Jordan v UK* (2003) 37 EHRR 2, para 101. Full copies of the submission are available from the Commission itself.

[256] ibid.

[257] (2002) 35 EHRR 23.

[258] (2003) 37 EHRR 29. See Rolston (2000); Lawyers Committee for Human Rights (2003); O'Brien (2005).

loyalist paramilitaries in 1989 in circumstances strongly suggesting collusion on the part of British army intelligence officers.

The bigger question remaining after the delivery of all of these judgments, however, was how would the government go about implementing them?[259] It is one thing for the European Court to declare what human rights standards have been violated, but how effective is it in ensuring that the State concerned makes the necessary alterations to its law, policy, and practice in order to ensure that justice is done for the particular applicants? That question has been a focus of attention for the Council of Europe's Committee of Ministers during the intervening eight years and, unfortunately, the Committee is still not entirely satisfied that the UK government has done all that it needs to do in this context.

On the positive side, the following changes to law and practice, which are listed in chronological order, *have* occurred:[260]

- as a result of a series of changes to practice begun in 1996, information relevant to inquests is now disclosed to all parties in advance, although some disclosure may still not take place in the interests of national security;
- since 1996 the Chief Constable in Northern Ireland has had statutory power to ask police officers from other forces in Great Britain to investigate an incident in Northern Ireland that is placing special demand on the PSNI's resources;[261]
- since 1999 it has been judges, not ministers, who have decided whether the content of documents is so sensitive as to entitle them to be protected from disclosure under 'public interest immunity certificates';
- in 2000 the office of the Police Ombudsman for Northern Ireland was created, to conduct completely independent investigations of complaints against the police;
- in 2002 the rules applicable to inquests in Northern Ireland were changed so that witnesses suspected of involvement in a death could be compelled to attend the inquest, although they could not be compelled to give self-incriminating answers;[262]
- in 2002 the Prosecution Service in Northern Ireland explained that it would from then on give reasons for not prosecuting in cases where death is, or may have been, occasioned by the conduct of agents of the State;[263]

[259] See, generally, Anthony and Mageean (2007).

[260] This summary is based on the information provided to the Committee of Ministers and appended to that Committee's Interim Resolution CM/ResDH(2005)20 (adopted 23 February 2005); Interim Resolution CM/ResDH(2007)73 (adopted 6 June 2007); and Interim Resolution CM/ResDH(2009)44 (adopted 19 March 2009). These documents are all available on the website of the European Court. In this context one might also cite the Northern Ireland (Location of Victims' Remains) Act 1999, which allows immunity from suit to be granted to persons who disclose information about the location of people who were 'disappeared' by republican terrorists. Police training on human rights has also contributed greatly to better accountability under Article 2 and other provisions, although O'Rawe argues that there are still flaws in the training process: O'Rawe, M (2005). For a more generous appraisal see Starmer (2007).

[261] Police Act 1996, s 98(1).

[262] Coroners (Practice and Procedure) (Amendment) Rules (NI) 2002 (SR 37).

[263] See now the Code for Prosecutors of the Public Prosecution Service of Northern Ireland, at para 4.12.4 (effective from June 2005), available on the PPS's website. For further discussion see ch 8 above, 186–8.

- in 2003 the Chief Constable of the PSNI established the Serious Crimes Review Team 'to review a number of unsolved major crimes, including murder and rape, where it is thought that new evidential leads may be developed', and in 2005 the work of this team was taken over by the Historical Enquiries Team;
- also in 2003 the Lord Chancellor established a statutory scheme (further to an already existing *ex gratia* scheme) to provide for legal representation at certain exceptional inquests in Northern Ireland, where the applicant had a sufficiently close relationship to the deceased;[264]
- in a case decided in 2004[265] the House of Lords ruled that in order to provide an Article 2-compliant investigation, an inquest is required, when examining 'how' a deceased came by his or her death, to determine not only 'by what means' but also 'in what circumstances' the death occurred;
- in 2006 a new Coroners Service was launched in Northern Ireland, with a view to expediting the holding of inquests.[266]

On the negative side, the Committee of Ministers, even in March 2009, was unhappy that one 'general measure' required by the judgments of 2001 had still not been taken, namely ensuring that retired police officers could be investigated by an independent body such as the Police Ombudsman. 'Individual measures' relevant to each of the four 2001 cases still needed to be taken too: the UK government had not brought to an end the ongoing investigations into these killings. In the *McKerr* case, the government was still considering whether to disclose parts of the Stalker/Sampson papers;[267] in the case of *Kelly and others*, further inquiries still needed to be carried out before the Historical Enquiries Team could deliver a summary report to the families; in the case of *Shanaghan*, the Historical Enquiries Team was still preparing a final summary report and an investigation by the Police Ombudsman was still incomplete; and as regards the *Jordan* case, an inquest into the killing had still not been reopened.[268] On the other hand, the Committee of Ministers has closed its examination of the individual measures required in the *McShane* and *Finucane* cases, even though as regards the latter death no public inquiry has yet taken place, as recommended by ex-Canadian Supreme Court judge Peter Cory.[269] The Finucane family is unwilling to cooperate with an inquiry held under the Inquiries Act 2005, since on one view that Act was specifically enacted in order to thwart the disclosure of relevant information by the State, making any such inquiry in potential breach of Article 2 of the Convention.[270]

[264] The scheme was established under the Access to Justice (NI) Order 2003, art 12(8).

[265] *R (Middleton) v HM Coroner for the Western District of Somerset* [2004] UKHL 10, [2004] 2 AC 182.

[266] For further details of the current arrangements see <http://www.coronersni.gov.uk>.

[267] These are the papers collected by John Stalker and Colin Sampson for their investigations into alleged collusion between members of the security forces and loyalist paramilitaries: see 253 above.

[268] The Jordan family also instituted civil proceedings in 1992, but these have been suspended pending the outcome of the inquest.

[269] Cory (2004). See too Connolly (2007); Hegarty (2002–3).

[270] Requa (2007). See too Lundy (2009), who critiques police inquiries.

The major difficulty facing the families of people killed during the troubles in Northern Ireland is that, while they might be able to persuade the European Court of Human Rights that an investigation fully compliant with Article 2 of the Convention has not taken place, and may even receive compensation from the UK government for that failing, there is no obligation under domestic law to hold such an investigation. This was categorically asserted by the House of Lords in *Re McKerr*,[271] where their Lordships drew a sharp distinction between international and national legal obligations and where they refused to hold that under the common law there was a right to an investigation just as effective as that required under the Convention.[272] In so holding the House reversed the Court of Appeal of Northern Ireland,[273] which had managed to construe the duty to investigate as a continuing one, still existing when the Human Rights Act came into force on 2 October 2000. Anthony and Mageean portray the House's decision as illustrative of 'how core precepts of the UK constitution can be of questionable value in the Northern Ireland polity',[274] but the larger point is surely that the decision illustrates the more general defects in the dualist approach to international law adopted by the United Kingdom as a whole, a point which Lord Steyn, an enthusiastic internationalist, addressed in his judgment, concluding that '[a] critical re-examination of this branch of the law may become necessary in the future'.[275]

The *Jordan* case also made its way to the House of Lords following the European Court's decision, this time on whether coroners and juries at inquests in Northern Ireland, because of the special legislative provisions in force there,[276] could return verdicts of lawful or unlawful killing. By three to two their Lordships confirmed the widely held view that such verdicts were not possible.[277] However, the majority did concede that there was nothing to prevent coroners or juries finding facts directly relevant to the cause of death which might point to the existence of criminal liability. Moreover, in an appeal decided alongside the *Jordan* case, *McCaughey v Chief Constable of the PSNI*, the House held that the police were under a continuing statutory duty[278] to supply to the coroner such information as they had relating to the death.[279]

At the end of 2007 no fewer than five further cases involving alleged defective investigations into killings in Northern Ireland were decided by the European

[271] [2004] UKHL 12, [2004] 1 WLR 807. The death had been the subject of a much earlier appeal to the Lords relating to the scope of an inquest: *McKerr v Armagh Coroner* [1990] 1 WLR 649.

[272] On this point Lord Nicholls said, at [31]: 'The suggested new common law right is sought as a means of supplementing, or overriding, the statutory provisions relating to the holding of coroners' inquests. That is not an appropriate role for the common law.' See too Anthony (2005).

[273] [2003] NI 117 (Carswell LCJ, McCollum LJ, and Coghlin J).

[274] Anthony and Mageean (2007) 199.

[275] [2004] UKHL 12, [2004] 1 WLR 807, at [50].

[276] Coroners Act (NI) 1959, s 31(1) and Coroners (Practice and Procedure) Rules (NI) 1963, rr 15 and 16.

[277] *Jordan v Lord Chancellor* [2007] UKHL 14, [2007] 2 AC 226, affirming the Court of Appeal of Northern Ireland: [2005] NI 144.

[278] Under the Coroners Act (NI) 1959, s 8. On this the House reversed the Court of Appeal of Northern Ireland: [2005] NI 144.

[279] It has since been reported that Mr McCaughey's mother has lodged an application with the European Court of Human Rights claiming that her son's death was not properly investigated: *Irish News*, 14 August 2009.

Court,[280] but in all of these the only respect in which the applicants won was with regard to the absence of any truly independent element in the early stages of the investigation. Perhaps surprisingly, given the overlap in the membership of the bodies, the Court held that when the Police Service of Northern Ireland took over responsibility for investigating the killings from the Royal Ulster Constabulary in 2001, this remedied the lack of independence.

Inquests

Throughout the conflict in Northern Ireland the law relating to inquests was very similar to that applicable in England and Wales. But there were some important differences which meant that the human rights of the families of the deceased were not as well protected in Northern Ireland.[281] The three most important anomalies were brought to light in the quartet of cases decided by the European Court in May 2001, namely, that inquests took a very long time to be completed, that persons suspected of involvement in the killings could not be compelled to give evidence at the inquests, and that juries and coroners at inquests could not issue verdicts determining that a killing had been lawful or unlawful.[282] In addition, the inquest system suffered from defects which existed in England and Wales too—that the scope of the inquiry was very limited, that verdicts could not suggest some named person might be responsible for the death under civil or criminal law, that legal aid was not available to pay for the family of the deceased to be legally represented at an inquest, and that documents could be withheld from inquests if covered by a 'public interest immunity certificate'.

It took quite some time for these various anomalies to be rectified, but this reforming process was certainly accelerated by the comments of the European Court in the 2001 cases. The Court was not of course insisting that Article 2 implicitly entailed a right to an inquest in relation to every death, for most European countries know nothing of such a procedure at all, nor was it suggesting that an inquest would always by itself be a way of satisfying the procedural requirements of Article 2, but the Court was saying that every unexplained death had to be thoroughly investigated—not just when an agent of the State is allegedly implicated but also in other cases. In common law systems inquests can often fulfil that investigative obligation, especially as coroners have the power to refer findings to the public prosecutor for consideration of whether criminal proceedings should then be issued. However, despite the reforms to Northern Ireland's inquest system already alluded to,[283] some inquests into

280 *Brecknell v UK* (2008) 46 EHRR 42; *O'Dowd v UK* App 34622/04, decision of 27 November 2007; *McCartney v UK* App 34575/04, decision of 27 November 2007; *Reavey v UK* App 34640/04, decision of 27 November 2007; *McGrath v UK* App 34651/04, decision of 27 November 2007.

281 See, generally, Ní Aoláin (2000) ch 3.

282 A further anomaly was that inquests on bodies found outside Northern Ireland could not be held in Northern Ireland, but this was of no real importance during the conflict. It did mean, though, that inquests into the deaths of three IRA members in Gibraltar could not be held in Northern Ireland.

283 See 271–2 above. For earlier reform proposals see Hadden (1992).

disputed killings dating back many years are *still* outstanding. There may yet be further applications to Strasbourg relating to the failure of Northern Ireland law to comply fully with the duty to thoroughly investigate a suspicious death as developed by the European Court.

Conclusion

Cases emerging out of the conflict in Northern Ireland have had a profound effect on the development of the European Court's approach to Article 2 of the Convention. They largely initiated the Court's adherence to standards concerning the control and organization of operations that result in deaths and to standards relating to the investigation of deaths. While each of these sets of standards appears to apply *ex post facto*—after a death has occurred—their long-term effect is to ensure that the risk of deaths occurring in similar circumstances in the future is reduced. Ultimately, despite what might initially be thought, the standards are preventative rather than reactive in nature. They have been applied many times in cases arising out of conflicts elsewhere in Europe, especially those in Turkey (concerning the rights of Kurds) and in Russia (concerning the governance of Chechnya). There are also signs that the standards are being increasingly applied in non-conflict situations, such as prison suicides and hospital deaths. The fact that Article 2 is a non-derogable right, even though it is actually expressed in qualified terms, has gone a long way towards rendering it immune from manipulation by member States, yet in both domestic and Strasbourg jurisprudence it is clear that some interests, particularly those of national security, can override even the right to life. As on so many other occasions highlighted in this book, the coming of age of Article 2 occurred rather late in the day to guarantee better protection of the right to life within Northern Ireland itself, but applications originating in that jurisdiction played a far from negligible role in enhancing protection of the right all across Europe for future generations.

10

The Right to a Private and Family Life

Article 8 is one of the European Convention's most flexible provisions, and even today its potential for development is far from being fully realized. In decades to come the European Court might well turn it into the equivalent of Article 21 of the Indian Constitution which, although ostensibly dealing with the right to life,[1] has been unashamedly exploited by the Indian Supreme Court as the foundation for a huge range of rights far beyond the foresight of any of the drafters of the country's 1950 Constitution. In Northern Ireland Article 8 issues first came to the fore in the context of disputes within the prisons, where the conflict that otherwise manifested itself on the province's streets was played out in a much more confined and pressurized environment. Only belatedly was Article 8 cited in challenges to security force search operations, when the police or army would close off entire streets and systematically rummage through every room of every house while looking for equipment or documents that might implicate the residents in terrorist activity. Northern Ireland's conflict was never 'about' privacy and family life, but aspects of how it unfolded certainly impinged upon those rights, at times quite severely. In addition, Article 8 played a vital role in ensuring that homosexuals in Northern Ireland acquired protection from discrimination, though it cannot honestly be claimed that prejudice against gay and lesbian people was a salient aspect of the conflict in Northern Ireland.

Prison conditions

The European Convention has been invoked very frequently by prisoners all across Europe, on a wide range of issues.[2] Indeed the first judgment issued against the United Kingdom by the European Court was in a case brought by a prisoner[3] and in 1977 two Irish republican prisoners held in England, one of them (Patrick Fell) a Catholic priest, launched a further application.[4] In September 1976 they had engaged, with others, in a sit-down protest in the corridor of Albany prison on the Isle of Wight. They were each later charged with serious disciplinary offences including, in Campbell's case, mutiny and doing gross personal violence to an officer, but

[1] It reads: 'No person shall be deprived of his life or personal liberty except according to procedure established by law.'

[2] Reid (2008) 464–80.

[3] *Golder v UK* (1978–80) 1 EHRR 524.

[4] *Campbell and Fell v UK* (1984) 7 EHRR 165.

they were denied legal representation at the disciplinary hearing before the Board of Visitors and were 'awarded', amongst other things, loss of remission (570 days in Campbell's case). When they later asked permission to consult with lawyers about taking a civil action against the prison officers who had allegedly ended the sit-down protest very roughly, Fell was told that he could consult his lawyers only within the sight and hearing of a prison officer.

The European Commission of Human Rights delivered its report on the admissibility and merits of the applicants' claims in May 1982 and upheld most of the complaints.[5] Likewise, the European Court held, by a unanimous vote, that Father Fell's rights under Article 6(1) had been breached, by five to two that Campbell's rights under Article 6 (1) had been breached in that the Board of Visitors had not made its decision public, and by four to three that Campbell's rights under Article 6(3)(b) and (c) had been breached because of his inability to obtain legal assistance or legal representation for the hearing with the Board of Visitors. The Court additionally held, unanimously, that there had been a breach of both applicants' rights under Articles 6(1) and 8 when their attempts to get legal advice in connection with their personal injuries claim were interfered with. This case had little to do with the Northern Ireland conflict *per se*, but the Court's ruling did go a long way towards helping prisoners across the continent get access to legal assistance when defending accusations that they had broken the prison's rules or when considering other litigation.[6] The decision also illustrates how the values protected by Article 8 of the Convention significantly overlap with those protected by other provisions such as Article 6.

Throughout the 1970s and 1980s there were persistent complaints from detainees and prisoners in Northern Ireland that the conditions in which they were being held were unacceptably harsh.[7] Many of these complaints, especially those raised by detainees (ie people who were interned, or held in police holding centres while being interrogated), were challenges based on Article 3,[8] but some, especially those raised by convicted prisoners, were based on Article 8. While some of the conditions faced by prisoners were indubitably harsh, it must also be remembered that many prisoners, especially republicans, saw propaganda value in raising complaints over restrictions that in reality were not serious. Terrorists in Germany did the same in the early 1970s, and were given short shrift by the European Commission.[9]

Initially, all prisoners convicted in Northern Ireland of crimes connected with the conflict were not classified in any special way, but in July 1972, just before the introduction of juryless Diplock courts, the then Conservative government under Prime Minister Ted Heath and Secretary of State William Whitelaw allowed such prisoners

[5] Available on the website of the European Court.

[6] Harlow and Rawlings (1992) 256 pay tribute to the role played by the NGO Interights in this case, saying that Commission lawyers referred the case to that organization at a late stage when the applicants wanted to change their lawyers. They then say that Interights helped to negotiate a friendly settlement, 'a fact not recorded in the official report'. The case did nevertheless result in a European Court judgment.

[7] For an insightful account of containment policy in Northern Ireland see Gormally, McEvoy, and Wall (1993).

[8] See ch 7 above.

[9] *Baader, Meins, Meinhof and Grundmann v Federal Republic of Germany* App No 6166/73, decision of 30 May 1975.

to hold so-called 'Special Category Status'. This status was supposedly granted in order to ward off a hunger strike by up to 40 IRA prisoners, but some see it as part of a bigger political negotiation process at the time.[10] The consequence of according this status was that these prisoners did not have to wear prison uniform or do any prison work. They were housed in compounds separate from the other cells and were allowed additional privileges, including extra visits and food parcels. By the end of 1974 the number of special category prisoners had risen to 1,065.

While stopping short of labelling the prisoners 'prisoners of war', it was still an extraordinary concession for a British Conservative government to make and in retrospect has been viewed by most as a policy blunder. Even in 1975, in its first annual report, the newly created Standing Advisory Commission on Human Rights in Northern Ireland came out strongly against special category status.[11] It supported the Gardiner Committee's recommendation that the status should be ended at 'the earliest practical opportunity'[12] because it:

> makes a mockery of fair prison practices by granting privileges to convicted prisoners claiming political motivation which are not available to other convicted prisoners. All concerned should be subject to the same Prison Rules, thereby removing a genuine sense of grievance felt by other convicted prisoners and demonstrating that claims of political motivation in no sense either justify the offences or reduce the gravity with which they are viewed.[13]

In 1976, after a review of Britain's overall policy approach to the conflict in Northern Ireland, the then Labour government and its Secretary of State for Northern Ireland, Merlyn Rees, decided to treat people convicted in connection with the conflict as ordinary criminals. Wisely, the change of policy was not made retrospective,[14] so prisoners who already enjoyed the special category status were allowed to retain it until their sentences expired. Anyone convicted after 1 March 1976, on the other hand, was not given the status. At the same time the government secured the passing of the Treatment of Offenders (NI) Order 1976, effectively a *quid pro quo* for the removal of special category status, which increased the maximum remission a prisoner could earn from one-third of his or her sentence to one-half. Notwithstanding this 'concession' the immediate reaction of the IRA to the change of policy on political status was first to threaten and then to murder off-duty prison officers. The first such killing occurred in April 1976 and over the next 17 years a further 28 prison officers were murdered.[15]

Within the prisons the republican response was to initiate what was called 'the blanket protest', whereby republican prisoners refused to wear prison uniforms and instead

[10] See McEvoy (2001) 217, citing the autobiography of Gerry Adams (current President of Sinn Féin) and the memoirs of the then Secretary of State for Northern Ireland, William Whitelaw. Whitelaw admitted that granting special category status 'did establish a practice which caused my successors considerable trouble. I conclude today that its immediate impact was limited and it was later found to have been a misguided decision': Whitelaw (1989) 94.

[11] SACHR (1975) para 35.

[12] Gardiner (1975) paras 105–8.

[13] ibid.

[14] SACHR regretted this: SACHR (1977a) para 21.

[15] Ryder (2000a) 161. For further details see <http://www.palacebarracksmemorialgarden.org/Northern%20Ireland%20Prison%20Service.htm>.

draped themselves with prison blankets.[16] The first such 'blanketman' was Kieran Nugent, who adopted his stance on 14 September 1976. By the end of that year there were some 40 such protestors. Attempts to resolve the impasse failed and in March 1978 the protest was ratcheted up when some prisoners refused to leave their cells to shower or use the toilet. Wash-hand basins were then installed in the cells, but not showers. Following a fight between a prisoner and a prison officer, and the alleged beating of that prisoner while he was in solitary confinement, prisoners smashed the furniture in their cells. To prevent the prisoners from using parts of the furniture as weapons, all furniture was then removed from the cells, leaving the prisoners with just blankets, mattresses and chamber pots. Prisoners then refused to leave their cells to 'slop-out' and what had been a 'blanket protest' escalated into a 'dirty protest', as the prisoners began smearing their own excrement on the walls of their cells. When the prison authorities forcibly removed prisoners and hosed down their cells the protest would resume when the prisoners were back in the cells. By August 1978 there were about 300 prisoners participating in the dirty protest. Then, in January 1980, the protestors clarified their position by making 'five demands', which they framed as rights, although not as human rights, and not with reference to any provision in the European Convention:

- the right not to wear a prisoner uniform;
- the right to free association with republican political prisoners;
- the right not to do prison work;
- the right to organize their own educational and recreational facilities; and
- the right to one weekly visit, letter, and parcel.

The prisoners also wanted full restoration of any remission they would otherwise lose as a result of engaging in the protest. A month later, more than 30 female prisoners in Armagh Women's Prison adopted the same protest tactics.

Meanwhile, four of the male dirty protestors, including Kieran Nugent, had lodged applications with the European Commission of Human Rights,[17] and on 15 May 1980 the Commission pronounced its views. In *McFeeley, Nugent, Huntley and Campbell v United Kingdom*[18] there were several allegations that the conditions under which the applicants were living in the Maze Prison amounted to a breach of Article 3 of the Convention. As regards breaches of Article 8, the prisoners complained about having to 'slop-out' and use chamber-pots within the sight of their cell mates, having to wash and use toilet facilities within the sight of prison officers, being restricted to one family visit per month, having to wear prison uniform during such visits, having restrictions placed on their incoming and outgoing mail, and being given limited writing facilities. To the disappointment of the applicants and their lawyers the European Commission declared all of these complaints to be inadmissible, except for those regarding alleged interference with mail, which were adjourned for later consideration pending the outcome of the Commission's deliberations on

[16] See, generally, McEvoy (2001) 82–93; Bishop and Mallie (1987) ch 3; Kelley (1982) ch 8.

[17] Their legal representatives were Francis Keenan (a solicitor in Belfast) and Kevin Boyle, who by then had moved from Queen's University Belfast to become a Professor of Law at University College, Galway.

[18] (1981) 3 EHRR 161.

other applications by prisoners in England—applications which resulted in *Silver v United Kingdom*, where the European Court established that routine interference with prisoners' mail was a breach of Article 8 (though not of Article 10).[19] It later transpired that the applicants failed to pursue these adjourned complaints and in 1984 the Commission struck the applications off the list, saying that the applicants had lost interest in them and that 'there are no reasons of a general character affecting the observance of the Convention which warrant further examination of the application'.[20]

As regards slopping-out and the use of chamber pots in cells, the European Commission found these to be attributable to the actions of the applicants themselves in the furtherance of their protest and not therefore amounting to interference by the State with their rights under Article 8(1):

> ... if they had to slop out either naked or covered only in a blanket or towel, it was because of their persistent refusal to wear prison clothes. In the same way, the use of a chamber pot in the cell both day and night is the direct result of their decision in early 1978 not to avail of the toilet facilities and to intensify their campaign.[21]

This is an explicit reaffirmation of the basic principle that no-one can deliberately refuse to 'enjoy' their basic human rights and then claim that the State is to blame. To try to exploit human rights law in such a way is to denigrate those genuine claimants who have indeed been denied their rights by the State.

As regards the complaints about surveillance by prison warders and searching procedures, the Commission said that these activities were justified because they were necessary to prevent disorder or crime. It had to have regard to the real security threat posed by such a large-scale protest campaign: 'The attempts to conceal dangerous objects and the previous disruptive behaviour of the prisoners ... make it inevitable that close surveillance and thorough searching takes place.'[22] In so far as the applicants complained that they were not permitted to associate with other prisoners, the Commission confirmed that the concept of private life in the Convention embraces to some extent the right to establish and develop relationships with other human beings and that this right existed even in a prison. The applicants' removal from association was therefore an interference with their right to privacy, but again it was a justifiable interference because its purpose was to prevent disorder. The Commission hinted that it was also justifiable because it was a punishment imposed with a view to bringing the prisoners' protest to an end, but that is surely a less acceptable justification because it amounts to saying that a person can be denied some rights in order to make sure that they enjoy other rights. Rights should not be seen as bargaining chips, and are not 'earned'. In any event, Article 17 of the Convention already provides a rationale for denying some rights:

> Nothing in this Convention may be interpreted as implying for any State, group or person any right to engage in any activity or perform any act aimed at the destruction of any of the rights

[19] (1983) 5 EHRR 347.
[20] Report of the Commission, adopted 2 October 1984, 4.
[21] (1981) 3 EHRR 161, 205, para 80.
[22] ibid, para 81.

and freedoms set forth herein or at their limitation to a greater extent than is provided for in the Convention.

The prisoners' complaint about restrictions on family visits was dealt with similarly to those about restrictions on association and, although the matter had not been specifically argued before it, the Commission also offered the view *ex cathedra* that a requirement to wear prison uniform was justified in the interests of public safety and in order to prevent crime.

On the more general issue of whether the prisoners should be entitled to 'political status' the European Commission said the following:

The Commission... must observe that the applicants are seeking to achieve a status of political prisoner which they are not entitled to under national law or under the Convention. Furthermore... the Commission does not consider that such an entitlement in the present context can be derived from existing norms of International Law. In this regard the Commission recalls its opinion that the applicants' convictions are not protected by the Convention or Article 9 in particular, and that their complaint under this provision has been rejected as incompatible ratione materiae. It follows from this that their protest cannot derive any legitimacy or justification from the Convention and cannot be attributed to any positive action on behalf of the respondent Government.[23]

The European Commission's decision was essentially an endorsement of the view of the UK government that the human rights of the prison protestors were not being infringed by the State, and the government was predictably pleased with it.[24] The conditions under which the prisoners were living were not a breach of Articles 3, 8 or any other provision in the European Convention. The outcome could not really have been a surprise to those who were active in the human rights movement at the time,[25] and Amnesty International said virtually nothing, not being in support of special status for any prisoners.[26] O'Malley recounts how Charles Haughey, the Irish Taoiseach, tried to persuade the sister of one of the prisoners, Bobby Sands, to lodge a complaint on her brother's behalf with the European Commission of Human Rights, but that it came to nothing because when a delegation from the Commission visited the prison Bobby Sands would not meet with it unless representatives of the IRA and Sinn Féin were present, and the prison authorities would not allow this.[27] Beresford then recounts how Haughey continued to look for a prisoner who would make the application that Sands had refused to make.[28]

[23] ibid, para 43.

[24] O'Malley (1990) 191 says the government embraced the Commission's findings 'with a relish bordering on exuberance'.

[25] It is no coincidence that the group which eventually became the leading non-governmental human rights organization in Northern Ireland (the Committee on the Administration of Justice) was formed in the midst of the hunger strikes in 1981, but although it worked on prison issues right from the start it did not campaign on behalf of the hunger strikers themselves.

[26] See O'Malley (1990) 24.

[27] ibid, 62. See too Kelley (1982) 337. A complaint was lodged in Strasbourg but was struck off after Bobby Sands died: *Sands v UK* App No 9338/81.

[28] Beresford (1987) 196. He adds that after Ireland's Foreign Minister visited Strasbourg in May 1980 'the European Commission announced that it was reopening the 1978 *McFeeley* case', but what he

The intransigence of the then British Prime Minister, Margaret Thatcher, was in stark contrast to the pragmatism displayed by her Conservative predecessor, Ted Heath, who had agreed to special category status being granted in 1972. At one point, however, the Commission did criticize the government for its rigidity:

> No doubt the authorities consider that to make concessions to the applicants will result in strengthening their resolve to continue their protest to a successful conclusion. However, the Commission must express its concern at the inflexible approach of the State authorities which has been concerned more to punish offenders against prison discipline than to explore ways of resolving such a serious deadlock. Furthermore, the Commission is of the view that, for humanitarian reasons, efforts should have been made by the authorities to ensure that the applicants could avail of certain facilities such as taking regular exercise in the open air with some form of clothing (other than prison clothing) and making greater use of the prison amenities under similar conditions. At the same time, arrangements should have been made to enable the applicants to consult outside medical specialists even though they were not prepared to wear prison uniform or underwear.[29]

This was a very rare example of a European Convention organ 'daring' to give direct advice to a State as to how best to resolve a difficult domestic issue and its utterance is an indication of how seriously the Commission considered the stalemate in the prison to be. By way of response the UK government did make an important concession in that it offered the prisoners more civilian-like clothes to wear. Otherwise, as McEvoy notes, the Commission's decision illustrates the limited potential for using the European Convention on Human Rights in a 'frontal assault' on political status for prisoners.[30] Ryder describes it as 'a deep and fundamental setback for the prisoners',[31] though he points out that in anticipation of adverse comments from the European Commission the government did change the rules on confinement to cells and on dietary punishments.[32]

Back in the H-blocks of the Maze Prison, the European Commission's ruling caused discord amongst the protesting prisoners. Some felt it was now right to give up the protest, and they did so. The Army Council of the Provisional IRA called for its termination too. But other prisoners considered the new clothes being offered as too similar to prison uniforms and they decided to continue their dirty protest. Shortly afterwards, a strategic decision was taken by the paramilitary commanders in the prison to raise the stakes even further by initiating a hunger strike. One of the four applicants in the failed attempt to provoke sympathy from the European Commission, Thomas McFeeley, was one of seven prisoners who began this hunger strike on 27 October 1980.[33] It lasted 53 days, with at least one of the strikers coming close to death, and ended just before Christmas only because the British government produced a document proposing a settlement and the head of the Catholic Church in

must be referring to here is the Commission's decision on 15 May 1980 to declare most of the complaints inadmissible and to adjourn its consideration of those relating to Arts 8 and 13.

[29] (1981) 3 EHRR 161, para 64.

[30] McEvoy (2001) 155.

[31] Ryder (2000a) 195.

[32] ibid, 193.

[33] The others were Leo Green, Brendan Hughes, Raymond McCartney, Tommy McKearney, Sean McKenna, and John Nixon.

Ireland appealed for its termination. However, in the New Year the prisoners decided they had been duped, because their five demands would not be met under the government's settlement, and on 1 March 1981 a new hunger strike began, this time with Bobby Sands being the first to refuse food. The only concession made by the prisoners was that they ended the dirty protest immediately after this second hunger strike commenced.

The strike led to 10 men dying of starvation between 5 May 1981 and 20 August 1981[34] and was not officially called off until 3 October 1981. The IRA Army Council was not supportive of it and insisted on continuing its armed struggle: during the 1981 hunger strike it killed 13 policemen, eight soldiers, five members of the UDR, and five civilians.[35] In the midst of his strike Bobby Sands was put forward as a candidate for a seat at the Westminster Parliament in a by-election in Fermanagh and South Tyrone, and he won (largely because no other nationalist politician would stand against him). Attempts were made by one or two groups to mediate between the British government and the prisoners, but to no avail. A delegation representing the Irish Commission for Justice and Peace met with officials in the Northern Ireland Office in June and July but when the discussions broke down the prisoners asked for government officials to meet directly with them, not through intermediaries. The International Committee of the Red Cross also tried to intervene, and visited the prison in July, but again the prisoners asked them not to make further efforts; as is the custom with the Red Cross, its views on the conditions in the Maze Prison were kept confidential. The strike finally ended when the then Secretary of State for Northern Ireland, James Prior, announced that the government was making various changes to prison policy, including allowing all paramilitary prisoners to wear their own clothes at all times, allowing prisoners to have free association with neighbouring wings of each H-Block, creating an exercise area and more recreation rooms, increasing the number of visits each prisoner was to be allowed, and restoring the right to 50per cent remission for good behaviour.[36]

As a postscript it should be noted that in *Martin v Northern Ireland Prison Service*[37] the plaintiff, who had been imprisoned in 2004, again complained about having to use a chamber pot in his cell (this time at Magilligan Prison) and also about having to slop-out each morning without the use of adequate cleaning materials. He argued that these practices amounted to violations of Articles 3 and 8 of the European Convention, relying in part on the decision of Lord Bonomy in the Scottish case of *Napier*,[38] where slopping-out at Barlinnie Prison had been held to be in breach of Article 3. Girvan J

[34] The 10 who died and the period during which they refused food were: Bobby Sands (66 days), Francis Hughes (59), Raymond McCreesh (61), Patsy O'Hara (61), Joe McDonnell (61), Martin Hurson (46), Kevin Lynch (71), Kieran Doherty (73), Thomas McElwee (62), and Michael Devine (60). For the full story of this hunger strike see Beresford (1987). Controversy still rages over the degree to which Sinn Féin allowed the strike to continue even after a compromise had been suggested by the British authorities: see, eg, O'Rawe, R (2005).

[35] Taylor (1997) 237.

[36] For an assessment of the long-lasting effects of imprisonment within the Republican community of Northern Ireland see Shirlow (2001).

[37] [2006] NIQB 1.

[38] *Napier v Scottish Ministers* [2005] CSIH 16.

held in the case before him that the situation was not serious enough to amount to degrading treatment for the purposes of Article 3 but that the plaintiff was entitled to a declaration that the Prison Service had failed to adequately respect his right to respect for his private life in relation to the arrangements made at Magilligan in respect of toileting and washing facilities. This is a further clear indication of how Convention rights grow and develop over time. Having not played a significant role in the prison protests of the early 1980s, they had come of age a generation later.

Strip-searches

Strange to relate, the practice of strip-searching in Northern Ireland's prisons, while widespread for a long time, was never made the subject of a successful court challenge, whether locally or wider afield in Strasbourg. The story of this particular phenomenon is, in a way, a microcosm of the wider story which this book seeks to relate, namely that human rights law played a belated and somewhat peripheral role in 'managing' Northern Ireland's conflict, and the belatedness and peripherality had more to do with the relative newness of the European Convention than with any conspiracy by judges or others to tolerate dubious practices which today would seem unacceptable. Human rights thinking has progressed so quickly in the last 20 to 30 years that it is difficult to cast oneself back to the mindset which officials, lawyers, and 'ordinary people' lived with in that era. Strip-searching was given scant attention in several relevant books published in the 1980s,[39] though it did feature in reports published by the National Council for Civil Liberites and Amnesty International in 1991.[40]

Strip-searching was conducted systematically in Northern Ireland from about February 1978, certainly in relation to male prisoners who were protesting against the refusal to recognize them as political prisoners. But it was used routinely in relation to female prisoners only from 1982, supposedly after a set of keys was found in a cell occupied by two female prisoners at Armagh Prison.[41] In 1983, a total of 1,218 strip searches were conducted on 358 women prisoners in that prison.[42] Even allowing for the inevitable propaganda quality of some of the literature in this field, the practice and consequences of strip-searching are well attested to in prisoner memoirs. However, these also reveal that the practice was by no means confined to prisons in Northern Ireland. Aíne and Eibhlin Gillespie, for example, write about how the practice was used in English gaols during their 15-year incarceration for IRA-related activity.[43] In 1985 the Irish Information Partnership published a report on

[39] eg Boyle, Hadden, and Hillyard (1980), though 'continuing complaints of excessive body searches' are mentioned at 90; Jennings (1988c); Hayes and O'Higgins (1990). There is an account of the experiences of some women prisoners in McCafferty (1981).

[40] NCCL (1986); Amnesty International (1991).

[41] Faul (1983); 'The stripping of women prisoners in Armagh gaol', *Irish News*, 22 December 1983.

[42] HC Deb, vol 72, col 142W (29 January 1985), per Nicholas Scott MP.

[43] Gillespie (1987). See too *Women in Struggle/Mna I Streachailt,* issued by Sinn Fein Women's Department.

the issue,[44] finding not only that strip-searches had failed to yield appreciable results but that they were in any event incapable of doing so:

If the purpose of the strip search is to discover material such as explosives or metal objects held externally by a prisoner and which would put in jeopardy the security of the prison, metal detectors and explosive detectors are available and could be used as a substitute to some degree. Metal detectors are, for instance, used during rub-down searches in Armagh and other prisons in Northern Ireland. By the British Government's own admission, the searches do not cover the orifices and thus forbidden material (including explosives or bullets concealed in the orifices) cannot be discovered by strip searches.

The report concluded that the real purpose of the strip search policy in Northern Ireland was 'equivocal' and that the need for it on security grounds was 'still unproven'. But in the same year a British government Minister, in response to a parliamentary question posed by the SDLP's John Hume asking for details of items found during strip-searches in each of the previous five years, said:

One of the most important aspects of any form of searching is its deterrent value. Whilst detailed records are not kept of all the items found during strip searches carried out at individual prison establishments, detonators, drugs, unauthorised cash and illicit letters have been among the items discovered.[45]

Strip-searching is not *per se* prohibited by the European Convention. Under Article 8(2) the practice is not a breach of the right to a private life if it is carried out in accordance with the law and is necessary 'in the interests of national security, public safety or the economic well-being of the country, for the prevention of disorder or crime, for the protection of health or morals, or for the protection of the rights and freedoms of others'. In *McFeeley, Nugent, Huntley and Campbell v United Kingdom*,[46] one of the complaints by the 'dirty protest' prisoners in Northern Ireland in the late 1970s related to so-called 'close body' searches, including anal inspections, which were conducted every week or so before and after the prisoners received visits and also before they were transferred to a different wing of the Maze Prison (which occurred every seven to 10 days to allow the occupied cells to be washed down). The searches took place in the presence of three prison officers and one senior officer, with no other prisoners being present. There was no physical contact with the prisoner unless he resisted. A mirror and sometimes a torch were used to examine the prisoner's rectum and a metal detector was used to check for metal objects. If the prisoner was suspected of concealing an article in his rectum he was examined by a prison doctor.

The government attempted to justify the searches on the basis that on previous occasions various prohibited objects had been discovered hidden in prisoners' rectums, including cigarette lighters, flints, razor blades, tobacco, cigarettes, cigars, cuttings, tablets, matches, chewing gum, and a metal comb.[47] In its report in the *McFeeley* case the European Commission of Human Rights found that the previous

[44] *Strip Searches at Her Majesty's Prison for Women. Armagh, Northern Ireland.*

[45] HC Deb, vol 72, col 141W (29 January 1985), per Nicholas Scott MP.

[46] (1981) 3 EHRR 161. This case is discussed in more detail at 279–81 above.

[47] ibid,176.

attempts to conceal dangerous objects made it inevitable that thorough searching had to take place in the prisons. Although an interference with the prisoners' right to respect for private life, the searches were deemed to be justifiable because they were in accordance with the law (ie the Prison Rules) and 'necessary in a democratic society for the prevention of disorder or crime':

> the Commission must have regard to the real security threat posed by such a large-scale protest campaign. The attempts to conceal dangerous objects and the previous disruptive behaviour of the prisoners... make it inevitable that close surveillance and thorough searching takes place.[48]

Some indication of the direction of travel of the European Court on the issue of strip-searching is apparent from its recent decision in *Wainwright v United Kingdom*,[49] which also illustrates the distance which law throughout the United Kingdom has still to go before it matches Strasbourg's standards. The case concerned a mother and son who had reluctantly consented to being strip-searched before visiting another member of their family in prison in Leeds. During the course of the strip-search of the son, who was 21 years old but had cerebral palsy and severe learning disabilities, a prison officer touched his penis, and a psychiatrist later reported that this had caused the son to suffer post-traumatic stress disorder. The mother, too, suffered emotional distress. They sued the Home Office for damages and won at the High Court level but lost in both the Court of Appeal[50] and House of Lords.[51] The Law Lords unanimously said that the common law did not recognize invasion of privacy as a tort. The facts of the case had occurred before the Human Rights Act 1998 came into force, but Lord Hoffmann intimated that even if the Act had been in force he would not have been inclined to find a breach of Article 8 if the invasion of privacy was merely negligent rather than intentional.[52] The mother and son then lodged an application with the European Court of Human Rights, which eventually held that, although the distress caused to the applicants was not serious enough to amount to a breach of Article 3 of the Convention, it did breach Article 8, as well as Article 13 (the right to an effective remedy for a breach of Convention rights). The search might have been for a legitimate aim (to stop drugs from being smuggled into the prison) but the manner in which it was carried out was not proportionate to that aim and so it could not be described as 'necessary in a democratic society'. Each applicant was awarded 3,000 euros as compensation. One could deduce from this decision that if strip-searching were today to be conducted in Northern Ireland's prisons in the same systemic and undignified way in which it was carried out during the 1970s and 1980s, it would clearly be a breach of Article 8, and possibly also of Article 3.

This is borne out by recent decisions of the European Court relating to other countries.[53] In *Valašinas v Lithuania*[54] the Court held that a particular body search of a male prisoner, during which he was required to strip naked in front of a female

[48] ibid, para 81.
[49] (2007) 44 EHRR 40.
[50] [2001] EWCA Civ 2081, [2002] QB 1334.
[51] [2003] UKHL 53, [2004] 2 AC 406.
[52] ibid, [51]. Lords Bingham, Hope, Hutton, and Scott did not dissent from this intimation.
[53] Reid (2008) 472.
[54] (2001) 12 BHRC 266.

officer and squat so that his anus was visible, while the male officers present, without wearing gloves, handled his sexual organs and then touched some food that had been given to the prisoner, was a breach of Article 3 of the Convention, as it amounted to degrading treatment. And in *Iwańczuk v Poland*[55] the Court found (by six to one) there had again been degrading treatment within the meaning of Article 3 when a remand prisoner was required to be strip-searched before he was allowed to exercise his right to vote. In *Frérot v France*[56] a former member of the terrorist group *Action directe* was strip-searched more frequently and in different ways at one particular prison than at others and the Court held that the arbitrariness of the searching system was degrading treatment within the terms of Article 3 (but not inhuman), and that it was therefore unnecessary to consider whether Article 8 had been breached too.[57] In two further cases brought against the Netherlands, the European Court held that the weekly strip-searching of prisoners, combined with other very strict security measures, amounted to both degrading *and* inhuman treatment, but not, on the facts, to a breach of Article 8.[58] The unqualified nature of the right conferred by Article 3 means that on occasions it can protect the right to privacy in a way that even Article 8 cannot achieve, given the limitations permitted by Article 8(2).

Transfer of prisoners

When it comes to the rights of prisoners to be imprisoned in a place which is reasonably accessible by relatives who might want to visit them, the European Convention proved of no help whatsoever during the Northern Ireland conflict. There are at least 14 examples of applications to Strasbourg on this issue which were declared inadmissible by the European Commission, all of them taken by men imprisoned in England for their activities on behalf of the IRA there. The first was *McCotter v United Kingdom*,[59] where a republican prisoner in Leicester (who was categorized as 'an exceptional risk') wanted to visit his two brothers, who were each in prison in Northern Ireland for IRA activities. He also wanted a temporary transfer to a prison in Northern Ireland so that he could receive more visits from his other relatives who lived there or in the Republic of Ireland. But the Commission declared the application manifestly ill-founded and restated its established view on the location of imprisonment:

> The Commission has also had regard to its constant case-law according to which a prisoner has no right as such under the Convention to choose the place of his confinement and that a separation of a detained person from his family and the hardship resulting from it are the inevitable consequences of detention.[60]

[55] (2004) 38 EHRR 8.

[56] App No 70204/01, decision of 12 June 2007 (available only in French).

[57] The applicant was awarded 12,000 euros as compensation.

[58] *Van der Ven v Netherlands* (2004) 28 EHRR 46 and *Lorsé v Netherlands* (2004) 37 EHRR 3. But in the latter case no breach was found in relation to the strip-searching of prisoners' relatives.

[59] App No 18632/91, decision of 9 December 1992.

[60] ibid, 'The Law', para 2, citing *KPT v UK* App No 5229/71, 42 CD 14, decision of 5 October 1972; *X v UK* App No 5712/72, 46 CD 112, decision of 18 July 1974; and App No 9054/90, 30 DR 113, decision of 8 October 1982.

The Commission added that 'only in exceptional circumstances will the detention of a prisoner a long way from his home or family infringe the requirements of Article 8', suggesting that if a prisoner from the Bahamas were imprisoned in England and there were facilities for him to be accommodated in the Bahamas where all his relatives lived then Article 8 would be breached if he was not transferred.[61] In *McCotter* the applicant was not in such an isolated position: he had seven other siblings who were able to visit him in England and he had received 49 such visits over 34 days. The case was not the strongest with which to test the willingness of European Commissioners to recognize prisoners' rights.

In a series of nine further applications, all taken by the Belfast solicitor Peter Madden and decided by the Commission on 1 September 1993, the same rather thin reasoning was employed to reject them. At times the Irish prisoners in England were joined in their applications by family relatives living in the Republic of Ireland or Northern Ireland, but the Commission constantly emphasized why the applicants were in prison in the first place, stressing the (rather fanciful) dangers involved in moving prisoners around:

> The Commission notes that the first applicant is lawfully detained for serious offences committed against the background of a terrorist campaign. The applicant is apparently detained as a Category A prisoner and any transfer would arguably be highly dangerous, increasing the risk of escape.[62]

This consideration, coupled with the blunt assertion that the prisoners were detained in 'mainland' United Kingdom because they were arrested and tried there for offences committed there,[63] was used to outweigh any arguments for allowing a transfer, including the requirement contained within the European Prison Rules (another product of the Council of Europe, adopted in 1987) that 'every effort shall be made to ensure that the regimes of the institutions are designed and managed so as . . . to ensure and strengthen those links with relatives and the outside community that will promote the best interests of prisoners and their families'.[64]

Some of the Irish prisoners in England also complained that they were being discriminated against as far as transfer was concerned because other prisoners in England were treated more favourably and the regime in England for republican prisoners was much less agreeable than that in Northern Ireland.[65] But the Commission

[61] ibid, citing *X v UK* App 5712/72, 46 CD 112, 18 July 1974 (where the applicant, a Bahamian, wanted to be transferred to the Bahamas from England but the Commission held that he should not be returned there because a special facility would have had to be built to accommodate him).

[62] *Kinsella and Mulvaney v UK* App No 19200/91, decision of 1 September 1993.

[63] See, eg, *Holmes, McGeough and Holmes v UK* App No 19786/92, decision of 1 September 1993, 'The Law', para 1.

[64] Rule 65(c). A revised version of the European Prison Rules was issued in 2006. The equivalent provision there is rule 24.4, which reads: 'The arrangements for visits shall be such as to allow prisoners to maintain and develop family relationships in as normal a manner as possible'.

[65] Irish republican prisoners in England were allegedly segregated from one another unless they happened to be in the same prison because there were no other prisons available. They were generally held in solitary confinement, in isolation, and there was supposedly a policy of regular transfer from prison to prison, resulting in their being unable to settle into familiar surroundings and suffering ill-health.

said that neither of these grievances, even if sustained by evidence, amounted to a breach of Article 14 of the Convention (the right not to be discriminated against) because 'different considerations concerning security apply to different prisoners'.[66] And the government did not fall into the trap of adopting a blanket policy against transfer, knowing that that would have been an approach of which the Commission and Court would disapprove; very occasionally, therefore, a transfer application was accepted.[67] Moreover at this time the concept of 'positive obligations' was not highly developed at Strasbourg and in some of the cases on transfer of prisoners the Commission made it clear that it thought the greater ease and convenience for prison visitors from Ireland was 'insufficient to impose what in effect would have been a positive obligation on the respondent government to effect a transfer from mainland United Kingdom to Northern Ireland'.[68] Overarching all of these reasons, however, was the broader point that the Commission recognized that a margin of appreciation rested with the UK government:

> The disposition of [Irish republican] prisoners within the prison administration system raises special and sensitive considerations, given the history of conflict in Northern Ireland in respect of which the political situation is subject to continuing and complex pressures. To the extent therefore that there has been any difference of treatment, the Commission finds that it falls within the wide margin of appreciation enjoyed by the domestic authorities.[69]

Again we see a highly deferential attitude displayed by the Strasbourg enforcement organs. The 'politics of terrorism' played a role in how those organs interpreted the concept of human rights.

In 1983 the Council of Europe adopted a Convention on the Transfer of Sentenced Prisoners, and the United Kingdom was one of the first countries to ratify it in 1985, the year it came into force. But the Convention deals with the transfer of prisoners *between* countries, not *within* the same country, and the United Kingdom is regarded as one country for this purpose, even though it comprises three distinct legal systems. Spain and France also ratified the Convention quickly, but this has done little to ease the position faced by the many Basques who are imprisoned in those countries many hundreds of miles from where their families live.[70] As in the Northern Ireland conflict, it seems that making prison visits difficult for families is part and parcel of the 'politics of terrorism' in the Basque territory and something which the European Convention on Human Rights is powerless to control.

[66] *McCombe v UK* App No 19785/92, decision of 1 September 1993, 'The Law', para 2.

[67] eg Marion and Dolours Price, and Gerry Kelly (now a Minister in the Northern Ireland Executive), imprisoned in England for planting car bombs in London in 1973, were transferred to a prison in Northern Ireland in 1975 after going on hunger strike.

[68] *Vella v UK* App No 23958/94, decision of 28 November 1994, 'The Law', para 1 (one of two decisions on this issue by the Plenary Commission—25 Commissioners—delivered on the same day: see also *McKenny v UK* App No 23956/94).

[69] *McKenny v UK* ibid, 'The Law', para 2.

[70] Idoiaga (2006) 8, who sees this fact as a major obstacle to a peace settlement in the Basque territory. See too HRW (2005) 62–4.

Other prison issues

Amongst the variety of other prison issues that have raised Convention points relevant to the conflict in Northern Ireland is that of force-feeding.[71] It seems that at no point during the hunger strikes in 1980–81 did the Northern Ireland Office seriously consider force-feeding the prisoners, doubtless because its view of the legal position at that time was that such force-feeding was neither a positive obligation nor, indeed, permissible at all unless the prisoner could be shown not to have the mental capacity to take a rational decision whether to continue with the hunger strike. In the early years of the troubles Irish republican prisoners in England who went on hunger strike *were* forcibly fed,[72] but this practice was quickly abandoned, though without explicit reference to the requirements of the European Convention.[73] The Convention was not invoked by the prisoners to stop the force-feeding or to claim that their hunger strike was caused by the State's inhuman or degrading treatment of republican prisoners.[74] It is often forgotten that two IRA prisoners died on hunger strike in England in the mid 1970s.[75] In the much more recent case of *Nevmerzhitsky v Ukraine*[76] the European Court held that the manner in which the force-feeding of a prisoner was conducted, even though prescribed by decree, could amount to torture within Article 3 of the European Convention, if there was no medical necessity for the feeding. The applicant in that case was successful in proving a lack of medical necessity and the Court therefore found a violation of Article 3. In a different context the European Court has ruled (though only by a slender majority) that using force to pump the stomach of a man who was suspected of having swallowed drugs to conceal his involvement in their trading was also a violation of Article 3.[77]

[71] For a brief discussion of this issue in relation to Art 2 of the Convention, see ch 9 above, at 226–7.

[72] For an account of what was involved see Suzanne Breen's interview with the IRA prisoner Marion Price in *The Village*, 4 December 2004: <http://irishfreedomcommittee.net/NEWS/december_2004.htm#Marian_Price_interviewDec04>, last visited 16 August 2009. See too Lanham (1974).

[73] HC Deb, vol 877, cols 451–5 (17 July 1974), per Roy Jenkins MP. Mr Jenkins said (at col 452): '[T]he future practice should, in my view, be that if a prisoner persists in refusing to accept any form of nourishment, the medical officer should first satisfy himself that the prisoner's capacity for rational judgment is unimpaired by illness, mental or physical. If the medical officer is so satisfied, he should seek confirmation of his opinion from an outside consultant. If the consultant confirms the opinion of the prison medical officer, the prisoner should be told that he will continue to receive medical supervision and advice and that food will be made available to him. He should be informed that he will be removed to the prison hospital if and when this is considered appropriate. But it should be made clear to him that there is no rule of prison practice which requires the prison medical officer to resort to artificial feeding, whether by tube or intravenously. Finally, he should be plainly and categorically warned that the consequent and inevitable deterioration in his health may be allowed to continue without medical intervention, unless he specifically requests it.'

[74] The Convention was equally irrelevant during a large-scale hunger strike by prisoners in Turkey in the 2000–2; more than 40 prisoners starved themselves to death.

[75] Michael Gaughan died in 1974 (from complications arising out of his being force-fed: Gillespie (1987) 101) and Frank Stagg died in 1976. See Zellick (1976).

[76] (2006) 43 EHRR 32. The vote on Art 3 was ten to seven. The Court voted by 12 to five that no separate issue arose under Art 8.

[77] *Jalloh v Germany* (2007) 44 EHRR 32.

Placing a prisoner in solitary confinement, even for quite long periods, and whether for reasons of discipline or security, is usually not a violation of Article 3 or of Article 8.[78] In *Re Conlon's Application*[79] a prisoner who had been confined in the Punishment and Segregation Unit of Maghaberry Prison in Northern Ireland complained that the restrictions on his association with other prisoners contravened the European Convention, but the Court of Appeal, relying on two previous decisions of the European Commission on Human Rights,[80] rejected the claim. In such situations there is not even a breach of Article 11 (the right to freedom of assembly and association) because Article 11(2) specifically permits restrictions on that right in the interests of, amongst other things, national security, public safety, or the prevention of disorder or crime.

A ban on wearing what are deemed to be sectarian symbols associated with paramilitary groupings, such as Orange lilies or Easter lilies, has been held not to be a breach of the Convention, although in these cases the applicants have tended to rely much more on Article 10 of the Convention than on Article 8.[81] In *Re McCrory's Application*[82] Kerr J, as he then was, held that new identification procedures put in place at Magilligan Prison (requiring all visitors, including solicitors, to be photographed and finger scanned) did not violate Article 8 because they were 'necessary in a democratic society' within the terms of Article 8(2). We saw in the previous chapter that an applicant who wanted to be transferred to the separate accommodation made available for loyalist prisoners in Maghaberry Prison failed in his request: the court had little difficulty in rejecting his arguments based on Article 2 of the Convention, and he does not seem to have relied on Article 8 (or on Article 11—the right to freedom of association).[83]

Throughout the conflict in Northern Ireland no prisoner, or sexual partner of a prisoner, petitioned a court to claim the right to a conjugal visit in the prison. This was either not deemed to be an important issue for the prisoners or they were advised that the current state of European Convention law would not support any such claim. In fact the right of prisoners and their partners to have their family life protected in this context was not fully examined by the European Court until the Grand Chamber decided the English case of *Dickson v United Kingdom* in 2007, where the applicant prisoner complained about the refusal of access to artificial insemination facilities. A Chamber of the Court had held by four votes to three that neither Article 8 nor Article 12 (which protects the right to marry) had been breached,[84] but the

[78] *Ramirez Sanchez v France*, decision of 4 July 2006, where the European Court held that France had not violated Art 3 by holding the terrorist better known as Carlos the Jackal in solitary confinement from the moment he was first taken into custody in 1994 until 2002, and again from March 2004 to January 2006.

[79] [2002] NIJB 35.

[80] *Dhoest v Belgium* App No 10448/83, decision of 14 May 1987, and *Kröcher and Möller v Switzerland* (1983) 34 DR 24.

[81] *Re Byer's Application* [2004] NIQB 23; *Re McCafferty's Application* (9 February 2007; unreported); *Re Donaldson's Application* [2009] NICA 25 (all cases on Easter lilies, and all decided with reference to Art 10 of the Convention, not Art 8).

[82] June 2001, unreported.

[83] *Re Anderson's Application* [2005] NIQB 61 (Weatherup J).

[84] (2007) 44 EHRR 21.

Grand Chamber held by 12 votes to five[85] that there had in fact been a violation of Article 8 and unanimously that it was not then necessary to consider the position under Article 12.[86]

Interference with prisoners' correspondence in Northern Ireland was raised by the applicants in an early case, *X and Y v UK*,[87] where a man who had previously lodged a complaint about his internment in Long Kesh, complained, together with his legal representative (James Heaney, from the USA), that correspondence between them had been opened and censored by UK authorities, in violation of Articles 5, 6, 8, and 11. The Commission, however, declared the application inadmissible for the simple reason that no actual evidence of censoring had been adduced by the applicants. Even if it had been, said the Commission, such interference with mail was allowed under Article 8(2) because in Northern Ireland it was 'prescribed by law'[88] and had taken place 'in the interests of national security' or 'for the prevention of disorder or crime'. In *McFeeley, Nugent, Huntley and Campbell v United Kingdom*, discussed above, a complaint was again raised about interference with correspondence, but despite indications that the Commission was more interested in this than in any of the other complaints in that case the applicants chose not to pursue the matter and the complaint was struck off the list.[89] Cases taken by prisoners in England established that the right to correspond is considered to be quite fundamental in Strasbourg. Consequently, the European Court found a violation of Article 8 in *Faulkner v United Kingdom*,[90] when a letter written by a prisoner in Northern Ireland to an address in Scotland was returned to him undelivered.

The rights of unconvicted prisoners to have their private lives protected came up for consideration in the leading case on port powers discussed in Chapter 4, *McVeigh, O'Neill and Evans v United Kingdom*.[91] The Commission held there that searching and fingerprinting the detainees did not breach their Article 8 rights, and that retaining these records could be justified under Article 8(2) on the basis that it was in the interests of public safety and the prevention of crime. The Commission saw the interferences with privacy as 'relatively slight' when weighed against 'the pressing necessity to combat terrorist activity'.[92] One commentator suggests that this means that a State might never have to rely on a derogation notice under Article 15 when interfering with rights protected by Articles 8 to 11 of the Convention for the purposes of combating terrorism.[93]

[85] Sir Nicolas Bratza, the UK judge, changed his mind between the Chamber and the Grand Chamber hearing, for reasons he explained in a note to his separate concurring opinion in the Grand Chamber decision.

[86] (2008) 46 EHRR 41.

[87] 40 CD 7, decision of 23 March 1972.

[88] reg 13(2) of the Special Powers Act Regulations provided that no communications may be sent or received by a person interned under the regulations except such as have been examined and passed by the competent officer.

[89] Report of the Commission, adopted 2 October 1984. See 279–80 above.

[90] App No 37471/97, decision of 4 June 2002.

[91] (1983) 5 EHRR 71.

[92] ibid, para 231.

[93] Warbrick (1983a) 763.

Searches of property

During times of insurgency the State's security forces need to be able to conduct searches. These may be searches for the insurgents themselves, for people who may be aiding them, or for the things used by the insurgents such as guns, ammunition, explosives, maps, clothing, etc. To allow such searches to be conducted lawfully the State's ordinary law usually needs to be amended, because that law will probably permit searches only where reasonable suspicion exists that (for example) stolen property or other prohibited goods are in a certain location. And under long-established common law principles searches of private property can be conducted only if the police first obtain a warrant, signed by a magistrate, to do so. The old phrase, 'an Englishman's home is his castle', sums up the legal position that was established after a series of cases decided by the English courts in the eighteenth century, the most famous being *Entick v Carrington*,[94] where the house of John Entick, who was suspected of writing seditious pamphlets, was searched on the basis of a warrant issued by the Secretary of State, Lord Halifax. In the Court of Common Pleas Lord Camden ruled that the search had been unlawful because it was not expressly permitted by statute or precedent:

> By the laws of England, every invasion of private property, be it ever so minute, is a trespass. No man can set his foot upon my ground without my license, but he is liable to an action, though the damage be nothing; which is proved by every declaration in trespass, where the defendant is called upon to answer for bruising the grass and even treading upon the soil. If he admits the fact, he is bound to show by way of justification, that some positive law has empowered or excused him.[95]

Just 25 years later the principle established in *Entick v Carrington* was deemed important enough to find its way into the US Bill of Rights, the first 10 amendments to the US Constitution. The Fourth Amendment reads as follows:

> The right of the people to be secure in their persons, houses, papers, and effects, against unreasonable searches and seizures, shall not be violated, and no Warrants shall issue, but upon probable cause, supported by Oath or affirmation, and particularly describing the place to be searched, and the persons or things to be seized.

Regulations made under the Civil Authorities (Special Powers) Acts (NI) 1922–43 authorized the Royal Ulster Constabulary to conduct searches, and the Northern Ireland (Emergency Provisions) Act 1973, which replaced those Acts, did likewise.[96]

[94] (1765) 95 Eng Rep 807. See too the case won by the radical MP John Wilkes: *Wilkes v Wood* (1763) 98 Eng Rep 489.

[95] Writing in 1980 Raymond Wacks noted that there were 'at least 188 statutory provisions severely restricting this supposedly sacred right': Wacks (1980) 49.

[96] EPA 1973, s 10(2) (searches of places by the police for suspected terrorists); s 11(2) (searches of places by the police for other suspected offenders); s 12(3) (searches of places by the army for suspected offenders); s 13 (searches of places by the police or army for munitions); s 14 (searches of persons by 'explosive inspectors'); s 15 (searches by the police or army for persons unlawfully detained). These powers were mirrored in the EPA 1978, ss 11 and 13–17 (later amended by the EPA 1987); EPA 1991, ss 16–21; EPA 1996, ss 17–23; Terrorism Act 2000, 81–6.

The job of searching is difficult, because searches are by definition invasive, and in the course of the search a lot of people will be inconvenienced, or possessions disturbed, even though they have nothing at all to do with the insurgency. The 'strike rate' may be very low, with perhaps hundreds of searches having to be conducted before one proves productive. Naturally this can build up resentment on the part of those entirely innocent people whose private property is examined; if this happens more than once the resentment will be multiplied.

One of the provisions in the 1973 Act[97] allowed a member of Her Majesty's forces on duty to arrest without warrant, and detain for not more than four hours, any person whom he or she suspected of committing, having committed or being about to commit any offence. For the purpose of arresting a person under this provision a member of Her Majesty's forces was authorized to enter and search any premises or other place (a) where that person was, or (b) if that person was suspected of being a terrorist or of having committed an offence involving the use or possession of an explosive, explosive substance or firearm, where that person was suspected of being. The 1973 provision was reviewed by both the Gardiner Committee in 1975 and Sir George Baker in 1984. Neither suggested that the search power needed to be reformed, except that Baker proposed making the power dependent upon there being 'reasonable' suspicion (without referring directly to the Convention).[98]

The European Convention, unlike the US Bill of Rights, does not make specific provision for searches. Instead it subsumes the topic within the broader right of respect for a private and family life, protected by Article 8, and in Article 1 of Protocol 1 it protects the right to peaceful enjoyment of one's possessions. At times the latter can provide greater protection to the victim of a search (especially if it relates to business rather than residential premises), but at other times the converse can be the case (especially if what is affected is not property but personal privacy).[99] Amazingly, the first application to be lodged in Strasbourg concerning security force searches in Northern Ireland does not have seemed to have arrived until 1988, when Mrs Margaret Murray, together with her husband and four children, complained about a search of their home in Belfast (and about Mrs Murray's arrest). All six applicants argued that the entry into, and search of, their home by the British Army, including the 'confinement' of five of the applicants for a short while in one room, violated Article 8. The British government's lawyers[100] argued that the actions taken were justified under Article 8(2) as being lawful measures necessary in a democratic society for the prevention of crime in the context of the fight against terrorism in Northern Ireland. Sir George Baker had noted in his 1984 report that he knew of one civil action in which damages had been awarded when the army kept all the occupants of a house in one room while the rest of the house was searched and he recommended

[97] EPA 1973, s 12(3), later EPA 1978, s 14(3) (later amended by the EPA 1987); EPA 1991, s 18(3); EPA 1996, s 19(3); Terrorism Act 2000, s 83(3) and (4).

[98] Baker (1984).

[99] For more on this distinction and overlap see Stone (2008) ch 5, and Stone (2005) chs 6 to 9.

[100] One of whom was Ronald Weatherup QC, later a High Court judge in Northern Ireland. The two barristers for the applicants were Reg Weir QC and Seamus Treacy, both of whom were also later appointed as High Court judges in Northern Ireland.

that the legislation be amended to make it clear that such a power existed.[101] But the government had not implemented this recommendation.

In the Court of Appeal of Northern Ireland the search of the Murrays' house was held to be lawful, as there was a sufficient basis for it in the Northern Ireland (Emergency Provisions) Act (EPA) 1978.[102] The taking of Mrs Murray's photograph was also deemed lawful, because under the general common law of Northern Ireland, as in England and Wales, it is lawful to take a photograph of someone without their consent. Section 11(4) of the 1978 Act, for the avoidance of doubt, expressly conferred on the *police* a power to photograph an arrested person, and went on to confer a power to take an arrested person's finger and palm prints; it expressly added that a police officer could use such reasonable force as may be necessary for these purposes. The Court of Appeal also held that, as a practical necessity, the authority granted to the army under section 14 included a power to record personal particulars and details concerning a person's arrest and detention. The standard record form used—the 'screening proforma'—was found to contain no information which might have been irrelevant to determining whether the suspicion relating to the person arrested was justified. The power of search was used only to facilitate the arrest and to obtain incriminating evidence. The House of Lords confirmed the Court of Appeal's views, holding in particular that the short period of restraint endured by Mrs Murray's husband and children when they were asked to assemble in one room was a necessary and proper part of the procedure of arrest of Mrs Murray.[103]

On 17 February 1993 the European Commission found by 13 votes to one that there had been no violation of Article 8, unanimously that there had been no violation of Article 13 in relation to the entry and search of Mrs Murray's home, and by 10 votes to four that there had been no violation of Article 13 in relation to the taking and keeping of a photograph and personal details of Mrs Murray.[104] When the case reached the European Court it was considered important enough to be referred 'forthwith' to the Grand Chamber, comprising (at that time) 18 judges. On 28 October 1994 the European Court endorsed the Commission's decision, holding by 15 votes to three that there had been no breach of Article 8 in respect of any of the applicants.[105] Everything turned, thought the Court, on whether the measures taken were necessary in a democratic society and whether the means employed were proportionate to the legitimate aim pursued. As so often before, the Court noted that it was not for it to substitute its own assessment for that of the national authorities as to what might be the best policy in the field of investigating terrorist crime: 'A certain margin of appreciation in deciding what measures to take both in general and in particular cases should be left to the national authorities'.[106] It mentioned again the

[101] Baker (1984) para 367.

[102] s 14(3).

[103] [1988] 2 All ER 521.

[104] Art 13, of course, protects the right to an effective remedy for a breach of a Convention right. The main parts of the Commission's opinion (including the three partly dissenting opinions) are extracted within the Court's judgment at (1995) 19 EHRR 193, 209–22.

[105] (1995) 19 EHRR 193.

[106] ibid, para 90.

responsibility of an elected government in a democratic society to protect its citizens and its institutions against the threats posed by organized terrorism and the special problems involved in the arrest and detention of persons suspected of terrorist-linked offences. In view of these points, the Court accepted that 'there was in principle a need both for powers of the kind granted by section 14 of the 1978 Act and, in the particular case, to enter and search the home of the Murray family in order to arrest Mrs Murray'.[107] The Court also recognized as legitimate the dangerous environment in which, as Lord Griffiths had pointed out in the House of Lords, arrests of suspected IRA members had to be carried out in Northern Ireland.[108] Moreover:

> Neither can it be regarded as falling outside the legitimate bounds of the process of investigation of terrorist crime for the competent authorities to record and retain basic personal details concerning the arrested person or even other persons present at the time and place of arrest. None of the personal details taken during the search of the family home or during Mrs Murray's stay at the Army centre would appear to have been irrelevant to the procedures of arrest and interrogation... Similar conclusions apply to the taking and retention of a photograph of Mrs Murray at the Army centre.[109]

The three dissenting judges[110] did not think there was sufficient suspicion to justify Mrs Murray's arrest in the first place, and therefore held that the measures taken by the Army which interfered with Mrs Murray's private life could not be regarded as necessary in a democratic society for the prevention of crime in accordance with Article 8(2).

The *Margaret Murray* case encapsulates the dilemma facing governments and law enforcement bodies when they are trying to deal with organized crime and terrorism: what lengths can they go to when searching for evidence of involvement in such activities without at the same time violating human rights and, in particular, to what extent can those authorities rely upon public expectations as to what is reasonable and proportionate in this context being altered by the fact that society at large has a huge interest in detecting and punishing those involved in such activities? For innocent people whose lives are seriously (though temporarily) disrupted by searches which in the end prove groundless, the public interest may not seem that important. But for the vast majority of other people in society the 'sacrifice' made by those innocent people may seem a small price to pay for the sake of society's greater reassurance that steps are being taken to put an end to nefarious actions.

In the years following this judgment the annual reviewers of the emergency laws in Northern Ireland commented on the way in which the search powers were exercised, but the conclusions they drew were inevitably based more on impressions than on hard facts.[111] No further adjustments were made to the legislation prior to its demise

[107] ibid, para 92.

[108] ibid, Lord Griffiths had said: 'It is in everyone's best interest that the arrest is peaceably effected and I am satisfied that the procedures adopted by the Army are sensible, reasonable and designed to bring about the arrest with the minimum of danger and distress to all concerned.' [1988] 2 All ER 521, 527j.

[109] (1995) 19 EHRR 193, para 93.

[110] Judges Loizou (Cyprus), Morenilla (Spain), and Makarczyk (Poland).

[111] See, eg, the rather exiguous remarks by John Rowe in his report on the operation of the EPA 1996 during 1998, paras 65–71.

in 2007. The European Court never again had to consider in detail the legality of searches in Northern Ireland. The Court has taken pre-arrest searches sufficiently seriously, however, to rule that the search of a person's home (or the seizure of certain of his or her goods) may trigger the start of a 'trial' period, during which the requirements of fairness stipulated in Article 6 of the European Convention must be complied with.[112] In future cases this may be an argument that applicants can develop if they feel that their private life has been interfered with by searches but who are advised that Article 8 is not a sufficient protection for them.

Sexual issues

While nearly all of the cases taken from Northern Ireland to Strasbourg in the 1970s and 1980s had some fairly obvious connection with the conflict, there was at least one outstanding exception—*Dudgeon v United Kingdom*.[113] This was an application taken by a gay man who argued that the criminalization of homosexual conduct between consenting male adults was a breach of his right to a private life. The Unionist government of Northern Ireland had refused to decriminalize homosexuality at the time when this occurred in England and Wales in 1967,[114] in the wake of the Wolfenden Report 10 years earlier.[115] The European Court held in Jeff Dudgeon's favour, by 15 votes to four, and within a year the Homosexuality (NI) Order 1982 had been passed to bring Northern Ireland's law into line with the Convention. Some would try to argue that the oppression of homosexuals in Northern Ireland in the 1960s and 1970s was indeed an aspect of the troubles, but that is far-fetched. Members of society such as gay and lesbian people were undoubtedly marginalized, as they had been in England and Wales, but the antipathy to homosexual practices was strong in both the Protestant and the Catholic communities—it was not a sectarian repression. It is worth recalling that male homosexuality in the Republic of Ireland was not decriminalized until 1993,[116] again following a decision of the European Court of Human Rights, in *Norris v Ireland*.[117]

In an interesting case that recently went from Northern Ireland to the House of Lords it was decided that unmarried couples, including partners of the same sex,

[112] *Eckle v Germany* (1983) 5 EHRR 1, paras 12 and 74; *Diamantides v Greece* App No 60821/00, decision of 23 October 2003, para 21 (in French only); *Lopez Sole y Martin de Vargas v Spain* App No 61133/00, decision of 28 October 2003, para 26 (in French only).

[113] (1981) 4 EHRR 149. For a personalized account of this important decision, and its progeny, see Goldhaber (2007) 33–47.

[114] By the Sexual Offences Act 1967, s 1. This applied only to men aged 21 or over. The age of consent for homosexuality was reduced to 18 throughout the UK by the Criminal Justice and Public Order Act 1994, s 145; it was further reduced to 16 for England, Wales and Scotland and to 17 in Northern Ireland by the Sexual Offences (Amendment) Act 2000, s 1(2)–(4); it was not reduced to 16 in Northern Ireland until the Sexual Offences (NI) Order 2008, art 16, decriminalized most consensual sexual activity between persons of that age or over. In the Republic of Ireland the age of consent for homosexual and heterosexual sex remains at 17.

[115] Wolfenden (1957). Mr Justice Diplock, as he then was, was a member of this committee.

[116] Criminal Law (Sexual Offences) Act 1993, s 2.

[117] (1988) 13 EHRR 186.

should be allowed to apply to adopt children. A legislative prohibition on such applications was declared by their Lordships—reversing the judges in Northern Ireland—to be a violation of Article 8 of the Convention, even though the European Court itself has not yet decided that the right to adopt is a right recognized by the Convention.[118] This is a rare example of British judges being a step ahead of their Strasbourg counterparts.

Conclusion

Article 8 has not been of great significance to people who have claimed to be the victims of human rights abuses in Northern Ireland during the years of conflict there. It rarely assisted prisoners to get a more humane regime in their prison, but by and large it did protect their right to correspond with persons in the outside world. It did not greatly protect people whose home, car, or other property was regularly searched, sometimes very intensely and repeatedly, nor did it help them when they claimed the right not to have information collected and stored relating to their identity, movements and proclivities. The one aspect of private life which *was* effectively protected was homosexuality.

In 1999 it came to light that for a number of years prominent organizations that were campaigning for better protection of human rights in Northern Ireland were themselves the object of covert surveillance by the intelligence services in England. Liberty (formerly the National Council for Civil Liberties, the London-based organization which decades earlier had issued a damning report on the Special Powers Act in Northern Ireland),[119] British Irish Rights Watch (also London-based), and the Irish Council for Civil Liberties (Dublin-based) all complained that telephone calls, faxes, and emails passing between them between 1990 and 1997 had been intercepted by a listening station in Cheshire. A complaint was first lodged with the Interception of Communications Tribunal, which investigated the matter but declared that it was satisfied there had been no contravention of the Interception of Communications Act 1985. The Tribunal would not reveal whether any interceptions had in fact taken place. Further complaints were then lodged with the police, who eventually replied to say that their inquiries had not revealed any offence under the 1985 Act. Yet another complaint was then considered by the newly established Investigatory Powers Tribunal, which concluded that the complainants were not entitled to know more details about why and how the interceptions were conducted: they were carried out 'in accordance with law', which was precise enough as far as the Tribunal was concerned.

It was this point which was then taken by the three organizations to the European Court of Human Rights. They argued that it would not compromise national security if the government were to describe the arrangements in place for filtering and disseminating intercepted material, and they pointed out that such information had

[118] *In re G (Adoption: Unmarried Couple)* [2008] UKHL 38, [2008] 3 WLR 76. See Kavanagh (2009).
[119] NCCL (1936).

already been published by other countries, such as the United States of America, Australia, and Germany. The European Court agreed that the UK government had interfered with the applicants' Article 8 rights in a way that was not 'in accordance with law' because at the relevant time that law did not indicate with sufficient clarity 'the scope or manner of exercise of the very wide discretion conferred on the State to intercept and examine external communications'.[120] More specifically, the law did not set out 'in a form accessible to the public any indication of the procedure to be followed for selecting for examination, sharing, storing and destroying intercepted material'.[121] This decision was a notable victory for the campaigning organizations, and it will have to lead to a change in UK procedures in this context, but of course it was a somewhat hollow victory because the organizations are still in the dark as to which of their communications were in fact intercepted, including perhaps legally privileged or otherwise confidential material. That the British government feels it necessary to intercept communications between civil liberties organizations in these islands on the ground that national security may be at stake is surely a very sad reflection of its general attitude, and that of its intelligence services, towards human rights work in this country. Article 8 has ridden to the rescue, but rather belatedly and only to a partial extent.

[120] *Liberty and others v UK* (2009) 48 EHRR 1, para 69.
[121] ibid.

11

Freedom of Expression, Belief, and Assembly

The law relating to the freedoms protected by Articles 9 to 11 of the European Convention—freedom of speech, belief, assembly, and association—has in Northern Ireland always been similar to that applying in England and Wales. During the years of conflict it has been a key element in a number of important controversies. This chapter looks in turn at broadcasting bans, freedom of expression during electoral and parliamentary processes, freedom of belief claims such as those put forward by people seeking to join the police, and the freedom to march, together with a miscellany of other relatively minor issues. Until 2000, of course, the European Convention was not part of the domestic law of any part of the United Kingdom (nor of Ireland until 2004), so persons or organizations with grievances about their right to freedom of speech, belief, and assembly had to take their complaints to Strasbourg if they wanted Convention standards to be directly applied. This happened rarely, and when it did, applicants tended to discover that this was yet another field in which the enforcement organs of the Convention system were quite content to confer a wide margin of appreciation on States.

Bans on broadcasting and reporting

Undoubtedly the most notorious infringement of free speech in Northern Ireland during the conflict was the so-called broadcasting ban. This was imposed on 19 October 1988, in the wake of some particularly horrific IRA atrocities, which also gave rise to changes to the law on the right to silence,[1] and it remained in force until lifted by Prime Minister John Major a few days after the announcement of the IRA ceasefire on 31 August 1994.[2] Technically the ban was imposed through instructions issued by the then Home Secretary, Douglas Hurd, to the BBC and the Independent Broadcasting Association, in exercise of a power conferred on him by, respectively,

[1] See ch 8 above, at 199. Mrs Thatcher referred at the time to the need to deprive terrorists and their supporters of the 'oxygen of publicity'. She has since written that the broadcasting ban was effective: '[The broadcasting ban] immediately provoked cries of censorship: but I have no doubt that not only was it justified but that it has worked, and there is reason to believe that the terrorists think so too.' See Thatcher (1993) 412.

[2] The best account of how the ban worked in practice (and of related incidents of censorship) is that by Moloney (1991). More generally on the dilemmas facing journalists who report on terrorists, see Clutterbuck (1983) chs 9–13.

the BBC's Licence[3] and the Broadcasting Act 1981.[4] The instruction stated that the two organizations should:

> refrain at all times from sending any broadcast matter which consists of or includes any words spoken, whether in the course of an interview or discussion or otherwise, by a person who appears or is heard on the programme in which the matter is broadcast (a) where the person speaking the words represents or purports to represent an organisation specified below, or (b) the words support or solicit or invite support for such an organisation.

The instruction then listed a variety of specified organizations. Some of these, including the Irish Republican Army, the Irish National Liberation Army, the Ulster Volunteer Force, the Ulster Freedom Fighters, and the Red Hand Commandos, were already proscribed. Three others were not—Sinn Féin, Republican Sinn Féin and the Ulster Defence Association (this last was eventually proscribed only in 1992). The ban was debated and approved in the House of Commons on 2 November 1988;[5] the House of Lords also debated and 'took note' of the ban on 8 December 1988.[6]

It quickly became clear that the ban was slightly farcical, partly because it was not draconian enough. In an explanatory letter dated 24 October 1988, the Home Office itself indicated that the ban did not mean that pictures could not be shown of a person speaking while someone else voiced his or her words. Actors then began to perfect the accents and vocal mannerisms of individual representatives, the result being that many casual viewers tended to pay *more* regard to what was being said than would otherwise have been the case, and the interviewees often came across as more articulate than if they had been shown speaking their own words. In this respect the ban in Northern Ireland was not as far-reaching as that in the Republic of Ireland. The ban there, issued under the Broadcasting Authority Act 1960,[7] had been in place since 1971. It applied even during election periods, contained no so-called 'ventriloquism clause', and had been strengthened by the then Minister for Posts and Telegraphs, Conor Cruise O'Brien, in 1976 so that it could allow the banning of any matter if the minister was of the opinion that broadcasting it 'would be likely to promote, or incite to, crime or would tend to undermine the authority of the State'.[8]

The operation of the 1988 ban in the United Kingdom was challenged before the domestic courts, as far as the House of Lords, but unsuccessfully. The House decided that under the common law the Home Secretary had not acted 'unreasonably'.[9] Livingstone saw this decision as further evidence of 'a lack of judicial willingness to engage with the human rights issues which the situation in Northern Ireland poses'.[10]

[3] Cl 13(4). The then version of the licence dated from 2 April 1981. All television broadcasters, except the BBC, now operate under licences granted under the Communications Act 2003 by the Office of Communications (Ofcom). The BBC operates under a Royal Charter and its regulation is therefore extra-statutory.

[4] s 29(3).

[5] By 243 votes to 179. See HC Deb, vol 139, cols 1073–155.

[6] See HL Deb, vol 502, cols 676–719.

[7] s 31.

[8] s 31(1) of the 1960 Act as substituted by the Broadcasting Authority (Amendment) Act 1976, s 16.

[9] *R v Secretary of State for the Home Department, ex p Brind* [1991] 1 AC 696.

[10] Livingstone (1994) 348–9 (speaking principally of the judges in the House of Lords).

The television producer who failed in the Lords, together with five other broadcast journalists (including the renowned John Pilger) lodged an application in Strasbourg in March 1991, but just a month later the European Commission ruled that a challenge to the more extensive broadcasting ban operating in the Republic of Ireland was inadmissible.[11] The key issue for the Commission had been whether the Irish government's interference with the right to freedom of expression was 'necessary in a democratic society'.[12] It noted that the European Court had consistently held that State parties to the Convention have a certain margin of appreciation in assessing whether a pressing social need exists. It was therefore not the Commission's task:

> to determine whether other measures would have been more appropriate for achieving the intended purpose... nor to assess the expediency and efficacy of the measures taken by the Minister. In view of the Government's margin of appreciation, the Commission's sole task is to examine whether the reasons underlying the Section 31 Order are relevant and sufficient under Article 10(2)... i.e. whether the Minister had convincing reasons for assuming the existence of a pressing social need for imposing the impugned restrictions on the applicants.[13]

The Commission then determined, in terms indicating a realistic appreciation of the difficulties facing democracies in these situations, that a pressing social need did indeed exist:

> ... the defeat of terrorism is a public interest of the first importance in a democratic society. In a situation where politically motivated violence poses a constant threat to the lives and security of the population and where the advocates of this violence seek access to the mass media for publicity purposes, it is particularly difficult to strike a fair balance between the requirements of protecting freedom of information and the imperatives of protecting the State and the public against armed conspiracies seeking to overthrow the democratic order which guarantees this freedom and other human rights.[14]

The applicants in the *Brind* case must have realized as soon as they read the decision in the *Purcell* case that their own chances of persuading the Commission to find a violation of the Convention in the UK's broadcasting ban were slim indeed. And this proved to be the case, even though it took the Commission until May 1994 to express its views.[15] It again noted that the struggle against terrorism was a very important area of domestic policy, citing what the European Court had said in this regard in two other cases from Northern Ireland.[16] As in *Purcell*, the Commission indicated

[11] *Purcell v Ireland* (1991) 70 DR 262, (1991) 12 HRLJ 254. One of the counsel for the applicants was Kevin Boyle. For an account by the principal applicant of how the ban operated in the Republic see Purcell (1991). The Irish Supreme Court had already held that the ban did not breach the Irish Constitution: see *The State (Lynch) v Cooney* [1982] IR 337, reversing O'Hanlon J in the High Court (whose judgment is to be found at [1982] IR 343). The case was brought by a member of Sinn Féin who had been denied the right to make an election broadcast; he was represented by Sean McBride SC and Patrick MacEntee SC.

[12] Art 10(2) of the Convention.

[13] *Purcell v Ireland* (1991) 70 DR 262, 278; (1991) 12 HRLJ 254, 260.

[14] ibid. The Commission also declared the complaints under Arts 13 and 14, and Art 3 of Prot 1, to be manifestly ill-founded.

[15] *Brind and McLaughlin v UK* (1994) 77-A DR 42.

[16] *Brogan v UK* (1989) 11 EHRR 117 and *Brannigan and McBride v UK* (1994) 17 EHRR 539. The Commission also rejected the complaint under Art 13 as manifestly ill-founded.

that the restrictions imposed on the journalists, while inconvenient, were not that far-reaching.

Human rights activists tended to be disappointed at the outcome of the *Purcell* and *Brind* cases, but in doing so they may have been underestimating the impact of broadcasts with supporters of violence. Today, though, the law on freedom of speech in the United Kingdom has veered towards disapproving the kind of restrictions contained in the earlier bans. A provision in the Human Rights Act 1998,[17] specifically inserted in the original draft Bill as a result of special pleading by newspaper editors,[18] now requires courts to:

> ... have particular regard to the importance of the Convention right to freedom of expression and, where the proceedings relate to material which the respondent claims, or which appears to the court, to be journalistic, ... to (a) the extent to which (i) the material has, or is about to, become available to the public; or (ii) it is, or would be, in the public interest for the material to be published; (b) any relevant privacy code.[19]

Strictly speaking this provision applies only when a court is considering whether to grant any relief (such as an injunction) which might affect the exercise of the Convention right to freedom of expression,[20] but the spirit of the section is likely to influence the exercise of a court's discretion in other situations where the right to freedom of expression is at issue.[21] In the recent decision of the House of Lords in *Cream Holdings Ltd v Banerjee*,[22] where both at first instance and in the Court of Appeal a company succeeded in obtaining an interlocutory injunction against the Liverpool Echo, restraining it from publishing any further confidential information passed to it by a recently dismissed employee of the company, the House held that, when deciding *not* to grant such interlocutory relief:

> There can be no single, rigid standard governing all applications ... Rather ... the court is not to make an interim restraint order unless satisfied the applicant's prospects of success at the trial are sufficiently favourable to justify an order being made in the particular circumstances of the case. As to what degree of likelihood makes the prospects of success 'sufficiently favourable', the general approach should be that courts will be exceedingly slow to make interim

[17] s 12.

[18] 'The concern was that, applying the conventional *American Cyanamid* approach [*American Cyanamid Co v Ethicon Ltd* [1975] AC 396], orders imposing prior restraint on newspapers might readily be granted by the courts to preserve the status quo until trial whenever applicants claimed that a threatened publication would infringe their rights under Article 8. Section 12(3) was enacted to allay these fears. Its principal purpose was to buttress the protection afforded to freedom of speech at the interlocutory stage. It sought to do so by setting a higher threshold for the grant of interlocutory injunctions against the media than the *American Cyanamid* guideline of a "serious question to be tried" or a "real prospect" of success at the trial.' *Cream Holdings Ltd v Banerjee* [2004] UKHL 44, [2005] 1 AC 253 at [15] (per Lord Nicholls).

[19] s 12(4).

[20] s 12(1).

[21] See the comments by the then Home Secretary, Jack Straw: 'We have taken the opportunity to enhance press freedom in a wider way than would arise simply from the incorporation of the Convention into our domestic law.' HC Deb, vol 315, col 535 (2 July 1998).

[22] [2004] UKHL 44, [2005] 1 AC 253.

restraint orders where the applicant has not satisfied the court he will probably ('more likely than not') succeed at the trial.[23]

The House allowed the newspaper's appeal, on the basis that the lower courts had failed to note that the principal happenings which the Echo wished to publish were matters clearly of serious public interest. In this context one should also be mindful of the role of the internet, which was not a factor in the 1980s: courts may be particularly reluctant to ban broadcasts or press articles when they realize that people may in any event be easily able to access the material through their personal computers.[24]

A further legal development which may make it easier to challenge any repeat of a broadcasting ban is the readiness of the courts to examine the proportionality of a measure. In *Brind*[25] the House of Lords rejected the applicability of such a test within the context of an application for judicial review, but in cases involving human rights the House has since moved away from that position[26] and UK courts are now perfectly willing to consider whether, to use a colloquial phrase, a sledgehammer has been used to crack a nut. Gagging the media is today regarded by the law as a ploy that needs to be reserved for really extreme situations, such as when national security or public safety are genuinely at stake. One can imagine the government successfully imposing a ban on the publication of details of ongoing covert anti-terrorist surveillance, but not, say, on reports of press conferences organized by persons claiming to know the latest thinking of the UDA or the Real IRA.

One can also imagine bans being upheld in situations where there are countervailing rights to consider, such as those which are protected by Article 8 of the European Convention.[27] In at least three cases the English High Court has already issued purportedly worldwide bans prohibiting the broadcasting (or reporting) of information relating to the identity or whereabouts of particular criminals. These were the cases of Mary Bell (convicted of murdering two young boys in 1968),[28] Robert Thompson and Jon Venables (convicted of murdering two-year-old Jamie Bulger in 1993),[29] and Maxine Carr (convicted of conspiring to pervert the course of justice during the inquiry into the murders of 10-year-old Jessica Chapman and Holly Wells in 2002).[30] In the last case internet service providers were also banned from soliciting information about Carr. We have already noted in an earlier chapter that a judge in Northern Ireland issued a comprehensive injunction banning the publication of the whereabouts of an

[23] ibid, [22] (per Lord Nicholls).

[24] The saga in the 1980s over Peter Wright's book *Spycatcher* shows that publishing material outside the UK can render ineffective any injunction issued domestically. See *Observer and Guardian v UK* (1991) 14 EHRR 153.

[25] [1991] 1 AC 696.

[26] *R v Secretary of State for the Home Department, ex p Daly* [2001] 2 AC 532; Lester, Pannick and Herberg (2009) para 3.10; Gearty (2004) 99–107.

[27] Art 8 protects everyone's right to respect for his or her private and family life, home and correspondence.

[28] *Re X (A Minor) (Wardship Proceedings: Injunction)* [1984] 1 WLR 1422.

[29] *Venables v News Group Newspapers; Thompson v News Group Newspapers* [2001] 2 WLR 1038.

[30] A temporary injunction was issued in May 2004 and was made permanent by Eady J on 24 February 2004: *Daily Telegraph* (25 February 2005; Joshua Rozenberg). See also Sereny (1999) and (on the Jamie Bulger case) Lee (2003).

alleged IRA informer.[31] In another Northern Ireland case, not connected to the conflict, the Court of Appeal found no difficulty in continuing a court order banning the reporting of a case, at least until an appeal had been heard in the case.[32] Most recently, however, in *In re S (A Child)*[33] the House of Lords has held that newspapers should not be prevented from referring to the family name of a woman awaiting trial for the murder of one of her children simply because this could lead to another of her children being identified. Lord Steyn referred with approval to four propositions which he said could be deduced from the previous examination of the interplay between Articles 8 and 10 by the House of Lords in *Campbell v MGN Ltd*:[34]

> First, neither article has as such precedence over the other. Secondly, where the values under the two articles are in conflict, an intense focus on the comparative importance of the specific rights being claimed in the individual case is necessary. Thirdly, the justifications for interfering with or restricting each right must be taken into account. Finally, the proportionality test must be applied to each.[35]

This decision represents one of the very rare instances where the rights of a child have been trumped by another, even more important, right. It has been rightly welcomed as a rejection of the automatic paramountcy of the concept of child welfare and as an endorsement of the value in 'presumptive equality' of rights.[36]

A different form of broadcasting ban was at issue before the European Court of Human Rights in *United Christian Broadcasters Ltd v United Kingdom*,[37] where a charity whose main objective is to promote national religious broadcasting in the United Kingdom and Ireland complained that, because of the UK's statutory ban on the award of a national radio licence to a body whose objects are wholly or mainly of a religious nature,[38] its Article 10 rights had been breached (whether in conjunction or not with Articles 9 and 14). The charity is active in Northern Ireland, where there is likely to be more of an audience for religious broadcasting, and the Northern Ireland Human Rights Commission (NIHRC) agreed to make an application to

[31] See ch 9, 238. The case is *Scappaticci v Independent News and Media Ltd*; see *Belfast Telegraph*, 30 June 2006, and *Irish News*, 30 June 2006, each reporting on the decision of Weir J. For a copy of the court order, supplied by Mr Scappaticci's solicitor, see *http://cryptome.org/scappaticci-gag.htm*, last visited 16 August 2009.

[32] *R v Lees* [2001] NI 233.

[33] [2004] UKHL 47, [2005] 1 AC 593.

[34] [2004] UKHL 22, [2004] 2 AC 457.

[35] [2004] UKHL 47, [2005] 1 AC 593 at [17].

[36] Fenwick (2004). Writing before the House of Lords confirmed the Court of Appeal's decision in *In re S (A Child)*, Fenwick states (at 925): 'The idea that publicity is almost always harmful is an out-of-date one that in itself may be inimical to welfare since it tends to stifle a debate that could otherwise flourish.' For a more recent example of the same principle at work, see the lifting of the injunction which prevented publication of the names of the killers of Baby P in 2007: <http://news.bbc.co.uk/1/hi/england/london/8194873.stm>, last visited 16 August 2009.

[37] App No 44802/98, decision of 7 November 2000.

[38] Broadcasting Act 1990, Sch 2, Pt II, para 2(1)(a). There is also a ban on 'a body whose objects are wholly or mainly of a political nature': Sch 2, Pt II, para 1(1)(d). These provisions were left unchanged by the Communications Act 2003 and were the subject of a further dispute which reached the House of Lords: *R (Animal Defenders International) v Secretary of State for Culture, Media and Sport* [2008] UKHL 15, [2008] 1 AC 1312. See too *Murphy v Ireland* (2004) 38 EHRR 13, esp para 73.

intervene in the European Court proceedings had the charity's application been deemed admissible: the NIHRC felt that a blanket ban on such broadcasting licences was unjustifiable.

The UK government argued that for technical reasons the capacity for national radio services in the United Kingdom was very limited and that the aim of the disqualification of religious broadcasters was to promote the efficient use of scarce resources in order to safeguard pluralism in the media and avoid discrimination between the many different religions practised in the United Kingdom. The charity responded by arguing that the ban was not necessary to achieve this aim because other statutory provisions already required the Radio Authority to award licences in the manner best calculated to facilitate the provision of a wide range of quality programmes appealing to a variety of tastes and interests. Despite ruling that the necessity for any restriction on applications for broadcasting licences 'must be convincingly established', the European Court went on to hold that the restriction in this case could not be said to be arbitrary or to fall outside the State's margin of appreciation. It noted that the charity and other religious organizations could still apply for and be awarded licences for *local* radio broadcasting. The application was therefore rejected as being manifestly ill-founded.[39] As the case did not proceed further, the NIHRC's written intervention was not formally considered by the European Court. Religious broadcasting in Northern Ireland remains as restricted now as it was during the darkest years of the troubles. Given that religion was, and remains, a significant factor in the divisions in Northern Ireland society, there may be a greater public interest in keeping religious views off the air waves in that part of Europe than there is in other less conflicted European societies.

Freedom of expression and elections

The 1988 broadcasting ban in Northern Ireland (unlike the one in the Republic of Ireland) was expressly excluded from operating during election periods or when constituency matters were being debated. Elections are obviously features of a democratic society which must be the very last to be interfered with if the essence of democracy is not to be destroyed. Nevertheless, in Northern Ireland Article 10 rights have to some extent been compromised even in that context.

In the area of arrangements for voting at elections the European Court is almost always unwilling to interfere with a State's preferred choices. Back in 1921, when Northern Ireland was first created as a separate political entity, one of the first actions of the new unionist government was to insist upon first-past-the-post elections for

[39] The Court cited *Brook v UK* App No 38218/97, decision of 11 July 2000, where the applicant complained that the failure by the government to grant him a shortwave broadcasting licence was an unjustified interference with his right to impart information. The Court held the application to be manifestly ill-founded because the purported interference with the applicant's freedom of expression could be said to have been necessary in a democratic society, pursuing, in a proportionate manner, the aim of protecting the rights and freedoms of others, namely those who receive shortwave broadcasts and whose clarity of reception is endangered by authorizing too many broadcasters.

local council elections,[40] and a few years later elections for the Northern Ireland Parliament itself were also firmly based on that system.[41] Matters were made worse for nationalists by the fact that to some extent the right to vote was made dependent on the value of the land one owned, a practice previously common elsewhere in Britain but by then abandoned. One of the demands of the Northern Ireland Civil Rights Association in the late 1960s was the right to 'one man one vote', and after the imposition of direct rule by the government in London proportional representation was reintroduced for local council elections in 1972.[42] It has been used for every Northern Ireland Assembly election since then too,[43] and for all elections to the European Parliament,[44] but the first-past-the-post system is still used for elections to the House of Commons.

The right to lodge petitions in Strasbourg was extended to people living anywhere in the United Kingdom in 1966, but very few petitions have been lodged in connection with electoral issues in Northern Ireland, no doubt because the Convention has precious little to say about such matters. Article 3 of Protocol 1 (ratified by the United Kingdom in 1952, and in force from 1954) merely says that States 'undertake to hold free elections at reasonable intervals by secret ballot, under conditions which will ensure the free expression of the opinion of the people in the choice of the legislature'. We saw in Chapter 3 that complaints were made about the rules on who could vote, the way in which seats were allocated to each constituency, and the fact that only 12 MPs could be elected to serve at Westminster.[45] The European Commission declared the application inadmissible because the word 'legislature' in Article 3 of Protocol 1 did not embrace bodies with as few law-making powers as Northern Ireland's local councils.[46] As regards the number of MPs to be elected for Westminster,[47] the Commission accepted that the UK government enjoyed a margin of appreciation on this matter and it did not think the government had strayed outside what was justifiable. The claim that the electoral arrangements were discriminatory against Catholics, in violation of Article 14 of the Convention, failed too, because to succeed it needed to be able to piggy-back on some other violation or potential violation of a Convention right, and there was none.

Some years later, when a challenge was made in Strasbourg to the fact that in Northern Ireland a proportional representation system of voting was used in elections for the European Parliament, while in Great Britain a first-past-the-post system was used, this was held not to be an infringement of Article 10 or of any other provision in

[40] Method of Voting and Redistribution of Seats Act (NI) 1922. Proportional representation had been introduced only three years earlier, by the Local Government (Ireland) Act 1919.

[41] House of Commons (Method of Voting and Redistribution of Seats) Act 1929. For further details see Hennessey (1997) 43–53.

[42] Electoral Law (NI) Order 1972.

[43] These have occurred in 1973, 1982, 1998, 2003, and 2007. For details see <http://www.ark.ac.uk/elections>, last visited 17 August 2009.

[44] These began in 1979 and have occurred at five year intervals since then. In Great Britain PR has been used for European elections only since 1999 but the system used there (d'Hondt) is still different from that used in Northern Ireland (Single Transferable Vote).

[45] Reported under both *MM v UK* and *X, Y and Z v UK* (1976) 6 DR 13.

[46] ibid.

[47] Analyses conducted by Barritt and Carter led them to conclude that gerrymandering did not have a large influence on Parliamentary elections: Barritt and Carter (1972) 42.

the European Convention.[48] A claim by the same applicant (a former unionist MP in the Northern Ireland Parliament) that Article 10 and other provisions were breached by the arrangements made for the 1996 Forum elections in Northern Ireland was also declared inadmissible by the Commission.[49]

Electoral rules (leaving voting systems to one side) are virtually identical throughout the United Kingdom,[50] but in Northern Ireland there is a special legislative provision[51] which requires candidates who are standing for election to a district council or to the Northern Ireland Assembly—not to the Westminster Parliament—to sign a declaration when submitting their nomination papers and to sign again, if elected, before taking their seats. The declaration is in the following terms:

> If elected, I will not by word or deed express support for or approval of (a) any proscribed organisation, or (b) acts of terrorism (that is to say, violence for political ends) connected with the affairs of Northern Ireland.

It would seem that all candidates for council and Assembly elections since 1989 have felt able to sign such a declaration, even Sinn Féin candidates prior to the IRA's ceasefire in 1994 and Progressive Unionist Party candidates prior to the Ulster Volunteer Force (UVF) ceasefire a few weeks later. High Court proceedings can be initiated by a fellow elected representative, or by an elector, if he or she suspects that a person who signed the declaration is actually in breach of it, but no such proceedings have yet been taken. It is probable that any challenge under the Human Rights Act 1998, or in Strasbourg, to the requirement to sign the declaration would fail, since if it is deemed to be an interference with the right to freedom of expression at all it would be held to be necessary in the interests of public safety (under Article 10(2)) and not disproportionate.

The right to stand for election is obviously an important feature of a democracy and in both parts of Ireland there is a long history of persons standing not because they want to take a seat in the elected body in question but because they want their supporters to be able to register a protest vote.[52] The most notorious example of this during the recent conflict is when Bobby Sands, a republican prisoner on hunger strike in the Maze Prison, stood for election to the Westminster Parliament in 1981. At that time there was no law preventing a convicted prisoner from standing for election, although somewhat paradoxically there was a law preventing such a person from voting. After Sands had been duly elected[53] the UK Parliament passed the very short Representation of the People Act 1981. This disqualified from standing for election any person serving a prison sentence in the United Kingdom or the Republic of

[48] *Lindsay v UK* [1979] 3 CMLR 166. The disparity in election systems derived from the European Assembly Elections Act 1978.

[49] *Lindsay v UK* App No 31699/96, decision of 17 January 1997. The Forum elections were held to elect delegates to a body that would operate alongside the peace talks on-going in Northern Ireland, a kind of proto-Assembly.

[50] For slight differences regarding election broadcasts see the information provided by the official watchdog, Ofcom at: <http://www.ofcom.org.uk/tv/ifi/guidance/ppbrules/>, last visited 17 August 2009.

[51] Elected Authorities (NI) Act 1989. For discussion of alternatives see Walker (1988).

[52] In the 1918 general election for the Westminster Parliament, 36 of the 73 Sinn Féin candidates who were elected were still in prison: see Feeney (2002) 109–12.

[53] Sands received 51 per cent of the vote—30,492 votes. He later died as a result of his hunger strike.

Ireland of more than one year. The Act was strongly and unanimously opposed by the Standing Advisory Commission on Human Rights, which thought it did 'nothing to ameliorate the situation in Northern Ireland', was 'offensive in principle and defective in effect', and 'may well assist the terrorist campaign against democracy'.[54] It also doubted whether the Act was compatible with Article 3 of Protocol 1 to the European Convention, although it gave no specific reasons for coming to this conclusion.[55] It is submitted here that any challenge in Strasbourg would have been likely to fail, since the European Commission and Court would probably have viewed the restriction as pursuing a legitimate aim, necessary, and proportionate. Some support for such a view can be gleaned from the European Commission's decision in *Mallon v United Kingdom*, where Seamus Mallon, a nationalist member of the Northern Ireland Assembly who had also been appointed to the Irish Seanad (Senate),[56] complained about a domestic law which disqualified him from being a member of the Assembly while at the same time being a member of the Parliament of a non-Commonwealth country.[57] The Commission considered such a disqualification to be justifiable within the margin of appreciation doctrine.[58]

The rules on civil servants standing for election in Northern Ireland did not seem to provoke any resentment during the worst years of the troubles but they have recently been challenged in the courts.[59] Ryan McKinney, an administrative officer in the Child Support Agency in Belfast, wanted to stand for election to the Northern Ireland Assembly in 2003. The Northern Ireland Assembly Disqualification Act 1975[60] disqualifies *all* civil servants from membership of the Assembly, and the Civil Service (Parliamentary and Assembly Candidature) (Amendment) Order (NI) 1998[61] states that no civil servant can announce him- or herself as a candidate for election to the Assembly. McKinney argued that the restrictions on his election ambitions were a breach of his human rights under Article 10. He noted that industrial and non-office grade civil servants *are* allowed to be candidates for elections to the Assembly and are guaranteed reinstatement in their jobs after they have served as members of the Assembly. He felt that as an 'intermediate' grade civil servant he should benefit from the same regime. Weatherup J, however, dismissed his application for judicial review, holding that the restrictions imposed on intermediate grade civil servants were proportionate and impaired the rights conferred by Articles 10 and 11 as minimally as

[54] SACHR (1981) para 21.

[55] ibid, para 18.

[56] He later served as an MP and became the deputy First Minister of Northern Ireland from 1999 to 2001 in the first Executive to be formed after the Belfast (Good Friday) Agreement 1998.

[57] Northern Ireland Assembly Disqualification Act 1975, s 1(1)(e); there was a similar provision for membership of the House of Commons: House of Commons Disqualification Act 1975, s 1(1)(e).

[58] (1984) 37 DR 129. The rules on disqualification were altered in 2000 so as to make it acceptable for someone to be a member of both the Oireachtas and the House of Commons or Northern Ireland Assembly. For more details see Gay (2000).

[59] *Re McKinney* [2004] NIQB 73.

[60] s 1(1)(b).

[61] The 1998 Order amends an Order of the same name made in 1990. Both were made by the Secretary of State in exercise of powers conferred by Letters Patent of Her Majesty (ie under Crown prerogative). The 1990 Order also makes it clear that employees in the Northern Ireland civil service (except for those in industrial and non-office grades) cannot stand for election to the Westminster or European Parliaments.

possible. In coming to this conclusion he applied the European Court's reasoning in *Ahmed v United Kingdom*.[62]

In *Ahmed v United Kingdom* four local government employees in England complained that their Article 10 rights had been breached by the Local Government Officers (Political Restrictions) Regulations 1990, made under the Local Government and Housing Act 1989,[63] which empowered the Secretary of State for the Environment to restrict the political activities of certain categories of local government officers. By six votes to three, the judges of the European Court held that the Regulations did not breach Article 10, because the interference in question was 'necessary in a democratic society'. Four particular features of the Regulations seemed to impress the majority: (a) their focus on the need to preserve the impartiality of carefully defined categories of officers whose duties involve the provision of advice to a local authority council or to its operational committees, or who represent the council in dealings with the media, (b) their inclusion of a procedure whereby categories of officers could apply to be exempted from the restrictions, (c) their prohibition not of all comments on political matters but only of those which could be considered as espousing or opposing a party political view, and (d) their prohibition not of all political activities by local government officers but only those which would be likely to link a politically restricted post-holder, in the eyes of the public or council members, with a particular party political line: there was no restriction on the officers' rights to join a political party or to engage in activities within a party other than those which would involve participating in its general management or representing it in its dealings with others. In *Ahmed* the European Court also stressed[64] that, in measuring the proportionality of a measure taken, it had to have regard to the fact that, whenever the right to freedom of expression of public servants is in issue, the 'duties and responsibilities' referred to in Article 10(2) assume a special significance.[65] This justifies leaving to the authorities of the respondent State a clear margin of appreciation when determining whether the impugned interference is proportionate to the aim as stated.

The prohibition on the right of prisoners to vote in Northern Ireland and elsewhere in the United Kingdom is also under examination in Whitehall at present, given that the Grand Chamber of the European Court of Human Rights held in *Hirst v United Kingdom (No 2)*[66] that the prohibition is much too widely stated. The applicant, a discretionary lifer serving a sentence for manslaughter who had already served his tariff period, complained that he did not have the right to vote in elections. His claim under the Human Rights Act 1998 was rejected by the Divisional Court in England but the European Court held that there had been a breach of

[62] (1998) 29 EHRR 1.

[63] s 1(5).

[64] (1998) 29 EHRR 1, para 61. This approach also derives from *Vogt v Germany* (1995) 21 EHRR 205.

[65] Art 10(2) begins: 'The exercise of these freedoms, since it carries with it duties and responsibilities, may be subject to such formalities, conditions, restrictions or penalties as are prescribed by law and are necessary in a democratic society...'

[66] (2006) 42 EHRR 41. No compensation was awarded. Five of the 17 judges dissented.

Article 3 of Protocol 1.[67] It said that no separate issue arose under Articles 10 or 14 of the Convention, but it is likely that, had Article 3 of Protocol 1 not been applicable, those provisions would have been. According to the European Court, the current UK law[68] is disproportionate, even though it does not deny the right to vote to those imprisoned for contempt of court, for not paying a fine, or while on remand in custody. The Court accepted that national legislatures should be accorded a wide margin of appreciation when determining whether restrictions on prisoners' right to vote could still be justified in modern times and, if so, how a fair balance was to be struck, but it said there were limits to such freedom of action:

> It is, however, for the Court... to satisfy itself that the conditions do not curtail the rights in question to such an extent as to impair their very essence and deprive them of their effectiveness; that they are imposed in pursuit of a legitimate aim; and that the means employed are not disproportionate. In particular, any conditions imposed must not thwart the free expression of the people in the choice of the legislature—in other words, they must reflect, or not run counter to, the concern to maintain the integrity and effectiveness of an electoral procedure aimed at identifying the will of people through universal suffrage.[69]

The European Court referred to *Holland v Ireland*[70] as being the previous Strasbourg case closest to *Hirst v United Kingdom*, but it was able to distinguish that decision on the basis that there the European Commission of Human Rights omitted to address the legitimacy of the aim being pursued and the proportionality of the measure taken. In *Hirst*, said the Court, the margin of appreciation had been overstepped:

> ...section 3 of the 1983 Act remains a blunt instrument. It strips of their Convention right to vote a significant category of persons and it does so in a way which is indiscriminate. The provision imposes a blanket restriction on all convicted prisoners in prison. It applies automatically to such prisoners, irrespective of the length of their sentence and irrespective of the nature or gravity of their offence and their individual circumstances. Such a general, automatic and indiscriminate restriction on a vitally important Convention right must be seen as falling outside any acceptable margin of appreciation...[71]

The Court deliberately gave no guidance to the UK government on how it should go about distinguishing between prisoners who should be given the right to vote and those who should not. There was, it said, a number of different ways of doing so, as a survey of European State practice revealed.

[67] On this provision more generally, see Harris et al (2009) 711–33; Lester, Pannick, and Herberg (2009) 687–701; Reid (2007) 290–300; Mowbray (2007) 973–88; Ovey and White (2006) 388–99. See also the studies conducted by the Venice Commission for Democracy.

[68] Representation of the People Acts 1983 (s 3) and 2000.

[69] (2006) 42 EHRR 41, para 62.

[70] (1998) 93 DR 15, where a prisoner serving a seven-year term for possession of explosives was denied the right to vote and the European Commission declared his application to be inadmissible because the denial was not arbitrary. Moreover, in *Breathnach v Ireland* [2001] 3 IR 230, the Irish Supreme Court held that such prohibitions did not infringe the Irish Constitution.

[71] (2006) 42 EHRR 41, para 82. Cf the over-wide nature of the ban on prisoners giving face-to-face interviews to professional journalists, which was 'read down' by the House of Lords in the *Simms* case, discussed later in this chapter.

Prisoners in Northern Ireland have long been aware of their inability to vote in elections and shortly after the *Hirst* decision two such prisoners claimed that their Convention rights were being violated because they were unable to vote in the Northern Ireland Assembly elections in March 2007. But the High Court of Northern Ireland held that the government was justified in taking more time before deciding how best to respond to the decision in *Hirst*.[72] At the time of writing the government has just completed the second stage of its consultation process on how best to proceed, but both the Parliamentary Joint Committee on Human Rights[73] and the Council of Europe's Committee of Ministers[74] have urged the government to ensure that new legislation is in place before the next UK general election, which has to occur before June 2010. It seems very unlikely that the government will meet that deadline.

Election law in Northern Ireland has also been affected by one other decision of the European Court in a case taken from England, and by a recent decision of the House of Lords. The former is *Bowman v United Kingdom*,[75] where Phyllis Bowman, the Executive Director of the Society for the Protection of the Unborn Child, arranged to have 1,500,000 leaflets distributed in constituencies throughout the United Kingdom prior to the 1992 general election. The leaflets gave information about local candidates' views on abortion and embryo experimentation. Bowman was charged, under the Representation of the People Act 1983,[76] with spending more than £5 on conveying information to electors with a view to promoting or procuring the election of a candidate. The Crown Court judge directed her acquittal because the summons charging her had not been issued within a year (as required by the 1983 Act) but the proceedings were reported in the press and she applied to the European Court arguing that her Article 10 rights had been violated. The Grand Chamber of the Court held, by 14 votes to six, that there had indeed been a violation of Article 10.[77] The majority view was that the 1983 Act operated, for all practical purposes, as a total barrier to the applicant's publishing information with a view to influencing voters. It was not 'necessary' to limit spending to £5 in order to achieve the otherwise legitimate aim of securing equality between candidates, especially as there were no restrictions on the freedom of the press to support or oppose the election of any candidate or on political parties to advertise generally. The restriction in question was thus disproportionate to the aim pursued. The UK judge, Sir John Freeland, again voted in favour of his own country's stance. He argued that the 1983 Act did not totally prevent Bowman from informing voters of her views or from encouraging them to question candidates—it merely required her to spend no more than £5 in

[72] *Re Toner's Application* [2007] NIQB 18 (Gillen J).

[73] 13th Report, 2005–6, HL 133 / HC 954, paras 51–3; 16th Report, 2006–7, HL 128 / HC 728, paras 67–79; 31st Report, 2007–8, HL 173 / HC 1078, paras 47–63; 4th Report, 2008–9, HL 23 / HC 204, paras 1.10–1.19; Press Release No 58, 30 July 2009 (disclosing a letter from the chairman of the Committee to the Secretary of State for Justice, dated 21 July 2009).

[74] CM/Del/Dec(2009)1059 8 June 2009, 1059th (DH) meeting, accessible on the Council of Europe's website.

[75] (1998) 26 EHRR 1.

[76] s 75.

[77] The judges unanimously agreed that no compensation should be awarded for the violation.

relation to a particular candidate! With respect, this seems a very weak justification for rejecting the application; the majority view is greatly to be preferred.

The House of Lords' decision concerns the images that can be banned from broadcast at election time. In *R v BBC, ex parte ProLife Alliance*[78] it was held that the right to broadcast in this context is far from absolute. ProLife Alliance is a political party registered under the Political Parties, Elections and Referendums Act 2000.[79] It campaigns for 'absolute respect for innocent human life from fertilisation until natural death' and one of its principal policy goals is the prohibition of abortion. In May 2001 the party put up sufficient candidates for the June 2001 UK general election to entitle it to make one party election broadcast in Wales. The broadcasters, however, refused to transmit what was offered to them because in their opinion it offended good taste and decency. An application for judicial review of this decision failed, but an appeal was successful. The Court of Appeal[80] made a declaration that the refusal to broadcast ProLife Alliance's party election broadcast was unlawful. The House of Lords, with one dissenting voice (Lord Scott of Foscote), restored the High Court's decision. In doing so the majority emphasized that freedom of political speech is a freedom of the very highest importance in any country which lays claim to being a democracy and restrictions on such freedom need to be examined rigorously by all concerned.[81] However—rather strangely it is submitted—they maintained at the same time that the primary right protected by Article 10 is the right of every citizen not to be *prevented* from expressing his opinions.[82] In the present case, said Lord Hoffmann, that primary right was not engaged:

> There was nothing that the Alliance was prevented from doing. It enjoyed the same free speech as every other citizen. By virtue of its entitlement to a [party election broadcast] it had more access to the homes of its fellow citizens than other single-issue groups which could not afford to register as a political party and put up six deposits.[83]

The court pointed out that there is no human right to use a television channel. Parliament has rightly authorized broadcasters to allow political parties to broadcast, but subject to certain conditions. Qualifying conditions are essential because it would be impossible to give every grouping which registers as a political party the time to make a party broadcast. In support of this position Lord Hoffmann cited the decision by the European Commission of Human Rights in the application brought by the right-wing Austrian politician Jörg Haider,[84] whose complaint that a television

[78] [2003] UKHL 23, [2004] 1 AC 185.

[79] See <http://prolife.org.uk>, last visited 29 August 2009.

[80] [2002] EWCA Civ 297, [2004] 1 AC 185.

[81] [2003] UKHL 23, [2004] 1 AC 185, [6] (per Lord Nicholls).

[82] The right is to 'receive and impart information and ideas without *interference* by public authority' (emphasis added): ibid, [55] (Lord Hoffmann).

[83] ibid, [56].

[84] *Haider v Austria* (1995) 83 DR 66. The Commission specifically addressed the nature of political speech: '... freedom of political debate is at the very core of the concept of a democratic society which prevails throughout the Convention. The limits of acceptable criticism are accordingly much wider with regard to a politician acting in his public capacity than in relation to a private individual. The former inevitably and knowingly lays himself open to close scrutiny of his every word and deed by both journalists and the public at large, and he must display a greater degree of tolerance, especially when he himself

channel had not given his opinions enough time and had not portrayed them objectively was rejected as manifestly ill-founded. The position is also consistent with that adopted by Sir John Freeland in *Bowman v United Kingdom*, as noted above. However, the fact that Sir John's view was a dissenting one in the European Court lends some support to the suggestion that the decision of the majority in the House of Lords is out of step with prevailing Strasbourg jurisprudence.[85] It seems to focus unduly on the fact that ProLife could make an election broadcast, ignoring the fact that the party's complaint was rather about what they could say in that broadcast.

The one dissenting voice in the Lords was that of Lord Scott, who reminded his colleagues of the precise wording of Article 10(2) of the Convention, which allows certain restrictions on Article 10(1) rights. He stressed their comprehensive character and said: 'The application of restrictions allegedly in the public interest but not justifiable under any of these heads would, in my opinion, constitute a breach of Article 10 rights'.[86] There is, with respect, much force in this position, since it is surely stretching beyond breaking point the phrase 'for the protection of health or morals' to suggest that the sort of material which the ProLife Alliance wished to broadcast was risking people's health or morals. In fact a good case could be made for saying exactly the opposite—that the material was *promoting* health and morals. It was certainly aimed at promoting the value of life. Lord Scott might also have stressed that, although Article 10(1) says that the right to freedom of expression 'includes' the right to impart information and ideas without interference by public authority, this is just one example of the general scope of the right. The opening sentence of Article 10(1) is otherwise unequivocal: 'Everyone has the right to freedom of expression'. If political parties in Northern Ireland were to attempt to use images of devastation caused by bombs and bullets in the past in an attempt to denigrate the electability of rival candidates in an election today, there is a chance, if the decision in the *ProLife* case is relied upon, that broadcasters would be entitled to refuse to show those images.

Freedom of expression and parliamentary processes

The compatibility of the doctrine of Parliamentary privilege with the European Convention was at issue in *A v United Kingdom*, not itself a case from Northern Ireland but one with definite implications for the conflict there.[87] The applicant

makes public statements that are susceptible of criticism . . . The Commission also finds that with regard to interviews of politicians it is in the interest of freedom of political debate that the interviewing journalist may also express critical and provocative points of view and not merely give neutral cues for the statements of the interviewed person, since the latter can reply immediately.' Haider had also been one of the original applicants in the case of *Informationsverein Lentia v Austria* (1993) 17 EHRR 93, where a group of co-owners and residents of a housing development successfully relied upon Art 10 to challenge the Austrian State monopoly on broadcasting.

[85] It appears that the ProLife Alliance has not lodged an application in the European Court of Human Rights to challenge the decision by the House of Lords.

[86] [2003] UKHL 23, [2004] 1 AC 185, [88].

[87] (2003) 36 EHRR 917.

alleged that the absolute Parliamentary immunity which prevented her from taking legal action in respect of statements made about her in Parliament violated her right of access to justice under Article 6(1) of the Convention, as well as her right to privacy under Article 8. She also said she was being discriminated against contrary to Article 14. She did not argue on the basis of Article 10(1), because her own right to freedom of expression was not at issue and the respondent State did not therefore have to justify its law in terms of Article 10(2).[88] The European Court permitted interventions to be made by the governments of Austria, Belgium, Finland, France, Ireland, Italy, the Netherlands, and Norway. Needless to say, all of these supported to a greater or lesser extent the principle of Parliamentary immunity. The European Court consequently held, albeit with Judge Loucaides dissenting, that there had been no breach of Articles 6(1) or 8 and, unanimously, that there had been no breach of Article 14. It ruled that the parliamentary immunity enjoyed by MPs in the United Kingdom pursued the legitimate aims of protecting free speech in Parliament and maintaining the separation of powers between the legislature and the judiciary.[89] The Court also said that a rule of Parliamentary immunity that generally reflected recognized practice within European States and inter-State assemblies could not be regarded as imposing a *disproportionate* restriction on the right of access to justice as embodied in Article 6(1).[90] The decision acknowledges, once again, that individual human rights sometimes have to take second place to even greater values. This can surely be justified, however, only if Parliaments are themselves willing to police the behaviour of their members in an appropriate way. Serious harm can be caused to individuals if Parliamentarians are allowed a completely free rein to say what they like under the cover of Parliamentary immunity.

Shortly before this decision in Strasbourg a similar case had come before the High Court in Belfast. In *Reavey v Century Newspapers Ltd*[91] Sheil J, as he then was, rejected an application that the publishers of the News Letter, a daily newspaper, and the Rev Dr Ian Paisley MP (who had spoken about the matter in Parliament) should reveal the source for their stories that certain named individuals were members of the IRA. As regards the newspaper publishers, who relied on section 10 of the Contempt of Court Act 1981[92] as well as on Article 10 of the Convention, the judge held that the public interest in protecting a newspaper's source in order to ensure free communication of information to and through the press outweighed the specific legitimate interest of the plaintiffs in having the source identified so that he or she could be sued for

[88] At [72], ibid, the European Court noted that freedom of speech in Parliament must, as in local government and other contexts, carry with it duties and responsibilities, as confirmed by Art 10(2) of the Convention.

[89] ibid, [77].

[90] ibid, [83].

[91] [2001] NI 187.

[92] This states that: 'No court may require a person to disclose, nor is any person guilty of contempt of court for refusing to disclose, the source of information contained in a publication for which he is responsible, unless it be established to the satisfaction of the court that disclosure is necessary in the interests of justice or national security or for the prevention of disorder or crime.' This provision was part of the UK government's response to the decision of the European Court of Human Rights in *Sunday Times v UK (No 1)* (1979–80) 2 EHRR 245.

defamation or malicious falsehood.[93] Sheil J relied heavily on the seminal decision of the European Court in *Goodwin v United Kingdom*,[94] which effectively overturned the decision of the House of Lords in the same matter,[95] and also on various English cases subsequent to the Human Rights Act 1998 in which section 10 of the 1981 Act had been analysed, particularly the Court of Appeal's decision in *Ashworth Hospital Authority v MGN Ltd*.[96] As regards the position of Dr Paisley, the judge held that Article 9 of the Bill of Rights 1689[97] had to be interpreted in the light of the Human Rights Act 1998 but that on the facts before him the resort to a claim of Parliamentary privilege was not disproportionate. It is worth emphasizing that the plaintiffs in this case did not provide evidence that their right to life or any other human right was at risk of being violated as a result of the statements made about them, although the judge did take judicial notice of the fact that:

> during the last 30 years of 'The Troubles' in Northern Ireland people have been murdered by reason of allegations made against them, such allegations frequently being based on mere rumour or suspicion, often ill-founded.[98]

Had there been such evidence, the judge would have had to weigh the importance of the right to freedom of expression against the right to life and the right not to be subjected to torture or inhuman or degrading treatment. The judge added that if the privilege accorded by Article 9 of the Bill of Rights 1689 is abused by a member of Parliament, what should be done about it is a matter entirely within the jurisdiction of the House of Commons. The disappointed claimant in this case did not then lodge an application in Strasbourg, presumably on the strength of legal advice that it would have been to no avail.

The same position was adopted in the first of two further Northern Ireland cases where the relevance of Article 10 in a Parliamentary setting was at issue. Both involved representatives of Sinn Féin. First, Martin McGuinness MP[99] argued that it was a breach of his Article 10 rights to require him to swear an oath of allegiance to Queen Elizabeth II before taking his seat at Westminster.[100] He sought judicial review of the decision taken by the then Speaker of the House of Commons, Betty Boothroyd, who had ruled that an MP who had not taken his or her seat could not avail of any of the services or facilities within the House of Commons.[101] Kerr J, as he then was, held that 'the Speaker's action

[93] The right of journalists to keep their sources secret is considered in more detail later in this chapter.

[94] (1996) 22 EHRR 123.

[95] *X Ltd v Morgan-Grampian (Publishers) Ltd* [1991] 1 AC 1.

[96] [2001] 1 WLR 515. This decision was affirmed by the House of Lords: [2002] UKHL 29, [2002] 1 WLR 2033.

[97] Art 9 reads: 'That the freedom of speech, and debates or proceedings in parliament, ought not to be impeached or questioned in any court or place out of parliament.'

[98] [2001] NI 187, 205d.

[99] Currently the deputy First Minister of Northern Ireland.

[100] The oath is as follows: 'I [name] do swear that I will be faithful and bear true allegiance to Her Majesty Queen Elizabeth II, her heirs and successors, according to law. So help me God.' See Parliamentary Oaths Act 1866, s 1, as amended by the Promissory Oaths Act 1868. It should be noted that the official position of Sinn Féin is that, even if the requirement to make such an oath were abolished, their MPs would still refuse to take their seats.

[101] There is an account of the matter in Boothroyd (2001).

lies squarely within the realm of internal arrangements of the House of Commons and is not amenable to judicial review'.[102] The judge also held that the court had no jurisdiction to review the validity of primary legislation such as the Parliamentary Oaths Act 1866[103] and that the Speaker's decision was protected by Article 9 of the Bill of Rights 1689.[104] There was no appeal against Kerr J's decision but an application was made to Strasbourg.

In holding Mr McGuinness's application to be inadmissible the European Court clearly let it be known that, although freedom of expression is especially important for elected representatives of the people, it is not an absolute right. Inhibitions on the right, however, need to be strictly justified. Did the inhibition in question pursue a legitimate aim and was it necessary in a democratic society? In this case the Court answered each of these questions affirmatively. 'Protecting the rights of others'—an allowable exception to the right to freedom of expression under Article 10(2) of the Convention—can embrace 'the protection of the constitutional principles which underpin a democracy', and imposing the condition in question was 'an integral part of the respondent state's constitutional order'. More particularly, although somewhat circularly, the Court added:

> ...the requirement that elected representatives to the House of Commons take an oath of allegiance to the reigning monarch can be reasonably viewed as an affirmation of loyalty to the constitutional principles which support, inter alia, the workings of representative democracy in the respondent State.[105]

On whether the impugned measure was necessary in a democratic society the Court said that the applicant could not claim with justification that it had a disproportionate effect on his right to freedom of expression. But that, with respect, is surely not the applicable test in this context. The onus is not on the applicant to prove that the measure is disproportionate but rather on the State to prove that it is proportionate. The fact that the applicant could still express the views of his constituents and party in other contexts, including at meetings outside the House of Commons in which government ministers and other MPs were participating, is hardly of relevance if the particular denial of his right to take his parliamentary seat and use the parliamentary facilities available to all other MPs is still 'unnecessary'. Can it reasonably be argued in a modern European democracy that its Parliament should be allowed to admit as elected members only those persons who are prepared to swear allegiance to the country's Head of State? Is this concept of allegiance not entirely outmoded? Would it not be much more sensible to require, as is the case for local and Assembly elections in Northern Ireland, that persons elected must swear not to use or support the use of violence for political ends? In McGuinness's case a safer ground for rejecting his application would surely have been that he had not demonstrated that he actually wanted to take his seat in Parliament, given that he had been elected on a

[102] Decision of 3 October 1997, cited by the European Court of Human Rights in *McGuinness v UK* App No 38511/98, decision of 8 June 1999.

[103] Even after the commencement of the Human Rights Act on 2 October 2000, courts in the UK do not have the power to declare primary legislation to be *invalid*: all they can do is declare it to be *incompatible* with one or more Convention rights, leaving it to Parliament to amend the legislation if and when it so desires.

[104] See n 97 above.

[105] *McGuinness v UK* App No 38511/98, decision of 8 June 1999, at 6.

manifesto which promised abstentionism. His application could have been described as an abuse of the application process.

In the second of this brace of cases, Sinn Féin again alleged a denial of their representatives' right to freedom of expression, with some apparent justification. Under the Political Parties, Elections and Referendums Act 2000[106] policy development grants (PDGs) can be made to 'represented' registered political parties in order to assist them with the development of policies for inclusion in a party election manifesto. 'Represented' in this context is stated to mean that 'there are at least two Members of the House of Commons belonging to the party who have made and subscribed the oath required by the Parliamentary Oaths Act 1866'.[107] Sinn Féin sought a declaration from the High Court in Belfast that the 2000 Act was incompatible with Article 10 of the European Convention, read in conjunction with Article 14 (the non-discrimination provision). At first instance Coghlin J rejected the application, mainly on the basis that Sinn Féin had not proved any restriction on its members' ability to hold or express opinions or receive or impart information.[108] This decision was affirmed by the Court of Appeal of Northern Ireland,[109] the rationale being that 'the basic object of the provision of PDGs was to give resources for undertaking policy formulation to parties whose Members of Parliament were too taken up with the daily work of Parliament to be able to afford the time required for that'.[110] But it is not immediately apparent either from the High Court decision or the Court of Appeal's where the evidence for such a statement lies. In July 2004 the House of Lords granted Sinn Féin leave to appeal but in March 2005, no doubt on legal advice, the party indicated that it would not be proceeding with the appeal.[111]

Comparing and contrasting the decisions relating to the role of Article 10 in electoral and Parliamentary matters, it is tempting to conclude that the four traditional tests for assessing the validity of a restriction to the right to freedom of expression are not nuanced enough to take account of all the relevant factors. 'Prescribed by law', 'in pursuit of a legitimate aim', 'necessary in a democratic society', and 'proportionate' are all quite blunt instruments when it comes to differentiating between restrictions which in overall terms are justifiable and those which are not. It would seem, moreover, that a very wide margin of appreciation is accorded to States as regards what is or is not acceptable within the Parliamentary process, with the European Court being reluctant to interfere with certain traditions even if there is little objective justification for maintaining them. Following the European Court's decision in *McGonnell v United Kingdom*,[112] however, where the constitutional position of the Bailiff in Guernsey was held to be incompatible with Article 6 of the European Convention, the UK government did make changes to

[106] s 12.

[107] s 12(1)(b)(i).

[108] *Re Sinn Féin's Application* [2003] NIQB 27.

[109] *Re Sinn Féin's Application* [2004] NICA 4.

[110] ibid, [13]. Sinn Féin MPs do not in any event involve themselves in the daily work of Parliament.

[111] This occurred a month after the party lost a comparable case in the High Court of Northern Ireland where it had challenged findings of the International Monitoring Commission and the Secretary of State's direction not to pay money to the party under the Financial Assistance for Political Parties Act (NI) 2000: *Re Sinn Féin's Application* [2005] NIQB 10.

[112] (2000) 30 EHRR 289.

the role of the Lord Chancellor and to the appointment system for judges throughout the United Kingdom.[113] The government has also moved the most senior judges (the Law Lords) out of a chamber of Parliament (the House of Lords) and into a new Supreme Court of the United Kingdom.[114] These developments are some indication that the European Court, and States themselves, are beginning to realize that the European Convention's requirement for a fair hearing, with all that that means for free speech, is capable of permeating even into the deepest recesses of a country's constitutional traditions. But whether these developments are yet advanced enough to contribute to the detailed regulation of societies that are deeply divided along political lines is still unclear. Political developments in Northern Ireland certainly did not come about as a result of pressure exerted through decisions of the European Court of Human Rights.

Treason, sedition, and incitement to disaffection

The principal driver behind much of the violence which was a constant feature of the conflict in Northern Ireland was, of course, the ideology of the IRA and other republican paramilitary groups. They did not want Northern Ireland to be part of the British State and they reserved particular hatred for anything connected with the British Crown, including the Royal family itself. But at no point in the conflict, with one exception, was anyone suspected of republican activities in Northern Ireland, whether violent or otherwise, charged with the offence of treason, the definition of which includes 'compassing or imagining' the death of the monarch and 'levying war' against the monarch in his or her realm.[115] Plenty of anti-monarchical articles were published in republican newspapers such as An Phoblacht, but the prosecuting authorities did not think it was worthwhile trying to stop these publications through bringing treason proceedings. Nor, again with one exception, was anyone charged with sedition, the almost obsolete common law offence of making a statement which brings the Queen or her heirs, the government and constitution, either House of Parliament, or the administration of justice, 'into hatred or contempt', or which 'promotes discontent among or hostility between British subjects'.[116]

[113] The Lord Chancellor no longer sits as a judge or Speaker of the House of Lords, but he also holds the office of Secretary of State for Constitutional Affairs. A Commission for Judicial Appointments was created under the Crown prerogative in 2001 and in 2006 this body was replaced by the Judicial Appointments Commission, created under the Constitutional Reform Act 2005, one of its members being John Simpson, the Commissioner for Judicial Appointments in Northern Ireland. A full-blown Judicial Appointments Commission is now up and running in Northern Ireland, thanks to the Justice (NI) Act 2004, ss 1–3. The Constitutional Reform Act 2005, s 124, provides for the appointment of a Northern Ireland Judicial Appointments Ombudsman. In England and Wales ss 61–2 of the 2005 Act provide respectively for a Judicial Appointments Commission and a Judicial Appointments and Conduct Ombudsman.

[114] This is provided for in the Constitutional Reform Act 2005, Pt 3. See generally Le Sueur (2004) and the collection of articles in the journal *Legal Studies* (2004, issues 1 and 2).

[115] The quoted words are taken from the Treason Act 1351, still partly in force. The suggestion that treason might be revived in England and Wales was allegedly floated within the Home Office in the aftermath of the bombings in London on 7 July 2005.

[116] Thomas Paine was convicted of sedition after he published his *Rights of Man* in 1792. An attempt was made to force a prosecution of Salman Rushdie for his novel *Satanic Verses* in 1988, but it failed.

The exception referred to above relates to a prosecution brought in 1972 against three people who were charged in England with 'treason felony',[117] 'seditious conspiracy', and sedition for attempting to recruit people to travel to Northern Ireland to join in the fight of local Catholics against loyalists and British security forces.[118] The most serious charges were eventually not proceeded with, but the accused were convicted of uttering seditious words and of public order offences, and were given suspended prison sentences. This appears to be the last occasion on which anyone has been charged with treason or sedition in the United Kingdom and these defendants did not subsequently lodge a complaint in Strasbourg. As far back as 1977 the Law Commission of England and Wales recommended reform of the treason law and abolition of the offence of sedition,[119] but to date neither reform has occurred. However in a debate on the Coroners and Justice Bill in the House of Lords in July 2009 a government Minister promised that the crime of sedition *will* be abolished, including in Northern Ireland.[120] Lord Lester of Herne Hill QC, for his part, said that abolishing the laws would encourage the European Court of Human Rights to 'adopt a robust position in reviewing such laws and their operation'.[121]

Strangely, however, the compatibility of the treason laws with the European Convention did arise five years after the Belfast (Good Friday) Agreement, but in England itself. In *R v Attorney General, ex parte Rusbridger*[122] the editor of *The Guardian* and the journalist Polly Toynbee argued that their Article 10 rights were breached by the fact that, in conducting a press campaign advocating the peaceful and constitutional replacement of the monarchy by a republican form of government, they might be committing an offence under section 3 of the Treason Act 1848, which reads (in part):

> If any person whatsoever shall, within the United Kingdom or without, compass, imagine, invent, devise, or intend to deprive or depose our Most Gracious Lady the Queen, . . . from the style, honour, or royal name of the imperial crown of the United Kingdom, or of any other of her Majesty's dominions and countries . . . and such compassings, imaginations, inventions, devices, or intentions, or any of them, shall express, utter, or declare, by publishing any printing or writing, . . . or by any overt act or deed, every person so offending shall be guilty of felony, and being convicted thereof shall be liable, . . . to be transported beyond the seas for the term of his or her natural life . . . [123]

The Court of Appeal in England allowed the editor to proceed with his claim for a declaration on the proper construction of section 3 of the 1848 Act and with his

[117] Treason felony, an offence under the Treason Felony Act 1848, is comparable to treason but has never carried a mandatory death penalty.

[118] See Law Commission Working Paper No 72: Codification of the Criminal Law—Treason, Sedition and Allied Offences 1977, para 47.

[119] ibid, para 78; the Commission thought not only that there was a sufficient range of other offences covering conduct amounting to sedition but also that it was better in principle to rely on these other offences than on one which has the implication that the conduct in question is 'political': ibid.

[120] HL Deb, vol 712, col 850, 9 July 2009 (Lord Bach).

[121] ibid, col 845.

[122] [2003] UKHL 38, [2004] 1 AC 357.

[123] Under the Criminal Law Act 1967, s 1, the reference in s 3 of the 1848 Act to 'felony' is to be read as a reference to an offence. Under the Penal Servitude Act 1857 and the Criminal Justice Act 1848 the penalty under s 3 is now imprisonment for life or any shorter period.

alternative claim for a declaration that the section was incompatible with Article 10 of the European Convention. But the House of Lords disagreed. Quite apart from the fact that it was reluctant to make an exception to the normal rule that courts will not make declarations *in abstracto* as to whether certain future conduct would be lawful,[124] their Lordships thought the litigation was unnecessary. Lord Steyn stated the position with admirable pithiness:

> The part of section 3 of the 1848 Act which appears to criminalise the advocacy of republicanism is a relic of a bygone age and does not fit into the fabric of our modern legal system. The idea that section 3 could survive scrutiny under the Human Rights Act is unreal.[125]

And in the words of Lord Scott:

> [T]he United Kingdom is a mature democracy and in a mature democracy people do not get prosecuted for advocating political change by peaceful and constitutional means.[126]

Such clarity is of course to be welcomed, and should indeed have been expected, but it remains uncertain what attitude the courts would adopt if they were faced with slightly more difficult circumstances. What, for instance, if the facts of *Arrowsmith v United Kingdom*[127] were to recur? The applicant there, a pacifist, was convicted under the Incitement to Disaffection Act 1934 and given a seven-month prison sentence for distributing leaflets at an army camp encouraging soldiers to leave the army rather than go and fight in Northern Ireland. The Court of Appeal upheld the conviction and the European Commission of Human Rights also held that Article 10 had not been breached.[128] The Commission accepted that, in view of the applicant's manifest intention to continue her action unless stopped by prohibitive measures, the decision to prosecute her was necessary for the protection of national security and the prevention of disorder in the army. One would hope that today a more robust approach would be taken by both the domestic and the European Court. Cannot soldiers be expected to resist such calls for their desertion? Is not criminalizing such advocacy just as much a relic of a bygone age as criminalizing advocacy of the abolition of the monarchy?

It may be that the prosecution of Pat Arrowsmith is best explained by the fact that she was distributing her leaflets in Wiltshire, England. The authorities in Northern Ireland, to their credit, have not been quick to resort to such strong-arm tactics in the fight against views they do not happen to like. Even the offences of inviting support for a proscribed organization,[129] or displaying an article arousing reasonable suspicion of support for such an organization,[130] have not been vigorously prosecuted. Conversely, no-one has seriously argued that proscribing organizations such as the

[124] Lord Steyn thought this was an exceptional case [25], but Lord Rodger did not [57].

[125] [2003] UKHL 38, [2004] 1 AC 357, [28].

[126] ibid, [46]. Lord Walker added: 'It is inconceivable that [s 3] could be invoked in the 21st century in order to punish anyone who advocates that a republican form of government should be established by peaceful means.' [60]

[127] (1978) 3 EHRR 218.

[128] There was a convincing dissent from Torkel Opsahl of Norway.

[129] Now an offence under the Terrorism Act 2000, s 12(1).

[130] Terrorism Act 2000, s 13(1).

IRA and UVF is an unjustifiable denial of anyone's right to freedom of expression,[131] and the House of Lords has recently upheld the proscription of the Real IRA even though the legislation did not on its face seem to extend that far.[132] It has, off and on, been an offence to fail to disclose information to the police or army which might be of assistance in preventing an act of terrorism or in apprehending someone involved in such an act,[133] but here again there have been few prosecutions. The 'ordinary' law in Northern Ireland also makes it an offence to fail to give the police information about an arrestable offence committed by some other person,[134] but this too is virtually a dead letter. In England and Wales the comparable offence requires the concealer of information to have accepted some consideration in exchange for not disclosing it.[135]

One might have thought that, in the context of so many street protests in Northern Ireland, there would have been a number of cases where persons have challenged their conviction for public order offences on the basis that these infringed their right to freedom to express themselves or to manifest their beliefs. But if this has occurred it is not recorded in the law reports. However, the formerly common procedure of binding someone over 'to be of good behaviour' has been held by the European Court to contravene Article 10, primarily because it leaves so vague what is or is not permissible under the order.[136] There is equally little evidence to suggest that the laws prohibiting incitement to hatred in Northern Ireland are being systematically enforced, even in the face of a rising incidence of racial attacks. The Public Order (NI) Order 1987[137] makes it an offence to use or display threatening, abusive or insulting words or behaviour, with intent to stir up hatred or fear of a section of the Northern Ireland community, or where such fear or hatred is likely to be stirred up. The fear or hatred must be directed against a group of persons defined by religious belief, sexual orientation, disability, colour, race, nationality, or ethnic or national origins.[138] It is not an offence to use such words or behaviour in a private dwelling, provided that the person concerned has no reason to suppose that the words or behaviour will be seen or heard outside. It is similarly an offence under the 1987 Order[139] to publish, distribute, play, or show written or taped material which is threatening, abusive, or insulting, with the intention of stirring up fear or hatred or where such fear or hatred is likely to be aroused. And it is an

[131] Although this still appears to be the position of the Committee on the Administration of Justice, a human rights NGO based in Belfast. The Proscribed Organisation Appeals Commission has been established to hear complaints about refusals to de-proscribe an organization: Terrorism Act 2000, s 5 and Sch 3.

[132] *R v Z* [2005] UKHL 35, [2005] 2 AC 645.

[133] See, currently, Terrorism Act 2000, s 38B, inserted by the Anti-terrorism, Crime and Security Act 2001, s 117.

[134] Criminal Law Act (NI) 1967, s 5.

[135] Criminal Law Act 1967, s 5(1).

[136] *Steel v UK* (1999) 28 EHRR 603 and *Hashman and Harrap v UK* (1999) 30 EHRR 241.

[137] art 9.

[138] ibid, art 8, as amended by the Criminal Justice (No 2) (NI) Order 2004, art 3. In England and Wales the Public Order Act 1986 contains similar, but not identical, offences. The Racial and Religious Hatred Act 2006 extends the 1986 Act to religious hatred. There was fierce opposition to this, even among many religious groups, and a number of amendments were passed by Parliament, including a protection for freedom of expression (s 29K).

[139] arts 10 and 11.

offence to possess such material with a view to publishing, displaying, or distributing it.[140] Finally, under the Criminal Justice (No 2) (NI) Order 2004, courts in Northern Ireland are able to increase the sentence imposed upon someone for an offence if the offence was aggravated by hostility based on the victim's actual or presumed racial group, religious belief, sexual orientation, or disability.[141] Official statistics on how frequently the offences listed above have been charged in Northern Ireland, or how many convictions have been obtained, appear to be unavailable. If the laws on incitement were enforced it is possible that defendants could successfully rely on their Article 10 rights,[142] although the European Court may well conclude that in a conflicted society such as Northern Ireland the authorities must be given an even wider margin of appreciation than normal. By the same token, there is probably little that can be done under the European Convention to insist that such prosecutions be initiated in the first place.

Prisoners and journalists

One of the commonest varieties of judicial review applications in Northern Ireland is those made by prisoners. In recent years a few of these have raised points under Articles 9, 10, or 11. In *Re Dowdall's Application*[143] a convicted sex offender argued that the prison's refusal to put him on an 'enhanced' regime unless he admitted his guilt of a sexual crime and agreed to take part in an Offender Behaviour Programme was a breach not just of his Article 9 right to freedom of belief but also of his Article 10 right to freedom of expression. Not surprisingly, the Court of Appeal rejected both suggestions. We saw in Chapter 10, on the right to a private life, that courts have more than once rejected prisoners' claims to be able to wear certain symbols, the restrictions being deemed to be justifiable within the terms of Article 10(2). But the most significant decision in recent years regarding prisoners' rights to free speech (apart from *Hirst v United Kingdom*, on the right to vote, discussed above) is that of the House of Lords in *R v Secretary of State for the Home Department, ex parte Simms*,[144] where it was held that the Home Secretary's policy of imposing a blanket ban on prisoners giving face-to-face interviews to journalists about whether their convictions were safe or not (in the absence of undertakings from the journalists not to publish the results of the conversations) was unlawful. In interpreting the relevant Prison Standing Order,[145] their Lordships applied the 'principle of legality', whereby legislation, even if it is not ambiguous, has to be construed in a way that upholds fundamental or basic rights.[146] This important ruling affects prisoners and journalists

[140] art 13.

[141] art 2(3).

[142] As did the applicants, successfully, in *Sadik Ahmet v Greece* App No 18877/91, decision of 4 April 1995, and *Incal v Turkey* App No 22678/93, decision of 9 June 1998.

[143] [2003] NICA 8.

[144] [2000] 2 AC 115.

[145] paras 37 and 37A of Standing Order 5A, issued under the Prison Act 1952, s 47.

[146] Lord Steyn, who gave the leading speech, cited the examples given by Lord Browne-Wilkinson, and by himself, in *R v Secretary of State for the Home Department, ex p Pierson* [1998] AC 539, 573G-575D and 587C–590A.

in Northern Ireland as well as those elsewhere in the United Kingdom. Once again we see the impact of changing times on human rights standards: during the worst years of the conflict in Northern Ireland it would have been inconceivable that any paramilitary prisoner would have been allowed to give face-to-face interviews to a journalist.

Journalists continue to want to keep their sources confidential, at least in most situations, and they claim this right on the basis of Article 10 of the Convention. They argue that their freedom of expression would be unduly compromised—and democracy considerably weakened as a result—if they could be forced to divulge who told them what. In *Re Clements' and Moloney's Applications*, at first instance,[147] the Recorder of Belfast was prepared to order journalists to disclose notes of meetings they had held with their sources. He saw no incompatibility between the statutory authority for such an order, which was part of the anti-terrorist laws,[148] and Article 10 of the European Convention. On appeal, however, the Divisional Court found it unnecessary on the facts to make such a disclosure order.[149] In the more recent case of *Re Detective Inspector Galloway's Application* the current Recorder of Belfast, Judge Burgess, refused to order Sunday Tribune journalist Suzanne Breen to disclose her interview notes and other related information concerning an article she had written about the Real IRA after its murder of two British soldiers in Antrim in March 2009.[150] The judge said that Ms Breen's life would be at real and immediate risk if she released the information in her possession, though he was careful to say that a journalist's right to keep his or her sources confidential is not an absolute one. The decision is certainly not a basis on which to argue that the relevant anti-terrorism measure allowing disclosure to be compelled is incompatible with Article 10 of the European Convention.[151]

In 2001 the journalist Martin O'Hagan paid with his life for his investigative journalism in Northern Ireland, even though he had *not* revealed his sources.[152] His murder illustrates the immense dangers facing some journalists in Northern Ireland but, unlike after the murder of Veronica Guerin in Ireland in 1996, there has not been a comparable degree of outrage in the North. The Police Service of Northern Ireland has not yet been successful in bringing anyone to justice for the killing. To make matters worse, the PSNI showed scant regard for the rights of journalists when, in 2003, they raided the home of two journalists, Liam Clarke and Kathryn

[147] 2 September 1999: <http://www.courtsni.gov.uk/en-gb/judicial+decisions/judgments/j_j_ruling19990902.htm>.

[148] At the time of the case the legislation was the Prevention of Terrorism (Temporary Provisions) Act 1989, Sch 7, para 3(5); today it is the Terrorism Act 2000, Sch 5, para 6(3). This states that one of the conditions which has to be satisfied before a judge will order journalistic material to be disclosed is that there are reasonable grounds for believing that it is in the public interest that the material should be produced having regard... (b) to the circumstances under which the person concerned has any of the material in his possession, custody or power.

[149] [2000] NIJB 195.

[150] [2009] NICty 4.

[151] Other decisions emanating from Strasbourg seem to endorse the non-absolute status of a journalist's right to protect sources: see Brady (2004) 14–21 and *Financial Times Ltd and others v UK* App No 821/03, decision of 15 December 2009.

[152] He was shot dead by loyalist paramilitaries on 28 September 2001.

Johnston, as well as the Belfast offices of *The Sunday Times*, following the publication of the paperback edition of Clarke and Johnston's biography of Martin McGuinness, which included transcripts of private telephone conversations between McGuinness and a government spokesman.[153] The journalists were arrested for alleged breaches of the Official Secrets Act 1989. An investigation by the Police Ombudsman concluded in October 2004 that the search of the journalists' home was 'poorly led and…an unprofessional operation'.[154] She upheld complaints that the particular search warrant used by the police did not authorize them to seize material held for journalistic reasons—surely an elementary mistake for a police service to make in the context of a highly sensitive investigation? But the Police Ombudsman did not substantiate complaints about the need for the journalists' arrest, the disproportionate timing of their arrest, or the legality of their detention. She made disciplinary recommendations in respect of eight officers involved in the operation, ranging in rank from Constable to Chief Superintendent.

Journalists have also sought to protect their sources during the Saville Tribunal of Inquiry into the events on Bloody Sunday in 1972. Alex Thomson and Lena Ferguson, two reporters with Channel Four News, refused to disclose the source of their information about the original Widgery Inquiry into Bloody Sunday, which they had broadcast in a series of reports in 1997 and 1998. In 2002 the journalists were told by Lord Saville that they would face contempt proceedings, but in 2004 he reversed this ruling, saying: 'it is unlikely that any further action will produce new information of real value…'.[155] It remains to be seen whether the unverifiability of the information supplied by the journalists will make the report of the Tribunal, now due for publication in March 2010, any less convincing.

Given the context, it is perhaps a little surprising that sources were not voluntarily revealed during the Bloody Sunday Inquiry. For journalists can, of course, waive their right to secrecy, as Jacky Rowland and Martin Bell of the BBC did in 2002 during the trial of Slobodan Milosevic for crimes against humanity at the UN's International Criminal Tribunal for the former Yugoslavia in The Hague.[156] A journalist with *The Washington Post*, Jonathan Randal, took the opposite position during the trial of former Bosnian Serb Deputy Prime Minister Radoslav Brdjanin; he was at first ordered by the Tribunal to testify, but the Appeals Chamber set aside the subpoena.[157] In doing so, it was careful to limit its judgment to the case of war reporters. With respect, one would have thought that the more serious the crime (and it is difficult to think of crimes more serious than those against humanity itself) the more indefensible is the 'right' of journalists reporting it not to disclose information to a court or tribunal of inquiry. Admittedly there will always be difficult borderline

[153] Clarke and Johnston (2001).

[154] See Police Ombudsman press release dated 3 October 2004.

[155] See <http://www.channel4.com/news/articles/politics/domestic_politics/bloody+sunday+inquiry+rules+in+favour+of+itn/254193>, last visited 17 August 2009.

[156] Ed Vulliamy of *The Observer* also testified during the trial of General Blaškić.

[157] *Prosecutor v Brdjanin* (Decision on Interlocutory Appeal) IT-99–36 (11 December 2002): <http://www.icty.org/x/cases/brdanin/acdec/en/randall021211.htm>.

cases,[158] but the right of journalists to preserve the secrecy of their sources must, like virtually all rights, be a limited one.

Belief and identity issues

In *Re Treacy's and Macdonald's Applications*[159] two prominent barristers claimed that their Article 10 rights had been breached by the requirement that before being accepted as Queen's Counsel in Northern Ireland they would have to declare that they would serve the Queen. Kerr J, as he was then, held that the requirement had no impact on their freedom of expression:

> They are not required to express or to refrain from the expression of any political view by making the declaration. They are merely required to confirm that they will supply a suitable professional service to the Queen if they choose to accept instructions from the Crown. This undertaking involves no expression of political opinion whatever. No breach of Article 10 arises, therefore.[160]

Five years earlier another barrister from Northern Ireland had complained to Strasbourg about the same oath (without taking any domestic proceedings), but his application was declared inadmissible on the rather flimsy ground that, as he had not yet been offered the position of Queen's Counsel and not therefore asked to swear any oath, his Article 9 and 10 rights had not come into play.[161] Notwithstanding these court defeats, the wording of the required declaration was soon altered to take account of the barristers' concerns. It seems that the Lord Chancellor, Lord Irvine, had not previously been aware that the senior judges in Northern Ireland had not been consulted by the Lord Chief Justice, Sir Robert Carswell, about the need for a change. Unlike the declaration used in Great Britain, it now simply reads: 'I do sincerely promise and declare that I will well and truly serve all whom I may lawfully be called upon to serve in the office of one of Her Majesty's Counsel learned in the law according to the best of my skill and understanding'.[162] By legislation adopted in 2002 a change was also made to the oath to be taken by judges, magistrates, and most tribunal members in Northern Ireland. It now reads: 'I [name] do swear that I will well and faithfully serve in the office of [eg judge of the High Court] and that I will do right to all manner of people without fear or favour, affection or ill-will according to the laws and usages of this realm.'[163] The version used in England and Wales is: 'I

[158] Such as that of the New York Times journalist Judith Miller, who in 2005 spent 85 days in prison for refusing to disclose the source for information about an undercover CIA operative found in one of her notebooks.

[159] [2000] NI 330.

[160] ibid, para 131.

[161] *Magee v UK* App No 24892/95, decision of 6 April 1995. A more enlightened approach to the position of potential victims of human rights violations was taken by the European Commission and Court in *Dudgeon v UK* (1981) 4 EHRR 149, the case on homosexuality in Northern Ireland (see ch 10 above, 297).

[162] HL Deb, vol 614, col 622, 26 June 2000 (Lord Irvine LC).

[163] Justice (NI) Act 2002, s 19(2).

[name] do swear by Almighty God that I will well and truly serve our Sovereign Lady Queen Elizabeth the Second in the office of [eg judge of the High Court], and I will do right to all manner of people after the laws and usages of this realm, without fear or favour, affection or ill will'. In 2007 one of the applicants in the case highlighted above was himself appointed as a judge of the High Court and took the new oath.[164]

Just as some people in Northern Ireland are keen to make their religious or political background clear, others prefer to keep it hidden, to have a mixed identity, or to be classified as neither Protestant nor Catholic, neither nationalist nor unionist. The domestic fair employment legislation, however, does not allow them complete freedom to make this choice. It requires all firms employing more than 10 people to register with the Equality Commission, and all registered employers, together with all public authorities, are required to monitor the composition of their workforce in terms of the workers' 'community background'.[165] The employer can directly ask the employee whether he or she comes from a Protestant or Catholic background, but if this question is not answered the employer can use a residuary method for ascertaining that background.[166] This method can include consideration of the employee's name, the primary school he or she attended, and the clubs or societies he or she belongs to.[167] An employer can treat an employee as if the community to which he or she belongs cannot be determined only if the other methods for determining that community fail. Employers have to tell their employees which community they have been categorized as belonging to and, while employees have seven days in which to challenge this categorization, employers can persist with it if they think they have not made a mistake.[168] Once a year the information collected by employers in this way is returned to the Equality Commission so that it can identify and keep under review patterns and trends of employment in Northern Ireland.[169] The information supplied to the Commission must be treated confidentially both by the employer[170] and by the Commission,[171] but on the basis of what it finds the Commission can issue directions to employers to take steps to improve 'fair participation' in its workforce through affirmative action.[172]

The monitoring system was obviously put in place to help to ensure that employers in Northern Ireland would be aware of the need not to discriminate against people from one or other of the community backgrounds. Religious and political discrimination in the workplace had been one of the most regrettable features of Northern Ireland society prior to the outbreak of the troubles in 1968.[173] But one can see that the current system runs the danger of entrenching divisions by effectively

[164] Seamus Treacy. He also accepted the knighthood that customarily accompanies such an appointment (no oath of allegiance is required for such an honour).

[165] Fair Employment and Treatment (NI) Order 1998, arts 48(1), 48(2) and 52–4.

[166] Fair Employment (Monitoring) Regs (NI) 1999, reg 8(1) and Sch 2, Pt I.

[167] ibid, regs 11(1), 11(3) and Sch 3.

[168] ibid, regs 12 and 13.

[169] Fair Employment and Treatment (NI) Order 1998, art 10.

[170] Fair Employment (Monitoring) Regs (NI) 1999, reg 16.

[171] Fair Employment and Treatment (NI) Order 1998, art 18.

[172] ibid, arts 12–14.

[173] Though some academics remain sceptical: Hewitt (1981), Gudgin (1999).

forcing people to be designated as coming from one particular community background or another even though for very many years they may have ceased to have any significant affiliation to that, or either, community. People who switch religions, or who give up all religious belief, or who are children from a mixed marriage and went to an integrated school, all have grounds for feeling that they are being treated as a member of a group that they do not want to belong to. It seems, though, that there is nothing in the European Convention to prevent this labelling process occurring. No individual's freedom of belief or of association is affected by the monitoring system, because even when an employee or job applicant happens to be of the background whose representatives the employer in question wants to boost, it would be a breach of the discrimination laws to allocate a post to that person on that basis alone, even in a 'tie-break' situation where there are two otherwise indistinguishable applicants and only one of them is from the under-represented community.[174]

Many would applaud the fact that the European Convention is flexible enough to accommodate the monitoring arrangements. Others think this is a rather undesirable flexibility because it does not encourage Northern Ireland to make community background a totally irrelevant factor in employment. They fear what Amartya Sen has referred to as the 'miniaturization' of people through labelling.[175] These critics point to another human rights treaty produced by the Council of Europe—the Framework Convention on National Minorities, agreed in 1995—which provides that: 'Every person belonging to a national minority shall have the right freely to choose to be treated or not to be treated as such'.[176] But it is difficult to use this provision to challenge the fair employment monitoring regulations in Northern Ireland. First, the Framework Convention speaks only of national *minorities*, which leaves open the question whether a group in a particular part of a State can be a minority even though it is part of a majority if the State is looked at as a whole. Second, the Convention does not define the term *national* minority, although it does refer to the duty on States to preserve the essential elements of the minority's identity, namely its religion, language, traditions, and cultural heritage, which suggests that religious communities can form 'national' minorities. Third, the Framework Convention only confers the right not to be *treated* as belonging to a national minority, and it is questionable whether the use made by the Equality Commission of the monitoring information confidentially supplied by employers amounts to 'treatment', even though the monitoring regulations themselves repeatedly refer to employers 'treating' employees as belonging to a community.

[174] The Equality Bill currently proposed for Great Britain (but not Northern Ireland) may permit this kind of positive action: see cl 158.

[175] Sen (2006) xiii: 'When the prospects of good relations among different human beings are seen (as they increasingly are) primarily in terms of "amity among civilizations," or "dialogue between religious groups," or "friendly relations between different communities" (ignoring the great many different ways in which people relate to each other), a serious miniaturization of human beings precedes the devised programs for peace.' At 13 and 160 he is disparaging about segregated schooling in Northern Ireland.

[176] Art 3(1). The UK ratified the Framework Convention in 1998 and it came into force later that same year.

The Northern Ireland Human Rights Commission, in its 2001 and 2004 draft Bills of Rights, tried to ensure that people had the right not to be treated as members of a community if they did not want to be,[177] but this met with some opposition.[178] In its 2008 advice to the UK government on what should be contained in a Bill of Rights for Northern Ireland the NIHRC no longer pressed the point.[179]

Recruitment to the police

One of the features of the governance of Northern Ireland after the partition of the island in 1920 was that the composition of the police force became ever more Protestant. While this might well have been the result, to some extent, of direct religious discrimination on the part of the recruiting authorities, it was also partly due, especially during the three decades of the most recent conflict period, to intimidation by republican paramilitary groups, who viewed Catholics[180] who joined the police as collaborators with the enemy. Many members of the police were killed merely because they were Catholics. A major challenge for those who were asked to consider how to reform the police, in the wake of the Belfast (Good Friday) Agreement of 1988, was how to increase the proportion of Catholics in the police so that it was fairly close to that in the population as a whole (ie around 40–45 per cent). The solution hit upon was that of positive discrimination. The rules governing recruitment were drafted so that 50 per cent of each new batch of recruits has to profess to be Catholics, even if this means that better qualified non-Catholics are denied a position.[181]

Such a solution is a drastic one, so much so that the UK government had to negotiate with its fellow governments in the European Union a special exemption for the provision in EU laws on religious discrimination.[182] The question then arose whether such positive discrimination was compatible with European Convention law. On the face of it one would have thought not, because it is surely a basic human right not to be discriminated against merely because of one's religious belief. But in fact the Convention tolerates such discrimination quite easily, for two main reasons. First, it does not directly confer on anyone a right to a job, so Article 14 of the Convention (which protects people from being discriminated against in their enjoyment of 'the rights and freedoms set forth in this Convention') is of no assistance to disap pointed job-seekers. We will see in the following chapter how the European Court

[177] NIHRC (2001b) 21–4; NIHRC (2004) 29–33.

[178] eg McCrudden (2007b).

[179] The explanatory section on 'The right to identity and culture' refers (at 101) to Art 3(2) of the Framework Convention ('Persons belonging to national minorities may exercise the rights and enjoy the freedoms flowing from the principles enshrined in the present Framework Convention individually as well as in community with others') but not to Art 3(1): NIHRC (2008) 101. See too Harvey and Schwartz (2009) 193–9 and Craig (2009) 210–1.

[180] Ryder (2000b).

[181] Police (NI) Act 2000, s 46. The measure was initially due to last just three years, but it has been twice renewed since then for further three-year periods.

[182] EU Framework Directive for Equal Treatment in Employment and Occupation, 2007/78/EC, Art 15(2).

has managed to sidestep this obstacle by relying on Article 6 of the Convention to give a remedy to applicants who have been denied jobs or contracts because they are supposedly a security risk, but when the reason for non-appointment is not some inscrutable national security consideration but an overt State policy to construct a more representative police service for the whole community, Article 6 does not seem to be engaged. Second, while Article 9 of the Convention gives everyone the right to freedom of thought, conscience, and religion, including the freedom to manifest his or her religion or belief in worship, teaching, practice, and observance, it says nothing about guaranteeing people of different religions or beliefs the right to equal opportunity in the workplace.

Hence, when a Protestant man who had been denied entry as a trainee officer in the Police Service of Northern Ireland claimed that his rights under the Convention had been violated, he lost.[183] The domestic courts had no real difficulty in upholding the new law and in declaring it to be compatible with the Convention. The disappointed litigant does not seem to have lodged an application in Strasbourg, no doubt because his legal advisers told him that his chances of succeeding there would be virtually nil. In 2001, when the Police Service of Northern Ireland replaced the Royal Ulster Constabulary, the percentage of Catholics in the police was just 8 per cent. By October 2009 it was 27.58 per cent.[184] Given that the target set for Catholic membership of the police when the positive discrimination system was initiated was 30 per cent, the special rules may need to be kept in place for one more year when the current period expires in 2010.[185]

Parades

Undoubtedly one of the most contentious aspects of the troubles in Northern Ireland has been the use of marches or parades by different sections of the community to demonstrate their identity and allegiances. On the Protestant side this is most clearly manifested in the processions organized by the Orange Order; on the Catholic side there are processions (much fewer in number) organized by the Ancient Order of Hibernians, as well as various commemorative parades by republicans marking anniversaries such as the introduction of internment in 1971 or the hunger strikes in 1981. The fact that the unrest which broke out in the late 1960s is associated in most people's minds with the civil rights marches of those days is further reason to see freedom of assembly as a very sensitive issue in Northern Ireland.

One might reasonably have expected that in the regulating of parades the standards deducible from the European Convention would have played a significant

[183] *Re Parsons' Application* [2003] NICA 20, [2004] NI 38.

[184] Northern Ireland Office, Consultation Paper, *Police (NI) Act 2000—Review of Temporary Recruitment Provisions*, 2. On aspects of policing and human rights in Northern Ireland since 1998, see Dickson (2006b).

[185] This is what the Northern Ireland Office is currently proposing (see consultation paper in n184).

role.[186] The truth is that it soon became apparent that the Convention's standards were not yet sophisticated enough to allow for a generally acceptable solution to marching disputes to be reached. The Convention's guarantee of the right to freedom of assembly in Article 11 is perhaps too absolute to allow for a nuanced approach to the regulation of contentious marches: while the Article may give people a wide-ranging right to march, the practical consequences of exercising that right in a deeply divided society may be such that it is folly for an adjudicating or law-enforcement body to insist upon the right's vindication at virtually all times.

For most of the 1970s and 1980s violence regularly flared at predictable times, usually around 12 July, when the Orange Order commemorates the victory of King William III over King James II at the Battle of the Boyne, a river flowing north of Dublin, in 1690. While it was possible to ban the holding of parades connected with Northern Ireland in other jurisdictions, it was just not feasible to do so in Northern Ireland itself, where the potential for wide-scale civil unrest attendant on any such ban was very great. In 1995, in *Rai, Allmond and 'Negotiate Now' v United Kingdom*,[187] the European Commission upheld a ban on demonstrations relating to Northern Ireland in London's Trafalgar Square. The applicants had wished to hold a rally there, for about 1,000 people, to be addressed by speakers who would be calling for the government to open negotiations with Sinn Féin (who had not yet renounced their support for violence) to try to agree a settlement to the conflict in Northern Ireland. The police had no objection to the rally but the government's Department of National Heritage refused to permit it[188] because of government policy concerning meetings in Trafalgar Square on issues related to Northern Ireland. This policy had been in place since 1972 and had been applied by all governments since then with rare exceptions, such as when the Peace People wanted to hold an event in the Square in 1976.[189] The European Commission decided that the ban pursued a legitimate aim, namely the prevention of disorder:

> ...in the circumstances of Northern Ireland where sensitive and complex issues arise as to the causes of the conflict and any possible solutions, the Government can be considered in its general policy of banning demonstrations concerning the subject to be pursuing the aim of preventing disorder and protecting the rights and freedoms of others.[190]

The Commission then went on to hold that the ban was both 'necessary in a democratic society' and 'proportionate'. The assessment as to whether the applicants' desire

[186] For details on the domestic law of Northern Ireland on the right to freedom of assembly see Dickson and Hamilton (2003), and also the equivalent chapters in earlier editions of that book published in 1990, 1993, and 1997.

[187] 81-A DR 146, decision of 6 April 1995. The applicants were represented by John Wadham, of the NGO Liberty.

[188] Its permission was required under the Trafalgar Square Act 1844, the Parks Regulation (Amendment) Act 1926, s 2(1), and the Trafalgar Square Regulations 1952, para 3.

[189] Other exceptions were made for the Apprentice Boys of Derry in 1984, the Irish Congress of Trade Unions in 1978, and 'Peace '93' in 1993. Rev Ian Paisley had made a political speech at the Apprentice Boys' meeting, which the government later said was a breach of the agreement with that organization and a basis for the government's intention of 'avoiding any repetition of that sort of incident': 81-A DR 146, 150.

[190] ibid,151.

to push for unconditional negotiations over the future of Northern Ireland was controversial was said to be within the government's margin of appreciation. Moreover the Commission rejected the applicants' ingenious argument that the rarely invoked Article 18 of the Convention could assist them. This article provides that: 'The restrictions permitted under this Convention to the said rights and freedoms shall not be applied for any purpose other than those for which they have been prescribed'. The applicants contended that the Trafalgar Square ban was applied to them because their views shocked or offended the government, a reason which the European Court had previously ruled would not be enough to justify a restriction on free speech.[191] But the Commission felt that the evidence showed that the government had not acted with this motive.[192]

The decision in the *Negotiate Now* case, which provoked little if any comment at the time, is indicative of the width of the margin of appreciation which the Convention organs were prepared to allow to State parties when devising policies to deal with serious civil unrest. While at one level the underlying rationale for a hands-off approach may be understandable, the consequence was that the Convention organs were not able to be a positive force for change in the Northern Ireland conflict. If an international treaty on human rights cannot even guarantee the right of campaigners to hold a rally calling for a negotiated settlement to a long-running internal conflict in a distant part of the State, it is surely failing in a crucial respect.

In the 1990s the intercommunal violence attendant upon some Orange Order marches within Northern Ireland became focused on one particular march—that to the Church of Ireland in Drumcree, County Armagh. On the way back from the church the Orange Order wanted to walk along a road which they had traditionally used but on which many more Catholics now resided than before, 'the Garvaghy Road'. To avoid the risk of violent clashes the police ordered the march to be re-routed and took steps to enforce this decision, calling in the army to assist.[193] There was frequent and serious violence over a number of summers.[194] Eventually, in the period when inter-party talks were commencing in the run-up to the Belfast (Good Friday) Agreement, the government appointed an English legal academic, Dr Peter North, to prepare a report with recommendations as to how best to regulate marches in the future.[195] As a result of this report Westminster passed the Public Processions (NI) Act 1998 and put on to a statutory footing[196] a Parades Commission for Northern Ireland.[197] The Commission took over from the police the responsibility for deciding whether to reroute marches,[198] the hope being that a quango whose membership was 'as far

[191] *Handyside v UK* (1979–80) 1 EHRR 737, para 49.

[192] On the same ground a complaint based on Art 14 of the Convention (the right not to be discriminated against) was rejected.

[193] See, generally, Hadden and Donnelly (1997); Bryan (1998); Jarman (1999); Bryan (2000).

[194] Ryder and Kearney (2001).

[195] North (1997).

[196] The Parades Commission was brought into being in February 2007 on a non-statutory basis, but with mediation and conciliation functions only. See McAuley (1998).

[197] Dickson (2005b) 451–5.

[198] The police were not able to ban marches, only to re-route them. Bans were, and still are, the prerogative of the Secretary of State: see Dickson and Hamilton (2003) 174–5.

as is practicable... representative of the community in Northern Ireland'[199] would stand a greater chance of gaining widespread community acceptance. In fact, the Commission became the *bête noire* of the Orange Order,[200] some elements of which to this day refuses to meet with the Commission in direct talks. Nationalists, too, were sceptical. A challenge was raised to the first set of appointments by a nationalist residents' group from the Ormeau Road, in Belfast,[201] but it failed.[202] A later application for judicial review brought on gender grounds[203] by a female resident of the Garvaghy Road in Portadown also failed, one indicator of the prevailing judicial mindset at the time being that the Lord Chief Justice, Sir Robert Carswell, intimated in his judgment that he thought 'representative of the community' in this context meant representative of Catholics and Protestants, not of men and women.[204] There was nothing in the European Convention that the applicant could point to which promoted the claim of women in this regard.[205]

One of the controversial aspects of the new statutory scheme for regulating processions was that it gave the Parades Commission the right to impose conditions on processions not only if public disorder or damage to property might otherwise result[206] but also if there might be disruption to the life of the community or an impact on relationships within the community.[207] It could also have regard to a person's failure to comply with the Commission's Code of Conduct and to the desirability of continuing to allow processions to be held along a customary route.[208] These might seem like sensible factors to take into account, but their compatibility with Article 11 of the European Convention is potentially problematic because Article 11(2), as interpreted by the enforcement organs, does not seem to embrace them. When the Northern Ireland Human Rights Commission was brought into existence in 1999, just a few months after the Human Rights Act 1998 was enacted (but some 18 months before it would come fully into force), one of the first questions it was asked was, what exactly did the European Convention allow and/or require in this context? At a meeting between representatives of the Parades and Human Rights Commissions it was clear that the former believed that the latter could give guidance on this issue which would help to

199 Public Processions (NI) Act 1998, Sch 1, para 2(3). There are valuable annotations to this Act by Imelda McAuley in Current Law Statutes.

200 Kaufmann (2007) 236–65.

201 The Lower Ormeau Concerned Community.

202 *Re Armstrong's Application* (1998, unreported; Kerr J).

203 All seven members appointed to the Commission at that time were men.

204 *Re White's Application* [2000] NI 432, 440a–g. But in *In re Duffy* [2008] UKHL 4, [2008] NI 152 the House of Lords ruled that it was improper of the Secretary of State for Northern Ireland to appoint two members of the Orange Order to the Parades Commission. The Court of Appeal of Northern Ireland had held otherwise.

205 The Northern Ireland Human Rights Commission had been allowed to make a written (but not oral) intervention in the case, and tried to argue that various international human rights treaties (if not the European Convention) strongly suggested that public bodies should be gender-balanced, but this received short shrift from the Lord Chief Justice (ibid, 445e–g): 'I do not consider that any of the provisions of the several conventions cited by the Human Rights Commission adds anything of consequence to those of domestic law.

206 Public Processions (NI) Act 1998, s 8(6)(a).

207 ibid, s 8(6)(b) and (c). For further insights on this see Hamilton (2005).

208 ibid, s 8(6)(d) and (e).

ensure a resolution of the marching disputes in Northern Ireland.[209] Alas, that was wishful thinking, because the jurisprudence on Article 11 was not, and is still not, sufficiently nuanced to allow such guidance to be formulated. The NIHRC commissioned a study on the matter from academic experts[210] but this too, while thorough and clear, could not conjure out of the air guidance that simply did not exist in any of the decisions already taken in Strasbourg. At one point the Northern Ireland Office consulted the NIHRC on whether the provisions of the Human Rights Act 1998 should be commenced earlier than planned (in the spring of 2000) so as to allow challenges to be made to decisions of the Parades Commission based on Convention rights, but the NIHRC advised against this on the basis that commencing the Act early in such a specific way would be detrimental to the reputation of the Human Rights Act more generally.[211] In the end the government decided not to commence the Act early.

Representatives of the Orange Order and like-minded groups[212] engaged with the NIHRC, arguing strongly that at several locations around Northern Ireland their basic right to freedom of assembly was being denied to them because of restrictions imposed on proposed processions by the Parades Commission. Yet challenges brought against decisions of the Parades Commission in judicial review proceedings consistently failed,[213] and it would appear that at no point was any application lodged in Strasbourg. It is interesting to speculate what the attitude of the European Court would have been if it had been asked to adjudicate on, say, the refusal to allow the Orange Order to march down the Garvaghy Road in Portadown in early July. Very likely it would have ruled that re-routing such a march was an interference with the right to march that was perfectly legitimate and proportionate in the circumstances and that the State had not exceeded its margin of appreciation in so determining. But the Court might have been less sympathetic to the Parades Commission in relation to other decisions where the principal underlying reason for the decision to re-route a local march was the need to avoid the possibility of disorder flaring up elsewhere in Northern Ireland. The Court might have been of the view that such an approach by the Commission to a human rights claim was in effect supporting those who sought to prevent others from exercising their human rights by threatening or using violence if they did so. That would have been a failure by the State to apply Article 17 of the Convention.[214] The European Court has not made significant use of Article 17 to

[209] For a summary of the debates within the NIHRC on the relevance of the European Convention to the Parades Commission see Dickson (2007a) 215.

[210] Hamilton, Jarman and Bryan (2001).

[211] See Dickson (2007a) 211.

[212] eg Ulster Human Rights Watch.

[213] *Re Patricia Pelan's Application* (1998); *Re Kevin Farrell's Application* (1999); *Re Joseph McConnell's Application* (1999); *Re Rachel Campbell's Application* (2000); *Re David Tweed's Application* (2000). These are all unreported judgments mentioned in Hamilton, Jarman and Bryan (2001). The Court of Appeal of Northern Ireland later affirmed the High Court's decisions in three of these cases: *Re McConnell's Application* [1999] NICA 9; *Re Tweed's Application* [2001] NI 165; *Re Pelan's Application* [2001] NICA 35. These appeal decisions can be accessed on the website of the British and Irish Legal Information Institute (<http://www.bailii.org>).

[214] Art 17 reads: 'Nothing in this Convention may be interpreted as implying for any State, group or person any right to engage in any activity or perform any act aimed at the destruction of any of the rights and freedoms set forth herein or at their limitation to a greater extent than is provided for in the Convention.'

date,[215] no doubt because it fears that to do so could unduly restrict the way it might in future wish to interpret the limitations on rights listed in the second paragraphs of Articles 8, 9, 10, and 11, but it did use it to reject a complaint brought by a British National Party activist in England who had been charged with a public order offence after displaying a highly provocative poster on the window of his house.[216] Very provocative 'speech' by extreme loyalists or republicans in Northern Ireland should be treated similarly.

The issue of whether the current law governing determinations by the Parades Commission of Northern Ireland was compatible with the European Convention did eventually come before the Court of Appeal of Northern Ireland in *Re Tweed's Application (No 5)*.[217] On the specific question of the compatibility of the provision allowing the Commission to impose conditions on a parade because of the impact it may have on relationships within the community, Girvan LJ explained that it is compatible if the power is used to attain one of the purposes listed in Articles 9(2), 10(2), or 11(2) of the Convention. Those purposes include the prevention of disorder and the protection of the rights of others. Though he admitted that 'Strasbourg and domestic case law has not fully or finally established the full parameters of what constitute rights and freedoms to which regard may properly be had',[218] he concluded that:

> Where the impact on relationships within the community brings into play enhanced risks of public disorder, damage to property, criminality (which may fall short of public disorder but of its nature impacts on the rights and freedoms of others) or other types of interference with the legitimate rights and freedoms of others then that impact on relationships within the community would be a proper matter to which the Commission could have regard when exercising its section 8 powers.[219]

The learned judge went on to mention that the European Court has already said that in the context of religious opinions there is an obligation under Article 10 of the Convention to avoid as far as possible expressions that are gratuitously offensive to others,[220] and that the State is under a duty to take steps to protect people against anti-social behaviour or nuisances which subject them to significant interference with the enjoyment of their home environment.[221] He also held that the decision taken by the Parades Commission was not disproportionate nor procedurally unfair.

A further avenue open to those who feel that their right to assemble has been violated is to argue that their right to a fair hearing in relation to the matter has been breached. This is indeed what a leading member of the Orange Order did when challenging the restrictions imposed by the Parades Commission on a procession planned for Easter Sunday 2004 along a 325-yard stretch of road in Dunloy, a predominantly Catholic village in County Antrim.[222] He contended that unless he was given sight

[215] Reid (2008) 344; Van Dijk et al (2006) 750–5.
[216] *Norwood v UK* (2004) 40 EHRR SE111. See Wadham et al (2007) 238–9.
[217] [2009] NICA 13. See also the recommendations in SRP (2008).
[218] ibid, para 9.
[219] ibid. See too para 24, per Sir Anthony Campbell.
[220] ibid, para 10, citing *Otto Preminger v Austria* (1994) 19 EHRR 3.
[221] ibid, para 10, citing *Moreno Gomez v Spain* (2005) 41 EHRR 40.
[222] The 2001 census suggested that 97 per cent of the residents in the village were Catholic.

of the full documents (and not just summaries prepared by the Parades Commission) which had been supplied to the Commission by the police and other assessors, and based to some extent on information conveyed confidentially, he could not satisfactorily present his case for the restrictions not to be imposed. In interlocutory (ie preliminary) proceedings Girvan J ordered the documents to be disclosed under the proportionality doctrine implicit in the European Convention, but the Parades Commission successfully appealed to the Court of Appeal of Northern Ireland. The Law Lords, however, restored the decision of the judge, with Lord Carswell, a former Lord Chief Justice of Northern Ireland, giving the principal judgment.[223] He quoted extensively from Lord Steyn's seminal judgment on proportionality in *R (Daly) v Secretary of State for the Home Department*,[224] and was careful to say that he would apply the new approach to disclosure whether it was Article 9(2), 10(2), or 11(2) of the Convention that was at issue. Lord Brown added, for good measure:

> ... the courts may be expected to show a somewhat greater readiness than hitherto to order disclosure of the main documents underlying proportionality decisions, particularly in cases where only a comparatively narrow margin of discretion falls to be accorded to the decision-maker (*a fortiori* the main documents underlying decisions challenged on the ground that they violate an *unqualified* Convention right, for example under Article 3).[225]

Thus has the conflict in Northern Ireland again given rise to a new, more human rights friendly approach, to the adjudication of disputes over Convention rights throughout the United Kingdom.

One more example of this occurring emerges from an even more contentious episode during the conflict in Northern Ireland, again one that post-dates the Belfast (Good Friday) Agreement. This was when, in 2001, loyalist protestors tried to prevent girls from attending a Catholic primary school in north Belfast because they were discontent at what they saw as the increasing dominance of Catholics in the locality. The police initially required the children and their adult companions to approach the school using a different road, but they then decided it was better to allow the usual route to be used and they sought to contain the protestors so that none of the children or adults would be injured by the protestors. The mother of a child who felt that the police were not doing enough to protect her and her daughter brought judicial review proceedings challenging the Chief Constable's decisions in relation to the policing arrangements.[226] Interestingly, her lawyers claimed a breach of Article 3 of the Convention (the right not to be subjected to ill-treatment)[227] and do not seem to have relied upon Article 11,[228] perhaps fatally so because the applicant lost in all of the courts which considered the case, with none of the nine judges

[223] *Tweed v Parades Commission for Northern Ireland* [2006] UKHL 53, [2007] 1 AC 650.

[224] [2001] 2 AC 532, [27] and [28].

[225] [2006] UKHL 53, [2007] 1 AC 650, [57].

[226] The NIHRC agreed to support the applicant in her proceedings, although this led to considerable upheaval within the Commission itself.

[227] There is therefore discussion of the case in ch 7 above, at 164–5.

[228] In the High Court and Court of Appeal they did also rely on Arts 2 and 14, and on Art 2 of Prot 1, but the judges rejected those claims too.

thinking the police had violated Article 3.[229] The reasoning of the judges, though, is perhaps a little odd, for they all justified not interfering with the police's decision on the basis that the police were in a better position than anyone else to assess whether more forceful policing near the Holy Cross School in North Belfast would have led to outbreaks of violence elsewhere in Northern Ireland. At first instance, for example, Kerr LCJ said:

> Those who had to decide how to deal with this protest were obliged to have regard to the effect that their decisions might have in the wider community. It is not difficult to understand that an aggressive, uncompromising approach to the protest might have been the catalyst for widespread unrest elsewhere. It is precisely because the Police Service is better equipped to appreciate and evaluate the dangers of such secondary protests and disturbances that an area of discretionary judgment must be allowed them, particularly in the realm of operational decisions.[230]

A better reason for not interfering with the police's decision, it is respectfully submitted, is that more forceful policing of this protest could have significantly enhanced the risks to the lives and safety of the children and adults walking to this particular school. In the words of Baroness Hale:

> ...I do not think it has been demonstrated that, had the police behaved at the outset in the way in which it is now said that they should have behaved, the children's experience would have been any better. Indeed, it could have been a great deal worse. They were in very real physical danger at the beginning. On 5 September [2001] an explosive device was thrown into the road where they were walking but thankfully injured no one. The difficulties and dangers to them in doing what it is now suggested should have been done cannot be ignored.[231]

Granting the police a wider discretion to police in a certain way because violence might be committed by others elsewhere is, one could argue, tantamount to allowing threats of violence to diminish the exercise of the right to march, to protest, or simply to walk to school or the shops. While it is appropriate to defer to the views of experienced police officers when they are seeking to control a crowd or determining how best to deploy their resources, it is not appropriate to sacrifice basic human rights in the interests of political expediency more generally. The European Court has not pronounced on this issue to any great extent in its judgments to date, but it appears that the applicant in the Holy Cross case has since lodged an application in Strasbourg, so some guidance may be forthcoming soon.

The House of Lords did correct the lower courts in one respect in the Holy Cross case. It said that the test to be applied when assessing police behaviour had been altered, by the House itself, in its 2007 decision in *Huang v Secretary of State for*

[229] *E v Chief Constable of the Royal Ulster Constabulary* [2004] NIQB 35 (Kerr LCJ); [2006] NICA 37 (Campbell and Sheil LJJ, and Gillen J); [2008] UKHL 66, [2008] 2 WLR 1208 (Lords Hoffmann, Scott, Carswell, and Brown, and Lady Hale).

[230] [2004] NIQB 35, [46]. For comparable remarks in the Court of Appeal and House of Lords see [2006] NICA 37, [89] per Campbell LJ, and [2008] UKHL 66, [2008] 2 WLR 1208, [58] per Lord Carswell.

[231] [2008] UKHL 66, [2008] 2 WLR 1208, [14].

the Home Department.[232] Rather than the courts looking to see whether the public authority's decision was unreasonable, in the sense that it was beyond the range of responses open to a reasonable decision-maker bearing in mind the degree of interference with human rights it entailed,[233] they now have to make their own assessment of whether a public authority has acted incompatibly with Convention rights. But the House said that this change of test did not mean that the actual outcome of the lower court's analysis in the Holy Cross case had to be changed too.[234]

Conclusion

As the concepts of 'belief', 'expression', and 'association' in Articles 9 to 11 of the Convention are all flexible, it is likely that in the years ahead lawyers in Northern Ireland will deploy even greater ingenuity than heretofore in arguing that an aspect of their client's rights guaranteed by these provisions has been put in question by some initiative.[235] To date, however, the articles have not been very effective in preventing the State in Northern Ireland from imposing restrictions on broadcasting rights, voting and electioneering rights, rights to demonstrate, and even rights to express one's identity.

The area is ripe for further development. We could well see the argument raised that requiring someone to adopt a certain position on an issue (for example, that he or she knows certain things, or pledges to do or not do certain things) is itself a denial of the right to freedom of expression. To date such mandated speech has been regulated only by reference to other articles in the European Convention, such as Article 6, which protects the right to a fair trial,[236] or Article 8, which protects the right to a private and family life. But the ever-present danger from terrorists—whether 'home-grown' or imported—will doubtless also mean that restrictions will continue to be

232 [2007] UKHL 11, [2007] 2 AC 167.

233 This was the test laid down by the Court of Appeal in England in *R v Ministry of Defence, ex p Smith* [1996] QB 517 (the 'gays in the army' case), but it had been found by the European Court to be inadequate to ensure compliance with Art 6 of the Convention: *Smith and Grady v UK* (1999) 29 EHRR 493, para 138.

234 Understandably, this was the positive dimension to the House's decision which the NIHRC chose to highlight in its press release issued on 12 November 2008.

235 Cf *Re Misbehavin' Ltd's Application* [2004] NIQB 61, where applicants who had been refused sex establishment licences in Belfast resorted to relying on Art 10 arguments. Weatherup J had little difficulty in holding that any interference there may have been with Art 10(1) had been justified under Art 10(2). His decision was reversed by the Court of Appeal of Northern Ireland ([2005] NICA 35) but restored by the House of Lords ([2007] UKHL 19, [2007] 1 WLR 1420), where it was stressed that the relevant question on judicial review was not whether the council had given proper consideration to the applicant's Convention rights but whether those rights had actually been violated.

236 See, eg, the discussion in ch 8 above of *Saunders v UK* (1996) 23 EHRR 313; *IJL, GMR and AKP v UK* (2000) 33 EHRR 225; and *R v Lyons* [2002] UKHL 44, [2003] 1 AC 976. See too *Shannon v UK* (2006) 42 EHRR 31, discussed in ch 8 at 202–3, and *Clinton v Bradley* [2000] NI 196, where the accused had not already been charged with an offence when he was interviewed by the police. In *Brown v Stott* [2003] 1 AC 681 the requirement on a car owner in Scotland to identify the driver of his or her car at any particular time was held by the Privy Council not to infringe Art 6, and the European Court reached a similar conclusion in *O'Halloran and Francis v UK* (2008) 46 EHRR 21 (15 v 2).

placed on Article 10 and 11 rights. The UK's Terrorism Act 2006 already outlaws statements intended to be, and likely to be understood as, 'a direct or indirect encouragement or other inducement to the commission, preparation or instigation of acts of terrorism',[237] and statements glorifying the commission of such acts, whether in the past, in the future, or generally, are to be taken as outlawed under this heading if members of the public could reasonably be expected to infer that the conduct 'should be emulated by them in existing circumstances'.[238] At least one commentator has suggested that the phrase 'in existing circumstances' may be too vague to satisfy the European Court's insistence on certainty in the law.[239] The general approach to Article 10 adopted by the European Court in the early case of *Handyside v United Kingdom*[240] will, one hopes, generally be maintained in the face of such new laws, although without the same degree of deference to State discretion under the guise of the doctrine of margin of appreciation. In *Handyside* the Court upheld the British ban on 'The Little Red Schoolbook', but in doing so it emphasized that Article 10 *is* intended to protect information and ideas 'that offend, shock, or disturb the State or any sector of the population'.[241] Criminalizing speech is extremely dangerous in a democracy. Liberty thrives in a free thinking, expressive, and associating society.[242]

[237] s 1(1).

[238] s 1(3)(b).

[239] Hoffmann (2006).

[240] (1979–80) 1 EHRR 737. See too *Hertel v Switzerland* App No 25181/94, decision of 25 August 1998, [46]. The approach in *Handyside* was approved by the then UK Home Secretary, Jack Straw, in HC Deb, vol 315 col 539 (2 July 1998).

[241] (1976) 1 EHRR 737 [49]. These governing principles were confirmed by the European Court in *Vogt v Germany* (1995) 21 EHRR 205.

[242] One good sign in this context is the decision by the European Court in *Steel and Morris v UK* (2005) 41 EHRR 403 (the 'McLibel case'), where it took the opportunity to strongly reaffirm just how important free speech is for the proper functioning of a fully healthy democracy. The Court held that the lack of procedural fairness and equality experienced by two campaigning defendants who were sued for defamation by the fast-food chain McDonald's was a breach not only of Art 6 of the Convention but also of Art 10. The denial of legal aid to the defendants, and the size of the compensation awards made against them in the English courts (£76,000 in total), were cited as evidence of the unfairness. The Court said (at para 95): 'The more general interest in promoting the free circulation of information and ideas about the activities of powerful commercial entities, and the possible "chilling" effect on others are also important factors to be considered in this context, bearing in mind the legitimate and important role that campaign groups can play in stimulating public discussion.'

12

Freedom from Discrimination

As explained in Chapter 2, the conflict in Northern Ireland has to a very large extent been about discrimination. Discrimination in granting employment, in giving access to housing, in making arrangements for voting, and in tolerance of cultural practices and political ideas. To a degree such discrimination was inevitable because Northern Ireland was founded on the understanding that unionist Protestants would be allowed to dominate the political scene: this was the inevitable by-product of partition, which divided Ireland on the basis of the national allegiance and religious beliefs of the vast majority of the people living in the two parts of the island. Of course this did not have to mean that the groups in power in each part would actively work to disempower the minority groups, but in practice such disempowerment was always going to occur to some extent. It was part and parcel of the 1920 settlement. Politicians at the time must have realized this, but were content to let partition proceed on the basis that it was the lesser of two evils. It would avoid an immediate bloody civil war (although a pretty bad civil war occurred anyway, mainly in the South of the island) and would provide for relative political stability, at least temporarily.

The potential for discrimination to occur in both parts of Ireland on the grounds of religious belief was clearly foreseen in the 1920 settlement because section 5(1) of the Government of Ireland Act 1920 provided that:

> In the exercise of their power to make laws under this Act neither the Parliament of Southern Ireland nor the Parliament of Northern Ireland shall make a law so as either directly or indirectly to establish or endow any religion, or prohibit or restrict the free exercise thereof, or give a preference, privilege, or advantage, or impose any disability or disadvantage, on account of religious belief or religious or ecclesiastical status, or make any religious belief or religious ceremony a condition of the validity of any marriage, or affect prejudicially the right of any child to attend a school receiving public money without attending the religious instruction at that school, or alter the constitution of any religious body except where the alteration is approved on behalf of the religious body by the governing body thereof, or divert from any religious denomination the fabric of cathedral churches, or, except for the purpose of roads, railways, lighting, water, or drainage works, or other works of public utility upon payment of compensation, any other property, or take any property without compensation.
>
> Any law made in contravention of the restrictions imposed by this subsection shall, so far as it contravenes those restrictions, be void.

This provision restricting Parliamentary authority was mirrored by section 8(6) of the Act, which dealt with executive authority:

> In the exercise of power delegated to the Lord Lieutenant[1] in pursuance of this section no preference, privilege, or advantage shall be given to, nor shall any disability or disadvantage be imposed upon, any person on account of religious belief except where the nature of the case in which the power is exercised itself involves the giving of such a disability or disadvantage.

Brigid Hadfield has pointed out that sections 5(1) and 8(6) are to some extent based on provisions which had been included in the constitutions of other former British possessions, in particular the First Amendment to the US Constitution and section 9 of the Commonwealth of Australia Constitution.[2] But Hadfield also reminds us that no Act of the Northern Ireland Parliament was ever deemed to be void for contravention of the principle of religious equality and that in 1981 the then Under-Secretary of State for Northern Ireland admitted in answer to a Parliamentary question at Westminster that he was not aware of any provisions which discriminated between persons or classes of persons on the ground of religious belief.[3] The unionist government in Northern Ireland certainly believed its legislation was always constitutional:

> I do not know any case offhand—I may be wrong in this—in which our legislation has been condemned as unconstitutional. There were two occasions in the Court of Appeal in Northern Ireland in which that result has arisen but they are, I think, now generally recognised to be questionable in view of the most recent decision of the House of Lords in the O D Cars case.[4]

The part of section 5 which gave rise to most litigation was the part prohibiting the taking of any property without compensation, which was interpreted by the Northern Ireland courts as protecting *all* property and not just ecclesiastical property.[5] It was repealed by the Northern Ireland Act 1962,[6] an Act which extended the powers of the Parliament of Northern Ireland in several other respects as well. It relaxed the restrictions imposed by the 1920 Act so as to permit the Northern Ireland Parliament to compulsorily acquire land belonging to a religious denomination or educational institution for the purposes of housing, slum clearance, or development.[7] But that was not a discriminatory provision.

In the common law world the 1960s was an era when the realization dawned that the law could do a lot more to make societies more equal places. The starting location for this appreciation was the United States, where momentous decisions of the Supreme Court in the 1950s, especially *Brown v Board of Education*,[8] paved the way in ensuing years for a whole host of 'civil rights' litigation—and legislation. In the United Kingdom this trend was manifested by the enactment of measures such as the Race Relations Acts in

[1] In Northern Ireland this post became that of the Governor.

[2] Hadfield (1989) 79.

[3] ibid, 78. See HC Deb, vol 14, cols 376–7 (3 December 1981) per John Patten MP.

[4] HC Deb (NI), vol 54, col 2027 (16 June 1964), per the Attorney General, Ted Jones. The case he mentions is *OD Cars Ltd v Belfast Corp* [1960] AC 490.

[5] In *O'Neill v NIRTB* [1938] NI 104 and *Robb v Electricity Board for NI* [1937] NI 103.

[6] s 14.

[7] s 13(1)(a) and (b).

[8] 347 US 483 (1954).

1965 and 1968 and the Parliamentary Commissioner Act in 1967. The latter was complemented in Northern Ireland by the Parliamentary Commissioner Act (NI) 1969 and the Commissioner for Complaints Act (NI) 1969 which, among other things, allowed people to lodge complaints about discrimination allegedly practised by public bodies in Northern Ireland and required these to be investigated by Ombudsmen. In fact these officials did not then encounter too many instances of religious discrimination in their work,[9] though this may be because victims of such discrimination were unwilling to put their heads above the parapet or because the difficulties of proving on the balance of probabilities that decisions were taken for a sectarian motive were just too great.[10] This was also the decade in which judges in England and Wales began to develop the principles whereby they were prepared to review the decisions of public bodies. The House of Lords issued seminal rulings in this area in *Ridge v Baldwin*,[11] *Padfield v Minister of Agriculture, Fisheries and Food*,[12] *Conway v Rimmer*,[13] and *Anisminic Ltd v Foreign Compensation Commission*.[14]

Religious and political discrimination

Following the imposition of direct rule in 1972 a new system of devolved government in Northern Ireland was provided for by the Northern Ireland Constitution Act 1973.[15] It operated for only five months in 1974,[16] but other provisions of the 1973 Act dealing with discrimination remained in force until replaced by those in the Northern Ireland Act 1998, which provided for yet another system of devolved government. Section 17 of the 1973 Act mirrored section 5 of the Government of Ireland Act 1920 in that it rendered void any legislative provision applying in Northern Ireland to the extent that it discriminated against any person or class of person on the ground of religious belief or political opinion. Section 19 made it unlawful for public or local bodies to discriminate against any person or class of persons on the ground of religious belief or political opinion. The term 'discrimination' is defined in wide terms in the Act,[17] as meaning treating a person less favourably than another person 'in any circumstances', which would embrace indirect as well as direct discrimination. Moreover the Act makes it explicit that the victim of religious or political discrimination perpetrated by a public or local body can sue for compensation.[18] And

[9] eg, in 1972 the Commissioner for Complaints received 431 complaints, but only 11 of these alleged religious or political discrimination. During that year he also investigated 11 cases but found no evidence of discrimination in any of them.

[10] Carroll (1973) 52–5.

[11] [1964] AC 40.

[12] [1968] AC 997.

[13] [1968] AC 910.

[14] [1969] 2 AC 147. For a discussion of the significance of these cases see Griffith (1993) 79–109 and Blom-Cooper and Drewry (2009).

[15] See Hadfield (1999b).

[16] It was brought down by the Ulster Workers' Council strike. See Fisk (1975).

[17] s 23.

[18] s 19(2).

a special body was established to advise the Secretary of State on whether the law on religious and political discrimination was working effectively to prevent it and to provide redress when it occurred. So important was the topic that this body was called the Standing Advisory Commission on Human Rights, not the Standing Advisory Commission on Discrimination. SACHR, as it became known, was to continue in existence for 25 years and was to broaden its remit considerably during that time.[19]

For the present study it is unnecessary to examine just how widespread was the religious discrimination practised in Northern Ireland during 'the unionist era' from 1921 to 1972.[20] The most respected analysis of that issue was conducted by John Whyte,[21] who concluded that there was indeed discrimination, particularly West of the River Bann (in Counties Fermanagh and Tyrone). He said it was most evident in the fields of electoral practices, private *and* public employment, policing, public housing, and regional policy. Whether the discrimination was ever so serious as to justify the use of violence is, of course, a different question.[22]

The extent and effects of, and the efforts to combat, religious discrimination in Northern Ireland after direct rule from Whitehall and Westminster was imposed in 1972 have been valuably explored by Cormack and Osborne in two edited collections.[23] In an overview of the evolution of policies designed to deliver equality of employment opportunities,[24] they point in particular to the report of the Working Party chaired by a junior government minister, William van Straubenzee, in 1973, which led to the enactment—at Westminster—of the Fair Employment (NI) Act 1976, which itself created the Fair Employment Agency (FEA). In conducting investigations of employment practices to see whether they accorded with principles of equality of opportunity the Fair Employment Agency was required to follow a government document called the *Guide to Manpower Policy and Practice*, published in 1978. The 1976 Act also permitted the Agency to direct employers to put in place affirmative action programmes (sometimes involving the use of goals and timetables) if they had been found not to have afforded equality of opportunity.

The 1976 Act and the work of the FEA were subjected to much criticism, though sometimes the Agency was blamed for the limitations imposed on it by the Act itself, a matter beyond its control. McCrudden was probably the harshest critic,[25] with more measured assessments being made by Appleby and Ellis[26] and by SACHR.[27]

[19] See also ch 2 above, at 17–20.

[20] See generally Schmitt (1976).

[21] Whyte (1983). John Whyte was a highly respected political scientist at Queen's University Belfast from 1966 to 1984.

[22] Hewitt (1981), Hewitt (1991). At the end of the latter piece (at 37) Hewitt says: 'Although Catholics had legitimate reasons to complain about the situation, their grievances do not seem sufficient to explain the kind of mass violence that was provoked by the civil rights campaign. Instead the evidence suggests that the civil rights movement was essentially nationalist inspired, seeking not the reform but the overthrow of the northern Irish state.'

[23] Cormack and Osborne (1983); Cormack and Osborne (1991).

[24] Cormack and Osborne (1991) ch 1.

[25] McCrudden (1983).

[26] Appleby and Ellis (1991) ch 9; cf the performance of similar bodies in Great Britain: Appleby and Ellis (1984).

[27] SACHR (1987).

Smith and Chambers say that regulation under the 1976 Act was 'ineffective'.[28] It was in 1985 that the then Secretary of State for Northern Ireland, Douglas Hurd, announced a review of the existing approach to equality of opportunity. Cormack and Osborne identify the main drivers of this review as being the report of the Fair Employment Agency's investigation of the Northern Ireland Civil Service published in 1983, the production of the so-called MacBride Principles in 1984,[29] the publication in 1985 of the government's Continuous Household Survey which revealed that unemployment rates for Catholic men and women were still much higher than for Protestant men and women, and the pressure exerted by the Irish government in the wake of the Anglo-Irish Agreement of November 1995.

The MacBride Principles, drafted in the USA to mirror the Sullivan Principles applicable to South Africa, were designed to increase the commitment of those US pension funds which were considering investing in US companies operating in Northern Ireland to do so only if the firms they invested in abided by proper fair employment practices. Although the principles, in Cormack's and Osborne's terms, were 'relatively innocuous', the British government consistently opposed them, as did the unionist parties and the nationalist Social and Democratic Labour Party (SDLP). The only local political party to support them was Sinn Féin, which at the time was still refusing to condemn the use of violence to counter the British presence in Northern Ireland. The fact that the Principles were named after a former 1930s Chief of Staff of the IRA, albeit someone who had since shared the Nobel Peace Prize in 1974[30] and become a respected member of the Republic of Ireland's legal profession, did not enhance their attractiveness to many in the North. Moreover, there was a doubt about whether applying all of the Principles would be legal in Northern Ireland, since Principle 8 required 'the establishment of procedures to assess, identify and actively recruit minority employees with potential for further advancement'. This looked suspiciously like positive discrimination, which the 1976 Act did not countenance (and nor did any other anti-discrimination legislation in the UK or Ireland at the time). It might also have been contrary to European Community law, which had already emerged as the leading engine of change regarding discrimination in the employment context, though as yet still focused on discrimination based on gender. Although this particular MacBride principle was 'amplified' two years later to make it clear that it was not intended to imply 'that such procedures should not apply to all employees equally', it did little to placate opponents of the Principles in general.

The review of the government's approach to equality of opportunity was undertaken by SACHR, which reported in 1987.[31] In seeking to find the cause of the differences between the employment profiles of the Protestant and Catholic communities SACHR reviewed the possible influence of regional factors, differential labour markets, class differences, differences in education, differences in attitudes to work, age, family size, the chill factor (ie people not wanting to work in places considered

[28] Smith and Chambers (1991) 372.

[29] These are discussed in the next paragraph.

[30] This was for his international peace work, especially in Namibia.

[31] SACHR (1987).

hostile), security occupations, and the black economy. Having decided that these factors did not account for all of the differences, and in the absence of other plausible explanations, SACHR concluded that the remaining differences were probably due to religion.[32] In one of the research studies published alongside SACHR's report the author, David Smith, went further and suggested that all the differences which could not be accounted for by other factors must be the result of religious discrimination.[33]

The SACHR report did result in new legislation, the Fair Employment (NI) Act 1989, the innovative features of which were the replacement of the Fair Employment Agency with the Fair Employment Commission and the addition of a statutory duty on the enforcement body to promote affirmative action to help redress existing imbalances in the workforce. The government also undertook to commission yet another review of the legislation after five years, again giving this responsibility to SACHR. It was actually eight years before the outcome of this further review was published,[34] but it too led to a government White Paper and to legislation, the Fair Employment and Treatment (NI) Order 1998. This Order added to the earlier legislation by authorizing the use of positive discrimination to help the long-term unemployed and by extending the prohibition on religious and political discrimination from the employment context to that of access to goods, facilities, and services. Later in 1998, in the Northern Ireland Act implementing the Belfast (Good Friday) Agreement, the government legislated for the merger of the Fair Employment Commission with other anti-discrimination bodies in Northern Ireland to form the Equality Commission,[35] and it conferred upon that new body the duty to monitor the operation of section 75 of the Act, which requires all public bodies in Northern Ireland to produce 'equality schemes' showing how they will promote equality of opportunity between different groups in society, including different religious groups and people of different political opinions. There was some opposition to this merger, especially from the smaller existing bodies, which felt that the resources allocated to their issues would be reduced if a merger took place. The Equality Commission for Northern Ireland nevertheless came into being on 1 October 1999.

The relevance of the European Convention

During the whole of the period which has just been reviewed the role of the European Convention on Human Rights was minimal. Why was this? If religious and political discrimination was so important in the conflict in Northern Ireland, why could the

[32] '[I]t is reasonable to suppose that religion is the most likely explanatory factor which accounts for at least some if not most of the residual element': ibid, 35.

[33] Smith (1987). Cormack and Osborne took issue with Smith's conclusion, accusing him of using the term 'discrimination' too loosely; see Cormack and Osborne (1991) 24–5. See too Smith and Chambers (1991), who say with respect to the difference between Protestant and Catholic male unemployment rates that, 'after discounting the joint effects of five factors (age, socio-economic group, number of children, qualifications, and area of residence)... [i]t must be concluded that Protestant and Catholic men have substantially unequal opportunities for employment in Northern Ireland' (at 371).

[34] SACHR (1997); Magill and Rose (1997).

[35] Northern Ireland Act 1998, ss 73–4 and Sch 8.

European Convention not do anything to counter it? Given that the Second World War had developed out of repellent discrimination exercised against Jews and others in Germany, and that one of the aims of the Convention had been to ensure that this kind of mass human rights abuse could not happen again in Europe, why was the Convention so ineffective in Northern Ireland?

There are perhaps two answers to this conundrum, one contextual, the other technical. The contextual argument is that the discrimination which was experienced in Northern Ireland was already addressed by the local law but the victims of the practice had difficulty in proving discrimination to the satisfaction of a judicial body. It was only after a number of years that campaigners for better discrimination laws realized that, just as important as the substance of the laws is the procedure available to enforce them. If, for example, the burden lies on the complainant to produce evidence that he or she has been discriminated against, this requires him or her to obtain information from the employer or other alleged discriminator concerning the exact practices used by that organization when acting prejudicially. Moreover, showing that particular influences are the cause of the discrimination is also difficult and too often the more likely causes are not within the power of the alleged discriminator to do anything about (for example, the reputation of the neighbourhood where the workplace is situated, or the lack of qualified applicants available within the minority pool).

The technical reason for the irrelevance of the Convention was that its discrimination provision—Article 14—is limited to protecting people against the way in which 'the enjoyment of the rights and freedoms set forth in this Convention shall be secured'. True, it goes on to list 11 grounds on which such discrimination can be challenged, not forgetting the catch-all phrase at the end—'or other status', but these grounds can be invoked only in relation to the differential enjoyment of 'the rights and freedoms set forth in this Convention'.[36] The sorts of 'rights' which were at issue in the discrimination claims emerging from Northern Ireland were rights to a job, to social housing, to fair electoral boundaries, and to impartial administration. These were not rights 'set forth' in the Convention. The European Convention was less progressive in this respect than the UN's International Covenant on Civil and Political Rights of 1966, which contains a more general anti-discrimination provision, a provision which in fact confers a positive right to equality as well as a negative right not to be discriminated against.[37] Moreover the European Convention does not contain a provision protecting 'group rights', unlike the International Covenant,[38] and, even if it had done so, such a provision might not have availed the victims of discrimination in Northern Ireland because for the most part they were not complaining about

[36] Art 14. See generally Livingstone (1997).

[37] Art 26 reads: 'All persons are equal before the law and are entitled without any discrimination to the equal protection of the law. In this respect, the law shall prohibit any discrimination and guarantee to all persons equal and effective protection against discrimination on any ground such as race, colour, sex, language, religion, political or other opinion, national or social origin, property, birth or other status.'

[38] Art 27 reads: 'In those States in which ethnic, religious or linguistic minorities exist, persons belonging to such minorities shall not be denied the right, in community with the other members of their group, to enjoy their own culture, to profess and practise their own religion, or to use their own language.'

denial of their right to collectively enjoy their culture, to profess and practise their religion, or to use their language.

Article 14 also makes no reference to indirect as opposed to direct discrimination and for a long while it was not clear whether the Strasbourg bodies would interpret it as protecting against the former.[39] The breakthrough did not come until 2000, a year or so after the European Court became a full-time institution. In *Thlimmenos v Greece* the Court said that '[t]he right not to be discriminated against in the enjoyment of the rights guaranteed under the Convention is also violated when States without an objective and reasonable justification fail to treat differently persons whose situations are significantly different'.[40] Two years later, in one of the Northern Irish cases that went to Strasbourg concerning the right to life, the applicant argued that the high number of killings of Catholics and members of republican paramilitary groups by the security forces and police, compared with a disproportionately low number of prosecutions and convictions, indicated that the security forces were using lethal force against civilians and members of paramilitary groups in a highly discriminatory fashion.[41] The Court rejected the claim, but conceded that it was one which, if supported by credible evidence, might fall within the purview of Article 14:

> Where a general policy or measure has disproportionately prejudicial effects on a particular group, it is not excluded that this may be considered as discriminatory notwithstanding that it is not specifically aimed or directed at that group. However, even though statistically it appears that the majority of people shot by the security forces were from the Catholic or nationalist community, the Court does not consider that statistics can in themselves disclose a practice which could be classified as discriminatory within the meaning of Article 14. There is no evidence before the Court which would entitle it to conclude that any of those killings, save those cases which resulted in convictions, involved the unlawful or excessive use of force by members of the security forces.[42]

Early drafts of Article 14 had qualified the protection it granted against discrimination on the basis of political or other opinion by saying that it applied only if such opinion was professed without violence.[43] But this qualification was removed by 12 votes to three (with one abstention) at the sitting of the relevant Committee of the Consultative Assembly on 30 August 1949.[44] During the debates of the Committee on Legal and Administrative Questions a proposal was made by Mr Lannung, from Denmark, on the need for wider protection of the rights of national minorities (he had in mind the Danes who then lived in South Schleswig, in Germany). The Committee decided that it should confine its proposed list of fundamental rights to those which appeared suitable for inclusion in an immediate international guarantee, rather than including fundamental rights which must be defined in a general declaration, but it

[39] Lester, Pannick and Herberg (2009) 606–9.

[40] (2001) 31 EHRR 15, para 44.

[41] *McShane v UK* (2002) 35 EHRR 23, para 133.

[42] ibid, para 135.

[43] See, eg, the summary of the Convention's content contained in the proposals made at the sitting on 29 August 1949 of the Council of Europe's Consultative Assembly's Committee on legal and administrative questions: *Travaux Préparatoires* (1975), vol 1, 168.

[44] ibid, 178.

added that the attention of the Committee of Ministers should be drawn to the need for the rights of national minorities to be subsequently examined and defined.[45] In its report the Committee's non-discrimination clause read as follows:

> The fundamental rights and liberties enumerated above shall be guaranteed without any distinction based on race, colour, sex, language, religion, political or other opinion, national or social origin, membership of national minority, fortune or birth.[46]

In the draft European Convention on Human Rights prepared by the European Movement and submitted to the Consultative Assembly of the Council of Europe, freedom from discrimination (albeit only on the grounds of religion, race, national origin, or political or other opinion) was included as a free-standing right, not one which was parasitic on other rights.[47]

In the late 1960s, as we saw in Chapter 3, the deficiencies of the Convention as regards protecting people in Northern Ireland against discrimination in voting arrangements, the allocation of social housing, or the awarding of jobs, were all too apparent. The Irish government tried to have these rectified by proposing to the Council of Europe's Consultative Assembly[48] that it request the Council of Ministers to instruct the Committee of Experts on Human Rights to draft an additional Protocol to the Convention which would prohibit discrimination on any grounds in those fields (and also in the field of law enforcement).[49] The Assembly did indeed issue such a recommendation[50] and the Committee of Experts produced a report on the matter, but the Committee of Ministers, no doubt after pressure had been exerted by the United Kingdom's delegation, resolved only that Council of Europe States should take steps at the national level to repeal discriminatory laws and promote anti-discriminatory practices.[51] No other meaningful steps were taken by the Committee of Ministers vis-à-vis discrimination in Northern Ireland.

In a volume which reviews the main case law of the European Court of Human Rights from its first decision in 1960 to the end of 1987,[52] Vincent Berger, a senior legal officer at the Court's Registry, cites no case in which alleged religious discrimination featured. This is an aspect of a wider problem with the Court's approach to Article 14, namely, that it has been unwilling to develop the Article even within the constraints imposed by its wording. This neglect has been particularly unfortunate for those parts of Europe where the discrimination in question has been part of a

[45] ibid, 54, 200. Mr Lannung had proposed that the European Charter (as it was then called) should contain a provision saying 'National minorities should be assured a free life with a free enjoyment of their own cultural development': ibid, 182.

[46] Draft Article 5: ibid, 208. When the Consultative Assembly came to consider this report at its 15th sitting on 5 September 1949 the wording of the last line had changed to 'affiliation to a national minority, fortune or birth': ibid, 230.

[47] This draft ECHR is published as an Appendix to the *Travaux Préparatoires* (1975) vol 1, 296.

[48] In 1994 the Council's Committee of Ministers decided to rename the body 'the Parliamentary Assembly'.

[49] Consultative Assembly, 21st session, 29 September to 30 October 1969 (Doc 2653).

[50] Rec 583/70.

[51] Res (72)22.

[52] Berger (1989); this summarizes 117 decisions of the Court and supplies useful references to secondary literature on the decisions.

wider picture reflecting a deep-seated sectarianism in the society. In the words of Philip Leach:

> It has been the stated practice of the Court not to examine a complaint under Article 14 where a substantive breach of the substantive Article [on which Article 14 is 'parasitic'] has been found, unless a clear inequality of treatment is a fundamental aspect of the case.[53] In the many cases against Turkey brought since the mid-1990s, concerning a wide range of violations of the rights of the Kurdish community in Turkey, the Court has declined to find violations of Article 14. That was the position too in the earlier Roma cases brought against Bulgaria...[54]

In some of the early cases taken to Strasbourg from Northern Ireland efforts were made to claim a breach of Article 14, usually on the basis that the alleged breach of the substantive right was one which was more likely to be inflicted on members of the Catholic or nationalist community than on members of the Protestant or unionist community. These all failed. The argument was also rejected in *Jordan v United Kingdom*,[55] one of the important cases on the extent of the State's obligation to conduct a thorough inquiry into a mysterious death, where the applicant argued that the so-called 'shoot-to-kill' policy of the police in Northern Ireland was targeted disproportionately at nationalists. The Court said that the claim, as with all previous attempts to raise it, had not been supported by sufficient evidence.

It is regrettable that, even when the European Court was given a clear opportunity to develop its application of Article 14 in a non-troubles related case from Northern Ireland, *Dudgeon v United Kingdom*,[56] it failed to do so. Having found a breach of Article 8, because the State was criminalizing private sexual conduct between adult consenting males, the Court, by 14 votes to five, said that it was unnecessary to say anything about Article 14. Jeff Dudgeon had complained that he was subject to greater interference with his private life than were male homosexuals in other parts of the United Kingdom or heterosexuals and female homosexuals in Northern Ireland. He argued, in particular, that Article 14 required the age of consent to be the same for all forms of sexual relations throughout the United Kingdom. But the Court said that it fell in the first instance to the national authorities to fix the age under which young people should have the protection of the criminal law and that only when a minimum age had been established for lawful male homosexual acts in Northern Ireland would the Court be willing to pronounce upon the broader discrimination issue. More generally on Article 14, the Court said:

> Where a substantive Article of the Convention has been invoked both on its own and together with Article 14 and a separate breach has been found of the substantive Article, it is not generally necessary for the Court also to examine the case under Article 14, though the position is otherwise if a clear inequality of treatment in the enjoyment of the right in question is a fundamental aspect of the case.[57]

[53] Citing *Dudgeon v UK* (1982) 4 EHRR 149, para 67 (see ch 10 above, 297–8).
[54] Leach (2005) 346. But for a more generous view see Gilbert (2002).
[55] (2003) 37 EHRR 2.
[56] (1982) 4 EHRR 149.
[57] ibid, para 67. The Court cited *Airey v Ireland* (1979–80) 2 EHRR 305, para 30.

The Court then held that this 'clear inequality' criterion had not been met in the *Dudgeon* case, either as regards the alleged discrimination resulting from the existence of different laws concerning male homosexual acts in various parts of the United Kingdom or as regards the existence in Northern Ireland of legislation which makes certain homosexual acts punishable under the criminal law in all circumstances. The latter complaint was, in effect, the same complaint that the Court had already considered in relation to Article 8 and so it could not be said that a clear inequality of treatment *remained* a fundamental aspect of the case.[58]

In *Quinn v United Kingdom*[59] a man working in the Northern Ireland Passport Office had been dismissed and when he complained to the Fair Employment Tribunal (FET) the Secretary of State issued a certificate under the Fair Employment (NI) Act 1976[60] claiming that the decision to dismiss him had been taken on national security grounds. The European Commission held the application to be inadmissible, on the basis that a dispute between a civil servant and the State as employer does not involve 'civil rights' within the meaning of Article 6 of the Convention.[61] Two years later, in *Pellegrin v France*,[62] the Grand Chamber of the European Court changed its stance on which category of public servants could claim the protection of Article 6, thereby embracing a lot more potential claimants. But this change came too late for the numerous victims of discrimination in public sector employment in Northern Ireland. So did the change regarding challenges to national security grounds.

Tinnelly & Son Ltd and McElduff v United Kingdom

Having failed to successfully invoke Article 14 via Article 8, or indeed via Articles 2 or 3, it was left to applicants who invoked Article 14 in conjunction with Article 6 to eventually succeed in getting the European Court to apply Article 14 to a case from Northern Ireland. This was in *Tinnelly & Son Ltd and McElduff v United Kingdom* in 1998.[63] Tinnelly & Son Ltd submitted a bid to demolish a power station at Ballylumford in County Antrim and to purchase the resulting scrap. Their bid was the lowest and was recommended for acceptance by Northern Ireland Electricity Services (NIE), but about six weeks later the firm received a letter saying its tender had not been successful. In their complaint to Northern Ireland's FEA the applicants stated that they had learned that they had been the favourites to obtain the Ballylumford contract but were not awarded it because the trade unions at Ballylumford would not allow employees of Tinnelly access to the site as 'there was no way they were going to have IRA sympathisers working with them'. When the FEA began to investigate Tinnelly's

[58] ibid, paras 68–9.

[59] App No 33694/96, decision of 23 October 1997.

[60] s 42.

[61] The Court relied on *Neigel v France* App No 18725/91, judgment of 17 March 1997.

[62] (1999) 31 EHRR 651. The test has since been altered again by the European Court, in *Vilho Eskelinen v Finland* (2007) 45 EHRR 43 (Grand Chamber).

[63] (1999) 27 EHRR 249. The Court's decision was issued some six years after the applications were lodged in Strasbourg. The applications were declared admissible on 20 May 1996, more than four years before the decision was eventually issued.

complaint the NIE asked the Secretary of State for Northern Ireland to issue a certificate under the Fair Employment (NI) 1976 Act[64] to the effect that the decision not to grant the contract to Tinnelly was 'an act done for the purpose of safeguarding national security or of protecting public safety or public order'. The Secretary of State duly issued such a certificate a few days later. Under the Act, this certificate was 'conclusive evidence' that the act was done for the stated purpose.[65]

The FEA brought judicial review proceedings to try to have the Secretary of State's decision to issue the section 42 certificate quashed. During the course of these proceedings the Secretary of State issued a 'public interest immunity certificate' (PIIC) on the basis that full disclosure of the information at its disposal would be injurious to the public interest because it would possibly reveal to those who are engaged in unlawful activities, including acts of terrorism, the source from which it originated, putting that source's life in danger. Nicholson J, as he then was, declared that as a judge he was competent to decide whether a document might involve national security but he accepted that, if disclosure might imperil national security, it was for a minister, not a judge, to balance national security against other considerations of public interest. He then accepted the validity of the PIIC in relation to 14 of the 19 documents in question, but rejected it in relation to the remaining five. The main case was then heard before a different judge, McCollum J, who decided that there was no evidence that the section 42 certificate had been applied for in bad faith. The FEA decided not to appeal this decision.

In the complaint brought by the McElduffs, the applicants had tendered for a joinery subcontract with a building contractor who was building premises for the Department of the Environment for Northern Ireland in Omagh, County Tyrone. The contractor accepted the tender and the applicants were told that they could start the work, subject to security clearance from the Department of the Environment. Some six weeks later they were informed that they had not been granted security clearance, a refusal which was based on information supplied by the police. The applicants believed that they had been discriminated against on the grounds of religious belief or political opinion. They knew they would be perceived as having nationalist views, but they maintained that they were not engaged in any form of political activity, unlike another family of the same name in their area. Their complaint to the Fair Employment Tribunal was again resisted on the ground that the Department was safeguarding national security, and the Secretary of State issued a section 42 certificate. On counsel's advice the applicants withdrew their application to the FET.

Tinnelly & Son Ltd and the McElduffs both lodged petitions in Strasbourg.[66] SACHR was granted leave to submit written observations in which it argued that

[64] s 42, which reads: '(1) This Act shall not apply to an act done for the purpose of safeguarding national security or of protecting public safety or public order. (2) A certificate signed by or on behalf of the Secretary of State and certifying that an act specified in the certificate was done for a purpose mentioned in subsection (1) shall be conclusive evidence that it was done for that purpose. (3) A document purporting to be a document such as is mentioned in sub-section (2) shall be received in evidence and, unless the contrary is proved, shall be deemed to be such a certificate.'

[65] s 42(2).

[66] SACHR (1998a). Amongst the barristers acting for the government were Ronald Weatherup QC and Bernard McCloskey, two future High Court judges in Northern Ireland. Lord Lester QC was one of the barristers acting for the applicants.

the present system did not provide for effective judicial scrutiny of whether an act had in fact been done to safeguard national security or protect public safety or public order. SACHR suggested that section 42 of the 1976 Act should be repealed and a new system devised whereby the person affected by the decision in question would be provided with much fuller information. The extent to which this could be done could be decided at a private or *ex parte* hearing at the Fair Employment Tribunal.

The applications were first considered by the European Commission (the changes effected by Protocol 11 not yet having kicked in[67]), which held unanimously in 1997 that there had been a violation of Article 6 of the Convention and that it was not necessary to determine whether there had also been a breach of Articles 8, 13, or 14. The key issue for the European Court,[68] therefore, was whether Article 6 applied to the facts of this case. The UK government argued that the proceedings instigated by the applicants under the fair employment legislation did not involve the determination of 'civil rights' within the meaning of Article 6(1) because there was no free-standing right in the Convention not to be subjected to unlawful discrimination and the applicants did not have any contractual rights as their bids for the contracts in question had never been accepted. They also knew that acceptance of their tenders would always be conditional on security clearance. The government even contended that the 'public law nature' of the contracts was sufficient in itself to exclude the applicability of Article 6(1) and that in any event no substantive right existed under the fair employment legislation because section 42(1) of the 1976 Act changed the acts in question from acts of unlawful discrimination to acts done for the protection of national security. For good measure the government relied heavily on the difficult security situation in Northern Ireland, saying that 'the issues of religious belief and political opinion were intertwined with the intercommunal violence and the terrorist threat to national security, public safety and public order in Northern Ireland'.[69] It would not be appropriate to involve the judiciary in making national security assessments because 'in Northern Ireland the standing of the judiciary is a matter of critical importance and it is essential that public confidence in the administration of justice be maintained and that the independence of the judiciary be upheld in dealing with secret data on terrorist activity'.[70] This was the argument which the government had successfully deployed on a previous occasion when trying to persuade the Strasbourg enforcement bodies that judges in Northern Ireland could not be involved in determining how long a suspected terrorist should be held in pre-charge detention.[71]

But this time the Court had little hesitation in unanimously rejecting the government's arguments: 'The fact that the contracts in issue were public procurement contracts or that the applicants' offers were never accepted cannot prevent that right [not to be discriminated against on grounds of religious belief or political opinion in the job market]

[67] Prot 11 abolished the European Commission of Human Rights and made the European Court into a full-time body.

[68] Before the Court the European Commission was represented by Ms Jane Liddy, the Commissioner from Ireland, who was later a member of the Irish Human Rights Commission.

[69] (1999) 27 EHRR 249, para 68.

[70] ibid.

[71] See ch 6 above, 124–9.

from being considered a 'civil right' for the purposes of Article 6(1).'[72] Having decided that Article 6 was engaged, the Court then confirmed that Article 6 embodied the 'right to a court', one aspect of which was the right to institute court proceedings in civil matters. It conceded that this right was not absolute, but noted that any limitations on the right must not restrict or reduce access to a court in such a way as to impair the very essence of the right. The limitations must also pursue a legitimate aim and there must be a reasonable relationship of proportionality between the means employed and the aim sought to be achieved by the limitations. In a memorable phrase the Court said: 'The right guaranteed to an applicant under Article 6... cannot be displaced by the *ipse dixit* of the executive.'[73] It was also not persuaded that adjustment of procedures under the fair employment legislation to allow consideration of national security concerns need in any way undermine the independence of the judiciary in Northern Ireland or impair public confidence in the administration of justice in the province. In fact the Court thought that such adjustments which allowed judges to examine, in complete cognizance of all relevant evidence, the merits of the submissions of both sides on national security arguments could *enhance* public confidence.[74] The issue by the Secretary of State of section 42 certificates therefore constituted a disproportionate restriction on the applicants' right of access to a court or tribunal, and the Court awarded Tinnelly & Son Ltd and McElduff £15,000 and £10,000 respectively as compensation.

The approach of the European Court in the *Tinnelly and McElduff* case marks a significant development in its attitude to Article 14, but it also stands in stark contrast to the approach adopted by the Court five years earlier in *Brannigan and McBride v United Kingdom*,[75] where it totally deferred to the UK's assertion that national security considerations required judges in Northern Ireland to be kept well away from decisions regarding the detention of people who were suspected terrorists. It is almost as if the Court was flexing its muscles in the knowledge that a few months later it would become a full-time body with a lot more constitutional significance in Europe. The decision also reverberated through the Northern Ireland Office and led to the almost immediate repeal of section 42 of the 1976 Act. This was just at the time when the government, having secured the Belfast (Good Friday) Agreement on 10 April 1998, was implementing parts of that Agreement by passing the Northern Ireland Act 1998. It decided to deal with the European Court's decision by inserting a provision in that Act to allow appeals to be lodged against such certificates.[76] Under the Northern Ireland Act Tribunal (Procedure) Rules 1999[77] an appellant may exercise his or her right of appeal to the tribunal by giving notice within 14 days of learning that a certificate has been issued. The tribunal must ensure that information is not

[72] (1999) 27 EHRR 249, para 61. The Court comprised nine judges, including the usually conservative UK judge, Sir John Freeland.

[73] ibid, para 77.

[74] ibid, para 78.

[75] (1993) 17 EHRR 539.

[76] s 91. As well as s 42 certificates (which by then were provided for by art 80 of the Fair Employment and Treatment (NI) Order 1998) the Tribunal deals with appeals against certificates issued under s 90 of the Northern Ireland Act 1998 itself, art 53ZA of the Sex Discrimination (NI) Order 1976, and art 41A of the Race Relations (NI) Order 1997.

[77] r 7.

disclosed contrary to the interest of national security, public safety or public order, or in any other circumstances where disclosure is likely to harm a public interest.[78] In 2000 the Committee of Ministers of the Council of Europe accepted that the UK government had fully complied with the European Court's judgment.[79] It seems that the tribunal envisaged by the 1998 Act has never in fact sat, which calls into question the need for section 42 certificates in the first place.

By this time two further applications from Northern Ireland on the same topic were already wending their way through the Strasbourg system—*Devlin v United Kingdom*[80] and *Devenney v United Kingdom*.[81] In the former, the applicant was represented in Strasbourg by a lawyer working for the Equality Commission for Northern Ireland. He had applied for a position as an administrative assistant with the Northern Ireland Civil Service in 1991 but, after being told that he was being recommended for appointment 'subject to the satisfactory outcome of various pre-appointment enquiries', he was informed in 1992 that he had been unsuccessful. Believing his rejection to have been based on the fact that he was a Catholic and a member of an association known as the Irish National Foresters,[82] he lodged a complaint with the Fair Employment Tribunal alleging religious or political discrimination. The Northern Ireland Civil Service confirmed at this point that his rejection had been based on security grounds and in 1993 the Secretary of State for Northern Ireland certified under the Fair Employment (NI) Act 1976 that the refusal of employment was an act 'done for the purpose of safeguarding national security and of protecting public safety'. An application for judicial review failed before Kerr J, as he then was, because of the precedent set by McCollum J in the *Tinnelly & Son Ltd* case four years earlier.

When the *Devlin* application reached Strasbourg the British government, relying on *Quinn v United Kingdom*,[83] argued that the present application should be distinguished from *Tinnelly & Son Ltd and McElduff* because it concerned access to the civil service rather than a dispute about a works contract, and access to the civil service had always been a matter to which special considerations applied. But the European Court pointed out in reply that its approach to civil service employment disputes had moved on since *Quinn v United Kingdom*, particularly in the light of its decision in *Pellegrin v France*.[84] Applying the test laid down there, the Court easily concluded that 'the post of administrative assistant (which is described as the lowest grade in the non-industrial civil service) is not a post where it can be said the incumbent was wielding "a portion of the State's sovereign power."'[85] This meant

[78] r 3(1).

[79] Resolution DH (2000) 49 (14 April).

[80] (2002) 34 EHRR 43.

[81] (2002) 35 EHRR 24.

[82] This is a nationalist organization which was formerly a thriving 'friendly society', a savings club.

[83] See text at n 59 above. Oddly, *Quinn v UK* was not discussed by the European Court in *Tinnelly and McElduff v UK*.

[84] See text at n 62 above.

[85] (2002) 34 EHRR 43, para 26.

that the case was indistinguishable from *Tinnelly & Son Ltd and McElduff*, and on this occasion the Court awarded the applicant £10,000 as compensation.[86]

In the second of the two post-*Tinnelly* cases, *Devenney v United Kingdom*,[87] the applicant had been summarily dismissed just 10 weeks after starting a job as a silver service waiter in one of Northern Ireland's top hotels, the Culloden at Cultra in County Down. The police had apparently told his employers that he was a 'suspect', but the applicant was never shown any evidence to substantiate that.[88] He also believed that he was the only Catholic amongst all the full-time and permanent staff in the restaurant where he worked. As the application was so similar to that dealt with by the Court in *Tinnelly*, neither side even bothered to file observations on the merits. Predictably, the Court decided it in the same way as the *Tinnelly* case and, again, awarded the applicant £10,000 as compensation.[89]

There is no doubt, then, that the European Court did eventually 'come good' as far as protecting people against discrimination on 'political opinion' grounds in Northern Ireland is concerned. There is also cause for hope that, unlikely though it might be, if any kind of lustration law were to be put in place in Northern Ireland (eg banning former police officers, or advocates of violence, from certain posts) the European Court would prevent its enforcement. In this context one can point to decisions taken in cases emerging from Lithuania. In *Sidabras v Lithuania*,[90] two men were dismissed from public employment because they had previously served as KGB agents. For the first time, the European Court ruled that banning someone from a wide range of employment is an action that falls within the ambit of Article 8 of the Convention: the ban affects the ability to earn a living and thus indirectly affects enjoyment of a private life. Employment bans that are based on any of the grounds listed in Article 14, including political opinion, national origin, or association with a national minority, can therefore be challenged on the basis of combining Article 14 with Article 8. In *Zickus v Lithuania*[91] suspected collaborators with the Communist security service had been given an opportunity to confess their collaborator status to a commission. If they confessed, their confessions had to be kept secret. If they did not confess, they were excluded from specified jobs. The European Court criticized the blanket nature of the rule, pointing out that the lustration law could

[86] The Court then held that it was not necessary to examine the applicant's further complaints made under Arts 8, 9, 10, 13, and 14 of the Convention. The Committee of Ministers resolved on 24 February 2003 that the UK government had fully complied with this judgment: Resolution DH (2003) 9.

[87] (2002) 35 EHRR 24. The application was lodged on 12 April 1994. Sir Nicolas Bratza, the UK judge at the Court, withdrew from the case when it reached the Court, presumably because he had been a member of the European Commission when it held the application admissible on 24 February 1997. The UK government appointed Judge Pellonpää, from Finland, to replace him. These steps were permitted by Rules 28 and 29 of the Rules of the Court.

[88] The Court's judgment states, at para 9, that Liam Devenney and 13 of his 15 siblings were not involved in any politically related activity.

[89] Again the Committee of Ministers later resolved that the UK government had fully complied with the Court's judgment: Resolution DH (2004) 9 (24 February 2004).

[90] (2004) 42 EHRR 104.

[91] App No 26652/02, judgment of 7 April 2009.

have distinguished between different types of collaborators and taken into account the actual security risk posed by each individual.[92]

Other grounds of discrimination

During the conflict in Northern Ireland no cases reached Strasbourg alleging discrimination on the grounds of sex, race, colour, language, property, or birth. This is very surprising, especially when one realizes that it was only on 4 August 1997 that racial discrimination became unlawful in Northern Ireland, by virtue of the Race Relations (NI) Order 1997. There had long been a campaign to get such legislation put in place,[93] because it had existed in the rest of the United Kingdom since 1976,[94] and the UK government could easily have been condemned at Strasbourg had a victim of racial discrimination in Northern Ireland not been able to obtain an adequate domestic remedy. The 1997 Order is very similar to the Race Relations Act 1976, but even in this context the government felt it necessary to include a special provision allowing it to issue a certificate analogous to section 42 certificates under the Fair Employment (NI) Act 1976 in case it wished to stop challenges to an allegedly discriminatory act because of national security considerations.[95] No doubt this was inserted because the government feared that a Catholic nationalist who was stymied by the Fair Employment (NI) Act 1976 would seek to evade that obstacle by bringing a claim instead under the Race Relations (NI) Order 1997, relying on his or her race, nationality, or ethnic or national origins.[96]

The absence of any challenge to the absence of race discrimination laws is all the more startling when one bears in mind that throughout the conflict in Northern Ireland the principle was adhered to that some senior positions in the civil service could be occupied only by British citizens, thereby rendering ineligible any person born and living in Northern Ireland who identified themselves as Irish rather than British.[97] The European Convention is again of limited help in such situations because of the parasitic nature of Article 14: it applies only if the substantive right violated is 'within the ambit of a Convention right'. A better tool for attacking such discrimination may be European Union law. The topic came before the High Court of Northern Ireland in *Re O'Conor's Application*,[98] where the applicant, an Irish national, had been rejected for the post of legal assistant in the office of the Director of Public Prosecutions because she was not a UK national. The position had been designated by the Northern Ireland Office as

[92] ibid, [30–3]. See too *McConkey v The Simon Community* [2009] UKHL 24.

[93] For one of the earliest efforts see NISLL (1969) 6–11.

[94] Race Relations Act 1976.

[95] See Race Relations (NI) Order 1997, art 66. The Disability Discrimination Act 1995, which applies throughout the UK, does not provide for such certificates, but s 59(3) says that nothing in the Act makes unlawful any act done for the purpose of safeguarding national security.

[96] These are the grounds embraced by 'racial grounds' in the Order: see art 5.

[97] Under the Irish Nationality and Citizenship Act 1956 (Ir), ss 6 and 7, all persons born in Northern Ireland since 1921 had a right to claim Irish nationality, and under the British Nationality Act 1948 (UK), s 4, all persons born in Northern Ireland had the right to claim British nationality.

[98] [2005] NIQB 11.

a 'public service post' under the Treaty of Rome,[99] and the Department of Finance and Personnel in Northern Ireland had set out the nationality requirements in directions issued under the Civil Service (NI) Order 1999. Bizarrely, the equivalent posts in England's Crown Prosecution Service and the Police Service of Northern Ireland were not designated as public service posts and so European and Commonwealth nationals were eligible to apply for them. Girvan J, as he then was, nevertheless held that Ms O'Conor's application must fail, because in his view the government had no discretion to treat the post in question as open to non-nationals once it had been designated as a public service post under the Treaty of Rome,[100] a designation which could not be described as 'unreasonable, untenable or unlawful'.[101] He added that it was the English CPS that was out of step in opening its post to non-UK nationals.[102] The European Convention was not even mentioned in the judgment.

Claims of sex discrimination emanating from Northern Ireland have also not featured in Strasbourg, notwithstanding that Northern Ireland is generally considered to be a less progressive environment than many other parts of the United Kingdom when it comes to the acceptance of women as fully equal citizens. One significant case did reach the European Court of Justice—*Johnston v Chief Constable of the RUC*[103]—and this has been referred to once or twice by the European Court of Human Rights in its jurisprudence.[104] In *Johnston* 31 female police reservists in Northern Ireland challenged the decision of the Chief Constable, Sir John Hermon, not to renew their contracts. Sir John tried to justify his decision on national security grounds, saying that all police reservists would have to carry firearms and that women would not be able to handle these as easily as men. The matter was referred to the European Court of Justice by an industrial tribunal and the European Court ruled in favour of the women reservists, relying in part on Articles 6 and 13 of the European Convention in the process.[105] Compensation of £1.2 million was agreed and the Sex Discrimination (Amendment) (NI) Order 1988 was passed so as to remove from the Sex Discrimination (NI) Order 1976 the provision which allowed reliance on national security to automatically obstruct a claim based on sex discrimination. In *Tinnelly & Son Ltd and McElduff v United Kingdom* the Court of Human Rights referred to the Sex Discrimination (Amendment) (NI) Order 1988 as an example of how steps *could* be taken to allow an industrial tribunal to determine whether a particular act was done on grounds of national security or not, while still ensuring that there were appropriate safeguards in place to protect national security, public safety, and public order. It noted that, following the preliminary ruling of the Court of Justice in *Johnston*, the industrial tribunal which heard the complaint took evidence from one witness in camera for reasons of national security.[106]

[99] Art 39(4).

[100] Applying the decision of the Court of Appeal of Northern Ireland in *Re O'Boyle* [1999] NI 126.

[101] [2005] NIQB 11, [26].

[102] ibid, [28].

[103] [1986] ECR 1651; [1987] QB 129.

[104] eg in *Tinnelly & Son Ltd and McElduff v UK* (1998) 27 EHRR 249, para 47; *Bosphorus Hava Yollari Turizm Ve Ticaret Anonim Sirketi v Ireland* (2006) 42 EHRR 1, para 73; *Vilho Eskelinen v Finland* (2007) 45 EHRR 43.

[105] [1986] ECR 1651, para 18.

[106] (1999) 27 EHRR 249, paras 49 and 78.

There have been some applications in Strasbourg where, in addition to the main complaints, the applicants have alleged discrimination under Article 14 in that, as Irish republicans, they have been treated less well than British people or than other foreigners. They have, in other words, relied on the Article 14 grounds of 'national or social origin, association with a national minority, or other status'. We have already seen how these allegations fared in the early cases alleging discrimination in housing and voting rights,[107] and also in cases concerning the transfer of prisoners[108] and the right to life.[109] The Irish government initially refused to lodge an inter-State application because it did not think Article 14 covered the kind of discriminatory practices that were so common in Northern Ireland[110] and, when it did eventually raise them in relation to breaches of Articles 5 and 6, it managed to persuade only two of the 17 judges to support its arguments (one of these being the Irish judge).[111] On the other hand we have seen applicants from the loyalist community in Northern Ireland argue (usually impliedly) that they too have been discriminated against because of their national minority status in the United Kingdom as a whole.[112] Applicants have frequently asserted, but always unsuccessfully, that the catch-all phrase 'other status' at the end of Article 14 allows them to benefit from the right not to be discriminated against purely because they have been treated differently from some other group of people. It is abundantly clear from the Strasbourg jurisprudence that 'other status' is to be narrowly interpreted, the most salient of the statuses so far recognized being those based on physical or mental disability, sexual orientation, and age.[113] It certainly does not allow people living in one part of a State to argue that their Convention rights must be protected in exactly the same way as the Convention rights of people living elsewhere in the State. This is what an applicant from Northern Ireland tried to argue in a right to silence case,[114] his point being that terrorist suspects detained in England and Wales were granted access to a solicitor much sooner than terrorist suspects detained in Northern Ireland. In holding that any such difference in treatment did not amount to discriminatory treatment for the purposes of Article 14 the European Court observed:

in the constituent parts of the United Kingdom there is not always a uniform approach to legislation in particular areas. Whether or not an individual can assert a right derived from legislation may accordingly depend on the geographical reach of the legislation at issue and the individual's location at the time. For the Court, in so far as there exists a difference in treatment of detained suspects under the 1988 Order and the legislation of England and Wales on the matters referred to by the applicant, that difference is not to be explained in terms of personal characteristics, such as national origin or association with a national minority, but on the geographical location where the individual is arrested and detained. This permits legislation to take account of regional differences and characteristics of an objective and reasonable

[107] Ch 3 above, 42–8.
[108] Ch 10 above, 287–9.
[109] See text at n 41 above.
[110] Ch 3 above, 46.
[111] Ch 4 above, 66–8.
[112] eg *Orchin v UK* (1984) 6 EHRR 391 (ch 7 above, 211) and *Lindsay v UK* [1979] 3 CMLR 166 (ch 11 above, 308).
[113] Harris et al (2009) 584–5.
[114] *Magee v UK* (2001) 31 EHRR 35. See ch 8 above, 200.

nature. In the present case, such a difference does not amount to discriminatory treatment within the meaning of Article 14 of the Convention.[115]

Housing and education issues

Notwithstanding the developments in discrimination law resulting from the interpretation placed by the European Court of Human Rights on the access to justice provision in Article 6 of the Convention, Article 14 remains a relatively unused tool in this context. In particular, discrimination in the allocation of public housing and in the enjoyment of education rights, which were two of the problems that helped to trigger the troubles in Northern Ireland in the 1960s,[116] has still not been brought within the ambit of Article 14 in any systematic way.[117] Article 8 has not yet been interpreted so as to enhance the right to be given a home (as opposed to the right to have one's existing home protected),[118] and Article 14 has not been used to help ensure that the housing policies of member States are non-discriminatory in their impact. One would like to think that, if complaints of religious or political discrimination in the allocation of public housing were to arise in Northern Ireland today in the same manner as they did back in 1964, when the Campaign for Social Justice got nowhere in Strasbourg because the United Kingdom had not yet accepted the right of individual petition,[119] the chances of success would be greater. But there is no guarantee that this would be so.

One positive development is the European Court's decision in *DH v Czech Republic*,[120] where it held that, in allowing a disproportionate number of Roma children to be educated in 'special schools', which were designed for children with mental deficiencies, the member State had not done enough to justify the discriminatory effect of its policy (even if the discrimination was unintended). This is evidence that the European Court is prepared to take a stricter line with member States when confronted with social or economic inequality in which the different strata seem to be distinguishable on one or more of the grounds listed in Article 14. But of course a lot will turn on the particular facts brought to the attention of the Court. Thus, in *Doğan v Turkey*,[121] people who allegedly had been evicted from their village in south-eastern Turkey relied (*inter alia*) on Article 14, in conjunction with Articles 6, 8, and 13 of the Convention and Article 1 of Protocol 1, on the basis that they had been discriminated against because of their birthplace. But the European Court considered the complaints to be unsubstantiated by evidence and therefore declared them to be manifestly ill-founded.[122] Likewise,

[115] ibid, para 50.

[116] For good accounts see Wilson (1989) chs 13 and 14.

[117] O'Connell (2008). For earlier radical thinking see Cassese (1991).

[118] Kenna (2008), who argues that there is considerable potential in the Convention in this context, if only the European Court would have greater regard for the relevant opinions of the Council of Europe's Committee on Social Rights. He is also critical of the way in which the European Court has protected the rights of corporations in the housing context.

[119] See ch 3, 43.

[120] (2008) 47 EHRR 3 (Grand Chamber). See Hobcraft (2009); O'Connell (2008) 221 and 227–9.

[121] App Nos 8803–11/02, 8813/02 and 8819/02, decision of 29 June 2004.

[122] ibid, paras 128–130.

in *Oršuš v Croatia* the Court found no violation of the Convention when Roma-only classes were organized at a primary school: it thought that the difference in treatment was a result of the Roma children's poor ability in the Croatian language, not because of their race or ethnicity.[123]

In Northern Ireland an attempt was made in the late 1970s to persuade the European Commission of Human Rights that the UK government was violating Article 2 of Protocol 1 by not being more supportive of those parents in Northern Ireland who wanted their children to be educated in an integrated school, not in a school that was run in accordance with a Catholic ethos or in one that, by default, had a Protestant ethos.[124] But the Commission rejected the application because Article 2 of Protocol 1 merely affirms that no-one must be denied the right to education and that the State must, when exercising functions in relation to education, 'respect the right of parents to ensure such education and teaching in conformity with their own religious and philosophical convictions'. This does not mean that States must deal with different types of school in exactly the same way, nor that they must provide funding for any school. The Commission added, unfortunately, that a strong belief on the part of parents in Northern Ireland that their children, and society as a whole, would be much better off if they were educated alongside children of the 'other' community, did not amount to a 'philosophical conviction'. Parents who belong to small religious communities in Northern Ireland (Jews or Muslims, for example) can therefore benefit from the Convention's provisions on education, but thousands of parents who understandably feel that much of Northern Ireland's sad history can be explained by the fact that its children are educated separately depending on their religious background cannot.

Unless and until the European Court moves towards interpreting Article 14 as granting protection of a free-standing right to equality, there will continue to be instances where differences of treatment go unregulated by domestic legal systems. The Council of Europe has been very aware of this for years and for that reason it has been encouraging member States to ratify another Protocol to the Convention—Protocol 12—which radically supplements Article 14. Agreed in 2000, and coming into force for those States which had by then ratified it in 2005, this Protocol does two important things. First, it effectively amends Article 14 of the Convention by removing its 'parasitic' quality: protection against discrimination will apply to 'the enjoyment of any right set forth by law', not just to 'the enjoyment of the rights and freedoms set forth in this Convention'.[125] This means that whatever rights a member State's legal system confers on people, whether they are Convention rights or not, these have to be enjoyed equally by everyone. Second, the Protocol provides that '[n]o one shall be discriminated against by any public authority on any ground such as those mentioned in paragraph 1'. This means that public authorities have to act in a non-discriminatory way not just as regards how people enjoy their rights but in all other respects as well. Moreover, the Preamble to the Protocol makes it clear that 'the principle of non-discrimination does not prevent States from taking measures in

[123] App No 15766/03, decision of 17 July 2008.
[124] *X v UK* App No 7782/77, 14 DR 179 (1978).
[125] Prot 12, Art 1(1).

order to promote full and effective equality, provided that there is an objective and reasonable justification for those measures', which is an attempt to preserve the legality of justifiable affirmative action, or even positive discrimination. The placing of this provision in the Preamble rather than in the body of the Protocol is strange, but the European Court will probably treat it as just as binding.

Regrettably, neither the United Kingdom nor Ireland has yet ratified this Protocol 12,[126] and the UK government seems implacably opposed to doing so, having not even signed the document.[127] The most recently proposed domestic legislation on discrimination, the Equality Bill 2009, does not do much to establish a right to equality as such in the United Kingdom because, although it strengthens the duties on public authorities to pay due regard to the need to promote equality of opportunity,[128] it does not accompany these duties with enforceable rights for individuals. In any event this Bill does not extend to Northern Ireland.[129]

Conclusion

Rosalyn Higgins, then a Professor of International Law at the London School of Economics, and later a judge and President of the International Court of Justice at The Hague, argued in 1994 that it is important to make clear distinctions between the right of self-determination, the right of non-discrimination, and the rights of minorities.[130] All of these issues have been part and parcel of the human rights dimension to the conflict in Northern Ireland since 1968 but only one of them—the right not to be discriminated against—has had any resonance with the European Convention on Human Rights, and then only belatedly and partially. The main reasons for the Convention's 'irrelevance' in this context have been the scant reference to social and economic rights in the Convention or its Protocols and the fact that Article 14 does not confer a free-standing right to be treated equally. In addition, the enforcement organs in Strasbourg have become so fixated on delivering justice to individual claimants that they have lost sight of one of the reasons why the Convention was drafted in the first place—to prevent the oppression of minority or unpopular sections of society. We still await a florescence of Strasbourg jurisprudence in the domain of group rights, and there are small signs that that might be in the offing. It will come too late for Northern Ireland where, with only a few exceptions, injustices resulting from discriminatory practices have had to be dealt with through other means than by invoking Convention rights.

[126] By 31 August 2009 only 17 Council of Europe States had ratified, the most prominent being Finland, the Netherlands, and Spain.

[127] See HL Deb, vol 616, col 169WA (27 September 2000), per Baroness Scotland. Denmark, France, Sweden, and Switzerland have also not signed.

[128] Even requires regard to be paid to socio-economic inequalities.

[129] Since 2001 the Northern Ireland Executive has pledged to introduce a 'Single Equality Bill', but this is a commitment which, like many others, has since been de-prioritized, if not completely shelved: *Programme for Government 2001–04*, 16.

[130] Higgins (1994).

13

The Final Picture

The contribution of the Convention in Northern Ireland

This book has told the story of the part played by the European Convention on Human Rights in the conflict which began in Northern Ireland in 1968 and is still not completely over even today. It is a convoluted story in that the Convention has featured at many different times and on many different topics during the past 40 years, yet the influence it has had is difficult to characterize. If one had to be brutally summative one would conclude that the Convention was very largely irrelevant both to the way the conflict was managed while it was raging and to the way it was largely resolved through the Belfast (Good Friday) Agreement of 1998. The Convention's political role, in other words, was minimal. Apart from during the very early days, when the operation of the Special Powers Act was a cause of great dismay to many, leading to a call for it to be amended so as to be compatible with the European Convention, the Convention has not featured as a political bargaining chip during any of the negotiations between different sides to the conflict. It has been a focus of attention when the need for a Bill of Rights in Northern Ireland has been debated, but even then very few politicians have deemed it important enough to form the basis of manifesto pledges. When the Convention became part of the domestic law of Northern Ireland through the Human Rights Act 1998—which did not come fully into force until October 2000—some politicians in Northern Ireland might have viewed the development as a beneficial by-product of the Agreement reached in April of that year, but the reality is that the Human Rights Act would have been passed at Westminster anyway, even if the Belfast Agreement had not been reached, and it would have applied in Northern Ireland just as much as in the rest of the United Kingdom.

Generally speaking, the Convention functioned as a tool which people with grievances about real or perceived injustices in Northern Ireland turned to on very many occasions. They were encouraged in this by lawyers who, at least after the first few years of fumbling with the Convention, became well versed in the Convention's wording and in the jurisprudence of the European Commission and Court. Signal successes in cases taken to Strasbourg from other parts of the United Kingdom, and from the Republic of Ireland, raised the hopes of lawyers and litigants in Northern Ireland. Victims of injustice there would have identified with the victims of the thalidomide tragedy in England, who, with the backing of *The Sunday Times*, secured a great blow for transparency and accountability when they obtained a ruling from the European Court preventing the manufacturer of thalidomide from silencing its critics in the run-up to litigation over the drug.[1] People who were frustrated at the lack of remedies in the domestic law of Northern Ireland for basic human rights abuses would also have taken heart from the victory of Mrs Airey in 1979 when the European Court ruled that Ireland was violating Article 6 of the Convention by not making legal aid available to people who, while unable to obtain a divorce, wanted a decree of judicial separation.[2] And the triumph of local man Jeff Dudgeon, in his fight to get homosexuality decriminalized in Northern Ireland by complaining to the European Court, was also inspirational.[3]

Unfortunately, though, many petitions were lodged with the registry in Strasbourg more in hope than in expectation. Lawyers would have been only too aware of the various limitations in the Convention system—the demanding admissibility and standing criteria, the margin of appreciation doctrine, the qualifications to rights in the text of the Convention itself, the tendency (in the early years at least) for the Court's judges to be even more conservative and partisan in their approach than the Commission's commissioners, and, above all, the inability of the Convention's enforcement organs to provide truly effective remedies to those whose rights had been violated.[4] The enforcement organs would not consider challenges to laws *in abstracto*, they would not often engage in their own fact-finding exercises, they would not readily translate individuals' rights into States' duties, and they would not develop the content of human rights unless there already appeared to be a consensus to do so within the domestic law of the States throughout the Council of Europe.

Inestimable damage was done to the credibility of the Convention when, in the two cases where the acceptability of internment was up for consideration, first in the Republic of Ireland[5] and then in Northern Ireland,[6] the European Court deferred almost unctuously to the governments of the member States concerned. In the latter case, the damage was compounded by the failure of the European Court to support the finding by the European Commission—in spite of impressive evidence substantiating that finding—that the United Kingdom's security forces had used torture against Irish republican detainees.[7] An opportunity was missed at that time, 1978, to set the threshold for what was acceptable treatment of detainees at a much higher level. And for a long time thereafter, even if the mistreatment of detainees in Northern Ireland was moderated, the Convention was powerless to stop very many individuals being convicted of serious crimes on the basis of confessions they had produced in highly dubious circumstances. The practice of arresting large numbers of people, interrogating them over several days, and then releasing them without charge, also continued, and was not terminated even after the European Court ruled

[1] *Sunday Times v UK* (No 1) (1979–80) 2 EHRR 245.
[2] *Airey v Ireland* (1979–80) 2 EHRR 305.
[3] *Dudgeon v UK* (1982) 4 EHRR 149.
[4] Churchill and Young (1991).
[5] *Lawless v Ireland* (1979–80) 1 EHRR 115.
[6] *Ireland v UK* (1979–80) 2 EHRR 25.
[7] ibid.

that seven-day detentions authorized by a government minister were a violation of Article 5 of the Convention[8]—the UK government simply devised a fresh derogation notice under Article 15 of the Convention and the Court meekly accepted the need for that derogation when it was confronted by a challenge from a new group of detainees.[9] We have also seen how the Convention was of no help in ensuring that detainees were given immediate access to a solicitor when they were arrested, at any rate not until, almost by accident, this 'concession' was achieved because the UK government had put a law in place which permitted inferences to be drawn from a detainee's silence in the face of police questioning.[10] In the words of one commentator of an avowedly unionist persuasion who has briefly reviewed the most prominent Northern Ireland cases before the European Court, 'the UK got a relatively easy ride at Strasbourg in the 1970s, 1980s and 1990s'.[11]

There were successes in Strasbourg too, but they came rather late in the day. When arrest powers were eventually subjected to a 'reasonableness' test, the domestic law had already been changed in that direction.[12] When the Court insisted that counter-insurgency operations had to be controlled and organized in a way which considered all other alternatives besides the one which might lead to the death of the insurgents, the intensity of the conflict was already much less than it had been, indeed the major paramilitary groupings in Northern Ireland had already announced their ceasefires more than a year earlier.[13] And when the Court began to impose exacting standards for effective and thorough investigations of killings, especially those carried out by agents of the State, the ink on the Belfast (Good Friday) Agreement had already been dry for three years.[14] The Court's first attack on national security certificates as a method for obstructing challenges to alleged religious or political discrimination in the employment field occurred at a time when national security concerns were drastically reduced compared with the 1970s and 1980s.[15]

It is as if, like most of the people living in Northern Ireland at the time, the European Court was initially so shocked at the intensity of the conflict that it could not bring itself to wave the flag of human rights very vigorously. The human rights abuses committed by the IRA, INLA, the UVF, and the UDA (amongst others) were enough to sicken even the staunchest defenders of the mantra 'human rights for all'. But human rights activists in Northern Ireland, from the Campaign for Social Justice and the Northern Ireland Civil Rights Association, through the Association for Legal Justice and the Northern Ireland Association of Socialist Lawyers, to the Committee on the Administration of Justice, were always ahead of the game in that they could see that serious abuses were being committed by the State as well as by

[8] *Brogan v UK* (1989) 11 EHRR 117.
[9] *Brannigan and McBride v UK* (1994) 17 EHRR 539.
[10] *Murray (John) v UK* (1994) 19 EHRR 193.
[11] Morgan (2009) 172.
[12] *Fox, Campbell and Hartley v UK* (1990) 13 EHRR 157.
[13] *McCann v UK* (1996) 21 EHRR 97.
[14] *Jordan v UK* (2003) 37 EHRR 2; *Kelly v UK* App No 30054/96, decision of 4 May 2001; *McKerr v UK* (2002) 34 EHRR 20; *Shanaghan v UK* App No 37715/97, decision of 4 May 2001.
[15] *Tinnelly & Son Ltd and McElduff v UK* (1999) 27 EHRR 249.

paramilitaries. The members of those groups were often very unpopular for the stand they took and it is regrettable that their efforts were not mirrored by those of the enforcement organs in Strasbourg at an earlier stage and at a more frequent rate.

A Bill of Rights for Northern Ireland?

In the first chapter of this book reference was made to the attempts by some MPs in the old Northern Ireland Parliament to get a Bill of Rights enacted. The aspirations of these pioneers were low, because they focused on the need to put in place guarantees against religious and political discrimination, without paying much attention to other issues such as police brutality, unfair electoral practices, socio-economic inequality, and curbs on freedom of movement and expression. Excellent work on whether a Bill of Rights should be enacted for Northern Ireland was conducted by the Standing Advisory Commission on Human Rights in the late 1970s, but it came to nothing legislatively, the focus having shifted to the need for specific anti-discrimination legislation. As various reforms were put in place to deal with particular injustices the demands for an over-arching Bill of Rights were somewhat muted.[16] Political parties and human rights organizations did not let the idea rest, however, and they continued to press for a Bill of Rights in the 1990s, the most thorough work being done by the Committee on the Administration of Justice.[17] The need for a Bill seemed all the more urgent given the rising number of articles, books, and reports severely criticizing the UK government for its human rights record in Northern Ireland.[18] The idea was kept alive in government circles too, with a reference in the Anglo-Irish Agreement of 1985 to the need for consideration to be given to 'the advantages and disadvantages of a Bill of Rights in some form in Northern Ireland',[19] though by the time of the Framework Documents of 1995 the phrase 'Bill of Rights' had been replaced by 'an explicit undertaking... to ensure... the systematic and effective protection of common specified civil, political, social and cultural rights'.[20] Then, in 1998, a reference to the possibility of a Bill of Rights for Northern Ireland was included in the Belfast (Good Friday) Agreement,[21] and a Northern Ireland

[16] Bailey (1988).

[17] CAJ (1990). An excellent overview of the state of human rights in the UK as a whole in the early 1990s can be found in Palley (1991).

[18] eg Hunt and Dickson (1983); Shoot to Kill (1985); Jennings (1988a); Amnesty International (1988); Hellerstein (1988); Helsinki Watch (1991); Lawyers Committee for Human Rights (1993); NIHRA (1993); Amnesty International (1994).

[19] Art 5(a); Hadden and Boyle (1989) 30–4.

[20] *A New Framework for Agreement*, para 50.

[21] para 5 in the section headed 'Rights, Safeguards and Equality of Opportunity' in Strand Three of the Agreement reads: 'The new Northern Ireland Human Rights Commission will be invited to consult and to advise on the scope for defining, in Westminster legislation, rights supplementary to those in the European Convention on Human Rights, to reflect the particular circumstances of Northern Ireland, drawing as appropriate on international instruments and experience. These additional rights to reflect the principles of mutual respect for the identity and ethos of both communities and parity of esteem, and—taken together with the ECHR—to constitute a Bill of Rights for Northern Ireland. Among the issues for consideration by the Commission will be the formulation of a general obligation on government and public bodies fully to respect, on the basis of equality of treatment, the identity and ethos of both

Human Rights Commission was promised as a replacement for the Standing Advisory Commission on Human Rights.[22] Almost at the same time the European Convention on Human Rights was incorporated into UK domestic law by the Human Rights Act 1998, which slightly took the shine off the Bill of Rights concept because it meant that any Bill of Rights for Northern Ireland needed to start from the basis of the European Convention and then add rights addressing 'the particular circumstances' of Northern Ireland.[23] The Human Rights Act has itself had a significant impact in Northern Ireland, as have many other features of the post-1998 landscape of Northern Ireland.[24]

It was the Northern Ireland Human Rights Commission that was given the task of compiling advice for the UK government on what might be contained in a Bill of Rights for Northern Ireland. Undeterred by the political and constitutional difficulties involved in producing a document that needed to be founded on cross-community consensus, the Commission launched its efforts in March 2000. After consulting on what should be contained in the document it produced a first draft of its advice in September 2001.[25] By that time a considerable head of steam in favour of a very comprehensive Bill of Rights had been built up, particularly within certain sectors of civil society, so much so that, even though the Commission's draft was possibly the most all-embracing Bill of Rights ever devised, it still did not satisfy grassroot campaigners and some academics.[26] The Commission took on board the comments made and produced a second draft of the proposed Bill of Rights in April 2004.[27] Less attention was paid to that document, partly because the Commission's credibility had been weakened by a series of resignations from the Commission. The revised document was still a very ambitious one, but it did not meet with the approval of the unionist parties in Northern Ireland, nor of the British and Irish governments.

When a largely new Human Rights Commission was formed in September 2005 it inherited a third version of the previous Commission's draft Bill which had been finalized in February 2005.[28] The new Commission decided to take the matter forward by supporting calls, initially made by the Social and Democratic Labour Party, for a Forum to be established at which interested parties, but especially political representatives, could try to thrash out their differences over what should be contained in a Bill of Rights. The UK government went along with those calls and a Forum was set up in December 2006. It sat throughout 2007 and produced a report at the end of March

communities in Northern Ireland; and a clear formulation of the rights not to be discriminated against and to equality of opportunity in both the public and private sectors.' See generally O'Leary (2001).

[22] Dickson (1999b); Livingstone (1999).

[23] Livingstone (2001).

[24] McEvoy and McGregor (2008); Besson (2008); Carmichael, Knox and Osborne (2007); Dickson (2007a); McCrudden (2007a); Cox, Guelke and Stephen (2006); McGarry and O'Leary (2004); Campbell, Ní Aoláin, and Harvey (2003); Tonge (2002); Harvey (2001); Mallie and McKittrick (2001); Livingstone and Doak (2000). Allamby (2007), Besson (2008). Beylefeld (1995) argued that the European Convention could be treated as part of UK law even before the Human Rights Act was passed in 1998, but that was a minority position.

[25] NIHRC (2001b).

[26] McCrudden (2001), Kavanagh (2004).

[27] NIHRC (2004).

[28] NIHRC (2005).

2008.[29] The main participants were 14 representatives from five political parties and 14 representatives from civil society, with an independent (Australian) chairperson.[30] The Forum's report was submitted to the Human Rights Commission, which then pondered over its recommendations, very far from consensus-based, and produced its own final advice to the Secretary of State in December 2008.[31] Like the 2001 and 2004 documents the 2008 advice takes as its starting point the rights in the European Convention on Human Rights and proceeds to build upon them very significantly. If the advice were accepted by the UK government and enacted as legislation it would undoubtedly constitute one of the most far-reaching Bills of Rights in the world.

In November 2009 the government responded to the Commission's advice by issuing a consultation paper proposing a much less radical Bill of Rights. It clearly felt that the Commission's proposals were too ambitious, and not politically realistic. The two main stumbling blocks are, first, the opposition to a far-reaching Bill of Rights from the overtly unionist parties which, in the last test of the electorate's views (the European Parliament elections in June 2009) gained 49 per cent of the first preference votes in Northern Ireland.[32] Second, the UK government is extremely reluctant to put in place a law which will guarantee to people living in one part of the United Kingdom a host of rights (particularly those relating to health care, housing, and standards of living) which people living elsewhere in the United Kingdom will not enjoy. The Irish government is equally nervous because under the terms of the Belfast Agreement it would have to match in the Republic of Ireland any rights protection put in place in Northern Ireland.[33] The main opposition parties in the two countries are sceptical too, and the fact that both islands have been experiencing a deep recession for the past year or so has not made it easy to suggest that they can 'afford' a far-reaching Bill of Rights. The position has also been complicated by the move on the part of the Labour and Conservative parties in Great Britain to push for a 'British' Bill of Rights, one that would ensure that values and processes which some see as particularly important to the British way of life (jury trial, for example) are covered in the document. There is a growing consensus in political circles in Great Britain, moreover, that a Bill of Rights should contain some reference to responsibilities (which the advice from the NIHRC omits). The European Convention is not popular amongst many elected Parliamentarians because it is perceived to be an undue constraint on government discretion and a document which is tainted by 'Europe', even though, of course, the European Convention is *not* a product of the European Union. The EU does have its own Charter of Fundamental Rights, which is part of the Treaty of Lisbon and is now in force for all EU countries (except the Czech Republic, Poland, and the United Kingdom) from 1 December 2009. The Charter contains significant guarantees regarding social and economic rights.

[29] Bill of Rights Forum (2008). See too <http://www.billofrightsforum.org>, last visited 17 August 2009.

[30] Chris Sidoti, a former Human Rights Commissioner in Australia.

[31] NIHRC (2008).

[32] In the Northern Ireland Assembly elections of 2007 they obtained 54 per cent, and in the 2005 general election 51 per cent.

[33] para 8 of the 'Rights, Safeguards and Equality of Opportunity' section in Strand Three of the Agreement.

For those involved in campaigning for a Bill of Rights for Northern Ireland for many years it is obviously uncomfortable to have to face the prospect of no such Bill emerging in the foreseeable future, at least one that is worth the name. One has to recall, on the other hand, that a lot of rhetoric has been built up in recent times to encourage people to support the principle of a Bill of Rights, and there is a danger of that rhetoric getting in the way of an honest debate about the practical differences a far-reaching Bill of Rights could make to the particular circumstances of Northern Ireland. As the prominent Canadian politician and intellectual Michael Ignatieff has argued, campaigners for human rights should be wary of becoming idolatrous. This book has attempted to show that even the world's most widely used and admired international human rights treaty—the European Convention—was not able to do much to lessen the consequences of the conflict in Northern Ireland after 1968 or to contribute towards the search for a settlement to that conflict. Rights might exist on paper but, as Jeremy Bentham famously said, unless they are backed by real actions on the ground they are 'nonsense on stilts'.[34] The 64,000 dollar question is, if there had been a wide-ranging Bill of Rights in place for Northern Ireland in 1968, would it have done much to reduce the conflict and hasten a settlement? Abuses by the State may have been curtailed, yes, but only provided domestic judges did not take advantage of the qualifications and limitations that would inevitably have been contained in the Bill of Rights, as their Strasbourg counterparts have done. Human rights abuses by non-State agents, the paramilitaries, would probably have continued unabated. Northern Irish society might have been fairer and more just, but it would not necessarily have been more safe. And would a far-reaching Bill of Rights put in place now or in the next two or three years help to ensure that the conflict will not break out again in Northern Ireland? In theory, yes, because there will be fewer grievances left undealt with by the legal system and the need to resort to violence for political ends should therefore diminish to vanishing point. But Bills of Rights do not put an end to criminality or to all politically motivated violence, nor do they guarantee greater investment and prosperity. There is little if any empirical evidence to show that, in a territory where there are deep divisions between half of the people who want the territory to be considered as part of State A and half who want it to be considered as part of State B, the likelihood of violence breaking out between extremists in those two factions is any less significant because of the presence of a comprehensive Bill of Rights in the territory. Moreover, there are many different ways in which human rights can be effectively protected other than through entrenched Bills of Rights—the common law, 'ordinary' legislation, and executive action can all play a very constructive role too.[35] A Bill of Rights can supplement the protection

[34] For an excellent account of Bentham's views on human rights, and how they relate to the European Convention, see Dembour (2006) 30–67. For comparable pragmatism see Ignatieff (2001).

[35] See generally Alston (1999), esp ch 1 on the common law (J Doyle and B Wells), ch 2 on Basic Laws in Israel (D Kretzmer), ch 5 on Parliamentary scrutiny (D Kinley), and ch 13 on comparative perspectives (M Raddow and P Alston). Australia is one of the few common law countries not to have a Bill of Rights (see Campbell, Goldsworthy, and Stone, (2006)), but a national consultation process has recently culminated in a report calling for a Human Rights Act for the nation: see <http://www.humanrightsconsultation.gov.au>, last visited 8 November 2009. For a sceptical approach see Tham and Ewing (2007).

of rights and is desirable *per se*, but it needs to be tailored to the constitutional, legal and cultural traditions of the society it serves. And so that it does not lead to disillusionment after it has been enacted, it must not be over-sold as a cure for all ills. The Belfast (Good Friday) Agreement does not *require* a Bill of Rights, and nor do peace and non-violence in Northern Ireland need to be predicated upon one, but a carefully worded Bill of Rights would have a reassuring and inspiring effect and would, at the absolute minimum, *do no harm*.[36]

The Convention and conflicts in other European societies

Bearing in mind the objectives of those who drafted the European Convention in the late 1940s, it is permissible to ask whether its potential to manage, if not reduce, conflict in European societies has been realized. The short answer, based on the survey conducted for this book, is probably no. Numerous conflicts have flourished throughout Europe during the life of the Convention to date, most notably in Spain (over the status of the Basque territory), in Turkey (over the rights of the Kurds), and in Russia (over the governance of Chechnya). The Balkan wars took place in the early 1990s at a time when none of the former Yugoslav republics was a party to the Convention, but the Convention has been incorporated into the various peace agreements that have been reached for that region, in particular the Dayton Agreement of 1996 in relation to the conflict between Bosnia and Herzegovina, Croatia, and Serbia. Mol has expressed the hope that the centrality of the Convention to that Agreement will help to ensure that in the post-conflict period human rights are impartially upheld in the region.[37] There have also been international disputes in Europe, such as between Romania and Moldova over Transdnistria and between Russia and Georgia over South Ossetia and Abkhazia. Several leading European democracies—Germany, France, and Italy—have experienced sustained periods during which serious terrorist campaigns were waged, not by people fighting on nationalistic or ethnic grounds but by groups who were fervently anti-capitalist.[38] Right-wing extremism has turned violent even in countries such as the Netherlands, and we have seen how Islamic extremists have reacted in the United Kingdom, Spain, and elsewhere to the involvement of Western military forces in Iraq and Afghanistan, not to mention the response in some quarters to the Danish government's tolerance of offensive cartoons of the prophet Mohammed.

However, the conflict which is worth looking at in a little more detail, in order to put in perspective the role played by the European Convention in Northern Ireland during the last 40 years, is the conflict in Cyprus, another 'partitioned' island where political divisions run very deep.[39] The island became a full British Crown

[36] The Agreement also envisages the Northern Ireland and Irish Human Rights Commissions collaborating on a possible Charter of Rights for the island of Ireland, though it seems to envisage a political rather than a legal document; see Egan and Murray (2007). For a more general analysis of the human rights dimension to the Agreement see Wartchow (2005).

[37] Mol (1998).

[38] Lodge (1988).

[39] For an excellent overview of the Cyprus 'problem', see Harbottle (1976).

Colony in 1925, and when the United Kingdom ratified the European Convention in 1953 it was content for it to apply in Cyprus too. But there was a strong movement within Cyprus for the island to be united with Greece ('enosis') and when this led to serious violence in 1955 the United Kingdom issued a notice derogating from the Convention's application in Cyprus.[40] Greece, too, had ratified the Convention in 1953 but, like the United Kingdom, did not at that time accept the right of individual petition or the compulsory jurisdiction of the Court. This was no impediment, however, to Greece lodging two inter-State applications against the United Kingdom in 1956 and 1957. The first alleged that the UK's derogation was invalid and that some of the emergency laws and practices adopted in Cyprus were incompatible with the Convention, such as the use of whipping and collective punishment. The second application alleged that 49 individuals in Cyprus had been tortured by British soldiers. While the Commission investigated these complaints the Greek and British governments began peace talks, and when the Commission referred the applications to the Committee of Ministers (they could not be referred to the Court because the UK had not yet accepted its jurisdiction in any matter) the Committee decided that no further action was called for and the two governments agreed that the file should be closed.[41] That both of these applications, which raised such serious issues, could be so easily swept under the carpet for reasons of political expediency tells us a great deal about the politicization of the Council of Europe's human rights organs at this time. It did not augur well for the future.

Cyprus was granted its independence in 1960, but there continued to be antagonism between the Greek-speaking majority and the Turkish-speaking minority. Few thought that the fragile peace settlement would last. Writing in 1968, with remarkable prescience, Moses Moskowitz predicted that difficulties would arise because of the one-sided nature of the country's 1960 Constitution:

> The Constitution is patently weighted in favour of the Turkish minority. It provides an elaborate system of checks, balances and divided powers between the two communities and vests in the Turkish minority a virtual veto over all important acts of state in the field of foreign and domestic policy, defense and security . . . A constitution which institutionalized these [ethnic, religious and sociological] differences, not only could not facilitate a process of integration around a common Cypriot nationality, but also checked the natural process of majority and minority accommodation.[42]

After a number of violent incidents the Turkish government took matters into its own hands by boldly launching an invasion of the northern part of the island in 1974, and it has occupied that territory (amounting to some 40 per cent of the island's land area) ever since, despite its right to be there not being recognized by any other nation in Western Europe. In the immediate aftermath of the Turkish invasion, and no doubt inspired by the fact that both Greece and Ireland had already taken inter-State cases against the United Kingdom, the Cypriot government lodged two applications against

[40] For the text of the thinly worded *Note Verbale* see (1956–57) 1 Ybk 49.

[41] *Greece v UK* (1956–57) 1 Ybk 128; (1958–59) 2 Ybk 174.

[42] Moskowitz (1968) 131 and 132.

Turkey in Strasbourg.[43] The European Commission reported on these applications in May 1976,[44] even though Turkey had refused to participate in the proceedings beyond arguing that they were inadmissible because Turkey had no jurisdiction over what was 'the Turkish Federate State of Cyprus'. The Commission's report found that the Turkish security forces had killed a substantial number of people in Cyprus, raped and ill-treated both detainees and non-detainees, displaced people from their homes and not allowed them to return, held more than 2,000 Cypriots in detention centres, and deprived many people of their property. Moreover, the Commission noted that 'the acts violating the Convention were exclusively directed against members of one of the two communities in Cyprus, namely the Greek Cypriot community' and it concluded, by 11 votes to three, 'that Turkey has thus failed to secure the rights and freedoms set forth in these Articles without discrimination on the grounds of ethnic origin, race and religion as required by Article 14 of the Convention'.[45] One of the dissenters was Dr Daver, the Turkish Commissioner, whose separate opinion disagrees with virtually every aspect of the Commission's work on the case and upbraids the other majority Commissioners for not concerning themselves with the reasons which led to Turkey 'intervening' in Cyprus in the first place. When the Commission's report was referred to the Committee of Ministers the latter requested the Turkish government to take measures to put an end to the violations identified by the Commission and urged the parties to resume 'intercommunal talks'. Nearly two years later, in 1979, a full year after the European Court's decision in *Ireland v United Kingdom*,[46] the Committee of Ministers further noted, with regret, that its request had not been taken up by the parties concerned. It nevertheless repeated its call, this time suggesting that the talks be held under the auspices of the Secretary General of the United Nations. Very regrettably, it then stated that this action completed its consideration of *Cyprus v Turkey*. In other words, the Committee of Ministers showed itself to be pusillanimous in the face of serious human rights violations committed by one member State of the Council of Europe on the territory of another. It was a black day for human rights throughout the Continent.

Meanwhile, however, Cyprus had lodged a third application against Turkey, in 1977, the complaints being similar to those raised in the earlier applications.[47] Again Turkey would not participate in the proceedings, at least when the merits were being discussed. The Commission presented its report on the merits in 1983, though the Committee of Ministers did not permit this to be published until more than eight years later.[48] The report found once more that Turkey had committed several serious violations, including of the rights protected by Articles 5 and 8 and Article 1 of Protocol 1, but there was again a strongly worded dissent from the Turkish

[43] Turkey had ratified the Convention in 1954, but did not recognize the competence of the European Commission to receive petitions from individuals or non-governmental organizations until 1987, or the automatic competence of the European Court until 1990. Cyprus ratified in 1962.

[44] *Cyprus v Turkey* (1982) 4 EHRR 482.

[45] ibid, para 503.

[46] (1979–80) 2 EHRR 25.

[47] *Cyprus v Turkey* (1979) 13 DR 85.

[48] The Commission's report is most easily accessed through (1992) 13 HRLJ 154.

Commissioner.[49] The report was transmitted to the Committee of Ministers but still no action was taken by Turkey to redress the identified violations and the Committee did little to put pressure on the Turkish government. In the 1992 resolution by which it eventually authorized publication of the Commission's report, the Committee said that the resolution completed its consideration of the case.[50] Reviewing the record of the European Convention system after these first three applications in connection with Turkish actions in Cyprus, one can only agree with Nowak that they 'clearly show the limits of the international protection of human rights'.[51] The Committee of Ministers, above all, displayed a political approach which was quite antithetical to human rights. Inter-State applications, like that brought by the United Kingdom against Ireland, were proving mostly inefficacious.

But there was still one further inter-State application by Cyprus against Turkey to come, in 1994, and this time the issues could at last be referred to the European Court, because by then Turkey had accepted the Court's competence. The matters raised concerned missing persons, displaced persons, living conditions for Greek Cypriots in Northern Cyprus, and the rights of Turkish Cypriots and Gypsies. The Commission adopted its report on the merits in 1999[52] and the case then went to the Court. Cyprus objected to two of the individuals selected to serve as Turkey's judge on the Court and Turkey, in turn, objected to Mr Loukis Loucaides, the Cypriot judge, who had acted for Cyprus in relation to its application lodged against Turkey in 1977. The Grand Chamber of the Court eventually delivered a very full judgment (126 pages if the dissents are included) in 2001, less than a week after its seminal decisions in the quartet of Northern Irish cases on the duty to investigate killings.[53]

It is neither possible nor necessary to provide full details here of all of the Court's conclusions. Suffice it to say that, in respect of missing persons, it held unanimously that there had been no breach of Articles 2 or 5 by reason of any violation of substantive obligations under those Articles but, by 16 votes to one, that there had been a continuing violation of Articles 2, 3, and 5 in that Turkish authorities had failed to conduct effective investigations into the whereabouts and fate of Greek-Cypriot missing persons who had disappeared in life-threatening circumstances. By the same voting margin there were held to be continuing violations of Articles 8 and 13 and of Article 1 of Protocol 1 in respect of displaced persons. But as for Article 14, all 17 judges agreed that in relation to displaced persons there was no need to examine whether it had been violated in conjunction with other articles, nor whether the alleged discriminatory treatment of Greek-Cypriot displaced persons gave rise to a

49 'The Commission's Report, unfortunately like the previous one, is incomplete, lacking in many crucial facts relevant to the case, arrives at conclusions without the counter evidence and omits some important factual and legal issues indicated above. I consider that the content and the presentation of the Report as such do not reflect in an accurate and complete way the historical, factual and legal situation in Cyprus... For these reasons, I am against the Report as a whole, and I am opposed to the conclusions of the Commission therein.' ibid, 171.

50 Resolution DH (92) 12; (1992) 13 HRLJ 181.

51 Nowak (1989) 99.

52 This is published as an Annex to the report of the European Court's judgment printed in *Reports of Judgments and Decisions*.

53 *Cyprus v Turkey* (2002) 35 EHRR 731.

breach of Article 3. In relation to living conditions, again by 16 votes to one, there were found to be breaches of Articles 8, 9, 10 and 13, and of Articles 1 or 2 of Protocol 1, but again it was deemed unnecessary to consider Article 14. The consistently dissenting voice in these votes was that of Judge Fuad, the *ad hoc* judge from Turkey. The Committee of Ministers, in 2005 and 2007,[54] adopted interim resolutions welcoming the progress made by the Turkish government in complying with the 2001 judgment, expressed itself satisfied on some counts (eg as regards the means taken to comply with Articles 9 and 10, and Article 2 of Protocol 1) but called for more information in relation to the remaining issues.

After Turkey accepted the right of individual petition in 1990 there were several applications lodged in Strasbourg relating to the 1974 invasion of Cyprus. The best known of these resulted in the judgment in *Loizidou v Turkey*,[55] where a Greek Cypriot claimed that she owned property in northern Cyprus and that Turkish forces were preventing her from returning to it. She alleged that Turkey was therefore responsible for continuing violations of Article 1 of Protocol 1 and of Article 8 of the Convention. On the preliminary point of whether the application could refer to events occurring before 1990, the Court held by 11 votes to six that it could, drawing support for this from its own previous rulings in two cases brought against Greece. [56] On the substance of the matter the Court then held, again by 11 votes to six, that there had been a breach of Article 1 of Protocol 1 but, unanimously, that there had been no breach of Article 8.[57] The applicant lost on Article 8 because she did not have a home on the land in question but merely proposed to build one there. In a very recent decision, *Varnava and others v Turkey*,[58] involving applications by individuals relating to the disappearance of nine Cypriot nationals during Turkish military operations in Cyprus in the summer of 1974, the Court was satisfied that, having regard to the exceptional situation brought about by the international conflict, the applicants had acted with reasonable expedition, even though they had brought their complaints *three years* after Turkey accepted the right of individual petition. Notwithstanding the time lapse (and Turkey's acceptance of the work being carried out by the UN's Committee of Missing Persons) the Court concluded that Turkey was in continuing breach of its duty under Article 2 of the European Convention to effectively investigate the disappearances. The rights of the relatives of the disappeared not to be ill-treated under Article 3 were also violated. Only one judge dissented—*ad hoc* Judge Erönen from Turkey.

[54] Interim Resolution CM/ResDH (2007) 25.

[55] (1997) 23 EHRR 513. See too *Demades v Turkey* App No 16219/90, decision of 31 July 2003.

[56] *Papamichalopoulos v Greece* (1993) 16 EHRR 440, para 46, and *Agrotexim v Greece* (1996) 21 EHRR 250, para 58.

[57] One of the dissenters, needless to say, was Judge Gölcüklü from Turkey. He was joined by the judges from France, Germany, Hungary, Portugal, and Slovenia, all of whom doubted whether Turkey could be held responsible under principles of public international law. Judge Pettiti from France said: 'The movement of displaced persons from one zone to another, an exodus which affected both communities, was the consequence of international events for which responsibility cannot be ascribed on the basis of the facts of the *Loizidou* case but has to be sought in the sphere of international relations.'

[58] App No 16064/90 et al, decision of 18 September 2009 (Grand Chamber).

The lesson to be drawn from the way in which cases involving human rights abuses associated with the conflict in Cyprus have been dealt with is surely that effective monitoring has really become possible only with developments in the *modus operandi* of the European Convention's enforcement organs. The Committee of Ministers, above all, initially displayed a political approach which was quite unhelpful. But in 1998 the Commission of Human Rights was abolished, the Court became more accessible and more professional, and the role of the Committee of Ministers became less significant. As a result, the recent 'policing' of the Cypriot conflict, in human rights terms, has been more transparent, even if a lot more still needs to be done to ensure full accountability of the Turkish authorities. Loukis Loucaides, the Cypriot judge who was barred from sitting in the Court's hearing of Cyprus' fourth inter-State application, has since observed that the case dealt with human rights violations on a much greater scale than those examined in *Ireland v United Kingdom*,[59] but he adds: 'The Court has proved once more that it can act judicially and defend the public order of Europe in situations where the violations are intertwined with political issues leading to them.'[60] The recent decisions involving Cyprus, although not cited by him in this connection, do tend to support Nico Krisch's argument that the European Convention operates as a 'pluralist order' wherein 'mutual accommodation and convergence have been the norm, facilitated by the flexible and responsive strategies of the courts involved, and especially of the [European Court] itself'.[61] This approach reflects even more obviously the experience of Northern Ireland vis-à-vis the Convention, given that national courts in the United Kingdom have 'inter-played' with the European Court to a much greater extent than have courts in Cyprus or Turkey.

The fate of the attempts to use the European Convention to identify and remedy human rights violations in Cyprus shows that the experience of applicants complaining of human rights violations in Northern Ireland was not unique. The Cypriot efforts were focused primarily on inter-State applications, while the efforts relating to Northern Ireland were a mixture of inter-State and individual applications, although predominantly the latter. Inter-governmental political sensitivities bedevilled the satisfactory resolution of many of the issues, at least during the worst years of the conflicts, and breakthroughs were achieved only when the Court in Strasbourg gained enough self-confidence to strike out on its own as a truly independent and rights-focused institution. As regards the resort by States to notices of derogation, however, the Court has still to apply more rigorous criteria and, as a result, it is still perceived as too subservient and deferential to the policy choices made by State governments. There is still a residue of what looks like bias on the part of certain national judges, who are unable to see the situation in their own country with truly objective eyes. The Committee of Ministers also still lacks the teeth to be able to ensure that Court judgments are adhered to quickly and completely.

59 Loucaides (2007) 108. 60 ibid, 119. 61 Krisch (2008) 215.

The future

There is every chance that the European Court will continue to provide strong support for individual human rights on a Europe-wide basis for the foreseeable future. Notwithstanding its huge workload problems,[62] it will seek to reaffirm its pre-eminence as the leading international human rights court in the world. To maintain that position, however, it may have to shift towards providing 'constitutional' justice rather than justice in every individual case.[63] It will also have to engage more earnestly with the interface between the protection of human rights and the prevention of terrorism, as there seems to be no let-up in the threat from that quarter.[64] To do so it may need to develop still further the concept of positive obligations, along the lines of those already adopted in the leading Article 2 cases concerning deaths connected with Northern Ireland's conflict.[65] It will also need to be more assertive on a range of rights over and above the so-called 'absolute' rights in Articles 2, 3, 4, and 7 of the Convention. When governments are faced with conflicts in their societies they will be tempted to cut corners even on non-derogable human rights in order to preserve public order. The Court must not allow this to occur unless the justification for doing so is absolutely clear and compelling. Too often in the past the enforcement organs at Strasbourg did not adopt a strict enough approach when considering applications arising out of Northern Ireland's conflict. Failure to do so helped to prolong that conflict. In the future the Court and Committee of Ministers will need to be more aggressive with recalcitrant governments. Arold has claimed that already '[t]he Court breaks century old traditions in national legal systems and replaces them with its own interpretation of the law of the Convention',[66] but the evidence from Northern Ireland does not suggest that that is true across all European jurisdictions. Unless the Court is bolder and less deferential than it has been to date regarding the protection of human rights during times of severe societal unrest, it will lose credibility as the foremost standard-bearer for human rights in the world today.

[62] Bernhardt (1995); Greer (2006) 38–41.

[63] ibid, 165–74. See too Jackson (1997) and Letsas (2007) esp 99–119.

[64] Bonner (2007); Russell (2007); Guelke (2006); Wilkinson (2006); Warbrick (2002); Bonner (2000).

[65] See nn 13 and 14 above.

[66] Arold (2007) 34.

APPENDIX

Applications lodged in Strasbourg relating to the conflict in Northern Ireland

Applications are listed in the order of the application number allocated to them in Strasbourg. While attempts have been made to make the list as comprehensive as possible, it is likely that some lesser-known applications have been omitted because of the difficulties involved in tracing applications on the basis of the applicant's place of residence. For the pages in the book where these applications are discussed or mentioned, see the Table of Cases. Note that from 2001 references to the EHRR are to case numbers, not page numbers.

Name, number, and date of introduction of the application (when known)	Summary of Commission, Court, and Committee of Ministers decisions in Strasbourg
Lawless v Ireland App 352/57 8 November 1957	Commission: 30 August 1958; 2 Ybk 308: declared admissible 19 December 1959: report adopted 13 April 1960: case submitted to the Court Court: 3–4 October 1960: oral hearings at the Court 14 November 1960 (A1); (1979–80) 1 EHRR 1 (6 v 1): held that the European Commission of Human Rights could, prior to the Court hearing, provide a copy of its report on the application to persons directly concerned in the case. 7 April 1961 (A2); (1979–80) 1 EHRR 13 (7 v 0): held that the European Commission of Human Rights, when making its observations on the application to the Court, could take account of the views of the applicant on the issues involved. 1 July 1961 (A3); (1979–80) 1 EHRR 15 (7 v 0): held that Ireland had not violated Art 5 by interning the applicant because its derogation notice was valid; there was a public emergency threatening the life of the nation and internment was a proportionate response to that emergency.
A and others v UK App 3625/68	December 1970; (1970) Ybk 340: held by the Commission that the applications complaining about the Special Powers Act, electoral law, and discrimination, should be struck out because the applicants had failed to settle who would represent them and had omitted to make supplementary submissions when requested to do so.

Devlin v UK (*also known as X v UK*) App 4607/70	3 February 1971; (1971) Ybk 634; 37 DR 1 Commission held that the application alleging violation of the right to a fair trial was inadmissible because the Convention gives a wide latitude to States to decide what evidence can or cannot be admitted in court proceedings.
X v UK *aka MM v UK* App 5155/71 20 August 1971	12 July 1976; 6 DR 13 Complaints about the lack of local government elections since 1969, and the electoral system used up to then, held inadmissible by the Commission because local elections are not covered by Art 3 of Prot 1.
Ireland v UK App 5310/71 16 December 1971 App 5451/72 6 March 1972	Commission: 16 December 1971; (1971) 14 Ybk 100: application lodged 1 October 1972; (1972) 15 Ybk 76: declared admissible 9 February 1976; (1976) 19 Ybk 512: Commission's report Court: 18 January 1978 (A25); (1979–80) 2 EHRR 25 16 v 1: the 'five techniques' were inhuman and degrading treatment 17 v 0: there was a practice of inhuman treatment at Palace Barracks 13 v 4: the 'five techniques' were not torture 14 v 3: the practice at Palace Barracks was not torture 15 v 2: no violation of Art 3 in relation to other places 17 v 0: there was a public emergency threatening the life of the nation 16 v 1: the steps taken did not exceed what was required under Art 5 17 v 0: the steps taken did not exceed what was required under Art 6 15 v 2: no violation of Art 14 taken together with Arts 5 or 6
X and Y v UK App 5459/72 10 March 1972	23 March 1972; 40 CD 7 The applicant who brought App 5155/71 (an internee in Long Kesh), and his legal representative (James Heaney, from the USA), complained that correspondence between them was opened and censored by UK authorities, in violation of Arts 5, 6, 8, and 11. The Commission said no evidence of censoring had been adduced, and that interference with mail was justified under Art 8(2) as it was 'prescribed by law' (reg 13(2) of the Special Powers Act Regulations) and was 'in the interests of national security' or 'for the prevention of disorder or crime'. The Commission found no basis for a violation of Arts 5, 6, or 11: in those respects, the application was declared inadmissible as manifestly ill-founded.
Donnelly and others v UK App 5577/72–5583/72	14 July 1972 Commission decided to expedite its handling of the application, but could not issue a temporary injunction. 5 April 1973; (1973) Ybk 212; 43 CD 122 Complaints admissible even though little evidence of victimhood or of exhaustion of domestic remedies. 15 December 1975; (1975) 4 DR 4 Complaints held inadmissible in so far as they alleged specific acts in violation of Art 3. All the other admissible applications were rejected.

X, Y and Z v UK App 5727/72, 5744/72, 5857/72	12 July 1978; 14 DR 5 Complaints of violations of Arts 5, 6, 14, and 15 in relation to the applicants' arrest, detention, and internment under the Special Powers Act held inadmissible by the Commission, following *Ireland v UK*.
JPB v Ireland (aka X v Ireland) App 6040/73 12 February 1973	20 July 1973; 16 Ybk 388 Commission found the applicant's complaints under Arts 2, 5, 8, and 14 to be manifestly ill-founded. He had complained that the State was not properly protecting him against threats to his life from the IRA.
X v UK App 6406/73	8 March 1979; (1981) 3 EHRR 302 Commission found the applicant's complaints inadmissi. His arrest under the Special Powers Act was lawful because of the UK's derogation notice (citing *Ireland v UK*), and his complaint about the retrospectivity of the Northern Ireland Act 1972 was ill-founded because he had not exhausted his domestic remedies on that point.
Arrowsmith v UK App 7050/75	16 May 1977; 8 DR 123 Complaints by woman convicted of inciting British soldiers not to agree to serve in Northern Ireland declared admissi. 12 October 1978; (1981) 3 EHRR 218 Complaints not accepted on their merits by the Commission. 15 v 0: no violation of Arts 5 or 9 11 v 1: no violation of Art 10 11 v 0 (and 1 abstention): no violation of Art 14 taken with Arts 9 or 10 Prosecution of the applicant was 'necessary for the protection of national security and the prevention of disorder in the army'. 12 June 1979: Committee of Ministers agreed that there had been no violation of the Convention: ResDH(79) 4.
Dudgeon v UK App 7525/76 22 May 1976	Commission: 13 March 1980; (1980) 3 EHRR 40 Applicant complaining that the criminalization of homosexuality violated his Convention rights. 9 v 1: violation of Art 8 in respect of persons aged over 21 8 v 2: no violation of Art 8 in respect of persons aged under 21 9 v 1: no need to consider Art 14 Court: 23 September 1981 (A45); (1981) 4 EHRR 149 15 v 4: violation of Art 8 14 v 5: no need to consider Art 14 24 February 1983 (A59); (1983) 5 EHRR 573 7 v 0: no compensation awarded
X v UK App 7782/77	2 May 1978; 14 DR 179 (1978) Complaint of violation of Art 2 of Prot 1, and of Art 14, over lack of integrated education in Northern Ireland, held inadmissible by the Commission.
Campbell and Fell v UK App 7819/77 and 7878/77 4 and 31 March 1977	6 May 1978, 9 October 1980, and 14 and 19 March 1981: 22 Ybk 268 (1979); 24 Ybk 110 (1981) Commission held complaints by two Irish republican prisoners in England partly admissible. 12 May 1982: Commission's decision on the merits: Regarding Campbell's application:

- the proceedings before the Board of Visitors involved a violation of Art 6 (9 v 3 abstentions)
- the delay in allowing him to obtain legal advice involved violations of Arts 6(1) and 8(1) (unanimously)
- no violation of Art 6(1) arose from the refusal to allow him facilities for an independent medical examination (unanimously).

Regarding Father Fell's application:

- the delay in allowing him to obtain legal advice involved violations of Arts 6(1) and 8(1) (unanimously)
- no violation of Art 6(1) arose from the refusal to allow him facilities for an independent medical examination (unanimously)
- the refusal to allow him to consult in private with his lawyer was a violation of Art 6(1) and it was not necessary to consider whether it also violated Art 8 (unanimously)
- the refusal to allow him to correspond with two nuns was a violation of Art 8 (unanimously)
- no effective remedy was available to him for his complaints under Art 8 and so there was a violation of Art 13 (unanimously).

28 June 1984 (A80); (1985) 7 EHRR 165; Court held:

Regarding Campbell's application:

- Art 6 was applicable (4 v 3)
- there was no violation of Art 6(1) by reason of the fact that the Board of Visitors did not conduct its adjudication in public (4 v 3)
- there was a violation of Art 6(1) in that the Board did not make public its decision (5 v 2)
- Campbell's inability to obtain legal assistance or legal representation was a violation of Art 6(3)(b) and (c) (5 v 2)
- there was a violation of Arts 6(1) and 8 as regards his access to legal advice in connection with his personal injuries claim (unanimously).

Regarding Father Fell's application:

- there was a violation of Art 6(1) as regards the conditions for visits by his solicitors, and it was not necessary to examine Art 8 on this (unanimously)
- there was a violation of Art 8 as regards his personal correspondence (unanimously)
- there was a violation of Arts 6(1) and 8 as regards his access to legal advice in connection with his personal injuries claim (unanimously)
- there was a violation of Art 13 (unanimously).

Byrne, McFadden, McCluskey and McLarnon v UK
App 7879/77, 7931/77, 7935/77, and 7936/77
1 April 1977, 21 May 1977 (2), and 23 May 1977

51 DR 5

Applicants complained of their inability, while in prison in England, to consult their solicitors out of the sight and hearing of any prison officer. The first applicant also complained about the refusal to allow him access to a doctor of his choice. Held by the Commission:

13 v 0: violation of Art 6(1) concerning the lack of private consultation with solicitors

12 v 1: no violation of Art 6(1) concerning access to a doctor

13 v 0: violation of Arts 6(1) and 8 when the first applicant's correspondence with his solicitor was interfered with

20 March 1987; 51 DR 17: Committee of Ministers' Resolution DH (87) 7

McVeigh, O'Neill and Evans v UK App 8022/77, 8025/77, and 8027/77 29 July 1977	8 December 1979; 18 DR 66 Complaints over the detention and searching of travellers at ports declared admissible by the Commission (*sub nom X, Y and Z v UK*). 18 March 1981; (1983) 5 EHRR 71; (1981) 25 DR 15 Complaints unsuccessful on the merits before the Commission. 13 v 1: no violation of Art 5(1) or (3) 13 v 0 (+ 1 abstention): no violation of Art 5(2) 12 v 0 (+ 2 abstentions): no violation of Art 5(4) 13 v 0 (+ 1 abstention): no violation of Art 5(5) 14 v 0: the measures such as fingerprinting had not violated Art 8 11 v 1 (+ 2 abstentions): retention of records after release had not violated Art 8 14 v 0: the fact that two of the applicants had been prevented from joining their wives did not violate Art 8 12 v 2: the alleged failure to allow two of the applicants to contact their wives violated Art 8. The case was not referred to the European Court (by either the Commission or the UK government), so it was considered instead by the Committee of Ministers. By a Resolution dated 24 March 1982 the Committee endorsed the Commission's views and, because of the changes introduced by s 62 of the Criminal Law Act 1977, it decided that no further action needed to be taken.
X v UK App 8065/77	3 May 1978; 14 DR 246 Complaint by the wife of a republican prisoner in England that her Art 8 rights were violated because there was a partition between her and her husband when she visited and the constant presence of a prison officer. Commission held that the interference with Art 8(1) rights was justified under Art 8(2).
X, Y and Z v UK App 8158/78, 8159/78, and 8462/78	10 July 1980; 21 DR 95 Applicant serving life imprisonment for IRA terrorist offences complained of assault by police officers in England when en route to the police station and while there; his injuries required treatment in hospital. He was also held in solitary confinement for 760 days. The Commission believed the police evidence that he was injured during a struggle, and the solitary confinement, while 'for an unusual and undesirable length of time', was not arbitrary nor of such severity as to fall within the scope of Art 3. Application rejected as manifestly ill-founded.
X and Y v Ireland App 8299/78 16 June 1974	10 October 1980; 22 DR 51 Two brothers complained that they did not get a fair trial, that their extradition proceedings in England were held *in camera* and were based on an affidavit sworn by Ireland's Attorney General stating that their offences were not of a political character, yet they were tried by the Special Criminal Court, and that the conditions of their imprisonment in Ireland were a violation of Art 3. The Commission declared the applications inadmissible because there was no unfairness on the facts, the application should have been brought against the UK in relation to the extradition proceedings there, the Special Criminal Court was lawfully established, and the applicants had not exhausted their domestic remedies in relation to the prison conditions.

McFeeley, Nugent, Hunter and Campbell v UK App 8317/78 9 August 1978	15 May 1980; (1981) 3 EHRR 161; 20 DR 44 17 v 0: complaint over conditions in which prisoners were being held in the Maze Prison held inadmissible by the Commission because the conditions were self-imposed. 2 October 1984: 17 v 0: remaining complaints under Arts 8 and 13 struck off the list because the applicants had failed to pursue them.
Lindsay v UK App 8364/78	8 March 1979; 15 DR 247 (1979); [1979] 3 CMLR 166 15 v 0: complaint of violation of Art 3 of Prot 1, and of Art 14, over use of a different electoral system in Northern Ireland for European elections, held inadmissible because a proportional representation electoral system must be seen as making it easier for the people of Northern Ireland to express their opinions freely and because it was not discriminatory; nor was there any 'degrading treatment' under Art 3.
Orchin v UK App 8435/78 1 September 1978	9 October 1982; 26 DR 18 Complaint held admissible 27 October 1983; (1984) 6 EHRR 391 Commission's report on the merits: 13 v 1: violation of Art 6(1) because the applicant had been held on bail for 4 years in connection with alleged firearms offences 14 v 0: no violation of Arts 3 or 14. Committee of Ministers resolved not to take any further action because the UK government had already announced the steps it had taken to ensure that the abuse would not occur again.
Farrell v UK App 9013/80	11 December 1982; (1983) 5 EHRR 466; 30 DR 96 Complaint that Art 2 had been violated when the applicant's husband was shot dead by British soldiers because they thought he was in the process of planting a bomb, held admissible, but complaints under Arts 6(1) and 13 held manifestly ill-founded. A friendly settlement ensued.
Sands v UK App 9338/81	Complaints by hunger striker Bobby Sands relating to Arts 2, 3, and 10. Struck off the list after the applicant died in prison while on hunger strike in 1981.
W v UK App 9348/81 and *X v Ireland* [same applicant] App 9360/81	(1983) 5 EHRR 504 The UK could not be held responsible in relation to a death occurring in the Republic of Ireland, even if the victim had travelled there from Northern Ireland for a brief visit. Complaint under Art 2 manifestly ill-founded.
X v Ireland App 9742/82	2 March 1983; 32 DR 251 Applicant complained that the length of extradition proceedings against him was a violation of Art 6. Held inadmissible by the Commission because the applicant was himself responsible for the delays, having broken the bail conditions imposed on him when he was arrested in London for handling stolen electric detonators.
X v UK and Ireland App 9825/82	(1986) 8 EHRR 49 As against the UK, the applicant was outside the 6-month time limit in respect of her husband's death, and no issue arose under any article in relation to herself. As against Ireland all complaints were inadmissible *ratione personae*.

H v UK and Ireland App 9833/82 3 December 1981	7 March 1985; 42 DR 53 Commission declared the complaint inadmissible because it was outside the 6-month time limit. The applicant had complained that the UK and Ireland had not done enough to prevent terrorists from killing her daughter in 1977.
M v UK and Ireland App 9837/82	4 March 1986; 47 DR 27 Applicant complained, on behalf of herself and her dependent children, of violations of Art 2 in respect of the murder of her husband in Armagh in 1980. The Commission applied its decision in *H v UK* (7 March 1985) and held the application to be manifestly ill-founded because the UK was not required to take further measures to protect the applicant's husband.
Stewart v UK App 10044/82	(1985) 7 EHRR 453 Complaints alleging violation of Arts 2, 3, and 14 over fatal shooting of 13-year-old boy by plastic baton round. Held inadmissible by the Commission because the action was lawfully taken for the purpose of quelling a riot.
Mallon v UK App 10316/83	7 March 1984; 37 DR 129 (1984) No violation of Art 3 of Prot 1 in the ban on a person being a member of a British Parliamentary body as well as of a foreign Parliamentary body (the Irish Senate). Application declared manifestly ill-founded by the Commission.
M v UK App 10386/83 12 May 1983	12 March 1986 Commission declared inadmissible the complaint by an Irish republican prisoner in England that his rights under Art 6 were violated by the fact the governments of the UK and Ireland had passed legislation enabling persons accused of committing crimes in the UK to be tried in Ireland and vice versa. He had no standing to appear before the Irish Court of Criminal Appeal when the British DPP applied there for access to certain exhibits (in use at a trial of another man there). Nor could he get legal aid in respect of those proceedings. The Commission said the application was inadmissible *ratione materiae* because the proceedings in Ireland did not 'determine his civil rights or obligations' under Art 6(1) and the UK could not confer a right of audience in an Irish court. There was in any event no allegation that the exhibits transferred from and to Ireland were contaminated in any way.
M and others v UK App 11208/84 9 October 1984 *William McQuiston* *William Ritchie* *Thomas Harris* *Elmer Stevenson* *Alan McKenzie*	4 March 1986; 46 DR 182 14 v 0: complaints by loyalist prisoners who had taken part in an abortive hunger strike to achieve segregation from republican prisoners at Magilligan Prison, from 19 August to 18 September 1984, declared inadmissible. Complaints under Arts 2 and 3 were declared inadmissible because of a failure to exhaust domestic remedies. Further complaints under Art 3 were declared manifestly ill-founded because the applicants were alone responsible for their condition. Complaints under Art 5 were declared inadmissible because the 'right to security' has never been interpreted by the Court in the way suggested. Complaints under Art 14 were declared inadmissible too.

Brogan v UK App 11209/84 18 October 1984 *Coyle v UK* App 11234/84 22 October 1984 *McFadden v UK* App 11266/84 22 November 1984 *Tracey v UK* App 11365/85 8 February 1985	Commission: 11 July 1986: joint hearing on admissibility and merits; all complaints about not being brought promptly before a court held admissible 14 May 1987; (1987) 9 EHRR 378 10 v 2: applications by Brogan (detained for 5 days 11 hours) and Coyle (6 days and 16.5 hours) upheld 8 v 4: applications by McFadden (4 days 6 hours) and Tracey (4 days 11 hours) rejected Court: 29 November 1988 (A145); (1989) 11 EHRR 117 12 v 7: all applications upheld in relation to violation of Art 5(3) 13 v 6: all applications upheld in relation to violation of Art 5(5) 30 May 1989 (A152) 18 v 0: the judgment already issued was held to be just satisfaction, so no compensation was awarded.
M v UK App No 11517/85	3 March 1986 Complaint against applicant's exclusion from Great Britain held inadmissible as 'manifestly ill-founded' because it was not a penalty, so Arts 6 and 7 were not engaged, and there was no violation of Arts 8, 9, or 13.
Lyttle v UK App 11650/85	(1987) 9 EHRR 381 Complaint over the detention and searching of travellers at ports, held inadmissible. No violation of Art 5(1), (2), or (4), following *McVeigh and others v UK*, or of Art 13.
Fox v UK App 12244/86 16 June 1986 *Campbell v UK* App 12245/86 16 June 1986 *Hartley v UK* 12383/86 8 September 1986	Commission: 10 May 1988; 15 v 0: complaints declared admissible 4 May 1989: 7 v 5: the applicants' arrest and detention were not justified under Art 5(1)(c) 7 v 5: the applicants were not informed promptly of the reasons for their arrest, in violation of Art 5(2) 9 v 3: there was no violation of Art 5(4) 7 v 5: there was a violation of Art 5(5) 12 v 0: no separate issue arose under Art 13. Court: 30 August 1990 (A182); (1990) 13 EHRR 157 4 v 3: violation of Art 5(1) 7 v 0: no violation of Art 5(2) 4 v 3: violation of Art 5(5) 7 v 0: unnecessary to examine the complaints under Arts 5(4) and 13 27 March 1991 (A190-B): Court decided by 6 v 1 not to award any compensation because the principal judgment in itself constituted sufficient just satisfaction for the purposes of Art 50.
K and F v The Netherlands App No 12543/86 18 November 1986	2 December 1986; 51 DR 272 Commission declared inadmissible claims by potential extraditees from the Netherlands that they would be ill-treated in the Maze prison if returned there.

Clinton v UK App 12690/87 27 January 1987 Also: *Simpson v UK* 12731/87, *Maguire v UK* 12823/87, *McGeown v UK* 12900/87 *Murray v UK* 13032/87 *Campbell v UK* 13033/87 *Smyth v UK* 13246/87 *Breslin v UK* 13231/87 *Connolly v UK* 13232/87 *McGuinness v UK* 13233/87 *L v UK* 13310/87 *M v UK* 13553/88 *N v UK* 13555/88	Commission: 31 May 1991: held admissible 14 October 1991: decision on the merits: 7 v 2: violation of Art 5(1) in all applications, following *Fox, Campbell and Hartley v UK* (lack of reasonable suspicion). Unnecessary, therefore, to consider the applicants' argument that their arrest had been merely for the purposes of interrogation. 9 v 0: violation of Art 5(2) in the case of Kieran Smyth, who had been kept overnight without being given any substantial explanation for his detention other than an initial reference to the EPA 1978, and whose interviews began 14 hours 50 minutes after his arrest 7 v 2: violation of Art 5(5) in the cases of the first seven applicants 11 January 1995: Committee of Ministers expressed satisfaction with the friendly settlement reached by the UK government with the parties whereby the government paid their agreed costs and expenses. The statutory test for arrest had also been changed by the EPA 1987.
Murray (Margaret) App 14310/88 28 September 1988	17 February 1993 Commission decided complaints raised by a family during a house search by the Army: 11 v 3: violation of Art 5(1) and 5(5) 10 v 4: violation of Art 5(2) 13 v 1: no violation of Art 8 10 v 4: no violation of Art 13 in relation to the keeping of a photograph and personal details 14 v 0: no violation of Art 13 in relation to the entry and search of the applicant's home. Court: 28 October 1994 (A300); (1995) 19 EHRR 193 14 v 4: no violation of Art 5(1) 13 v 5: no violation of Art 5(2) or 5(5) 15 v 3: no violation of Art 8 18 v 0: no violation of Art 13.
Sean and Kathleen McEldowney v UK App 14550/89 13 January 1989 and 11 other applicants: *Gerard Burns* *Sean McGovern* *Michael Fox*	Commission: 5 March 1991 9 v 0: App 14550/89 held admissible as regards Arts 5(3) and 5(5), but not 5(2), following *Fox, Campbell and Hartley v UK.* 14 October 1991 9 v 1: violation of Arts 5(3) and 5(5), applying *Brogan v UK*; the applicants had been held under s 12 of the PTA 1984 between August and October 1988 for between 4 days 6 hours and 6 days 20 hours. 4 May 1994: Committee of Ministers' Resolution accepted that the

Michael Mullin *Kevin Mullin* *Mark Mullin* *Arthur McNally* *Francis McKeown* *Peter Hughes* *Patrick O'Hagan* *Raymond Larmour*	UK government had paid the applicant's costs and expenses, nothing else having been claimed, and had entered a notice a derogation after the decision in *Brogan v UK*.
McShane v UK App 14552/89 16 December 1988	26 February 1991 Commission referred the application to the Second Chamber of the Commission, having awaited the Court's decision in *Fox, Campbell and Hartley v UK*. 5 March 1991 Second Chamber found the complaint ('by a majority' of the 9 Commissioners) to be manifestly ill-founded since the applicant had been detained for 3 days and 11 hours on suspicion of involvement in the murder of a UDR soldier the previous month (ie within the 4-day maximum) and had given contradictory accounts of his movements on that day.
Brannigan and McBride v UK App 14553/89 and 14554/89 19 January 1989	Commission: 28 February 1991: complaints declared admissible 3 December 1991: by 8 v 5 the Commission held on the merits that, since the requirements of Art 15 had been met, there was no violation of Art 5(3) or 5(5) when the applicants were held in pre-charge detention for more then 4 days. Court: 26 May 1993 (A258); (1993) 17 EHRR 539 22 v 4: the UK's derogation satisfied the requirements of Art 15 and therefore the applicants could not validly complain of a violation of Art 5(3) 22 v 4: no violation of Art 5 (5) 22 v 4: no violation of Art 13.
Malachy Mullin v UK App 14707/89 13 February 1989	5 March 1991 Complaint that applicant, having been arrested on suspicion of involvement in planting a bomb near Ballygawley which killed eight British soldiers in 1988, was unlawfully detained for one day and 14 hours in violation of Art 5(3). Held inadmissible in the light of the European Court's decision in *Brogan v UK* that detention for up to 4 days before being brought before a court was justifiable.
Callaghan and others v UK App No 14739/89 13 October 1988	9 May 1989; 60 DR 296 Complaints by the 'Birmingham Six' that Arts 6 and 13 were violated because the Court of Appeal in England had considered the new evidence in the case without ordering a retrial in front of a jury: declared inadmissible by the Commission (17 v 0).
O'Hagan v UK App 14765/89 27 February 1989	5 March 1991 Commission declared admissible a complaint under Art 5(3) and (5) that the applicant had been arrested and detained for 4 days 6 hours and 41 minutes under the same provisions as in *Brogan v UK*, without being brought before a judge or other officer authorized by law to exercise judicial power.
McGlinchey (Dominic) v Ireland App 14774/89	4 September 1989 Application declared inadmissible by the Commission (referred to in App 16751/90, below).

McGlinchey (Paul), Quinn and Barrow v UK App 15096–15098/89 29 March 1989	2 July 1990 Commission, following *Brogan v UK*, declared admissible complaints by three applicants that they had been detained at Stranraer for 4 days and 20½ hours (from 29 September to 4 October 1988) before being issued with exclusion orders excluding them from Great Britain. 7 December 1990 Commission unanimously held that there had been a violation of Art 5(3) and (5). 28 January 1997 Committee of Ministers resolved that it would accept the UK government's response to the case (viz the lodging of a further notice of derogation under Art 15 of the Convention).
Purcell v Ireland App 15404/89 11 August 1989	16 April 1991; (1991) 12 HRLJ 254 Application challenging the broadcasting ban declared inadmissible, by a majority. Cf *Brind v United Kingdom* (App 18714/91).
McGlinchey (Dominic) v Ireland App 16751/90 19 January 1990	5 March 1991 Application by Dominic McGlinchey challenging his arrest and extradition to Northern Ireland declared inadmissible because it was lodged outside the 6-month time limit; the Commission said it was in any event unfounded because there was no evidence to show that the arrest or extradition were unlawful .
O'Neill (Anne-Marie) v UK App 17441/90 19 November 1990	4 September 1992 Commission declared application complaining about house search procedures to be inadmissible because of a failure to exhaust domestic remedies.
Kelly v UK App 17579/90 4 December 1990	13 January 1993; (1993) 16 EHRR CD20 Complaint over the fatal shooting of a teenage joyrider by a British soldier, inadmissible because the use of force was justified in the circumstances (by a majority of the 17 Commissioners).
Kelly (Gerard) v UK App 17711/91 14 December 1990	4 September 1992 Complaint held inadmissible ('by a majority') for non-exhaustion of domestic remedies; the applicant complained about being stopped in a car and required to accompany it to the Maze prison for a thorough search, all of which took almost 3 hours.
McCotter v UK App No 18632/91 26 July 1991	(1993) 15 EHRR CD98; 9 December 1992 Commission declared inadmissible a complaint by an Irish republican prisoner in Leicester that the Home Secretary would not allow him to be temporarily transferred to a Northern Ireland prison to facilitate visits from his family. A later application by the same applicant was also declared inadmissible (see App No 20479/92).
Brind (David) v UK App 18714/91 12 March 1991 and 6 other applicants: *Fred Emery* *Alex Graham* *Victoria Leonard* *Scarlett McGwire* *Thomas Nash* *John Pilger*	9 May 1994; 77 DR 42 Complaint alleging that the broadcasting ban operating in the UK was a violation of the right to freedom of expression under Art 10, held inadmissible by the Commission ('by a majority' of the 20 Commissioners). Cf *Purcell v Ireland* (App 15404/89).

Murray (John) v UK App 18731/91 16 August 1991	Commission: 18 January 1994: complaints about the denial of access to a solicitor and the drawing of inferences from the applicant's silence declared admissible. 27 June 1994: report published 15 v 2: no violation of Art 6(1) and (2) 13 v 4: violation of Art 6(1) in conjunction with (3)(c) 14 v 3: unnecessary to consider Art 14. Court: 8 February 1996; (1996) 22 EHRR 29 14 v 5: no violation of Art 6(1) and (2) arising out of the drawing of adverse inferences from the applicant's silence 12 v 7: violation of Art 6(1) in conjunction with Art 6 (3)(c) as regards the applicant's lack of access to a lawyer during the first 48 hours of detention 19 v 0: unnecessary to consider Art 14 19 v 0: no compensation awarded.
McCann, Farrell and Savage v UK App 18984/91 14 August 1991	Commission: 3 September 1993: complaints about the shooting dead of three alleged terrorists in Gibraltar declared admissible. 4 March 1994: merits; (1996) 21 EHRR 97 at 135–159 11 v 6: no violation of Art 2. Court: 27 September 1995 (A324); (1996) 21 EHRR 97 10 v 9: violation of Art 2. 22 March 1996: Resolution of Committee of Ministers.
PK, MK and BK v UK App 19085/91 15 October 1991	(1993) 15 EHRR CD106 Complaints by a life sentence prisoner in England and his mother and sister in Northern Ireland that the refusal to transfer him to a prison in Northern Ireland was a violation of the applicants' rights under Art 8, and that the treatment of Irish republican prisoners in English prisons was a violation of the right not to be discriminated against under Art 14. The Commission held that the refusal to transfer was a justifiable interference with Art 8 rights and that the differential treatment of Category A prisoners convicted of terrorist offences was justifiable under Art 14.
O'Neill (Peter) v UK App 19748/92 30 January 1992	5 May 1993 Complaint about the delay involved in releasing the applicant from detention under the PTA while an application for an exclusion order was dealt with, held inadmissible because it was not brought within the 6-month time limit.
Tinnelly v UK App 20390/92 27 May 1992 *McElduff Ltd v UK* App 21322/92 6 August 1992	Commission: 20 May 1996: complaints declared admissible, 'by a majority' 8 April 1997: 17 v 0: violation of Art 6(1) and not necessary to decide claims based on Arts 8, 13, and 14. Court: 10 July 1998; (1999) 27 EHRR 249 9 v 0: violation of Art 6(1) when firms of contractors had been denied the chance to challenge in a domestic court the validity of a statutory 'national security certificate' issued by the Secretary of State for

	Northern Ireland to prevent an inquiry into alleged discrimination on grounds of religious belief or political opinion. Not necessary to consider the claims under Arts 8, 13, or 14. 10 April 2000: Resolution by Committee of Ministers expressed satisfaction that the Northern Ireland Act Tribunal (Procedure) Rules 1999 had come into force.
Vella v UK App 20482/92 3 July 1992	See the same applicant's later application: App 23958/94.
O'Dwyer v UK App 20487/92 3 July 1992	1 September 1993 Complaint that not transferring one prisoner from England to Northern Ireland was a violation of her and her family's rights under Art 8, declared inadmissible; also a complaint that there was discrimination under Art 14 because Irish republican prisoners were treated differently from other prisoners, but this was held inadmissible too.
X v UK App 20657/92	(1993) 15 EHRR CD113 One individual tried and convicted for the murder of two British corporals in a filmed incident in Belfast in 1988 complained that at his trial he was unable to see witnesses from the press because they were screened off from him and from the public. The Commission held there was no violation of Art 6(1) or of Art 6(3)(d). The applicant's legal representative had been able to see the witnesses (as had the judge and the prosecution) and to put all the questions he wished to them. In any event the evidence in question had not implicated the applicant at all.
Hamill v United Kingdom App 21656/93 15 April 1993	Complaint that the inferences drawn against the applicant pursuant to the Criminal Evidence (NI) Order 1988 deprived him of his right to a fair trial and his right to be presumed innocent, citing Art 6(1), (2), and (3). He also complained that the admission of a woman's statement in writing only, with no opportunity for cross-examination, was a violation of Art 6(3)(d). 10 October 1994: Commission adjourned the application pending the outcome of *Murray (John) v UK*. 21 October 1996: Commission held admissible the first complaint but held the complaint about the written statement to be inadmissible because it was raised beyond the 6-month limitation rule. 2 December 1997: Commission found no violation (31 v 1).
Walsh, Holmes, Armstrong, Walsh, Walsh and Walsh v UK App 21681/93 10 March 1993	11 January 1994 Complaints by three Irish prisoners in Maghaberry, and the wife and children of one of them, that their sentences had been fixed by a decision of the Secretary of State rather than by a judicial hearing, in violation of Art 5(4), declared inadmissible because out of time. Complaints by all six applicants that their family life had not been respected because of the failure to transfer the prisoners from England to Northern Ireland also declared inadmissible because the first three applicants were no longer victims. The complaint about discrimination on the basis of the prisoners' identification with the Irish republican movement did not have to be considered.
Hardy v Ireland	29 June 1994 Commission unanimously declared inadmissible a complaint that

App 23456/94 14 September 1993	s 4 of the Explosive Substances Act 1883 violated the presumption of innocence guaranteed by Art 6(2).
Quinn (Dermot) v United Kingdom App 23496/94 30 September 1993	20 May 1995: Commission adjourned the case pending the European Court's judgment in *Murray (John) v UK.* 21 October 1996: declared the complaints admissible (27 v 0) 11 December 1997: Commission held: 30 v 2: no violation of Art 6(1) in respect of the drawing of adverse inferences 30 v 2: no violation of Art 6(2) 30 v 2: a violation of Art 6(1) in conjunction with Art 6(3)(c) as regards the applicant's lack of access to a solicitor 29 v 3: no violation of Art 6(1) in conjunction with Art 6(3)(d) as regards the admission of written statements in evidence 11 June 2002: Committee of Ministers regretted that, more than 2 years after the adoption of Interim Resolution DH(2000)26, the amendments to the Youth Justice and Criminal Evidence Act 1999 (in particular the new s 58) and the Criminal Evidence (NI) Order 1999 had still not entered into force: Interim Resolution ResDH(2002)85.
Vella v UK App 23958/94 11 April 1994	28 November 1994 Plenary Commission declared inadmissible a complaint by an Irish republican prisoner in Durham that the Home Secretary would not agree to transfer him to a Northern Ireland prison to facilitate visits from his family in Ireland. An earlier application by the same applicant was also declared inadmissible (see App No 20482/92), though it was made clear in the later application that the applicant had at that time been mis-categorized as a Category A prisoner when he was actually a Category B prisoner (and was now a Category C prisoner).
Devenney v UK App 24265/94 12 April 1994	24 February 1997: Complaint declared admissible by the Commission. 19 March 2002; (2002) 35 EHRR 24: Court found a violation of Art 6 when the applicant was denied the chance to challenge in a domestic court the validity of a statutory 'national security certificate' issued by the Secretary of State for Northern Ireland to prevent an inquiry into alleged discrimination on grounds of religious belief or political opinion. 24 February 2004: information given by the UK to the Committee of Ministers, viz the entry into force on 29 July 1999 of the Northern Ireland Act Tribunal (Procedure) Rules 1999.
Caraher v UK App 24520/94 22 June 1994	11 January 2000; (2000) 29 EHRR CD119 Complaint that payment of £50,000 for death of the applicant's husband was not an adequate remedy, rejected. Also, there was no evidence that the UK was operating an administrative practice, contrary to Art 2, whereby it offered compensation to the families of victims shot by the security forces to buy them off.
Jordan v UK App 24746/94 13 May 1994	4 April 2000: complaint about the failure properly to investigate the death of the applicant's son, shot dead by RUC officers in 1992, held admissible (7 v 0). 4 May 2001; (2003) 37 EHRR 2 Court held by 7 v 0 that there had been a violation of Art 2 in respect of failings in the investigative procedures concerning the death, but that there had been no violation of Arts 13 or 14. £10,000 was awarded as compensation to the applicant. 23 February 2005; 6 June 2007; 19 March 2009: Resolutions by

	Committee of Ministers expressing dissatisfaction with the UK government's response to the judgment. See also *McKerr v UK* App 28883/95, *Kelly and others v UK* App 30054/96, and *Shanaghan v UK* App 37715/97.
McCullough v UK App 24889/94 28 March 1994	12 September 1997; (1998) 25 EHRR CD34 Complaint about the use of exclusion orders held inadmissible, by a majority (19 Commissioners). Complaint under Art 6 rejected as incompatible *ratione materiae.* Complaint under Art 8 manifestly ill-founded because the UK did not show a lack of respect for the applicant's family life. No evidence of discrimination to ground a complaint under Art 14.
Magee (Philip) v UK App No 24892/95 29 March 1994	6 April 1995 Commission held the application inadmissible (11 v 0) because the applicant had not yet been asked to make the QC's oath to which he was objecting, so he was not a victim.
Rai, Allmond and 'Negotiate Now' v UK App 25522/94 18 October 1994	6 April 1995; 81 DR 146 (1995) Complaint over a ban on demonstrations relating to Northern Ireland in London's Trafalgar Square, held inadmissible.
Adams (David) v UK App 25526/94 24 August 1994	29 June 1998 Commission held that the application should be struck off the list since David Adams had already had his rights vindicated through a High Court decision in Belfast; he had been awarded compensation for the injuries inflicted on him by RUC officers during and after his arrest.
McDaid v UK App 25681/94 17 August 1994	9 April 1996; (1996) 22 EHRR CD197; 85 DR 134 Applications by relatives of those killed by the British army on Bloody Sunday (30 January 1972), held inadmissible because out of time (27 v 0).
Garland and others v UK App 28120/95 7 July 1995 *Stephen McMullan* *Hugh McLaughlin* *Michael Beck* *Brendan McCrory* *Daniel Pettigrew* *Ciaran McAllister*	27 November 1996 The seven applicants had been arrested in relation to an attack on a police patrol in 1991. The Commission held the application was inadmissible as regards complaints of ill-treatment in Castlereagh Holding Centre because they were lodged more than 2½ years out of time. Complaints about not being released on bail early enough were also too late. Some complaints relating to Art 6 were rectified by the applicants' acquittal by the domestic court, but complaints about an unreasonable period of time elapsing before the trial were declared admissible, as were complaints that the judge's statement that the applicants' acquittal was not 'a resounding vindication of their innocence' violated their right to be presumed innocent under Art 6(2). 2 February 1999 The Court struck the application off the list because the applicants had not submitted observations in response to those submitted by the UK government.
Magee (Gerard) v UK App 28135/95 22 May 1992	14 September 1999; (2001) 31 EHRR 35 Complaints about alleged mistreatment in Castlereagh Holding Centre and the drawing of inferences from silence held partly admissible. 6 June 2000 Court held there was a violation of Art 6(3)(c) with respect to the drawing of inferences from the applicant's silence in the absence of any access to a solicitor, but not of any other articles.

McKerr v UK App 28883/95 7 March 1993	4 April 2000 Court declared the application by the son of a man shot dead by RUC officers in 1982 near Lurgan, County Armagh, admissible. 4 May 2001; (2002) 34 EHRR 20 Court held by 7 v 0 that there had been a violation of Art 2 in respect of failings in the investigative procedures concerning the death, but that there had been no violation of Arts 13 or 14. £10,000 was awarded as compensation to the applicant. 23 February 2005; 6 June 2007; 19 March 2009: Resolutions by Committee of Ministers expressing dissatisfaction with the UK government's response to the judgment.
Adams and Benn v UK App 28979/95 and 30343/96 29 March 1994	13 January 1997; 88 DR 137 Commission held that complaints about the exclusion order placed on Gerry Adams preventing him from speaking at a meeting organized by Tony Benn MP were inadmissible.
Finucane v UK App 29178/95 5 July 1995	2 July 2002: complaints about the failure properly to investigate the murder of a solicitor held admissible 1 July 2003; (2003) 37 EHRR 29: violation of Art 2.
Devlin v UK App 29545/95 30 November 1995	11 April 2001: held admissible 30 October 2001; (2002) 34 EHRR 43: violation of Art 6(1) when the applicant was denied the chance to challenge in a domestic court the validity of a statutory 'national security certificate' issued by the Secretary of State for Northern Ireland to prevent an inquiry into alleged discrimination on grounds of religious belief or political opinion 24 February 2003: information given by the UK to the Committee of Ministers, viz the entry into force on 29 July 1999 of the Northern Ireland Act (Tribunal (Procedure) Rules 1999
Kelly (Vincent) and others v UK App 30054/96 5 October 1995 *Kevin McKearney* *Amelia Arthurs* *Letitia Donnelly* *Mary Kelly* *Annie Gormley* *Patrick O'Callaghan* *Carmel Lynagh* *Brigid Hughes*	4 April 2000 Court declared the applications by the next-of-kin of 9 men shot dead by the security forces at the entrance to Loughgall police station in 1987 admissible. 4 May 2001 Court held by 7 v 0 that there had been a violation of Art 2 in respect of failings in the investigative procedures concerning the deaths of the applicants' relatives, but that there had been no violation of Arts 6(1), 13, or 14. £10,000 was awarded as compensation to each applicant. 23 February 2005; 6 June 2007; 19 March 2009: Resolutions by Committee of Ministers expressing dissatisfaction with the UK government's response to the judgment.
O'Kane v UK App No 30550/96 12 December 1995	6 July 1999 Complaint that the applicant did not receive a fair trial in that the court had relied upon confession evidence obtained in the course of police interviews at which his solicitor was not permitted to be present and in circumstances where he had been cautioned that inferences might be drawn from his silence under the Criminal Evidence (NI) Order 1988. Court held 7 v 0 that there was no violation of Art 6(1) taken in conjunction with Art 6(3)(c).

McElhinney v Ireland and UK App 31253/96 16 April 1996	(1) 9 February 2000; (2000) 29 EHRR CD214; Grand Chamber Complaint that reliance by the UK and Ireland on sovereign immunity was a violation of Art 6 when the applicant failed in his suit against a British soldier for injuries suffered in the Republic of Ireland: inadmissible ('by a majority') for failure to exhaust domestic remedies. Complaint that the applicant was refused access to a court in Ireland and was discriminated against held admissible ('by a majority'). (2) 21 November 2001: no violation of Art 6(1) in the complaint against Ireland (12 v 5), because the doctrine of state immunity applied.
Lindsay and others v UK App 31699/96 14 April 1996	Complaint that the 1996 elections to a Forum in Northern Ireland were in violation of Art 3 of Prot 1, and of Art 14, because not all political parties were allowed to contest the elections. Held inadmissible because the Forum was a negotiating body, not a legislative body, and the six applicants were individuals, not excluded political parties.
Heaney and McGuinness v Ireland App 34720/97 17 January 1997	21 September 1999: held admissible. 21 December 2000; (2001) 33 EHRR 12: violation of Art 6(1) and (2), but no separate issue arising under Arts 8 or 10. Each applicant was awarded IR£4,000 as compensation. Cf *Quinn v Ireland* (App 36887/97).
Averill v UK App 36408/97 24 March 1997	6 July 1999: complaints about the drawing of inferences from the suspect's silence held admissible by the Court. 6 June 2000; (2000) 31 EHRR 36 Court's decision on the merits: 6 v 1: no violation of Art 6(1) arising out of the drawing of inferences from the applicant's silence 6 v 1: no violation of Art 6(2) 7 v 0: violation of Art 6(1) taken in conjunction with Art 6(3)(c) as regards the applicant's lack of access to a solicitor during the first 24 hours of his detention. 11 June 2002: Committee of Ministers expressed regret that legislation to rectify the defect in England's and Northern Ireland's law was still not in force.
Quinn v Ireland App 36887/97 6 March 1997	21 December 2000. Court found a violation of Arts 6(1) and (2), but no separate issue arose under Art 10. It awarded IR£4,000 to the applicant as compensation. Cf *Heaney and McGuinness v Ireland* (App 34720/97).
Faulkner v UK App 37471/97 8 August 1996	8 September 2001: declared partly admissible. 4 June 2002: violation of Art 8 when a letter written by a prisoner was returned to him undelivered.
O'Hara v UK App 37555/97 20 May 1997	14 March 2000: complaint held partly admissible. 16 October 2001; (2002) 34 EHRR 32. Violation of Art 5(3) in that the applicant had been detained for more than 4 days without being brought before a judicial officer, at a time when there was no derogation notice in place.

Shanaghan v UK App 37715/97 3 October 1996	4 April 2000 Court declared the application by the mother of a man shot dead by loyalist gunmen in 1991 admissible. 4 May 2001 Court held by 7 v 0 that there had been a violation of Art 2 in respect of failings in the investigative procedures concerning the death, but that there had been no violation of Arts 13 or 14. £10,000 was awarded as compensation to the applicant. 23 February 2005; 6 June 2007; 19 March 2009: Resolutions by Committee of Ministers expressing dissatisfaction with the UK government's response to the judgment.
McGuinness v UK App 39511/98 20 October 1997	8 June 1999 Complaint that the requirement that all MPs must swear an oath of allegiance to the Queen before being allowed to avail of normal facilities at Westminster held inadmissible: no violation of Arts 9, 10, and Art 3 of Prot 1.
Brennan v UK App 39846/98 27 January 1998	Commission: 9 January 2001: complaints admissible (7 v 0). Court: 16 October 2001; (2002) 34 EHRR 18 Violation of Art 6(3)(c) if a police officer is in the hearing of a detainee's consultation with his or her solicitor, but otherwise the right of access to a solicitor can be restricted for good cause (for example, during police interviews).
Kerr v UK App 40451/98 8 January 1998	(1) 7 December 1999; (2000) 29 EHRR CD184 Complaint under Art 3 manifestly ill-founded because although the applicant's detention in Castlereagh police station was 'austere' he had not disclosed any physical or mental ill-treatment such as to attain the minimum level of severity required for a violation of Art 3. Complaint under Art 5(2) inadmissible because the reason for his arrest should have been obvious to the applicant from the questions posed during his interrogation. Complaint under Art 5(3) inadmissible because the applicant had not earlier applied for the domestic remedy of bail. Complaint under Art 5(4) manifestly ill-founded because the applicant could have lodged habeas corpus proceedings. Complaints under Art 5(3) and (5) adjourned to give notice of them to the UK government. (2) 10 July 2001: Complaint under Art 5(3) declared inadmissible because brought outside the 6-month limitation period.
Marshall v UK App 41571/98 5 March 1998	10 July 2001 7 v 0: Complaint that derogation notice relating to the emergency in Northern Ireland was invalid under Art 15 rejected by the Commission.
McShane v UK App 43290/98	12 December 2000 Complaint over failure to properly investigate a man's death during a riot in Derry held admissible by the Court. 28 May 2002; (2002) 35 EHRR 23

3 October 1996	Court held by 7 v 0: - a violation of Art 2 in respect of failings in the investigative procedures concerning the death of Dermot McShane - no violation of Art 6(1) - no violation of Art 14 - no violation of Article 13 of the Convention - a failure by the UK government to comply with its obligations under Art 34 of the Convention not to hinder in any way the effective exercise of the right of petition (the RUC had lodged a formal complaint with the Law Society of Northern Ireland concerning alleged breach of an undertaking of confidentiality by the applicant's solicitor in the inquest in this case; the alleged breach of confidentiality related to materials which the applicant's representatives before the European Court had included in their written observations to the Court) - the applicant was entitled to compensation of £8,000.
Kerr (Robert) v UK App 44071/98 1 October 1998	7 December 1999 No violation of Art 5(4) when the applicant, a mandatory life sentence prisoner released from prison on licence, was recalled to prison.
United Christian Broadcasters Ltd v UK App 44802/98 30 September 1998	7 November 2000 Complaints about the denial to the applicant of a licence to conduct religious broadcasting, in alleged violation of Art 10. Declared inadmissible, by an undisclosed majority of the seven judges.
Liberty and others v UK App 58243/00 9 September 1999	1 July 2008; (2009) 48 EHRR 1 Court found a violation of Art 8(2) in that the interferences with the rights of human rights organizations in the UK to communicate freely with a human rights organization in Ireland were not 'in accordance with law'.
McKay v UK App 543/03 9 December 2002	30 November 2004: complaint held admissible. 3 October 2006; (2007) 44 EHRR 41 16 v 1: no violation of Art 5(3) when the applicant was brought before a judicial officer who had no power to grant him bail.
Shannon v UK App 6563/03 5 February 2003	23 November 2004: declared admissible (7 v 0). No hearing 4 October 2005; (2006) 42 EHRR 31 7 v 0: violation of Art 6(1) because the applicant had been required to attend an interview with financial investigators and was compelled to answer questions in connection with events in respect of which he had already been charged with offences; this was not compatible with his right not to incriminate himself. Compensation of 1,750 euros awarded.
Brecknell v UK App 32457/04 10 September 2004	6 March 2007: held admissible. 27 November 2007; (2008) 46 EHRR 42: 27 November 2007: violation of Art 2 due to the lack of independence of the RUC during the initial stages of the investigation begun in 1999; not necessary to consider Art 13; 5,000 euros awarded as compensation. 9 January 2009: Resolution CM/ResDH(2009)19 adopted by the Committee of Ministers following information supplied by the UK government.

McCartney v UK App 34575/04 10 September 2004	6 March 2007: complaint held admissible. 27 November 2007: violation of Art 2 due to the lack of independence of the RUC during the initial stages of a homicide investigation begun in 1999; not necessary to consider Art 13; 5,000 euros awarded as compensation. 9 January 2009: Resolution CM/ResDH(2009)19 adopted by the Committee of Ministers following information supplied by the UK government.
O'Dowd v UK App 34622/04 10 September 2004	6 March 2007: complaint held admissible. 27 November 2007: violation of Art 2 due to the lack of independence of the RUC during the initial stages of a homicide investigation begun in 1999; not necessary to consider Art 13; 5,000 euros awarded as compensation. 9 January 2009: Resolution CM/ResDH(2009)19 adopted by the Committee of Ministers following information supplied by the UK government.
Reavey v UK App 34640/04 10 September 2004	6 March 2007: complaint held admissible. 27 November 2007: violation of Art 2 due to the lack of independence of the RUC during the initial stages of a homicide investigation begun in 1999; not necessary to consider Art 13; 5,000 euros awarded as compensation. 9 January 2009: Resolution CM/ResDH(2009)19 adopted by the Committee of Ministers following information supplied by the UK government.
McGrath v UK App 34651/04 10 September 2004	6 March 2007: complaint held admissible. 27 November 2007: violation of Art 2 due to the lack of independence of the RUC during the initial stages of a homicide investigation begun in 1999; not necessary to consider Art 13; 5,000 euros awarded as compensation. 9 January 2009: Resolution CM/ResDH(2009)19 adopted by the Committee of Ministers following information supplied by the UK government.
Gault v UK App 1271/05 5 January 2005	20 November 2007 Court declared the application admissible and found a violation of Art 5(3) as regards the denial of bail to the applicant pending her retrial for murder; no separate issue under Art 8; 7,500 euros awarded as compensation.
McBride v UK App 1396/06 23 December 2005	9 May 2006; (2006) 43 EHRR SE10 Complaint over refusal by Ministry of Defence to sack two soldiers convicted of murder in Northern Ireland held inadmissible because Art 2 was not engaged (nor, therefore, Art 14).

Bibliography

Addo, M and N Grief (1998) 'Some practical issues affecting the notion of absolute right in Article 3 ECHR' European Law Review (Human Rights Survey) 23: HR/17.

Alexander, Y and A O'Day (1984) *Terrorism in Ireland*, London and Canberra, Croom Helm; and New York, St Martin's Press.

Alston, P (1999) (Ed) *Promoting Bills of Rights through Bills of Rights: Comparative Perspectives*, Oxford, Oxford University Press.

Amnesty International (1972) *Report on an Enquiry into Allegations of Ill-treatment in Northern Ireland*, London, Amnesty International.

Amnesty International (1978) *Report of a Mission to Northern Ireland*, London, Amnesty International.

Amnesty International (1988) *Northern Ireland: Killings by Security Forces and 'Supergrass' Trials*, London, Amnesty International.

Amnesty International (1991) *Women in the Front Line*, London, Amnesty International.

Amnesty International (1994) *Political Killings in Northern Ireland*, London, Amnesty International British Section.

Anderson, D (1994) *14 May Days: The Inside Story of the Loyalist Strike of 1974*, Dublin, Gill and Macmillan.

Andrews, J (1978) 'The Northern Irish Case before the Court' European Law Review 3: 250.

Anthony, G (2005) 'Human rights in Northern Ireland after Re McKerr' European Public Law 11: 5.

Anthony, G (2008) *Judicial Review in Northern Ireland*, Oxford and Portland, Hart Publishing.

Anthony, G (2009) 'Positive Obligations and Policing in the House of Lords' European Human Rights Law Review 538.

Anthony, G and P Mageean (2007) 'Habits of Mind and "Truth-Telling": Article 2 ECHR in Post-Conflict Northern Ireland' in J Morison, K McEvoy, and G Anthony (Eds), *Judges, Transition and Human Rights*, Oxford, Oxford University Press, 181–200.

Appleby, G and E Ellis (1984) 'Formal Investigations: The Commission for Racial Equality and the Equal Opportunities Commission as Law Enforcement Agencies' Public Law 236.

Appleby, G and E Ellis (1991) 'Law and Employment Discrimination: The Working of the Northern Ireland Fair Employment Agency' in R J Cormack and R D Osborne (Eds), *Discrimination and Public Policy in Northern Ireland*, Oxford, Clarendon Press, ch 9.

Arold, N-L (2007) *The Legal Culture of the European Court of Human Rights*, Leiden and Boston, Martinus Nijhoff.

Ashworth, A and P Creighton (1990) 'The Right of Silence in Northern Ireland' in J Hayes and P O'Higgins (Eds), *Lessons from Northern Ireland,* Belfast, SLS Legal Publications (NI) 117–41.

Bailey, S (1988) (Ed) *Human Rights and Responsibilities in Britain and Ireland*, Basingstoke and London, Macmillan Press.

Bajwa, A N and B Duke (2006) 'Pre-charge detention in terrorism cases' New Law Journal 156: 1578.

Baker, Sir G (1984) *Review of the Operation of the Northern Ireland (Emergency Provisions) Act 1978*, London, Her Majesty's Stationery Office, Cmnd 9222.

Barritt, D P and C F Carter (1962) *The Northern Ireland Problem: A Study in Group Relations*, Oxford, Oxford University Press; and (1972) 2nd edn.

Bates, E (2005) 'Supervising the Execution of Judgments Delivered by the European Court of Human Rights: The Challenges Facing the Committee of Ministers' in T A Christou and J P Raymond (Eds), *European Court of Human Rights: Remedies and Execution of Judgments*, London, British Institute of International and Comparative Law, 49–106.

Bates, E (2006) 'A "public emergency threatening the life of the nation"? The United Kingdom's derogation from the European Convention on Human Rights of 18 December 2001 and the "A" case' British Year Book of International Law 76: 245.

Becker, T (2006) *Terrorism and the State: Rethinking the Rules on State Responsibility*, Portland, Oregon, Hart Publishing.

Beddard, R (1967) 'The status of the European Convention on Human Rights in domestic law' International and Comparative Law Quarterly 16: 206.

Beddard, R (1993) *Human Rights and Europe*, London, Sweet & Maxwell, 3rd edn. Also 2nd edn (1980).

Belfast Agreement (1998) *The Belfast Agreement: An Agreement Reached at the Multi-Party Talks on Northern Ireland*, London, The Stationery Office, Cm 3883.

Bell, C (1997) 'Complying with European Court of Human Rights Decisions: An assessment of *McCann and Others v UK* ("Gibraltar Case") and *Murray v UK* ("Rights to Silence")' in *Annual Report of the Standing Advisory Commission on Human Rights 1996–97*, London, Her Majesty's Stationery Office, HC 402, 121–46.

Bell, C and J Keenan (2005) 'Lost on the Way Home? The Right to Life in Northern Ireland' Journal of Law and Society 32: 68.

Bell, J B (1993) *The Irish Troubles: A Generation of Violence 1967–1992*, Dublin, Gill and Macmillan.

Bell, J B (1997) *The IRA*, New Brunswick, New Jersey, Transaction Publishers, 3rd edn.

Bennett, Judge (1979) *Report of the Committee of Inquiry into Police Interrogation Procedures in Northern Ireland*, London, Her Majesty's Stationery Office, Cmnd 7497.

Beresford, D (1987) *Ten Men Dead: Story of the 1981 Irish Hunger Strike*, London, Grafton Books.

Berger, V (1989) *Case Law of the European Court of Human Rights*, Dublin, Round Hall Press.

Bernhardt, R (1995) 'Reform of the control machinery under the European Convention on Human Rights' American Journal of International Law 89: 144.

Besson, S (2008) 'The Reception Process in Ireland and the United Kingdom' in H Keller and A Stone Sweet, *A Europe of Rights: The Impact of the ECHR on National Legal Systems*, Oxford, Oxford University Press, 31–106.

Bew, P and G Gillespie (1993) *Northern Ireland: A Chronology of the Troubles 1968–1993*, Dublin, Gill and Macmillan.

Beyleveld, D (1995) 'The concept of a human right and incorporation of the European Convention on Human Rights' Public Law 577.

Bill of Rights Forum (2008) *Final Report: Recommendations to the Northern Ireland Human Rights Commission on a Bill of Rights for Northern Ireland*, Belfast, Bill of Rights Forum.

Birrell, D (1972) 'Relative deprivation as a factor in conflict in Northern Ireland' Sociological Review 20: 317.

Birrell, D and A Murie (1980) *Policy and Government in Northern Ireland: Lessons of Devolution*, Dublin, Gill and Macmillan; and New York, Barnes and Noble Books.

BIRW (2006) *Plastic Bullets: A Human Rights Perspective*, London, British Irish Rights Watch.

Bishop, J W (1978) 'Law in the control of terrorism and insurrection: the British laboratory experience' Law and Contemporary Problems 42: 140.

Bishop, P and E Mallie (1987) *The Provisional IRA*, London, Heinemann.

Black-Branch, J (2001) 'Powers of detention of suspected international terrorists under the United Kingdom Anti-Terrorism, Crime and Security Act 2001: dismantling the cornerstones of a civil society' European Law Review (Human Rights Survey) 27: HR/19.

Blom-Cooper, Sir L and G Drewry (2009) 'Towards a System of Administrative Law: The Reid and Wilberforce Era, 1945–82' in L Blom-Cooper, B Dickson, and G Drewry (Eds) (2009), *The Judicial House of Lords 1876–2009*, Oxford, Oxford University Press, 209–31.

Bonner, D (1978) 'Ireland v UK' International and Comparative Law Quarterly 27: 897.

Bonner, D (1984) 'The Baker Review of the Northern Ireland (Emergency Provisions) Act 1978' Public Law 348.

Bonner, D (1985) *Emergency Powers in Peacetime*, London, Sweet & Maxwell.

Bonner, D (1990) 'Freedom of Movement' in B Dickson (Ed), *Civil Liberties in Northern Ireland: the CAJ Handbook*, Belfast, Committee on the Administration of Justice, 1st edn.

Bonner, D (2000) 'The United Kingdom's Response to Terrorism: the Impact of Decisions of European Judicial Institutions and of the Northern Ireland "Peace Process"' in F Reinares (Ed), *European Democracies Against Terrorism: Governmental policies and international cooperation*, Aldershot, Ashgate Dartmouth, 31–71.

Bonner, D (2006) 'Responding to crisis: legislating against terrorism' Law Quarterly Review 122: 602.

Bonner, D (2007) *Executive Measures, Terrorism and National Security: Have the Rules of the Game Changed?* Aldershot, Ashgate Publishing.

Boothroyd, B (2001) *The Autobiography*, London, Century.

Bowen, R (1966) *Procedures for the Arrest, Interrogation and Detention of Suspected Terrorists in Aden*, London, Her Majesty's Stationery Office, Cmnd 3165.

Boyd, A (1972) *Brian Faulkner and the Crisis of Ulster Unionism*, Tralee, Anvil Books.

Boyd, A (1984) *The Informers: A Chilling Account of the Supergrasses in Northern Ireland*, Dublin and Cork, The Mercier Press.

Boyle, K (1972) 'The McElduff case and the law of arrest under the Special Powers Act' Northern Ireland Legal Quarterly 23: 334.

Boyle, K (1982–3) 'Human rights and political resolution in Northern Ireland' Yale Journal of World Public Order 9: 156.

Boyle, K, T Hadden, and P Hillyard (1974) *Law and State: The Case of Northern Ireland*, London, Martin Robertson.

Boyle, K, T Hadden, and P Hillyard (1980) *Ten Years On in Northern Ireland*, London, The Cobden Trust.

Boyle, K and H Hannum (1974) 'Individual applications under the European Convention on Human Rights and the concept of administrative practice: the Donnelly case' American Journal of International Law 68: 440.

Brady, R (2004) *Protecting our Sources of Information: Why journalists need to resist legal attacks*, Brussels, European Federation of Journalists.

Brandon, B (2004) 'Terrorism, human rights and the rule of law: 120 years of the UK's legal response to terrorism' Criminal Law Review 981.

Branick, M I (2001–2) 'Extradition and the conflict in Northern Ireland: the past, present and future of an intractable problem' Hastings International and Comparative Law Review 25: 169.

Brownlie, I (1972) 'Interrogation in depth: the Compton and Parker Reports' Modern Law Review 35: 501.

Bryan, D (1998) '"The Right to March": parading a loyal Protestant identity in Northern Ireland' International Journal on Minority and Group Rights 4:373.

Bryan, D (2000) 'Drumcree and "The Right to March": Ritual and Politics in Northern Ireland.' in T G Fraser (Ed), *We'll Follow the Drum: The Irish Parading Tradition*, Basingstoke, Macmillan.

Buckland, P (1981) *A History of Northern Ireland*, Dublin, Gill and Macmillan.

Burton, F (1978) *The Politics of Legitimacy: Struggles in a Belfast Community*, London, Henley and Boston, Routledge and Kegan Paul.

Byrne, S (1999) 'Israel, Northern Ireland, and South Africa at a crossroads: understanding intergroup conflict, peace-building, and conflict resolution' International Journal of Group Tensions 28: 231.

CAJ (1990) *Making Rights Count*, Belfast, Committee on the Administration of Justice (Pamphlet No 17).

CAJ (1993) *Allegations of Psychological Ill-treatment of Detainees Held under Emergency Legislation in Northern Ireland*, Belfast, Committee on the Administration of Justice.

Calvert, H (1968) *Constitutional Law in Northern Ireland: A study in regional government*, London and Belfast, Stevens & Sons Ltd and Northern Ireland Legal Quarterly.

Calvert, H (1970) 'The Republican Clubs Case' Northern Ireland Legal Quarterly 21: 191.

Cameron, I (2000) *National Security and the European Convention on Human Rights*, The Hague, London and Boston, Kluwer Law International.

Campbell, C (1989) 'Extradition to Northern Ireland: prospects and problems' Modern Law Review 52: 585.

Campbell, C (1994) *Emergency Law in Ireland 1918–1925*, Oxford, Clarendon Press.

Campbell, C (2005) 'Wars on terror and vicarious hegemonies: the UK, international law, and the Northern Ireland conflict' International and Comparative Law Quarterly 54: 321.

Campbell, C and I Connolly (2006) 'Making war on terror? Global lessons from Northern Ireland' Modern Law Review 69: 935.

Campbell C, F Ní Aoláin and C Harvey (2003) 'The frontiers of legal analysis: reframing the transition in Northern Ireland' Modern Law Review 66: 317.

Campbell, C M (1980) (Ed) *Do We Need a Bill of Rights?* London, Temple Smith.

Campbell, D (2009) 'The threat of terror and the plausibility of terrorism' Public Law 501.

Campbell, T, J Goldsworthy, and A Stone (2006) *Protecting Rights Without a Bill of Rights: Institutional Performance and Reform in Australia*, Aldershot, Ashgate Publishing.

Carlile, Lord (2008) *Report on the Operation in 2007 of the Terrorism Act 2000 and of Part 1 of the Terrorism Act 2006*, London, Home Office.

Carlton, C (1981) 'Judging without consensus: the Diplock courts in Northern Ireland' Law and Policy Quarterly 3: 225.

Carmichael, P, C Knox, and R Osborne (2007) (Eds) *Devolution and Constitutional Change in Northern Ireland*, Manchester and New York, Manchester University Press.

Carroll, W D (1973) 'The search for justice in Northern Ireland' New York University Journal of International Law and Politics 6: 28.

Carswell, Sir R (1999) 'Human rights and the rule of law' Journal of Clinical Forensic Medicine 6: 249.

Cassese, A (1991) 'Can the notion of inhuman and degrading treatment be applied to socio-economic conditions?' European Journal of International Law 2: 141.

Census (2002) *Northern Ireland Census 2001 Key Statistics*, Belfast, Northern Ireland Statistics and Research Agency.

CGP (2009) *Report of the Consultative Group on the Past*, Belfast.

Choudhury, S (2008) (Ed) *Constitutional Design for Divided Societies: Integration or Accommodation?* Oxford, Oxford University Press.

Churchill R R and J R Young (1991) 'Compliance with judgments of the European Court of Human Rights and decisions of the Committee of Ministers: The experience of the United Kingdom, 1975–1987' British Year Book of International Law LXII: 283.

Clapham, A (2006) *Human Rights Obligations of Non-State Actors*, Oxford, Oxford University Press.

Clarke, L and K Johnston (2001) *Martin McGuinness: From Guns to Government*, Edinburgh, Mainstream Publishing.

Clutterbuck, R (1975) *Living with Terrorism*, London, Faber and Faber.

Clutterbuck, R (1983) *The Media and Political Violence*, London, Macmillan, 2nd edn.

Colville, Viscount (1987) *Review of the Operation of the Prevention of Terrorism (Temporary Provisions) Act 1984*, London, Her Majesty's Stationery Office, Cm 264.

Colville, Viscount (1991) *Report on the Operation in 1991 of the Northern Ireland (Emergency Provisions) Act 1991*, London, Northern Ireland Office.

Compton, Sir E (1971) *Report of the Enquiry into Allegations against the Security Forces of Physical Brutality in Northern Ireland Arising Out of Events on the 9th August 1971*, London, Her Majesty's Stationery Office, Cmnd 4823.

Connelly, A (1982) 'Non-extradition for political offences: a matter of legal obligation or simply a policy choice?' Irish Jurist (new series) 17: 59.

Connelly, A (1985) 'Ireland and the political offence exception to extradition' Journal of Law and Society 12: 153.

Connelly, A (1997) 'Ireland and the European Convention' in B Dickson (Ed), *Human Rights and the European Convention: The Effects of the Convention on the United Kingdom and Ireland*, London, Sweet & Maxwell, ch 6.

Connolly, C K (2007) 'Seeking the final Court of Justice: the European Court of Human Rights and accountability for state violence in Northern Ireland' San Diego International Law Journal 9: 81.

Connolly, S J (1992) *Religion, Law, and Power: The Making of Protestant Ireland 1660–1770*, Oxford, Clarendon Press.

Coogan, T P (2002) *The IRA*, New York, Palgrave.

Cormack, R J and R D Osborne (1983) (Eds) *Religion, Education and Employment: Aspects of Equal Opportunity in Northern Ireland*, Belfast, Appletree Press.

Cormack, R J and R D Osborne (1991) *Discrimination and Public Policy in Northern Ireland*, Oxford, Clarendon Press.

Cory, P (2004), *Collusion Inquiry Reports* <http://www.nio.gov.uk/index/media-centre/media-detail.htm?newsID=9220> (for the deaths occurring in Northern Ireland: Pat Finucane, Robert Hamill, Rosemary Nelson, and Billy Wright).

Council of Europe (1952) *The European Convention on Human Rights*, Strasbourg Directorate of Information of the Council of Europe.

Council of Europe (1970) *Manual of the Council of Europe*, London, Stevens and Sons.

Cox, M, A Guelke, and F Stephen (2006) *A Farewell to Arms: Beyond the Good Friday Agreement*, Manchester, Manchester University Press, 2nd edn.

Craig, E (2009) 'The Framework Convention for the Protection of National Minorities and the Northern Ireland Bill of Rights process' Northern Ireland Legal Quarterly 60: 201.

Cunningham, M J (1991) *British Government Policy in Northern Ireland 1969–89: Its Nature and Execution*, Manchester and New York: Manchester University Press.

Currie, A (2004) *All Hell Will Break Loose*, Dublin, O'Brien Press.

Daintith, T C (1968) 'The protection of human rights in the UK' Human Rights Journal 1: 275 and 1: 407.

Darby, J (1976) *Conflict in Northern Ireland: The Development of a Polarised Community*, Dublin, Gill and Macmillan; and New York, Barnes and Noble Books.

Darby, J (1983) (Ed) *Northern Ireland: The Background to the Conflict*, Belfast, Appletree Press.

Davies, N (1999) *Ten Thirty-Three: The Inside Story of Britain's secret Killing Machine in Northern Ireland*, Edinburgh and London, Mainstream Publishing.

Davis, F F (2007) *The History and Development of the Special Criminal Court 1922–2005*, Dublin, Four Courts Press.

Dawkins, R (2006) *The God Delusion*, London, Transworld.

De Paor, L (1970) *Divided Ulster*, Harmondsworth, Penguin Books.

De Smith, S A (1972) 'Internment and Natural Justice' Northern Ireland Legal Quarterly 23: 331.

Delmas-Marty, M and C Chodkiewicz (1992) *The European Convention for the Protection of Human Rights: International Protection Versus National Restrictions*, Dordrecht, Boston and London, Martinus Nijhoff.

Dembour, M-B (2006) *Who Believes in Human Rights? Reflections on the European Convention*, Cambridge, Cambridge University Press.

Dickson, B (1991) 'The Legal Response to the Troubles in Northern Ireland' in P Roche and B Barton (Eds), *The Northern Ireland Question: Myth and Reality*, Aldershot, Avebury, 151–72.

Dickson, B (1992) 'Northern Ireland's emergency laws—the wrong medicine?' Public Law 592.

Dickson, B (1996a) 'The right to silence and legal advice under the European Convention' European Law Review 21: 424.

Dickson, B (1996b) 'The European Convention in Northern Irish Courts' European Human Rights Law Review 496.

Dickson, B (1997) (Ed) *Human Rights and the European Convention: The Effects of the Convention on the United Kingdom and Ireland*, London, Sweet and Maxwell.

Dickson, B (1999a) 'Miscarriages of Justice in Northern Ireland' in C Walker and K Starmer (Eds), *Miscarriages of Justice: A Review of Justice in Error*, London, Blackstone Press, 287–303.

Dickson, B (1999b) 'Creating an Effective Human Rights Commission for Northern Ireland' in *Annual Report of the Standing Advisory Commission on Human Rights 1998–99*, Belfast, The Stationery Office, HC 265, 109–45.

Dickson, B (2005a) 'Law versus terrorism: can law win?' European Human Rights Law Review 11.

Dickson, B (2005b) *The Legal System of Northern Ireland*, Belfast, SLS Legal Publications (NI), 5th edn.

Dickson, B (2006a) 'The House of Lords and the Northern Ireland conflict—a sequel' Modern Law Review 69: 383.

Dickson, B (2006b) 'Policing and Human Rights after the Conflict' in M Cox, A Guelke and F Stephen (Eds), *A Farewell to Arms? From 'long war' to long peace in Northern Ireland*, Manchester and New York, Manchester University Press, 2nd edn, 170–186.

Dickson, B (2007a) 'The Impact of the Human Rights Act in Northern Ireland' in J Morison, K McEvoy and G Anthony (Eds), *Judges, Transition and Human Rights*, Oxford, Oxford University Press, 201–22.

Dickson, B (2007b) 'The House of Lords' in Brice Dickson (Ed), *Judicial Activism in Common Law Supreme Courts*, Oxford, Oxford University Press, 363–414.

Dickson, B (2009a) 'The detention of suspected terrorists in Northern Ireland and Great Britain' University of Richmond Law Review 43: 927.

Dickson, B (2009b) 'Article 5 of the ECHR and 28-day pre-charge detentions of terrorist suspects' Northern Ireland Legal Quarterly 60: 231.

Dickson, B (2009c) 'A Hard Act to Follow: The Bingham Court, 2000–8' in L Blom-Cooper, B Dickson, and G Drewry (Eds), *The Judicial House of Lords 1876–2009*, Oxford, Oxford University Press, 255–75.

Dickson, B and M Hamilton (2003) 'Marches and Meetings' in B Dickson and M O'Brien (Eds), *Civil Liberties in Northern Ireland: the CAJ Handbook*, Belfast, Committee on the Administration of Justice, 4th edn, ch 8.

Dickson, B and M O'Brien (Eds) (2003) *Civil Liberties in Northern Ireland: the CAJ Handbook*, Belfast, Committee on the Administration of Justice, 4th edn.

Dillon, M (1992) *Killer in Clowntown: Joe Doherty, the IRA and the Special Relationship*, London, Arrow Books.

Dillon, M and D Lehane (1973) *Political Murder in Northern Ireland*, Harmondsworth, Penguin Books.

Diplock, Lord (1972) *Report of the Commission to Consider Legal Procedures to Deal with Terrorist Activities in Northern Ireland*, London, Her Majesty's Stationery Office, Cmnd 5185.

Doherty, F and P Mageean (2006) *Investigating Lethal Force Deaths in Northern Ireland*, Belfast, Northern Ireland Human Rights Commission.

Donohue, L K (2001) *Counter-Terrorist Law and Emergency Powers in the United Kingdom 1922–2000*, Dublin, Irish Academic Press.

Doolan, B (2001), *Lawless v Ireland (1957–1961): The First Case Before the European Court of Human Rights: An International Miscarriage of Justice?* Aldershot, Ashgate Publishing.

Doran, S (1987) 'The use of force by the security forces in Northern Ireland: a legal perspective' Legal Studies 7: 291.

Drzemczewski, A (1978) 'A "non-decision" of the Committee of Ministers under Article 32 of the European Convention on Human Rights: the East African Asians cases' Modern Law Review 41: 337.

Drzemczewski, A (1983) *European Rights Convention in Domestic Law: A Comparative Study*, Oxford, Clarendon Press.

Duffy, H (2005) *The 'War on Terror' and the Framework of International Law*, Cambridge, Cambridge University Press.

Duffy, P (1980) 'English law and the European Convention on Human Rights' International and Comparative Law Quarterly 29: 585.

Dyzenhaus, D (2005) 'An unfortunate outburst of Anglo-Saxon parochialism' Modern Law Review 68: 673.

Edwards, J Ll (1956a) 'Special powers in Northern Ireland' Criminal Law Review 7.

Edwards, J Ll (1956b) 'Capital punishment in Northern Ireland' Criminal Law Review 750.

Egan, S and R Murray (2007) 'A Charter of Rights for Ireland: an unknown quantity in the Belfast Agreement' International and Comparative Law Quarterly 56 :797.

Elliot, RSP and J Hickie (1971) *Ulster: A Case Study in Conflict Theory*, London, Longman.

Elliott, M (2003) 'United Kingdom: human rights—indefinite deprivation of liberty without trial under the Anti-terrorism, Crime and Security Act 2001' International Journal of Constitutional Law 1: 334.

Elliott, M (2006) 'Detention without trial and the "war on terror" ' International Journal of Constitutional Law 4: 553.

Elliott, S (1992) 'Voting Systems and Political Parties in Northern Ireland' in Brigid Hadfield (Ed), *Northern Ireland: Politics and the Constitution*, Buckingham, Open University Press, 76–93.

Ellison, G and J Smyth (2000) *The Crowned Harp: Policing Northern Ireland*, London, Pluto Press.

English, R (2003) *Armed Struggle: The History of the IRA*, London, Macmillan.

English, R (2006) *Irish Freedom: The History of Nationalism in Ireland*, London, Macmillan Ltd.

Evans, M D and R Morgan (1998) *Preventing Torture*, Oxford, Clarendon Press.

Faligot, R (1983) *Britain's Military Strategy in Ireland: The Kitson Experiment*, Dingle, County Kerry, Brandon Books.

Farrell, M (1976) *Northern Ireland: The Orange State*, London, Pluto Press; and 2nd edn (1980).

Farrell, M (1985) *Sheltering the Fugitive? The Extradition of Irish Political Offenders*, Cork, Mercier Press.

Faul, D and R Murray (1975), *The Shame of Merlyn Rees* (pamphlet) (no publisher given).

Faul, D (1983) *The Stripping Naked of Women Prisoners in Armagh Prison* (pamphlet) (no publisher given).

FCO (2005) *Counter-Terrorism Legislation and Practice: A Survey of Selected Countries*, London, Foreign and Commonwealth Office.

Feenan, D (2002) *Informal Criminal Justice*, London, Ashgate Publishing.

Feeney, B (2002) *Sinn Féin: A Hundred Turbulent Years*, Dublin, O'Brien Press.

Fenwick, H (2004) 'Clashing rights, the welfare of the child and the Human Rights Act' Modern Law Review 67: 889.

Fenwick, H (2007) *Civil Liberties and Human Rights*, Abingdon, Routledge Cavendish, 4th edn.

Finn, J (1991) *Constitutions in Crisis: Political Violence and the Rule of Law*, New York, Oxford University Press.

Finnie, W (1989) 'The Prevention of Terrorism Act and the European Convention on Human Rights' Modern Law Review 52: 703.

Finnie, W (1991) 'Anti-terrorist legislation and the European Convention on Human Rights' Modern Law Review 54: 288.

Fisk, R (1975) *The Point of No Return: The Strike which Broke the British in Ulster*, London, Times Books/Deutsch.

Flaherty, M (1994) 'Human rights violations against defense lawyers: the case of Northern Ireland' Harvard Human Rights Journal 7: 87.

Flynn, B (2009) *Soldiers of Folly: The IRA Border Campaign 1956–1962*, Wilton, Co Cork, The Collins Press.

Foley, T (1982) 'Public security and individual freedom: the dilemma of Northern Ireland' Yale Journal of World Public Order 8: 284.

Fredman, S (2006a) 'From deference to democracy: the role of equality under the Human Rights Act 1998' Law Quarterly Review 122: 53.

Fredman, S (2006b) *Human Rights Transformed: Positive Duties and Positive Rights*, Oxford, Oxford University Press.

Gallagher, F (1957) *The Indivisible Island: The History of the Partition of Ireland*, London, Victor Gollancz Ltd.

Gardiner, Lord (1975) *Report of a Committee to Consider, in the Context of Civil Liberties and Human Rights, Measures to Deal with Terrorism in Northern Ireland*, London, Her Majesty's Stationery Office, Cmnd 5847.

Gay, O (2000) *Disqualification Bill, Bill 41 of 1999–2000*, London, House of Commons Library, Research Paper 00/6.

Gearty, C (1993) 'The European Court of Human Rights and the protection of civil liberties' Cambridge Law Journal 89: 122.

Gearty, C (1997) 'The United Kingdom' in C Gearty (Ed), *European Civil Liberties and the European Convention on Human Rights: A Comparative Study*, The Hague, Martinus Nijhoff; ch 1.

Gearty, C (2004) *Principles of Human Rights Adjudication*, Oxford, Oxford University Press.

Gifford, Lord (1984) *Supergrasses: The Use of Accomplice Evidence in Northern Ireland*, London, The Cobden Trust.

Gilbert, G (1992) 'The Irish interpretation of the political offence exemption' International and Comparative Law Quarterly 41: 66.

Gilbert, G (2002) 'The burgeoning minority rights jurisprudence of the European Court of Human Rights' Human Rights Quarterly 24: 736.
Gillespie [Nic Giolla Easpaig], A and E (1987) *Sisters in Cells*, Westport, Co Mayo, Foilseacháin Náisiúnta Teoranta.
Gilmour, D R (1968) 'The sovereignty of Parliament and the European Commission on Human Rights' Public Law 62.
Goldhaber, M D (2007) *A People's History of the European Court of Human Rights*, New Brunswick, NJ and London, Rutgers University Press.
Golsong, H L (1986–7) 'The European Commission of Human Rights' Connecticut Journal of International Law 2: 285.
Gomien, D (1996) *Judgments of the European Court of Human Rights 1959–95: reference charts*, Strasbourg, Council of Europe Publishing (Human Rights Information Centre).
Gormally, B, K McEvoy, and D Wall (1993) *Criminal Justice in a Divided Society: Northern Ireland Prisons,* Crime and Justice 17: 51.
Graham, E (1982) *Ireland and Extradition: A Protection for Terrorists*, Belfast, Ulster Unionist Party (pamphlet).
Green, L C (1978) 'Derogations of human rights in emergency situations' Canadian Yearbook of International Law 16: 92.
Greenberg, K J and J L Dratel (2005) *The Torture Papers: The Road to Abu Ghraib*, Cambridge, Cambridge University Press.
Greer, D S (1973) 'Admissibility of confessions and the common law in times of emergency' Northern Ireland Legal Quarterly 24: 199.
Greer, D S (1980a) 'Legal control of military operations—a missed opportunity' Northern Ireland Legal Quarterly 31: 151.
Greer, D S (1980b) 'The admissibility of confessions under the Northern Ireland (Emergency Provisions) Act' Northern Ireland Legal Quarterly 31: 205.
Greer, S (1986) 'Supergrasses and the legal system in Britain and Ireland' Law Quarterly Review 102: 198.
Greer, S (1995) *Supergrasses: A Study in Anti-Terrorist Law Enforcement in Northern Ireland*, Oxford, Clarendon Press.
Greer, S (2006) *The European Convention on Human Rights: Achievements, Problems and Prospects*, Cambridge, Cambridge University Press.
Greer, S and A White (1986) *Abolishing the Diplock Courts,* London, The Cobden Trust.
Greer, S, T Hadden, and M O'Hagan (1985) 'Civil liberties in Northern Ireland: from special powers to Supergrasses' *Fortnight*, 18 February, No 214: 4.
Griffith, J (1993) *Judicial Politics since 1920: A Chronicle*, Oxford, Blackwell Publishers.
Grimes, A and D Bonner (1997) 'Freedom of movement' in B Dickson (Ed), *Civil Liberties in Northern Ireland: The CAJ Handbook*, Belfast, Committee on the Administration of Justice, 3rd edn.
Gross, O and F Ní Aoláin (2001), 'From discretion to scrutiny: revisiting the application of the margin of appreciation doctrine in the context of Article 15 of the European Convention on Human Rights' Human Rights Quarterly 23: 625.
Gross, O and F Ní Aoláin (2006) *Law in Times of Crisis: Emergency Powers in Theory and Practice*, Cambridge, Cambridge University Press.
Gudgin, G (1999) 'Discrimination in Housing and Employment under the Stormont Administration' in P J Roche and B Barton (Eds), *The Northern Ireland Question: Nationalism, unionism and partition*, Aldershot, Ashgate Publishing, 97–121.

Guelke, A (1985) 'International legitimacy, self-determination and Northern Ireland' Review of International Studies 11: 37.

Guelke, A (1988) *Northern Ireland: the International Perspective*, Dublin, Gill and Macmillan.

Guelke, A (2006) *Terrorism and Global Disorder: Political Violence in the Contemporary World*, London, IB Tauris & Co.

Hadden, T (1992) 'The law on inquests in Northern Ireland—proposals for reform' in *Annual Report of the Standing Advisory Commission on Human Rights 1991–92*, London, Her Majesty's Stationery Office, HC 54, 245–66.

Hadden, T (1993) 'Legal controls on the use of lethal force: options for reform', in *Annual Report of the Standing Advisory Commission on Human Rights 1992–93*, London, Her Majesty's Stationery Office, HC 739, 129–74.

Hadden, T and K Boyle (1989) *The Anglo-Irish Agreement: Commentary, Text and Official Review*, London, Edwin Higel and Sweet & Maxwell.

Hadden, T, K Boyle, and C Campbell (1988) 'Emergency Law in Northern Ireland: The Context' in A Jennings (Ed), *Justice Under Fire: The Abuse of Civil Liberties in Northern Ireland*, London, Pluto Press, 1–26.

Hadden, T and A Donnelly (1997) *The Legal Control of Marches in Northern Ireland*, Belfast, Community Relations Council.

Hadden, T and P Hillyard (1973) *Justice in Northern Ireland: A Study in Social Confidence*, London, The Cobden Trust.

Hadfield, B (1989) *The Constitution of Northern Ireland*, Belfast, SLS Legal Publications (NI).

Hadfield, B (1999a) '*R v Lord Saville of Newdigate, ex p. anonymous soldiers*: What is the purpose of a tribunal of inquiry?' Public Law 663.

Hadfield, B (1999b) 'The Northern Ireland Constitution Act 1973: lessons for minority rights' in P Cumper and S Wheatley (Eds), *Minority Rights in the 'New' Europe*, The Hague, Martinus Nijhoff, 129–46.

Hamilton, M (2005) 'Freedom of assembly, consequential harms and the rule of law: Liberty-limiting principles in the context of transition' Oxford Journal of Legal Studies 27: 75.

Hamilton, M, N Jarman, and D Bryan (2001) *Parades, Protests and Policing: A Human Rights Framework*, Belfast, Northern Ireland Human Rights Commission.

Hanlon, L (2008) *An Assessment of the Legitimacy of Internment in a Constitutional Democracy Based on the Rule of Law: Case Study Ireland*, doctoral thesis submitted to the University of Limerick.

Hannum, H and K Boyle (1972) 'Ireland in Strasbourg: an analysis of Northern Irish proceedings before the European Commission of Human Rights' Irish Jurist 7: 329.

Hannum, H and K Boyle (1977) 'The Donnelly case, administrative practice and domestic remedies under the European Convention: one step forward and two steps back' American Journal of International Law 71: 316.

Harbottle, M and E (1976) 'Cyprus: The Greek and Turkish Confrontation' in W Veenhoven (Ed), *Case Studies on Human Rights and Fundamental Freedoms*, The Hague, Martinus Nijhoff, vol 4, 497–533.

Hargie, O and D Dickson (2003) (Eds) *Researching the Troubles: Social science perspectives on the Northern Ireland conflict*, Edinburgh and London, Mainstream Publishing.

Harlow, C and R Rawlings (1992) *Pressure Through Law*, London and New York, Routledge.

Harrington, J (2009) 'Peace in Northern Ireland and the remaining issue of the "on the runs"' Human Rights Review 10: 5.

Harris, D (1994) 'The right to life under the European Convention on Human Rights' Maastricht Journal of European and Comparative Law 1: 122.

Harris, D, M O'Boyle, E P Bates, and C M Buckley (2009) *Harris, O'Boyle and Warbrick Law of the European Convention on Human Rights*, 2nd edn.

Harris, R (1972) *Prejudice and Tolerance in Ulster: A study of neighbours and 'strangers' in a border community*, Manchester, Manchester University Press.

Hartman, J F (1981) 'Derogations from human rights treaties in public emergencies' Harvard International Law Journal 22: 1.

Harvey, C (2001) (Ed) *Human Rights, Equality and Democratic Renewal in Northern Ireland*, Oxford and Portland, Hart Publishing.

Harvey, C and A Schwartz (2009) 'Designing a Bill of Rights for Northern Ireland' Northern Ireland Legal Quarterly 60: 181.

Harvey, R (1981) *Diplock and the Assault on Civil Liberties*, London, Haldane Society.

Hayes, J and P O'Higgins (1990) *Lessons from Northern Ireland*, Belfast, SLS Legal Publications.

Hayes, M (1997) *A Police Ombudsman for Northern Ireland? A Review of the Police Complaints System in Northern Ireland*, London, The Stationery Office.

Hegarty, A (2002–3) 'Government of memory: public inquiries and the limits of justice in Northern Ireland' Fordham International Law Journal 26: 1148.

Hellerstein, W E et al (1988) *Criminal Justice and Human Rights in Northern Ireland: A Report to the Association of the Bar of the City of New York*, New York, Association of the Bar of the City of New York.

Helsinki Watch (1991) *Human Rights in Northern Ireland*, New York, Helsinki Watch.

Helsinki Watch (1992) *Children in Northern Ireland: Abused by Security Forces and Paramilitaries*, New York and Washington DC, Helsinki Watch.

Hennessey, T (1997) *A History of Northern Ireland 1920–1996*, Dublin, Gill and Macmillan.

Hennessey, T (2007) *The Evolution of the Troubles 1970–72*, Dublin and Portland, Irish Academic Press.

Hewitt, C (1981) 'Catholic grievances, Catholic nationalism and violence in Northern Ireland during the civil rights period' British Journal of Sociology 3: 362.

Hewitt, C (1987) 'Explaining violence in Northern Ireland' British Journal of Sociology 38: 88.

Hewitt, C (1991) 'The roots of violence: Catholic grievances and Irish nationalism during the civil rights period' in P J Roche and B Barton (Eds) *The Northern Ireland Question: Myth and Reality*, Aldershot, Avebury, 17–39.

Hickman, T R (2005) 'Between human rights and the rule of law: indefinite detention and the derogation model of constitutionalism' Modern Law Review 68: 655.

Higgins, R (1994) 'Minority rights: discrepancies and divergencies between the International Covenant and the Council of Europe system' in R Lawson and M de Blois (Eds), *The Dynamics of the Protection of Human Rights in Europe: Essays in Honour of Henry G Schermers*, Dordrecht, Martinus Nijhoff, Vol III, 195–209.

Hill, C (1991) 'Video recording of interviews during police detention' in *Annual Report of the Standing Advisory Commission on Human Rights 1990–91*, London, Her Majesty's Stationery Office, HC 488, 109–16.

Hillyard, P (1993) *Suspect Community: People's Experience of the Prevention of Terrorism Acts in Britain*, London and Boulder, Colorado, Pluto Press in association with Liberty.

Hillyard, P and J Percy-Smith (1984) 'Converting terrorists: the use of supergrasses in Northern Ireland' Journal of Law and Society 11: 335.

Hobcraft, G (2008) 'Roma children and education in the Czech Republic: DH v Czech Republic: opening the door to indirect discrimination findings in Strasbourg?' European Human Rights Law Review 245.

Hoffmann, D (2006) *Annotations to the Terrorism Act 2006*, Current Law Statutes Annotated 2006, London, Sweet & Maxwell, vol 1.

Hoffmann, Lord (2009) 'The Universality of Human Rights' Judicial Studies Board Annual Lecture, available at <http://www.jsboard.co.uk/aboutus/annuallectures.htm>.

Hogan, G (2000) 'The Supreme Court and the Reference of the Offences against the State (Amendment) Bill 1940' Irish Jurist (ns) 35: 238.

Hogan, G and C Walker (1989) *Political Violence and the Law in Ireland*, Manchester, Manchester University Press.

Holland, J and H McDonald (1994) *INLA: Deadly Divisions*, Dublin, Torc.

Home Office and NIO (1998) *Legislation against Terrorism*, London, The Stationery Office, Cm 4178.

Hooper , Sir A (2009) 'Fair trial: "One Golden Thread"' in Sir L Blom-Cooper, B Dickson, and G Drewry (2009) (Eds), *The Judicial House of Lords 1876–2009*, Oxford, Oxford University Press, ch 33.

Houston, J (1978) (Ed) *Brian Faulkner: Memoirs of a Statesman,* London, Weidenfeld and Nicolson.

HRW (2005) *Setting an Example? Counter-Terrorism Measures in Spain*, New York, Human Rights Watch.

Hughes, M (1982) 'Terrorism and national security' Philosophy 57: 5.

Hull, R H (1976) *The Irish Triangle: Conflict in Northern Ireland*, Princeton, New Jersey, Princeton University Press.

Hunt, A (1997) 'Terrorism and reasonable suspicion by proxy' Law Quarterly Review 113: 548.

Hunt, P and B Dickson (1983) 'Northern Ireland's emergency laws and international human rights' Netherlands Quarterly of Human Rights 173.

ICJ (1969) 'Human rights in Northern Ireland' International Commission of Jurists Review 14.

ICJ (1983) *States of Emergency: Their Impact on Human Rights*, Geneva, International Commission of Jurists.

Idoiaga, G E (2006) *The Basque Conflict: New Ideas and Prospects for Peace*, Washington DC, US Institute of Peace.

Ignatieff, M (2001) *Human Rights as Politics and Idolatry*, Princeton, New Jersey, Princeton University Press.

Ishay, M R (2008) *The History of Human Rights*, Berkeley, Los Angeles and London, University of California Press.

Jackson, D W (1997) *The United Kingdom Confronts the European Convention on Human Rights*, Gainesville, University Press of Florida.

Jackson, J D (1985) 'The use of "supergrasses" as a model of prosecution in Northern Ireland' in *Annual Report of the Standing Advisory Commission on Human Rights for 1983–84*, London, Her Majesty's Stationery Office.

Jackson, J D (1986) 'Three judge courts in Northern Ireland' in *Annual Report of the Standing Advisory Commission on Human Rights for 1985–86*, London, Her Majesty's Stationery Office, HC 151, pp 63–76.

Jackson, J D (1988) 'The Northern Ireland (Emergency Provisions) Act 1987' Northern Ireland Legal Quarterly 39: 235.

Jackson, J D (1991) 'Curtailing the right of silence: lessons from Northern Ireland' Criminal Law Review 404.

Jackson, J D (2003) 'The rights of detainees' in B Dickson and M O'Brien (Eds), *Civil Liberties in Northern Ireland: the CAJ Handbook*, Belfast, Committee on the Administration of Justice, 4th edn, 68–89.

Jackson J D and S Doran (1992) 'Diplock and the presumption against jury trial: a critique' Criminal Law Review 755.

Jackson, J D and S Doran (1995) *Judge Without Jury: Diplock Trials in the Adversary System*, Oxford, Clarendon Press.

Jackson, J D (2005) 'The effect of human rights on criminal evidentiary processes: towards convergence, divergence or realignment?' Modern Law Review 68: 737.

Jaconelli, J (1980) *Enacting a Bill of Rights: The Legal Problems*, Oxford, Clarendon Press.

Janis, M W, R S Kay, and A W Bradley (2008) *European Human Rights Law: Text and Materials*, Oxford, Oxford University Press, 3rd edn.

Jarman, N (1999) 'Regulating rights and managing public order: parade disputes and the peace process, 1995–1998' Fordham International Law Journal 22: 1415.

Jellicoe, Earl (1983) *Review of the Operation of the Prevention of Terrorism (Temporary Provisions) Act 1976*, London, Her Majesty's Stationery Office, Cmnd 8803.

Jennings, A (1988a) 'Shoot to kill: the final courts of justice' in A Jennings (Ed), *Justice Under Fire: The Abuse of Civil Liberties in Northern Ireland*, London, Pluto Press, ch 5.

Jennings, A (1988b) 'Bullets above the law' in A Jennings (Ed), *Justice Under Fire: The Abuse of Civil Liberties in Northern Ireland*, London, Pluto Press, ch 6.

Jennings, A (1988c) (Ed) *Justice Under Fire: The Abuse of Civil Liberties in Northern Ireland*, London, Pluto Press.

Joseph, S (1996) 'Denouement of the deaths on the rock: the right to life of terrorists' Netherlands Human Rights Quarterly 14: 5.

Kaufmann, EP (2007) *The Orange Order: A Contemporary Northern Irish History*, Oxford, Oxford University Press.

Kavanagh, A (2004) 'The role of a bill of rights in reconstructing Northern Ireland' Human Rights Quarterly 26: 956.

Kavanagh, A (2009) 'Strasbourg, the House of Lords and elected politicians: Who decides about rights after *Re P*?' Modern Law Review 72: 828.

Kelley, K (1982) *The Longest War: Northern Ireland and the IRA*, Dingle, Brandon Book Publishers.

Kelly, J T (1992) 'The Empire Strikes Back: the taking of Joe Doherty' Fordham Law Review 61: 317.

Kelly, M (2005) *The Right to Life*, Belfast, Northern Ireland Human Rights Commission.

Kenna, P (2008) 'Housing rights: positive duties and enforceable rights at the European Court of Human Rights' European Human Rights Law Review 193.

Kennedy, L (1995) (Ed) *Crime and Punishment in West Belfast*, Belfast, The Summer School, West Belfast.

Kent, K D (2000) 'Basic rights and anti-terrorism legislation: can Britain's Criminal Justice (Terrorism and Conspiracy) Act 1998 be reconciled with its Human Rights Act?' Vanderbilt Journal of Transnational Law 33: 221.

Keown, J (2002) *Euthanasia, Ethics and Public Policy: An Argument Against Legalisation*, Cambridge, Cambridge University Press.

Kinley, D (1993) *The European Convention on Human Rights: Compliance Without Incorporation*, Aldershot, Dartmouth Publishing.

Kitson, F (1971) *Low Intensity Operations: Subversion, Insurgency, Peacekeeping*, London, Faber and Faber.

Knox, C and R Monaghan (2002) *Informal Justice in Divided Societies: Northern Ireland and South Africa*, Basingstoke and New York, Palgrave Macmillan.

Knox, C and P Quirk (2000) *Peace Building in Northern Ireland, Israel and South Africa: Transition, Transformation and Reconciliation*, Basingstoke, Macmillan Press.

Korff, D (1984) *The Diplock Courts in Northern Ireland: A Fair Trial?* Utrecht, Netherlands Institute of Human Rights.

Krisch, N (2008) 'The open architecture of European human rights law' Modern Law Review 71: 183.

Lanham, D J (1974) 'Feeding prisoners by force' Criminal Law Review 206.

Larkin, J and D Scoffield (2007) *Judicial Review in Northern Ireland: A Practitioner's Guide*, Belfast, SLS Legal Publications.

Law Enforcement Commission (1974), *Report of the Law Enforcement Commission*, London, Her Majesty's Stationery Office, Cmnd 5627.

Lawyers Committee for Human Rights (1993) *Human Rights and Legal Defense in Northern Ireland*, New York, Lawyers Committee for Human Rights.

Lawyers Committee for Human Rights (2003) *Beyond Collusion: The UK Security Forces and the Murder of Patrick Finucane*, New York, Lawyers Committee for Human Rights.

Leach, P (2005) *Taking a Case to the European Court of Human Rights*, Oxford, Oxford University Press, 2nd edn.

Leach, P, C Paraskeva, and G Uzelac (2009) *International Human Rights and Fact-Finding*, London, Human Rights and Social Justice Research Institute, London Metropolitan University.

Lee, S (1995) 'Self-determination: which self, determining what?' in *Annual Report of the Standing Advisory Commission on Human Rights 1994–95*, London, Her Majesty's Stationery Office, HC 506, 183–93.

Lee, S (2003) 'Child killers: uneasy mercy' in S Lee, *Uneasy Ethics*, London, Pimlico, 51–85.

Leigh, L H (1989) 'The Police and Criminal Evidence (NI) Order 1989: powers of arrest and detention' Northern Ireland Legal Quarterly 40: 363.

Lester, A (1968) *Democracy and Individual Rights*, London, Fabian Society, Fabian Tract 390.

Lester, A (1998) 'UK acceptance of the Strasbourg jurisdiction: what really went on in Whitehall in 1965' Public Law 237.

Lester, A, D Pannick, and J Herberg (2009) *Human Rights Law and Practice*, London, LexisNexis Butterworths, 3rd edn. And 2nd edn (2004).

Le Sueur, A (2004) (Ed) *Building the UK's New Supreme Court: National and Comparative Perspectives*, Oxford, Oxford University Press.

Letsas, G (2007) *A Theory of Interpretation of the European Convention on Human Rights* Oxford: Oxford University Press.

Livingstone, S (1989) 'A week is a long time in detention: *Brogan and others v United Kingdom*' Northern Ireland Legal Quarterly 40: 288.

Livingstone, S (1994) 'The House of Lords and the Northern Ireland conflict' Modern Law Review 57: 333.

Livingstone, S (1995) 'Reviewing Northern Ireland in Strasbourg 1969–1994' in G Quinn (Ed), *Irish Human Rights Yearbook*, Dublin, Round Hall, 15–30.

Livingstone, S (1997) 'Article 14 and the prevention of discrimination in the ECHR' European Human Rights Law Review 25.

Livingstone, S (1999) 'The Northern Ireland Human Rights Commission' Fordham International Law Journal 22: 1465.

Livingstone, S (2001) 'The need for a Bill of Rights in Northern Ireland' Northern Ireland Legal Quarterly 52: 269.

Livingstone, S and J Doak (2000) *Human Rights Standards and Criminal Justice*, Research Report No 14, Criminal Justice Review.

Lloyd, Lord (1996) *Inquiry into Legislation Against Terrorism*, London, The Stationery Office, Cm 3420.

Lodge, J (1988) (Ed) *The Threat of Terrorism*, Brighton, Wheatsheaf Books.

Lomas, O (1980) 'The executive and the anti-terrorist legislation of 1939' Public Law 16.

Loucaides, L (2007) 'The judgment of the European Court of Human Rights in the Case of *Cyprus v Turkey*' in L Loucaides, *The European Convention on Human Rights: Collected Essays*, The Hague and Leiden, Martinus Nijhoff, 107–20.

Lowry, D R (1975) 'Internment: detention without trial in Northern Ireland' Human Rights 5: 261.

Lowry, D R (1976) 'Internment in Northern Ireland' University of Toledo Law Review 8: 169.

Lubet, S (1987) 'Taking the terror out of political terrorism: the Supplementary Treaty of Extradition between the United States and the United Kingdom' Connecticut Law Review 19: 863.

Lucy, U (2003) 'Improper interference: the perils of defending suspected terrorists in Northern Ireland' Pace International Law Review 15: 411.

Lundy, P (2009) 'Exploring home-grown transitional justice and its dilemmas: a case study of the historical enquiries team, Northern Ireland' International Journal of Transitional Justice 3: 321.

MacDermott, Lord (1972) 'The decline of the rule of law' Northern Ireland Legal Quarterly 23: 475.

Magill, D and S Rose (1997) *Fair Employment Law in Northern Ireland: Debates and Issues*, Belfast, Standing Advisory Commission on Human Rights.

Maguire, J (2004) 'Internment, the IRA and the Lawless Case in Ireland: 1957–61' Journal of the Oxford University History Society, Michaelmas.

Maguire, P (1981) 'The Standing Advisory Commission on Human Rights 1973–1980' Northern Ireland Legal Quarterly 32: 31.

Mallie, E and D McKittrick (2001) *Endgame in Ireland*, London, Hodder & Stoughton.

Mangan, B (1988) 'Protecting human rights in national emergencies: shortcomings in the European system and a proposal for reform' Human Rights Quarterly 10: 372.

Mansergh, N (1991) *The Unresolved Question: The Anglo-Irish Settlement and its Undoing 1912–72*, New Haven and London, Yale University Press.

Marston, G (1993) 'The United Kingdom's part in the preparation of the European Convention on Human Rights 1950' International and Comparative Law Quarterly 42: 796.

McAuley, I (1998) 'Reforming the law on contentious parades in Northern Ireland' Public Law 44.

McBride, J (1999) 'Protecting life: a positive obligation to help' European Law Review (Human Rights Survey) 24: HR/43.

McBride, J (2000) 'Imperfect limits to unacceptable treatment' European Law Review (Human Rights Survey) 25: HR/31.

McBride, R (1995) *It's Part of Life Here: The Security Forces and Harassment in Northern Ireland*, Belfast, Committee on Administration of Justice.

McCafferty, N (1981) *The Armagh Women*, Dublin, Co-op Books.

McCall Smith, A and P Magee (1975) 'The Anglo-Irish Law Enforcement Report in historical and political context' Criminal Law Review 200.

McCann, E (1974) *War and an Irish Town*, Harmondsworth, Penguin Books.

McCluskey, C (1989) *Up Off Their Knees: A Commentary on the Civil Rights Movement in Northern Ireland*, Ireland, Conn McCluskey and Associates.

McCrudden, C (1983) 'The experience of the legal enforcement of the Fair Employment (Northern Ireland) Act 1976' in R J Cormack and R D Osborne (Eds), *Religion, Education and Employment: Aspects of Equal Opportunity in Northern Ireland*, Belfast, Appletree Press, 201–21.

McCrudden, C (2001) 'Not the way forward: some comments on the Northern Ireland Human Rights Commission's consultation document on a Bill of Rights for Northern Ireland' Northern Ireland Legal Quarterly 52. 372.

McCrudden, C (2007a) 'Northern Ireland and the British Constitution since the Belfast Agreement' in J Jowell and D Oliver (Eds), *The Changing Constitution*, Oxford, Oxford University Press, 6th edn, 227–70.

McCrudden (2007b) 'Consociationalism, equality and minorities in the Northern Ireland Bill of Rights Debate: the role of the OSCE High Commissioner on National Minorities' in J Morison, K McEvoy and G Anthony, *Judges, Transition, and Human Rights*, Oxford, Oxford University Press, 315–354.

McElrath, K (2000) *Unsafe Haven: The United States, the IRA and Political Prisoners*, London, Pluto Press.

McEvoy, K (2001) *Paramilitary Imprisonment in Northern Ireland: Resistance, Management and Release*, Oxford, Oxford University Press.

McEvoy, K and L McGregor (2008) (Eds) *Transitional Justice From Below: Grassroots Activism and the Struggle for Change*, Oxford and Portland, Hart Publishing.

McEvoy, K and R Rebouche (2007) 'Mobilizing the Professions: Lawyers, Politics and the Collective Social Conscience' in J Morison, K McEvoy, and G Anthony (Eds), *Judges, Transition and Human Rights*, Oxford, Oxford University Press, 275–314.

McGarry, J (2001) (Ed) *Northern Ireland and the Divided World*, Oxford, Oxford University Press.

McGarry, J and B O'Leary (1995) *Explaining Northern Ireland*, Oxford, Blackwell.

McGarry, J and B O'Leary (2004) *The Northern Ireland Conflict: Consociational Engagements*, Oxford, Oxford University Press.

McGrath, M (1983) 'Extradition: another Irish problem' Northern Ireland Legal Quarterly 34: 292.

McGuffin, J (1973) *Internment*, Tralee, Anvil Books.

McKeown, M (1989) *Two Seven Six Three: An Analysis of Fatalities Attributable to Civil Disturbances in Northern Ireland in the Twenty Years between July 13, 1969, and July 12,* 1989, Dublin, Murlough Press.

McKittrick, D, S Kelters, B Feeney, C Thornton, and D McVea (2004) *Lost Lives*, Edinburgh and London, Mainstream Publishing.

McKittrick, D and D McVea (2000) *Making Sense of the Troubles*, Belfast, Blackstaff Press.

McMahon, B (1979) 'Developments in the Irish Legal System since 1945' in J J Lee (Ed), *Ireland 1945–70*, Dublin, Gill and Macmillan, 83–95.

Merrills, J G (1994) '*Imbrioscia* case' British Year Book of International Law 65: 516.

Merrills, J G (1996a) '*McCann and others* case' British Year Book of International Law 67: 609.

Merrills, J G (1996b) '*Murray* case' British Year Book of International Law 67: 620.

Mikaelsen, L (1980) *European Protection of Human Rights: The Practice and Procedure of the European Commission of Human Rights on the Admissibility of Applications from Individuals and States*, Alphen aan den Rijn, The Netherlands, and Germantown, Maryland, Sijthoff and Noordhoff.

Millar, A (2006) *Socio-ideological Fantasy and the Northern Ireland Conflict: The Other Side*, Manchester and New York, Manchester University Press.

Millar, R, W H Rutherford, S Johnston, and V J Malhotra (1975) 'Injuries caused by rubber bullets: A report on 90 patients' British Journal of Surgery 62: 480.

Miller, C J and D J Feldman (1997) 'The law officers, contempt and judicial review' Public Law 113.

Moeckli, D (2007) 'Stop and search powers under the Terrorism Act 2000: a comment on *R (Gillan) v Commissioner of Police for the Metropolis*' Modern Law Review 70: 659.

Mol, N (1998) 'Implications of the special status accorded in the General Framework Agreement for Peace to the European Convention on Human Rights' in M O'Flaherty and G Gisvold (Eds), *Post-War Protection of Human Rights in Bosnia and Herzegovina*, The Hague, Martinus Nijhoff.

Moloney, E (1991) 'Closing Down the Media: The Story of the Broadcasting Ban' in B Rolston (Ed), *The Media and Northern Ireland: Covering the Troubles*, Basingstoke, Macmillan.

Moloney, Ed (2002) *A Secret History of the IRA*, London, Allen Lane.

Morgan, A (2000) *The Belfast Agreement: A Practical Legal Analysis*, London, The Belfast Press.

Morgan, A (2009) 'Northern Ireland terrorism: the legal response' in J Dingley (Ed), *Combating Terrorism in Northern Ireland*, Abingdon, Routledge.

Morison, J and S Livingstone (1995) *Reshaping Public Power: Northern Ireland and the British Constitutional Crisis*, London, Sweet and Maxwell.

Morrissey, M and M Smyth (2002) *Northern Ireland After the Good Friday Agreement: Victims, Grievance and Blame*, London and Sterling, Virginia, Pluto Books.

Morrisson, C (1981) *The Dynamics of Development in the European Human Rights System*, The Hague, Martinus Nijhoff.

Moskowitz, M (1968) *The Politics and Dynamics of Human Rights*, Dobbs Ferry, New York, Oceana Publications.

Mowbray, A (2002) 'Duties of investigation under the ECHR' International and Comparative Law Quarterly 51: 437.

Mowbray, A (2004) *The Development of Positive Obligations Under the European Convention on Human Rights by the European Court of Human Rights*, Oxford and Portland, Hart Publishing.

Mowbray, A (2007), *Cases and Materials on the European Convention on Human Rights*, Oxford, Oxford University Press, 2nd edn.

Moxon-Browne, E (1983) *Nation, Class and Creed in Northern Ireland*, Aldershot, Gower Publishing.

Mulloy, E (1986) *Dynasties of Coercion*, Derry/Londonderry, Field Day Theatre Co, Pamphlet 10.

Murdoch, J (2002) *Article 5 of the European Convention on Human Rights*, Strasbourg, Council of Europe Publishing.

Murray, R (1998) *State Violence in Northern Ireland 1969–1997*, Dublin, Mercier Press.

NCCL (1936) *Report of a Commission of Inquiry Appointed to Examine the Purpose and Effect of the Civil Authorities (Special Powers) Acts (NI) 1922 and 1933*, London, National Council for Civil Liberties.

NCCL (1986) *Strip Searches*, London, National Council for Civil Liberties and the Cobden Trust.

Newsinger, J (2002) *British Counter-Insurgency: From Palestine to Northern Ireland*, Basingstoke, Palgrave Macmillan.

Ní Aoláin, F (2000) *The Politics of Force: Conflict Management and State Violence in Northern Ireland*, Belfast, Blackstaff Press.

Ní Aoláin, F (2001) 'The evolving jurisprudence of the European Convention concerning the right to life' Netherlands Quarterly of Human Rights 19: 21.

Ní Aoláin, F (2002) 'Truth telling, accountability and the right to life in Northern Ireland' European Human Rights Law Review 571.

Nicol, D (2005) 'Original intent and the European Convention on Human Rights' Public Law 152–72.

NICS (2009) *Northern Ireland Court Service Judicial Statistics 2008*, Belfast, Northern Ireland Statistics and Research Agency.

NIHRA (1993) *Broken Covenants: Violations of International Law in Northern Ireland—Report of the Northern Ireland Human Rights Assembly*, London, Liberty.

NIHRC (2001a) *The Recording of the Use of Plastic Bullets in Northern Ireland*, Belfast, Northern Ireland Human Rights Commission.

NIHRC (2001b) *Making a Bill of Rights for Northern Ireland*, Belfast, Northern Ireland Human Rights Commission.

NIHRC (2002) *Compatibility of Key Person Protection Scheme with ECHR*, Belfast, Northern Ireland Human Rights Commission.

NIHRC (2003) *Baton Rounds: A Review of the Human Rights Implications of the Introduction and Use of the L21A1 Baton Round in Northern Ireland and Proposed Alternatives to the Baton Round*, Belfast, Northern Ireland Human Rights Commission.

NIHRC (2004) *Progressing a Bill of Rights for Northern Ireland—An Update*, Belfast, Northern Ireland Human Rights Commission.

NIHRC (2005) *Taking Forward a Bill of Rights for Northern Ireland*, Belfast, Northern Ireland Human Rights Commission.

NIHRC (2008) *A Bill of Rights for Northern Ireland: Advice to the Secretary of State for Northern Ireland*, Belfast, Northern Ireland Human Rights Commission.

NIO (2000) *Report of the Diplock Review*, London, Northern Ireland Office.

NIO (2006) *Replacement Arrangements for the Diplock Court System*, London, Northern Ireland Office.

NISLL (1969) *Discrimination—Pride for Prejudice*, Belfast, Northern Ireland Society of Labour Lawyers (pamphlet).

North, P (1997) *Independent Review of Parades and Marches*, Belfast, The Stationery Office.

Nowak, M (1989) 'The European Convention on Human Rights and its control system' Netherlands Quarterly of Human Rights 7: 99.

O'Ballance, E (1981) *Terror in Ireland: The Heritage of Hate*, Novato, California, Presidio Press.

O'Boyle, M P (1977a) 'Emergency situations and the protection of human rights: a model derogation provision for a Northern Ireland Bill of Rights' Northern Ireland Legal Quarterly 28: 160.

O'Boyle, M P (1977b) 'Torture and emergency powers under the European Convention on Human Rights: *Ireland v United Kingdom*' (1977) American Journal of International Law 71: 674.

O'Brien, G (2006), 'Capital punishment in Ireland, 1922–1964' in N M Dawson (Ed), *Reflections on Law and History*, Dublin, Four Courts Press in association with the Irish Legal History Society.

O'Brien, J (2005) *Killing Finucane: Murder in Defence of the Realm*, Dublin, Gill and Macmillan.

O'Connell, R (2009) 'Cinderella comes to the ball: Art 14 and the right to non-discrimination in the ECHR' Legal Studies 29: 211.

O'Connor, M P and C M Rumann (2002–3) 'Into the fire: how to avoid getting burned by the same mistakes made fighting terrorism in Northern Ireland' Cardozo Law Review 24: 1657.

Ó Dochartaigh, N (1997) *From Civil Rights to Armalites: Derry and the Birth of the Irish Troubles*, Cork, Cork University Press.

O'Duffy, B (1993) 'Containment or regulation? The British approach to ethnic conflict in Northern Ireland' in J McGarry and B O'Leary (Eds), *The Politics of Ethnic Regulation*, London, Routledge.

O'Higgins, P (1962) 'The Lawless case' Cambridge Law Journal 16: 234.

O'Higgins, P (1972) 'The Northern Ireland Act 1972' Modern Law Review 35: 295.

O'Leary, B (2001) 'The protection of human rights under the Belfast Agreement' Political Quarterly 72: 353.

O'Leary, B and J McGarry (1993) *The Politics of Antagonism: Understanding Northern Ireland*, London and Atlantic Highlands, New Jersey, Athlone Press.

Ó Longaigh, S (2006) *Emergency Law in Independent Ireland 1922–1948*, Dublin, Four Courts Press.

O'Malley, P (1990) *Biting at the Grave: The Irish Hunger Strikes and the Politics of Despair*, Boston, Massachusetts, Beacon Press.

O'Rawe, M (2005) 'Human rights and police training in transitional societies: exporting the lessons of Northern Ireland' Human Rights Quarterly 27: 943.

O'Rawe, R (2005) *Blanketmen: An Untold Story of the H-block Hunger Strike*, Dublin, New Island.

Oliver, J A (1978) *Working at Stormont*, Dublin, Institute of Public Administration.

Ormerod, D (2008) *Smith and Hogan Criminal Law*, Oxford, Oxford University Press, 12th edn.

Ovey, C and R C A White (2006) *The European Convention on Human Rights*, Oxford, Oxford University Press, 4th edn.

Palley, C (1972) 'The evolution, disintegration and possible reconstruction of the Northern Ireland Constitution' Anglo-American Law Review 1: 368.

Palley, C (1991) *The United Kingdom and Human Rights*, London, Stevens & Sons/Sweet & Maxwell.

Parker, Lord (1972) *Report of the Committee of Privy Counsellors Appointed to Consider Authorised Procedures for the Interrogation of Persons Suspected of Terrorism*, London, Her Majesty's Stationery Office, Cmnd 4901.

Parkinson, C (2007) *Bills of Rights and Decolonization*, Oxford, Oxford University Press.

Patten, C (1999) *A New Beginning: Policing in Northern Ireland: The Report of the Independent Commission on Policing for Northern Ireland*. No publisher given.

Philips, Sir C (1981) *Report of the Royal Commission on Criminal Procedure*, London, Her Majesty's Stationery Office, Cmnd 8092.

Philips, Sir C (1986) *Review of the Operation of the Prevention of Terrorism Act in 1985*, London, Home Office.

Pollak, A (1993) (Ed) *A Citizens' Inquiry: The Opsahl Report on Northern Ireland*, Dublin, The Lilliput Press.

Porter, H F (1963) 'The Lawless case: a beachhead for civil rights' American Bar Association Journal 49: 79.

Powell, J (2008) *Great Hatred, Little Room: Making Peace in Northern Ireland*, London, The Bodley Head.

Prince, S (2007) *Northern Ireland's '68: Civil Rights, Global Revolt and the Origins of the Troubles*, Dublin, Irish Academic Press.

Purcell, B (1991) 'The silence in Irish broadcasting' in B Rolston (Ed), *The Media and Northern Ireland: Covering the Troubles*, Basingstoke, Macmillan.

Purdie, B (1990) *Politics in the Streets: The Origins of the Civil Rights Movement in Northern Ireland*, Belfast, Blackstaff Press.

Rauch, E (1973) 'The compatibility of the Detention of Terrorists Order (Northern Ireland) with the European Convention for the Protection of Human Rights' New York University Journal of International Law and Politics 6: 1.

Rees, M (1985) *Northern Ireland: A Personal Perspective*, London, Methuen.

Reid, K (2008) *A Practitioner's Guide to the European Convention on Human Rights*, London, Thomson Sweet & Maxwell, 3rd edn.

Requa, M (2007) 'Truth, transition and the Inquiries Act 2005' European Human Rights Law Review 404.

Requa, M and G Anthony (2008) 'Coroners, controversial deaths and Northern Ireland's past conflict' Public Law 443.

Robertson, A H (1956) *The Council of Europe: Its Structure, Functions and Achievements*, London, Stevens & Sons Ltd (and 2nd edn, 1961).

Robertson, A H (1960) 'The first case before the European Court of Human Rights—*Lawless v Ireland*' British Year Book of International Law 343.

Robertson, R (1988) 'Deadly force and riot control in the United Kingdom' Public Law 13.

Roche, P M (1989–90) 'The United Kingdon's obligation to balance human rights and its anti-terrorism legislation: the case of Brogan and others' Fordham International Law Journal 13: 328.

Rolin, H (1965) 'Has the European Court of Human Rights a future?' Howard Law Journal 11: 442.

Rolston, B (2000) *Unfinished Business: State Killings and the Quest for Truth*, Belfast, Beyond the Pale Publications.

Rose, P (2000) *How the Troubles Came to Northern Ireland*, Basingstoke, Palgrave.

Rowan, B (2003) *The Armed Peace: Life and Death after the Ceasefires*, Edinburgh and London, Mainstream Publishing.

Rowe, J J (1995) *Review of the Northern Ireland (Emergency Provisions) Act 1991*, London, Her Majesty's Stationery Office, Cm 2706.

Rowe, P (2006) *The Impact of Human Rights Law on Armed Forces*, Cambridge, Cambridge University Press.

Russell, J (2007) *Terrorism Pre-Charge Detention Comparative Law Study*, London, Liberty.

Ryder, C (2000a) *Inside the Maze: The Untold Story of the Northern Ireland Prison Service*, London, Methuen.

Ryder, C (2000b) *The RUC 1922–2000: A Force Under Fire*, London, Arrow Books.

Ryder, C and V Kearney (2001) *Drumcree: The Orange Order's Last Stand*, London, Methuen.

SACHR (1975) *First Report of the Standing Advisory Commission on Human Rights: Annual Report for 1974–75*, London, Her Majesty's Stationery Office, HC 632.

SACHR (1977a) *Second Report of the Standing Advisory Commission on Human Rights: Annual Report for 1975–76*, London, Her Majesty's Stationery Office, HC 130.

SACHR (1977b) *The Protection of Human Rights by Law in Northern Ireland*, Standing Advisory Commission on Human Rights, London, Her Majesty's Stationery Office, Cmnd 7009.

SACHR (1978) *Annual Report for 1976–77*, Standing Advisory Commission on Human Rights, London, Her Majesty's Stationery Office, HC 199.

SACHR (1979) *Annual Report for 1977–78*, Standing Advisory Commission on Human Rights, London, Her Majesty's Stationery Office, HC 176.

SACHR (1980) *Annual Report for 1978–79*, Standing Advisory Commission on Human Rights, London, Her Majesty's Stationery Office, HC 433.

SACHR (1981) *Annual Report for 1979–80*, Standing Advisory Commission on Human Rights, London, Her Majesty's Stationery Office, HC 143.

SACHR (1982) *Annual Report for 1980–81*, Standing Advisory Commission on Human Rights, London, Her Majesty's Stationery Office, HC 202.

SACHR (1983) *Annual Report for 1981–82*, Standing Advisory Commission on Human Rights, London, Her Majesty's Stationery Office, HC 230.
SACHR (1984) *Annual Report for 1982–83*, Standing Advisory Commission on Human Rights, London, Her Majesty's Stationery Office, HC 262.
SACHR (1985) *Annual Report for 1983–84*, Standing Advisory Commission on Human Rights, London, Her Majesty's Stationery Office, HC 175.
SACHR (1986) *Annual Report for 1984–85*, Standing Advisory Commission on Human Rights, London, Her Majesty's Stationery Office, HC 394.
SACHR (1987) *Religious and Political Discrimination and Equality of Opportunity in Northern Ireland: Report on Fair Employment*, London, Her Majesty's Stationery Office, Cmnd 237.
SACHR (1988) *Annual Report for 1986–87*, Standing Advisory Commission on Human Rights, London, Her Majesty's Stationery Office, HC 298.
SACHR (1997) *Employment Equality: Building for the Future*, Belfast, Standing Advisory Commission on Human Rights.
SACHR (1998a) 'Amicus Brief to the European Court of Human Rights in the case of Tinnelly and Sons and Others and McIlduff and Others v United Kingdom' in *Annual Report for 1997–98*, Standing Advisory Commission on Human Rights, Belfast The Stationery Office, HC 863, 103–6.
SACHR (1998b) 'Amicus Brief of SACHR to the European Court of Human Rights in John Murray v United Kingdom' in *Annual Report for 1995–96*, Standing Advisory Commission on Human Rights, Belfast, The Stationery Office, HC 467, 109–11.
Scanlan, G and S Gale (1997) *Annotations to the Northern Ireland (Emergency Provisions) Act 1996*, Current Law Statutes Annotated 1996, London, Sweet & Maxwell, vol 1.
Scarman, Sir L (1972) *Violence and Civil Disturbances in Northern Ireland in 1969: Report of Tribunal of Inquiry*, Belfast, Her Majesty's Stationery Office, Cmnd (NI) 566.
Scarman, Sir L (1974) *English Law—The New Dimension*, London, Stevens and Sons (The Hamlyn Lectures).
Schabas, W (2007) 'Ireland, the European Convention on Human Rights, and the Personal Contribution of Seán McBride' in J Morison, K McEvoy, and G Anthony (Eds), *Judges, Transition and Human Rights*, Oxford, Oxford University Press, 251–73.
Schabas, W and A O'Sullivan (2009) 'Of politics and poor weather: how Ireland decided to sue the United Kingdom under the European Convention on Human Rights' Irish Yearbook of International Law for 2007, 2: 3.
Schmitt, D (1976) 'Discrimination and conflict in Northern Ireland' in W Veenhoven (Ed), *Case Studies on Human Rights and Fundamental Freedoms*, The Hague, Martinus Nijhoff, 5: 3.
Sen, A (2006) *Identity and Violence: The Illusion of Destiny*, London, Allen Lane.
Sereny, G (1999) *Cries Unheard: Why Children Kill—The Story of Mary Bell*, London, Macmillan.
Shackleton, Lord (1978) *Review of the Operation of the Prevention of Terrorism (Temporary Provisions) Acts 1974 and 1976*, London, Her Majesty's Stationery Office, Cmnd 7324.
Shaw, S (1999) 'The CPT's Visits to the United Kingdom' in R Morgan and M D Evans (Eds), *Protecting Prisoners: The Standards of the European Committee for the Prevention of Torture in Context*, Oxford, Oxford University Press, 265–71.

Shawcross, Sir H (1965) 'UK Practice on the European Convention on Human Rights' Revue belge de droit international 1–2: 297.

Shirlow, P (2001) *The State they are Still In. Republican Ex-Prisoners and their families*, available online at <http://cain.ulst.ac.uk/issues/prison/shirlow01.htm>.

Shoot to Kill (1985) *Shoot to Kill? International Lawyers Inquiry into the Lethal Use of Firearms by the Security Forces in Northern Ireland*, Dublin, Mercier Press.

Simmonds, K R (1966) 'The United Kingdom and the European Convention on Human Rights' International and Comparative Law Quarterly 15: 539.

Simpson, A W B (1995–6) 'Round up the usual suspects: the legacy of British colonialism and the European Convention on Human Rights' Loyola Law Rev 41: 629.

Simpson, A W B (2001) *Human Rights and the End of Empire: Britain and the Genesis of the European Convention*, Oxford, Oxford University Press.

Simpson, K (2009) *Truth Recovery in Northern Ireland: Critically Interpreting the Past*, Manchester and New York, Manchester University Press.

Smith, D J (1987) *Equality and Inequality in Northern Ireland, Part I: Employment and Unemployment*, London, Policy Studies Institute.

Smith, D J and G Chambers (1991) *Inequality in Northern Ireland*, Oxford, Clarendon Press.

Smith, Sir J (1994) 'The right to life and the right to kill in law enforcement' New Law Journal 144: 354.

Smyth, M and M-T Fay (2000) (Eds) *Personal Accounts from Northern Ireland's Troubles: Public Conflict, Private Loss*, London, Pluto Press.

Smyth, M and J Hamilton (2003) 'The human costs of the troubles' in O Hargie and D Dickson (Eds), *Researching the Troubles: Social Science Perspectives on the Northern Ireland Conflict*, Edinburgh and London, Mainstream Publishing.

Spjut, R J (1979) 'Torture under the ECHR' American Journal of International Law 73: 267.

Spjut R J (1986) 'Internment and detention without trial in Northern Ireland 1971–75: ministerial policy and practice' Modern Law Review 49: 712.

Spjut, R J (1987) 'Deadly force and riot control in Northern Ireland' Public Law 35.

SRP (2008) *Strategic Review of Parading in Northern Ireland: Interim Consultative Report*, Belfast, Strategic Review of Parading.

Stalker, J (1988) *Stalker*, London, Harrap.

Stannard, J E (1980) 'Lethal force in self-defence' Northern Ireland Legal Quarterly 31: 173.

Starmer, K (2007) 'Monitoring the performance of the PSNI in complying with the Human Rights Act 1998' Oxford Journal of Policing 1: 94.

Stone, R (2005) *The Law Relating to Entry, Search and Seizure* Oxford, Oxford University Press, 4th edn.

Stone, R (2008) *Textbook on Civil Liberties and Human Rights*, Oxford, Oxford University Press, 7th edn.

Sullivan, M (1999) *Women in Northern Ireland: Cultural Studies and Material Conditions*, Gainesville, Florida, University Press of Florida.

Sunday Times Insight Team (1972) *Ulster*, London, Penguin Press.

Sutton, M (1994) *Bear in Mind These Dead: An Index of Deaths from the Conflict in Ireland 1969–1993*, Belfast, Beyond the Pale Publications.

Taylor, P (1997) *Provos: The IRA and Sinn Féin*, London, Bloomsbury Publishing.

Tham, J-C and K D Ewing (2007) 'Limitations of a charter of rights in the age of counter-terrorism' Melbourne University Law Review 31: 462.

Thatcher, M (1993) *The Downing Street Years*, London, Harper Collins.

Thompson, W and B Mulholland (1995) 'Paramilitary punishments and young people in West Belfast: Psychological effects and the implications for education' in L Kennedy (Ed), *Crime and Punishment in West Belfast*, Belfast, The Summer School, West Belfast.

Tomkins, A (1997) 'Civil liberties in the Council of Europe: a critical survey', in C Gearty (Ed), *European Civil Liberties and the European Convention on Human Rights: A Comparative Study*, Kluwer, The Hague.

Tomkins, A (2005) 'Readings of *A v Secretary of State for the Home Dept*' Public Law 259.

Tonge, J (2002), *Northern Ireland: Conflict and Change*, Harlow, Essex, Pearson Education.

Townshend, C (1983) *Political Violence in Ireland*, Oxford, Oxford University Press.

Travaux Préparatoires (1975), *Collected Edition of the "Travaux Préparatoires" of the European Convention on Human Rights*, The Hague, Martin Nijhoff (8 volumes).

Tulkens, F, A Kovler, D Spielmann, and L Cariolou (2008) *Judge Loukis Locaides: An Alternative View on the Jurisprudence of the European Court of Human Rights—A Collection of Separate Opinions (1998–2007)*, Leiden and Boston, Martinus Nijhoff.

Twining, W (1973) 'Emergency powers and criminal process: the Diplock Report' Criminal Law Review 406.

Van Dijk, P, F van Hoof, A van Rijn, and L Zwaak (2006) (Eds) *Theory and Practice of the European Convention on Human Rights*, Intersentia, Antwerp and Oxford, 4th edn.

Van Voris, W H (1975) *Violence in Ulster: An Oral Documentary*, Amherst, University of Massachusetts Press.

Vercher, A (1992) *Terrorism in Europe: An International Comparative Legal Analysis*, Oxford, Clarendon Press.

Wacks, R (1980) *The Protection of Privacy*, London, Sweet & Maxwell.

Wadham, J, H Mountfield, A Edmundson, and C Gallagher (2007) *Blackstone's Guide to the Human Rights Act 1998*, Oxford, Oxford University Press, 4th edn.

Walker, C (1980) 'Shooting to kill—some of the issues in *Farrell*' Modern Law Review 43: 591.

Walker, C (1983) 'The Jellicoe Report on the Prevention of Terrorism (Temporary Provisions) Act 1987' Modern Law Review 46: 484.

Walker, C (1984) 'Irish republican prisoners—political detainees, prisoners of war or common criminals' Irish Jurist (new series) 19: 189.

Walker, C (1985) 'Emergency arrest powers' Northern Ireland Legal Quarterly 36: 145.

Walker, C (1986) *The Prevention of Terrorism in British Law*, Manchester, Manchester University Press.

Walker, C (1988) 'Political violence and democracy in Northern Ireland' Modern Law Review 51: 605.

Walker, C (1989) 'Army special powers on parade' Northern Ireland Legal Quarterly 40: 1.

Walker, C (1998) 'The Independent Commissioner for the Holding Centres: a review' Public Law 106.

Walker, C (1999) 'The bombs in Omagh and their aftermath: the Criminal Justice (Terrorism and Conspiracy) Act 1998' Modern Law Review 62: 879.

Walker, C (2009) *Blackstone's Guide to the Anti-Terrorism Legislation*, Oxford, Oxford University Press, 2nd edn.

Wallace, M (1971) *Northern Ireland: 50 Years of Self-Government*, Newton Abbot, David and Charles.

Wallace, M (1982) *British Government in Northern Ireland: From Devolution to Direct Rule,* Newton Abbot, Devon; London; and North Pomfret, Vermont.

Walsh, B (1986–7), 'The European Court of Human Rights' Connecticut Journal of International Law 2: 271.

Walsh, D P J (1983) *The Use and Abuse of Emergency Legislation in Northern Ireland*, London, The Cobden Trust.

Walsh, D P J (2000) *Bloody Sunday and the Rule of Law in Northern Ireland*, Basingstoke and London, Macmillan Press.

Warbrick, C (1983a) 'The European Convention on Human Rights and the prevention of terrorism' International and Comparative Law Quarterly 32: 82.

Warbrick, C (1983b) 'The Prevention of Terrorism (Temporary Provisions) Act 1976 and the European Convention on Human Rights: the *McVeigh* case' International and Comparative Law Quarterly 32: 757.

Warbrick, C (2002) 'The principles of the European Convention on Human Rights and the response of states to terrorism' European Human Rights Law Review 7: 287.

Wartchow, L (2005) 'Civil and human rights violations in Northern Ireland: effects and shortcomings of the Good Friday Agreement in guaranteeing protections' Northwestern University Journal of International Human Rights 3: 1 (online).

Watt, D (1981) (Ed) *The Constitution of Northern Ireland: Problems and Prospects*, London, Heinemann.

Weil, G L (1963) 'The evolution of the European Convention on Human Rights' American Journal of International Law 57: 804.

Whalley, R (2008) *Report of the Independent Reviewer, Justice and Security (NI) Act 2007*, London, Northern Ireland Office.

Whelan, L (1992) 'The challenge of lobbying for civil rights in Northern Ireland: the Committee on the Administration of Justice' Human Rights Quarterly 14: 149.

Whitelaw, W (1989) *The Whitelaw Memoirs*, London, Aurum Press.

Whyte, J (1983) 'How much discrimination was there under the unionist regime, 1921–68?' in T Gallagher and J O'Connell (Eds), *Contemporary Irish Studies*, Manchester, Manchester University Press.

Whyte, J (1990) *Interpreting Northern Ireland*, Oxford, Clarendon Press.

Wicks, E (2000) 'The United Kingdom Government's perceptions of the European Convention on Human Rights at the time of entry' Public Law 438.

Widgery, Lord (1972) *Report of the Tribunal Appointed to Inquire into the Events on Sunday, 30th January 1972, Which Led to Loss of Life in Connection with the Procession in Londonderry on that Day*, London, Her Majesty's Stationery Office, HL 101 / HC 220.

Wilkinson, P (1977), *Terrorism and the Liberal State*, London, Macmillan (2nd edn, 1986).

Wilkinson, P (2006) *Terrorism Versus Democracy: The Liberal State Response*, Abingdon, Routledge, 2nd edn.

Wills, C (2007) *That Neutral Island: A Cultural History of Ireland during the Second World War*, Cambridge, Massachusetts, Belknap Press.

Wilson, T (1989) *Ulster: Conflict and Consent*, Oxford, Basil Blackwell.

Wolfenden, Lord (1957) *Report of the Departmental Committee on Homosexual Offences and Prostitution*, London, Her Majesty's Stationery Office, Cmd 247.
Woodhouse, D (1996) 'Politicians and judges: a conflict of interest' Parliamentary Affairs 49: 423.
Zander, M (1997) *A Bill of Rights?* London, Sweet and Maxwell, 4th edn.
Zellick, G (1976) 'The forcible feeding of prisoners: an examination of the legality of enforced therapy' Public Law 153.
Zwart, T (1994) *The Admissibility of Human Rights Petitions: The Case Law of the European Commission of Human Rights and the Human Rights Committee*, Dordrecht, Boston and London, Martinus Nijhoff.

Index